The Dead Sea Scrolls
Study Edition

The Dead Sea Scrolls Study Edition

EDITED BY

Florentino García Martínez
&
Eibert J. C. Tigchelaar

VOLUME ONE 1Q1–4Q273

BRILL

LEIDEN • BOSTON • KÖLN

WILLIAM B. EERDMANS PUBLISHING COMPANY

GRAND RAPIDS, MICHIGAN

Copyright © 1997 (vol. 1), 1998 (vol. 2) by
Koninklijke Brill NV, Leiden, The Netherlands

First published 1997 (vol. 1), 1998 (vol. 2)
Paperback edition published jointly 2000 by
Koninklijke Brill NV
Leiden, The Netherlands
and by
Wm. B. Eerdmans Publishing Company
2140 Oak Industrial Drive NE, Grand Rapids, Michigan 49505
www.eerdmans.com

Library of Congress Cataloging-in-Publication Data

A catalog record for this book is available from the Library of Congress

Die Deutsche Bibliothek – CIP-Einheitsaufnahme

The Dead Sea Scrolls Study Edition / ed. by Florentino García Martínez
and Eibert J. C. Tigchelaar. – Leiden ; New York ; Köln ; Brill

Brill ISBN 978-90-04-11545-3 (Vol. 1)
Brill ISBN 978-90-04-11546-0 (Vol. 2)
Brill ISBN 978-90-04-11547-7 (Set)

Eerdmans ISBN 978-0-8028-7752-9 (Vol. 1)
Eerdmans ISBN 978-0-8028-7753-6 (Vol. 2)
Eerdmans ISBN 978-0-8028-4493-4 (Set)

Dedicated to
Adam S. van der Woude

CONTENTS

FOREWORD

This book is intended as a practical tool to facilitate access to the Qumran collection of Dead Sea Scrolls. As such, it is primarily intended for classroom use and for the benefit of specialists from other disciplines (scholars working on the Hebrew Bible, the New Testament or Rabbinic literature, specialists on Semitic languages, on the History of Judaism or on the History of Religions, among others) who need a reliable compendium of all the relevant materials found in this collection. As such, it is not intended to compete with, let alone to replace, the *editio princeps* of the materials published in the series *Discoveries in the Judaean Desert* or outside this series, or the preliminary publications of materials which have not yet appeared in the *DJD* Series. The plates printed in the critical editions, as well as the transcriptions, translations and commentaries of the first editors are, and will always remain, the basis of all serious work on the Scrolls.

Whereas the evidence of the biblical manuscripts from Qumran will be shortly available in *The Qumran Bible* by E. Ulrich, this book offers a fresh transcription and an English translation of all the relevant non-biblical texts found at Qumran, arranged by serial number from Cave 1 to Cave 11. By biblical scrolls we understand here the copies of the books that subsequently emerged as the traditional Hebrew Bible, as well as the remains of *tefillin* and *mezuzot* which only contain quotations of those biblical books. In several cases the distinction between biblical and non-biblical texts is not clear-cut. Thus, the so-called *Reworked Pentateuch* consists mainly of the biblical text of the pentateuchal books, be it sometimes in a different order, but also has some sections with material that is not included in the Hebrew Bible; likewise, we have included the non-biblical psalms from the *Psalms Scrolls* 4Q88, 11Q5 and 11Q6. Not included are the scant remains of *Ben Sira* from Cave 2. The inclusion in the edition of these 'additions' does not imply a judgment on their 'biblical' or 'non-biblical' character. In three cases we have included texts not found at Qumran, but related to manuscripts from Qumran; this goes for the remains of the mediaeval copies of the Damascus Document and the Aramaic Levi Document found in the Cairo Genizah, and for the copy of the Songs of the Sabbath Sacrifice recovered at Masada.

The transcriptions of the material included in this edition are fresh transcriptions made by the authors, though it is a very pleasant duty to recognize the debt to all previous work by teachers and colleagues. Our transcriptions rely not only on the identification and placement of the many tens of thousands of fragments achieved by the original editors of the non-biblical scrolls, who arranged the fragments for the photographs made by the Palestine Archaeological Museum in the

1950s and 1960s, and the subsequent editions of these materials by the original editors, but also on all the editions done by other scholars.

Although we have consulted the available editions of the individual manuscripts, the responsibility for the transcriptions here presented is entirely ours. We have checked all the proposed readings against the photographs accessible to us: the photographs provided by the published editions, the photographs included in the Brill microfiche edition and the photographs available in the Oxford-Brill's CD-ROM. In most cases one will find no or few significant differences from other transcriptions because these readings are imposed by the univocal manuscript evidence. In the case of ambiguous manuscript evidence, and in view of the practical purpose of this book, we have often adopted the suggestions of previous editors, rather than presenting alternative readings for the sake of originality and difference, even when such readings would be palaeographically or otherwise possible. The restorations of the text offered in the transcriptions are on the whole relatively sparse. The main exceptions are reconstructions based upon the preserved text of parallel copies of the same manuscript.

A considerable part of the materials was already accessible in translation in *The Dead Sea Scrolls Translated*. That translation has served as the base-text of the translations presented in this edition, but has been thoroughly checked and corrected by the authors. Of the greatest help for this revision was the Dutch translation by A.S. van der Woude included in F. García Martínez & A.S. van der Woude, *De Rollen van de Dode Zee Ingeleid en in het Nederlands vertaald* (Kampen: Kok, 1994, 1995). Although we have consulted most other translations of individual manuscripts, the responsibility for the translations here presented is also ours. The practical purpose of the book has shaped the final translation: to a large extent literal, neutral and close to the transcribed text, even if the outcome lacks finesse and is less fluent than some other presently available translations. On the whole the translation aims to be a translation of the transcribed text on the facing page. Exceptions have been made for texts like *Tobit*, *Jubilees* and *1 Enoch*, where the translation fills in the lacunae on the basis of the known non-Hebrew versions for the benefit of the readers. Although we have tried to be generally consistent in the translation of technical terms, we have not established a chart of translation-equivalents to avoid imposing an uniform meaning upon texts which may be of different origin or of different epochs. Other differences of translation, and also, to some extent, method of transcription, may be attributed to the procedure followed by the authors: each author prepared his own lot, and revised the lot of the other author.

The practical purpose of the book has also governed the selection and the presentation of the materials. We have selected the materials on the basis of their extensiveness and interest, discarding most of the minute fragments which add little to our knowledge. On some occasions we have hesitantly opted for the inclusion of very small and insignificant fragments, only to provide some idea of the material remains of certain compositions, and in order not to leave too many entries empty. On the other hand, larger but, in our opinion, less interesting fragments from manuscripts have been omitted. This means that, in general, we present the largest fragments of a manuscript, and a selection of the smaller ones. Even so, many Q numbers from the different caves are exclusively made up of unidentified or unclassified fragments, and we have not attempted to reproduce these snippets. In spite of this, we consider this edition relatively complete for the non-biblical scrolls, and as such it could be useful as a companion volume with transcriptions and translations for the users of the microfiche or the CD-ROM editions of the photographs of the manuscripts.

This same practical purpose has governed the presentation of the transcriptions. We have avoided all diacritical marks which indicate the degree of certainty of a reading. Readings which in our view are sufficiently assured or have a high degree of probability, even if the remains are minimal, are transcribed outside square brackets. When we are not reasonably assured of a reading, we have noted the letter within square brackets, as a reconstruction, or replaced it by one or more dots. We have not reproduced the extent of lacunae; three dots within square brackets ([...]) indicate any amount of missing text and three dots outside square brackets (]...[) any amount of unreadable (either undecipherable or meaningless) letters or words. Readings corrected by a copyist are indicated within accolades. The text printed within accolades ({...}) may represent erasures, letters with cancellation dots, or text otherwise marked by the copyist as not to be read. One particular type of scribal correction, the overwriting and reshaping of individual letters, has not always been presented in the transcription. The indication *vacat* in the transcription, and *Blank* in the translation, indicate any amount of space left blank in the manuscript, either intentionally (as indication of a new paragraph) or accidentally. Words written above the line or in Palaeohebrew characters in the manuscript are reproduced as such in our transcription. In only a limited number of cases we have indicated obvious mistakes in the text which have not been corrected by the copyist. Text presented within angled brackets (< >) was written in the manuscripts, but should, in our opinion, be read otherwise or be deleted. Text within round brackets either presents our addition to the text, or indicates our corrected reading of the preceding word or words.

The materials are arranged according to cave and serial number. For the materials which do not have a serial number (1QIsa^a, 1QIsa^b, 1QH^a, 1QM, 1QS, 1QapGen, 1QpHab, and the three included non-Qumranic texts) we have adopted the procedure of the *Companion Volume* to the microfiche edition, placing them in the immediate vicinity of the corresponding materials which do have a serial number.

Each entry is provided with a heading which contains a summary of essential information:

1 Cave number and number of the manuscript, short title (when available) and official or descriptive title; it should be noted that the titles of the not yet officially published manuscripts are still subject to change;
2 bibliographical data of the editio princeps or of the preliminary edition;
3 main PAM or SHR photographs of the manuscript;
4 place where the manuscript is kept and Inventory Number of the manuscripts in the Rockefeller Museum;
5 other copies of the composition from the same cave or from other caves, when extant;
6 when appropriate, other relevant bibliographical data.

In the entries corresponding to biblical manuscripts the heading is followed by the references of the texts preserved on the individual fragments as published in the *DJD* Series. For the biblical manuscripts from Cave 4 which have not yet been published in the *DJD* Series the contents are indicated without linking them to concrete fragments, because the precise numbering of the fragments has not yet been fixed. In the entries corresponding to non-biblical manuscripts, the headings are followed by the transcription of the fragments with the translation in the facing page.

Only the more relevant PAM photographs are indicated. The information on the photographs and Museum Inventory numbers is mainly based on the data given in *The Dead Sea Scrolls Catalogue. Documents, Photographs and Museum Inventory Numbers*, Compiled by Stephen A. Reed, Revised and Edited by Marilyn J. Lundberg with the collaboration of Michael B. Phelps (SBL Resources for Biblical Study 32; Atlanta: Scholars Press, 1994). This information has been checked and corrected when necessary with the *Companion Volume to the Dead Sea Scrolls Microfiche Edition*, Edited by Emanuel Tov with the Collaboration of Stephen Pfann, Second Revised Edition, Leiden: E.J. Brill - IDC, 1995, and with the information provided in the bibliographical database of *The Dead Sea Scrolls. Electronic Reference Library*, Volume I, Edited by Timothy H. Lim in consultation with Philip S. Alexander, (Oxford University Press & Brill Academic Publishers, 1997). We also wish to thank Emanuel Tov for providing us with a copy of his updated desk-copy of the inventory of photographs and museum inventory numbers. Only the photographs available in the microfiche edition or in the CD-ROM are indicated, not other extant photographic collections of DSS materials.

It is a pleasant duty to acknowledge the help and to thank accordingly the many institutions and individuals who have contributed to the completion of this volume. First and foremost all the original editors of the manuscripts whose names appear at the beginning of each entry: without their pioneering work this book would not have been possible. It would also not have been possible without the intensive work done for almost fifty years by a large community of scholars who dedicated their efforts to increasing our understanding of these texts. Although we have been forced to restrict to a minimum the bibliographical references, excluding many names and many contributions, we are deeply indebted to each and all of these scholars, and we gladly acknowledge the influence of their work on our transcriptions and translations.

Hans van der Meij, Pim Rietbroek and the technical staff of Brill Academic Publishers, have been very actively involved in all the phases of the production of this book; their interest and the constant care with which they have followed the whole process have been instrumental in the completion of the book; they have earned the thanks of the readers as well as our own.

It is also a pleasure to thank the "Dirección General de Investigación y Desarrollo" of the Spanish Ministry of Education and Science, which funded the stay for a sabbatical semester in 1997 of F. García Martínez at the Instituto Universitario de Ciencias de las Religiones de la Universidad Complutense, and to its Director Julio Trebolle Barrera, who allowed this editor to work undisturbed on this book. Likewise, we are indebted to the "Koninklijke Nederlandse Akademie van Wetenschappen" which granted E.J.C. Tigchelaar an academy fellowship for a Qumran research project.

Finally, we acknowledge and thank the unfailing support of the Theological Faculty of the Rijksuniversiteit Groningen, our academic home base, which, with its Qumran Instituut, has established the ideal conditions for research. It is a pleasure to present this book as a token of the contribution of our Qumran Instituut in Groningen to the celebrations of the fiftieth anniversary of the Scrolls, and to dedicate it to A.S. van der Woude, the founder and former Director of the Qumran Instituut, on the occasion of his seventieth birthday.

The Authors
Groningen, October 1997

PREFACE TO THE PAPERBACK EDITION

As stated in the foreword to the hardcover edition, the *Dead Sea Scrolls Study Edition* (DSSSE) was primarily intended for classroom use. We are therefore very pleased that the publishers have agreed to print an even more affordable paperback edition. The short period which elapsed between the first publication of DSSSE and the present paperback edition (DSSSE2) has precluded us from thoroughly revising the work. Nevertheless, this edition contains numerous small improvements on the hardcover edition. All typing errors, typographical inconsistencies, and accidental omissions which we ourselves observed or which were brought to our attention have been corrected. Occasionally we have modified the transcriptions and translations on the basis of our own research, or in recognition of suggestions graciously put forward by several colleagues all over the world. In order to facilitate the use of the book we have indicated in the running heads the numbers of the columns in those documents which extend over many pages. The list of abbreviations has been somewhat expanded in order to include works that are frequently quoted in short form in the bibliographical headings, and some of those bibliographies have been updated with references to recent publications. On the basis of recent authoritative publications some of the numbers of lines, fragments, or columns have been changed, especially in 4Q255 to 4Q264, and most of the titles given to the manuscripts have been brought into line with those of the latest version of the desk-copy of Emanuel Tov's inventory. A very limited number of changes involves the reallocation of fragments among manuscripts or addition of fragments (some changes in the listing of the 4QPsalms manuscripts; 4Q177 19 has been deleted; 4Q392 and 4Q393 are now listed as one manuscript; the same goes for 4Q509 and 4Q505; 4Q556 now includes the transcription of one fragment). Due to all these different kinds of changes some pages have been considerably modified, whereas others are still exactly the same as in the hardcover edition. On the whole the page numbers of this paperback edition correspond to those of the earlier one, though occasionally the insertion or deletion of text has caused some text to flow from one page to another.

Finally, we wish to acknowledge our debt to Martin Meijer of Bookman, Leiden, who took care of the layout of this work. Annemieke van der Kolk and Bauke Koole helped us with the typing of a large part of the Hebrew text in these volumes. Martin Baasten, of Leiden University, called our attention to many typographical errors in the first edition. Anke Dorman, one of our students, checked all the PAM and ROC numbers by comparing them to those mentioned in other works.

The Authors
Groningen, April 1999

ABBREVIATIONS

BNP   Bibliothèque Nationale de Paris
DAJ   Department of Antiquities of Jordan
IAA   Israel Antiquities Authority
PAM   Palestine Archaeological Museum
ROC   Rockefeller Museum
SHR   Shrine of the Book

The most important editions of texts are always quoted by the short title which precedes the full title in the following list. Other often quoted works are generally quoted in full, but sometimes in abbreviated form. In the case of multiple copies of a composition, full bibliographical details are usually presented in the headings of the first manuscript, whereas abbreviated titles are given in the headings of the other copies. Full titles of often abbreviated works are presented below.

ATTM:	K. Beyer, *Die aramäischen Texte vom Toten Meer samt den Inschriften aus Palästina, dem Testament Levis aus der Kairoer Genisa, der Fastenrolle und den alten talmudischen Zitaten* (Göttingen: Vandenhoeck & Ruprecht, 1984)
ATTME:	K. Beyer, *Die aramäischen Texte vom Toten Meer. Ergänzungsband* (Göttingen: Vandenhoeck & Ruprecht, 1994)
Book of Giants:	L.T. Stuckenbruck, *The Book of Giants from Qumran. Texts, Translation and Commentary* (TSAJ 63; Tübingen: Mohr Siebeck, 1997)
Books of Enoch:	J.T. Milik, *The Books of Enoch. Aramaic Fragments of Qumrân Cave 4* (Oxford: Clarendon, 1976)
Catalogue:	*The Dead Sea Scrolls Catalogue. Documents, Photographs and Museum Inventory Numbers*, Compiled by S.A. Reed, Revised and Edited by M.J. Lundberg, with the collaboration of M.B. Phelps (SBL Resources for Biblical Study 32; Atlanta, Georgia: Scholars Press, 1994)
Concordance:	*A Preliminary Concordance to the Hebrew and Aramaic Fragments from Qumran Cave II-X Including Especially the Unpublished Material from Cave 4.* Printed from a card index prepared by R.E. Brown,

	J.A. Fitzmyer, W.G. Oxtoby and J. Teixidor, prepared and arranged for printing by Hans-Peter Richter. Privately printed 1988
Croyance des Esséniens:	É. Puech, *La Croyance des Esséniens en la Vie Future: Immortalité, Résurrection, Vie éternelle? Histoire d'une Croyance dans le Judaïsme Ancien I et II* (Études Bibliques Nouvelle série 21-22; Paris: Gabalda, 1993)
DJD I:	*Qumran Cave I*, by D. Barthélemy, O.P. and J.T. Milik, with contributions by R. de Vaux, O.P., G.M. Crowfooot, H.J. Plenderleith, G.L. Harding (Discoveries in the Judaean Desert I; Oxford: Clarendon, 1955)
DJD III:	*Les 'Petites Grottes' de Qumrân. Exploration de la falaise. Les grottes 2Q, 3Q, 5Q, 6Q, 7Q à 10Q. Le rouleau de cuivre*, par M. Baillet, J.T. Milik et R. de Vaux, O.P., avec une contribution de H.W. Baker (Discoveries in the Judaean Desert of Jordan III; Oxford: Clarendon, 1962)
DJD IV:	*The Psalms Scroll of Qumran Cave 11 (11QPsᵃ)*, by J.A. Sanders (Discoveries in the Judaean Desert of Jordan IV; Clarendon: Oxford 1965)
DJD V:	*Qumran Cave 4. I (4Q158-4Q186)*, by J.M. Allegro, with the collaboration of A.A. Anderson (Discoveries in the Judaean Desert of Jordan V; Oxford: Clarendon, 1969)
DJD VI:	*Qumran grotte 4. II (4Q128-4Q157)*, par R. de Vaux et J.T. Milik (Discoveries in the Judaean Desert VI; Oxford: Clarendon, 1977)
DJD VII:	*Qumran grotte 4. III (4Q482-4Q520)*, par M. Baillet (Discoveries in the Judaean Desert VII; Oxford: Clarendon, 1982)
DJD IX:	*Qumran Cave 4. IV: Palaeo-Hebrew and Greek Manuscripts*, by P.W. Skehan, E. Ulrich, J. Sanderson (Discoveries in the Judaean Desert IX; Oxford: Clarendon, 1992)
DJD X:	*Qumran Cave 4. V: Miqṣat maʿaśe ha-Torah*, by E. Qimron and J. Strugnell, in consultation with Y. Sussmann, and with contributions by Y. Sussmann and A. Yardeni (Discoveries in the Judaean Desert X; Oxford: Clarendon, 1994)

DJD XI:	*Qumran Cave 4. VI: Poetical and Liturgical Texts. Part 1* by E. Eshel, H. Eshel, C. Newsom, B. Nitzan, E. Schuller and A. Yardeni, in consultation with J. VanderKam and M. Brady (Discoveries in the Judaean Desert XI; Oxford: Clarendon, 1998)
DJD XII:	*Qumran Cave 4. VII: Genesis to Numbers*, by E. Ulrich, F.M. Cross (Discoveries in the Judaean Desert XII; Oxford: Clarendon, 1995)
DJD XIII:	*Qumran Cave 4. VIII: Parabiblical Texts, Part 1*, edited by H. Attridge, T. Elgvin, J. Milik, S. Olyan, J. Strugnell, E. Tov, J. VanderKam, S. White, in consultation with J. VanderKam (Discoveries in the Judaean Desert XIII; Oxford: Clarendon, 1994)
DJD XIV:	*Qumran Cave 4. IX: Deuteronomy, Joshua, Judges, Kings*, by E. Ulrich, F.M. Cross, S. White Crawford, J.A. Duncan, P.W. Skehan, E. Tov, J. Trebolle Barrera (Discoveries in the Judaean Desert XIV; Oxford: Clarendon, 1995)
DJD XV:	*Qumran Cave 4. X: The Prophets*, by E. Ulrich, F.M. Cross, R.E. Fuller, J.E. Sanderson, P.W. Skehan, E. Tov, with the collaboration of C.M. Murphy, C. Niccum (Discoveries in the Judaean Desert XV; Oxford: Clarendon, 1997)
DJD XVI:	*Qumran Cave 4. XI: Psalms to Chronicles*, by F.M. Cross, P. Flint, P. Skehan, E. Tov, J. Trebolle Barrera and E. Ulrich (Discoveries in the Judaean Desert XVI; Oxford: Clarendon, forthcoming)
DJD XVIII:	*Qumran Cave 4. XIII: The Damascus Document (4Q266-273)*, by J.M. Baumgarten, on the basis of transcriptions by J.T. Milik, with contributions by S. Pfann and A. Yardeni (Discoveries in the Judaean Desert XVIII; Oxford: Clarendon, 1996)
DJD XIX:	*Qumran Cave 4. XIV: Parabiblical Texts, Part 2,* edited by M. Broshi, E. Eshel, J. Fitzmyer, E. Larson, C. Newsom, L. Schiffman, M. Smith, M. Stone, J. Strugnell, and A. Yardeni, in consultation with J. VanderKam (Discoveries in the Judaean Desert XIX; Oxford: Clarendon, 1995)
DJD XX:	*Qumran Cave 4. XV: Sapiential Texts, Part 1*, edited by T. Elgvin, M. Kister, T. Lim, B. Nitzan, S. Pfann, E. Qimron, L.H. Schiffman, A. Steudel, in consulta-

tion with J.A. Fitzmyer, partially based on earlier transcriptions by J.T. Milik and J. Strugnell (Discoveries in the Judaean Desert XX; Oxford: Clarendon, 1997)

DJD XXII: *Qumran Cave 4. XVII: Parabiblical Texts, Part 3*, edited by G. Brooke, J. Collins, T. Elgvin, P. Flint, J. Greenfield, E. Larson, C. Newsom, É. Puech, L.H. Schiffman, M. Stone, and J. Trebolle Barrera, in consultation with J. VanderKam (Discoveries in the Judaean Desert XXII; Oxford: Clarendon, 1996)

DJD XXIII: *Qumran Cave 11. II: 11Q2-18, 11Q20-31* by F. García Martínez, E.J.C. Tigchelaar, A.S. van der Woude, incorporating earlier editions by J.P.M. van der Ploeg, O.P., with a contribution by E. Herbert (Discoveries in the Judaean Desert XXIII; Oxford: Clarendon, 1998)

DJD XXV: *Qumrân Grotte 4. XVIII: Textes hébreux (4Q521-4Q528, 4Q576-4Q579)* par Émile Puech (Discoveries in the Judaean Desert XXV; Oxford: Clarendon, 1998)

DJD XXVI: *Qumran Cave 4. XIX: 4QSerekh Ha-Yaḥad and Two Related Texts*, by P.S. Alexander and G. Vermes (Discoveries in the Judaean Desert XXVI; Oxford: Clarendon, 1998)

DJD XXVII: *Aramaic, Hebrew and Greek Documentary Texts from Naḥal Ḥever and Other Sites. With an Appendix Containing Alleged Qumran Texts (The Seiyâl Collection II),* by H.M. Cotton and A. Yardeni (Discoveries in the Judaean Desert XXVII; Oxford: Clarendon, 1997)

DSSHU: E.L Sukenik, אוצר המגילות הגנוזות (Jerusalem: Mosad Bialik/The Hebrew University, 1954) = *The Dead Sea Scrolls of the Hebrew University* (Jerusalem: Magnes Press/The Hebrew University, 1955)

DSSSMM I: *The Dead Sea Scrolls of St. Mark's Monastery. Volume I*: The Isaiah Manuscript and the Habakkuk Commentary, edited by M. Burrows with the assistance of J.C. Trever and W.H. Brownlee (New Haven: The American Schools of Oriental Research, 1950)

DSSSMM II: *The Dead Sea Scrolls of St. Mark's Monastery. Volume II.* Fascicle 2: Plates and Transcription of the

Manual of Discipline, edited by M. Burrows with the assistance of J.C. Trever and W.H. Brownlee (New Haven: The American Schools of Oriental Research, 1951)

DSSU: R. Eisenman, M. Wise, *The Dead Sea Scrolls Uncovered* (Shaftesbury, 1992)

Écrits préesséniens: J.T. Milik, 'Écrits préesséniens de Qumrân: d'Hénoch à Amram', in M. Delcor (ed.), *Qumrân: Sa piété, sa théologie et son milieu* (BETL 46; Paris-Gembloux: Duculot, 1978) 91-106

Legal Texts: M. Bernstein *et al.* (eds.), *Legal Texts and Legal Issues. Proceedings of the Second Meeting of the International Organization for Qumran Studies Cambridge 1995. Published in Honour of Joseph M. Baumgarten* (STDJ 23; Leiden: Brill, 1997)

MPAT: J.A. Fitzmyer, D.J. Harrington, *A Manual of Palestinian Aramaic Texts* (Biblica et Orientalia 34; Rome: Biblical Institute Press, 1978)

Madrid Qumran Congress: J. Trebolle Barrera, L. Vegas Montaner (eds.), *The Madrid Qumran Congress on the Dead Sea Scrolls 18-21 March 1991* (STDJ 11; Leiden: E.J. Brill, 1993)

Microfiche: *The Dead Sea Scrolls on Microfiche. A Comprehensive Facsimile Edition of the Texts from the Judean Desert*, edited by E. Tov with the collaboration of S.J. Pfann (Leiden: E.J. Brill – IDC, 1993)

Midrasch: A. Steudel, *Der Midrasch zur Eschatologie aus der Qumrangemeinde (4QMidrEschata,b). Materielle Rekonstruktion, Textbestand, Gattung und traditionsgeschichtliche Einordnung des durch 4Q174 ('Florilegium') und 4Q177 ('Catena A') repräsentierten Werkes aus den Qumranfunden* (STDJ 13; Leiden: E.J. Brill, 1994)

'Milkî-ṣedeq': J.T. Milik, 'Milkî-ṣedeq et Milkî-reša' dans les anciens écrits juifs et chrétiens', *JJS* 23 (1972) 95-144

Minor Prophets: R.E. Fuller, *The Minor Prophets Manuscripts from Qumrân, Cave 4* (Diss. Harvard 1988)

'Notes': J. Strugnell, 'Notes en marge du volume V des "Discoveries in the Judaean Desert of Jordan"', *RevQ* 7/26 (1970) 163-276, pls. I-VI

Notre Dame Symposium:	E. Ulrich, J. VanderKam (eds.), *The Community of the Renewed Covenant. The Notre Dame Symposium on the Dead Sea Scrolls* (Notre Dame, 1994)
Pesharim:	M.P. Horgan, *Pesharim: Qumran Interpretations of Biblical Books* (CBQMS 8; Washington, D.C.: Catholic Biblical Association, 1979)
Pomegranates:	D. Wright *et al.* (eds.), *Pomegranates and Golden Bells: Studies in Biblical, Jewish, and Near Eastern Ritual, Law, and Literature in Honor of Jacob Milgrom* (Winona Lake, Ind.: Eisenbrauns, 1995)
Provo Conference:	D.W. Parry, E. Ulrich (eds.), *The Provo International Conference on the Dead Sea Scrolls: Technological Innovations, New Texts, and Reformulated Issues* (STDJ 30; Leiden; Boston; Köln: Brill, 1999)
PTSDSSP 1:	*The Dead Sea Scrolls. Hebrew, Aramaic, and Greek Texts with English Translations. Volume 1: Rule of the Community and Related Documents*, edited by J.H. Charlesworth with F.M. Cross, J. Milgrom, E. Qimron, L.H. Schiffman, L.T. Stuckenbruck and R.E. Whitaker (Tübingen – Louisville: J.C.B. Mohr - Westminster John Knox Press, 1994)
PTSDSSP 2:	*The Dead Sea Scrolls. Hebrew, Aramaic, and Greek Texts with English Translations. Volume 2: Damascus Document, War Scroll and Related Documents*, edited by J.H. Charlesworth, with J.M. Baumgarten, M.T. Davis, J. Duhaime, Y. Ofer, H.W.L. Rietz, J.J.M. Roberts, D. Schwartz, B.A. Strawn, and R.E. Whitaker (Tübingen - Louisville: J.C.B. Mohr – Westminster John Knox Press, 1995)
PTSDSSP 4A:	*The Dead Sea Scrolls. Hebrew, Aramaic, and Greek Texts with English Translations. Volume 4A: Pseudepigraphic and Non-Masoretic Psalms and Prayers*, edited by J.H. Charlesworth and H.W.L. Rietz with P.W. Flint, D.T. Olson, J.A. Sanders, E.M. Schuller, and R.E. Whitaker (Tübingen – Louisville: J.C.B. Mohr - Westminster John Knox Press, 1997)
Qumran and Apocalyptic:	F. García Martínez, *Qumran and Apocalyptic. Studies on the Aramaic Texts from Qumran* (STDJ 9; Leiden: E.J. Brill, 1992)
Qumrân: Sa piété:	M. Delcor (ed.), *Qumrân: Sa piété, sa théologie et son milieu* (BETL 46; Paris-Gembloux: Duculot, 1978)

'Qumranica I':

G. W. Nebe, 'Qumranica I: Zu unveröffentlichten Handschriften aus Höhle 4 von Qumran', *ZAW* 106 (1994) 315-322

"Regola":

C. Martone, *La "Regola della Comunità". Edizione critica* (Quaderni di Henoch 8; Torino: Silvia Zamorani, 1995)

Scribes and Scrolls:

H.W. Attridge *et al.* (eds.), *Of Scribes and Scrolls: Studies on the Hebrew Bible, Intertestamental Judaism and christian Origins, Presented to John Strugnell on the Occasion of his Sixtieth Birthday* (Resources in Religion 5; Lanham: University Press of America, 1990)

Solving Riddles:

Z. Zevit *et al.* (eds.), *Solving Riddles and Untying Knots. Biblical, Epigraphic, and Semitic Studies in Honor of Jonas C. Greenfield* (Winona Lake, Indiana: Eisenbrauns, 1995)

Travail d'édition:

J. Starcky, 'Le travail d'édition des fragments manuscrits de Qumrân', *RB* 63 (1956) 66-67

Textual Development:

S. Metso, *The Textual Development of the Qumran Community Rule* (STDJ 21; Leiden: E.J. Brill, 1997)

Textual Studies:

J.C. VanderKam, *Textual and Historical Studies in the Book of Jubilees* (Missoula, Mont.: Scholars Press, 1977)

Wacholder-Abegg 1:

A Preliminary Edition of the Unpublished Dead Sea Scrolls. The Hebrew and Aramaic Texts from Cave Four. Fascicle One, Reconstructed and edited by B.Z. Wacholder and M.G. Abegg (Washington, D.C.: Biblical Archaeology Society, 1991)

Wacholder-Abegg 2:

A Preliminary Edition of the Unpublished Dead Sea Scrolls. The Hebrew and Aramaic Texts from Cave Four. Fascicle Two, Reconstructed and edited by B.Z. Wacholder and M.G. Abegg (Washington, D.C.: Dead Sea Scroll Research Council/Biblical Archaeology Society, 1992)

Wacholder-Abegg 3:

A Preliminary Edition of the Unpublished Dead Sea Scrolls. The Hebrew and Aramaic Texts from Cave Four. Fascicle Three, Reconstructed and edited by B.Z. Wacholder and M.G. Abegg, Based on a Reconstruction of the Original Transcriptions of J.T. Milik and J. Strugnell (Washington, D.C.: Biblical Archaeology Society, 1995)

KEY TO SYMBOLS IN THE TRANSCRIPTION

] אאא [

legible text of varying degrees of certainty, preserved in the manuscript

[אאא]

text restoration, sometimes minimally preserved in the manuscript

] . [or] ... [

one or more illegible traces or meaningless letters in the manuscript

[...]

lacuna of unspecified length in the manuscript

{אאא} or {...}

legible or illegible text erased or corrected by the copyist

<אאא>

text written in the manuscript which should be deleted according to the editors

(אאא)

reading suggested by the editors, either as addition, or in stead of preceding word(s)

vacat

space left blank in the manuscript

****

four dots in the manuscript to represent the tetragrammaton

KEY TO SYMBOLS IN THE TRANSLATION

] XXX [

legible text of varying degrees of certainty, preserved in the manuscript

[XXX]

text restoration, sometimes minimally preserved in the manuscript

] … [

one or more illegible traces or untranslatable readings in the manuscript

[…]

lacuna of unspecified length in the manuscript

{XXX} or {…}

legible or illegible text erased or corrected by the copyist

<XXX>

text written in the manuscript which should be deleted according to the editors

‹XXX›

translation of corrected text

Blank

space left blank in the manuscript

****

four dots in the manuscript to represent the tetragrammaton

(XXX)

explanation required for the meaning of the English text

/XXX/ or /…/

legible or illegible text inserted between the lines by the copyist

1Q1 (1QGen) *1QGenesis*

D. Barthélemy, *DJD I*, 49-50, pl. VIII
PAM 40.442, 40.481, 40.484
BNP
2Q1, 4Q1, 4Q2, 4Q3, 4Q4, 4Q5, 4Q6, 4Q7, 4Q8, 4Q8a, 4Q8b, 4Q8c, 4Q9, 4Q10, 4Q11, 4Q12, 4Q482?, 4Q483?, 4Q576, 6Q1, 8Q1

Frag. 1	Gen 1:18-21	Frag. 4	Gen 23:17-19
Frag. 2	Gen 3:11-14	Frag. 5	Gen 24:22-24
Frag. 3	Gen 22:13-15	Frag. 6-19	?

1Q2 (1QExod) *1QExodus*

D. Barthélemy, *DJD I*, 50-51, pl. VIII
PAM 40.485, 40.486, 40.491, 40.503, 40.538
BNP
2Q2, 2Q3, 2Q4, 4Q11, 4Q13, 4Q14, 4Q15, 4Q16, 4Q17, 4Q18, 4Q19, 4Q20, 4Q21, 4Q22

Frag. 1	Exod 16:12-16	Frag. 5-6	Exod 20:25 - 21:1
Frag. 2-3	Exod 19:24 - 20:1	Frag. 7	Exod 21:4-5
Frag. 4	Exod 20:5-6	Frag. 8-13	?

1Q3 (1QpaleoLev) *1QLeviticus*

D. Barthélemy, *DJD I*, 51-54, pls. VIII-IX
PAM 40.495, 40.496, 40.536, 40, 541, 40.542, 40,545, 40.550, 42.141
BNP
2Q5, 4Q23, 4Q24, 4Q25, 4Q26, 4Q26a, 4Q26b, 6Q2, 11Q1, 11Q2

Frag. 1	Lev 11:10-11	Frag. 8	Num 1:48-50
Frag. 2	Lev 19:30-34	Frag. 9	Num 36:7-8?
Frag. 3-4	Lev 20:20-24	Frag. 10-21	?
Frag. 5-6	Lev 21:24 - 22:6	Frag. 22	Lev 27:30-31?
Frag. 7	Lev 23:4-8	Frag. 23-24	?

Barthélemy accepts the possibility that there are three or four separate manuscripts, to which fragments 1-15, 16-21, 22-23 and 24 respectively belonged.
M. D. McLean, *The Use and Development of Paleo-Hebrew in the Hellenistic and*

Roman Period (Diss. Harvard 1982) 41-42, distinguishes three different MSS: 1QpaleoLev[a]: fragments 1-8.10-15; 1QpaleoLev[b]: fragments 22-23; 1Qpaleo-Num: fragments 16-21

1Q4 (1QDeut[a]) *1QDeuteronomy[a]*

D. Barthélemy, *DJD I*, 54-57, pl. IX
PAM 40.481, 40.482, 40.501, 40.507
BNP
1Q5, 2Q10, 2Q11, 2Q12, 4Q28, 4Q29, 4Q30, 4Q31, 4Q32, 4Q33, 4Q34, 4Q35, 4Q36, 4Q37, 4Q38, 4Q38a, 4Q39, 4Q40, 4Q41, 4Q42, 4Q43, 4Q44, 4Q45, 4Q46, 5Q1, 6Q3, 11Q3

Frag. 1	Deut 1:22-25	Frag. 9	Deut 13:4-6
Frag. 2	Deut 4:47-49	Frag. 10	Deut 13:13-14
Frag. 3	Deut 8:18-19	Frag. 11	Deut 14:21
Frag. 4	Deut 8:19?	Frag. 12	Deut 14:24-25
Frag. 5	Deut 9:27-28	Frag. 13	Deut 16:4
Frag. 6	Deut 11:27-30	Frag. 14	Deut 16:6-7
Frag. 7-8	Deut 13:1-4	Frag. 15-58	?

1Q5 (1QDeut[b]) *1QDeuteronomy[b]*

D. Barthélemy, *DJD I*, 57-62, pl. X
PAM 40.506, 43.751
ROC 673
1Q4, 2Q10, 2Q11, 2Q12, 4Q28, 4Q29, 4Q30, 4Q31, 4Q32, 4Q33, 4Q34, 4Q35, 4Q36, 4Q37, 4Q38, 4Q38a, 4Q39, 4Q40, 4Q41, 4Q42, 4Q43, 4Q44, 4Q45, 4Q46, 5Q1, 6Q3, 11Q3

Frag. 1	Deut 1:9-13	Frag, 10	Deut 28:44-48
Frag. 2	Deut 8:8-9	Frag. 11	Deut 29:9-11
Frag. 3	Deut 9:10	Frag. 12-13 i	Deut 29:12-20
Frag. 4	Deut 11:30-31	Frag. 13 ii	Deut 30:19 - 31:6
Frag. 5	Deut 15:14-15	Frag. 14	Deut 31:7-10
Frag. 6	Deut 17:16	Frag. 15	Deut 31:12-13
Frag. 7	Deut 21:8-9	Frag. 16	Deut 32:17-21
Frag. 8	Deut 24:10-16	Frag. 17	Deut 32:21-22
Frag. 9	Deut 25:13-18	Frag. 18-19	Deut 32:22-29

Frag. 20	Deut 33:12-17	Frag. 23	Deut 33:24
Frag. 21	Deut 33:18-19	Frag. 24-50	?
Frag. 22	Deut 33:21-23		

1Q6 (1QJudg) *1QJudges*

D. Barthélemy, *DJD I*, 62-64, pl. XI
PAM 40.489, 40.546
BNP
4Q49, 4Q50

Frag. 1	Judg 6:20-22	Frag. 7	Judg 9:40-42
Frag. 2	Judg 8:1?	Frag. 8	Judg 9:40-43
Frag. 3	Judg 9:1-4	Frag. 9	Judg 9:48-49
Frag. 4	Judg 9:4-6	Frag. 10-40	?
Frag. 5-6	Judg 9:28-31		

1Q7 (1QSam) *1QSamuel*

D. Barthélemy, *DJD I*, 64-65, pl. XI
PAM 40.522, 40.541
BNP
4Q51, 4Q52, 4Q53

Frag. 1	1 Sam 18:17-18	Frag. 3-7 (= 3)	2 Sam 21:16-18
Frag. 2-3 (= 2)	2 Sam 20:6-10	Frag. 8 (= 4)	2 Sam 23:19-12

1QIsaᵃ *1QIsaiahᵃ*

M. Burrows, *DSSSMM I*, pl. I-LIV
SHR 7001-7054
SHR
1QIsaᵇ (+ 1Q8), 4Q55, 4Q56, 4Q57, 4Q58, 4Q59, 4Q60, 4Q61, 4Q62, 4Q62a, 4Q63, 4Q64, 4Q65, 4Q66, 4Q67, 4Q68, 4Q69, 4Q69a, 4Q69b, 5Q3
Bibliography: E.Y. Kutscher, *The Language and Linguistic Background of the Isaiah Scroll (1QIsaᵃ)* (STDJ 6-6a; Leiden: E.J. Brill, 1974); A. van der Kooij, *Die alten Textzeugen des Jesajabuches: ein Beitrag zur Textgeschichte des Alten Testaments* (Göttingen: Vandenhoeck & Ruprecht, 1981); D.W. Parry, E. Qimron, *The Great Isaiah Scroll (1QIsaᵃ). A New Edition* (STDJ 32; Leiden: Brill, 1999)

Col. I	Isa 1:1-26	Col. XXVIII	Isa 34:1 - 36:2
Col. II	Isa 1:26 - 2:21	Col. XXIX	Isa 36:3-20
Col. III	Isa 2:21 - 3:24	Col. XXX	Isa 36:20 - 37:24
Col. IV	Isa 3:24 - 5:14	Col. XXXI	Isa 37:24 - 38:8
Col. V	Isa 5:14 - 6:7	Col. XXXII	Isa 38:8 - 40:2
Col. VI	Isa 6:7 - 7:15	Col. XXXIII	Isa 40:2-28
Col. VII	Isa 7:15 - 8:8	Col. XXXIV	Isa 40:28 - 41:23
Col. VIII	Isa 8:8 - 9:11	Col. XXXV	Isa 41:23 - 42:17
Col. IX	Isa 9:11 - 10:14	Col. XXXVI	Isa 42:18 - 43:20
Col. X	Isa 10:14 - 11:12	Col. XXXVII	Isa 43:20 - 44:23
Col. XI	Isa 11:12 - 14:1	Col. XXXVIII	Isa 44:23 - 45:21
Col. XII	Isa 14:1-29	Col. XXXIX	Isa 45:21 - 47:11
Col. XIII	Isa 14:29 - 16:14	Col. XL	Isa 47:11 - 49:4
Col. XIV	Isa 16:14 - 18:7	Col. XLI	Isa 49:4 - 50:1
Col. XV	Isa 18:7 - 19:23	Col. XLII	Isa 50:1 - 51:13
Col. XVI	Isa 19:23 - 21:15	Col. XLIII	Isa 51:13 - 52:12
Col. XVII	Isa 21:15 - 22:24	Col. XLIV	Isa 52:13 - 54:4
Col. XVIII	Isa 22:24 - 24:4	Col. XLV	Isa 54:4 - 55:8
Col. XIX	Isa 24:4 - 25:5	Col. XLVI	Isa 55:8 - 57:2
Col. XX	Isa 25:5 - 26:18	Col. XLVII	Isa 57:2 - 58:6
Col. XXI	Isa 26:19 - 28:2	Col. XLVIII	Isa 58:6 - 59:17
Col. XXII	Isa 28:2-24	Col. XLIX	Isa 59:17 - 61:4
Col. XXIII	Isa 28:23 - 29:21	Col. L	Isa 61:4 - 63:4
Col. XXIV	Isa 29:21 - 30:20	Col. LI	Isa 63:4 - 65:4
Col. XXV	Isa 30:20 - 31:4	Col. LII	Isa 65:4-18
Col. XXVI	Isa 31:5 - 33:1	Col. LIII	Isa 65:19 - 66:14
Col. XXVII	Isa 33:1-24	Col. LIV	Isa 66:14-24

1QIsaᵇ *1QIsaiahᵇ*

E.L. Sukenik, *DSSHU*, 30-34, pl. 1-15
SHR 4287, 4352-4364
SHR
1QIsaᵃ, 4Q55, 4Q56, 4Q57, 4Q58, 4Q59, 4Q60, 4Q61, 4Q62, 4Q62a, 4Q63, 4Q64, 4Q65, 4Q66, 4Q67, 4Q68, 4Q69, 4Q69a, 4Q69b, 5Q3
Bibliography: G. Garbini, '1QIsaᵇ et le texte d'Esaïe', *Henoch* 6 (1984) 17-21; É. Puech, 'Quelques aspects de la Restauration du Rouleau des Hymnes (1QH)', *JJS* 39 (1988) 55 note 40

Frag. 1 i	Isa 10:17-19	Frag. 3 i	Isa 16:7-11
Frag. 2 i	Isa 13:16-19	Frag. 4	Isa 19:20 - 20:1

Frag. 5	Isa 22:24 - 23:4	Col. IV	Isa 44:21 - 45:13
Frag. 6 i	Isa 26:1-5	Col. V	Isa 46:3 - 47:13
Frag. 6 ii	Isa 28:15-20	Col. VI	Isa 47:17 - 49:15
Frag. 7	Isa 29:1-8	Col. VII	Isa 50:7 - 51:10
Frag. 8	Isa 30:10-14	Col. VIII	Isa 52:7 - 54:6
Frag. 9	Isa 30:21-26	Col. IX	Isa 55:2 - 57:4
Frag. 10	Isa 35:4-5	Col. X	Isa 57:17 - 59:8
Frag. 11	Isa 37:8-12	Col. XI	Isa 59:20 - 61:2
Col. I + Frag. 12	Isa 38:12 - 39:8; 40:2-3	Col. XII	Isa 62:2 - 64:8
Col. II	Isa 41:3-23	Col. XIII	Isa 65:17 - 66:24
Col. III + Frag. 13	Isa 43:1-13; 23-27		

1Q8 (1QIsa^b) *1QIsaiah^b*

D. Barthélemy, *DJD I*, 66-68, pl. XII
PAM 41.983, 43.752
ROC 677
1QIsa^a, 4Q55, 4Q56, 4Q57, 4Q58, 4Q59, 4Q60, 4Q61, 4Q62, 4Q62a, 4Q63, 4Q64, 4Q65, 4Q66, 4Q67, 4Q68, 4Q69, 4Q69a, 4Q69b, 5Q3
Part of the foregoing manuscript (1QIsa^b) published by Sukenik

Frag. 1	Isa 7:22 - 8:1	Frag. 5	Isa 22:11-18
Frag. 2	Isa 12:3 - 13:8	Frag. 6	Isa 24:18 - 25:8
Frag. 3	Isa 15:3 - 16:2	Frag. 7	?
Frag. 4	Isa 19:7-17		

1Q9 (1QEzek) *1QEzekiel*

D. Barthélemy, *DJD I*, 68-69, pl. XII
PAM 41.983, 43.752
ROC 677
3Q1, 4Q73, 4Q74, 4Q75, 11Q4

Frag. 1	Ezek 4:16 - 5:1	Frag. 2	?

1Q10 (1QPs^a) *1QPsalms^a*

D. Barthélemy, *DJD I*, 69-70, pl. XIII
PAM 40.492, 40.502, 40.504, 40.516, 40.547

1Q11, 1Q12, 2Q14, 3Q2, 4Q83, 4Q84, 4Q85, 4Q86, 4Q87, 4Q88, 4Q89, 4Q90, 4Q91, 4Q92, 4Q93, 4Q94, 4Q95, 4Q96, 4Q97, 4Q98, 4Q98a, 4Q98b, 4Q98c, 4Q98d, 4Q236, 5Q5, 6Q5, 8Q2, 11Q5, 11Q6, 11Q7, 11Q8, 11Q9

Frag. 1	Ps 86:5-8	Frag. 6-7	Ps 119:31-34
Frag. 2	Ps 92:12-14	Frag. 8-10	Ps 119:43-48
Frag. 3-4	Ps 94:16	Frag. 11	Ps 119:77-79
Frag. 5	Ps 95:11 - 96:2	Frag. 12-22	?

1Q11 (1QPs^b) *1QPsalms^b*

D. Barthélemy, *DJD I*, 71, pl. XIII
PAM 40.438, 40.446, 40.491, 40.535
1Q10, 1Q12, 2Q14, 3Q2, 4Q83, 4Q84, 4Q85, 4Q86, 4Q87, 4Q88, 4Q89, 4Q90, 4Q91, 4Q92, 4Q93, 4Q94, 4Q95, 4Q96, 4Q97, 4Q98, 4Q98a, 4Q98b, 4Q98c, 4Q98d, 4Q236, 5Q5, 6Q5, 8Q2, 11Q5, 11Q6, 11Q7, 11Q8, 11Q9

| Frag. 1 | Ps 126:6 | Frag. 6 | Ps 128:3 |
| Frag. 2-5 | Ps 127:1-5 | | |

1Q12 (1QPs^c) *1QPsalms^c*

D. Barthélemy, *DJD I*, 71-72, pl. XIII
PAM 40.504, 40.537, 42.141
1Q10, 1Q11, 2Q14, 3Q2, 4Q83, 4Q84, 4Q85, 4Q86, 4Q87, 4Q88, 4Q89, 4Q90, 4Q91, 4Q92, 4Q93, 4Q94, 4Q95, 4Q96, 4Q97, 4Q98, 4Q98a, 4Q98b, 4Q98c, 4Q98d, 4Q236, 5Q5, 6Q5, 8Q2, 11Q5, 11Q6, 11Q7, 11Q8, 11Q9

Frag. 1	Ps 44:3-5	Frag. 5-6	Ps 44:23-24
Frag. 2	Ps 44:4	Frag. 7	Ps 44:25
Frag. 3	Ps 44:7	Frag. 8-9	?
Frag. 4	Ps 44:9		

1Q13 (1QPhyl) *1QPhylactery*

D. Barthélemy, *DJD I*, 72-76, pl. XIV
PAM 40.458-40.466, 40.468-40.470
DAJ

4Q128, 4Q129, 4Q130, 4Q131, 4Q132, 4Q133, 4Q134, 4Q135, 4Q136, 4Q137, 4Q138, 4Q139, 4Q140, 4Q141, 4Q142, 4Q143, 4Q144, 4Q145, 4Q146, 4Q147, 4Q148, 5Q8

Frag. 1-18	Deut 5:1-22	Frag. 26-27	Deut 11:12
Frag. 19	Deut 5:23-27	Frag. 28-29	Exod 13:2-3
Frag. 20	Deut 10:17-18	Frag. 30-31	Exod 13:7-9
Frag. 21-22	Deut 10:21 - 11:1	Frag. 32-58	?
Frag. 23-25	Deut 11:8-11		

1Q14 (1QpMic) *1QPesher to Micah*

J.T. Milik, *DJD I*, 77-80, pl. XV
PAM 40.437, 40.536, 40.537, 40.545, 40.548
BNP
4Q168?

Frags. 1-5   1 [...]ה[וֹ]ה[ר]ר[אדוני יהי]ה בכם   2 [לעד אדוני מהיכל
קודשו כיא הנ[ה]ה ה[ר]ה[ו] יוצא מ[מ]קומו   3 [וירד על במ]ותי האר[ץ ונמסו
ההרי[ם תח]תיו והעמקים ית[בקעו]   4 [כדו]נג מפנ]י הא[ש כ]מים מוגרים
במורד בפשע יעקו[ב כול   5 [זוא]ת ובחט[אות בית ישראל ...]

Frag. 6   1 [...].[...]   2 [... ב]אחרית [הימים ...]   3 [...] כבודו[
[... אש]ר עברו[...]   4

Frag. 7   1 [...] .[...]   2 [...] .[הלוא]   3 [...]. הפתא[ים ...]
4-5 [...]...[...]

Frags. 8-10   3 [... ומה במות יהודה הלוא יר[ושל]ם ושמתי שומרון[
4 לעי שדה למטעי כרם *vacat* [פשרו על מטיף הכזב   5 [אשר הואה יתעה
ה]פתאים *vacat* ומה במות יהודה   6 [הלוא ירושלם פשרו ע]ל מורה הצדק
אשר הואה   7 [יורה התורה לעצתו] ולכו[ל]ול המתנדבים לוסף על בחירי
8 [אל עושי התורה [בעצת היחד אשר ינצל[ו] מיום   9 [המשפט ...].[...].[...]
10 [... ואשר אמר ושמתי שומרון ל]עי שדה   11 [...].[...].[...]

Frag. 11   1 [ואיללה פשרו על כוהני ירו[של]ם אשר יתעו[...]
2 [...]אויביו שלל ועו[רום *vacat*   3 [... נגע ע[ד] שער עמי ע[ד ירושלם
[...]4 [פשרו על מורה הצדק אשר י[דין אויבי]ו ...   5 [...]. יבגוד [...]
6 [...]...[...]

1Q14

1Q14 (1QpMic) *1QPesher to Micah*

Bibliography: J. Carmignac, 'Notes sur les Peshârîm', *RevQ* 3/12 (1962) 505-538; M. Horgan, *Pesharim: Qumran Interpretations of Biblical Books* (Washington, D.C.: Catholic Biblical Association, 1979) 55-63. Part I. Texts, 10-12; É. Puech, *La Croyance des Esséniens en la Vie Future: Immortalité, Résurrection, Vie éternelle?*, vol. 2 (Paris: Gabalda, 1993) 599-600

Frags. 1 - 5   *1* [*Mic 1:2-5* ... the Lord Y]HWH [will b]e *2* [a witness] against you, [the Lord, from his holy temple. For beho]ld, YH[WH leaves] his place *3* [and descends upon the he]ights of the ear[th. The mountain]s benea[th him] melt, [and the valleys sp]lit apart, *4* [like w]ax befo[re the fi]re, like [water poured down a slope.] All [because of Jaco]b's [crime,] *5* because of the si[ns of the House of Israel ...]

Frag. 6   *1* [...] ... [...] *2* [... in the] last [days ...] *3* [...] ... his glory [...] *4* [... wh]o have trespassed [...]

Frag. 7   *1* [...] ... [...] *2* [...] is not [...] *3* [...] the simple [...] *4-5* [...] ... [...]

Frags. 8 - 10   *3* [... *Mic 1:5-6* What are the high places of Judah? Is it not Je]rusa[lem? I will reduce Samaria *4* [to a country ruin, to a plot of vines. *Blank*] Its interpretation concerns the Spreader of the Lie *5* [who has misdirected the] simple. *Blank Mic 1:5* What are the high places of Judah? *6* [Is it not Jerusalem? Its interpretation con]cerns the Teacher of Righteousness who *7* [teaches the law to] his [council] and to a[l]l those volunteering to join the chosen of *8* [God, observing the law] in the council of the Community, those who will be saved from the day of *9* [judgment ...] ... [...] *10* [... As for what he says: *Mic 1:6-7* I will reduce Samaria to] a country ruin *11* [...] ... [...]

Frag. 11   *1* [*Mic 1:8* and I will wail. Its interpretation concerns the priests of Jeru]sa[le]m, who misdirect [...] *2* [...] his enemies. *Blank Mic 1:8-9* Barefoot and na[ked, ...] *3* [... has reached as] far as the gate of my people, as far [as Jerusalem...] *4* [Its interpretation concerns the Teacher of Righteousness, who will] judge [his] enemies [...] *5* [...] he will act treacherously [...] *6* [...] ... [...]

Frag. 12 1 [...]...[...] 2 [...]... כבודו משעיר] ... [3 ...] כי[א יצא

ᴸ╤ מ][...] 4 [...]...[...]

Frags. 17-18 1 [... בקרבכ]ה ותשוג] ולוא תפלט ואשר] 2 [תפלט

לחרב אתן אתה תזרע ולוא [תקצור את]ה תדרוך זית] 3 [ולוא תסוך שמן

ותירוש ולו[א תשתה] י]ין וי[שתמר חוקות עומרי] 4 [וכול מעשה בית

אחאב ותל]כו במועצותם ל[מען תתי אותך לשמה] 5 [וישביה לשרקה

פשרו] על הדור ה[א]חרו]ן [...] 6 [...]...[...]

1QpHab *1QPesher to Habakkuk*

M. Burrows, *DSSSMM I*, pl. LV-LVI
SHR 7201-7214
SHR
Bibliography: K. Elliger, *Studien zum Habakuk-Kommentar vom Toten Meer* (Tübingen: J.C.B. Mohr, 1953); W.H. Brownlee, *The Text of Habakkuk in the Ancient Commentary from Qumran* (Philadelphia, Pa, 1959); W.H. Brownlee,

Col. I 1 [המשא אשר חזה חבקוק הנביא עד אנה ק╤ו ╡ שועתי ולוא

2 [תשמע אזעק אליך חמס ולוא תושיע פשרו על תו]חלת דור [... 3

הבא]ות עליהם 4 [... יז]עקו על 5 [... למה תראני און וע]מל תביט

vacat 6 [פשרו ...] אל בעשק ומעל 7 [ושוד וחמס לנגדי ויהי ריב ומדון

ישא] *vacat* 8 [פשרו ...] וגז]י]לי ה]...[.[...]. וריב 9 [... מ]ריבה וח]שב]ו

הואה 10 [...] על כן תפוג תורה 11 [פשרו ...] אשר מאשו בתורת אל

12 [ולוא יצא לנצח משפט כיא רשע מכתי]ר את הצדיק *vacat* 13 [פשרו

הרשע הוא הכוהן הרשע והצדי]ק] הוא מורה הצדק 14 [... ע]ל כן יצא

המשפט 15 [מעוקל פשרו ...] ולוא מ]...[16 [... ראו בוגדים והביטו]

17 [והתמהו תמהו כיא פעל פועל בימיכם לוא תאמינו כיא]

Frag. 12   *1* […] *2* […] his glory from Seir […] *3* [… becau]se God will go out from […] *4* […] … […]

Frags. 17 - 18   *1* [… *Mic 6:14-15* in you]r [midst;] you shall turn away, [but not escape; and whoever] *2* [escapes, I will turn over to the sword. You shall sow and not] reap, yo[u shall tread olives] *3* [and not anoint yourself, tread grapes and no]t drink [w]ine. [The laws of Omri] are [kept] *4* [and all the procedures of the House of Ahab; you beha]ve according to their counsels; t[hus I shall destroy you] *5* [and hand over its inhabitants to insult. Its interpretation] concerns the [l]ast generation […] *6* […] … […]

1QpHab *1QPesher to Habakkuk*

The Midrash Pesher of Habakkuk (Missoula, Mont.: Scholars Press, 1979); M. Horgan, *Pesharim: Qumran Interpretations of Biblical Books* (Washington, D.C.: Catholic Biblical Association, 1979) 1-55; Part I: Texts, 1-9; B. Nitzan, *Pesher Habakkuk: A Scroll from the Wilderness of Judaea (1QpHab)* (Jerusalem: Bialik, 1986) [Hebrew]

Col. 1   *1* [*Hab 1:1-2* Oracle received by the prophet Habakkuk in a vision. For how long, YHWH] do I ask for help without *2* [you hearing (me); do I shout: Violence! to you without you saving (me)? The interpretation of this concerns the beg]inning of the generation *3* [… which will com]e upon them *4* […they] will [sh]out against *5* [… *Hab 1:3a* Why do you show me misdeeds and] do you behold [to]il? *Blank* *6* [The interpretation of this … of] God with persecution and betrayal. *7* [*Hab 1:3b* You set destruction and violence in front of me and brawls occur and quarrels arise]. *Blank* *8* [The interpretation of this …] ro[bbe]ry of […] and brawls *9* [… ar]gument and they th[ink] destruction *10* […] *Hab 1:4a* For the Law falls into abeyance. *11* [The interpretation of this …] that they have rejected the Law of God. *12* [*Hab 1:4bc* And justice does not emerge as the winner, for the evildoer accos]ts the upright man. *Blank 13* [Its interpretation: the evildoer is the Wicked Priest and the upright man] is the Teacher of Righteousness *14* [… *Hab 1:4d* This] is why justice emerges *15* [distorted. The interpretation of this …] and not […] *16* [… *Hab 1:5* Look, traitors, and behold,] *17* [be astonished, shocked, for in your time a work is done which you would not believe if]

Col. II 1 vacat ‏[... פשר הדבר על]הבוגדים עם איש 2 הכזב
כי לוא[האמינו בדברי] מורה ‏הצדקה מפיא 3 אל ועל הבוג[דים בברית
‏[החדשה כ]י[א לוא 4 האמינו בברית אל [ויחללו] את ש[ם]קודשו 5 וכן
vacat פשר הדבר] על הבו[ג]דים לאחרית <א> 6 הימים המה עריצ[י
הבר]ית אשר לוא יאמינוא 7 בשומעם את כול הבא[ות ע]ל הדור האחרון
מפי 8 הכוהן אשר נתן אל ב[תוך העד]ה לפשור את כול 9 דברי עבדיו
הנביאים[אשר]בידם ספר אל את 10 כול הבאות על עמו יש[ראל]כיא
הנני מקים את 11 הכשדאים הגוי המר[והנמ]הר vacat 12 פשרו על
הכתיאים א[שר המ]ה קלים וגבורים 13 במלחמה לאבד רבים[...]
בממשלת 14 הכתיאים ירש[ו]ארצות רבו[ת ולוא יאמינו 15 בחוקי]
א[ל ...] ההולך למרחבי ארץ] 16 ל[רשת משכנות לוא לו פשרו ...]
17 [...]

Col. III 1 ובמישור ילכו לכות ולבוז את ערי הארץ 2 כיא הוא אשר
אמר לרשת משכנות לוא לו איום 3 ונורא הוא ממנו משפטו ושאתו יצא
vacat 4 פשרו על הכתיאים אשר פחדם ואמת‏ᵐ על כול 5 ‏הגואים ובעצה
כול מחשבתם להרע ובנכל ומרמה 6 ילכו עם כול העמים וקול (וקלו)
מנמרים סוסו וחדו 7 מ‏ᵓאבי ערב vacat פשו ופרשו פרשו מרחוק 8 יעופו
כנשר חש לאכול כול[ו] לחמס יבוא מגמת 9 פניהם קדים vacat פ[שר]ו על
הכתיאים אשר 10 ידושו את הארץ בסוס[יהם] ובבהמתם וממרחק
11 יבואו מאיי הים לאכול[את]כול העמים כנשר 12 ואין שבעה ובחמה
יכ[מרו וב]חרן אף וזעף 13 אפים ידברו עם כול[העמים כי]א הוא אשר
14 אמר מגמ[ת פניה]ם קדים ויאסוף כח[ול שבי 15 [פש]רו ...] 16 [...]
17 [... והוא במלכים]

Col. IV 1 יקלס ורזנים משחק לו vacat פשרו אשר 2 ילעיגו על
רבים ובזו על נכבדים במלכים 3 ושרים יתעתעו וקלסו בעם רב והוא
4 לכול מבצר ישחק ו‏ᵓצבור עפר וילכדהו 5 פשרו על מושלי הכתיאים
אשר יבזו על 6 מבצרי העמים ובלעג ישח[ו]קו עליהם 7 ובעם רב

12

Col. II   *1* it was reported. *Blank* [… The interpretation of the word concerns] the traitors with the Man of *2* the Lie, since they do not [believe in the words of] the Teacher of Righteousness from the mouth of *3* God; and (it concerns) the traito[rs of the] new [covenant] si[n]ce they did not *4* believe in the covenant of God [and dishonoured] his holy na[me]. *5* Likewise: *Blank* The interpretation of the word [concerns the trai]tors in the last *6* days. They are violator[s of the coven]ant who will not believe *7* when they hear all that is going [to happen t]o the final generation, from the mouth of *8* the Priest whom God has placed wi[thin the Commun]ity, to foretell the fulfilment of all *9* the words of his servants, the prophets, [by] means of whom God has declared *10* all that is going to happen to his people Is[rael]. *Hab 1:6* For see, I will mobilize *11* the Chaldaeans, a cruel [and deter]mined people. *Blank 12* Its interpretation concerns the Kittim, wh[o ar]e swift and powerful *13* in battle, to slay many [...] in the kingdom of *14* the Kittim; they will take possession [of many countries] and will not believe *15* in the precepts of [Go]d [... *Hab 1:6* They go across the earth] *16* to [take possession of dwellings not theirs. Its interpretation …] *17* [...]

Col. III   *1* and they will advance over the plain, to destroy and pillage the cities of the country. *2* For this is what he has said: *Hab 1:6* « To take possession of dwellings not theirs ». *Hab 1:7* It is dreadful *3* and terrible; his judgment and his exaltation arise from himself. *Blank 4* Its interpretation concerns the Kittim, the fear and dread of whom are on all *5* /the peoples;/ all their thoughts are premeditated to do evil, and with cunning and treachery *6* they behave towards all the nations. *Hab 1:8* Their horses are swifter than panthers; they are keener *7* than wolves at night. *Blank* Their war-horses paw the ground, galop, from afar *8* they come flying like an eagle, hastening to eat. *Hab 1:9* All of them come to use violence; the breath of *9* their faces is like the East wind. *Blank* Its inter[pretation] concerns the Kittim, who *10* trample the land with [their] horse[s] and their animals *11* and come from far off, from the islands of the sea, to devour all the nations, like an eagle, *12* insatiable. With fury they are he[ated, and with] burning wrath and livid *13* faces they will speak to all [the nations. Fo]r this is what *14* he has said: *Hab 1:9* The brea[th of their faces is like the East wind. And he gathers] captives [like sa]nd. *15* Its [interpreta]tion [...] *16* [...] *17* [... *Hab 1:10a* At kings]

Col. IV   *1* it sneers and leaders it mocks. *Blank* Its interpretation: *2* they deride the powerful and despise the honoured men; at kings *3* and princes they jeer, and sneer at a huge army. *Hab 1:10b* And he *4* laughs at every strong fortress, piles up earth and captures it. *5* The interpretation of this concerns the leaders of the Kittim, who despise the *6* fortresses of the peoples and with derision laugh at them, *7* they surround them with a huge army to capture them. And through

יקיפום לתפושם ובאמה ובפחד   8   ינתנו בידם והרסום בעוון היושבים
9 בהם אז חלף רוח ויעבר וישם זה כוחו   10   לאלוהו *vacat* פשרו על[ע]ל
מושלי הכתיאים   11   אשר בעצת בית האשמ[ים]יעבורו איש   12   מלפני
רעהו מושלי[הם ז]ה אחר זה יבואו   13   לשחית את הא[רץ וישם]זה כוחו
לאלוהו   14   פרשו[... כו]ל העמים   15   ל[...]   16   [... הלוא אתה]
17 [מקדם ⊐וⴲ⊐ אלוהי קודשי לוא נמות ⊐וⴲ⊐]

1   *Col.* v   למשפט שמתו וצור למוכיחו יסדתו טהור ע[ינים   2   מראות
ברע והבט אל עמל לוא תוכל *vacat*   3   פשר הדבר אשר לוא יכלה אל את
עמו ביד הגוים   4   וביד בחירו יתן אל את משפט כול הגוים ובתוכחתם
5   יאשמו כל רשעי עמו אשר שמרו את מצוותו   6   בצר למו כיא הוא אשר
אמר טהור עינים מראות   7   ברע *vacat* פשרו אשר לוא זנו אחר עיניהם
בקץ   8   הרשעה למה תביטו בוגדים ותחריש בבלע   9   רשע צדיק ממנו
vacat   פשרו על בית אבשלום   10   ואנשי עצתם אשר נדמו בתוכחת מורה
הצדק   11   ולוא עזרוהו על איש הכזב *vacat* אשר מאס את   12   התורה
בתוך כול עצתם ותעש אדם כדגי הים   13   כרמש למשל בו כול[ה בח]כה
יעלה ויגרהו בחרמו   14   ויספהו במכ[מרתו על כן יזב]ח לחרמו על כן
ישמח   15   [ויגי]ל[ ]ויקטר למכמרתו כיא בהם] שמן חלקו   16   [ומאכלו ברי
[...]   17   [...

1   *Col.* vi   הכתיאים ויוסיפו את הונם עם כול שללם   2   כדגת הים
ואשר אמר על כן יזבח לחרמו   3   ויקטר למכמרתו *vacat* פשרו אשר המה
4   זבחים לאותותם וכלי מלחמותם המה   5   מוראם כיא בהם שמן חלקו
ומאכלם ברי   6   פשרו אשר המה מחלקים את עולם ואת   7   מסם מאכלם על
כול העמים שנה בשנה   8   לחריב ארצות רבות על כן יריק חרבו תמיד
9   להרוג גוים ולוא יחמל   10   *vacat* פשרו על הכתיאים אשר יאבדו רבים
בחרב   11   נערים אשישים וזקנים נשים וטף ועל פרי   12   בטן לוא ירחמו
על משמרתי אעמודה   13   ואתיצבה על מצורי ואצפה לראות מה ידבר

dread and fear *8* they surrender to their hands, and they demolish them because of the wickedness of those who dwell *9* in them. *Hab 1:11* Then the wind changes and goes on; and this one has made his might *10* his God. *Blank* Its interpretation [con]cerns the leaders of the Kittim, *11* who on the advice of a house of guilty [people] go by, one *12* before the other. [Their] leaders, [o]ne after another, will come *13* to raze the ea[rth. *Hab 1:11* And] this one [has made] his might his God. *14* Its interpretation [... al]l the nations *15* [...] *16* [... *Hab 1:12-13a* Are you not] *17* [from of old, YHWH my holy God. We will not die. YHWH,]

Col. V *1* you have appointed him to judge; Rock, you have installed him to rebuke him. Your eyes are too pure *2* to look at evil, you can not stare at calamity. *Blank 3* The interpretation of the word: God is not to destroy his nation at the hand of the peoples, *4* but in the hand of his chosen ones God will place the judgment over all the peoples; and by their reproof *5* all the evildoers of his people will be pronounced guilty, (by the reproof) of those who kept his commandments *6* in their hardship. For this is what he has said: *Hab 1:13a* «Your eyes are too pure to look *7* at evil». *Blank* Its interpretation: they have not run after the desire of their eyes in the era of *8* wickedness. *Hab 1:13b* Why do you stare, traitors, and remain silent when *9* a wicked person consumes someone more upright than himself? *Blank* Its interpretation concerns the House of Absalom *10* and the members of their council, who kept silent when the Teacher of Righteousness was rebuked, *11* and did not help him against the Man of the Lie, *Blank* who rejected *12* the Law in the midst of their whole Council. *Hab 1:14-16* You made man like fish of the sea, *13* like a reptile, to rule over it. All of [them] he hauls up [with a fish]-hook, catches in his net *14* and gathers in [his] tr[awl. This is why he offers sacri]fices to his net; this is why he rejoices *15* [and is hap]py [and burns incense to his trawl; since by them] his portion is fat *16* [and his food rich ...] *17* [...]

Col. VI *1* of the Kittim, and they gather their wealth with all their loot *2* like fish of the sea. And what it says: *Hab 1:16a* This is why he offers sacrifices to his net *3* and burns incense to his trawl. *Blank* Its interpretation: they *4* offer sacrifices to their standards and their weapons are *5* the object of their worship. *Hab 1:16b* Since by them his portion is fat and his food rich. *6* Its interpretation: they distribute their yoke and *7* their burden, which is their food, among all the peoples, year after year, *8* ravaging many countries. *Hab 1:17* For this he continually unsheathes his sword *9* to kill peoples without pity. *Blank 10* Its interpretation concerns the Kittim who will cause many to die by the edge of the sword, *11* youths, adults and old people, women and children; not even *12* children at the breast will they pity. *Hab 2:1-2* I will stand firm in my sentry-post, *13* I will position myself in my fortress, and I will look out to see what he

14 בי ומה] ישיב ע[ל תוכחתי ויענני 𐤉𐤅𐤄𐤉 15 [ויומר כתוב חזון ובא]ר על
הלוחות למען ירוץ 16 [הקורא בו ...]...[... 17 [...]

Col. VII 1 וידבר אל ᵃˡ חבקוק לכתוב את הבאות על <על> הדור 2
האחרון ואת גמר הקץ לוא הודיעו 3 *vacat* ואשר אמר למען ירוץ הקורא בו
4 פשרו על מורה הצדק אשר הודיעו אל את 5 כול רזי דברי עבדיו
הנבאים כיא עוד חזון 6 למועד יפיח לקץ ולוא יכזב *vacat* 7 פשרו אשר
יארוך הקץ האחרון ויתר על כול 8 אשר דברו הנביאים כיא רזי אל
להפלה 9 אם יתמהמה חכה לו כיא בוא יבוא ולוא 10 יאחר *vacat* פשרו
על אנשי האמת 11 עושי התורה אשר לוא ירפו ידיהם מעבודת 12 האמת
בהמשך עליהם הקץ האחרון כיא 13 כול קיצי אל יבואו לתכונם כאשר
חקק 14 להם ברזי ערמתו הנה עופלה לוא יושרה 15 [נפשו בו *vacat*
פשרו אשר יכפלו עליהם 16 ...] ו[ל]וא [ירצו במשפטם ...] 17 [...]
וצדיק באמונתו יחיה]

Col. VIII 1 פשרו על כול עושי התורה בבית יהודה אשר 2 יצילם אל
מבית המשפט בעבור עמלם ואמנתם 3 במורה הצדק ואף כיא הון יבגוד
גבר יהיר ולוא 4 ינוה אשר הרחיב כשאול נפשו והוא כמות לוא ישבע
5 ויאספו אלו כול הגוים ויקבצו אלו כול העמים 6 הלוא כולם משל עליו
ישאו ומליצי חידות לו 7 ויומרו הוי המרבה ולוא לו עד מתי יכביד עלו
8 עבטט *vacat* פשרו על הכוהן הרשע אשר 9 נקרא על שם האמת בתחלת
עומדו וכאשר משל 10 בישראל רם לבו ויעזוב את אל ויבגוד בחוקים
בעבור 11 הון ויגזול ויקבוץ הון אנשי חמס אשר מרדו באל 12 והון
עמים לקח לוסיף עליו עון אשמה ודרכי 13 ת[וע]בות פעל בכול נדת
טמאה הלוא פתן] אום ויקומו 14 {ו}{נ}[ש]כיך ויקיצו מזעזעיכה והיתה
למשיסות למו 15 כי אתה שלותה גוים רבים וישלוכה כול יתר עמים
16 *vacat* פ]שר הדבר [על הכוהן אשר מרד 17 [...].ר חוקי[ן אל ...]...[...]

says *14* to me, and what [he answers t]o my reproof. YHWH answered me *15* [and said: Write the vision; inscr]ibe it on tablets so that may run *16* [the one who reads it …] … […] *17* […]

Col. VII *1* And God told Habakkuk to write what was going to happen to *2* <to> the last generation, but he did not let him know the consummation of the era. *3 Blank* And as for what he says: *Hab 2:2* «So that /may run/ the one who reads it». *4* Its interpretation concerns the Teacher of Righteousness, to whom God has made known *5* all the mysteries of the words of his servants, the prophets. *Hab 2:3* For the vision has an appointed *6* time, it will have an end and not fail. *Blank 7* Its interpretation: the final age will be extended and go beyond all that *8* the prophets say, because the mysteries of God are wonderful. *9 Hab 2:3b* Though it might tarry, wait for it; it definitely has to come and will not *10* delay. *Blank* Its interpretation concerns the men of truth, *11* those who observe the Law, whose hands will not desert the service *12* of truth when the final age is extended beyond them, because *13* all the ages of God will come at the right time, as he established *14* for them in the mysteries of his prudence. *Hab 2:4* See, it is conceited and does not give way *15* [his soul within him.] *Blank* Its interpretation: they will double upon them *16* [… and] find [no] mercy at being judged. […] *17* [… *Hab 2:4b* But the righteous man will live because of their loyalty to him.]

Col. VIII *1* Its interpretation concerns all observing the Law in the House of Judah, whom *2* God will free from the house of judgment on account of their toil and of their loyalty *3* to the Teacher of Righteousness. *Hab 2:5-6* Surely wealth will corrupt the boaster, and not *4* will he last, he who widens his throat like the abyss, and he, like death can not be satisfied. *5* All the peoples ally against him, all the nations come together against him. *6* Are they not all going to chant verses against him, explaining riddles at his expense? *7* They shall say: Ah, one who amasses the wealth of others! How long will he load himself *8* with debts? *Blank* Its interpretation concerns the Wicked Priest, who *9* was called loyal at the start of his office. However, when he ruled *10* over Israel his heart became proud, he deserted God and betrayed the laws for the sake of *11* riches. And he robbed and hoarded wealth from the violent men who had rebelled against God. *12* And he seized public money, incurring additional serious sin. *13* And he performed re[pul]sive acts by every type of defiling impurity. *Hab 2:7-8* Will not suddenly *14* your cre[di]tors get up, and those who shake you wake up? You will be their prey. *15* Since you pillaged many peoples all the rest of the nations will pillage you. *16 Blank* The in[terpretation of the word] concerns the Priest who rebelled *17* […] the precepts of [God …] … […]

Col. IX 1 נגועו במשפטי רשעה ושערוריות מחלים 2 רעים עשו בו
ונקמות בגוית בשרו ואשר 3 אמר כי אתה שלותה גוים רבים וישלוכה כול
4 יתר עמים *vacat* פשרו על כוהני ירושלם 5 האחרונים אשר יקבוצו הון
ובצע משלל העמים 6 ולאחרית הימים ינתן הונם עם שללם ביד 7 חיל
הכתיאים *vacat* כיא המה יתר העמים 8 מדמי אדם וחמס ארץ קריה וכול
יושבי בה *vacat* 9 פשרו על הכוהן ה[ר]שע אשר בעוון מורה 10 הצדק
ואנשי עצתו נתנו אל ביד אויביו לענ'תו 11 בנגע לכלה במרורי נפש
בעבור א[שר הרשיע 12 על בחירו הוי הבוצע בצע רע לביתו לשום
13 במרום קנו לנצל מכף רע יעצתה בשת 14 לביתכה קצוות עמים רבים
וחוטי[ן נפ]שכה כיא 15 אב[ן]מקיר תזעק [ו]כפיס מעץ יע[נ]נה [...]
16 [פשר הדב]ר על הכ[והן] אשר .[...] 17 [...]...[...]

Col. X 1 להיות אבניה בעשק וכפיס ע'צה (עצ'ה) בגזל ואשר 2 אמר
קצוות עמים רבים וחוטי נפשכה *vacat* 3 פשרו הוא בית המשפט אשר יתן
אל את 4 משפטו בתוך עמים רבים ומשם יעלנו למשפט 5 ובתוכם
ירשיענו ובאש גופרית ישפטנו הוי 6 בונה עיר בדמים ויכונן קריה בעולה
הלוא 7 הנה מעם ⊐ו⊐⋷ צבאות יגעו עמים בדי אש 8 ולאומים בדי ריק
ייעפו *vacat* 9 פשר הדבר על מטיף הכזב אשר התעה רבים
10 לבנות עיר שוו בדמים ולקים עדה בשקר 11 בעבור כבודה לוגיע
רבים בעבודת שוו ולהרותם 12 במ[ע]שי שקר להיות עמלם לריק בעבור
יבואו 13 למשפטי אש אשר גדפו ויחרפו את בחירי אל 14 כיא תמלא
הארץ לדעת את כבוד ⊐ו⊐⋷ כמים 15 יכסו על הים *vacat* פשר הדבר]
אש]ר 16 בשובם [...] 17 [...]

Col. XI 1 הכזב ואחר תגלה להם הדעת כמי 2 היים לרב הוי משקה
רעיהו מספח 3 חמתו אף שכר למען הבט אל מועדיהם *vacat* 4 פשרו על
הכוהן הרשע אשר 5 רדף אחר מורה הצדק לבלעו בכעס 6 חמתו אבית
גלותו ובקץ מועד מנוחת 7 יום הכפורים הופיע אליהם לבלעם

18

Col. IX   *1* afflicting him with the punishments of sin; the horrors of *2* terrifying maladies they have acted upon him, as well as vengeful acts on his fleshly body. And what *3* it says: *Hab 2:8a* «Since you pillaged many peoples all the *4* rest of the nations will pillage you». *Blank* Its interpretation concerns the last priests of Jerusalem, *5* who will accumulate riches and loot from plundering the nations. *6* However, in the last days their riches and their loot will be given into the hands *7* of the army of the Kittim. *Blank* For they are *Hab 2:8a* «the rest of the nations». *8 Hab 2:8b* For the human blood (spilt) and the violence (done) to the country, the city and all /who dwell/ in it. *Blank 9* Its interpretation concerns the [Wi]cked Priest, whom, for the wickedness against the Teacher of *10* Righteousness and the members of his council, God delivered into the hands of his enemies to disgrace him *11* with a punishment, to destroy him with bitterness of soul for having acted wickedly *12* against his elect. *Hab 2:9-11* Woe to anyone putting ill-gotten gains in his house, placing *13* his perch high up to escape the power of evil! You have planned things that will bring disgrace *14* to your house, destroying many nations and sinning against your [so]ul. For *15* the sto[ne] will shout from the wall, the wooden beam will an[swer ...] *16* [The interpretation of the wor]d concerns the pr[iest] who [...] *17* [...]

Col. X   *1* for its stones to be by oppression and the beam of its wood by pillage. And what *2* it says: *Hab 2:10* «Destroying many nations and sinning against your soul». *Blank 3* Its interpretation: it is the house of judgment, for God will give *4* his judgment among many nations and from there will lead him to punishment. *5* And in their midst he will proclaim him guilty and will punish him with sulphurous fire. *Hab 2:12-13* Woe *6* to him who builds a city with blood and founds a town on wickedness! Does *7* this not stem from YHWH of Hosts that the nations wear themselves out for fire *8* and the peoples are exhausted for nothing? *Blank 9* The interpretation of the word concerns the Spreader of the Lie, who has misdirected many, *10* building a useless city with blood and erecting a community with deceit *11* for his own glory, wearing out many by useless work and teaching them *12* a[c]ts of deceit, so that their labours are for nothing; so that *13* those who derided and insulted God's chosen will go to the punishment of fire. *14 Hab 2:14* For the earth will become full of the knowledge of YHWH's glory just as water *15* fills the sea. *Blank* The interpretation of the word: *16* in his return [...] *17* [...]

Col. XI   *1* the Lie. Afterwards, knowledge will be revealed to them, as plentiful as the water *2* in the sea. *Hab 2:15* Woe to anyone making his companion drunk, spilling out *3* his anger, or even making him drunk to look at their festivals! *4 Blank* Its interpretation concerns the Wicked Priest who *5* pursued the Teacher of Righteousness to consume him with the heat *6* of his anger in the place of his banishment. In festival time, during the rest *7* of the day of Atone-

8 ולכשילם ביום צום שבת מנוחתם שבעתה   9 קלון מ(כ)בוד שתה גם
אתה והרעל   10 תסוב עליכה כוס ימין 𐤉𐤄𐤅𐤄 וקיקלון   11 על כבודכה
12 *vacat* פשרו על הכוהן אשר גבר קלונו מכבודו   13 כיא לוא מל את
עורלת לבו וילך בדרכי   14 הרויה למען ספות הצמאה וכוס חמת   15 א[ל
תבלענו לוסיף] ... ק[ל]ל[ו]נו ומכאוב   16 [...]   17 [כיא חמס לבנון יכסכה
ושוד בהמות]

1 יחת(כ)ה מדמי אדם וחמס ארץ קריה וכול יושבי בה   *Col.* XII
2 פשר הדבר על הכוהן הרשע לשלם לו את   3 גמולו אשר גמל על אביונים
כיא הלבנון הוא   4 עצת היחד והבהמות המה פתאי יהודה עושה   5 התורה
אשר ישופטנו אל לכלה   6 *vacat* כאשר זמם לכלות אביונים ואשר אמר
מדמי   7 קריה וחמס ארץ פשרו הקריה היא ירושלם   8 אשר פעל בה
הכוהן הרשע מעשי תועבות ויטמא את   9 מקדש אל וחמס ארץ המה ערי
יהודה אשר   10 גזל הון אביונים מה הועיל פסל כיא פסל יצרו   11 מסיכה
ומרי שקר כיא בטח יצר יצריו עליהו   12 לעשות אלילים אלמים פשר
הדבר על כול   13 פסלי הגוים אשר יצרום לעובדם ולשתחות   14 להמה
והמה לוא יצילום ביום המשפט הוי   15 הו[י אומר]לעץ הקיצה ע[ורי
ל]א[בן דומם   16 [הוא יורה הנה הוא תפוש זהב וכסף וכול]   17 [רוח אין
בקרבו ו𐤉𐤄𐤅𐤄 בהיכל קודשו]

1 הס מלפניו כול ה(א)רץ פשרו על כול הגוים   2 אשר עבדו   *Col.* XIII
את האבן ואת העץ וביום   3 המשפט יכלה אל את כול עובדי העצבים
4 ואת הרשעים מן הארץ   *vacat*   5-15 *vacat*

1Q15 (1QpZeph) *1QPesher to Zephaniah*

J.T. Milik, *DJD I*, 80, pl. XV
PAM 40.497
BNP

20

ment, he appeared to them, to consume them *8* and make them fall on the day of fasting, the sabbath of their rest. *Hab 2:16* You are more glutted *9* with disgrace than with glory. Drink up also and stagger! *10* The cup of YHWH's right hand will turn against you and disgrace come *11* upon your glory. *Blank 12* Its interpretation concerns the Priest whose disgrace exceeded his glory *13* because he did not circumcise the foreskin of his heart and has walked on paths of *14* excessiveness to slake his thirst; but the cup of *15* [Go]d's anger will consume him, increasing […]his [dis]grace. And the pain *16* […] *17* [*Hab 2:17* For the violation of Lebanon will cover you, and the destruction of animals]

Col. XII   *1* will appal you, owing to the human blood and the violence (done to) the country, the city and all who dwell there. *2* The interpretation of the word concerns the Wicked Priest, to pay him the *3* reward for what he did to the poor. Because Lebanon is *4* the Council of the Community and the animals are the simple folk of Judah, those who observe *5* the Law. God will sentence him to destruction, *Blank 6* exactly as he intended to destroy the poor. And as for what he says: *Hab 2:17* «Owing to the blood *7* of the city and the violence (done to) the country». Its interpretation: the city is Jerusalem *8* in which the /Wicked/ Priest performed repulsive acts and defiled *9* the Sanctuary of God. The violence (done to) the country are the cities of Judah which *10* he plundered of the possessions of the poor. *Hab 2:18* What use is the sculpture which the craftsman carves, *11* (or) the cast effigy and sham oracle, in whom their craftsman trusts, *12* to make dumb idols? The interpretation of the word concerns all the *13* idols of the peoples which they made, to serve them and bow down *14* for them. But they will not save them on the day of Judgment. *Hab 2:19-20* Woe, *15* wo[e, to anyone saying] to wood: Wake up! and to a silent [st]one: G[et up!] *16* [Can it instruct? It is covered with gold and silver, but no] *17* [spirit at all is therein. But YHWH is in his holy Temple.]

Col. XIII   *1* Silence in his presence, all the world! Its interpretation concerns all the peoples *2* which serve stone and wood. However, on the day *3* of judgment God will destroy all the worshippers of idols, *4* and the wicked, from the earth. *Blank 5-15 Blank*

1Q15 (1QpZeph) *1QPesher to Zephaniah*

Bibliography: M. Horgan, *Pesharim: Qumran Interpretations of Biblical Books* (Washington, D.C.: Catholic Biblical Association, 1979) 63-65; Part I: Texts, 13

1 [... ובאש קנ]אתו תאכ[ל כול הארץ כיא כלה אך] 2 [נבהלה יעשה את
כול יוש[בי ה]א[רץ התקו[ש]ש[ו ו]ק[ושו הגוי לוא נכסף] 2a [בטרם לדת
חוק [כמץ עבר [י]ום 3 [בטרם לוא יבוא עליכ]ם חרון אף [זוֹזֵזֹ
4 [בטרם לוא יבוא עליכם יום א[ף זוֹזֵזֹ פשר [הדבר על ...] 5 [...] כול
יושבי] ארץ יהודה *vacat* אש[ר ...] 6 [...]ר [...]היו ל[...].

1Q16 (1QpPs) *1QPesher to Psalms*

J.T. Milik, *DJD I*, 81-82, pl. XV
PAM 40.436, 40.443, 40.478, 40.533, 40.540
BNP

Frags. 3-4 1 [...]...[...] 2 [...]...[...ב]...הכירו... [...] 3 [...]שמרו[...]
... מלכי צבאות ידו[דון ידודון ונות בית תחלק שלל] פשרו ב[ית היא ...
4 [...]...[...ת]פארת [...] 5 [...]. אשר יחלקו[ן ...] 6 [...]...[...]

Frag. 8 1 [...]...[...] 2 ... [בתוך עלמות תופפו]ת במקהלות ברכו
אלוה[ים יהוה ממקור] 3 [ישראל פשרו ... בר]כת המקו[ר] לברך את
[...].

Frag. 9 1 [מהיכלך על ירושלים לך יובילו מלכי]ם שי פשרו על כול
מ.[...]. 2 [...] לפניו בירושלים *vacat* גערת [חיית קנה] 3 [עדת אבירים
בעגלי עמים מתרפס ברצי]כסף פשרו חיית [קנה היא] 4 [... ה]כתיאים
ל[...]...[...] 5 [...]...[...].

1Q17 (1QJubᵃ) *1QJubilees*ᵃ

J.T. Milik, *DJD I*, 82-83, pl. XVI
PAM 40.540, 43.753
DAJ

22

1 [*Zeph 1:18* ... with the fire of] his [ze]al [all the earth] will be consu[med; because unquestionably he will cause the devastation,] *2* [the obliteration of all the inha]bitants of the [ea]rth. *Zeph 2:1-2* Ga[th]er together and hu[ddle up, people, without shame,] *2a* [before you scatter] like chaff which passes in one [d]ay *3* [before] the fire of the YHWH's wrath [overtakes you,] *4* [before the day of] Y]HWH's [wr]ath [overtakes you.] The interpretation of [the word concerns] *5* [... all the inhabitants of] the land of Judah, *Blank* since [...] *6* [...] will be ... [...]

1Q16 (1QpPs) *1QPesher to Psalms*

4Q171, 4Q173, 4Q173a
Bibliography: M. Horgan, *Pesharim*, 65-70; Part I: Texts, 13-15

Frags. 3 - 4 *1* [...] ... [...] *2* [...] ... they acknowledged ...[...] they observed [...] *3* [...] ... *Ps 68:13* the kings of the armies go fl[eeing, go fleeing; she who lives at home shares out the loot.] Its interpretation: the ho[me is ...] *4* [...] ... [the gr]andeur [...] *5* [...] which they share out [...] *6* [...] ... [...]

Frag. 8 *1* [...] ... [...] *2* [... *Ps 68:26-27* In the middle are the girls playing tambourin]es. Bless God in choirs, [YHWH the source of] *3* [Israel. Its interpretation ... the ble]ssing of the sour[ce] to bless ...[...]

Frag. 9 *1* [*Ps 68:30* On account of your temple at Jerusalem, kings bring] gifts [to you]. Its interpretation concerns all the ...[...] *2* [...] before him in Jerusalem. *Blank Ps 68:31* Rebuke the [beasts of the reedbed;] *3* [the herd of bulls are the calves of the nations, who proceed (?) with ingots (?) of] silver. Its interpretation: the beast of the [reedbed is] *4* [... the] Kittim for ...[...] *5* [...] ... [...]

1Q17 (1QJub^a) *1QJubilees^a*

1Q18, 2Q19, 2Q20, 3Q5, 4Q176a,b, 4Q216, 4Q217, 4Q218, 4Q219, 4Q220, 4Q221, 4Q222, 4Q223-4Q224, 4Q482?, 4Q483?, 11Q12
Bibliography: J.C. VanderKam, *Textual Studies*, 75-81

Frag. 1   1 [...] *vacat* [...]   2 [ויצא יעקוב מבאר שבע לל]כת חרן
באחד [שנה לשבוע השנית ביובל ארבעים]   3 [וארבעה ויבוא אל לוז
א]שר בהר היא בית אל] בראש החודש הראשון לשבוע]   4 [הזואת ויבוא
למק]ום] בער]ב ויט מן הדרך לימ]ה בלילה הזואת וילן שם]   5 [כיא
בא השמש ויק]ח מאבני המקום] הזה וישי]מנ]ה מראשותיו תחת העץ ...[
6 [... הואה] לבדו היה הול]ך ...[

1Q18 (1QJubᵇ) *1QJubilees*ᵇ

J.T. Milik, *DJD I*, 83-84, pl. XVI
PAM 40.540, 43.753
DAJ

Frags. 1-2   1 [... ע]מי על מותך *vacat* [...]   2 [ותבוא אל יצחק ותאמר
אליו אחת בקש]ה אב]ק]ש ממך השבע את עשו אשר ל]וא]   3 [ירע את
יעקב אחיו ולוא ירדפנו] באיבה כי י]וד]ע אתה את יצר עשו אשר הו]א]
4 [רע מנעוריו ואתה יודע כול אשר עש]ה מיום ל]כת אחיו י]עקב אל חרן
[עד היום]

1Q19 + 1Q19bis (1QNoah) *1QBook of Noah*

J.T. Milik, *DJD I*, 84-86, 152, pl. XVI; J.C. Trever, 'Completion of the Publi-
cation of Some Fragments from Qumran Cave I', *RevQ* 5 (1965) 334, pl. VII
PAM 40.476, 40.536, 43.753
DAJ (frag. 1, 3), Athanasius Samuel (frag. 2), ROC 647 (frag. 4-21)

Frag. 1   1 [...] וי]הי הוא]...[2 [...]ם גברו בארץ ו]...[3 [... כי
השחית כול בשר א]ת דרכו על הארץ] ...[4 [... תבוא צעק]תם לפני אל
[...] 5-6 [...]...[...]ו

Frag. 1 (= *Jub* 27:19-21)   *1* […] *Blank* […] *2* [And Jacob left Beersheba to g]o to Haran in the first [year of the second week of the forty-fourth jubilee] *3* [and reached Luz wh]ich is on the mountain - it is Bethel - [on the first (day) of the first month of this week.] *4* [And he reached the pl]ace [in the eve]ning and he moved off the path, to the rig[ht, that night and spent the night there,] *5* [because the sun had set. And he to]ok one of the stones of that place [and pla]ced [it as a pillow under the tree …] *6* [… for he] trav[elled] alone. […]

1Q18 (1QJub^b) *1QJubilees^b*

1Q17, 2Q19, 2Q20, 3Q5, 4Q176a,b, 4Q216, 4Q217, 4Q218, 4Q219, 4Q220, 4Q221, 4Q222, 4Q223-4Q224, 4Q482?, 4Q483?, 11Q12
Bibliography: J.C. VanderKam, *Textual Studies*, 81-88, 99

Frags. 1 - 2 (= *Jub* 35:8-10; 4Q223-224 *Unit* 2 1)   *1* [… wi]th me about your death. *Blank* […] *2* [And she fled to Isaac and said to him: One reque]st I a[s]k of you. Make Esau swear that *3* [he will] n[ot harm Jacob, his brother and that he will not persecute him] with enmity, for you k[no]w Esau's inclination which i[s] *4* [evil from his youth and you know all that he has do]ne from the day on which [his brother J]acob we[nt] to Haran [right till today.]

1Q19 + 1Q19bis (1QNoah) *1QBook of Noah*

Bibliography: K. Beyer, *ATTM*, 225-258; F. García Martínez, *Qumran and Apocalyptic. Studies on the Aramaic Texts from Qumran* (STDJ 9; Leiden: E.J. Brill, 1992) 24-44; L.T. Stuckenbruck, *The Book of Giants from Qumran* (TSAJ 62; Tübingen: J.C.B. Mohr, 1997) 219, 231-232

Frag. 1   *1* [… and] he [w]as […] *2* […] they increased in number upon the earth and […] *3* [… because all flesh had corrupted] its path on the earth […] *4* [… and] their [cry came] before God and […] *5-6* […] … […]

Frag. 2 1 [...] קדוש[י הש]מים [...] 2 [...] לאמר גלו מש[פטנו לפ]ני
עליון [...] 3 [...] ולא תחתך [...] 4 [...] רפ[א]ל וגבריאל [...] 5 [...]
אדון] אדונים וגב[ור גבורים ... [...] 6 [...] עלמי]ם [...]

Frag. 3 1 [...]...[...] 2 [...]... השתמ]מו ... [...] 3 ... ב]כור הולד כי
נכבדים [...] 4 [...]אביהו וכאשר ראה למך את[...] 5 [...] את חדרי
הבית כחדודי השמש [...] 6 [...]ל לבעת את [...] 7 [...]...[...]

Frag. 13 1 [...]. כי כבוד זוך .[...] לכבוד אל ב .[...] 2 [...] י]נשא
בהדר כבוד ותפארת[...] 3 [...]. יכבד בתוך [...]

1Q20 (1QapGen ar) *1QGenesis Apocryphon*

J.T. Milik, *DJD I*, 86-87, pl. XVII
PAM 43.753

Frag. 1 ı 1 [...]ם רגזך תתסך ותתקיים ומן הוא 2 [...]ם חמת רגזך
3 *vacat* [...]תיא וכביא ושפליא דאלין ... [...] 4 [...] וכען הא אניתי אסירין
5 [...]... 6 [...] *vacat* 7 ... [...]ק[דישא רבא 8 [...]...ודיא כול
9-10 [...]...

Frag. 1 ıı 1-2 ...[...] 3 יום .[...]... 4 כול ...[...] 5 ...[...]
6 ארעא ...[...] 7 עובדא די ...[...] 8 וביישתא למק...[...] 9-10 ...[...]

Frag. 2 1 [...]... 2 [...]... ומתמחין מן אחרהון ... 3 [...] *vacat*
4 [...]ין מת.תנין [...]... 5 [...]. קודם מרה עלמא *vacat* 6 [...]...[...]

Frag. 2   *1* [... Holy One]s of the hea[ven ...] *2* [... saying: Present] our [ca]se to [the Most High ...] *3* [...] and not under you [...] *4* [... Rapha]el and Gabriel [...] *5* [... Lord] of Lords and Migh[ty One of Mighty Ones ...] *6* [...] of the centuries [...]

Frag. 3   *1* [...] ... [...] *2* [...] ... were aston[ished ...] *3* [... (not like the children of men) the fir]st-born is born, but the glorious ones [...] *4* [...] his father, and when Lamech saw [...] *5* [...] the chambers of the house like the beams of the sun [...] *6* [...] to frighten the [...] *7* [...] ... [...]

Frag. 13   *1* [...] because the glory of your splendour [...] for the glory of God in [...] *2* [... he will] be exalted in the splendour of the glory and the beauty [...] *3* [...] he will be honoured in the midst of [...]

1Q20 (1QapGen ar) *1QGenesis Apocryphon*

DAJ

Frag. 1 col. I   *1* [...] of your anger is poured out and is established and who is he *2* [...] the fury of your anger. *Blank 3* [...] ... and those who have been wiped out and those who have fallen, bereft and ... *4* [...] and now, look, I have oppressed the prisoners *5* [...] ... *6* [...] *Blank 7* [...] the Great [H]oly One *8* [...] ... all *9-10* [...] ...

Frag. 1 col. II   *1-2* ... [...] *3* day of [...] *4* all ... [...] *5* ... [...] *6* land of ... [...] *7* the deed which ... [...] *8* and the evil for ... [...]

Frag. 2   *1* [...] ... *2* [...] ... and they were struck from behind ... *3* [...] *Blank 4* [...] ... [...] *5* [...] in front of the Lord of the Universe. *Blank. 6* [...] ... [...]

1QapGen ar *1QGenesis Apocryphon*

N. Avigad, Y. Yadin, *A Genesis Apocryhon. A Scroll from the Wilderness of Judaea* (Jerusalem: Magnes Press/Heikhal ha-Sefer, 1956); J.C. Greenfield, E. Qimron, 'The Genesis Apocryphon Col. XII', in T. Muraoka (ed.), *Studies in Qumran Aramaic* (Abr-Nahrain Supplement 3; Leuven: Peeters, 1992) 70-77; M. Morgenstern, E. Qimron, D. Sivan, 'The hitherto unpublished Columns of the Genesis Apocryphon', *Abr-Nahrain* 33 (1995) 30-54
SHR 3847-3865, 4444-4453, 7301-7322
SHR
Bibliography: E.Y. Kutscher, 'The Language of the 'Genesis Apocryphon': A Preliminary Study', *Scripta Hierosolymitana* 4 (1958) 1-35; J.A. Fitzmyer, *The*

Col. I   1 [...]... [...] 2 אף רז רשעא די ...[...] 3 ...[...] ...ועם נצבתא
4 ורזא די [...]... לא תדעון 5-9 [...]... 10 [...] מן קצת
24-11 [...]... 25 [...]... ולקלל לכול בשרא 26 [...]רה ובמשלהן לכון
שלה הוא 27 [...]לארעא ולמחת להא ... 28 [... לא יד]עין מא למעבד
אנשא לארעא 29 [...] להון עבד ואף לכול בשרא

Col. II   1 הא באדין חשבת בלבי די מן עירין הריאתא ומן קדישין
הריא ולנפיל[י]ן 2 ולבי עלי משתני על עולימא דנא *vacat* 3 באדין אנה
למך אתבהלת ועלת על בתאנוש אנתתי [ואמרת] 4 [הא] אנה מועד בעליא
במרה רבותא במלך כול ע[ולמים ... 5 [...]. בני שמין עד כולא בקושטא
תחויני הן[... 6 [...] תחויני ולא בכדבין הדא ...[...]. 7 במלך כול
עלמים עד בקושט עמי תמללין ולא בכדבין [...] 8 אדין בתאנוש אנתתי
בחלץ תקיף עמי מללת וב...[...]. 9 ואמרת יא אחי ויא מרי דכרלך על
עדינתי א...[...]. 10 בחום ענתא ונשמתי לגו נדנהא ואנה בקושט כולא
אחוינך [...] 11 [...]... שגי לבי עלי אדין אשתני *vacat* 12 וכדי חזת
בתאנוש אנתתי די אשתני אנפי עלי ...[...]. 13 באדין אנסת רוחהא ועמי
תמלל ולי תאמר יא מרי ויא אחי [דכרלך] 14 עדינתי יאמ̇י̇א̇ אנה לך
בקדישא רבא במלך שמ[י]א ...[...]. 15 די מנך זרעא דן ומנך הריונא דן
ומנך נצבת פריא[דן ... 16 ולא מן כול זר ולא מן כול עירין ולא מן כול

1QapGen ar *1QGenesis Apocryphon*

Genesis Apocryphon of Qumran Cave 1: A Commentary (Rome: Pontifical Biblical Institute Press, 1966, 1971²); J.A. Fitzmyer, D.J. Harrington, *MPAT*, 100-127; T. Muraoka, 'Notes on the Aramaic of the Genesis Apocryphon', *RevQ* 8/29 (1972) 7-51; K. Beyer, *ATTM*, 165-186; R.T. White, *The Qumran Genesis Apocryphon. A Review* (Sheffield: Sheffield Academic Press, 1988); R.C. Steiner, 'The Heading of the *Book of the Words of Noah* on a Fragment of the Genesis Apocryphon: New Light on a "Lost" Work', *DSD* 2 (1995) 66-71; M.J. Bernstein, 'Re-Arrangement, Anticipation and Harmonization as Exegetical Features in the Genesis Apocryphon', *DSD* 3 (1996) 37-57

Col. I   *1* […] … and with the planting *2* […] … moreover the mystery of evil which *3* […] … and the mystery which *4* […] … you do not know *5-9* […] … *10* […]   part of *11-24* […] … *25* […] … and to curse all flesh *26* […] … and when they are at ease, you will be safe *27* […] to the earth and to strike it … *28* [… they do not kn]ow what to do. Man to the earth *29* […] he does for them and also for all flesh

Col. II   *1* Behold, then, I thought in my heart that the conception was (the work) of the Watchers, and the pregnancy of the Holy Ones, and it belonged to the Nephil[in] *2* and my heart within me was upset on account of this boy. *Blank* *3* Then I, Lamech, was frightened and turned to Bitenosh, my wife, [and said:] *4* [Behold,] I adjure you by the Most High, by the Great Lord, by the King of all A[ges, …] *5* […] the sons of heaven, that you tell me in truth everything, whether […] *6* […] Tell me without lies whether this … […] *7* by the King of all Ages that you are speaking to me frankly and without lies […] *8* Then Bitenosh, my wife, spoke to me very harshly, and … […] *9* and said: Oh my brother and lord! Remember my sexual pleasure … […] *10* in the heat of intercourse, and the gasping of my breath in my breast. I shall tell you everything accurately […] *11* […] … very much my heart within me and I was still upset. *Blank* *12* When Bitenosh, my wife, realized that my countenance had altered … […] *13* then she suppressed her anger, speaking to me and saying to me: O my lord and brother! [Remember] *14* my sexual pleasure. I swear to you by the Great Holy One, by the King of the hea[ven]s … […] *15* that this seed comes from you, that this pregnancy comes from you, that the planting of [this] fruit comes from you, […] *16* and not from any foreigner nor from

בני שמ]ין למא צלם [17 אנפיך כדנא עליך שנא ושחת ורוחך כדן עליבא

[...] ארי אנה] 18 בקושט ממללא עמך [...] vacat 19 באדין אנה למך רטת

על מתושלח אבי וכולא לה חו]ית ... חנוך] 20 אבוהי וכולא מנה ביצבא

ינדע בדי הוא רחים ורעי] אלהא ועם קדישיא] 21 עדבה פליג ולה מחוין

כולא vacat וכדי שמע מתושל]ח פתגמיא אל]ן 22 רט לחנוך אבוהי למנדע

מנה כולא בקושטא ...[...] 23 רעותה ואזל לארקבת לפרוין ותמן אשכחה

לחנוך [אבוהי ...] 24 [ו]אמר לחנוך אבוהי יא אבי ויא מרי די אנה לך

את]ית ... [...] 25 [...]ואמר לך דאל תרגז עלי די להכא אתית ל[...]ך.[...]

26 דחיל לעליך [...] 27 [...]...

Col. v 1 וכתב [...] ...[vacat 2 ולך מתושלח ב]רי ... ל[די עולימא

3 דן הא כדי אנה חנוך ...[...] ו]ל]א [מן בני 4 שמין להן מן למך ברך [...]

5 ומדמא לא הווא [...] 6 ...[...] מן] 7 חזוה דחל למך ברך ... [...]

8 בקושט מהימן די ... vacat [...] 9 וכען לכ{א} אנה אמר ברי ולך אנה

מחוה ...[...] 10 אזל אמר ללמך ברך ...[...] 11 [.]מוהי בארעא וכול

עובד ...[...] 12 לאנפוהי נסבא בי ודנחא עינוהי כש]משא ...

13 עולימא דן נור והוא ל...[...] 15-14 ...[...] 16 הא באדין אשתבשון

...[...] 17 עלמא יהבין ...[...] 18 עבדין חמס שגי יעבדון עד די[...]

19 ... וכול שבילי ...[...] 20 וכען לך אנה מחוה ברז ...[...] 21 ברך

אחוי ברזא דנא ...[...] 22 ...[...] 23 מברך למרה כולא ...[...] 24 וכדי

שמע מתושלח ל]ו...[25 ועם למך ברה ברז מלל [...] 26 וכדי אנה למך

...[...] 27 די מני אנפיק ...[...] 28 vacat 29 [...] כתב מלי נוח[...]

30 [...]...[...]

Col. vi 1 מן עול ובכור הורתי יעית לקושט וכדי נפקת מן מעי אמי

לקושט נציבת 2 וקושטא כול יומי דברת והוית מהלך בשבילי אמת עלמא

ועמי קדי]ש...[...] 3 במסלי אוחת קושט ולאזהרותני מן נתיב שקר די אזלן

לחשוך [...] 4 ...[...]...[וחצי אסרת בחזין קושטא וחכמתא במעיל ...[...]

5 [...]כ]ול שבילי חמס vacat 6 ב]אדי]ן הוית אנה נוח גבר ואחדת בקושטא

ואתקפת ב...[...] 7 ... ולאמזרע ברתה לי לאנתה נסבת והרת מני וילדת

any of the watchers or sons of heav[en. Why is the expression] *17* of your face so changed and distorted, and your spirit so depressed? [... Behold I] *18* speak truthfully to you. *Blank* [...] *19* Then I, Lamech, /ran/ to my father, Methuselah, and to[ld] him everything, [... Enoch,] *20* his father and would know everything for certain from him, since he is the beloved and the favourite [of God, and with the holy ones] *21* his inheritance is found and they show him everything. *Blank* When Methusela[h] heard [these things] *22* [he ran] to Enoch, his father, in order to know everything reliably ... [...] *23* his will. And he left for the higher level, to Parvaim, and there he met Enoch, [his father ...] *24* He said to Enoch, his father: O my father and lord, to whom I have co[me ...] *25* [...] I say to you: Do not be annoyed with me because I came here to [...] you [...] *26* fear (?) before you ... [...] *27* ... [...]

Col. v *1* and he wrote ... [...] *2 Blank* And to you Methuselah [my] s[on ...] of this boy. *3* Behold, when I, Enoch ... [... and] n[ot] from the sons of *4* heaven but from Lamech your son [...] *5* and he does not resemble [...] *6* ... [...] *7* and Lamech your son is afraid of his appearance ... [...] *8* in veritable truth that ... *Blank 9* Now I tell you my son, and I let you know ... [...] *10* Go, tell Lamech, your son ... [...] *11* his [...] on the earth, and every deed ... [...] *12* his face has lifted to me and his eyes shine like [the] s[un ...] *13* (of) this boy is a flame and he ... [...] *14-15* ... [...] *16* then they were confounded ... [...] *17* eternal they give ... [...] *18* using enormous violence, they will do until [...] *19* ... and all the paths of ... [...] *20* And now, I make known to you the mystery of ... [...] *21* your son make known this mystery ... [...] *22* ... [...] *23* Praise the Lord of all ... [...] *24* When Methuselah heard [...] *25* and with Lamech, his son he spoke in secret [...] *26* When I, Lamech ... [...] *27* ... which he brought out of me ... [...] *28 Blank 29* [...] book of the words of Noah [...] *30* [...] ... [...]

Col. vi *1* from injustice, and in the crucible of her who was pregnant with me I burst forth for truth, and when I emerged from my mother's interior, I was planted for truth, *2* and all my life I behaved in truth, and walked in the paths of eternal verity, and with me the hol[y ...] *3* /on/ my tracks truth hastened, and to caution me against the path of falsehood which lead to darkness ... [...] *4* [...] ... and I girded my loins in the vision of truth and wisdom. In a robe (?) ... [...] *5* [...] all the paths of violence. *Blank 6* T[he]n I, Noah, became a man, and I held fast to truth and clung to ... [...] *7* ... and I married Amzara his

לי בנין ת[לת]ה[...] 8 ... לבני נשין נסבת מן בנת אחי ובנתי לבני אחי

יהבת כדת חוק עלמא 9 [...]ה עליא לבני אנשא *vacat* וביומי כדי שלמו לי

לחשבון די חשבת 10 [...]... יובלין עשרה באדין שלם לבני למסב להון

נשין ל... 11 [...] שמיא בחזיון חזית ואחואׁ[ת] ואודעת בעובד בני שמין ומא

כול 12 [...]... וטמרת רזא דן בלבבי ולכול אנוש לא אחויתה *vacat*

13 [...]... עלי בעירא רבא ׁעׁלי בציר ובמשלחת קדישא ... 14 [...]...

ובחזיון עמי מלל ולקובלי קם ... 15 [...]מ[שלחת קדישא רבא לי קל

אשמע לך אמרין יא נוח 16 [...] ... וחשבת בי כול לכת בני ארעא ידעת

וחוית כול[...] 17 [...]...קל יצלחון ... 18 [...] שבועין תרין ובאדין

מסתם ...[...] 19 [...] ... דמא די אשדו נפיליא שפית וקוית עׁד די ׁק[...]

20 [...] ... קדישין די עם בנת אנו[שא ... [...]...[...] 22-21

23 [...ואש]כחת אנה נוח חן [...]...[...] 25-24 [...] 26 ...[...]

לאנשא ולבעירא ולחיותא לעופא ו[...] 27 [...]...[...]

Col. VII 1 ...[...] עליהון ארעא וכול די עליהא בימיא ובטוריא

2 [...]...דא כול מזלת שמיא שמשא שהרא וכוכביא ועיריא 4-3 [...]...

5 [...]... אנה משלם לך 6 [...] *vacat* 7 [...] קדישא רבא וחדית למלי

מרה שמיא ואציחת 8-23 [...]...

Col. X 1 רבא *vacat* באדין ... כולא די בני מן [...]... 2 לנוח ...[...]

3 בליליא ...[...] 7-4 [...]...[...] 8 ... והללו ושבחו ... 9 ... כולכון למרכון

... 10 למלך כול עלמיא לעלם ולעד עד כול עלמים *vacat* 11 באדין ...

ונסב מן ... 12 [...]...תבותא נחת חד מן טורי הוררט ונור עלמא

13 [...]...]ועל כול ארעא כולהא כפרת ... 14 [...] ... לקדמין [...]...[...]...

ותרבא על נורא אקטרת ותניאנא ... 15 ... דמהון לׁׁאׁיסוד מדבחא ... וכול

בשרהון על מדבחא אקטרת ותליתי לבני שפנינא 16 ... על מדבחא קרבנא

...הון עליה יהבת סולת נשיפא פילא במשח עם לבונא למנחא 17 ...

בכלהון מלחא הוית יהב ורח מקטורתי ל[ש]מיא סלק *vacat* 18 באדין

עליא ...[...]

daughter, and she became pregnant from me and bore me th[ree] sons [...] *8* ... for my sons I took wives from my brother's daughters, and my daughters I gave to my brother's sons, according to the eternal law *9* [...] the Highest one to the sons of man. *Blank* And in my days, when there had been completed for me - according to the calculation that I calculated — *10* [...] ... ten jubilees, then my sons finished taking wives for themselves for ... *11* [...] the heavens. In a vision I saw, was shown and informed of the deed of the sons of heaven and how all *12* [...] ... and I hid this mystery in my heart and did not make it known to anyone. *Blank 13* [...] ... to me by a great watcher, /to/ me by a messenger, by an emissary of the Holy One ... *14* [...] ... and in visions he spoke to me, and he was standing before me ... *15* [... an e]missary of the Great Holy One called out to me: To you, o Noah, they say *16* [...] ... and I considered by myself all the behaviour of the sons of the earth, and I knew and demonstrated all [...] *17* [...] ... voice, they will succeed ... *18* [...] two weeks. And then sealed ... [...] *19* [...] ... the blood which the Nephilin spilled. And I waited /until/ [...] *20* [...] ... the holy ones with the daughters of m[en ...] *21-22* [...] ... [...] *23* [... and] I, Noah, [fou]nd grace ... [...] *24-25* [...] ... [...] *26* [...] ... to the people and the cattle, and to the beasts, to the birds and [...] *27* [...] ... [...]

Col. VII   *1* ... [...] upon them, the earth and all there is upon it, in the seas and on the mountains *2* [...] ... all the constellations of the heaven, the sun, the moon, and the stars. And the Watchers *3-4* [...] ... *5* [...] ... I will give to you *6* [...] *Blank 7* [...] the Great Holy One. And I was happy at the words of the Lord of the heavens and I cried out *8-23* [...] ...

Col. X   *1* great. *Blank* Then ... all of my sons from ... [...] *2* to Noah ... [...] *3* in the night ... [...] *4-7* ... [...] *8* ... and sang and praised ... *9* ... you all to your Lord ... *10* to the King of all ages, for ever and for all eternity, for all ages. *Blank 11* Then ... and he took from ... *12* ... [...] the ark settled [on] one of the mountains of Hurarat. And eternal fire *13* [...] I atoned for all the whole earth ... *14* [...] ... first ... [...] ... and I burned the fat on the fire, and secondly ... *15* ... their blood to the base of the altar ... and I burned all their flesh on the altar, and thirdly the turtledoves *16* ... on the altar, an offering ... on it I put fine flour mixed in oil together with frankincense, as a meal-offering *17* ... on all of them I placed salt, and the scent of my burnt-offering ascended to the [he]aven. *Blank 18* Then the Highest ... [...]

Col. XI   1 [...] אנה נוח הוית בתרע ת'בותא ...   2-10 [...]...[...]

12 ... [...] אדין אנ]ה נוח נפקת והלכת בארעא לאורכהא ולפותיהא 11
עליהא עדן בעליהון ובאנבהון וארעא כולהא מליא דתא ועשב ועבור אדין
ברכת למרה [...]... 13 לעלם הוא ולה תשבחתא ותבת וברכת די רחם על
ארעא ודי אעדי ואבד מנהא 14 כול עבדי חמסא ורשעא ושקרא ופלט ...
בדילה vacat 15 ... מלל עמי ולי אמר אל תדחל יא נוח עמך אנה ועם בניך
די להון כואתך לעלמים 16 ... ארעא ושלט בכולהון ...יהא ובמדבריהא
ובטוריהא ובכול די בהון והא אנה 17 יהב לך ולבניך כולא למאכל בירקא
ועשבא די ארעא ברם כול דם לא תאכלון אימתכון ודחלתכון 18-24
[...]...

Col. XII   1 [...] והואת לי לאת בעננה ולמ... 2 [...]...[...]...[...]
[א]רעא 3 [...] ... אתחזיאת לי 4-5 [...] 6 [...]. vacat 7 [...]
8 [...] ... בטורי הוררט ומן בתר כן נחתת לשפולי טורא דן אנה ובני ובני
בני [...] 9 ארו צדיתא הואת שגיא בארעא ויל]ידו [ל]... ב]נן מן בתר
מבולא [לשם ברי]רבא יליד לה בר לקדמין ארפכשד תרתין שנין בתר 10
מבולא [והוו]א כול בני שם כולהון 11 [עילם ואש]ור ארפכשד לוד וארם
ובנן נקבן חמש vacat ו]בני חם כוש ומצרי]ן ופוט וכנען ובנן 12 נקבן
שבע vacat ובנ]י] יפת גומר ומגוג ומדי ויוון ותובל ומשוך ותירס ובנן נקבן
ארבע vacat 13 [ו]שרית אנה ובני כולהון למפלח בארעא ונצבת כרם רב
בלובר טורא ולשנין ארבע עבד לי חמר ... vacat 14 ... כול ... וכדי ... רגלא
קדמיא ביום חד לרגלא קדמיא די בחודשא 15 [...]...[די כרמי כומרא דן
פתחת ושרית למשת'ה ביום חד לשתא חמישיתא 16 [...]... ביומא דן
קרית לבני ולבני בני ולנשי בני ולבנתהון ואתכנשנא כחדא ואזלנא
17 [...]...א והוית מברך למרה שמיא לאל עליון לקדישא רבא די פלטנא מן
אבדנא 18-35 [...]...[...]

Col. XIII   1-7 [...] 8 [...]... וחיות ברא ... ורחש יבישתא ...
9 [...] אבניא וחספיא הוא קצין ונסבין להון מנה חזה הוית לדהביא
ולכס]פי]א 10 [...] פרזלא ולאילניא כולהון קצין ונסבין להון מנה חזה

34

Col. XI   *1* [...] I, Noah, was in the door of the ark ... *2-10* [...] ... [...] *11* [Then I,] Noah went out and walked through the land, in its length and its breadth [...] *12* ... upon it; pleasure in their leaves and fruit. And all the land was filled with grass, herbs and grain. Then I praised the Lord of *13* [...] ... he is eternal, and he is entitled to praise. And I once more blessed because he had mercy on the earth and because he had removed and destroyed from it *14* all the workers of violence, wickedness and deceit, but has saved ... for his sake. *Blank 15* ... talked with me, and said to me: Do not be afraid, Noah, I am with you and with your sons, who will be like you, forever *16* ... of the earth, and rule over all of them, over its ... and its deserts and its mountains, and over all that is in them. And behold, I *17* give to you and your sons everything to eat of the vegetables and herbs of the earth, but you shall eat no blood of any kind. The fear and dread for you *18-24* [...] ...

Col. XII   *1* [...] ... [...] ... and it was for me a sign in the cloud and ... *2* [...] ... the [e]arth *3* [...] ... was revealed to me *4-5* [...]... *6* [...] *Blank 7* [...] ... *8* [...] ... in the mountains of Hurarat; afterwards I descended to the base of this mountain, I, my sons and my grandsons *9* [...] for desolation was great in the earth, and there were bo[rn] to [... daugh]ters after the flood. *10* [To Shem, my] oldest [son] was born first a son, Arpachsad, two years after the flood. [And these are] all the sons of Shem, all of them: *11* [Elam and Ash]ur, Arpachshad, Lud and Aram, and five daughters. *Blank* And [the sons of Ham: Cush, Mizrai]n, Put and Canaan and seven *12* daughters. *Blank* And the son[s of] Japhet: Gomer, Magog, Madai, Yavan, Tubal, Mosok, Tiras and four daughters. *Blank 13* I, and all my sons began to till the earth and I planted a huge vineyard on Mount Lubar and four years later it produced wine for me. *14* ... all ... *Blank* And when the first feast ..., on the first day of the first feast of the [...] month, *15* [...] ... of my vineyard; I opened this pitcher and began to drink it on the first day of the fifth year. *16* [...] ... On that day I called my sons, and my grandsons, and all our wives and their daughters and we got together and we went *17* [...] ... And I blessed the Lord of the Heavens, the God Most High, the Great Holy One, who saved us from destruction *18-35* [...] ... [...]

Col. XIII   *1-7* ... [...] *8* [...] ... and the wild beasts ... and the creeping creatures of the dry land ... *9* [...] stones and clay were cutting down, and taking from it for themselves. And I watched those of gold and sil[ver] *10* [...] iron, and they were cutting down all the trees, and taking of it for themselves. And I watched

הוית לשמשא ולשהרא   11 ולכוכביא קצין ונסבין להון מנה חזה הוית עד
די אסיפוהי שרץ ארעא ושרץ מיא וסף   12 מיא וסף   *vacat*   13 ואתפנית
למחזה זיתא וארו הא זיתא גבר ברומא ושען שגיאן ועוב עופיא שגיאן ...
אנ[ב]ין ברב   14 ... ומתחזה בהן מתבונך הוית בזיתא דן וארו הא משגית
עלוהי ...   15 ... קשרן בה והוית תמה על זיתא דן ועלוהי שגי לחדא תמהת
...   16 [ארבע רוחי שמיא נשבן בתקוף חבלא בזיתא דן ומענפן לה ויתברן
לה לקדמין ...   17 רוחא מערב וחבטתה ואתרת מן עלוהי ומן אנבה
ובדרתה לרוחיא ובתרה ...   34-18 [...]...

...

קאם ... רב ארזא הוא אנתה ושמע ...[...]   9 [...]...   8-1   Col. xiv
עד ואמא מנה נפקא די חלפא   10 [...]... טורים ראיש על בחלם לקובלך
ואעא ... ארזא בגדם דבקא קדמיתא לחלפתא   11 ... נ]י[ב תלתת רמה
... ש]מ[ך יתקרה ובזרעה מנך יפרש לא יומוהי כול   12 [...]...[...]... מנה
ודי לעלמים קאם ...[...]   14 [...] לכול קושט לנצבת יפוק   13 [...]...
לחלפתא חזיתה ודי   15 [...]... ארזא] ב]גד[ם ב דבקא לחלפתא חזיתא
... נ]י[ב תרין קדמיתא נוף בגו עלל נופהן קצת מן ...   16 ?*vacat*   [...]...
נוף בגו עלל נופהן קצת מן חזית ודי ... לשמאל ... [א]רעא מן ...[...]   17
...[...]   34-18   קדימיתא

...

משגיתהון יסורון ן[...] כולהון חזיתא ודי ...   9   [...]...   8-4   Col. xv
ונורא בידה מגלא ארעא ימין מן אתה לגברא   10 חזיתה ודי רשיעין להון
ירמי ורשעא[...   12 [...]... ארעא ימין מן יתה די הוא ...   11 ... עמה
חזיתה ודי   [...]... בין ויתה   13 [...] פש]... כול נורא על
[...]...[...]   22-15   [...] מלאכין ארבעא ...[...]...[...]   14

...

נהרא טינה עד מעין ראיש ביניהון מן די לשנה   9 [...]...   8-1   Col. xvi
תחומא [ו]עבר   11 ... ל דבק די עד כולהא צפונא ארע כול   10 ... בעין ...ו
ולבנוהי ליפת בעדב חלק   12 ... רא]לג[די דבק די עד רבא ימא מי דן
תניאנא עדבא נפק [ו]לשם   14   *vacat*   13   *vacat*   עלמים ירות למירת
נהרא ... 16   [...]...נהרא טינה מי ...[...]   15 ... ולבנוהי לה למירת

the sun and moon *11* and the stars cutting down and taking of it for themselves. And I watched until the creeping animals of the land and the creeping
animals of the waters had consumed it, and the waters were finished, *12* and it
was finished. *Blank 13* And I turned to watch the olive tree, and behold the olive
tree grew in height, and many hours (?), and a ramification of many leaves ...
14 and fr[uit]s in abundance ... and it appeared amongst them. I considered
this olive tree, and /behold/ the abundance of its leaves ... *15* ... they tied with
it. And I wondered greatly about this olive tree and its leaves, I wondered
immensely ... *16* [the four] winds of the heaven blowing with a destructive
strength against this olive tree, tearing off its branches, and breaking it. First
... *17* Western wind and struck it and shook off its leaves and fruit, and scattered it to the winds, and after it ... *18-34* [...] ...

Col. XIV   *1-8* [...] ... *9* [...] ... and hear: you are the great cedar ... standing
before you in a dream on the top of the mountains *10* [...] the willow that
emerges from it, and rises to a height: three s[on]s ... *11* ... the first willow,
joined to the stump of the cedar, ... and wood from it ... [...] *12* [...] ... all his
days he shall not depart from you, and by his progeny your na[me] shall be
called ... *13* [...] ... shall emerge for a righteous planting for all [...] *14* [...] ...
standing for always. And what you saw, the willow joined to the [stum]p of
[the cedar ...] *15* [...] ... and what you saw, the willow ... [...] *16 Blank?* ...
part of their branch entering in the branch of the first: two s[on]s ... *17* [...] ...
from the [ea]rth ... to the North ... and what you saw, part of their branch
entering in the branch of the first *18-34* [...] ...

Col. XV   *4-8* ... [...] *9* ... and what you saw, all of them [...] will pass, most of
them will be wicked. And what you saw, *10* the man coming from the South of
the land, with a sickle in his hand and fire with him ... *11* ... it is ... who come
from the South of the land [...] ... *12* [...] and wickedness. He will cast on the
fire all ... [...] *13* and he will come between ... and what you saw ... [...]
14 [...] ... [...] ... Four angels [...] *15-22* [...] ... [...]

Col. XVI   *1-8* [...] ... *9* the inlet which is between them, the riverhead until the
river Tina and ... *10* all the land of the North, all of it, until it reaches ...
11 [and] this area goes past the waters of the Great Sea until it reaches Ga[di]r
... *12* he apportioned in a lot for Japhet and his sons to inherit as an eternal
inheritance. *Blank 13 Blank 14* [And] for Shem emerged the second lot to inherit
for him and his sons ... *15* [...] ... the waters of the river Tina ... [...] *16* ... the

17 [ל]ים מלחא רבא ואזל תחומא דן כעין מן [...] [...] 18 [...] די פנה
למערב ועבר [...] 19 ... עד די דבק ל... 20 ... למדנחא 21-34 ...

Col. XVII 1-5 [...]... 6 [...]... *vacat* 7 [ו]שם פ[ל]ג [חו]לקה בין
בנוהי ונפל לקדמין ל[עי]ל[ם] בצפונא ליד מי חדקל נהרא עד דדבק לימא
8 ש[מו]קא לראישה די בצפונא וסחר למערבא לאשור עד דבק לחדקל ...
ובתרה 9 לארם ארעא די בין תרין נהריא עד די דבק לראיש ... 10 נפל
טור תורא דן ועבר חולקא ואזל מערבה עד דבק למגוג ... מדנחא
11 בצפונא די מחען לשנא דן דעל ראיש תלתת חולקיא ליד ימא דן
לארפכשד ... 12 ... די פנה לדרומא כול ארעא די משקה פורת וכול
[...]... 13 [...]... כול בקעאתא ומישריא די ביניהון ואיא די בגו לשנא
14 ... ואמנא ...[...]... 15 ... חולקא די פלג לה ויהב לה נוח אבוהי *vacat*
16 [ו]יפת פלג בין בנוהי לגמר יהב לקדמין בצפונא עד די דבק לטינה נהרא
ובתרה למגוג ובתרה 17 למדי וליון כול נגאותא דיליד לוד ובין
לשנא ... 18 [...]... ולמשך ...[...]... 19 [...]... בני חם ... *vacat*

Col. XIX 6 ...[...].[...]... 7 [...].[...]. וקרית תמן ב[שם [אל]הא]
ואמרת אנתה הוא 8 אל[הי א]ל[ה ע]ל[ה עד כען לא דבקתה]
לטורא קדישא ונגדת 9 ל... והוית אזל לדרומא ... ואתית עד די דבק
לחברון ול[ה זמנא] אתב[נ]יאת חברון ויתבת 10 [תרתין שנין ת]מן *vacat*
והוא כפנא בארעא דא כולא ושמעת די ע[בו]רא ה[וא] במצרין ונגדת
11 ל[מ]על לארע מצרין [...]...[...]... עד די דבק]ת לכרמונא נהרא חד מן
12 ראשי נהרא ...[...]... [כען אנחנא ... ארענא [וח]לפת שבעת ראשי נהרא דן
די ...[...]א 13 כען חלפנא ארענא ועלנא לארע בני חם לארע מצרין
14 *vacat* וחלמת אנה אברם חלם בלילה מעלי לארע מצרין וחזית בחלמי
[וה]א ארז חד ותמרא ... 15 חדא ...[...]... [וב]נ[י] אנוש אתו ובעון למקץ
ולמעקר ל[א]רזא ולמשבק תמר[ת]א בלחודיהה 16 ואכליאת תמרתא
ואמרת אל תקוצו ל[א]רזא ארי תרינא מן שרש...א ... ושביק ארזא בטלל
תמרתא 17 ולא [אתקץ] *vacat* ואתעירת בליליא מן שנתי ואמרת לשרי
אנתתי חלם 18 חלמת [אנה וא]דחל [מן] חלמא דן ואמרת לי אשתעי לי

river ... *17* [to] the Great Salt Sea, and this boundary runs as a spring from ... [...] *18* [...] ... which turns to the west and passes [...] *19* ... until it reaches ... *20* ... to the East *21-34* ...

Col. XVII   *5* [...] ... *6* [...] ... *Blank 7* [And] Shem di[vi]ded his [por]tion between his sons, and the first fell to [E]l[am] in the North, by the waters of the river Tigris, until it reaches the R[e]d Sea *8* to its source, which is in the North, and turning towards the West, towards Ashur, until it reached the Tigris ... and after him *9* (fell) to Aram, the land between the two rivers, until it reaches the upper part of ... *10* fell this mountain of the Bull, and the portion passes on and goes further westwards until it reaches Magog ... the East; *11* in the North of the bosom of this branch which is at the head of the three portions by this sea to Arpachsad ... *12* ... which is directed to the South, all the land that the Euphrates irrigates and all ... [...] *13* ... all the valleys and the plains that are between them, and the island in the midst of the bay ... [...] *14* ... and Amana ... [...] *15* the portion which his father Noah apportioned for him and gave to him. *Blank 16* [And] Japeth divided between his sons. To Gomer he gave first, in the North until it reaches the river Tina, and after him to Magog, and after him *17* to Madai, and after him to Javan, all the islands which are close to Lydia, and between the bay ... *18* [...] ... to Meshek ... [...] *19* [...] ... the sons of Ham ... *Blank*

Col. XIX   *6* ... [...] ... [...] ... *7* ... [...] and I called on the [name] of G[od] there and said: You are *8* [my] Go[d, the et]er[nal God ...] ... Up till now I had not reached the holy mountain, so I set out *9* for ... and kept on walking towards the South ... and I went until I reached Hebron. At [that time] Hebron had been bu[il]t, and I lived *10* [two years th]ere. *Blank* However, a famine occurred in this whole country. I heard that there w[as] gr[ai]n in Egypt, and left *11* to [enter] the land of Egypt [...] ... [... until] I [reached] the river Carmon, one of the *12* branches of the river ... [...] now we ... our land. [And] I [cro]ssed the seven branches of this river which *13* ... [...] Then we crossed our land and we entered the land of the sons of Ham, the land of Egypt. *14 Blank* I, Abram, dreamt a dream, on the night of my entry into Egypt. And in my dream I saw a cedar and a palm-tree *15* ... [...] Some men arrived intending to cut and uproot the [ce]dar, and to leave the palm-tree by itself. *16* But the palm-tree shouted and said: Do not hew down the [ce]dar, because both of us are from root .... And the cedar was saved thanks to the palm-tree, *17* and was not [hewn down.] *Blank* I woke up from my slumber during the night and said to Sarai, my wife: I have had *18* a dream [and] I am alarmed [by] this

חלמך ואנדע ושרית לאשתעיא לה חלמא דן   19 [וחוית] ל[ה פשר] חלמא
[דן ו]אמ[רת] ... די יבעון למקטלני ולכי למשבק [ב]רם דא כול טבותא
20 [די תעבדין עמי] בכול אתר די [נהך לה אמרי] עלי די אחי הוא ואחי
בטליכי ותפלט נפשי בדיליכי   21 [... יבעון] לאע[ד]יותכי מני ולמקטלני
ובכת שרי על מלי בליליא דן   22 [...]...[...] ופרעו צ[ען ... שרי למפנה
לצען   23 [עמי והסתמרת י]תירא בנפשה די לא יחזנה כול [אנש חמש
שני]ן ולסוף חמש שניא אלן   24 [... אתו] תלתת גברין מן רברבי מצרי]ן
[... די פרעו] צע[ן] על מל[י] ועל אנתתי והווא יהבין   25 [לי מתן שגיאן
ובעו] ל[י] ל[אודעא] טבתא וחכמתא וקושטא וקרית קודמיהון ל[כתב] מלי
חנוך   26 [...] בכפנא די [...] ... ולא ...ין למקם עד די ... מלי
27 [...]ל[...]במאכל שגי ובמשתה]   28-30 [חמרא ...] [...]...[...]

Col. xx   1 ...[...]... 2 ...[...]... כמה ... ושפיר לה צלם אנפיהא וכמא
3 [נ]עים וכמא רקיק לה שער ראישה כמא יאין להון לה עיניהא ומא רגג
הוא לה אנפהא וכול נץ ... אנפיהא   4 כמא יאא לה חדיה וכמא שפיר לה
כול לבנהא דרעיהא מא שפירן וידיהא כמא   5 כלילן וחמיד כול מחזה
יד[י]הא כמא יאין כפיהא ומא אריכן וקטינן כול אצבעת ידיהא רגליהא
6 כמא שפירן וכמא שלמא להן לה שקיהא וכל בתולן וכלאן די יעלן לגנון
לא ישפרן מנהא ועל כול   7 נשין שופר שפרה ועליא שפרהא לעלא מן
כולהן ועם כול שפרא דן חכמא שגיא עמהא ודלידיהא   8 יאא וכדי שמע
מלכא מלי חרקנוש ומלי תרין חברוהי די פם חד תלתתהון ממללין שגי רחמה
ושלח   9 לעובע דברהא וחזהא ואתמה על כול שפרהא ונסבהא לה לאנתא
ובעא למקטלני ואמרת שרי   10 למלכא דאחי הוא כדי הוית מתגר על
דילהא ושביקת אנה אברם בדילהא ולא קטילת ובכית אנה   11 אברם בכי
תקיף אנה ולוט בר אחי עמי בליליא כדי דבירת מני שרי באונס *vacat*
12 בליליא דן צלית ובעית ואתחננת ואמרת באתעצבא ודמעי נחתן
בריך אנתה אל עליון מרי לכול   13 עלמים די אנתה מרה ושליט על כולא
ובכול מלכי ארעא אנתה שליט למעבד בכולהון דין וכען   14 קבלתך מרי
על פרעו צען מלך מצרין די דברת אנתתי מני בתוקף עבד לי דין מנה ואחזי
ידך רבתא   15 בה ובכול ביתה ואל ישלט בליליא דן לטמיא דן אנתתי מני

dream. She said to me: Tell me your dream so that I may know it. And I began to tell her the dream, *19* [and I told her the interpretation] of th[is] dream. [I] sai[d:] … they want to kill me and leave you alone. This favour [o]nly *20* [must you do for me]: in every place [we reach, say] about me: He is my brother. And I shall live under your protection and my life will be spared because of you. *21* [… they will try] to se[p]arate you from me and kill me. Sarai wept because of my words that night. *22* […] … […] the Pharaoh Z[oan …] Sarai to go to Zoan *23* [with me, because she gr]eatly [feared] within herself that any[body] could see her, [five years long.] After these five years *24* […] three men of the princes of Egyp[t came …] from Phara[oh] Zoa[n] on account of [my] words and of my wife. They gave *25* [me many presents expecting from me] goodness, wisdom and truth. I read in front of them the [book] of the words of Enoch *26* […] concerning the famine which […] … and not … to stay until … the words of *27* […] with much eating and drinking […] wine […] *28-30* […] … […]

Col. xx   *1* … […] … *2* … […] How … and pretty is the shape of her face, and how *3* [lo]vely and how smooth the hair of her head! How lovely are her eyes; how pleasant her nose and all the blossom *4* of her face … How graceful is her breast and how lovely all her whiteness! How beautiful are her arms! And her hands, how *5* perfect! How alluring is the whole appearance of her hand[s]! How pretty are the palms of her hands and how long and supple all the fingers of her hands! Her feet, *6* how lovely! How perfect her thighs! No virgin or wife who enters the bridal chamber is more beautiful than her. Above all *7* women her beauty stands out; her loveliness is far above them all. And with all this beauty there is in her great wisdom. And everything she does with her hands *8* is perfect. When the king heard the words of Hirqanos and the words of his two companions, which the three of them spoke in unison, he desired her greatly and sent *9* immediately for her to be fetched. He saw her and was amazed at all her beauty, and took her for himself as a wife. He wanted to kill me, but Sarai said *10* to the king: He is my brother, so that I could profit at her expense. I, Abram, was spared on her account and I was not killed. But I wept *11* bitterly that night, I, Abram, and my nephew Lot with me, because Sarai had been taken away from me by force. *Blank 12* That night I prayed, pleaded and entreated and said in (my) distress, while my tears flowed: Blessed are you, O God Most High, my Lord, for all *13* ages. For you are Lord and Master of everything and rule all the kings of the earth, to judge them all. Now *14* I lodge a complaint before you, my Lord, against Pharaoh Zoan, king of Egypt, because my wife has been taken away from me by force. Do justice for me against him and show your mighty arm *15* against him, and against all his house. During this night, may he not be able to defile my wife, separated from

ויⁱⁱדעוך מרי די אנתה מרה לכול מלכי   16 ארעא ובכית וחשית בליליא דן

שלח לה אל עליון רוח מכדש למכתשה ולכול אנש ביתה רוח   17 באישא

והואת כתשא לה ולכול אנש ביתה ולא יכל למקרב בהא ואף לא ידעהא

והוא עמה   18 תרתין שנין ולסוף תרתין שנין תקפו וגברו עלוהי מכתשיא

ונגדיא ועל כול אנש ביתה ושלח   19 קרא לכול חכימ[י] מצרין ולכול

אשפיא עם כול אסי מצרין הן יכולון לאסיותה מן מכתשה דן ולאנש

20 ביתה ולא יכלו כול אסיא ואשפיא וכול חכימיא למקם לאסיותה ארי

הוא רוחא כתש לכולהון   21 וערקו   *vacat*

באדין אתה עלי חרקנוש ובעא מני די אתה ואצלה על   22 מלכא ואסמוך

ידי עלוהי ויחא ארי ב[ח]לם חז[ני] ואמר לה לוט לא יכול אברם דדי לצליא

על   23 מלכא ושרי אנתתה עמה וכען אזל אמר למלכא וישלח אנתתה מנה

לבעלהא ויצלה עלוהי ויחה

vacat 24 וכדי שמע חרקנוש מלי לוט אזל אמר למלכא כול מכתשיא

ונגדיא   25 אלן די מתכתש ומתנגד מרי מלכא בדיל שרי אנתת אברם יתיבו

נה לשרי לאברם בעלה   26 ויתוך מנכה מכתשא דן ורוח שחלניא וקרא

מ[ל]ל[כ]א לי ואמר לי מא עבדתה לי בדיל [שר]י ותאמר   27 לי די אחתי

היא והיא הואת אנתתך ונסבתהא לי לאנתה הא אנתתך דברה אזל ועדי לך

מן   28 כול מדינת מצרין וכען צלי עלי ועל ביתי ותתגער מננה רוחא דא

באישתא וצלית על [ד]י [ית]רפא   29 הו וסמכת ידי על [רא]י[ש]ה ואתפלי

מנה מכתשא ואתגערת [מנה רוחא] באישתא וחי וקם ויהב   30 לי מלכא

ב[יומא] דנא מנתנ[ן] שגיאן וימא לי מלכא במומה די לא [...]....]הא ואתיב

לי   31 לשרי ויהב לה מלכא [כסף וד]הב שגיא ולבוש שגי די בוץ וארגואן

ו[...]   32 קודמיהא ואף להגר וא[ש]למה לי ומני עמי אנוש די ינפקונני

ול... מן מצרין   *vacat* 33 *vacat* ואזלת אנה אברם בנכסין שגיאין לחדא ואף

בכסף ודהב וסלקת מן [מצרין] [ולוט]   34 בר אחי עמי ואף לוט קנה לה

נכסין שגיאין ונסב לה אנתה מן בנת [מצרין] והוית ש[רא עמה]

[ב]כל אתר משריאתי עד די דבקת לבית אל לאתרא די   1   *Col.* xxi

בנית תמן בה מדבחא ובניתה תניאני   2 [ו]אקרבת עלוהי עלואן ומנחה לאל

עליון וקרית תמן בשם מרה עלמיא והללת לשם אלהא וברכת   3 אלהא

me, so that it be known about you, my Lord, that you are the Lord of all the kings *16* of the earth. And I wept and stayed silent. That night, the God Most High sent him a chastising spirit, to afflict him and all the members of his household, an evil spirit *17* that kept afflicting him and all the members of his household. And he was unable to approach her, let alone to have sexual intercourse with her, in spite of being with her *18* for two years. At the end of two years, the punishments and plagues, against him and against all the members of his household, increased and intensified. And he sent *19* for all the wise men [of] Egypt to be called, and all the wizards as well as all the healers of Egypt, (to see) whether they could heal him of that disease, (him) and the members *20* of his household. However, all the healers and wizards and all the wise men were unable to rise up to heal him. For the spirit attacked all of them *21* and they fled. *Blank* Then Hirqanos came to me and asked me to come and pray for *22* the king, and lay my hands upon him so that he would recover. For he had seen [me] in a [dr]eam. But Lot said to him: Abram, my uncle, cannot pray for *23* the king while Sarai, his wife, is with him. Go, now, and tell the king to send back his wife to her own husband and he will pray for him and he will recover. *24 Blank* When Hirqanos heard Lot's words, he went and said to the king: All these plagues and punishments *25* with which the king my Lord is afflicted and punished are on account of Sarai, Abram's wife. They should return Sarai, then, to Abram, her husband, *26* and this plague and the spirit of purulent evils will cease to afflict you. The [ki]n[g] called me and said to me: What have you done to me with regard to [Sara]i? You told me: *27* She is my sister, when she is your wife; so that I took her for myself for a consort. Here is your wife; take her away! Go! Depart from *28* all the cities of Egypt! But now pray for me and for my household so that this evil spirit will be banished from us. I prayed that [he might be] cured *29* and laid my hands upon his [hea]d. The plague was removed from him; the evil [spirit] was banished [from him] and he recovered. The king got up and gave *30* me on that [day] many gifts, and the king swore an oath to me that (he had) not ... [...] her. Then, they [brought back to] me *31* Sarai. The king gave her much [silver and go]ld and many clothes of fine linen and purple and [...] *32* in front of her and also Hagar. He h[an]ded her to me, and appointed men to escort me and to ... out of Egypt. *Blank 33 Blank* I, Abram, went with much cattle and also with silver and gold. I left [Egyp]t. [And Lot,] *34* my brother's son, (was) with me. Lot, too, had acquired many flocks and had taken for himself a wife from among the daughters [of Egypt.] I ca[mped with him]

Col. XXI   *1* [in] all my (old) camp-sites until I reached Bethel, the place where I had built an altar, and I built it once again. *2* Upon it I offered holocausts and an offering to the God Most High, and invoked the name of the Lord of the Universe there; I praised God's name and blessed *3* God. I gave thanks there

ואודית תמן קודם אלהא על כול נכסיא וטבתא די יהב לי ודי עבד עמי טב
ודי אתיבני 4 לארעא דא בשלם *vacat*

5 בתר יומא דן פרש לוט מן לואתי מן עובד רעותנא ואזל ויתב לה
בבקעת ירדנא וכול נכסוהי 6 עמה ואף אנה אוספת לה על דילה שגי והוא
רעה נכסוהי ודבק לה עד סודם וזבן לה בסודם בי 7 ויתב בה ואנה הוית יתב
בטורא די בית אל ובאש עלי די פרש לוט בר אחי מן לואתי *vacat*

vacat 8 ואתחזי לי אלהא בחזוא די לילא ואמר לי סלק לך לרמת חצור
די על שמאל 9 ביתאל אתר די אנתה יתב ושקול עיניך וחזי למדנחא
ולמערבא ולדרומא ולצפונא וחזי כול 10 ארעא דא די אנה יהב לך ולזרעך
לכול עלמים וסלקת למחרתי לרמת חצור וחזית ארעא מן 11 רמתא דא
מן נהר מצרין עד לבנן ושניר ומן ימא רבא עד חורן וכול ארע גבל עד קדש
וכול מדברא 12 רבא די מדנח חורן ושניר עד פורת ואמר לי לזרעך אנתן
כול ארעא דא וירתונה לכול עלמים 13 ואשגה זרעך כעפר ארעא די לא
ישכח כול בר אנוש לממניה ואף זרעך לא יתמנה קום הלך ואזל 14 וחזי
כמן ארכהא וכמן פתיהא ארי לך ולזרעך אנתננה אחריך עד כול עלמיא

vacat

15 ואזלת אנה אברם למסחר ולמחזה ארעא ושרית למסחר מן גיחון
נהרא ואתית ליד ימא עד די 16 דבקת לטור תורא וסחרת מן לי[ד]ימא
רבא דן די מלחא ואזלת ליד טור תורא למדנחא לפותי ארעא 17 עד די
דבקת לפורת נהרא וסחרת ליד פורת עד די דבקת לימא שמוקא למדנחא
והוית אתה לי ליד 18 ימא שמוקא עד די דבקת ללשן ים סוף די נפק מן
ימא שמוקא וסחרת לדרומא עד די דבקת גחון 19 נהרא ותבת ואתית לי
לביתי בשלם ואשכחת כול אנשי שלם ואזלת ויתבת באלוני ממרה די
בחברון 20 כלמדנח צפון חברון ובנית תמן מדבח ואסקת עלוה]י[עלא
ומנחא לאל עליון ואכלת ואשתית תמן 21 אנה וכול אנש ביתי ושלחת
קרית לממרא ולערנם ולאשכול ת\[לתת אחיא אמוראא רחמי ואכלו כחדא
22 עמי ואשתיו עמי *vacat*

23 קדמת יומיא אלן אתה כדרלעומר מלך עילם אמרפל מלך בבל אריוך
מלך כפתוך תדעל מלך גוים די 24 הוא בין נהרין ועבדו קרב עם ברע מלך
סודם ועם ברשע מלך עומרם ועם שנאב מלך אדמא 25 ועם שמיאבד מלך

in God's presence for all the flocks and wealth which he had given me, because he had acted well towards me, and because he had returned me *4* in peace to this land. *Blank 5* After that day, Lot parted from me on account of the behaviour of our shepherds. He went and settled in the Jordan Valley (taking) all his flocks *6* with him. And I even added many to his. He pastured his flocks and reached Sodom and bought himself a house in Sodom *7* and lived there, while I lived in the mountain of Bethel. It distressed me that Lot, my brother's son, should have parted from me. *Blank 8 Blank* God appeared to me in a night vision and said to me: Go up to Ramat Hazor, which is to the North of *9* Bethel, the place where you are living; raise your eyes and look to the East, to the West, to the South and to the North. Look at all *10* this land, which I am giving you and your descendants for ever. The following morning I went up to Ramat Hazor and looked at the land from *11* that height, from the River of Egypt up to Lebanon and Senir, and from the Great Sea up to Hauran, and all the land of Gebal up to Qadesh, and all the *12* Great Desert which there is to the East of Hauran and Senir as far as the Euphrates. And he said to me: I shall give all this land to your descendants and they will inherit it forever. *13* I will multiply your descendants like the dust of the earth which no-one can count. In the same way, your descendants will be innumerable. Get up, walk and go, *14* and see how great is its length and how great is its width. For I shall give it to you, to you and to your descendants after you, for all the ages. *Blank 15* I, Abram, went out to traverse and see the land. I began the traverse at the River Gihon. I went along the shore of the sea until *16* I reached the mountain of the Bull. I walked from the sh[ore] of this Great Sea of Salt, skirting the mountain of the Bull towards the East, through the breadth of the land, *17* until I reached the River Euphrates. I proceeded towards the East along the bank of the Euphrates, until reaching the Red Sea. I continued walking along the shore *18* of the Red Sea until arriving at the branch of the Sea of Reeds which issues from the Red Sea, and continued towards the South until I reached the *19* River Gihon. Then I turned back and arrived at my house in peace and found all my people well. I went and settled at the oaks of Mamre, at Hebron, *20* to the North-east of Hebron. There I built an altar, and upon i[t] I offered a holocaust and an offering to the God Most High. And I ate and drank there, *21* I and all the people of my household. I invited Mamre, Arnem and Eshkol, the three Amorite brothers, my friends, and they ate together *22* with me and drank with me. *Blank 23* Before those days there came Chedorlaomer, king of Elam, Amraphel, king of Babylonia, Arioch, king of Cappadocia, Tidal, king of Goiim, which *24* is Mesopotamia, and they declared war on Bera, king of Sodom, Birsha, king of Gomorrah, Shinab, king of Admah, *25* Shemiabad,

צביין ועם מלך בלע כול אלן אזדמנו כחדא לקרב לעמקא די סדיא ותקף
מלך   26 עילם ומלכיא די עמה למלך סודם ולכול חברוהי ושויו עליהון
מדא תרתי עשרה שנין הווא   27 יהבין מדתהון למלך עילם ובשנת תלת
עשרה מרדו בה ובשנת ארבע עשרה דבר מלך עילם לכול   28 חברוהי
וסלקו ארחא די מדברא והווא מחין ובזין מן פורת נהרא ומחו לרפאיא די
בעשתרא   29 דקרנין ולזו̇מזמיא די בעמן ולאימיא ד[י ב]שוה הקריות
ולחוריא די בטורי גבל עד דבקו לאיל   30 פרן די במדברה ותבו ומחו
ל[...] בחצצן תמר *vacat*

31 ונפק מלך סודם לעורעהון ומלך [עומרם ... וֹמ]לך אדמא ומלך
צבואין ומלך בלע ... קרבא   32 בעמקא ד[י סדיא] לקובלי כדרל[עומר
מלך עילם ומלכיא] די עמה ואתבר מלך סודום וערק ומלך עומרים
33 נפל בעגיאין [די ...]... ובז מלך עילם כול נכסיא די סודם ודי
34 [עו]מר[ם] [...]...[...]... ושבו לוט בר אחוי

Col. xxii   1 די אברם די הוא יתב בסודם כחדא עמהון וכול נכסוהי
ואתה חד מן רעה   2 ענה די יהב אברם ללוט די פלט מן שביא על אברם
ואברם באדין הוא   3 יתב בחברון וחויה די שבי לוט בר אחוהי וכול נכסוהי
ולא קטיל ודי   4 נגדו מלכיא ארחא חלתא רבתא למדיתון ושבין ובזין
ומחין וקטלין ואזלין   5 למדינת דרמשק ובכא אברם על לוט בר אחוהי
ואתחלם אברם וקם   6 ובחר מן עבדוהי גברין בחירין לקרב תלת מאא
ותמניאת עשר וערנם   7 ואשכול וממרה נגדו עמה והוא רדף בתרהון עד
דבק לדן ואשכח אנון   8 שרין בבקעת דן ורמה עליהון בליליא מן ארבע
רוחיהון והווא קטל   9 בהון בליליא ותבר אנון והוא רדף להון וכולהון
הווא ערקין מן קודמוהי   10 עד דבקו לחלבון די שימא על שמאל דרמשק
ואצל מנהון כול די שבוא   11 וכול די בזו וכול טבתהון ואף ללוט בר
אחוהי פצא וכול נכסוהי וכול   12 שביתא די שבאו ואתיב ושמע מלך סודם
די אתיב אברם כול שביתא   13 וכול בזתא וסלק לעורעה ואתה לשלם היא
ירושלם ואברם שרא בעמק   14 שוא והוא עמק מלכא בקעת בית כרמא
ומלכיצדק מלכא דשלם אנפק   15 מאכל ומשתה לאברם ולכול אנשא די
עמה והוא הוא כהן לאל עליון וברך   16 ל[א]ברם ואמר בריך אברם לאל

king of Zeboiim and the king of Bela. All these had formed an alliance to wage war in the Valley of Siddim. However, the king of *26* Elam and the kings allied with him were victorious over the king of Sodom and all his allies, and they imposed tribute on them. Over twelve years they continued *27* paying their tribute to the King of Elam but in the thirteenth they revolted against him. In the fourteenth year, the king of Elam positioned himself at the head of all *28* his allies, they went up the desert road and were ravaging and laying waste from the river Euphrates. They routed the Rephaites of Ashteroth-*29* karnaim, the Zumzumites of Ammon, the Emim o[f] Shaveh-kiriathaim and the Horites of Mount Gebal until they reached El- *30* paran, in the desert. They returned and struck ... [...] in Hazazon-tamar. *Blank 31* The king of Sodom went out to encounter him, together with the king [of Gomorrah, ... the ki]ng of Admah, the king of Zeboiim and the king of Bela. ... battle *32* in the Valley o[f Siddim] against Chedorla[omer, king of Elam, and the kings] who were with him. But the king of Sodom was defeated and fled; the king of Gomorrah *33* fell in pits [of ...] ... The king of Elam pillaged all the property of Sodom and of *34* [Go]mor[rah ...] ... and they captured Lot, the son of the brother

Col. XXII *1* of Abram, who was living in Sodom, together with them and all his cattle. One of the shepherds of *2* the flock which Abram had given Lot, who had escaped captivity, came to Abram - at that time Abram was *3* living in Hebron - and told him that Lot, the son of his brother and all his flocks had been captured, but that he was not dead, and that *4* the kings had taken the road of the Great Valley towards their territory, taking prisoners, ravaging, smiting, killing and proceeding *5* as far as the city of Damascus. Abram wept for Lot, the son of his brother. Abram braced himself, stood up *6* and chose from among his servants those fit for war: three hundred and eighteen. Arnem, *7* Eshkol and Mamre were with him. He went in pursuit of them until he reached Dan and found them *8* camped in the Valley of Dan. He fell upon them by night from their four sides. He killed *9* some during the night. He defeated them and chased them and they were all fleeing before him *10* until they reached Helbon which lies north of Damascus. He retrieved from them all that they had captured, *11* all that they had looted and all their own goods. He also saved Lot, his brother's son, and all his flocks and brought back all *12* the captives they had taken. The king of Sodom heard that Abram had brought back all the captives *13* and all the loot and went up to meet him. He went to Salem, which is Jerusalem. Abram was encamped in the Valley of *14* Shaveh, which is the Valley of the King, the Valley of Bet ha-Kerem. Melchizedek, king of Salem, brought out *15* food and drink for Abram and for all the men there were with him. He was a priest of the Most High God. He

עליון מרה שמיא וארעא ובריך אל עליון 17 די סגר שנאיך בידך ויהב לה
מעשר מן כול יכסיא די מלך עילם וחברוהי

18 vacat באדין קרב מלכא די סודם ואמר לאברם מרי אברם 19 הב לי
נפשא די אʼתי לי די שביא עמך די אצלתה מן מלך עילם ונכסיא 20 כולהון
שביקין לך vacat

אדין אמר אברם למלך סודם מרים אנה 21 ידי יומא דן לאל עליון מרה
שמיא וארעא אן מן חוט עד ערקא דמסאן 22 אן אסב מן כול די איתי לך
דלʼא תהוה אמר vacat דמן נכסי כול עתרה די 23 אברם ברא מן די אכלו
כבר עולימי די עמי וברא מן חולק תלתת גבריא די 24 אזלו עמי אנון
שליטין בחולקהון למנתן לך ואתיב אברם כול נכסיא וכול 25 שביתא
ויהב למלך סודם וכול שביא די הואת עמה מן ארעה דא שבק 26 ושלח
כולהון vacat

27 בתר פתגמיא אלך אתחזי{ו} אלהא לאברם בחזוא ואמר לה הא עשר
שנין 28 שלמא מן יום די נפקתה מן חרן תרתין עבדתה תנה ושבע במצרין
וחדא 29 מן די תבת מן מצרין וכען בקר ומני כול די איתי לך וחזי כמן
כפלין שגיו מן 30 כול די נפקו עמך ביום מפקך מן חרן וכען אל תדחל אנה
עמך ואהוה לך 31 סעד ותקף ואנה מגן עליך ואספרך לך לתקיף ברא מנך
עתרך ונכסיך 32 ישגון לחדא vacat

ואמר אברם מרי אלהא שגי לי עתר ונכסין ולמא לי 33 כול אלן ואנה
כדי אמות ערטלי אהך די לא בנין וחד מן בני ביתי ירתנני 34 אליעזר
בר[...]לד [יʼ]רתני ואמר לה לא ירתנך דן להן די יפוק

CTL (CTLevi ar) *Cairo Geniza Testament of Levi*

H.L. Pass, J. Arendzen, 'Fragment of an Aramaic Text of The Testament of
Levi', *JQR* 12 (1899-1900) 651-661; R.H. Charles, A. Cowley, 'An Early
Source of the Testaments of the Patriarchs', *JQR* 19 (1906-7) 566-583 (One
Plate)
Cambridge University Library and Oxford Bodleian Library
1Q21, 4Q213, 4Q213a, 4Q213b, 4Q214, 4Q214a, 4Q214b, 4Q540, 4Q541

blessed *16* [A]bram and said: Blessed be Abram by the Most High God, Lord of heaven and earth and blessed be the Most High God, *17* who has delivered your enemies into your hands. And he (Abram) gave him a tithe of all the wealth of the king of Elam and his allies. *18 Blank* Then, the king of Sodom approached and said to Abram: My Lord Abram, *19* give me the people who are mine, who are captive with you, whom you have rescued from the king of Elam, but all the wealth, *20* keep for yourself. *Blank* Then Abram answered the king of Sodom: I swear *21* this day by the Most High God, Lord of heaven and earth, that I will not accept a thread or a sandal thong *22* or anything of what belongs to you so that you will not say: *Blank* From my wealth do all Abram's riches (come), *23* apart from what my boys who escort me have eaten, and apart from the share of the three men who *24* came with me; they are owners of their share to give to you. Abram gave back all the wealth and *25* all the captives and gave (them) to the king of Sodom. And all the prisoners who were with him from that area he released *26* and freed them all. *Blank 27* After these events, God appeared to Abram in a vision and said to him: See, ten years *28* have passed since the day you left Haran; you have spent two years here, seven in Egypt and one *29* since you came back from Egypt. Now inspect and count up all you possess and see how *30* everything which left with you on the day of your move from Haran has increased double. Now, do not fear, I am with you and for you I shall be *31* support and strength. I shall be your shield and your buckler against one stronger than you. Your riches and your flocks *32* shall increase enormously. *Blank* Abram replied: My Lord God, great are my riches and my flocks; but what use is all this to me? *33* When I die I shall go naked and without sons. One of my servants will inherit from me, *34* Eliezer, son […] … will inherit me. But he answered him: Not this one shall inherit from you, but one who shall come forth

---

CTL (CTLevi ar) *Cairo Geniza Testament of Levi*

Bibliography: M.E. Stone, J.C. Greenfield, 'Remarks on the Aramaic Testament of Levi from the Geniza', *RB* 86 (1979) 214-230 (two plates); reprinted in M.E. Stone, *Selected Studies in Pseudepigrapha & Apocrypha. With Special Reference to the Armenian Tradition* (SVTP 9; Leiden: E.J. Brill, 1991) 228-244; K. Beyer, *ATTM*, 188-208

Cambridge Col. a   14-1 [...]   15 [...]...   16 על [...]   [...א] דברת די כל א[...]
17 למעבד כדין בכ.[...]   18 יעקב אבי ורא[ובן אחי ...]   19 ואמרן להון
ב[...]נה דן[...]   20 צביין אינון בברתן ונהוי כולן א[חין]   21 וחברין גזרו
ערלת בשרכון   22 והתחמיין כו[א]ת[ן] ותהון חתימין   23 כואתן במילת
ט[...] ונהוי לכ[ון]

Cambridge Col. b   14-1 [...]   15 [...]   16 אחי בכל עדן [...]   א[...] די
הוו בשכם   17 [...]אחי ואחוי דן   18 [...]בשכם ומה   19 מ...[...]...עב[די
חמסא ואחוי   20 אינון יהודה די אנה ושמעון   21 אחי אזלנא לה[.]דד
לראובן   22 אחונן די למד[נח א]שר ושור   23 יהודה קדמא [למ]שבק
עאנא

Bodleian Col. a   1 שלמא וכל חמדת בכורי ארעא   2 כולה למאכל
ולמלכות חרבא פגשא   3 וקרבא ונחשירותא ועמלא   4 ונצפתא וקטלא
וכפנא זמנין תאכול   5 וזמנין תכפן וזמנין תעמול וזמנין   6 תנוח וזמנין
תדמוך וזמנין תנוד   7 שנת עינא בען חזי לך הכין רבינך   8 מן כולה והיך
יהבנא לך רבות שלם   9 *vacat* ונגדו שבעתין מן לותי   10 ואנה
אתעירת מן שנתי אדין   11 אמרת חזוא הוא דן וכדן אנה   12 מתמה די יהוי
לה כל חזוה וטמרת   13 אף דן בלבי ולכל איניש לא גליתה   14 ו[ע]לנא על
אבי יצחק ואף הוא כדן   15 *vacat* [ברכ]ני אדין כדי הוה יעקב   16 [אבי
מ]עשר כל מה די הוה לה כנדרה   17 [וכען]אנה חוית קדמי בראש
18 [כהונת]ה ולי מכל בנוהי יהב קרבן   19 [מעשר]לאל ואלבשי לבוש
כהונתא   20 ומלי ידי והוית כהין לאל עלמיא   21 וקרבית כל קרבנוהי
וברכת לאבי   22 בחיוהי וברכת לאחי אדין כולהון   23 ברכוני ואף אבא
ברכני ואשלמית

Bodleian Col. b   1 להקרבה קורבנוהי בבית אל ואזלנא   2 מבית אל
ושרינא בבירת אברהם   3 אבונן לות יצחק אבונה והוא (וחזא)   4 יצחק
אבונא לכולנא וברכנא   5 וחדי וכדי ידע די אנה כהין לאל   6 עליון למארי
שמיא שארי   7 לפקדה יתי ולאלפא יתי דין   8 כהנותא *vacat* ואמר לי לוי

Cambridge Col. a (= 1Q21 3) *1-14* [...] *15* ... [... be-] *16* cause all [...] *17* to act correctly with ... [...] *18* Jacob my father, and Re[uben my brother ...] *19* and we said to them [...] ... [...] *20* they desire our daughters, and we will all be br[others] *21* and friends. Circumcise the foreskin of your flesh *22* and you shall look li[k]e [us], and you shall be sealed *23* like us with the circumcision of [...] and we shall be to y[ou]

Cambridge Col. b *1-14* [...] *15* [...] my brothers at all times *16* [...] who were in Shechem *17* [...] my brothers. And Dan told *18* [...] in Shechem and what *19* ... [... do]ers of violence and *20* Judah told them that I and Simeon *21* my brother had gone to ... (to) Reuben *22* our brother, who was ea[st of A]ser, and *23* Judah jumped up forward [to] leave the flock

Bodleian Col. a (= 4Q213b) *1* peace, and all the pleasantness of the first fruits of the land, *2* all of it, for food and for dominion: the sword, fight *3* and battle and slaughter, and labour *4* and rage and murder and famine. Sometimes it shall eat *5* and sometimes it shall be hungry, and sometimes it shall labour and sometimes *6* it shall rest, and sometimes it shall sleep, and sometimes *7* the sleep of the eye shall depart. See then how he has made you greater *8* than all, and how we have given you the anointment of eternal peace». *9* *Blank* And those seven departed from me, *10* and I awoke from my dream. Then *11* I thought: «This vision is like the other one. I *12* am amazed that the whole vision is to come.» And I hid *13* this (vision) too, in my heart and to no one did I reveal it. *14* And we [w]ent to my father Isaac, and he also *15* [blessed] me likewise. *Blank* Then, when Jacob *16* [my father] tithed everything he had, according to his vow, *17* [then] I served for the first time at the head of *18* the [priesthood,] and to me, among all his sons, he gave the offering *19* [of the tithe] to God, and he clothed me with the clothing of the priesthood *20* and filled my hand, and I became a priest for God of eternity *21* and I offered all his offerings, and blessed my father *22* during his life, and I blessed my brothers. Then they all *23* blessed me, and father also blessed me, and I finished

Bodleian Col. b *1* to offer his offerings in Bethel, and we went *2* from Bethel and camped in the fortress of Abraham *3* our (grand)father, with Isaac our father, and *4* our father Isaac saw us all and blessed us *5* and rejoiced. And when he knew that I was a priest of God *6* Most High, of the Lord of Heaven, he began *7* to instruct me and to teach me the judgment of *8* the priesthood

אזדהר 9 לך ברי ברי מן כל טומאה ומן 10 כל חטא דינך רב הוא מן כל
11 בישרא vacat וכען ברי דין 12 קושטא אחזינך ולא אטמר 13 מינך כל
פתגם לאלפותך דין 14 כהנותא לקדמין היזדהר לך 15 ברי מן כל פחז
וטמאה ומן כל 16 זנות ואנת אנתתא מן משפחתי 17 סב לך ולא תחל
זרעך עם זניאן 18 ארי זרע קדיש אנת וקדיש 19 זרעך היך קודשא ארו
כהין 20 קדיש אנת מתקרי לכל זרע 21 אברהם קריב אנת ל]אל ו]קריב
22 לכל קדישוהי כען אזדכי 23 בבשרך מן כל טומאת כל גבר

1 וכדי תהוי קאים למיעל לבית אל 2 הוי סחי במיא   *Bodleian Col.* c
ובאדין תהוי לביש 3 לבוש כהנותא וכדי תהוי לביש 4 הוי תאיב תוב
ורחיע ידיך 5 ורגליך עד דלא תקרב למדבחא 6 כל דנה וכדי נסב
להקרבה 7 כל די חזה להנסקה למדבחה 8 הוי עוד תאב ורחע ידיך
ורגליך 9 ומהקריב אעין מהצלחין ובקר 10 אינון לקודמין מן תולעא
11 ובאדין הסק אינון ארי כדנה 12 חזיתי לאברהם אבי מיזדהר 13 מן
כל תריעשר מיני אעין אמר 14 לי די חזין להסקה מינהון למדבחה 15 די
ריח תננהון בשים סליק ואלין 16 אינון שמהתהון ארזא ודפרנא
17 וסגדא ואטולא ושוחא ואדונה 18 ברותא ותאנתא ואע משחא 19 ערא
והדסה ואעי דקתא אלין 20 אינון די אמר לי די חזין להסקה 21 מנהון
ל]תח]ות עלתא על מדבחה 22 וכדי [הסקת] מן אעי אלין על 23 מדבחה
ונורא ישרא להדלקא

1 בהון והא באדין תשרא למזרק דמא 2 על כותלי   *Bodleian Col.* d
מדבחה ועוד רחע ידיך 3 ורגליך מן דמא ושרי להנסקה אבריה
4 מליחי(ה) ואשה (ראשה) הוי מהנסק לקדמין 5 ועלוהי חפי תרבא ולא
יתחזה לה 6 דם נסבת תורא ובתרוהי צוארה 7 ובתר צוארה ידוהי ובתר
ידוהי 8 ניעא עם בן דפנא ובתר ידיא (ובתרהן) 9 ירכאתא עם שדרת
חרצא 10 ובתר ירכאתא רגלין רחיען עם 11 קרביא וכולהון מליחין
במלח כדי 12 חזה להון כמסתהון ובתר דנה נישפא 13 בליל במשחא
ובתר כולא חמר נסך 14 והקטיר עליהון לבונה וייהוון 15 עובדיך בסרך
וכל קורבניך [לרעו]א 16 לריח ניחח קודם אל עליון [וכל די] 17 תהוה

Blank And he told me: «Levi, beware, *9* my son, my son, of all defilement and of *10* all sin. Your judgment is greater than that of all *11* flesh. *Blank* And now, my son, *12* I will show you the judgment of the truth, and I will not hide *13* from you anything, to teach you the judgment *14* of the priesthood. First, beware, *15* my son, of all fornication and defilement and of all *16* uncleanness. But you, marry a woman from my family *17* and do not defile your seed with whores, *18* for you are a holy seed, and holy *19* is your seed like the sanctuary, for you are called a *20* holy priest for all the seed *21* of Abraham. You are close to God and close *22* to all his holy ones. Therefore keep yourself pure *23* in your flesh from all the defilement of all men.

Bodleian Col. c (= 4Q214b 2 - 6 1) *1* And when you stand up to enter the house of God, *2* bathe yourself in water, and dress yourself *3* with the clothes of the priesthood, and when you are dressed *4* go back again and wash your hands *5* and your feet before you offer on the altar *6* (anything) at all. When you take to offer *7* anything that is fitting to offer on the altar, *8* go and wash your hands and your feet again. *9* Offer the split logs; but examine *10* them first for worms, *11* and then offer them. For thus *12* I saw Abraham, my father, taking heed *13* of everything. Twelve kinds of wood he showed *14* me, which kinds are fitting to be offered upon the altar, *15* of which the smell of their smoke goes up pleasing. And these *16* are their names: cedar, juniper, *17* almond, tamarind, pine, ash, *18* cypress, fig, olive, *19* laurel, myrtle and balsam. These *20* are what he showed me, from which it is fitting to offer *21* be[nea]th the offering upon the altar. *22* When [you offer] any of these (kinds of) wood upon *23* the altar, and the fire starts to kindle

Bodleian Col. d (= 4Q214 2; 4Q214b 2 - 6 1) *1* them, then it is the moment to begin to sprinkle the blood *2* on the sides of the altar, and again wash your hands *3* and your feet from the blood, and begin to offer the salted portions. *4* Offer the head first, *5* and cover it with the fat, and not should be seen on it *6* blood of the offering of the cow. And after it the neck, *7* and after the neck, its forelegs, and after its forelegs *8* the breast with the ribs. And after them *9* the thighs and the spine of the loin. *10* And after the thighs, the hind-legs washed, with *11* the entrails. And all of them salted with salt, in the way which *12* is fitting for them, according to their need. And after this, flour *13* mixed with oil. And after everything, pour wine, *14* and burn incense over them so that *15* your works may be in order and all your offerings [be pleasi]ng, *16* to give an agree-

עביד בסרך הוי עב[יד במדה] 18 ובמתקל לא תותר צבו די לא [הזה]
19 ולא תחסר מן חושבן חזתא אע[ין] 20 חזיק (חזין) להקרבה לכל די
סליק למדב[חא] 21 לתורא רבא כבר (ככר) אעין ליה במתקל 22 ואם
תרבא בלחודוהי סליק שיתה 23 מנין ואם פר תורין הוא בתר די סליק

5 [וקרא]תי שמה [קהת וחזית]י די לה 6 [תהו]ה כנשת כל] עמא וד]י לה   *Cambridge Col. c*   3 [...]...[...]   2-1 [...]   4 [וה]רת עוד[...].
תהוה 7 כהנותא רבתא [לכל יש]ראל 8 *vacat* בשנת ארב[ע] ותל[תין לחיי
9 יליד בירחא קמ[אה בח]ד ליר[חא] 10 עם מדנח שמש[א] *vacat* ועוד
11 אוספת והיות ע[מה] ויילדת לי בר 12 תלית[ו]י וקראתי שמה מררי
ארי 13 מר לי עלוהי לחדה ארי כדי יליד 14 הוא מית והווה מריר לי
עלוהי 15 סגיא מן די ימות ובעית והתחננת 16 עלוהי והיה בכל מרר
vacat בשנת 17 ארבעין לחיי ילידת בييרחה תלית[י] 18 ועוד אוספת
והויתי עמהא והרת 19 ויילדת לי ברתא ושויתי שמהא 20 יוכבד אמ[רת
[כדי ילידת לי ליקר 21 ילידת לי לכבוד לישראל *vacat* 22 בשנת שתין
וארבע לי לחיי ויילדת 23 בחד בחודשא שביעיא מן בתר די

1 העל[נא ל]מצרים *vacat* בשנת שת 2 עש[רה   *Cambridge Col. d*
למ]עלינא לארע מצרים ולבני 3 [...]... בנת אחי לעדן אשויות 4 מבניהון
ו[יליד]ו להון בנין *vacat* שם בני 5 גרשון ל[בני ו]שמעי *vacat* ושם בני
6 ק[הת עמ]רם ויצהר וחברון ועוזיאל 7 [ושם] *vacat* בני מררי מחלי
ומושי 8 ונסב לה עמרם אנתא ליוכבד ברתי 9 עד די אנה חי בשנת
תשעין ואר[בע] 10 לחיי וקריתי שמה די עמרם כדי 11 יליד עמרם ארי
אמרת כדי יליד 12 דנה [...] עמא מן ארע] מצ]רים 13 *vacat* [כ]דן
יתקר[ר]א [שמה ...] ראמא 14 ביום חד י[לידו ו]הא הוא ויוכבד ברתי 15
בר שנין תמנה עשרה העלת 16 [לא]רע כנען ובר שנין [תמ]נה עשרה
17 כדי קטלית אנה לשכ[ם] *vacat* וגמרת 18 לעבדי חמסא ובר שנין תשע
19 עשרה כהנית ובר שנין תמנה 20 ועשרין נסבת לי אנתה *vacat* ובר
21 שנין תמנה וארבעין הויתי כדי 22 העלנא לארע מצרים ושנין
23 תמנין ותשע הויתי חי במצרי[ם]

able flavour before God Most High, [and all] *17* that you do, may you d[o] it in order, [in measure] *18* and in weight; do not add something that is not [fitting] *19* and do not omit (something) from the list of things that are fitting. The woo[d] *20* that is fitting to offer for all that goes up to [the] alta[r]: *21* for the large bull a talent of wood in weight, *22* and if only the fat is offered six *23* mina's; if it is a bull-calf that is offered

Cambridge Col. c (= 4Q214a 2 - 3 1)   *1-2* [...] *3* [...] ... [...] *4* [and] she [became pr]egnant once more [and gave birth to another son for me] *5* [and] I [called] him [Kohath and] I [saw] that to him *6* [would belo]ng the assembly of all [the nation, and th]at to him would belong *7* the high priesthood [of all Is]rael *8* *Blank* In the [thir]ty-four[th] year of my life *9* he was born, in the fir[st] month, [on the fir]st of [the] mon[th] *10* at sunrise. *Blank* And once *11* again I was wi[th her] and she gave birth *12* to a third son for me. And I called him Merari, for *13* I shed many bitter tears for him, for as soon as he was born *14* he seemed to die. And it was very bitter for me, *15* because he was dying. And I prayed and beseeched *16* for him, and it was altogether bitter. *Blank* In the *17* fortieth year of my life she gave birth in the third month, *18* and once again I was with her, and she became pregnant *19* and gave birth to a daughter for me. And I called her *20* Jochebed, [I] thou[ght:] «As she has given birth to me to (my) honour, *21* (thus) has she given birth to me to the glory of Israel». *Blank* *22* And in the sixty-fourth year of my life she gave birth *23* on the first day of the seventh month after

Cambridge Col. d   *1* [we] had en[tered] Egypt. *Blank* And in the six- *2* tee[nth] year [of] our [en]trance into the land of Egypt. And to my sons *3* [...] ... daughters of my brothers at the age when their development is complete. *4* And sons [were born] to them. *Blank* The name of the sons of *5* Gersom: Li[bnai and] Simei. *Blank* And the name of the sons of *6* Ko[hat: Am]ram and Izhar and Hebron and Uzziel *7* [*Blank* And the name of] the sons of Merari: Mahli and Musai. *8* And Amram married my daughter Jochebed *9* when I was living in the ninety-fou[rth] year *10* of my life. And I had called him Amram when *11* he was born, because I thought when he was born: «This one [...] the nation from the land of [Eg]ypt». *13* *Blank* [There]fore he was ca[l]led «El-evated [...]». *14* On one and the same day they [were] b[orn], he and Jochebed *15* my daughter. I was eight(een) years old when I entered *16* the [la]nd Canaan, and I was [eig]hteen years old *17* when I killed Shech[em] and anni-hilated *18* the workers of violence. *Blank* And I was nine- *19* teen years old when I became a priest, and twenty-eight years *20* when I married a wife. *Blank* And *21* I was forty-eight when *22* we entered the land of Egypt and *23* I lived ninety-eight years in Egyp[t.]

1 והוו כל יומי חיי שבע ות[ליתין ו]מאה   2 שנין   *Cambridge Col.* e

והזיתי לי בנין תל[יתאין] עד   3 די לא מיתת *vacat* ובש[נת מאה ות]מני

4 עשרה לחיי היא ש[נתא]די מית בה   5 יוסף אחי קרית לב[ני ו]לבניהון

6 ושריתי לפקדה הנון כל ד[י] הווה   7 עם לבבי ענית ואמרת לבני[שמעו]

8 למאמר לוי אבוכון והציתו לפקודי   9 ידיד אל אנה לכון מפקד בני ואנה

10 קושטא לכון מהחוי חביבי ראש   11 עובדיכון יהוי קושטא ועד

12 עלמ[א] י[הו]י קאים עמכון צדקה   13 וקוש[טא ... ...[... עלון   14 עללה

בריכה ו[זר]עא די זרע   15 טאב טאב מהנעל ודי זרע   16 ביש עלוהי תאיב

זרעה   17 *vacat*   וכען בני ספר מוסר   18 חוכמה אפילו (אליפו) לבניכון

ותהוי   19 חוכמתא עמכון ליקר עלם   20 די אליף חוכמתא ויקר היא

21 בה ודי שאיט חוכמתא לבשרון   22 *vacat* מתיהב   חזו בני ליוסף אחי

23 [ד]מאלפא ספר ומוסר חכמה

1-2 [...]   3 [...תשב].[...   4 לב[...]ן גבר ד[י]   *Cambridge Col.* f

5 אלף[ן] חכמה כל]יומוהו א[ריכין]   6 וסגה ל[ה שמ]עה לכל מא[נתה]

7 ומדינה[די אז]ל לה אח א...   8 הוי בה [לא כוא]ת נכר הוא בה   9 ולא

דמ]ה בה ל[נכרי ולא דמה   10 בה ל[כיל]י מ[ן די כולהון יהבי[ן]   11 לה בה

יקר] א[רי כולה צבין   12 למאלף מן חוכמתה רחמוה[י]   13 סגיאין ושאלי

שלמיה רברבין   14 ועל כורסי ייקר מהותבין לה   15 בדיל למשמע מילי

חוכמתה   16 עותר רב די יקר היא חוכמתה   17 וסימא טאבא לכל קניהא

הן   18 יאתון מלכין תקיפין ועם רב   19 וחיל ופרשין ורתיכין סגיאין

20 עמהון וינסבון נכסי מאת   21 ומדינה ויבוזון כל די בהון   22 אוצרי

חוכמתא לא יבוזון   23 ולא ישכחון מטמוריה ולא

1Q21 (1QTLevi ar) *1QTestament of Levi ar*

J.T. Milik, *DJD I*, 87-91, pl. XVII
PAM 40.537-541
ROC 647

Cambridge Col. e (= 4Q213 1 1)   *1* And all the days of my life have been hundred and t[hirty-]seven *2* years, and I have seen my gre[at-grand]children *3* before my death. *Blank* And in the ye[ar one hundred and ei]gh- *4* teen of my life, [the] ye[ar] in which *5* my brother Joseph died, I summoned [my] so[ns and] their sons, *6* and I began to instruct them all th[at] there was *7* in my heart. I began speaking and said to my sons: [«Listen] *8* to the word of Levi, your father, and pay attention to the precepts of *9* the beloved of God. I, to you my sons, give orders, and *10* to you I show the truth, my beloved ones. The principle of *11* all your deeds should be the truth, and *12* l[e]t justice and tru[th] stay with you for ever, *13* […] … upon them *14* a blessed harvest. The [sow]er that sows *15* goodness, harvests good, and whoever sows *16* evil, against him his seed turns. *17 Blank* But now, my sons, reading and instruction *18* and wisdom teach them to your sons, and *19* wisdom will be with you for eternal honour. *20* He who teaches wisdom will be honoured *21* by it, but he who despises wisdom, to insult *22* he will be given. *Blank* See then, my sons, my brother Joseph *23* [who] taught reading, and instruction of wisdom

Cambridge Col. f (= 4Q213 1 1 - 11 + 2; 4Q214a 2 - 3 11)   *1-2* […] *3* […] … […] *4* … […] man w[ho] *5* teaches [wisdom, all] his days will be len[gthened] *6* and multiplied will be his [reno]wn. In each re[gion] *7* and province to [which he go]es, a brother … *8* will be in it. He will [not be lik]e a foreigner in it, *9* and will not be li[ke a] stranger [in it,] nor be like *10* a scound[rel] in it. [Inst]ead, all shall give *11* him glory in it, [f]or all desire *12* to learn from his wisdom. Hi[s] friends *13* are many, and numerous those who wish him well. *14* And they shall seat him upon a throne of glory, *15* to listen to the words of his wisdom. *16* A great richness of glory is wisdom, *17* and a good treasure for all who acquire it. If *18* powerful kings come and a great people *19* and an army and horsemen and many chariots *20* with them, and they take the possessions of the region *21* and of the province and steal everything there is in them, *22* they cannot steal the treasure of wisdom, *23* nor will they find its secrets, nor

---

1Q21 (1QTLevi ar) *1QTestament of Levi ar*

CTL, 4Q213, 4Q213a, 4Q213b, 4Q214, 4Q214a, 4Q214b, 4Q540, 4Q541
Bibliography: J.T. Milik, 'Le Testament de Lévi en araméen. Fragment de la grotte 4 de Qumrân', *RB* 62 (1955) 398-399

Frag. 1   1 [...] מן די להוין תליתין [...]   2 [...]ביך מלכות כהנותא
רבא מן מלכות[...]...[...]   3 [...]...[...]

Frag. 3   1 [...] ולמלכות ח[ר]בא [...]   2 [... וזמנין] תעמל וזמנין
תנ[וח ...]   3 [... רבות ש]לם על[מא

Frag. 7 ı   1 [...]נתא עד אנתה   2 [...]תמלך עם די   3 [...]מ בעא

Frag. 8   1 [...] [ו]שלם *vacat* [...]ואנה[2 ...]שלם וכל אנש[...]
3 [...]ן אנה ל[...]   4 [...]...[...]

Frag. 30   1 [...]...[...]   2 [...]לא לזנו ...[...]   3 [...]בי להבעא
[...]צ   4 [...]...[...]

1Q22 (1QDM ["Dibrê Moshe"; "Dires de Moïse"]) *1QWords of Moses*

J.T. Milik, *DJD I*, 91-97, pls. XVIII-XIX
PAM 40.529, 40.530, 40.532
DAJ
1Q29?, 4Q375?, 4Q376?

Col. ı   1 [ויקרא] על מושה [אלוהי]ם [בארבעים] השנה לצא[ת בני
י]שר[אל מארץ מ]צרים בחו[דש ע]שתי   2 עש[ר] באחד ל[חו]דש לאמור
[הקהל א]ת כול הע[ד]ה ועלה א[ל הר נבו] ועמדתה [שמ]ה אתה
3 ואלע[זר ב]ן אהר[ון] *vacat* פש[ור] לראשי א[בות ללו]י[י]ם וכול
ה[כוהנים] וצויתה [א]ת בני   4 ישרא[ל ד]ברי התו[ר]ה אשר צויתי
אותכה] בהר ס[י]ני לצוות א[ותם קרא [באוזניה[ם] את הכול   5 היט[י]ב[
אשר א[עשו]ק מהם ו[העידותה ב]ם את [ה]שמים ואת [הארץ כ]י לוא
[יא]הבו   6 כאש[ר] צויתי [אותם ה]מה] ובני[הם כול] הימים אשר המה
[חיים על האד]מה [כי] מגיד   7 אנו[כי] אשר יעזבו]ני ויב[חר]ו בשקוצי
ה[גו]ים ותו[עבותיהם]וגל[ו]ליהם [ויעבדו] את   8 אלי[לי]ם והיו לפ[ח

Frag. 1 *1* [...] for they will be three [...] *2* [...] ... the sovereignty of the priest-hood will be greater than the sovereignty of [...] *3* [...] ... [...]

Frag. 3 (= CTL Bodleian *col.* a) *1* [... and for dominion:] the [sw]ord, [...] *2* [... sometimes] it shall labour and sometimes it sh[all rest ...] *3* [... the anoint-ment of] etern[al pe]ace [...]

Frag. 7 *col.* I *1* [...] ... until you *2* [...] you shall rule with who *3* [...] he seeks

Frag. 8 *1* [...] and peace. *Blank* And I [...] *2* [...] peace, and every man [...] *3* [...] I [...] *4* [...] ... [...]

Frag. 30 *1* [...] ... [...] *2* [...] not for fornication ... [...] *3* [...] ... to seek [...] *4* [...] ... [...]

―――――

1Q22 (1QDM ["Dibrê Moshe"; "Dires de Moïse"]) *1QWords of Moses*

Bibliography: J. Strugnell, 'Moses-Pseudepigrapha at Qumran: 4Q375, 4Q376 and Similar Works', in L.H. Schiffman (ed.), *Archaeology and History in the Dead Sea Scrolls* (Sheffield: JSOT, 1990) 221-256

Col. I *1* [And God spoke] to Moses in the year [forty] of the depart[ure of the children of I]sra[el from the land of E]gypt, in the eleventh mo[nth,] *2* the first day of the [mo]nth, saying: [Muster] all the con[gre]gation, climb [Mount Nebo] and stay [there,] you *3* and Elea[zar,] Aar[on's s]on. *Blank* Inter[pret for the heads of fam]ilies, for the levites and for all the [priests] and decree to the sons of *4* Israe[l the wo]rds of the Law which [I] commanded [you] on Mount S[i]nai to decree to th[em. Proclaim] in the[ir] ears everything *5* accura[tely,] for I will [requi]re it from them. [Take the] heavens and [the earth as witnesses against] them, [f]or they will not [lo]ve *6* wha[t] I have commanded [them,] th[ey] and [their] sons, [all] the days they [live upon the ea]rth. [However] I announce *7* that they will desert [me and ch]oose [the sins of the] peo[ples,] their [abo]minations [and] their [disre]putable acts [and will serve] *8* ido[l]s, who will become a tr[ap and] a snare. They will vio[late all the ho]ly [assem-

ו[מוקש ויע]ברו כול מקרא קו[דש ושבת הברית [ומועדים] את אשר
9 אנו[כי] מצוך היום [לע]שות אותם [להכו]ת אותם [מכה] רבה בקרב
[ה]ארץ א[שר המ]ה עוברים 10 את [הי]רדן שמה [לרש]תה והיה [א]שר
יבואו ע[לי]הם כול הקלל[ות] והשיגום ע[ד] אובדם ועד 11 הש[מד]ם
וידעו [כי] אמת נע[שתה] עמהם vacat ויקרא מושה לאלעזר בן
12 [אהרון] וליש[ו]ע בן נון ויאמר אלי[הם] דברו [כול דברי התורה עד]
לכלות א[ותם הסכת]

1 [י]שראל ושמע [היו]ם הזה [תהיה לע]ם לאלוהי [אלוהי]ך Col. II
וש[מרתה חוקי] ועדוותי [ומצוותי א]שר 2 [אנוכי] מצוך[הי]ום אשר
ת[עשה אותם כא]שר א[תה] עובר את ה[ירדן] ל[תת] לכה [ער]ים גדולות
3 [וטובו]ת ובת[י]ם מלאים כו[ל טוב כרמים וזיתים] אשר ל[וא נטעתה
ובו]רות חצוב[ים א]שר לו[א] 4 [ח]צבתה ואכל[ת]ה ושבעתה [השמר]
למה ירום [לב]בכה ושכ[חתה א]שר אנוכי [מצו]ך היום 5 [כי] הוא
חי[יכה] ואורך ימ[יכה] vacat [ויקרא] מושה ו[יאמר לבני י]שראל [זה]
ארבעים 6 [שנה מ]יום צ[את]נו מארץ [מצרים והיום הזה [אלו]הי
אלוה[ינו הוציא את הדב]רים [הא]לה מפיהו] 7 [את כול מש]פטיו <[וא]ת
כול מש]פטיו> אי[כה [אשא לבדי] טרחכם [ומש[א]כם וריבכם] ויהיה
8 [אשר בכלו]תני ל[...]ברית ולצוו[ת את] הד[רך אש]ר תלכו בה [הבו
לכם חכמים אשר י]עשו לבאר 9 [לכם ולבני]כם [את] כול דברי הת[ורה]
האלה הש[מרו מא]דה לנפשותיכם [לעשו]ת [אותם למה יב]עׁר וחרה אף
10 [אלוהיכם] בכם [ו]עצר את השמים [ממ]עלה להמטר ע[לי]כ]ם מטר ואת
ה[מים] למ[טה לארץ ל]תת לכם את 11 [התבו]אה vacat ו[יוסף לדב]ר
מושה אל בנ[י ישרא]ל אל[ה] מצ[וות אשר] צוה אל[ו]הים] לעשות אותם
[...]...[...] 12

1 [מקץ שבע ש]נים את שבת [הארץ תעשה ושבת ה]אר]ץ Col. III
תהיה לכה] לאכלה ל[כה ולבהמה ולחית] הש[דה] 2 [תהיה לאכו]ל [אשר
יו]תר ל[אביונים מן אחי]כה אשר ב[ארץ ושדהו לו]רע וכרמו לו[א]
יזמור אי[ש] 3 [ואת ספיחי קצירו לוא יקצור איש ולוא י]אסוף ל[ו] מאומה

blies], the sabbath of the covenant, [the festivals] which *9* I command you today [to k]eep. [This is why I will stri]ke them with a great [blow] in the midst of [the] land [for] *10* [the con]quest of whi[ch th]ey are going to cross [the Jo]rdan there. And [w]hen all the curse[s] happen t[o] them and overtake them un[til] they die and until *11* they are de[stroyed], then they will know [that] the truth has been ca[rried out] on them. *Blank* And Moses called Eleazar, son of *12* [Aaron] and Joshu[a, son of Nun, and said to] them: Speak [all the words of the Law, without] leaving any [out. Be silent,]

Col. II   *1* [I]srael, and listen! This [da]y [you are becoming the na]tion of God, your [God.] K[eep my rules], my stipulations, [my commandments wh]ich *2* [tod]ay [I] command you [to carry out. And wh]en y[ou] cross the [Jordan] I shall [give] you large [and good citie]s, *3* houses full of eve[ry wealth, vine-yards and olive groves] which [you did] n[ot plant, wel]ls bored [wh]ich you did no[t] *4* [d]ig, and you will eat and become replete. [Beware] of raising your [he]art and forget[ting wh]at I [command] you today; *5* [for] it is [your] life and [your] old age. *Blank* [And] Moses [spoke] and [said to the sons of I]srael: Forty *6* [years] have passed [from the] day of our dep[arture] from the land [of Egypt, and] to[day Go]d, [our] God, [has caused the]se [wo]rds [to issue] from h[is] mouth *7* [all] his [pre]cepts <[and] all [his] pre[cepts>. Ho]w [shall I alone carry] your burden, [your weig]ht, [your quarrels?] When *8* I [have finish]ed to [...] the covenant and to decree the pa[th] on [whi]ch you must] walk, [choose for yourselves wise men who will] have the task to ex-plain *9* [to you and to] your [sons] all these words of the L[aw.] Be [ve]ry ca[reful,] for your lives, [to observ]e [them, lest] the wrath *10* [of your God be en]kindled and break out against you, [and] he closes the skies [ab]ove, which make rain fall u[pon yo]u, and the [water] from under[neath the earth which] gives you *11* [the harv]est. *Blank* And Moses [continued spea]king to the son[s of Israe]l: The[se] are the command[ments which] Go[d] commands you to observe *12* [...]... [...]

Col. III   *1* [After seven ye]ars [you shall keep] the sabbath [of the land, and the yield of the sabbath of the] lan[d may be used by you] for food, by [you and your animals and the beasts of] the fi[eld.] *2* [it may be used for fo]od. [What rem]ains will be for [the poor from among] your [brothers] who are in [the land. N]o-on[e] will s[ow his field] nor prune [his vine.] *3* [No-one will har-vest what grows of it's own accord nor] gather [anything. Keep] al[l the]s[e

ושמרתה א[ת כו]ל דברי ה[ב]רית ה[א][ל]ה] 4 [לעשות אותם ו]יהי כי [...]

לעשות [...] ושמטתה [י]דכה בש[נ]ה הזא[ת] 5 [כול בעל משה ידו א]שר

[ישה מאומה ב]איש ו[אשר יהיה לו את אחיו] יש[מיט ידו בר]עהו כי

6 [תקרא שמטה] ל[א]ל[ו]הי אלוהיכ[ם את הנ]וכרי יגוש ואת אחיו ל[ו]א

[יגוש איש] כי בשנ[ה] 7 [הזאת יברככם אלו]הים [לכפר לכם] את

עוונ]ותיכם ...[...] 8 ...[...]...[...]ה בשנה [...] לחודש [...]...[...]ת ביום

הזה] ... כי ה[יו שטים 10 [במדבר אבו]תיכם עד יום] עש[ור לחודש

{ה[...]}ה [ביום ע]שר לחודש] 11 [כול עבודה ת]אסר וביום ע[שר ל]חודש

יכופר [...] לחודש [...] 12 ... וי]קחו [...]

1 ובעדת אלים [ובסוד קד]ושים וב[...]הם [בעד בני ישר]אל *Col.* IV

ובעד הא[רץ] 2 [ו]ל[קח] מן [דמו וי]שפך בארץ [...]...[...]

3 [...]צנה]...[ויכ]ופר להם בו [...] וידבר] מושה [לאמור] תעשו [...]

4 [...]ם חוקו]ת עול[ם לדורות]יכם [...]...[...]...[...] וביום [...]...[...]

יקח ה[...]בני ישראל 6 ...וכו]ל אשר [...]שמם לכ[ו]ל[...]ים לשנה

[...]הנפש אשר ה[ואה] 8 [...] על ספר [...]אני הכוהן [...] 9 [...] ו]סמך

את יד]יו ... [...] את כול אלה [...] 10 [...] ובשנה ה[...]ם האלה 11 [...] מן שני

השׂ[עירים ... [...] 12

1Q23 (1QEnGiants[a] ar) *1QEnoch Giants[a] ar*

J.T. Milik, *DJD I*, 97-98, pl. XIX
PAM 40.441, 40.447, 40.477, 40.538
DAJ
1Q24, 2Q26, 4Q203, 4Q530, 4Q531, 4Q532, 4Q533?, 4Q556, 6Q8
Bibliography: J.T. Milik, 'Turfan et Qumrân. Livre des Géants juif et
manichéen', in G. Jeremias, H.-W. Kuhn, H. Stegemann (eds.), *Tradition und
Glaube* (Göttingen: Vandenhoeck & Ruprecht, 1971) 117-127; J.T. Milik, The

1 [...]...[...] מאתין] 2 חמרין מאתין ערדין מאתי]ין ... *Frags.* 1+6

מאתין דכרין די] 3 ען מאתין תישין מאתי]ין ... חות] 4 ברא מן כל חוה

מן כ]ל עוף [...] 5 על מזג [...]

words of the] covenant *4* [to observe them, and] when [...] in order to do [...] And [in] thi[s y]ear you shall grant a release. *5* [Every creditor w]ho [has lent something to] someone, or [who possesses something from his brother,] will grant a re[lease to] his [fell]ow for *6* [a release] for [G]o[d, yo]ur [God, has been proclaimed. One may demand restitution] from the fore[igner, but from one's brother] no-[one shall demand restitution,] for in [that] year *7* [Go]d [will bless you, forgiving you your] sin[s ...] ... *8* [...] in the year [...] of the month of *9* [...] ... [...] on this day [... For] your [father]s wandered *10* [in the wilderness] until the [te]nth day of the month {the [... on the te]nth [day] of the month} *11* [You shall] refrain [from all work.] And on the te[nth] day [of the] month, atonement shall be made [...] of the month *12* [... and] they shall take [...]

Col. IV   *1* in the congregation of the gods [and in the council of the ho]ly ones, and in their [..., in favour of the sons of Isra]el and on behalf of the la[nd] *2* [And] ta[ke] from [its blood and] pour (it) on the earth [...] ... [...] *3* [...] ... [and atone]ment [shall be made] for them by it [... And] Moses [spoke saying:] Observe [...] *4* [... etern]al precepts for [your] generations [...] ... [...] And on the [...] day *5* [...] ... [...] he will take [...] the children of Israel [...] *6* [... and al]l that which [...] ... for a[ll] *7* [...] of the [...] year [...] the person who *8* [...] upon the book [...] ... the priest [...] *9* [...] he will lay [his] hands [...] all this *10* [...] in the [...] year [...] these *11* [...] of the two he-[goats ...] *12* [...]

1Q23 (1QEnGiants[a] ar) *1QEnoch Giants[a] ar*

Books of Enoch. Aramaic Fragments of Qumrân Cave 4 (Oxford: Clarendon, 1976) 302; K. Beyer, *ATTM*, 266-267; J.C. Reeves, *Jewish Lore in Manichaean Cosmogony: Studies in the Book of Giants Traditions* (Cincinnati: Hebrew Union College, 1991); F. García Martínez, 'The Book of Giants', in *Qumran and Apocalyptic. Studies on the Aramaic Texts from Qumran* (STDJ 9; Leiden: E.J. Brill, 1992) 97-115; L.T. Stuckenbruck, *The Book of Giants from Qumran* (TSAJ 63; Tübingen: Mohr Siebeck, 1997) 43-59

Frags. 1 + 6   *1* [...] ... [... two hundred] *2* donkeys, two hundred wild asses, two hund[red ... two hundred rams of the] *3* flock, two hundred he-goats, two hund[red ... wild] *4* animals, of each animal, of ea[ch bird ...] *5* of dilute wine [...]

Frags. 9+14+15   1 [...].[...]   2 [... ור]זי וידעו   3 [...].ה רבה

[...].בה וקטלו לשגי]א ...   5 [...]גברין מ[...].ל דין [...]   4 [...]בארעא

6 [...]...[...]

1Q24 (1QEnGiants^b ar) *1QEnoch Giants^b ar*

J.T. Milik, *DJD I*, 99, pl. XX
PAM 40.442, 40.443, 40.445, 40.538, 40.548
BNP

Frag. 1   1 [...]ן ורוח[...]   2 [...].שין ובחשין ו[...]   3 [...]ל...יא

[...] ולנה[...]   4 [...]תיא ולחמריא ו[...]   5 [...]א *vacat* ולכול [...]

6 [...].פיא *vacat* ולמ.[...]   7 [...]א ולברקיא [...]   8 [...]...[...]

Frag. 7   1 [...]. יום קץ[...]   2 [...]כולא גמירת[...]   3 [...]ע[ליהון

די[...]

Frag. 8   1 [...]...[...]   2 [...]לא שלם לכון[...]

1Q25 *1QApocryphal Prophecy*

J.T. Milik, *DJD I*, 100-101, pl. XX
PAM 40.536, 40.548

Frag. 1   1-2 ...[...]   3 וירא ...[...]   4 חקקתי להם [...]   5 להמה

וישי]מו ...[6 ובשומרון ישים [...]   7 בוז על נדיבים [...]   8 ל[ע]ב

בציו]ן [...]   9 [...]ירימו [...]

Frag. 4   1 [...]...[...]   2 [...]ממצוקותיהם [...]   3 [...]תח ואל יעוזו

ב[...]   4 [...]]וכופרם [...]   5 [...] אשר לו אמ[...]   6 [...]נאצו ולוא [...]

7 [...]שחו והשפלה [...]   8 [...]...[...]

Frags. 9 + 14 + 15 *1* […] *2* […] and they knew the mys[teries …] *3* […] a great […] on the earth […] *4* […] … and they killed a lot of […] *5* […] the giants […] which […] *6* […] … […]

1Q24 (1QEnGiants[b] ar) *1QEnoch Giants[b] ar*

1Q23, 2Q26, 4Q203, 4Q530, 4Q531, 4Q532, 4Q533?, 4Q556, 6Q8
Bibliography: L.T. Stuckenbruck, *Book of Giants*, 59-62; cf. 1Q23

Frag. 1 *1* […] and wind […] *2* […] … and hot ashes and […] *3* […] for the … and for … […] *4* […] the […] and for the donkeys and [for …] *5* […] *Blank* And for all […] *6* […] the … […] *Blank* And for … […] *7* […] and for the lightnings […] *8* […] … […]

Frag. 7 *1* […] day of the end […] *2* […] all of it, the consummation of […] *3* [… up]on those who […]

Frag. 8 *1* […] … […] *2* […] you will not have peace […]

1Q25 *1QApocryphal Prophecy*

BNP

Frag. 1 *1-2* … […] *3* and he saw … […] *4* I have engraved for them … […] *5* for them, and [t]he[y] pla[ced …] *6* and in Samaria he places […] *7* contempt for the noble ones […] *8* […] mo[ck]ery of Zio[n …] *9* […] they will elevate […]

Frag. 4 *1* […] … […] *2* […] from their afflictions […] *3* […] … and they shall not take refuge in […] *4* […] and their ransom […] *5* […] which he has. If […] *6* […] they reject, and not […] *7* […] … and the lowliness […] *8* […] … […]

Frag. 6 1 [...]...[...] 2 [...]בבהמות ו[...] 3 [...]קומה ולחכו[...]

4 [...]להביא מ[...]...[...]

1Q26 *1QInstruction*

J.T. Milik, *DJD I*, 101-102, pl. XX
PAM 40.449, 40.472
BNP

Frags. I+2 1 [...] 2 [...]ברז נה[י]ה וכן התהלך ו[כול תבואתכה ...]
3 [...]לם המזו[ן... אחוז]ת ארץ ועל פיהו [הרתה כול ...] 4 [...]תבואתכה
הג[... עם ראשית] פרי בטנכה ו[בכור כול ...] 5 [...] כאשר גלה אוזנכה
ברז נהי]ה לאמר וקדשתי ... [...] ... 6 [...]. לכה השמר לכה למה תכבדכה
ממנו ו[...] 7 [... בעבודתכה] ונארותה בכול תבואתכה ונ[כל]מתה בכול
מעשיכה במ[...] 8 [...]. ריבכה ובידו פקד [...] ואמר לו אני חל[...] 9
[...]לל[א ת]גדלכה נגד כול[...]כול [...] 10 [...]...[...]

1Q27 (1QMyst) *1QMysteries*

J.T. Milik, *DJD I*, 102-107, pls. XXI-XXII
PAM 40.523-40.528

Frag. 1 i 1 [...]כ[ול ...].[...] 2 [...]...[...]... רזי פשע 3 [...] כול
[חוכ[מת]מה ולוא ידעו רז נהיה ובקדמוניות לוא התבוננו ולוא 4 ידעו מה
אשר יבוא עליהמה ונפשממה לוא מלטו מרז נהיה *vacat* 5 וזה לכם האות כי
יהיה בהסגור מולדי עולה וגלה הרשע מפני הצדק כגלות [ח]ושך מפני
6 אור וכתום עשן וא[יננ]ו עוד כן יתם הרשע לעד והצדק יגלה כשמש תכון
7 תבל וכול תומכי רזי פלא אינמה עוד ודעה תמלא תבל ואין שם לע[ד]

Frag. 6   *1* […] … […] *2* […] by the animals and […] *3* […] arise and lick up […]
    4 […] to bring […] *5* […] … […]

1Q26 *1QInstruction*

4Q415, 4Q416, 4Q417, 4Q418, 4Q418a, 4Q423
Bibliography: D.J. Harrington, 'Wisdom at Qumran', in *Notre Dame Symposium*,
137-152

Frags. 1 + 2 (= 4Q423 3 + 4)   *1* […] … […] *2* […] by the mystery of exist[ence,
and thus walk. And] all your crops […] *3* […] … [… propert]y of land, and at
his command [it conceives all …] *4* […] your crops [… with the first] fruits of
your womb and [the firstborn of all …] *5* […] as he as opened your ears
through the mystery of existen[ce saying: I have sanctified …] *6* […]… for
you. Watch yourself lest you glorify yourself more than him and […] *7* […in
your work,] and you become cursed in all your crops, and you become
[asha]med in all your works by […] *8* […] your lawsuit, and through his hand
he visits […] and says to him: I am … […] *9* […] you will not glorify yourself
before all […] all […] *10* […] … […]

1Q27 (1QMyst) *1QMysteries*

DAJ
4Q299, 4Q300, 4Q301?

Frag. 1 *col.* 1 (= 4Q299 1; 4Q300 3)   *1* […] all […] *2* […] mysteries of sin *3* […
all] their wisd[om]. And they do not know the mystery of existence, nor understand ancient matters. And they do not *4* know what is going to happen to
them; and they will not save their souls from the mystery of existence. *Blank*
5 And this will be for you the sign /that this is going to happen./ When those
born of sin are locked up, evil will disappear before justice as [da]rkness disappears before *6* light. As smoke vanishes, and n[o] longer exists, so will evil
vanish for ever. And justice will be revealed like the sun which regulates *7* the
world. And all those who curb the wonderful mysteries will no longer exist.
And knowledge will pervade the world, and there will ne[ver] be folly there.

אולת 8 נכון הדבר לבוא ואמת המשא ומזה יודע לכמה כי לוא ישוב אחור

הלוא כול 9 העמים שנאו עול וביד כולמ[ה] יתהלך הלוא מפי כול לאומים

שמע האמת 10 היש שפה ולשון מחזקת בה מי גוי חפץ אשר יעושקנו חזק

ממנו מי 11 יחפץ כי יגזל ברשע הונו מי גוי אשר לוא עשק רעה[ו] איפה

עם אשר לוא 12 גזל הו[ן] ל[אחר...]...הו ותוצאות ית[...]

Frag. 1 II 1 [...]   2 [...]...[לו]לו שוו חשבונו[ת ...]   3 מנך [...]...[.] מה

הוא היותר ל[...]   4 כי אם המטיב והמרע אם יו.[...]   5 לוא יצלח לכול כן

כול טוב ממונו ברו[...]יגל]   6 בלוא הון ונמכר בלוא מחיר כי ...[...]   7 מה

מ[...]מחים כי אם כול [...]   8 דמי וכ[ול מח]יר לוא ישוה ב.[...]   *vacat* 9

10 לכול העמים ונ.ס.[...]   11 ידע כול מ[...]   12 [...]...[...]

1Q28 1QS title

J.T. Milik, *DJD I*, 107-108, pl. XXII
PAM 40.077

Title   [...] סר]ך היחד ומ[ן ...]

1QS (1QS) *1QRule of the Community*

M. Burrows, *DSSSMM II*
SHR 7101-7112
SHR
4Q255, 4Q256, 4Q257, 4Q258, 4Q259, 4Q260, 4Q261, 4Q262, 4Q263,
4Q264, 5Q11, 11Q29?
Bibliography: J. Licht, *The Rule Scroll: A Scroll from the Wilderness of Judaea-1QS,
1QSa, 1QSb: Text, Introduction and Commentary* (Jerusalem: Bialik, 1957) [He-
brew]; P. Wernberg-Møller, *The Manual of Discipline: Translated and Annotated
with an Introduction* (STDJ 1; Leiden: E.J. Brill, 1957); M. Weise, *Kultzeiten und
kultischer Bundesschluß in der 'Ordensregel' vom Toten Meer* (SP-B 3; Leiden:
E.J. Brill, 1961); H. Goedhart, *De Slothymne van het Manual of Discipline. A
theological-exegetical Study of 1QS X,9-XI,22* (Rotterdam, 1965); A.R.C.

8 This word will undoubtedly happen, the prediction is truthful. And by this he will show you that it is irrevocable: Do not all *9* nations loathe sin? And yet, it is about by the hands of all of them. Does not praise of truth come from the mouth of all nations? *10* And yet, is there perhaps one lip or one tongue which persists with it? What people would wish to be oppressed by another more powerful than itself? Who *11* would wish to be sinfully looted of its wealth? And yet, which is the people not to oppress its neighbour? Where is the people which has not *12* looted [another] of its wea[lth? ...] ... and the exits [...]

Frag. 1 *col.* II (= 4Q299 3) *1* [...] ... [...] *2* ... [...] for him schemes are advantageous [...] *3* ... [...] ... what benefit is there [...] *4* except he who does good and he who does evil. If ... [...] *5* He will have no success in anything. So all the good, his riches ... [...] *6* without wealth, and will be sold without them paying him, because ... [...] *7* What is [...] than life, except all [...] *8* value, and n[o pri]ce will be enough for [...] *9* *Blank* [...] *10* To all the nations ... [...] *11* God knows all [...] *12* [...] ... [...]

1Q28 1QS title

ROC 663

Title [... Ru]le of the Community and of [...]

1QS (1QS) *1QRule of the Community*

Leaney, *The Rule of Qumran and Its Meaning: Introduction, Translation and Commentary* (New Testament Library; London: SCM, 1966); J. Murphy-O'Connor, 'La genèse littéraire de la Règle de la Communauté', *RB* 76 (1969) 61-66; J.C. Trever, *Scrolls from Qumran Cave I* (Jerusalem: The Albright Institute of Archaeological Research and the Shrine of the Book, 1972) 126-127; J. Pouilly, *La Règle de la Communauté. Son évolution littéraire* (Cahiers de la Revue Biblique 17; Paris: Gabalda, 1976); M. Weinfeld, *The Organizational Pattern and the Penal Code of the Qumran Sect* (Fribourg/Göttingen: Vandenhoeck & Ruprecht, 1986); E. Qimron, J.H. Charlesworth, *PTSDSSP 1*, 1-51; C. Martone, *La "Regola della Comunità". Edizione critica* (Quaderni di Henoch 8; Torino: Silvio Zamorani, 1995); S. Metso, *The Textual Development of the Qumran Community Rule* (STDJ 21; Leiden: E.J. Brill, 1997)

1 ל[משכיל ...]שים לחיו [ספר ס]רך היחד לדרוש Col. I 2 אל
ב[כול לב ו]בכ[ול נפש]לעשות הטוב והישר לפניו כאשר 3 צוה ביד
מושה וביד כול עבדיו הנביאים ולאהוב כול 4 אשר בחר ולשנוא את כול
אשר מאס לרחוק מכול רע 5 ולדבוק בכול מעשי טוב ולעשות אמת
וצדקה ומשפט 6 בארץ ולוא ללכת עוד בשרירות לב אשמה ועיני זנות
7 לעשות כול רע ולהבי את כול הנדבים לעשות חוקי אל 8 בברית חסד
להיחד בעצת אל ולהתהלך לפניו תמים כול 9 הנגלות למועדי תעודותם
ולאהוב כול בני אור איש 10 כגורלו בעצת אל ולשנוא כול בני חושך איש
כאשמתו 11 בנקמת אל וכול הנדבים לאמתו יביאו כול דעתם וכוחם
12 והונם ביחד אל לברר דעתם באמת חוקי אל וכוחם לתכן 13 כתם
דרכיו וכול הונם כעצת צדקו ולוא לצעוד בכול אחד 14 מכול דברי אל
בקציהם ולוא לקדם עתיהם ולוא להתאחר 15 מכול מועדיהם ולוא לסור
מחוקי אמתו ללכת ימין ושמאול 16 וכול הבאים בסרך היחד י{א}עבורו
בברית {א}לפני אל לעשות 17 ככול אשר צוה ולוא לשוב מאחרו מכול
פחד ואימה ומצרף 18 נסוים בממשלת בליעל ובעוברם בברית יהיו
הכוהנים 19 והלויים מברכים את אל ישועות ואת כול מעשי אמתו וכול
20 העוברים בברית אומרים אחריהם אמן אמן vacat

21 vacat והכוהנים מספרים את צדקות אל במעשי גבורתום
22 ומשמיעים כול חסדי רחמים על ישראל והלויים מספרים 23 את
עוונות בני ישראל וכול פשעי אשמתם והטאתם בממשלת 24 בליעל
[וכו]ל העוברים בברית מודים אחריהם לאמור נעוינו 25 [פ]שענו
[חט]אנו הרשענו אנו ו[א]בותינו מלפנינו ב{ה}לכתנו 26 [...] אמת וצדיק[
...]משפטו בנו ובאבותינ[ו]

1 Col. II ורחמי חסדו גמל עלינו מעולם ועד עולם והכוהנים מברכים
את כול 2 אנשי גורל אל ההולכים תמים בכול דרכיו ואומרים יברככה

Col. I (= 4Q255 1; 4Q256 I, II)   *1* For [the Instructor ...] ... for his life, [book of the Ru]le of the Community: in order to seek *2* God with [all (one's) heart and] with a[ll (one's) soul;] in order to do what is good and just in his presence, as *3* he commanded by the hand of Moses and by the hand of all his servants the Prophets; in order to love everything *4* which he selects and to hate everything that he rejects; in order to keep oneself at a distance from all evil, *5* and to become attached to all good works; in order to do truth and justice and up-rightness *6* on earth and not to walk anymore in the stubbornness of a guilty heart and of lecherous eyes *7* performing every evil; in order to welcome all those who freely volunteer to carry out God's decrees *8* into the covenant of kindness; in order to be united in the counsel of God and walk in perfection in his sight, complying with all *9* revealed things concerning the regulated times of their stipulations; in order to love all the sons of light, each one *10* accord-ing to his lot in God's plan, and to detest all the sons of darkness, each one in accordance with his guilt *11* in God's vindication. All those who submit freely to his truth will convey all their knowledge, their energies, *12* and their riches to the Community of God in order to refine their knowledge in the truth of God's decrees and marshal their energies *13* in accordance with his perfect paths and all their riches in accordance with his just counsel. They shall not stray from any one *14* of all God's orders concerning their appointed times; they shall not advance their appointed times nor shall they retard *15* any one of their feasts. They shall not veer from his reliable precepts in order to go either to the right or to the left. *16* And all those who enter in the Rule of the Commu-nity shall establish a covenant before God in order to carry out *17* all that he commanded and in order not to stray from following him out of any fear, dread, or testing *18* (that might occur) during the dominion of Belial. When they enter the covenant, the priests *19* and the levites shall bless the God of victories and all the works of his faithfulness and all *20* those who enter the covenant shall repeat after them: «Amen, Amen». *Blank*

21 *Blank* The priests shall recite the just deeds of God in his mighty works, *22* and they shall proclaim all his merciful favours towards Israel. And the levites shall recite *23* the iniquities of the children of Israel, all their blameworthy offences and their sins during the dominion of *24* Belial. [And al]l those who enter the covenant shall confess after them and they shall say: «We have acted sinfully, *25* we have [trans]gressed, we have [si]nned, we have committed evil, we and our [fa]thers before us, inasmuch as we walk *26* [...] truth and just [...] his judgment upon us and upon o[ur] fathers;

Col. II (= 4Q256 II, III; 4Q257 II, III; 5Q11)   *1* but he has showered on us his merciful favour for ever and ever» And the priests will bless all *2* the men of God's lot who walk unblemished in all his paths and they shall say: «May he

בכול 3   טוב וישמורכה מכול רע ויאר לבכה בשכל חיים ויחונכה בדעת

עולמים 4   וישא פני חסדיו לכה לשלום עולמים *vacat* והלויים מקללים את

כול אנשי 5   גורל בליעל וענו ואמרו ארור אתה בכול מעשי רשע אשמתכה

יתנכה 6   אל זעוה ביד כול נוקמי נקם ויפקיד אחריכה כלה ביד כול משלמי

7 גמולים ארור אתה לאין רחמים כחושך מעשיכה וזעום אתה   8   באפלת

אש עולמים לוא יחונכה אל בקוראכה ולוא יסלח לכפר עווניך   9   ישא פני

אפו לנקמתכה ולוא יהיה לכה שלום בפי כול אוחזי אבות   10   וכול

העוברים בברית אומרים אחר המברכים והמקללים אמן אמן

vacat 11   והוסיפו הכוהנים והלויים ואמרו ארור בגלולי לבו לעבור

12 הבא בברית הזות ומכשול עוונו ישים לפניו להסוג בו והיה   13   בש'מעו

את דברי הברית הזות יתברך בלבבו לאמור שלום יהי לי   14   כיא

בשרירות לבי אלך ונספתה רוחו הצמאה עם הרויה לאין   15   סליחה אף אל

וקנאת משפטיו יבערו בו לכלת עולמים ידבקו בו כול   16   אלות הברית

הזות ויבדילהו אל לרעה ונכרת מתוך כול בני אור בהסוגו   17   מאחרי אל

בגלוליו ומכשול עוונו יתן גורלו בתוך ארורי עולמים   18   וכול באי הברית

יענו ואמרו אחריהם אמן אמן *vacat*

vacat 19   ככה יעשו שנה בשנה כול יומי ממשלת בליעל הכוהנים יעבורו

20 ברשונה בסרך לפי רוחותם זה אחר זה והלויים יעבורו אחריהם

21 וכול העם {.}יעבורו בשלישית בסרך זה אחר זה לאלפים ומאות

22 וחמשים ועשרות לדעת כול איש ישראל איש בית מעמדו ביחד אל

23 לעצת עולמים ולוא ישפול איש מבית מעמדו ולוא ירום ממקום גורלו

24 כיא הכול יהיו ביחד אמת וענות טוב ואהבת חסד ומחשבת צדק

25 איש לרעהו בעצת קודש ובני סוד עולמים וכול המואס לבוא

26 [בברית א]ל ללכת בשרירות לבו לוא [יעבור בי]חד אמתו כיא געלה

bless you with everything *3* good, and may he protect you from everything bad. May he illuminate your heart with the discernment of life and grace you with eternal knowledge. *4* May he lift upon you the countenance of his favour for eternal peace». *Blank* And the levites shall curse all the men of *5* the lot of Belial. They shall begin to speak and shall say: «Accursed are you for all your wicked, blameworthy deeds. May God hand you over *6* to terror by the hand of all those carrying out acts of vengeance. May he bring upon you destruction by the hand of all those who accomplish *7* retributions. Accursed are you, without mercy, according to the darkness of your deeds, and sentenced *8* to the gloom of everlasting fire. May God not be merciful when you entreat him. May he not forgive by purifying your iniquities. *9* May he lift the countenance of his anger to avenge himself on you, and may there be no peace for you by the mouth of those who intercede». *10* And all those who enter the covenant shall say, after those who pronounce blessings and those who pronounce curses: «Amen, Amen».

11 *Blank* And the priests and the levites shall continue, saying: «Cursed by the idols which his heart reveres *12* whoever enters this covenant, and places the obstacle of his iniquity in front of himself to fall over it. *13* When he hears the words of this covenant, he will congratulate himself in his heart, saying: «I will have peace, *14* in spite of my walking in the stubbornness of my heart». However, his spirit will be obliterated, the dry with the moist, without *15* mercy. May God's anger and the wrath of his verdicts consume him for everlasting destruction. May stick fast to him all *16* the curses of this covenant. May God separate him for evil, and may he be cut off from the midst of all the sons of light because of his straying *17* from following God on account of his idols and obstacle of his iniquity. May he assign his lot with the cursed ones for ever». *18* And all those who enter the covenant shall respond and shall say after them: «Amen, Amen». *Blank*

19 *Blank* They shall act in this way year after year, all the days of Belial's dominion. The priests shall enter *20* in order foremost, one behind the other, according to their spirits. And the levites shall enter after them. *21* In third place all the people shall enter in order, one after another, in thousands, hundreds, *22* fifties and tens, so that each Israelite may know his standing in God's Community *23* in conformity with an eternal plan. And no-one shall move down from his rank nor move up from the place of his lot. *24* For all shall be in a Community of truth, of proper meekness, of compassionate love and upright purpose, *25* towards each other, in a holy council, associates of an everlasting society. And anyone who declines to enter *26* [the covenant of Go]d in order to walk in the stubbornness of his heart shall not [enter the Com]munity of his truth, since

נפשו ביסורי דעת משפטי צדק לוא חזק למשוב חיו ועם   1   *Col. III*
ישרים לוא יתחשב   2   ודעתו וכוחו והונו לוא יבואו בעצת יחד כיא בסאון
רשע מחרשו וגואללים   3   בשובתו ולוא יצדק במתור שרירות לבו וחושך
יביט לדרכי אור בעין תמימים   4   לוא יתחשב לוא יזכה בכפורים ולוא
יטהר במי נדה ולוא יתקדש בימים   5   ונהרות ולוא יטהר בכול מי רחץ טמא
טמא יהיה כול יומי מאסו במשפטי   6   אל לבלתי התיסר ביחד עצתו כיא
ברוח עצת אמת אל דרכי איש יכופרו כול   7   עוונותו להביט באור החיים
וברוח קדושה ליחד באמתו יטהר מכול   8   עוונותו וברוח יושר וענו{ת}ה
תכופר חטתו ובענות נפשו לכול חוקי אל יטהר   9   בשרו להזות במי נדה
ולהתקדש במי דוכי ויהכין פעמיו להלכת תמים   10   בכול דרכי אל כאשר
צוה למועדי תעודתיו ולוא לסור ימין ושמאול ואין   11   לצעוד על אחד
מכול דבריו אז ירצה בכפורי ניחוח לפני אל והיתה לו לברית   12   יחד
עולמים   *vacat*

vacat 13   למשכיל להבין וללמד את כול בני אור בתולדות כול בני איש
14   לכול מיני רוחותם באותותם למעשיהם בדורותם ולפקודת נגועיהם עם
15   קצי שלומם מאל הדעות כול הויה ונהייה ולפני היותם הכין כול
מהשבתם (מחשבתם)   16   ובהיותם לתעודותם כמחשבת כבודו ימלאו
פעולתם ואין להשנות בידו   17   משפטי כול והואה יכלכלם בכול חפציהם
והואה ברא אנוש לממשלת   18   תבל וישם לו שתי רוחות להתהלך בם עד
מועד פקודתו

הנה רוחות   19   האמת והעול במעון אור תולדות האמת וממקור חושך
תולדות העול   20   וביד שר אורים ממשלת כול בני צדק בדרכי אור יתהלכו
וביד מלאך   21   חושך כול ממשלת בני עול ובדרכי חושך יתהלכו ובמלאך
חושך תעות   22   כול בני צדק וכול חטאתם ועוונותם ואשמתם ופשעי

Col. III (= 4Q255 2; 4Q257 III; 4Q262 1)   *1* his soul loathes the disciplines of knowledge of just judgments. He has not the strength to convert his life and shall not be counted with the upright. *2* His knowledge, his energy and his wealth shall not enter the council of the Community because he ploughs in the mud of wickedness and there are stains *3* on his conversion. He shall not be justified while he maintains the stubbornness of his heart, since he regards darkness as paths of light. In the source of the perfect *4* he shall not be counted. He will not become clean by the acts of atonement, nor shall he be purified by the cleansing waters, nor shall he be made holy by seas *5* or rivers, nor shall he be purified by all the water of ablution. Defiled, defiled shall he be all the days he spurns the decrees *6* of God, without allowing himself to be taught by the Community of his counsel. For it is by the spirit of the true counsel of God that are atoned the paths of man, all *7* his iniquities, so that he can look at the light of life. And it is by the holy spirit of the community, in its truth, that he is cleansed of all *8* his iniquities. And by the spirit of uprightness and of humility his sin is atoned. And by the compliance of his soul with all the laws of God *9* his flesh is cleansed by being sprinkled with cleansing waters and being made holy with the waters of repentance. May he, then, steady his steps in order to walk with perfection *10* on all the paths of God, as he has decreed concerning the appointed times of his assemblies and not turn aside, either right or left, nor *11* infringe even one of all his words. In this way he will be admitted by means of atonement pleasing to God, and for him it will be the covenant *12* of an everlasting Community. *Blank*

13 Blank The Instructor should instruct and teach all the sons of light about the nature of all the sons of man, *14* concerning all the ranks of their spirits, in accordance with their signs, concerning their deeds in their generations, and concerning the visitation of their punishments and *15* the times of their reward. From the God of knowledge stems all there is and all there shall be. Before they existed he established their entire design. *16* And when they have come into being, at their appointed time, they will execute all their works according to his glorious design, without altering anything. In his hand are *17* the laws of all things and he supports them in all their affairs. He created man to rule *18* the world and placed within him two spirits so that he would walk with them until the moment of his visitation: they are the spirits *19* of truth and of deceit. From the spring of light stem the generations of truth, and from the source of darkness the generations of deceit. *20* And in the hand of the Prince of Lights is dominion over all the sons of justice; they walk on paths of light. And in the hand of the Angel of *21* Darkness is total dominion over the sons of deceit; they walk on paths of darkness. From the Angel of Darkness stems the corruption of *22* all the sons of justice, and all their sins, their iniquities, their guilts and their offensive deeds are under his dominion

מעשיהם בממשלתי 23 לפי רזי אל עד קצו וכול נגועיהם ומועדי צרותם
בממשלת משטמתו 24 וכול רוחי גורלו להכשיל בני אור ואל ישראל
ומלאך אמתו עזר לכול 25 בני אור והואה ברא רוחות אור וחושך ועליהון
יסד כול מעשה 26 [ע]ל[ ] דרכ]יהן כול עבודה ועל דרכיהן [כו]ל[ ] ע[ב]ודה
אחת אהב אל לכול

Col. IV 1 [מ]ועדי עולמים ובכול עלילותיה ירצה לעד אחת תעב סודה
וכול דרכיה שנא לנצח vacat

vacat 2 ואלה דרכיהן בתבל להאיר בלבב איש ולישר לפניו כול דרכי
צדק אמת ולפחד לבבו במשפטי 3 אל ורוח ענוה וא'רך אפים ורוב רחמים
וטוב עולמים ושכל ובינה וחכמת גבורה מאמנת בכול 4 מעשי אל ונשענת
ברוב חסדו ורוח דעת בכול מחשבת מעשה וקנאת משפטי צדק ומחשבת
5 קודש ביצר סמוך ורוב חסדים על כול בני אמת וטהרת כבוד מתעב כול
גלולי נדה והצנע לכת 6 בערמת כול וחבא לאמת רזי דעת vacat אלה סודי
רוח לבני אמת תבל ופקודת כול הולכי בה למרפא 7 ורוב שלום באורך
ימים ופרות זרע עם כול ברכות עד ושמחת עולמים בחיי נצח וכליל כבוד
8 עם מדת הדר באור עולמים vacat

vacat 9 ולרוח עולה רחוב נפש ושפול ידים בעבודת צדק רשע ושקר
גוה ורום לבב כחש ורמיה אכזרי 10 ורוב חנף קצור אפים ורוב אולת
וקנאת זדון מעשי תועבה ברוח זנות ודרכי נדה בעבודת טמאה 11 ולשון
גדופים עורון עינים וכבוד אוזן קושי עורף וכובוד לב ללכת בכול דרכי
חושך וערמת רוע ופקודת 12 כול הולכי בה לרוב נגועים ביד כול מלאכי
חבל לשחת עולמים באף עברת אל נקמ{ו}ת לזעות נצח וחרפת 13 עד עם
כלמת כלה באש מחשכים וכול קציהם לדורותם באבל יגון ורעת מרורים
בהויות חושך עד 14 כלותם לאין שרית ופליטה למו vacat

23 in compliance with the mysteries of God, until his moment; and all their afflictions and their periods of grief are caused by the dominion of his enmity; *24* and all the spirits of his lot cause the sons of light to fall. However, the God of Israel and the angel of his truth assist all *25* the sons of light. He created the spirits of light and of darkness and on them established every deed, *26* [o]n their [path]s every labour ‹and on their paths [eve]ry [labo]ur›. God loves one of them for all

Col. IV (= 4Q257 v)   *1* eternal [a]ges and in all his deeds he takes pleasure for ever; the other one he detests, his counsel and all his paths he hates forever. *Blank*

2 Blank These are their paths in the world: to enlighten the heart of man, straighten out in front of him all the paths of true justice, establish in his heart respect for the precepts *3* of God; it is a spirit of meekness, of patience, generous compassion, eternal goodness, intelligence, understanding, potent wisdom which trusts in all *4* the deeds of God and depends on his abundant mercy; a spirit of knowledge in all the plans of action, of enthusiasm for the decrees of justice, *5* of holy plans with firm purpose, of generous compassion with all the sons of truth, of magnificent purity which detests all unclean idols, of careful behaviour *6* in wisdom concerning everything, of concealment concerning the truth of the mysteries of knowledge. *Blank* These are the foundations of the spirit of the sons of truth (in) the world. And the reward of all those who walk in it will be healing, *7* plentiful peace in a long life, fruitful offspring with all everlasting blessings, eternal enjoyment with endless life, and a crown of glory *8* with majestic raiment in eternal light. *Blank*

9 Blank However, to the spirit of deceit belong greed, sluggishness in the service of justice, wickedness, falsehood, pride, haughtiness of heart, dishonesty, trickery, cruelty, *10* much insincerity, impatience, much foolishness, impudent enthusiasm for appalling acts performed in a lustful passion, filthy paths in the service of impurity, *11* blasphemous tongue, blindness of eyes, hardness of hearing, stiffness of neck, hardness of heart in order to walk in all the paths of darkness and evil cunning. And the visitation *12* of all those who walk in it will be for an abundance of afflictions at the hands of all the angels of destruction, for eternal damnation by the scorching wrath of the God of revenges, for permanent terror and shame *13* without end with the humiliation of destruction by the fire of the dark regions. And all the ages of their generations (they shall spend) in bitter weeping and harsh evils in the abysses of darkness until *14* their destruction, without there being a remnant or a survivor for them. *Blank*

15 vacat באלה תולדות כול בני איש ובמפלגיהן ינחלו כול צבאותם
לדורותם ובדרכיהן יתהלכו וכול פעולת 16 מעשיהם במפלגיהן לפי נחלת
איש בין רוב למועט לכול קצי עולמים כיא אל שמן בד בבד עד קץ
17 אחרון ויתן איבת עולם בין מפלגות[◌] תועבת אמת עלילות עולה ותועבת
עולה כול דרכי אמת וקנאת 18 ריב על כול משפטיהן כיא לוא יחד יתהלכו
ואל ברזי שכלו ובחכמת כבודו נתן קץ להיות עולה ובמועד 19 פקודה
ישמידנה לעד ואז תצא לנצח אמת תבל כיא התגוללה בדרכי רשע בממשלת
עולה עד 20 מועד משפט נחרצה ואז יברר אל באמתו כול מעשי גבר יזקק
לו מבני איש להתם כול רוח עולה מתכמי 21 בשרו ולטהרו ברוח קודש
מכול עלילות רשעה ויז עליו רוח אמת כמי נדה מכול תועבות שקר
והתגולל 22 ברוח נדה להבין ישרים בדעת עליון וחכמת בני שמים
להשכיל תמימי דרך כיא בם בחר אל לברית עולמים 23 ולהם כול כבוד
אדם ואין עולה והיה לבושת כול מעשי רמיה עד הנה יריבו רוחי אמת ועול
בלבב גבר 24 יתהלכו בחכמה ואולת וכפי נחלת איש באמת יצדק וכן
ישנ{נ}א עולה וכירשתו בגורל עול ירשע בו וכן 25 יתעב אמת כיא בד
בבד שמן אל עד קץ נחרצה ועשות חדשה והואה ידע פעולת מעשיהן לכול
קצי 26 [עולמי]ם וינחילן לבני איש לדעת טוב[ורע ... ו]ל[ה]פיל גורלות
לכול חי לפי רוחו ב.[... עד מועד]הפקודה

Col. v 1 vacat וזה הסרך לאנשי היחד המתנדבים לשוב מכול רע
ולהחזיק בכול אשר צוה לרצונו להבדל מעדת 2 אנשי העול להיות ליחד
בתורה ובהון ומשובים על פי בני צדוק הכוהנים שומרי הברית ⌐על פי רוב
אנשי 3 היחד המחזקים בברית על פיהם יצא תכון הגורל לכול דבר לתורה
ולהון ולמשפט לעשות אמת יחד וענוה 4 צדקה ומשפט ואהבת חסד והצנע

15 Blank In these (lies) the history of all men; in their (two) divisions all their armies have a share for their generations; in their paths they walk; every deed *16* they do (falls) into their divisions, dependent on what might be the birthright of man, great or small, for all eternal times. For God has sorted them into equal parts until the *17* last time, and has put an everlasting loathing between /their/ divisions. Deeds of injustice are an abhorrence to truth and all the paths of truth are an abhorrence to injustice. (There exists) a violent *18* conflict in respect of all their decrees since they can not walk together. God, in the mysteries of his knowledge and in the wisdom of his glory, has determined an end to the existence of injustice and on the appointed time *19* of the visitation he will obliterate it for ever. Then truth shall rise up forever (in) the world, for it has been defiled in paths of wickedness during the dominion of injustice until *20* the time appointed for the judgment decided. Then God will refine, with his truth, all man's deeds, and will purify for himself the structure of man, ripping out all spirit of injustice from the innermost part *21* of his flesh, and cleansing him with the spirit of holiness from every wicked deeds. He will sprinkle over him the spirit of truth like lustral water (in order to cleanse him) from all the abhorrences of deceit and (from) the defilement *22* of the unclean spirit, in order to instruct the upright ones with knowledge of the Most High, and to make understand the wisdom of the sons of heaven to those of perfect behaviour. For those God has chosen for an everlasting covenant *23* and to them shall belong all the glory of Adam. There will be no more injustice and all the deeds of trickery will be a dishonour. Until now the spirits of truth and injustice feud in the heart of man: *24* they walk in wisdom or in folly. In agreement with man's inheritance in the truth, he shall be righteous and so abhor injustice; and according to his share in the lot of injustice, he shall act wickedly in it, and so *25* abhor the truth. For God has sorted them into equal parts until the appointed end and the new creation. He knows the result of their deeds for all times *26* [everlas]ting and has given them as a legacy to the sons of man so that they know good [and evil ... and] to cast the lots of every living being according to his spirit in [... until the time of] the visitation.

Col. v (= 4Q261 1; cf. 4Q256 IX; 4Q258 I, II)   *1 Blank* This is the rule for the men of the Community who freely volunteer to convert from all evil and to keep themselves steadfast in all he commanded in compliance with his will. They should keep apart from the congregation of *2* the men of injustice in order to constitute a Community in law and possessions, and acquiesce to the authority of the sons of Zadok, the priests who safeguard the covenant /and/ to the authority of the multitude of the men of *3* the Community, those who persevere steadfastly in the covenant. By their authority, decision by lot shall be made in every affair involving the law, property and judgment, to achieve together truth and humility, *4* justice and uprightness, compassionate love and

לכת בכול דרכיהם אשר לוא ילך איש בשרירות לבו לתעות אחר לבבו
5 ועינוהי ומחשבת יצרו (כ)יאאם למול ביחד עורלת יצר ועורף קשה ליסד
מוסד אמת לישראל ליחד ברית 6 עולם לכפר לכול המתנדבים לקודש
באהרון ולבית האמת בישראל והנלוים עליהם ליחד ולריב ולמשפט
7 להרשיע כול עוברי חוק ואלה תכון דרכיהם על כול החוקים האלה
בהאספם ליחד כול הבא לעצת היחד 8 יבוא בברית אל לעיני כול
המתנדבים ויקם על נפשו בשבועת אסר לשוב אל תורת מושה ככול אשר
צוה בכול 9 לב ובכול נפש לכול הנגלה ממנה לבני צדוק הכוהנים שומרי
הברית ודורשי רצונו ולרוב אנשי בריתם 10 המתנדבים יחד לאמתו
ולהתלך ברצונו ואשר יקים על נפשו להבדל מכול אנשי העול
ההולכים 11 בדרך הרשעה כיא לוא החשבו בבריתו כיא לוא בקשו ולוא
דרשוהי בחוקוהי לדעת הנסתרות אשר תעו 12 בם לאש<ש>מה והנגלות
עשו ביד רמה לעלות אף למשפט ולנקום נקם באלות ברית לעשות בם
{מ}שפטים 13 גדולים לכלת עולם לאין שרית *vacat*

אל יבוא במים לגעת בטהרת אנשי הקודש כיא לוא יטהרו 14 כי אם
שבו מרעתם כיא טמא בכול עוברי דברו ואשר לוא ייחד עמו בעבודתו
ובהו{וש}ו פן ישיאנו 15 עוון אשמה כיא ירחק ממנו בכול דבר כיא כן
כתוב מכול דבר שקר תרחק ואשר לוא ישוב איש מאנשׁ' 16 היחד על
פיהם לכול תורה ומשפט ואשר לוא יוכל מהונם כול ולוא ישתה ולוא יקח
מידם כול מאומ{א}ה 17 אשר לוא במחיר כאשר כתוב חדלו לכם מן האדם
אשר נשמה באפו כיא במה נחשב הואה כיא 18 כול אשר לוא נחשבו
בבריתו להבדיל אותם ואת כול אשר להם ולוא ישען איש הקודש על כול
מעשי 19 הבל כיא הבל כול אשר לוא ידעו את בריתו וכול מנאצי דברו
ישמיד מתבל וכול מעשיהם לנדה 20 לפניו וטמא בכול הונ{ו}ם וכיא יבוא

seemly behaviour in all their paths. No-one should walk in the stubbornness of his heart in order to go astray following his heart 5 and his eyes and the musings of his inclination. Instead he should circumcise in the Community the foreskin of his tendency and of his stiff neck in order to lay a foundation of truth for Israel, for the Community of the eternal 6 covenant. They should make atonement for all who freely volunteer for holiness in Aaron and for the house of truth in Israel and for those who join them for community, lawsuit and judgment, 7 to proclaim as guilty all those who trespass the decree. These are the regulations of their behaviour concerning all these decrees when they are enrolled in the Community. Whoever enters the council of the Community 8 enters the covenant of God in the presence of all who freely volunteer. He shall swear with a binding oath to revert to the Law of Moses, according to all that he commanded, with whole 9 heart and whole soul, in compliance with all that has been revealed of it to the sons of Zadok, the priests who keep the covenant and interpret his will and to the multitude of the men of their covenant 10 who freely volunteer together for this truth and to walk according to his will. He should swear by the covenant to be segregated from all the men of injustice who walk 11 along the path of wickedness. For they are not included in his covenant since they have neither sought nor examined his decrees in order to know the hidden matters in which they err 12 by their own fault and because they treated revealed matters with disrespect; this is why wrath will rise up for judgment in order to effect revenge by the curses of the covenant, in order to administer fierce 13 punishments for everlasting annihilation without there being any remnant. *Blank*

He should not go into the waters to share in the pure food of the men of holiness, for one is not cleansed 14 unless one turns away from ones wickedness, for he is unclean among all the transgressors of his word. No-one should associate with him in his work or in his possessions in order not to encumber him 15 with blameworthy iniquity; rather he should remain at a distance from him in every task, for it is written as follows (*Exod 23:7*): «You shall remain at a distance from every lie». None of the men 16 of the Community should acquiesce to their authority in any law or regulation. No-one should eat of any of their possessions, or drink or accept anything from their hands, 17 unless at its price, for it is written(*Isa 2:22*): «Shun the man whose breath is in his nostrils, for how much is he worth?» For 18 all those not numbered in his covenant will be segregated, they and all that belongs to them. No holy man should support himself on any deed of 19 futility, for futile are all those who do not know the covenant. And all those who scorn his word he shall cause to vanish from the world; all their deeds are uncleanness 20 before him and there is uncleanness in all {his} their possessions. And when someone enters the covenant to be-

בברית לעשות ככול החוקים האלה להיחד לעדת קודש ודרשו   21 את
רוחום ביחד בין איש לרעהו לפי שכלו ומעשיו בתורה על פי בני אהרון
המתנדבים ביחד להקים   22 את בריתו ולפקוד את כול חוקיו אשר צוה
לעשות ועל פי ר.}ב ישראל המתנדבים לשוב ביחד לבריתו   23 וכתבם
בסרך איש לפני רעהו לפי שכלו ומעשיו להשמע הכול איש לרעהו הקטן
לגדול ולהיות   24 פוקדם את רוחם ומעשיהם שנה בשנה להעלות איש לפי
שכלו ותום דרכו ולאחרו כנעוותו להוכיᵓ   25 איש את רעהו באמת וענוה
ואהבת חסד לאיש *vacat*

אל ידבר אלוהיהי (אל אחיהו) באף או בתלונה   26 או בעורף [קשה או
בקנאת] רוח רשע ואל ישנאהו [בעור]ל[ת]לבבו כיא ביומ}יו{ יוכיחנו ולוא

Col. VI   1 ישא עליו עוון וגם אל יביא איש על רעהו דבר לפני הרבים
אשר לוא בתוכחת לפני עדים ב}.{אᵓלה   2 יתהלכו בכול מגוריהם כול
הנמצא איש את רעהו וישמעו הקטן לגדול למלאכה ולממון ויחד יואכלו
3 ויחד יברכו }לה{ויחד יועצו ובכול מקום אשר יהיה שם עשרה אנשים
מעצת החיד (היחד) אל ימש מאתם איש   4 כוהן ואיש כתכונו ישבו לפניו
וכן ישאלו לעצתם לכול דבר והיה כיא יערוכו השול}חן{ לאכול או התירוש
5 לשתות הכוהן ישלח ידו לרשונה להברך בראשית הלחם <או התירוש
לשתות הכוהן ישלח ידו לרשונה   6 להברך בראשית הלחם> והתירוש ואל
ימש במקום אשר יהיו שם העשרה איש דורש בתורה יומם ולילה   7 תמיד
על יפות איש לרעהו והרבים ישקודו ביחד את שלישית כול לילות השנה
לקרוא בספר ולדרוש משפט   8 ולברך ביחד *vacat*

}ה{וזה הסרך למושב הרבים איש בתכונו הכוהנים ישבו לרשונה
והזקנים בשנית ושאר   9 כול העם ישבו איש בתכונו וכן ישאלו למשפט
ולכול עצה ודבר אשר יהיה לרבים להשיב איש את מדעו   10 לעצת היחד
vacat אל ידבר איש בתוך דברי רעהו טרם יכלה אחיהו לדבר *vacat* וגם אל

82

have in compliance with all these decrees, enrolling in the assembly of holiness, they shall examine *21* their spirits in the Community, one another, in respect of his insight and of his deeds in law, under the authority of the sons of Aaron, those who freely volunteer in the Community to set up *22* his covenant and to follow all the decrees which he commanded to fulfil, and under the authority of the majority of Israel, those who freely volunteer to return within the Community to his covenant. *23* And they shall be recorded in order, one before the other, according to one's insight and one's deeds, in such a way that each one obeys another, the junior the senior. And *24* their spirit and their deeds must be tested, year after year, in order to upgrade each one to the extent of his insight and the perfection of his path, or to demote him according to his failings. One should reproach *25* one another in truth, in meekness and in compassionate love for one's fellow-man. *Blank*

No-one should speak to his brother in anger or muttering, *26* or with a hard [neck or with passionate] spirit of wickedness, and he should not detest him [in the fore]sk[in] of his heart, but instead reproach him that day so as not

Col. VI (= 4Q256 XI; 4Q258 II, III; 4Q261 3; 4Q263)   *1* to incur a sin because of him. And in addition, no-one should raise a matter against his fellow in front of the Many unless it is with reproof in the presence of witnesses. In this way *2* shall they behave in all their places of residence. Whenever one fellow meets another, the junior shall obey the senior in work and in money. They shall eat together, *3* together they shall bless and together they shall take counsel. In every place where there are ten men of the Community council, there should not be missing amongst them *4* a priest. And every one shall sit according to his rank before him, and in this way shall they be asked for their counsel in every matter. And when they prepare the table to dine or the new wine *5* for drinking, the priest shall stretch out his hand as the first to bless the first fruits of the bread <or the new wine for drinking, the priest shall stretch out his hand as the first *6* to bless the first fruits of the bread> and the new wine. And in the place in which the Ten assemble there should not be missing a man to interpret the law day and night, *7* always, one relieving another. And the Many shall be on watch together for a third of each night of the year in order to read the book, explain the regulation, *8* and bless together. *Blank*

This is the Rule for the session of the Many. Each one by his rank: the priests will sit down first, the elders next and the remainder of *9* all the people will sit down in order of rank. And following the same system they shall be questioned with regard to judgment, all counsel and any matter referred to the Many, so that each can impart his knowledge *10* to the council of the Community. *Blank* No-one should talk during the speech of his fellow before his

ידבר לפני תכונו הכתוב 11 לפניו האיש הנשאל ידבר בתרו ובמושב
הרבים אל ידבר איש כול דבר אשר לוא להפץ (לחפץ) הרבים וכיא האיש
12 המבקר על הרבים וכול איש אשר יש אתו דבר לדבר לרבים אשר לוא
במעמד האיש השואל את עצת 13 היחד ועמד האיש על רגלוהי ואמר יש
אתי דבר לדבר לרבים אם יומרו לו ידבר וכולה מתנדב (וכול המתנדב)
מישראל 14 להוסיף על עצה היחד ידורשהו האיש הפקיד ברואש הרבים
לשכלו ולמעשיו ואם ישיג מוסר יביאהו 15 בברית לשוב לאמת ולסור
מכול עול והʰבינהו בכול משפטי היחד ואחר בבואו לעמוד לפני הרבים
ונשאלו 16 הכול על דבריו וכאשר יצא הגורל על עצה הרבים יקרב או
ירחק ובקורבו לעצת היחד לוא יגע בטהרת 17 הרבים עד אשר ידרושהו
לרוחו ומעשו עד מʰלואת לו שנה תמימה וגם הואה אל יתערב בהון הרבים
18 ובמולאת לו שנה בתוך היחד ישאלו הרבים על דבריו לפי שכלו ומעשיו
בתורה ואם יצא לו הגורל 19 לקרוב לסוד היחד על פי הכוהנים ורוב
אנשי בריתם יקר{י}בו גם את הונו ואת מלאכתו אל יד האיש 20 המבקר
{א}על מלאכת הרבים וכתבו בחשבון בידו ועל הרבים לוא יוציאנו אל יגע
במשקה הרבים עד 21 מולאת לו שנה שנית בתוך אנשי היחד ובמולאת לו
השנה השנית יפקודהו על פי הרבים ואם יצא לו 22 הגורל לקרבו ליחד
יכתובהו בסרך תכונו בתוך אחיו לתורה ולמשפט ולטוʰרה ולערב את הונו
ויה' עצתו 23 ליחד ומשפטו vacat

vacat 24 ואלʰ המשפטים אשר ישפטו בם במדרש יחד על פי הדברים
אם ימצא בם איש אשר ישקר 25 בהון והואה יודע ויבדילהו מתוך טהרת
רבים שנה אחת ונענשו את רביעית לחמו ואשר ישוב 26 רעהו בקשי
עורף ידבר בקוצר אפים לפרוע את יסוד עמיתו באמרות את פי רעהו
הכתוב לפנוהי 27 [וה]ושיעה ידו לוא ונ{א}ʰנעש שנה אח]ת ... וא[שר
יזכיר דבר בשם הנכבד על כול ה.].[...]

brother has finished speaking. *Blank* And neither should he speak before one whose rank is listed *11* before his own. Whoever is questioned should speak in his turn. And in the session of the Many no-one should utter anything without the consent of the Many, save the *12* Inspector of the Many. And anyone who has something to say to the Many but is not in the position of one who is asking questions to the Community council, *13* that man should stand up and say: «I have something to say to the Many». If they tell him to, he should speak. And anyone from Israel who freely volunteers *14* to enrol in the council of the Community, the man appointed at the head of the Many shall test him with regard to his insight and his deeds. If he suits the discipline he shall let him enter *15* into the covenant so that he can revert to the truth and shun all injustice, and he shall teach him all the precepts of the Community. And then, when he comes in to stand in front of the Many, they shall be questioned, *16* all of them, concerning his affairs. And depending on the outcome of the lot in the council of the Many he shall be included or excluded. When he is included in the Community council, he must not touch the pure food of *17* the Many until they test him about his spirit and about his deeds, until he has completed a full year; neither should he share in the possession of the Many. *18* When he has completed a year within the Community, the Many will be questioned about his affairs, concerning his insight and his deeds in connection with the law. And if the lot results in him *19* entering the inner council of the Community according to the priests and the majority of the men of their covenant, his possessions and his earnings will also be joined at the hand of the *20* Inspector of the earnings of the Many. And they shall credit it to his account, but they shall not use it for the Many. He must not touch the drink of the Many until *21* he completes a second year among the men of the Community. And when this second year is complete he will be examined by command of the Many. And if *22* the lot results in him joining the Community, they shall enter him in the order of his rank among his brothers for the law, for the judgment, for purity and for the placing of his possessions. And his advice will be *23* for the Community as will his judgment. *Blank*

24 Blank And these are the regulations by which they shall judge in an examination of the Community depending on the case. If one is found among them who has lied *25* knowingly concerning possessions, he shall be excluded from the pure food of the Many for a year and they shall withhold a quarter of his bread. And whoever retorts to *26* his fellow with stubbornness, (and) speaks with brusqueness, ruining the footing he has with him, defying the authority of his fellow who is enrolled ahead of him, *27* [he h]as taken the law into his own hands; and he will be punished for on[e] year [... Who]ever enunciates the Name (which is) honoured above all ... [...]

Col. VII 1 ואם קלל או להבעת מצרה או לכול דבר אשר לו {...} הואה
קורה בספר או מברך והבדילהו 2 ולוא ישוב עוד על עצה היחד vacat ואם
באחד מן הכוהנים הכתובים בספר דבר בחמה ונענש שנה 3 אחת ומובדל
{א}על נפשו מן טהרת רבים ואם בשגגה דבר ונענש ששה חודשים vacat
ואשר יכחס במדעו 4 ונענש ששה חודשים והאיש אשר יצחה בלו משפט
את רעהו בדעתא ונענש שנה אחת 5 ומובדל ואשר ידבר את רעהו במרום
או יעשה רמיה במדעו ונענש ששה חודשים ואם 6 vacat ברעהו יתרמה
ונענש שלושה חודשים vacat ואם בהון היחד יתרמה לאבדו ושלמו {...}
7 ברושו vacat 7a vacat 7b vacat

8 ואם לוא תשיג ידו לשלמו ונענש ששים יום ואשר יטו{.} לרעהו אשר
לוא {.}במשפט ונענש {ששה חודשים} שנה אחת 9 וכן לנוקם לנפשו כול
דבר ואשר ידבר בפיהו דבר נבל שלושה חודשים ולמדבר בתוך דברי רעהו
10 עשרת ימים ואשר ישכוב ויישן במושב הרבים שלושים ימים וכן לאיש
הנפ{ת}ר במושב הרבים 11 אשר לוא בעצה וחנם (והנם) עד שלוש
פעמים על מושב אחד ונענש עשרת ימים ואם יז{.}פו vacat
12 ונפטר ונענש שלושים יום ואשר יהלך לפני רעהו ערום ולוא היה אנוש
ונענש ששה חודשים 13 ואיש אשר ירוק אל תוך מושב הרבים ונענש
שלושים יום ואשר יוציא ידו מתוחת בגדו והואה 14 פוח ונר{ע}אתה
ערותו ונענש שלושים יום ואשר יש{ה}חק בסכלות להשמיע קולו ונענש
שלושים 15 יום והמוציא את יד שמאולו לשוח בה ונענש עשרת ימים
והאיש אשר ילך רכיל ברעהו 16 והבדילהו שנה אחת מטהרת הרבים
ונענש ואיש ברבים ילך רכיל לש{ו}לח הואה מאתם 17 ולוא ישוב עוד
והאיש אשר ילון על יסוד היחד ישלחהו ולוא ישוב ואם על רעהו ילון
18 אשר לוא במשפט ונענש ששה חודשים והאיש אשר תזוע רוחו מיסוד
היחד לבגוד באמת 19 וללכת בשרירות לבו אם ישוב ונענש שתי שנים
ברשונה {ו.}לוא יגע בטהרת הרבים vacat 20 vacat {...} ובשנית לוא יגע
ב{ט}הרת משקה הרבים ואחר כול אנשי היחד ישב ובמלואת 21 לו שנתים

86

Col. vii (= 4Q259 i-ii; 4Q261 5, 6; cf. 4Q265 1 i; 4Q266 10 ii; 4Q270 7 i; 11Q29 ?) *1* whether blaspheming, or suddenly overtaken by misfortune or for any other reason, {…} or reading a book, or blessing, will be excluded *2* and shall not go back ever to the Community council. *Blank* And if he has spoken angrily against one of the priests enrolled in the book, he will be punished for one *3* year and shall be excluded, under sentence of death, from the pure food of the Many. However, if he had spoken unintentionally, he will be punished for six months. *Blank* And whoever lies knowingly *4* shall be punished for six months. Whoever knowingly and for no reason insults his fellow will be punished for a year *5* and will be excluded. And whoever speaks to his fellow with deception or knowingly deceives him, will be punished for six months. And if *6 Blank* he is /negligent/ to his fellow he will be punished for three months. *Blank* However, if he is negligent with the possessions of the Community achieving a loss, he shall replace it {…} *7* in full. *Blank 7a Blank 7b Blank 8* And if he does not manage to replace it, he will be punished for /sixty days/. And whoever feels animosity towards his fellow for no cause will be punished for {six months} /one year/. *9* And likewise for anyone retaliating for any reason. Whoever utters with his mouth futile words, three months; and for talking in the middle of the words of his fellow, *10* ten days. And whoever lies down and goes to sleep in the session of the Many, thirty days. And the same applies to whoever leaves the session of the Many *11* without permission, or falls asleep up to three times during a session, he shall be punished ten days; however, if they raise up (?) *Blank 12* and he withdraws, he shall be punished for thirty days. And whoever walks about naked in front of his fellow, without needing to, shall be punished for six months. *13* And the person who spits in the course of a meeting of the Many shall be punished thirty days. And whoever takes out "his hand" from under his clothes, or if these are *14* rags which allow his nakedness to be seen, he will be punished thirty days. And whoever giggles inanely causing his voice to be heard shall be sentenced to thirty *15* days. And whoever takes out his left hand to gesticulate with it shall be punished ten days. And whoever goes round defaming his fellow *16* shall be excluded for one year from the pure food of the Many and shall be punished; however, whoever goes round defaming the Many shall be expelled from their midst *17* and will never return. And whoever complains against the foundation of the Community shall be expelled and will not return; however, if he complains against his fellow *18* without cause he will be punished six months. The person whose spirit turns aside from the foundation of the Community to betray the truth *19* and walk in the stubbornness of his heart, if he comes back, shall be punished for two years; during the first year he shall not approach the pure food of the Many. *Blank 20 Blank* {…} and during the second he shall not approach {the pure food} /the drink/ of the Many and shall sit at the back of all the men of the Community. *21* When the days of the two years are complete

ימים ישאלו הרבים *vacat* על דבריו ואם יקרבהו ונכתב בתכונו ואחר ישאל
אל המשפט 22 {...}יכול איש אשר יהיה בעצת היחד {...} על מלואת עשר
שנים *vacat* 23 *vacat* {...} *vacat* ושבה רוחו לבגוד ביחד ויצא מלפני *vacat*
24 הרבים ללכת בשרירות לבו לוא ישוב אל עצת היחד עוד ואיש מאנשי
היח[ד א]שר יתערב 25 עמו בטהרתו או בהונו אש[ר ...]הרבים והיה
משפטו כמוהו לשל[חו ...]

1 *Col.* VIII בעצת היחד שנים עשר איש וכוהנים שלושה תמימים
בכול הנגלה מכול 2 התורה לעשות אמת וצדקה ומשפט ואהבת חסד
והצנע לכת איש אם רעהו 3 לשמור אמונה בארץ ביצר סמוך ורוח נשברה
ולרצת עוון בעושי משפט 4 וצרת מצרף ולהתהלך עם כול ב{.}מדת האמת
ובתכון העת

בהיות אלה בישראל 5 נכונה {ה}עצת היחד באמת *vacat* {.} למ^טעת
עולם בית קודש לישראל וסוד קודש 6 קודשים לאהרון עדי אמת למשפט
ובנ}ח[']רי רצון לכפר בעד הארץ ולהשב 7 לרשעים גמולם *vacat* היאה
חומת הבחן פנת יקר בל *vacat* 8 יזדעזעו יסודותיהו ובל יחישו ממקומם
vacat מעון קודש קודשים 9 לאהרון בדעת כולם (עולם) לברית משפט
ולקריב ר^{יח} ניחוח ובית תמים ואמת בישראל 10 להקם {...} ברית
לח]ק^ות עולם והיו לרצון לכפר בעד הארץ ולחרוץ משפט רשעה {בתמים דרך} ואין
עולה בהכון אלה ביסוד היחד שנתים ימים בתמים דרך

11 יבדלו קודש בתוך עצת אנשי היחד וכול דבר הנסתר מישראל ונמצאו
לאיש 12 הדורש אל יסתרהו מאלה מיראת רוח נסוגה *vacat*
ובהיות אלה לי^{חד} בישראל 13 בתכונים האלה יבדלו מתוך מושב הנשי
(אנשי) העול ללכת למדבר לפנות שם את דרך הואהא 14 כאשר כתוב
במדבר פנו דרך **** ישרו בערבה מסלה לאלוהינו 15 היאה מדרש
התורה א[ש]ר צוה ביד מושה לעשות ככול הנגלה עת בעת 16 וכאשר גלו

the Many shall be questioned *Blank* concerning his affairs; if they admit him, he shall be enrolled in his rank; and later he will be questioned in connection with judgment. *22* {…} However, anyone who has been in the Community council {…} for ten full years. *Blank 23 Blank* {…} *Blank* and whose spirit reverts to betray the Community and go away from the presence *Blank 24* of the Many in order to walk in the stubbornness of his heart, will never return to the Community council. And the person among the men of the Commu[nity w]ho fraternizes *25* with him with regard to his purity or his goods, wh[o …] the Many, and his sentence will be like his, [he] shall be expe[lled …]

Col. VIII (= 4Q258 VI, VII; 4Q259 II-III)   *1* In the Community council (there shall be) twelve men and three priests, perfect in everything that has been revealed from all *2* the law to implement truth, justice, judgment, compassionate love and unassuming behaviour of one to another, *3* to preserve faithfulness in the land with firm purpose and repentant spirit in order to atone for sin by doing justice *4* and undergoing trials, and to walk with everyone in the measure of the truth and the regulation of the time.

When these things exist in Israel *5* the Community council shall be founded on truth, *Blank* to be an everlasting plantation, a holy house for Israel and the foundation of the holy of *6* holies for Aaron, true witnesses for the judgment and chosen by the will (of God) to atone for the land and to render *7* the wicked their retribution. *Blank* This (the Community) is the tested rampart, the precious cornerstone that does not *Blank 8* /whose foundations/ shake or tremble from their place. *Blank* (It will be) the most holy dwelling *9* for Aaron with eternal knowledge of the covenant of justice and in order to offer a pleasant /aroma/; and it will be a house of perfection and truth in Israel *10* in order to establish {/…/} a covenant in compliance with the everlasting decrees. /And these will be accepted in order to atone for the land and to decide the judgment of the wickedness {in perfect behaviour} and there will be no iniquity/. When these have been established in the foundation of the Community for two full years in perfect behaviour *11* /they will be segregated/ (like) holy ones in the midst of the council of the men of the Community. And every matter hidden from Israel but which has been found out by *12* the Interpreter, he should not keep hidden from them for fear of a spirit of desertion. *Blank* And when these have become /a community/ in Israel *13* /in compliance with these arrangements/ they are to be segregated from within the dwelling of the men of sin to walk to the desert in order to open there His path. *14* As it is written (*Isa 40:3*): «In the desert, prepare the way of ****, straighten in the steppe a roadway for our God». *15* This is the study of the law wh[i]ch he commanded through the hand of Moses, in order to act in compliance with all that has been revealed from age to age, *16* and according to what the prophets

הנביאים ברוח קודשו *vacat* וכול איש מאנשי היחד ברית   17 היחד אשר
יסור מכול המצוה דבר ביד רמה אל יגע בטהרת אנשי הקודש   18 ואל ידע
בכול עצתם עד אשר יזכו מעשיו מכול עול להלך בתמים דרך וקרבהו
19 בעצה על פי הרבים ואחר יכת{.}²   בתכונו וכמשפט הזה לכול הנוסף
ליחד

vacat 20 ואלה המשפטים אשר ילכו בם אנשי התמים קודש איש את
רעהו   21 כול הבא בעצת הקודש ההולכים בתמים דרך כאשר צוה כול
איש מהמה   22 אשר יעבר דבר מתורת מושה ביד רמה או ברמיה ישלחהו
מעצת היחד   23 ולוא ישוב עוד ולוא יתערב איש מאנשי הקודש בה[ו]נו ועם
עצתו לכול   24 דבר ואם בשגגה יעשה והובדל מן הטהרה ומן העצה ודרשו
המשפט   25 אשר לוא ישפוט איש ולוא [יש]אל על כול עצה שנתים ימים
אם תתם דרכו   26 במושב במדרש ובעצה [ע]ל[ ]פי [הרבים אם לוא שגג
עוד עד מולאת לו שנתים   27 ימים *vacat*

Col. IX 1 כיא על {...} שגגה אחת יענש שנתים ולעושה ביד רמה לוא
ישוב עוד אך השוגג   2 יבחן שנתים ימים לתמים דרכו ועצתו על פי הרבים
ואחר יכתוב בתכונו ליחד קודש   *vacat* 3 בהיות אלה בישראל ככול
התכונים האלה ליסוד רוח קודש לאמת   4 עולם לכפר על אשמת פשע
ומעל הטאת ולרצון לארץ מבשר עולות ומחלבי זבח ותרומת   5 שפתים
למשפט כניחוח צדק ותמים דרך כנדבת מנחת רצון

בעת ההיאה יבדילו אנשי   6 היחד בית קודש לאהרון להיחד קודש
קודשים ובית יחד לישראל ההולכים בתמים   7 רק בני אהרון ימשלו
במשפט ובהון ועל פיהם יצא והגורל לכול תכון אנשי היחד   8 והון אנשי
הקודש ההולכים בתמים אל יתערב הונם עם הון אנשי הרמיה אשר   9 לוא
הזכו דרכם להבדל מעול וללכת בתמים דרך ומכול עצת התורה לוא יצאו

have revealed through his holy spirit. *Blank* And anyone of the men of the Community, the covenant of *17* the Community, who insolently shuns anything at all commanded, cannot approach the pure food of the men of holiness, *18* and cannot know anything of their counsels until his deeds have been cleansed from every depravity, walking in perfect behaviour. Then they can include him *19* in the council under the authority of the Many and later they will enrol him according to his rank. And (they shall apply) this regulation to all who enter the Community.

20 Blank These are the regulations by which the men of perfect holiness shall conduct themselves, one with another. *21* All who enter the council of holiness of those walking in perfect behaviour as he commanded, anyone of them *22* who breaks a word of the law of Moses impertinently or through carelessness will be banished from the Community council *23* and shall not return again; none of the men of holiness should associate with his goods or his advice on any *24* matter. However if he acted through oversight he should be excluded from pure food and from the council and they shall apply the (following) regulation to him: *25* «He may not judge anyone and [he may] not [be a]sked any advice for two whole years». If his conduct is perfect *26* in the session, in the investigation, and in the council [ac]cor[ding to] the Many, if he has not sinned again through oversight until two full years have passed. *27 Blank*

Col. IX (= 4Q256 XVIII; 4Q258 VII, VIII; 4Q259 III, IV; 4Q260 I) *1* Because for {...} one sin of oversight he will be punished two years; but whoever acts impertinently shall not return again. Only someone who sins through oversight *2* shall be tested for two full years with respect to the perfectness of his behaviour and of his counsel according to the authority of the Many, and shall then be enrolled according to his rank in the Community of holiness. *3 Blank* When these exist in Israel in accordance with these rules in order to establish the spirit of holiness in truth *4* eternal, in order to atone for the guilt of iniquity and for the unfaithfulness of sin, and for approval for the earth, without the flesh of burnt offerings and without the fats of sacrifice - the offering of *5* the lips in compliance with the decree will be like the pleasant aroma of justice and the perfectness of behaviour will be acceptable like a freewill offering - at that moment the men of *6* the Community shall set apart a holy house for Aaron, in order to form a most holy community, and a house of the Community for Israel, those who walk in perfection. *7* Only the sons of Aaron will have authority in the matter of judgment and of goods, and their word will settle the lot of all provision for the men of the Community *8* and the goods of the men of holiness who walk in perfection. Their goods must not be mixed with the goods of the men of deceit who *9* have not cleansed their path to separate from injustice and walk in a perfect behaviour. They should not de-

ללכת 10 בכול שרירות לבם ונשפטו במשפטים הרשונים אשר החלו
אנשי היחד לתיסר בם 11 עד בוא נ^ביא ומשיחי אהרון וישראל *vacat*

vacat 12 אלה החוקים למשכיל להתהלך בם עם כול חי לתכון עת ועת
ולמשקל איש ואיש 13 לעשות את רצון אל ככול הנגלה לעת בעת ולמוד
את כול השכל הנמצא לפי העתים ואת 14 חוק העת להבדיל ולשקול בני
הצדוק *vacat* לפי רוחום ובבחירי העת להחזיק על פי 15 רצונו כאשר צוה
ואיש כרוחו כן לעשות משפטו ואיש כבור כפיו לקרבו ולפי שכלו
16 להגישו וכן אהבתו עם שנאתו *vacat* ואשר לוא להוכיח ולהתרובב עם
אנשי השחת 17 ולסתר את עצת התורה בתוך אנשי העול ולהוכיח דעת
אמת ומשפט צדק לביחרי 18 דרך איש כרוחו כתכון העת להנחותם בדעה
וכן להשכילם ברזי פלא ואמת בתוך 19 אנשי היחד לה{נ}לך תמים איש את
רעהו בכול הנגלה להם

{ה}היאה עת פנות הדרך 20 למדבר ולהשכילם כול הנמצא לעשות
בעת הזואת ו[ה]הבדל מכול איש ולוא הסר דרכו 21 מכול עול *vacat* ואלה
תכוני הדרך למשכיל בעתים האלה לאהבתו עם שנאתו שנאת עולם
22 עם אנשי שחת ברוח הסתר לעזוב למו הון ועמל כפים כעבד למושל בו
וענוה לפני 23 הרודה בו ולהיות איש מקנא לחוק ועתו ליום נקם לעשות
רצון בכול משלח כפים 24 ובכול ממשלו כאשר צוה וכול הנעשה בו ירצה
בנדבה וזולת רצון אל לו יחפץ 25 [וב]כול אמרי פיהו ירצה ולוא יתאוה
בכול אשר לוא צוה[ו]למשפט אל יצפה תמיד 26 [...] ובצו[קה]קה יברך
עושיו ובכול אשר יהיה יס[פר ... ותרומת] שפתים יברכנו

part from any counsel of the law in order to walk *10* in complete stubbornness of their heart, but instead shall be ruled by the first directives which the men of the Community began to be taught *11* until the prophet comes, and the Messiahs of Aaron and Israel. *Blank*

12 Blank These are the regulations for the Instructor by which he shall walk with every living being in compliance with the regulation of every period and in compliance with the worth of each man: *13* he should fulfil the will of God in compliance with all revelation for every period; he should acquire all the wisdom that has been gained according to the periods and the *14* decree of the period; he should separate and weigh the sons of Zadok *Blank* according to their spirits; he should keep hold of the chosen ones of the period according to his will, as he has commanded; he should carry out the judgment of each man in accordance with his spirit; he should include each one according to the purity of his hands and according to his intellect *16* promote him. And thus shall be his love and thus shall be his hatred. *Blank* He should not reproach or argue with the men of the pit *17* but instead hide the counsel of the law in the midst of the men of injustice. He should reproach (with) truthful knowledge and (with) just judgment those who choose *18* the path, each one according to his spirit, according to the regulation of the time. He should lead them with knowledge and in this way teach them the mysteries of wonder and of truth in the midst of *19* the men of the Community, so that they walk perfectly, one with another, in all that has been revealed to them.

This is the time for making ready the path *20* to the desert and he will teach them about all that has been discovered so that they can carry it out in this moment [and] so they will be detached from anyone who has not withdrawn his path *21* from all injustice. *Blank* And these are the regulations of behaviour for the Inspector in these times, concerning his love and his hatred. Everlasting hatred *22* for the men of the pit in clandestine spirit. To them he should leave goods and hand-made items like a servant to his master and like one oppressed before *23* someone domineering him. He should be a man enthusiastic for the decree and for its time, for the day of revenge. He should perform (God's) will in all that his hand should tackle *24* and in all that he controls, as he commanded. And all that happens to him he should welcome freely and be gratified by nothing except God's will. *25* He should relish all the words of his mouth, wish for nothing that he has not commanded [and] be ever alert to the precept of God. *26* [... and in distr]ess he shall bless his Creator and in all that happens he shall re[count ... and with the offering of] his lips he shall bless him

Col. x   1 עם קצים אש}ה{ר חקקא (חקק אל) ברשית ממשלת אור עם

תקופתו ובהאספו על מעון חוקו ברשית   2 אשמורי חושך כיא יפתח אוצרו

וישתהו עלת ובתקופתו עם האספו מפני אור באופיע   3 מאורות מזבול

קודש עם האספם למעון כבוד במבוא מועדים לימי חודש יחד תקופתם עם

4 מסרותם זה לזה בהתחדשם יום גדול לקודש קודשים ואות נ *vacat*

למפתח חסדיו עולם לראשי   5 מועדים בכול קץ נהיה *vacat* ברשית ירחים

למועדיהם וימי קודש בתכונם לזכרון במועדיהם   6 }.{תרומת שפתים

הברכנו כחוק חרות לעד בראשי }.{ שנים ובתקופת מועדיהם בהשלם חוק

7 תכונם יום משפטו זה לזה מועד קציר לקיץ ומועד זרע למועד דשא מועדי

שנים לשבועיהם   8 וברוש שבועיהם למועד דרור ובכול היותי חוק חרות

בלשוני לפרי תהלה ומנת שפתי }אשא{   9 }ש{ אזמרה בדעת וכול נגינתי

לכבוד אל וכנור נבלי לתכון קודשו וחליל שפתי אשא בקו משפטו   10 עם

מבוא יום ולילה אבו}ה{אה בברית אל ועם מוצא ערב ובוקר אמר חוקיו

ובהיותם אשים   11 גבולי לבלתי שוב ומשפטו אוכיח כנעוותי ופשעי לנגד

עיני כחוק חרות ולאל אומר צדקי   12 ולעליון מכין טובי מקור דעת ומעון

קודש רום כבוד וגבורת כול לתפארת עולם הבחרה באשר   13 יורני

וארצה כאשר ישופטני בר}.{שית משלח ידי ורגלי אברך שמו בראשית צאת

ובוא   14 לשבת וקום ועם משכב יצועי ארננה לו ואברכנו תרומת מוצא

שפתי במערכת אנשים   15 ובטרם אריע ידי להדשן בעדני תנובת תבל

ברשית פחד ואימה ובמכון צרה עם בוקה   16 אברכנו בהפלא מודה

ובגבורתו אשוחח ועל חסדיו אשען כול היום ואדעה כיא בידו משפט

17 כול חי ואמת כול מעשיו ובהפתח צרה אהללנו ובישועתו ארננה יחד

לוא אשיב לאיש גמול   18 רע וטוב ארדף גבר כיא את אל משפט כול חי

והואה ישלם לאיש גמולו לוא אקנא ברוח   19 רשעה והון חמס לוא תאוה

Col. x (= 4Q256 xix, xx; 4Q258 viii-x; 4Q260 ii-v) *1* during the periods which God decreed: at the commencement of the dominion of light, during its rotation and at its retirement to its appointed abode. At the commencement of *2* the vigils of darkness when he opens his store and stretches them upwards and during its rotation, when it retires before the light. When *3* the lights shine out of the holy vault, when they retire to the abode of glory. At the entry of the seasons in the days of the new moon together with their rotations during *4* their stations renewing each other. It is a great day for the holy of holies, and a sign *Blank* of the opening of his everlasting mercies for the beginnings of *5* the seasons in every future age. *Blank* At the commencement of the months in their seasons, and of the holy days in their sequence, as a reminder in their seasons. *6* With the offering of lips I shall bless him, in accordance with the decree recorded for ever. At the commencement of the years and in the turning of their seasons, when the decree of *7* their disposition is carried out, on its prescribed day, one after another; the season of the harvest up to summer, the season of seed-time up to the season of the grass, the seasons of the years up to their seven-year periods. *8* At the commencement of the seven-year periods up to the moment decided for deliverance. And in all my existence the precept will be engraved on my tongue to be a fruit of eulogy, and a portion (of offering) of my lips. {I shall tune} *9* I will sing with knowledge and for the glory of God shall all my music be, the playing of my harp according to his holy order, and the whistle of my lips I shall tune to its correct measure. *10* At the onset of day and night I shall enter the covenant of God, and when evening and morning depart I shall repeat his precepts; and by their existence I shall set *11* my limit without turning away. I acknowledge his judgment to be right according to my pervertedness; my sins are before my eyes, like an engraved decree. To God I shall say: «My justice», *12* and to the Most High: «Establisher of my well-being», «source of knowing», «spring of holiness», «peak of glory», «all-powerful one of eternal majesty». I shall choose what *13* he teaches me, I shall be pleased in how he might judge me. When I start to stretch out my hands and my feet I shall bless his name; when I start to go out and to come in, *14* to sit and to stand up, and lying down in my bed I shall extol him; I shall bless him with the offering that issues from my lips in the row of men. *15* And before stretching out my hand to get fat on the tasty fruit of the earth, at the onset of fright and dismay and in the place of distress and grief, *16* I shall bless him for (his) great marvels and shall meditate on his power and shall rely on his compassion the whole day. I realize that in his hand lies the judgment of *17* every living thing, and all his deeds are truth. When distress is unleashed I shall praise him, just as I shall sing to him for his deliverance. I shall not repay anyone with an evil reward; *18* with goodness I shall pursue man. For to God (belongs) the judgment of every living being, and it is he who pays man his wages. I shall not be jealous with a wicked *19* spirit, and my soul shall not

נפשי וריב אנש ᵂחת לוא א}טור באף לשבי{תפוש עד יום נקם ואפיא לוא

20 אשיב מאנשי עולה ולוא ארצה עד הכון משפט לוא אטור באף לשבי

פשע ולוא ארחם 21 על כול סוררי דרך לוא אנחם בנכאים עד תום דרכם

ובליעל לוא אשמור בלבבי ולוא ישמע בפי 22 נבלות וכחש עוון ומרמות

וכזבים לוא ימצאו בשפתי ופרי קודש בלשוני ושקוצים 23 לוא ימצא בה

בהודות אפתח פי וצדקות אל תספר לשוני תמיד ומעל אנשים עד תום

24 פשעם רקים אשבית משפטי נדות ונפתלות מדעת לבי בעצת תושיה

אסᵖ{ת}ר דעת 25 ובערמת דעת אשוך [בע]דה גבול סמוך לשמור אמנים

ומשפט עוז לצדקת אל אחלקה 26 חוק בקו עתים ו.[...]צדק אהבת חסד

לנוכנעים וחזוק ידים לנמהר[ים להודיע]

Col. XI 1 לתועי רוח בינה ולהשכיל רוכנים בלקח ולהשיב ענוה לנגד

רמי רוח וברוח נשברה לאנשי 2 מטה שולחי אצבע ומדברי און *vacat*

ומקני הון כיא אני לאל משפטי ובידו תום דרכי עם ישור לבבי

3 ובצדקותו ימח פשעי כיא ממקור דעתו פתח אורי ובנפלאותיו הביטה עיני

ואורת לבבי ברז 4 נהיה והויא עולם משען ימיני בסלע עוז דרך פעמי

מפני כול לוא יזד עזרע (יזדעזע) כיא אמת אל היאה 5 סלע פעמי וגבורתו

משענת ימיני וממקור צדקתו משפטי אור בלבבי מרזי פלאו בהויא עולם

6 הביטה עיני תושיה אשר נסתרה מאנᵂש דעה ומזמת ערמה מבני אדם

מקור צדקה ומקוה 7 גבורה עם מעין כבוד מסוד בשר לאשᵣ{.}ר בחר אל

נתנם לאוחזת עולם וינחיᶫ}י{ם בגורל 8 קדושים ועם בני שמים חבר סודם

לעצת יחד וסוד מבנית קודש למטעת עולם עם כול 9 קץ נהיה ואני לאדם

רשעה ולסוד בשר עול עוונותי פשעי חטאתי {...}עם נעוות לבבי 10 לסוד

crave wealth by violence; I {shall not sustain angry resentment for those who convert} /shall not be involved/ in any dispute with the men of the pit /until the day/ of vengeance. However, my anger I shall not 20 remove from unjust men, nor shall I be appeased, until he carries out his judgment. I shall not sustain angry resentment for those who convert from iniquity, but I shall have no mercy 21 for all those who deviate from the path. I shall not comfort the oppressed until their path is perfect. I shall not retain Belial within my heart. From my mouth shall not be heard 22 foolishness or wicked deceptions; sophistries or lies shall not be found on my lips. The fruit of holiness will be on my tongue, profanity 23 shall not be found on it. With hymns shall I open my mouth and my tongue will continually recount both the just acts of God and the unfaithfulness of men until their iniquity is complete. 24 I shall remove from my lips worthless words, unclean things and plotting from the knowledge of my heart. With prudent counsel {I shall hide} /I shall recount/ knowledge, 25 and with discretion of knowledge I shall enclose him with a solid fence to maintain faithfulness and staunch judgment according to the justice of God. I shall share out 26 the regulation with the cord of the ages and [...] justice (and) compassionate love with the oppressed, and to strengthen the hands of the dismay[ed, to teach]

Col. xi (= 4Q264)   *1* understanding to those with a stray spirit and to instruct in the teaching those who complain to reply with meekness to the haughty of spirit, and with a broken spirit to the men of *2* the bending (of the law), those who point the finger and speak evil, *Blank* and are keen on riches. As for me, to God belongs my judgment; in his hand is the perfection of my behaviour with the uprightness of my heart; *3* and with his just acts he cancels my iniquities. For from the source of his knowledge he has disclosed his light, and my eyes have observed his wonders, and the light of my heart the mystery of *4* existence. What always is, is support for my right hand, the path of my steps goes over firm rock, it does not waver before anything. For the truth of God is *5* the rock of my steps, and his might the support of my right hand. From the spring of his justice is my judgment and from the wonderful mystery is the light in my heart. My eyes have observed what always is, *6* wisdom that has been hidden from mankind, knowledge and prudent understanding (hidden) from the sons of man, fount of justice and well of *7* strength and spring of glory (hidden) from the assembly of flesh. To those whom God has selected he has given them as everlasting possession; and he has given them an inheritance in the lot of *8* the holy ones. He unites their assembly to the sons of the heavens in order (to form) the council of the Community and a foundation of the building of holiness to be an everlasting plantation throughout all *9* future ages. However, I belong to evil humankind, to the assembly of unfaithful flesh; my failings, my iniquities, my sins, {...} with the depravities of my heart, *10* be-

רמה והולכי חושך כיא ל(וא ל)אדם דרכו ואנוש לוא יכין צעדו כיא לאל
המשפט ומידו   11 תום הדרך ובדעתו נהיה כול וכ{ע}ול הויה במחשבתו
יכינו ומבלעדיו לוא יעשה *vacat* ואני אם   12 אמוט חסדי אל ישועתי לעד
ואם אכשול בעוון בשר משפטי בצדקת אל תעמוד לנצחים   13 ואם יפתח
צרתי וממשחת יחלץ נפשי ויכן לדרך פעמי ברחמיו הגישני ובחסדיו יביא
14 משפטי בצדקת אמתו שפטני וברוב טובו יכפר בעד כול עוונותי
ובצדקתו יטהרני מנדת   15 אנוש וחטאת בני אדם להודות לאל צדקו
ולעליון תפארתו

ברוך אתה אלי הפותח לדעה   16 לב עבדכה הכן בצדק כול מעשיו
והקם לבן אמתכה כאשר רציתה לבחירי אדם להתיצב   17 לפניכה לעד
כיא מבלעדיכה לוא תתם דרך ובלו רצונכה לוא יעשה כול אתה הוריתה
18 כול דעה וכול הנהיה ברצונכה היה ואין אחר זולתכה להשיב על עצתכה
ולהשכיל   19 בכול מחשבת קודשכה ולהביט בעומק רזיכה ולהתבונן בכול
נפלאותיכה עם כוח   20 גבורתכה ומי יכול להכיל את כבודכה ומה אף
הואה בן הֿאדם במעשי פלאכה   21 וילוד אשה מה יֿ(ח)שב לפניכה והואה
מעפר מגבלו ולחם רמה מדורו והואה מצירורק   22 חמר קורץ ולעפר
תשוקתו מה ישיב חמר ויוצר יד ולעצת מה יבין *vacat*

1Q28a (1QSa) *1QRule of the Congregation*

D. Barthélemy, *DJD I*, 107-118, pls. XXIII-XXIV
PAM 40.513, 42.141, 42.459, 42.926
DAJ
Bibliography: J. Licht, *The Rule Scroll: A Scroll from the Wilderness of Judaea-1QS,
1QSa, 1QSb: Text, Introduction and Commentary* (Jerusalem: Bialik, 1957) [He-
brew]; L.H. Schiffman, *The Eschatological Community of the Dead Sea Scrolls. A*

long to the assembly of worms and of those who walk in darkness. For to man (does not belong) his path, nor can a human being steady his step; since the judgment belongs to God, and from his hand *11* is the perfection of the path. By his knowledge everything shall come into being, and all that does exist he establishes with his calculations and nothing is done outside of him. *Blank* As for me, if *12* I stumble, the mercies of God shall be my salvation always; and if I fall in the sin of the flesh, in the justice of God, which endures eternally, shall my judgment be; *13* if my distress commences, he will free my soul from the pit and make my steps steady on the path; he will draw me near in his mercies, and by kindnesses set in motion *14* my judgment; he will judge me in the justice of his truth, and in his plentiful goodness always atone for all my sins; in his justice he will cleanse me from the uncleanness of *15* the human being and from the sin of the sons of man, so that I can give God thanks for his justice and The Highest for his majesty.

Blessed be you, my God, who opens *16* the heart of your servant to knowledge! Establish all his deeds in justice, and raise up the son of your handmaid to stand *17* everlastingly in your presence, as you have cared for the selected ones of humankind. For without you no behaviour is perfect, and without your will, nothing comes to be. You have taught *18* all knowledge and all that exists is so by your will. Beyond you there is no-one to oppose your counsel, to understand *19* any of your holy thoughts, to gaze into the abyss of your mysteries, to fathom all your marvels or the strength of *20* your might. Who can endure your glory? What, indeed, is the son of man, among all your marvellous deeds? *21* As what shall one born of woman be considered in your presence? Shaped from dust has he been, maggots' food shall be his dwelling; he is spat saliva, *22* moulded clay, and for dust is his longing. What will the clay reply and the one shaped by hand? And what advice will he be able to understand? *Blank*

1Q28a (1QSa) *1QRule of the Congregation*

Study of the Rule of the Congregation (SBL Monographs Series 38; Atlanta, GA: Scholars Press, 1989); J.H. Charlesworth, L.T. Stuckenbruck, *PTSDSSP 1*, 108-117; É. Puech, 'Préséance sacerdotale et Messie-Roi dans la Règle de la Congrégation (1QSa ii 11-22)', *RevQ* 16/63 (1994) 351-365; C. Hempel, 'The Earthly Essene Nucleus of 1QSa', *DSD* 3 (1996) 253-269

Col. I 1 וזה הסרך לכול עדת ישראל באחרית הימים בה(א)ספם] ליחד
להתה]לך 2 על פי משפט בני צדוק הכוהנים ואנושי בריתם אשר סר]ו
מלכת ב]דרך 3 העם המה אנושי עצתו אשר שמרו בריתו בתוך רשעה
לכפ]ר בעד האר]ץ 4 בבוא<י>ם יקהילו את כול הבאים מטף עד נשים
וקראו בא]וזניהמה]את 5 [כ]ול חוקי הברית ולהבינם בכול משפטיהמה פן
ישגו במ]שגותיהמ]ה

vacat 6 וזה ʰסרך לכול צבאות העדה לכול האזרח בישראל ומן נעו]רי]ו
7 [לל]מדהו בספר ההגי וכפי יומיו ישכילוהו בחוקי]י הברית ול]קחת[
8 [מו]סרו במשפטיהמה עשר שנים] י]בוא בט{ב}ף ובן[ן] עשרים שנ]ה
יעבר] 9 [על] הפקודים לבוא בגורל בתוך משפ]ח[תו ליחד בעד]ת] קודש
ולוא י]קרב] 10 אל אשה לדעתה למשכבי זכר כי אם לפי מילואת לו
עש]רי]ם שנה בדעתו] טוב] 11 ורע ובכן תקבל להעיד עליו משפטות
התורא ולהת]י]צב במשמע משפטים 12 ובמלוא בו vacat

ובן חמש ועשרים שנה יבוא להת]י]צב ביסודות עדת 13 הקודש לעבוד
את עבודה העדה ובן שלושים שנה יגש לריב ריב 14 ומ]ש]פט ולהתיצב
ברואשי אלפי ישראל לשרי מאות שרי ח]מ]שים 15 [שרי] עשרות
שופטים ושוטרים לשבטיהם בכול משפחותם [על פ]י בני 16 [אהר]ון
הכוהנים וכול {שׁ}רˢⁱ אבות העדה אשר יצא הגורל להתי]צב] בעבוד]ת
17 [לצא]ת ולבוא לפני העדה ולפי שכלו עם תום דרכו יחזק מתנו למעמ]ד
לצ]בואת 18 עבודת{ו} מעשו בתוך אחיו [בי]ן רוב למועט [זה על] זה
יכבדו איש מרעהו 19 וברובות שני איש לפי כוחו יתנו משאו בע]בו]דת
העדה וכול איש פותי 20 אל יבוא בגורל להתיצב על עדת ישראל לרי]ב
מ]שפט ולשאת משא עדה 21 ולהתיצב במלחמה להכניע גוים רק בסרך
הצבא יכתוב משפחתו 22 ובעבודת המס יעשה עבודתו כפי מעשו ובני לוי
יעמודו איש במעמדו 23 על פי בני אהרון להביא ולהוציא את כול העדה
איש בסרכו על יד ראשי 24 [א]בות העדה לשרים ולשופטים ולשוטרים
למספר כול צבאותם על פי בני צדוק הכוהנים 25 [וכול]ראשי אבות
העדה vacat

Col. I *1* And this is the rule of all the congregation of Israel in the final days, when they gather [in community to wa]lk *2* in accordance with the regulation of the sons of Zadok, the priests, and the men of their covenant who have turn[ed away from the] path *3* of the nation. These are the men of his counsel who have kept his covenant in the midst of wickedness to ato[ne for the ear]th. *4* When they come, they shall assemble all those who come, including children and women, and they shall read into [their] ea[rs] *5* [a]ll the precepts of the covenant, and shall instruct them in all their regulations, so that they do not stray in [the]ir e[rrors.] *6 Blank* And this is the rule for all the armies of the congregation, for all native Israelites. From [his] yo[uth] *7* [they shall edu]cate him in the book of HAGY, and according to his age, instruct him in the precept[s of] the covenant, and he will [receive] *8* his [ins]truction in their regulations; during ten years he will be counted among the children. At the a[ge] of twenty ye[ars, he will transfer] *9* [to] those enrolled, to enter the lot amongst his fam[il]y and join the holy commun[ity]. He shall not [approach] *10* a woman to know her through carnal intercourse until he is fully twe[nt]y years old, when he knows [good] *11* and evil. Then she shall be received to give witness against him (about) the regulations of the law and to take his [p]lace in the proclamation of the regulations. *12* And on his completion, *Blank* at the age of twenty-five years, he shall enter to take his place among the «foundations» of the holy *13* congregation to perform the service of the congregation. And at thirty years (of age) he shall approach to arbitrate in disputes *14* and ju[dg]ments, and to take his place among the chiefs of the thousand of Israel, the commanders of a hundred, commanders of fi[f]ty, *15* [commanders of] ten, the judges and the officials of their tribes in all their families, [according to the dec]ision of the sons of *16* [Aar]on, the priests. And every {chief} /head/ of clans of the congregation, for whom the lot comes out, to take his pl[ace] in the duties, *17* [to go ou]t and to come in before the congregation, in accordance with his intelligence and the perfection of his behaviour, shall gird his loins to remain steadfa[st, d]oing *18* his allotted duty among his brothers. [Depen]ding on whether (he has) much or a little, [one] will be more or less honoured [than] his fellow. *19* When the years of a man increase, they shall assign him a task in the ser[vi]ce of the congregation matching his strength. No man who is a simpleton *20* shall enter the lot to hold office in the congregation of Israel for dispute or judgment, or to perform a task of the congregation, *21* or to go out to war to subdue the nations; he shall only write his family in the army register, *22* and he will do his service in the chores to the extent of his ability. The sons of Levi shall each stay in his post, *23* under the authority of the sons of Aaron, to make all the congregation come in and go out, each one in his rank, under the direction of the heads of the *24* [c]lans of the congregation, as commanders, judges /and officials/, according to the number of all their armies, under the authority of the sons of Zadok, the priests, *25* [and of all] the heads of the clans of the congregation. *Blank* And if

ואם תעודה תהיה לכול הקהל למשפט או 26 לעצה יחד או לתעודת

מלחמה וקדשום שלושת ימים להיות כול הבא 27 עת]יד לע[ע]צה אלה

ה(א)נשים הנקראים לעצת היחד מבן עש *vacat* כול 28 ח]כמי [העדה

והנבונים והידעים תמימי הדרך ואנושי החיל עם 29 [שרי השב]טים וכול

שופטיהם ושוטריהם ושרי האלפים ושרי] למאות]

Col. II 1 ולחמשים ולעשרות והלויים בתו]ך מחל]קת עבודתו אלה

2 אנושי השם קוראי מועד הנועדים לעצת היחד בישראל 3 לפני בני צדוק

הכוהנים וכול איש מנוגע באחת מכול טמאות האדם אל יבוא בקהל אלה

וכול איש מנוגע באלה לבלתי 5 החזיק מעמד בתוך העדה וכול מנוגע

בבשרו נכאה רגלים או 6 ידים פסח או עור או חרש או אלם או מום מנוגע

בבשרו 7 לראות עינים או איש זקן כושל לבלתי התחזק בתוך העדה

8 אל יבו]או]אלה להתיצב [ב]תוך עדה א[נ]ושי השם כיא מלאכי 9 קודש

[בעד]תם ואם יש דב]ר לאחד מ]אלה לדבר אל עצת הקודש

10 [ו]דורש]והו] מפיהו ואל תוך [העדה לו]א יבוא האיש כיא מנוגע

11 [ה]וא ב]מו]שב אנשי השם [קוראי]מועד לעצת היחד אם יוליד

12 [אל] א[ת] המשיח אתם יבוא] הכוהן]רואש כול עדת ישראל וכול

13 א]חיו בני] אהרון הכוהנים [קרואי] מועד אנושי השם וישבו 14 ל]פניו

איש]לפי כבודו ואחר י]בוא מש]יח ישראל וישבו לפניו ראש` 15 א]לפי

ישראל אי]ש לפי כבודו כמ]עמדו] במחניהם וכמסעיהם וכול 16 ראשי

א]בות הע]דה עם חכמ]י ...]ישבו לפניהם איש לפי 17 כבודו ו[אם

לשול]חן יחד יועד]ו או לשתות הת]ירוש וערוך השולחן 18 היחד [ומסוך

ה]תירוש לשתות] אל ישלח] איש את ידו ברשת 19 הלחם ו]התירוש]

לפני הכוהן כיא] הוא מ]ברך את רשית הלחם 20 והתירו]ש ושלח [ידו

בלחם לפנים ואח]ר יש]לח משיח ישראל ידיו 21 בלחם [ואחר יבר]כו כול

עדת היחד א]יש לפי] כבודו וכחוק הזה יעש 22 לכול מע]רכת כיא יו]עדו

עד עשרא אנש]ים] *vacat*

there is a convocation of all the assembly for a judgment, or *26* for the community council, or for a convocation of war, they shall sanctify themselves during three days, so that every one who comes *27* is pre[pared for the cou]ncil. These are the men who are to be summoned to the community council from ... *Blank*: all *28* the wi[se men] of the congregation, the intelligent and those learned in perfect behaviour and the men of valour, together with *29* [the chiefs of the tri]bes and all their judges, their officials, the chiefs of thousands, the chiefs of [hundreds,]

Col. II *1* of fifties and of tens, and the levites, (each one) in the mid[st of his divi]sion of service. These *2* are the men of renown, those summoned to the assembly, those gathered for the community council in Israel *3* in the presence of the sons of Zadok, the priests. No man, defiled by any of the impurities *4* of a man, shall enter the assembly of these; and no-one who is defiled by these should be *5* established in his office amongst the congregation: everyone who is defiled in his flesh, paralysed in his feet or *6* in his hands, lame, blind, deaf, dumb or defiled in his flesh with a blemish *7* visible to the eyes, or the tottering old man who cannot keep upright in the midst of the assembly; *8* these shall not en[ter] to take their place [a]mong the congregation of the men of renown, for the angels *9* of holiness are among their [congre]gation. And if [one of] these has something to say to the holy council, *10* they shall question [him] in private, but the man shall [n]ot enter in the midst of [the congregation,] because [h]e is defiled. *11* At [a ses]sion of the men of renown, [those summoned to] the gathering of the community council, when [God] begets *12* the Messiah with them: [the] chief [priest] of all the congregation of Israel shall enter, and all *13* [his] br[others, the sons] of Aaron, the priests [summoned] to the assembly, the men of renown, and they shall sit *14* be[fore him, each one] according to his dignity. After, [the Mess]iah of Israel shall [enter] and before him shall sit the heads of the *15* th[ousands of Israel, each] one according to his dignity, according to [his] po[sition] in their camps and according to their marches. And all *16* the heads of the cl[ans of the congre]gation with the wise [men ...] shall sit before them, each one according *17* to his dignity. And [when] they gather [at the tab]le of community [or to drink the n]ew wine, and the table of *18* the community is prepared [and the] new wine [is mixed] for drinking, [no-one should stretch out] his hand to the first-fruit *19* of the bread and of [the new wine] before the priest, for [he is the one who bl]esses the first-fruit of bread *20* and of the new win[e and stretches out] his hand towards the bread before them. Afterwar[ds,] the Messiah of Israel [shall str]etch out his hands *21* towards the bread. [And afterwards, they shall ble]ss all the congregation of the community, each [one according to] his dignity. And in accordance with this precept one shall act *22* at each me[al, when] at least ten me[n are gat]hered. *Blank*

1Q28b (1QSb) *1QRule of Benedictions*

J.T. Milik, *DJD I*, 118-130, pls. XXV-XXIX; G.J. Brooke, *DJD XXVI*, 227-233, pl. XXIV
PAM 40.070, 40.071, 40.073, 40.471, 40.521, 40.534, 43.754
ROC 662, 663, 664, 1000; Schøyen Collection MS 1909
Bibliography: J. Licht, *The Rule Scroll: A Scroll from the Wilderness of Judaea-1QS,*

Col. I   1 דברי ברכ[ה] למשכיל לברך את ירא[י] אל עושי את] רצונו
שומרי מצו'תיו   2 ומחזקי בב[רי]ת קודשו והולכים תמים] בכול דרכי
אמ]תו ויבחר בם לברית 3 עולם א[שר ת]עמוד לעד יב{ר}רכמה}^{רככה} א]דוני
ממעון קודשו ואת] מקור ע[ו]לם 4 אשר ל[וא יכז]ב יפתח לכה מן השמ[ים
[...] 5 בידכה [... ויחו]ננכה בכול ברכ]ות ...]ה בעדת קדוש[ים   6 ...]ר
עולם ולוא י]...[.באים ואתה ...].   7 [...]יפ]לטכה מכול [...]שנאתה אין
ש]רית   8 [... כו]ל שטן [...ק]ודש יר]...[9 ...]...[... יע]מוד קודש[ו]
10 [...ק]ודשו .[...].

Col. II   1 [... ברית א]בותיכה   2 [...]יכה ישא   3 ...] י]חונכה יש[א]
4 [פניו אליכה ...]...[...עלכ]ה]   5 [...].ו אלים 21-6 [...] 22 [...] יחונכה
אדוני בו[... ובכול]   23 [גמו]לים ישעשעכה ויחונכ]ה [... 24 יחונכה
ברוח קודש וחס]ד [...   25 וברית עולם יחונכה וירנ]ינכה [...
26 ויחוננכה במשפט צדק [... לוא [תכשל]ל [...   27 ויחונכה בכול מעשיכה
[...]כה ובכול .[...] יחונכה]   28 [ב]אמת עולם] ... [על כול צאצ]איכה [...

Col. III   1 ישא אדוני פניו אליכה וריח ני[חוח זבחיכה יריח ובכו]ל
יושבי לכה]ונתכ]ה   2 יבחר ויפקוד כול קודש[י]כה ובמו[...]כול זרעכה]
יש]א   3 פניו אל כול עדתכה ישא ברושכה] ...[...].[...]בו 4 בכבו]ד עד
וי]קדש זרעכה בכבוד ע[ו]לם יש]א פניו ...[... 5 חני .]... עו]לם יתן לכה
ומלכות[...]   6 ...[...]ם מבשר ועם מלאכי ק[ודש ...]... 7 ילחם
[...]...[...]. 17 [...] 16-9 [...] מכולם [...] 8 [... ה]דור עול]ה

1Q28b (1QSb) *1QRule of Benedictions*

1QSa, 1QSb: Text, Introduction and Commentary (Jerusalem: Bialik, 1957) [Hebrew] 273-289; S. Talmon, 'The 'Manual of Benedictions' of the Sect of the Judaean Desert', *RevQ* 2/8 (1960) 475-500; J.H. Charlesworth, L.T. Stuckenbruck, *PTSDSSP 1*, 119-131

Col. I *1* Words of blessi[ng]. Of the Instructor. To bless those who fear [God, do] his will, keep his commandments, *2* remain constant in his holy co[ven]ant and walk with perfection [on all the paths of] his [tru]th, those he has chosen for an eternal covenant *3* wh[ich] endures for ever. May the L[ord] bless {them} /you/ [from his holy residence.] May he open the et[er]nal spring *4* which [does] n[ot dry] up for you. From the heaven[s ...] *5* in your hand [... May he be grac]ious to you in all bless[ings ...] in the congregation of the holy one[s.] *6* [...] eternal and not may he [...] ... And you, [...] *7* [... May he s]ave you from all [...] her hate, with no re[mnant.] *8* [... eve]ry foe [... of ho]liness ... [...] *9* [...] ... [... his] holiness [will re]main *10* [...] his holiness [...]

Col. II *1* [... the covenant with] your [f]athers *2* [...] of you. May he lift *3* [... May he] be gracious to you and lif[t] *4* [his face towards you ...] your ... *5* [...] gods *6-21* [...] *22* [...] May the Lord be gracious to you ... [... and with all] *23* [rew]ards may he delight you, may he be gracious to you [...] *24* May he be gracious to you with a spirit of holiness and (may) fav[our ...] *25* and the eternal covenant. May he be gracious to you and may he [cause you] to rej[oice ...] *26* May he be gracious to you with a just judgment [... so that] you do [not] stum[ble ...] *27* May he be gracious to you in all your works [...] your [...] and in all [... may he be gracious to you] *28* [in] everlasting truth [...] on all [your] descen[dants ...]

Col. III *1* May the Lord lift his face towards you, and the ple[asant] aroma [of your offerings may he smell, and al]l those who belong [yo]ur prie[sthood] *2* may he choose. And may he visit all your holy one[s], and in [...] all your descendants. [May he li]ft *3* his face towards all your community. May he place on your head [...] ... *4* in [perpetual] glor[y, and may he] make your descendants holy with eternal glory. May he lif[t his face ...] ... *5* ... [...] May he give you [eter]nal [...] and the kingship [...] *6* [...] from flesh. And with the h[oly] angels [...] *7* May he wage war [...] ... [...] cor[rupt] generation [...] *8* [...] of them all [...] *9-16* [...] *17* [...] ... [...] *18* [... to subd]ue for you ma[ny

18 [...] להכנ]יע לכה לא[ומי]ם ר[ב]ים ולוא [...] 19 [...] כול הון תבל
לה.[.].כה ממקור ...] 20 ת]דורשהו כיא אל הכין כול אושי
21 [...]...[...] יסד שלומכה לעולמי עד 22 *vacat* דברי ברכה למ]שכיל
לברך] את בני צדוק הכוהנים אשר 23 בחר בם אל לחזק בר'תו ל]עולם
ולב]חון כול משפטיו בתוך עמו ולהורותם 24 כאשר צוה ויקימו באמת]
את בריתו] ובצדק פקדו כול חוקיו ויתהלכו כאש[ר] 25 בחר יברככה
אדוני מ]מעון קו]דשו וישימכה מכלול הדר בתוך 26 קדושים וברית
כהונת] עולם יח]דש לכה ויתנכה מקומכה] במעון] 27 קודש ובמעשייכה
יש[פוט כו]ל נדיבים וממזל שפתיכה כול] שרי] 28 עמים ינחילכה רשית]
כול מעד]נים ועצת כול בשר בידכה יברך

1 ופע]מי רגל]יכה ירצה ו[...] [אנוש וקדושי]י [...] 2 ימנה   *Col.* IV
[אתו ל]התערב לו וכלי]ל ... א]נוש ובתענוג]ות בני אדם ...]ך 3 ברכות
[עול]ם עטרת רואשכה קוד]ש ...]ידיכה [...] [...] 4 [...]...[...]...[...]...[...]
5 [...]...[...] 6-19 [...] לו לבחון [...] 21 [...] סב]יב לו על פנ]י [...]
22 [...]כה ויצדיקכה מכול ...]...[בחר בכה]...] 23 ולשאת ברוש
קדושים ועמכה לב]...]כה ...ברת ידכה 24 אנשי עצת אל ולוא ביד שר
יד]...]באיש לרעהו ואתה 25 כמלאך פנים במעון קודש לכבוד אלהי
צבא]ות ... ות]היה סביב משרת בהיכל 26 מלכות ומפיל גורל עם מלאכי
פנים ועצת יחד] ... לעת עולם ולכול קצי נצח כיא 27 [אמת כול מ]שפטיו
וישימכה קוד]ש] בעמו ולמאור] ... לתבל בדעת ולהאיר פני רבים 28 [...]
וישימכה] נזר לקודש קודשים כיא] אתה תק]דש לו ותכבד שמו וקודשיו

[...]לוא הש[...] ... ו 3   [...] מ[ן הבדלתה 2   [...] *vacat* 1   *Col.* v
[...]...[...] 7   [...] רוחו עליכה 6   [...] וחדש לכה] 5   [...] מ]כה 4 רואיכה
ידיכה י]שר מלא [א...] 17   [...] 10-16 [...]...[...] 9   [...] ואדון [...]. 8
[א]ל 19   [וישים ...]י] לוא וכבודכה עד כול קצי עם ...]...[.] 18 [...]
פחדכה [על] כול שומעי שמעכה והדריכה [...] 20 *vacat* למשכיל לברך
את נשיא העדה אשר [...] 21 [...]תו וברית ה]י]חד יחדש לו להקים

natio]ns and not […] *19* […] all the wealth of the world, to […] you from the spring *20* [… you] will seek it, because God has established all the foundations of *21* […] he has established your peace for all the everlasting centuries. *22 Blank* Words of Blessing. Of the Ins[tructor. To bless] the sons of Zadok, the priests whom *23* God has chosen to strengthen his covenant, for [ever, to dis]tribute all his judgments in the midst of his people, to teach them *24* in accordance with his commandment. They have established [his covenant] in truth and have examined all his precepts in justice, and they have walked in accordance with wha[t] *25* he chooses. May the Lord bless you from his [ho]ly [residence]. May he set you as a glorious ornament in the midst of *26* the holy ones. [May he re]new the covenant of [eternal] priesthood for you. May he grant you your place [in the] holy [residence]. *27* May he j[udge al]l the nobles by your works and by what issues from your lips all the [princes of] *28* the nations. May he give you to inherit the first fruits of [all de]lights. And by your hand may he bless the counsel of all flesh.

Col. IV   *1* May he be pleased with the tre[ad of] your [fe]et and […] of man and of the holy one[s …] *2* may he count [with him, to] form a partnership with him. And the cro[wn … of m]an and in the pleasure[s of the sons of man …] *3* May [everlas]ting blessings be the crown of your head, hol[y …] your hands … […] *4* … […] … […] … […] *5-19* […] *20* […] to test […] *21* [… ar]ound him in front [of …] *22* […] … and may he justify you from all … […] he has chosen you […] *23* to raise above the heads of the holy ones, and with you to […] … of your hand *24* the men of the council of God and not by the hand of the prince of … […] one to his fellow. May you be *25* like an angel of the face in the holy residence for the glory of the God of the Hos[ts … You shall] be around, serving in the temple of the *26* kingdom, casting the lot with the angels of the face and the Council of the Community […] for eternal time and for all the perpetual periods. For *27* [all] his [ju]dgments [are truth.] And may he make you hol[y] among his people, like a luminary […] for the world in knowledge, and to shine on the face of the Many *28* [… And may he make you] a diadem of the holy of holies, because [you shall be made ho]ly for him and you shall glorify his name and his holy things.

Col. V (+ Schøyen MS 1909)   *1 Blank* […] *2* you have separated fr[om …] *3* … not … […] *4* those who see you […] *5* and renews for you […] *6* his spirit upon you […] *7* […] … […] *8* […] and Lord […] *9-16* […] *17* [… w]ho fills [your] ha[nds …] *18* … […] with all periods of eternity. And your glory may he not [… may] *19* [G]od [put] the dread of you [upon] all who hear speak of you, and your splendours […] *20 Blank* Of the Instructor. To bless the prince of the congregation, who […] *21* […] his […] And he will renew the covenant of the

מלכות עמו לעול[ם ולשפוט בצדק אביונים]   22   [ו]להוכיח במישור
ל[ע]נוי ארץ ולהתהלך לפניו תמים בכול דרכי [...]   23   ולהקים בריתו
קודש] ב[צר לדורשי]ו י[ש]א[כ]ה אדוני לרום עולם וכמגדל עו[ז] בחומה
24   נשגבה והייתה ע[...]   בעז [פי]כה בשבטכה תחריב ארץ וברוח שפתיכה
25   תמית רשע יתן[לכה רוח עצ]ה וגבורת עולם רוח דעת ויראת אל והיה
26   צדק אזור [מותניכה ואמונ]ה אזור חלציכה [ו]ישם קרניכה ברזל
ופרסותיכה נחושה   27   תנכה כפ]ר ... ותרמוס עמ[ם כטיט חוצות כיא אל
הקימכה לשבט   28   למושלים לפ]ניכה ... כול לא[ומים יעובדוכה ובשם
קודשו יגברכה   29   והייתה כא[ר]יה ...[כה טרף ואין משי[ב] ופרשו
[ק]ליכה על

1Q29 *1QLiturgy of the Three Tongues of Fire*

J.T. Milik, *DJD I*, 130-132, pl. XXX
PAM 40.437, 40.442, 40.481, 40.538, 40.539
ROC 663
4Q376 (1Q22, 4Q375)

Frag. 1   1 [...]   2 [...] האבן כאשר [...]   3 ... יאירוכה ויצא
[עמו בלשונות אש]האבן השמאלית אשר על צדו השמאלי תגלה]
4 [לעיני כול הקהל עד]כלות הכוהן לדבר [ואחר נעלה ... ואתה תשמור]
5 [ועשיתה כול אשר יד]בר אליכה והנב[י]א ... [...]   6 [...] המדבר שרה [...]
7 [... י]הוה אל[...]

Frag. 2   1 [...]...[...]   2 ... הא[בן הימנית בצאת הכו]הן [...
3 [...]שלוש לשונות אש מ[...]   4 ... [ואחר יעלה וננעל] [...
5 [...]...[...]

Frags. 3-4   1 [...]...[...]   2 ... י]הוה אלוהיכמה [...]   3 ... כו]ל
ישראל [...]   4 [...] בכולם שמכה [...]   5 [...]רוב כוח הנכבד]ים [...
6 [...]...[...]

108

[Com]munity for him, to establish the kingdom of his people for eve[r, to judge the poor with justice,] 22 to reproach the [hu]mble of the earth with upri[ghtness,] to walk in perfection before him on all the paths of [...] 23 to establish his covenant as holy [during] the anguish of those seeking [it. May] the Lord rai[se y]ou to an everlasting height, like a forti[fied] tower upon a raised rampart. 24 May you be [...] with the power of your [mouth.] With your sceptre may you lay waste the earth. With the breath of your lips 25 may you kill the wicked. May he give [you a spirit of coun]sel and of everlasting fortitude, a spirit of knowledge and of fear of God. May 26 justice be the belt of [your loins, and loyalt]y the belt of your hips. May he make your horns of iron and your hoofs of bronze. 27 May you gore like a bu[ll ... and may you trample the nation]s like mud of the streets. For God has raised you to a sceptre 28 for the rulers be[fore you ... all the na]tions will serve you, and he will make you strong by his holy Name, 29 so that you will be like a li[on ...] your the prey, with no-one to give it [back]. Your [fa]st ones will scatter over

---

1Q29 *1QLiturgy of the Three Tongues of Fire*

Bibliography: J. Strugnell, 'Moses-Pseudepigrapha at Qumran: 4Q375, 4Q376 and Similar Works', in L.H. Schiffman (ed.), *Archaeology and History in the Dead Sea Scrolls* (Sheffield: JSOT, 1990) 221-256

Frag. 1 (= 4Q376 1 II)   *1* [...] ... [...] *2* [...] the stone, like [...] *3* [... they will provide you with light and he will go out] with it with tongues of fire; [the stone of the left side which is at its left side will shine] *4* [to the eyes of all the assembly until] the priest finishes speaking. [And after it (the cloud?) has been removed ... and you shall keep] *5* [and do all that he te]lls you. And the proph[et ...] *6* [...] who speaks apostasy [...] *7* [... Y]HWH, God of [...]

Frag. 2   *1* [...] ... [...] *2* [... the] right [st]one when the prie[st] leaves [...] *3* [...] three tongues of fire [...] *4* [...] And after he shall go up and remove his shoes [...] *5* [...] ... [...]

Frags. 3 - 4   *1* [...] ... [...] *2* [... Y]HWH, your God, [...] *3* [... al]l Israel [...] *4* [...] with them all. Your name [...] *6* [...] the greatness of the power of the glorious one[s ...]

Frags. 5-7   1 [...] ה]דברים האלה על פי כול [...].   2 [...] ואח]ר
ידרוש הכוהן לכול רצונו כ]ול [... 3 [...] הקהל *vacat* [...]   4 [...] בני
י]ש]רא]ל שמורו את הדברים האלה [...]   5 [...] לע]שות כו]ל [...
6 [...]מספר המש]...[...]   7 [...]...יהם [...]

1Q30 *1QLiturgical Text (?)*

J.T. Milik, *DJD I*, 132-133, pl. XXX
PAM 40.436, 40.438

Frag. 1   1 [...].[...]   2 [...] [רוח הקודש]...[3 [...] ב]שלישית את
כול[...]   4 [... ס]פרים חומשים .[...]   5 [...]ויותר על ארבעת .[...].
6 [...] ופשריהם לפי]...[

1Q31 *1QLiturgical Text (?)*

J.T. Milik, *DJD I*, 133, pl. XXX
PAM 40.548

Frag. 1   1 [כ]ול אנשי היחד ישבו]... ועל]   2 פיהם ישסו כול [...]...[...]
3 [...]...[...]

Frag. 2   1 לאין כ.[...]   2 ובחירי]...[3 במחנים]...[4 למלח]מה
[...

1Q32 (1QNJ ar) *1QNew Jerusalem ar*

J.T. Milik, *DJD I*, 134-135, pl. XXXI
PAM 40.503, 40.538

Frags. 5 - 7   *1* [...] these words, according to all [...] *2* [... and afterwar]ds the priest will explain all he wishes, a[ll ...] *3* [...] the assembly. *Blank* [...] *4* [... Children of I]s[rae]l, keep these words [...] *5* [... to d]o al[l ...] *6* [...] the number of the ... [...] *7* [...] ... [...]

1Q30 *1QLiturgical Text (?)*

BNP

Frag. 1   *1* [...] ... [...] *2* [...] the holy spirit [...] *3* [... in] the third (place), all [...] *4* [... boo]ks, divided into five [...] *5* [...] and the remainder over four [...] *6* [...] and their interpretation according to [...]

1Q31 *1QLiturgical Text (?)*

BNP

Frag. 1   *1* [A]ll the men of the Community shall sit [... and at] *2* their order they shall plunder all ... [...] *3* [...] ... [...]

Frag. 2   *1* without ... [...] *2* and the elect of [...] *3* in the camps [...] *4* to the wa[r ...]

1Q32 (1QNJ ar) *1QNew Jerusalem ar*

BNP
2Q24, 4Q554, 4Q554a, 4Q555, 5Q15, 11Q18

Frag. 1   1 [...]ן תשוית עמוד[א ...   2 [...] ממע]ל לעמוד[א ...]

1QM (1QM) *1QWar Scroll*

E.L. Sukenik, *DSSHU*, 1-19, pls. 16-34, 47
SHR 3365-3407
SHR
1Q33, 4Q491, 4Q492, 4Q493, 4Q494, 4Q495, 4Q496, 4Q285? 11Q14?
Bibliography: J. Carmignac, *La Règle de la Guerre des Fils de Lumière contre les Fils de Ténèbres.* (Paris: Letouzey et Ané, 1958); J.P.M. van der Ploeg, *Le Rouleau de*

1Q33 (1QM) *1QWar Scroll*

J.T. Milik, *DJD I*, 135-136, pl. XXXI
PAM 40.487, 40.531

Col. I   1 למ[שכיל סרך] המלחמה ראשית משלוח יד בני אור להחל
בגורל בני חושך בחיל בליעל בגדוד אדום ומואב ובני עמון   2 וח[...
[פלשת ובגדודי כתיי אשור ועמהם בעזר מרשיעי ברית בני לוי ובני יהודה
ובני בנימין גולת המדבר ילחמו בם   3 ב[...] לכול גדודיהם בשוב גולת בני
אור ממדבר העמים לחנות במדבר ירושלים ואחד המלחמה יעלו משם
4 [...]... הכתיים במצרים ובקצו יצא בחמה גדולה להלחם במלכי הצפון
ואפו להשמיד ולהכרית את קרן   5 י[שראל והי]אה עת ישועה לעם אל וקץ
ממשל לכול אנשי גורלו וכלת עולמים לכול גורל בליעל והיתה מהומה
6 ג[דולה ב]בני יפת ונפל אשור ואין עוזר לו וסרה ממשלת כתיים להכניע
רשעה לאין שארית ופלטה לוא תהיה   7 ל[כול בנ]י חושך   *vacat*

8 ו[בני צ]דק יאירו לכול קצוות תבל הלוך ואור עד תום כול מועדי
חושך ובמועד אל יאיר רום גודלו לכול קצי ע[ולמים] לשלום וברכה
כבוד ושמחה ואורך ימים לכול בני אור וביום נפול בו כתיים קרב ונחשיר

Frag. 1   *1* [...] the base of [the] column [...] *2* [... abo]ve [the] column [...]

1QM (1QM) *1QWar Scroll*

la Guerre traduit et annoté (STDJ 2; Leiden: E.J. Brill, 1959); B. Jongeling, *Le rouleau de la guerre des manuscrits de Qumrân. Commentaire et traduction* (Studia Semitica Neerlandica 4; Assen: Van Gorcum, 1962); Y. Yadin, *The Scroll of the War of the Sons of Light against de Sons of Darkness* (Oxford: OUP, 1962); P.R. Davies, *IQM. The War Scroll from Qumran: Its Structure and History* (BibOr 32; Rome: Pontifical Biblical Institute, 1977); J. Duhaime, *PTSDSSP 2*, 80-203

1Q33 (1QM) *1QWar Scroll*

DAJ
1QM, 4Q491, 4Q492, 4Q493, 4Q494, 4Q495, 4Q496, 4Q285?, 11Q14?

Col. 1 (= 4Q496 2 + 1)   *1* For the Ins[tructor: The Rule of] the War. The first attack by the sons of light will be launched against the lot of the sons of darkness, against the army of Belial, against the band of Edom and of Moab and of the sons of Ammon *2* and [...] Philistia, and against the bands of the Kittim of Ashur, who are being helped by the violators of the covenant. The sons of Levi, the sons of Judah and the sons of Benjamin, the exiled of the desert, will wage war against them. *3* [...] against all their bands, when the exiled sons of light return from the desert of the nations to camp in the desert of Jerusalem. And after the war, they shall go up from there *4* ... [...] of the Kittim in Egypt. And in his time, he will go out with great rage to wage war against the kings of the North, and his anger wants to exterminate and cut off the horn of *5* I[srael. And th]is is a time of salvation for the nation of God and a period of rule for all the men of his lot, and of everlasting destruction for all the lot of Belial. There will be *6* g[reat] panic [among] the sons of Japhet, Ashur shall fall and there will be no help for him; the rule of the Kittim will come to an end, wickedness having been defeated, with no remnant remaining, and there will be no escape *7* for [any of the sons] of darkness. *Blank*

8 And [the sons of jus]tice shall shine to all the edges of the earth, they shall go on shining, up to the end of all the periods of darkness; and in the time of God, his exalted greatness will shine for all the et[ernal] times, *9* for peace and blessing, glory and joy, and length of days for all the sons of light. And on the day on which the Kittim fall, there will be a battle, and savage destruction

חזק לפני אל   10 ישראל כיא הואה יום יעוד לו מאז למלחמת כלה לבני
חושך בו יתקרבו לנחשיר גדול עדת אלים וקהלת   11 אנשים בני אור
וגורל חושך נלחמים יחד לגבורת אל בקול המון גדול ותרועת אלים
ואנשים ליום הווה והיאה עת   12 צרה ע]ל כו]ל עם פדות אל ובכול
צרותמה לוא נהיתה כמוה מחושה עד תומה לפדות עולמים וביום מלחמתם
בכתיים   13 יצא]ו ל]נחשיר במלחמה שלושה גורלות יחזקו בני אור לנגוף
רשעה ושלושה יתאזרו חיל בליעל למושב גורל   14 [אור ו]דגלי הבנים
יהיה להמס לבב וגבורת אל מאמצת ל]בב בני אור]ובגורל השביעי יד אל
הגדולה מכנעת   15 [בליעל וכו]ל מלאכי ממשלתו ולכול אנשי [גורלו]

vacat

16 [...] קדושים יופיע בעזרת [...] אמת לכלת בני חושך אז   17 [...]
גדול ...]...[ם יתנו יד בכל] ...

1   *Col.* II אבות העדה שנים וחמשים ואת ראשי הכוהנים יסרוכו אחר
כוהן הראש ומשנהו ראשים שנים עשר להיות משרתים   2 בתמיד לפני אל
וראשי המשמרות ששה ועשרים במשמרותם ישרתו ואחריהם ראשי
הלויים לשרת תמיד שנים עשר אחד   3 לשבט וראשי משמרותם איש
במעמדו ישרתו וראשי השבטים ואבות העדה אחריהם להתיצב תמיד
בשערי המקדש   4 וראשי משמרותם עם פקודיהם יתיצבו למועדיהם
לחודשיהם לשבתות ולכול ימי השנה מבן חמשים שנה ומעלה   5 אלה
יתיצבו על העולות ועל הזבחים לערוך מקטרת ניחוח לרצון אל לכפר בעד
כול עדתו ולהדשן לפניו תמיד   6 בשולחן כבוד את כול אלה יסרוכו במועד
שנת השמטה ובשלוש ושלושים שני המלחמה הנותרות יהיו אנשי השם
7 קרואי המועד וכול ראשי אבות העדה בחרים להם אנשי מלחמה לכול
ארצות הגוי'ם מכול שבטי ישראל יחלוצו   8 להם אנשי חיל לצאת לצבא
כפי תעודות המלחמה שנה בשנה ובשני השמטים לוא יחלוצו לצאת לצבא
כיא שבת   9 מנוח היאה לישראל בחמש ושלושים שני העבודה תערך
המלחמה שש שנים ועורכיה כול העדה יחד   10 ומלחמת המחלקות בעתש
(בתשע) ועשרים הנותרות ילחמו בשנה הראישונה בארם נהרים ובשנית

before the God of *10* Israel, for this will be the day determined by him since ancient times for the war of extermination against the sons of darkness. On this (day), the assembly of the gods and the congregation of men shall confront each other for great destruction. *11* The sons of light and the lot of darkness shall battle together for God's might, between the roar of a huge multitude and the shout of gods and of men, on the day of the calamity. It will be a time of *12* suffering fo[r al]l the nation redeemed by God. Of all their sufferings, none will be like this, hastening till eternal redemption is fulfilled. And on the day of their war against the Kittim, *13* [t]he[y] shall go out [to] destruction. In the war, the sons of light will be the strongest during three lots, in order to strike down wickedness; and in three (others), the army of Belial will gird themselves in order to force the lot of [light] to retreat. *14* There will be infantry battalions to melt the heart, but God's might will strengthen the he[art of the sons of light.] And in the seventh lot, God's great hand will subdue *15* [Belial, and al]l the angels of his dominion and all the men of [his lot.] *Blank 16* […] the holy ones, he will appear to assist the […] truth, for the destruction of the sons of darkness. Then *17* […] … great … […] shall stretch out the hand to […]

Col. II (= 4Q494; 4Q496 13)   *1* fathers of the congregation, fifty-two. They shall arrange the chiefs of the priests behind the High Priest and of his second (in rank), twelve chiefs to serve *2* in perpetuity before God. And the twenty-six chiefs of the divisions shall serve in their divisions and after them the chiefs of the levites to serve always, twelve, one *3* per tribe. And the chiefs of their divisions shall each serve in his place. The chiefs of the tribes, and after them the fathers of the congregation, shall take their positions in the gates of the sanctuary in perpetuity. *4* And the chiefs of the divisions with their enlisted shall take their positions at their feasts, their new moons, the sabbaths and all the days of the year - those of fifty years and upwards. *5* These shall take their positions at the holocausts and the sacrifices, in order to prepare the pleasant incense for God's approval, to atone for all his congregation and to satisfy themselves in perpetuity before him *6* at the table of glory. They shall arrange all /these/ during the appointed time of the year of release. During the remaining thirty-three years of the war, the men of renown, *7* those called at the assembly, and all the chiefs of the fathers of the congregation, shall choose for themselves men of war for all the countries of the nations; from all the tribes of Israel they shall equip *8* for themselves intrepid men, in order to go out on campaign according to the directives of war, year after year. However, during the years of release they shall not equip themselves in order to go out on campaign, for it is a sabbath of *9* rest for Israel. During the thirty-five years of service, the war will be prepared during six years; and all the congregation together will prepare it. *10* And the war of the divisions (will take place) dur-

בבני לוד בשלישית 11 ילחמו בשאר בני ארם בעוץ וחול תוגר ומשא
אשר בעבד פורת ברביעית ובחמישית ילחמו בבני ארפכשד
12 בששית ובשביעית ילחמו בכול בני אשור ופרס והקדמוני עד המדבר
הגדול בשנה השמינית ילחמו בבני 13 עילם בתשיעית ילחמו בבני
ישמעאל וקטורה ובעשר השנים אשר אחריהם תחלק המלחמה על כול בני
חם 14 למ[שפחותם במו]שבותם ובעשר השנים הנותרות תחלק המלחמה
על כול [בני יפ]ת במושבותיהם 15 *vacat* [*vacat*] *vacat* [*vacat*]

16 [סרך חצוצרות המקרא וחצוצר]ות התרועה לכול עבודתם ל[...]
לפקודיהם 17 [...] [...] ועושרות על ח[...]

1 *Col. III* {סדרי המלחמה והחצוצרות} סדרי המלחמה וחצוצרות מקראם
בהפתח שערי המלחמה לצאת אנשי הבנים וחצוצרות תרועות החללים
וחצוצרות 2 המארב וחצוצרות המדרף בהנגף אויב וחצו⸢צ⸣רות המאסף
בשוב המלחמה על חצוצרות מקרא העדה קרואי אל 3 ועל
חצוצרות מקרא ה{ס}שרים יכתובו נשיאי אל ועל חצוצרות המסורות
יכתובו סרך אל ועל חצוצרות אנשי 4 השם {יכתובו} ראשי אבות העדה
בהאספם לבית מועד יכתובו תעודות אל לעצת קודש ועל חצוצרות המחנות
5 יכתובו שלום אל במחני קדושיו ועל חצוצרות מסעיהם יכתובו גבורות
אל להפיץ אויב ולהניס כול משנאי 6 צדק ומשוב חסדים במשנאי אל ועל
חצוצרות סדרי המלחמה יכתובו סדרי דגלי אל לנקמת אפו בכול בני חושך
7 ועל חצוצרות מקרא אנשי הבנים בהפתח שערי המלחמה לצאת למערכת
האויב יכתובו זכרון נקם במועד 8 אל ועל חצוצרות החללים יכתובו יד
גבורת אל במלחמה להפיל כול חללי מעל ועל חצוצרות המארב יכתובו
9 רזי אל לשחת רשעה ועל חצוצרות המדרף בהנגף נגף אל כול בני חושך

ing the remaining twenty-nine years. During the first year they shall wage war against Aram-Naharaim; during the second, against the sons of Lud; during the third *11* they shall wage war against the remnant of the sons of Aram, against Uz and Hul, Togar and Mesha, who are beyond the Euphrates; during the fourth and fifth, they shall wage war against the sons of Arpachsad; *12* during the sixth and seventh they shall wage war against all the sons of Assyria and Persia, and the eastern nations up to the great desert; during the eighth year they shall wage war against the sons of *13* Elam; during the ninth they shall wage war against the sons of Ishmael and Ketura; and during the following ten years the war will be divided against all the sons of Ham, *14* according to [their] c[lans, in] their [dw]ellings; and during the remaining ten years the war will be divided against all [the sons of Japhe]t, in their dwellings. *Blank 15* [*Blank*] *Blank* [*Blank*]

16 [Rule of the trumpets of muster and the trumpet]s of alarm for all their services, for [...] for their enlisted men [...] *17* and tens above [...]

Col. III (= 4Q496 8, 3, 11, 10)   *1* {the battle formations and the trumpets} /the battle formations and the trumpets/ of their muster, when the gates of battle open for the men of the infantry to go out and the trumpets of alarm of the slain and the trumpets of *2* ambush, and the trumpets of pursuit, when the enemy is struck, and the trumpets of re-assembly, when they retreat from battle. On the trumpets of muster of the assembly they shall write: «Mustered by God». *3* On the trumpets of muster of the commanders they shall write: «Princes of God». And on the trumpets for enlisting, they shall write «Rule of God». And on the trumpets of *4* the men of renown, {they shall write} chiefs of the fathers of the congregation, when they meet in the meeting house, they shall write: «God's directives for the holy council». And on the trumpets of the camps *5* they shall write: «Peace of God in the camps of his holy ones». And on the trumpets of pulling them out they shall write: «God's mighty deeds to scatter the enemy and force all those who hate *6* justice to flee», and «Withdrawal of mercy from those who hate God». And on the trumpets of battle formations they shall write: «God's battle formations for avenging his wrath against all the sons of darkness». *7* And on the trumpets of the muster of the infantrymen when the gates of battle open so they can go out up to the enemy line they shall write: «Memorial of revenge at the moment appointed by *8* God». And on the trumpets of the slain they shall write: «God's mighty hand in the battle to fell all the slain of unfaithfulness». And on the trumpets of ambush they shall write: *9* «God's mysteries to destroy wickedness». And on the trumpets of pursuit they shall write: «God has struck all the sons of darkness, he shall not cause his wrath to return, until they are exterminated».

לוא ישוב אפו עד כלותם 10 ובשובם מן המלחמה לבוא המערכה יכתובו
על חצוצרות המשוב אסף אל ועל חצוצרות דרך המשוב 11 ממלחמת
האויב לבוא אל העדה ירושלים יכתובו גילות אל במשוב שלום *vacat*

vacat 12

13 סרך אותות כול העדה למסורותם על האות הגדולה אשר בראש כול
העם יכתובו עם אל ואת שם ישראל 14 ואהרון ושמות שנים עשר שב[טי
ישר]אל כתולדותם על אותות ראשי המחנות אשר לשלושת השבטים
15 יכתובו [...]... ע]ל אות השבט יכתובו נס אל ואת שם נשי הש[בט ...]
16 משפ]חותם ... א]ת שם הנשיא הרבוא ואת שמות שרי [... .17 [...]
מאיותיו ועל אות [...]

1 Col. IV ועל אות מררי יכתובו תרומת אל ואת שם נשי מררי ואת
שמות שרי אלפיו ועל אות האל[ל]ף יכתובו אף אל בעברה על 2 בליעל
ובכול אנשי גורלו לאין שארית ואת שם שר האלף ואת שמות שרי מאיותיו
ועל אות המאה יכתובו מאת 3 אל יד מלחמה בכול בשר עול ואת שם שר
המאה ואת שם שמות שרי עשרותיו ועל אות החמשים יכתובו חדל
4 מעמד רשעים [בב]גבורת אל ואת שם שר החמשים ואת שמות שרי
עשרותיו על אות העשרה יכתובו רנות 5 אל בנבל עשור ואת שם שר
העשרה ואת שמות תשעת אנשי תעודתו *vacat*

6 וב{כ}לכתם למלחמה יכתובו על אותותם אמת אל צדק אל כבוד אל
משפט אל ואחריהם כול סרך פרוש שמותם 7 ובגשתם למלחמה יכתובו
על אותותם ימין אל מועד אל מהומת אל חללי אל ואחריהם כול פרוש
שמותם 8 ובשובם מן המלחמה יכתובו על אותותם רומם אל גדל אל
תשבוחת אל כבוד אל עם כול פרוש שמותם *vacat*

9 סרך אותות העדה בצאתם למלחמה יכתבו על אות הראישונה עדת אל
על אות השנית מחני אל על השלישית 10 שבטי אל על הרביעית משפחות

10 And when they retreat from battle to return to the line, they shall write on the trumpets of retreat: «God has re-assembled». And on the trumpets of the path of return *11* from battle with the enemy, to go back to the congregation of Jerusalem, they shall write: «Exultations of God in a peaceful return». *Blank* *12 Blank*

13 Rule of the banners of all the congregation according to their formations. On the large banner which goes at the head of all the nation they shall write: «God's nation», and the name of Israel *14* and of Aaron and the names of the twelve tri[bes of Isra]el according to their births. Above the banner of the camp chiefs of the three tribes *15* they shall write: […] On the banner of the tribe they shall write: «God's flag», and the name of the prince of the tr[ibe …] *16* [their] cl[ans …] the name of the princes of the ten thousand and the names of the pri[nces of …] *17* […] his hundreds, and on the banner […]

Col. IV (= 4Q496 16)   *1* And on the banner of Merari they shall write: «God's offering» and the name of the prince of Merari and the names of the commanders of his thousands. And on the banner of the tho[us]and they shall write: «God's Fury unleashed against *2* Belial and against all the men of his lot so that no remnant (is left)» and the name of the commander of the thousand and the names of the commanders of his hundreds. And on the banner of the hundred they shall write: «From *3* God is the hand of battle against all degenerate flesh» and the name of the commander of the hundred and the names of the commanders of his tens. And on the banner of the fifty they shall write: «No longer *4* do the wicked rise, [due to] God's might», and the name of the commander of the fifty and the names of the commanders of his tens. On the banner of the ten they shall write: «Songs of jubilation of *5* God on the ten-string lyre» and the name of the commander of the ten and the names of the nine men under his command. *Blank 6* And when they go to battle they shall write on their banners: «God's truth», «God's justice», «God's glory», «God's judgment» and after these (names) all the ordered list of their names. *7* And when they approach for battle they shall write on their banners: «God's right hand», «Time appointed by God», «God's confusion», «God's slaughter», and after these the complete list of their names. *8* And when they retreat from battle, they shall write on their banners: «God's glorification», «God's greatness», «God's praise», «God's glory», with a complete list of their names. *Blank 9* Rule of the banners of the congregation. When they go out to battle they shall write on the first banner: «God's congregation»; on the second banner: «God's camps»; on the third, *10* «God's tribes»; on the fourth: «God's families»; on the fifth: «God's battalions»; on the sixth: «God's As-

אל על החמישית דגלי אל על הששית קהל אל על השביעית קריאי 11 אל
על השמינית צבאות אל ופרוש שמותם יכתובו עם כול סרכם ובגשתם
למלחמה יכתובו על אותותם 12 מלחמת אל נקמת אל ריב אל גמול אל
כוח אל שלומי אל גבורת אל כלת אל בכול גוי הבל ואת כול פרוש
שמותם יכתובו עליהם ובשובם מן המלחמה יכתובו על אותותם ישועות 13
אל נצח אל עזר אל משענת אל 14 שמחת אל הודות אל תהלת אל שלום
אל *vacat*

15 [מדות הא]ותות אות כול העדה אורך ארבע עשרה אמה אות
של[ושת השבטים אורך שלש וע]שרה אמה 16 [אות השבט]שתים עשרה
אמה אות הרבוא עשתי עש[רה אמה אות האלף]עשר אמות אות המ[א]ה תשע
אמות 17 [אות החמישים שמו]נה אמות אות העשרה שבע] אמות [*vacat*

Col. v 1 ועל מ[ג]ן נשיא כול העדה יכתבו שמו[ו]שם ישראל ולוי
ואהרון ושמות שנים עשר שבטי ישראל כתולדותם 2 ושמות שנים עשר
שרי שבטיהם *vacat*

3 סרך לסדר דגלי המלחמה בהמלא צבאם להשלים מ^ערכת פנים על
אלף איש תאסר המערכה ושבעה סדרי 4 פנים למערכה האחת סדו{ן}כ}ים
בסרך מעמד איש אחד איש וכולם מחזיקים מגני נחושת מרוקה כמעשה
5 מראת פנים והמגן מוסב מעשי גדיל שפה וצורת מחברת מעשה חושב
זהב וכסף ונחושת ממוזזים 6 ואבני חפץ אבדני רוקמה מעשה חרש
מחשבת אורך המגן אמתים וחצי ורוחבו אמה וחצי רמח ובידם 7 וכידן
אורך הרמח שבע אמות מזה הסגר והלוהב חצי האמה ובסגר שלושה
צמידים מפותחים כמעשי 8 גדיל שפה בזהב וכסף ונחושת ממוזזים
כמעשי צורה מחשבת ומחברת הצ[ו]רה מזה ומזה לצמיד 9 סביב אבני
חפץ בדני רוקמה מעשי חרש מחשבת ושבולת והסגד מחורץ בין הצמידים
כמעשי 10 עמוד מחשבת והלוהב ברזל לבן מאיר מעשי חרש מחשבת
ושבולת זהב טהור בתוך הלהב ושפוד אל 11 הראש והכידנים ברזל ברור
טהור בכור ומלובן כמראת פנים מעשי חרש מחשבת ומראי שבולת

sembly»; on the seventh: «Summoned by *11* God»; on the eighth: «God's armies»; and they shall write the list of their names in all their order. And when they approach for battle they shall write on their banners: *12* «God's battle», «God's revenge», «God's lawsuit», «God's reward», «God's might», «God's prize», «God's power», «God's destruction of every futile people», and all the list of *13* their names they shall write on them. And when they retreat from battle they shall write on their banners: «God's acts of salvation», «God's victory», «God's help», «God's support», *14* «God's joy», «God's thanksgiving», «God's praise», «God's peace». *Blank 15* [Sizes of the ban]ners: banner of the whole congregation, fourteen cubits long; banner of the th[ree tribes, thir]teen cubits long; *16* [tribal banner], twelve cubits; banner of the ten thousand, eleven [cubits; banner of the thousand, ten cubits; banner of the /hund]red/, nine cubits; *17* [banner of the fifty, eig]ht cubits; banner of the ten, seven [cubits. *Blank*]

Col. V   *1* And upon the sh[ie]ld of the Prince of the whole congregation they shall write his name [and] the name of Israel and Levi and Aaron and the names of the twelve tribes of Israel, according to their births, *2* and the names of the twelve commanders of their tribes. *Blank*

3 Rule of the formation of fighting battalions. When their army is complete, to fill a front line, the line will be formed of one thousand men, with seven forward *4* formations per line, each formation in its order, each man being behind the other. And all shall be armed with bronze shields, polished like *5* a mirror. And the shield will be surrounded by a plaited border and will have a pattern engraved, a work of art in gold, silver and copper blended together, *6* and precious stones, many-hued decorations, work of a skilful craftsman. Height of the shield: two and a half cubits; and its width, one and a half cubits. And in their hand, a spear *7* and a sword. Length of the spear: seven cubits, including the haft, and the tip of half a cubit. In the haft there will be three rings cut, with an border *8* plaited in gold, silver and bronze intermixed, like a work of art and an engraved pattern. On both parts of the ring, the pattern will be surrounded *9* with precious stones, many-hued decorations, work of a skilful craftsman, and an ear of wheat. And the haft will be engraved between the rings in the style of *10* an artistic column. The point will be of shining white iron, work of a skilful craftsman, and will have an ear of wheat, of pure gold, in the centre of the point pointing towards *11* the tip. The swords shall be of purified iron, refined in a crucible and whitened like a mirror, work of a skilful craftsman;

12 זהב טהור חוברת בו לשני עבריו וספות ישר אל הראוש שתים מזה
ושתים מזה אורך הכידן אמה   13 וחצי ורוחבו ארבע אצבעות והבטן ארבע
גודלים וארבעה טפחים עד הבטן והבטן מרוגלת הנה   14 והנה חמשה
טפחים ויד הכידן קרן ברורה מעשה חושב צורת רוקמה בזהב ובכסף ואבני
חפץ   15 *vacat*

16 ובעמוד ה[...]ה יסדרו שבע המערכות מערכה אחר מערכה
17 ורוח[... ש]לושים באמה אשר יעמודו שם אנש[י...]   18 [...]... הפנים
[...]...

1 *Col.* vi   שבע פעמים ושבו למעמדם ואחריהם יצאו שלושה דגלי
ביניב ועמדו בין המערכות הדגל הראישון ישליך אל   2 מערכת האויב
שבעה זרקות מלחמה ועל לוהב הזרק יכתובו ברקת חנית לגבורת אל ועל
השלט השני יכתובו   3 זיקי דם להפיל חללים באף אל ועל הזרק השלישי
יכתובו שלהובת חרב אוכלת חללי און במשפט אל   4 כול אלה יטילו שבע
פעמים ושבו למעמדם ואחריהם יצאו שני דגלי ביניב ועמדו בין שתי
המערכות הדגל   5 הראישון מחזיק חנית ומגן והדגל השני מחזיקי מגן
וכידן להפיל חללים במשפט אל ולהכניע מ^ערכת   6 אויב בגבורת אל לשלם
גמול רעתם לכול גוי הבל והיתה לאל ישראל המלוכה ובקדושי עמו יעשה
חיל   7 *vacat*

8 ושבעה סדרי פרשים יעמודו גם המה לימין המערכה ולשמאולה מזה
ומזה יעמודו סדריהם שבע מאות   9 פרשים לעבר האחד ושבע מאות לעבר
השני מאתים פרשים יצאו עם אלף מערכת אנשי הבינים וכן   10 יעמודו
לכול ע[ב]רי המחנה הכול שש מאות וארבעת אלפים ואלף וארבע מאות
רכב לאנשי סרך המע^רכות   11 חמשים למערכה [הא]חת ויהיו הפרשים על
רכב אנשי הסרך ששת אלפים חמש מאות לשבט כול הרכב היוצאים
12 למלחמה עם אנש[י]הבנים סוסים זכרים קלי רגל ורכי פה וארוכי רוח
ומלאים בתכון ימיהם מלומדי מלחמה   13 ובעולים לשמוע [ק]ולות ולכול
מראי דמיונים והרוכבים עליהם אנשי חיל למלחמה מלומדי רכב ותכון

and it will have shapes of an ear of wheat, *12* of pure gold, encrusted in it on both sides. And it will have two straight channels right to the tip, two on each side. Length of the sword: one cubit *13* and a half. And its width: four fingers. The scabbard will be four thumbs; it will have four palms up to the scabbard and diagonally, the scabbard from one part to *14* the other (will be) five palms. The hilt of the sword will be of select horn, craftwork, with a pattern in many colours: gold, silver and precious stones. *15 Blank*

16 And when the [...] stand up, they shall line up in seven lines, one line behind the other, *17* and the space [...] thirty cubits in which the me[n] shall stand *18* [...] the faces [...]

Col. VI *1* seven times and they shall return to their position. After them, three battalions of infantry shall go out and shall take up position between the lines. The first battalion will hurl against *2* the enemy line seven javelins of war. On the point of the javelin they shall write: «Sheen of the spear by God's might». On the second dart they shall write: *3* «Arrows of blood to fell the dead by God's wrath». And on the third javelin they shall write: «Flame of the sword devouring the wicked dead by God's judgment». *4* All these they shall hurl seven times and go back to their position. And after them, two infantry battalions shall go out and they shall take up position between the two lines. The first *5* battalion will be equipped with a spear and a shield and the second battalion will be equipped with a shield and a sword, to fell the dead by the judgment of God and to humiliate the enemy line *6* by God's might, to pay the reward of their evil towards every people of futility. For kingship belongs to the God of Israel and with the holy ones of his nation he will work wonders. *7 Blank*

8 And seven cavalry formations shall take up position, they also, on the right and on the left of the line. Their formations shall take up position on one side and the other, seven hundred *9* cavalry on one flank and seven hundred on the second flank. Two hundred cavalry shall go out with the thousand soldiers of the infantry of one line. And thus *10* shall they take up position on all the flanks of the camp. In all, four thousand six hundred; and fourteen hundred mounts for the men of the array of the lines, *11* fifty for [ea]ch line. The cavalry, including the mounts of the men of the array, will be six thousand, five hundred per tribe. All the mounts which go out *12* to the battle with the infantry-men shall be stallions, fleet of foot, tame of mouth, long in wind, in the fullness of their days, trained for battle *13* and disciplined to hearing [d]in and the sight of every display. And those who mount them shall be men, hardened

14 ימיהם מבן שלושים שנה עד בן חמש וארבעים ופרשי הסרך יהיו מבן
ארבעים שנה ועד בן חמשים והמה   15 ורכ]בם מ]ל[ובשים מ]צחות ובתי
ראשים ושוקים ומחזיקים בידם מגני עגלה ורמח ארוך שמונה אמ]ות[
16]... [וקשת וחצים וזרקות מלחמה וכולם עתודים בס]...[17   [...]ל[
ולשפוך דם חללי אשמתם אלה המה ה.[...]   18   [...] *vacat* [...]

1   *Col.* VII   ואנשי הסרך יהיו מבן ארבעים שנה ועד בן חמשים וסורכי
המחנות יהיו מבן {ארבעים} חמשים שנה ועד בן {חמשים} ששים
והשוטרים   2 יהיו גם הם מבן ארבעים שנה ועד בן חמשים וכול מפשיטי
החללים ושוללי השלל ומטהרי הארץ ושומרי הכלים   3 ועורך הצידה
כולם יהיו מבן חמש ועשרים שנה ועד בן שלושים וכול נער זעטוט ואשה
לוא יבואו למחנותם בצאתם   4 מירושלים ללכת למלחמה עד שובם וכול
פסח או עור או חגר או איש אשר מום עולם בבשרו או איש מנוגע בטמאת
5 בשרו כול אלה לוא ילכו אתם למלחמה כולם יהיו אנשי נדבת מלחמה
ותמימי רוח ובשר ועתודים ליום נקם וכול   6 איש אשר לוא יהיה טהור
ממקורו ביום המלחמה לוא ירד אתם כיא מלאכי קודש עם צבאותם יחד
ורוח יהיה   7 בין כול מחניהמה למקום היד כאלפים באמה וכול ערות דבר
רע לוא יראה סביבות כול מחניהם   8 *vacat*

9 ובסדר מערכות המלחמה לקראת אויב מערכה לקראת מערכה ויצאו
מן השער התיכון אל בין המערכות שבעה   10 כוהנים מבני אהרון לובשים
בגדי שש לבן כתונת בד ומכנסי בד וחוגרים באבנט בד שש משוזר תכלת
11 וארגמן ותולעת שני וצורת רוקמה מעשה חושב ופרי מגבעות
בראשיהם בגדי מלחמה ואל המקדש לוא   12 יביאום הכוהן האחד יהיה
מהלך על פני כול אנשי המערכה לחזק ידיהם במלחמה וביד הששה יהיו
13 חצוצרות המקרא וחצוצרות הזכרון וחצוצרות התרועה והצוצרות
המרדף וחצוצרות המאסף ובצאת הכוהנים   14 אל בין המערכות יצאו
עמהמה שבעה לויים ובידם שבעת שופרות היובל ושלושה שוטרים מן
הלויים לפני   15 הכוהנים והלויים ותקעו הכוהנים בשתי חצוצרות
המקרא]... מ]לחמה על חמשים מגן   16 וחמשים אנשי בינים יצאו מן

in battle, trained in horsemanship. The range of *14* their days will be from thirty up to forty-five years. The horsemen of the array shall be between forty and fifty years old. They *15* and [their] moun[ts shall be] at[tired in cu]irasses, helmets and greaves and shall hold in their hands circular shields and a spear of eight cu[bits] *16* [...] and a bow and arrows and war javelins. And all shall be ready ... [...] *17* [...] and to shed the blood of the fallen on account of their wickedness. These are the ones who [...] *18* [...] *Blank* [...].

Col. VII (= 4Q496 7) *1* The men of the array shall be between forty and fifty years (old). Those governing the camps shall be between {forty} fifty and {fifty} sixty years (old). The supervisors *2* shall also be between forty and fifty years (old). And all those who despoil the fallen and those who pillage the loot and those who cleanse the earth and those who protect the weapons *3* and those who prepare the supplies all shall be between twenty-five and thirty years (old). And no young boy or any woman at all shall enter the camps when they leave *4* Jerusalem to go to war, until they return. And no lame, blind, paralysed person nor any man who has an indelible blemish on his flesh, nor any man suffering from uncleanness *5* in his flesh, none of these will go out to war with them. All these shall be volunteers for war, perfect in spirit and in body, and ready for the day of vengeance. And every *6* man who has not cleansed himself of his 'spring' on the day of battle will not go down with them, for the holy angels are together with their armies. And there will be a space *7* between all their camps and «the place of the hand» of about two thousand cubits. And no immodest nakedness will be seen in the surroundings of all their camps. *8 Blank*

9 When they draw up the battle lines against the enemy, one line opposite another line, out from the central gate towards (the space) between the lines, shall go seven *10* priests of the sons of Aaron, robed with garments of white byssus, a linen tunic and linen trousers, and they shall gird on a belt of intertwined byssus, violet, *11* purple and crimson, with many-hued patterns, work of a craftsman, and upon their heads (they shall wear) turbans. (These are) the garments of war; they shall not bring them into the sanctuary. *12* The first priest will walk in front of all the men of the line, to strengthen their hands for battle. And the (other) six shall hold in their hand *13* the trumpets of muster, the memorial trumpets, the alarm trumpets, the pursuit trumpets and the trumpets of re-assembly. When the priests go out *14* towards (the space) between the lines, seven levites shall go out with them, with seven ram's horns in their hands. Three supervisors from among the levites (shall go) in front of *15* the priests and the levites. The priests will blow the two trumpets of muster [... of bat]tle upon fifty shields, *16* and fifty infantrymen shall go out of the first gate

השער האחד ו[...].[לויים שוטרים ועם 17 כול מערכה ומערכה יצאו ככול
הס[רך ... אנשי]בינים מן השערים 18 [ועמ]דו בין שתי המערכות
[...] ... [המל]חמה

Col. VIII 1 החצוצרות תהיינה מריעות לנצח אנשי הקלע עד כלותם
להשליך שבע 2 פעמים ואחר יתקעו להם הכוהנים בחצוצרות המשוב
ובאו ליד המערכה 3 הראישונה להתיצב על מעמדם ותקעו הכוהנים
בחצוצרות המקרא ויצאו 4 שלושה דגלי בינים מן השערים ועמדו בין
המערכות ולידם ואנשי הרכב 5 מימון ומשמאול ותקעו הכוהנים
בחצוצרות קול מרודד ידי סדר מלחמה 6 והראשים יהיו נפשטים
לסדריהם איש למעמדו ובעומדם שלושה סדרים 7 ותקעו להם הכוהנים
תרועה שנית קול נוח וסמוך ידי מפשע עד קורבם 8 למערכת האויב ונטו
ידם בכלי המלחמה והכוהנים יריעו בשש חצוצרות 9 החללים קול חד
טרוד לנצח מלחמה והלויים וכול עם השופרות יריעו 10 קול אחד תרועת
מלחמה גדולה להמס לב אויב ועם קול התרועה יצאו 11 זרקות המלחמה
להפיל חללים קול השופרות יחישו ובח[צו]צרות יהיו 12 הכוהנים
מריעים קול חד טרוד לנצח ידי מלחמה עד השליכם למערכת 13 האויב
שבע פעמים ואחר יתקעו להם הכוהנים בחצוצרות המשוב 14 קול נוח
מרודד סמון כסרך הזה יתקעו ה[כו]הנים לשלושת הדגלים ועם 15 הטל
הראישון יריעו ה[כוהנים והלויים וכול העם השופ]רות קול תרועה
16 גדולה לנצח מל[חמה ... יתקעו] להם הכוהנים 17 בחצו[צ]רות [...]
על מעמדם במערכת 18 [...]ם ועמד 19 [...] ח[ל]לים

Col. IX 1 יחלו ידם להפיל בחללים וכול העם יחשו מקול התרועה
והכוהנים יהיו מריעים בחצוצרות 2 החללים לנצח המלחמה עד הנגף
האויב והסבו עורפם והכוהנים מריעים לנצח מלחמה 3 ובהנגפם לפניהם
יתקעו הכוהנים בחצוצרות המקרא ויצאו אליהם כול אנשי הבינים מתוך
4 מערכות הפנים ועמדו ששה דגלים והדגל המתקרב כולם שבע מערכות
שמונה ועשרים אלף 5 אנשי מלחמה והרוכבים ששת אלפים כול אלה
ירדופו להמשיד אויב במלחמת אל לכלת 6 עולמים ותקעו להמה הכוהנים

[…] the officers of the levites. And with *17* each line they shall go out in accordance with this ru[le … the infan]trymen [shall go out] of the gates *18* [and take up po]sition between the two li[nes …] the ba[ttle]

Col. VIII *1* The trumpets shall continue sounding, to guide the slingers until they have finished throwing seven *2* times. After, the priests shall blow the trumpets of return for them, and they shall return to the flank of the first *3* line to remain in their position. And the priests shall blow the trumpets of muster and there shall go out *4* three battalions of infantry from the gates and they shall take up position between the lines; at their side, cavalrymen, *5* right and left. The priests shall blow the trumpets with a sustained blast, the signal for battle order. *6* And the columns shall deploy in their formations, each in his own position. When they are in three formations, *7* the priests shall blow for them a second blast, low and sustained, the signal to proceed, until they approach *8* the enemy line and take hold of their weapons of war. The priests shall blow the six trumpets *9* of the slain with a shrill, staccato blast, to direct the battle. And the levites and all the throng with ram's horns shall blow *10* a single blast, a deafening war alarm, to melt the heart of the enemy. And at the alarm blast *11* the war javelins shall fly, to bring down the slain. The blast of the ram's horns will stop, but with the tr[um]pets *12* the priests shall continue blowing a shrill staccato blast, to direct the fighting hands until they have thrown against the *13* enemy line seven times. Next, the [pr]iests shall blow for them the trumpets of retreat, *14* with a low blast, steady and continuous. According to this rule, the priests shall blow for the three battalions. When *15* the first throws, the [priests, the Levites and all the throng] shall blow the [rams-]horns, a *16* deafening war alarm to direct the bat[tle …] the priests [shall blow] *17* the trumpe[ts] for them […] in their positions in the line *18* […] and take up positions *19* [… /the sl]ain/

Col. IX *1* will begin to strike the fallen with their hands. And all the throng shall stop the alarm signal, but the priests shall continue blowing the trumpets *2* of the slain to direct the battle until the enemy has been routed and turns its back, and the priests shall continue blowing to direct the battle. *3* And when they have been routed in front of them, the priests shall blow the trumpets of muster, and all infantry-men shall go out towards them from the midpoint *4* of their front lines. Six battalions shall take up position together with the battalion which is fighting, seven lines in all, twenty-eight thousand *5* warriors and six thousand on horse. All these shall pursue the enemy to exterminate them in God's battle for *6* eternal destruction. The priests shall blow the trumpets of

בהצוצרות המרדוף ונחל]קו[על כול האויב לרדף כלה והרכב 7 משיבים
על ידי המלחמה עד החרם ובנפול החללים יהיו הכו]הנ[ים מריעים מרחוק
ולוא יבואו 8 אל תוך החללים להתגאל בדם טמאתם כיא קדושים המה
]לו[א יחלו שמן משיחת כהונתם בדם 9 גוי הבל *vacat*

10 סרך לשנות סדר דגלי המלחמה לערוך המעמד על ...].[...].[...]
גליל כפים ומגדלות 11 וקשת ומגדלות ועל דרוך מעט וראשים יוצאים
וכנפים] יוצאות]מ[שנ]י עברי המערכה]ל[המיס 12 אויב ומגני המגדלות
יהיו ארוכים שלוש אמות ורמחיהם א]ור[ך שמונה אמות והמג]ד[לות
13 יוצאים מן המערכה מאה מגן ומאה פני המגדל כו]לם י[סבו המגדל
לשלושת רוחות הפנים 14 מגנים שלוש מאות ושערים שנים למגדל אחד
ל]ימין ו[אחד לשמאול ועל כול מגני המגדלות 15 יכתובו על הראישון
מיכ]א[ל] על השני גבריאל על השלישי]שריאל על הרביעי רפאל
16 מיכאל וגבריאל לי]מין וישראל ורפאל לשמאול [... *vacat* 17 .[...]
לארבע]א...[אורב ישימ]ו[ל].[.[...] 18 ל].[...]

Col. x 1 מחנינו ול]ה[שמר מכול ערות דבר רע ואשר הגיד לנו כיא
אתה בקרבנו אל גדול ונורא לשול את כול 2 אויבינו לפ]נינ[ו וילמדנו מאז
לדורותינו לאמור בקרבכם למלחמה ועמד הכוהן ודבר אל העם 3 לאמור
שמעה ישראל אתמה קרבים היום למלחמה על אויביכמה אל תירא ואל ירך
לבבכמה 4 ואל תחפ]זו וא[ל תערוצו מפניהם כיא אלוהיכם הולך עמכם
להלחם לכם עם אויביכם להושיע 5 אתכמה ו]ש[וטרינו ידברו לכול עתודי
המלחמה נדיבי לב להחזיק בגבורת אל ולשוב כול 6 מסי לבב ולחזיק יחד
בכול גבורי חיל ואשר ד]בר[תה ביד מושה לאמור כיא תבוא מלחמה
7 בארצכמה על הצר הצורר אתכמה והריעות]מה [בחצוצרות ונזכרתמה
לפני אלוהיכם 8 ונושעתם מאויביכם

מיא כמוכה אל ישראל בש]מי[ם ובארץ אשר יעשה כמעשיכה הגדולים
9 וכגבורתכה החזקה ומיא כעמכה ישראל אשר בחרתה לכה מכול עמי
הארצות 10 עם קדושי ברית ומלומדי חוק משכילי בינ]ה[...].[...].[...].
ושומעי קול נכבד ורואי 11 מלאכי קודש מגולי אוזן ושומעי עמוקות] ...

pursuit for them, and [they] shall divi[de] for the pursuit to destruction of all the enemy. And the cavalry *7* will make them return to the battle fields, until their annihilation. When the slain fall, the prie[st]s shall continue blowing at a distance, and they shall not enter *8* in the midst of the slain so as not be defiled with their impure blood, for they are holy. They shall [no]t desecrate the oil of their priestly anointing with the blood *9* of futile people. *Blank 10* Rule for changing the array of the combat battalions. To establish the formation against [...] a semicircle with towers, *11* and an arc with towers and when it advances a little, the columns go out and the flanks [go out, on both] sides of the line, [to] crush *12* the enemy. The shields of the towers shall be three cubits long and the length of their spears will be eight cubits. When the towers *13* go out from the line, (they shall have) one hundred shields on each face of the towers, in all, each tower will be surrounded on its three forward faces, *14* three hundred shields. The tower will have two gates, one on [the right and] the other on the left. And on all the shields of the towers *15* they shall write: on the first: «Michael», [on the second: «Gabriel», on the third:] «Sariel», on the fourth: «Raphael»; *16* «Michael» and «Gabriel» on [the right, and «Sariel» and «Raphael» on the left ...] *Blank 17* [...] on the four [...] they shall set an ambush against [...] *18* [...] ... [...]

Col. x *1* our camps and to keep ourselves from any immodest nakedness. And also he told us that you, great and terrible God, will be in our midst to plunder all *2* our enemies be[fore u]s. And he taught us from ancient times for our generations, saying: *Dt 20:2-5* «When you approach for battle, the priest is to stand up and speak to the nation *3* saying: 'Listen Israel, today you are approaching the battle against your enemies. Do not be afraid, and may your heart not fail; *4* do not fe[ar and do no]t tremble in front of them, for your God goes with you to do battle for you against your enemies to save *5* you'». Our [of]ficers shall speak to all those in readiness for battle, to those with resolute hearts, to strengthen them with God's power, but to send away all (those) *6* whose heart melts, and to strengthen together all the intrepid heroes. For (this is) what you s[aid] by Moses' hand, saying: *Num 10:9* «When there is a war *7* in your land against the enemy who oppresses you, you shall blow the trumpets and you shall be remembered before your God, *8* and you shall be saved from your enemies.»

Who (is) like you, God of Israel, in the hea[ven]s or on earth, to do great deeds like your deeds, *9* marvels like your feats? And who (is) like your nation, Israel, whom you chose for yourself from among all the nations of the earth, *10* a nation of holy ones of the covenant, learned in the law, wise in knowledge, [...] hearers of the glorious voice, seers of *11* the holy angels, with

מפרש שחקים צבא מאורות   12   ומשא רוחות וממשלת קדושים אוצרות
כב[וד באפ]ל עבים הבורא ארץ וחוקי מפלגיה   13   למדבר וארץ ערבה
וכול צאצאיה עם פר[י]ם ...[.]ה חוג ימים ומקוי נהרות ומבקע תה[ו]מות
14   מעשי חיה ובני כנף תבנית אדם ותול[דות ...]עו בלת לשון ומפרד עמים
מושב משפחות   15   ונחלת ארצות[...] [מועדי קודש ותקופות שנים וקצי
16   עד ...[.]ה אלה ידענו מבינתכם אשר ...[...]   17   [...] אוזנ]כה אל
שועתנו כיא .[...]   18   [...] ... ביתו הכו]ל...]

1   כיא אם לכה המלחמה ובכוח ידכה רוטשו פגריהם לאין   *Col.* XI
קובר ואת גולית הגתי איש גבור חיל   2   הסגרתה ביד דויד עבדכה כיא בטח
בשמכה הגדול ולוא בחרב וחנית כיא לכה המלחמה ואת   3   פלשתיים
הכנ[י]ע פעמים רבות בשם קודשכה וגם ביד מלכינו הושעתנו פעמים רבות
4   בעבור רחמיכה ולוא כמעשינו אשר הרעונו ועלילות פשעינו לכה
המלחמה ומאתכה הגבורה   5   ולוא לנו ולוא כוחנו ועצום ידינו עשה חיל
כיא בכוחכה ובעוז חילכה הגדול כאשר הגדתה   6   לנו מאז לאמור דרך
כוכב מיעקוב קם שבט מישראל ומחץ פאתי מואב ו{כ}קרקר כול בני שית
7   וירד מיעקוב והאביד שריד מעיר והיה אויב ירשה וישראל עשה חיל וביד
משיחיכה   8   חוזי תעודות הגדתה לנו ק[צי] מלחמות ידיכה לה{ג}לחם{כ}בד
באויבינו להפיל גדודי בליעל שבעת   9   גוי הבל ביד אביוני פדותכה [בכו]ח
ובשלום לגבורת פלא ולב נמס לפתח תקוה ותעש להמה כפרעוה
10   וכשלישי מרכבותיו בים סו[ף] ונכאי רוח תבעיר כלפיד אש בעמיר
אוכלת רשעה לוא תשוב עד   11   כלות אשמה ומאז השמע]תנו מ[ועד
גבורת ידכה בכתיים לאמור ונפל אשור בחרב לוא איש וחרב   12   לוא אדם
תואכלנו   *vacat*

13   כיא ביד אביונים תסגיר] או]יבי כול הארצות וביד כורעי עפר
להשפיל גבורי עמים להשיב גמול   14   רשעים בראש אש[מתם] ולהצדיק
משפט אמתכה בכול בני איש ולעשות לכה שם עולם בעם
15   [...]המלחמות ולהתגדל ולהתקדש לעיני שאר הגוים לדעת[...]   16   [...]

opened ears, hearing profound things? [... *You created*] the dome of the sky, the army of luminaries, *12* the task of the spirits, the dominion of the holy ones, the treasures of glo[ry, in the darkness] of the clouds; (you are) creator of the earth and of the laws of its divisions *13* in desert and steppe, of all its products, with frui[ts ...,] of the circle of the seas, of the reservoirs of the rivers, of the chasm of the abyss, *14* of beasts and birds, of man's image, of the gener[ations of ...], of the confusion of tongues, of the separation of nations, of the dwelling of the clans, *15* of the inheritance of the lands, [...] of the sacred seasons, of the cycle of the years and the ages *16* of eternity [...] We have known this through your knowledge which [...] *17* [...] your [ear] to our cry, for [...] *18* [...] his house ... [...]

Col. XI   *1* For the battle is yours! With the might of your hand their corpses have been torn to pieces with no-one to bury them. Goliath from Gath, gallant giant, *2* you delivered into the hands of David, your servant, for he trusted in your powerful name and not in sword or spear. For the battle is yours! *3* The Philistines you humiliated many times for your holy name. By the hand of our kings, besides, you saved us many times *4* thanks to your mercy, and not by our own deeds by which we did wrong, nor by our sinful actions. For the battle is yours! And it is from you that power comes, *5* and not from our own being. It is not our might nor the power of our own hands which performs these marvels, except by your great strength and by your mighty deeds. Thus you taught *6* us from ancient times, saying: *Num 24:17-19* «A star will depart from Jacob, a sceptre will be raised in Israel. It will smash the temples of Moab, it will destroy all the sons of Seth. *7* It will come down from Jacob, it will exterminate the remnant of the city, the enemy will be its possession, and Israel will perform feats». By the hand of your anointed ones, *8* seers of decrees, you taught us the ti[mes of] the wars of your hands, to {fight} /to be glorious/ over our enemies, to fell the hordes of Belial, the seven *9* peoples of futility, by the hand of the poor, those you saved, [with stren]gth and success towards wonderful power, so that a melting heart became a door to hope. You shall treat them like Pharaoh, *10* like the officers of his chariots in the Red Sea. The stricken of spirit you shall set aflame, like a torch of fire in straw, devouring wickedness, without ceasing until, *11* the sin has been consumed. From of old [you] foretold [us the appoin]ted time of the power of your hand against the Kittim saying: *Isa 31:8* «Ashur will fall by the sword of not a man, the sword of *12* not a human being will devour it.» *Blank 13* For you will deliver into the hands of the poor the [ene]mies of all the countries, and in the hand of those prone in the dust in order to fell the powerful ones of the nations, to return the reward of *14* sin on [their] gui[lty] heads, and to pronounce the justice of your truthful judgment on every son of man, and to make an everlasting name for yourself among the people of *15* [...] the wars, in order to show yourself great and holy in the eyes of the remainder of the peoples, so

ע[שותכה שפטים בגוג ובכול קהלו הקלו הנק[ה]ל[י]ים ל[ו ...] 17 [... כי]א

תלחם בם מן השמ[י]ם.[.].[...] 18 [...]עליהם למהמה [...]

Col. XII 1 כיא רוב קדשים [א]לה בשמים וצבאות מלאכים בזבול

קודשכה לה[ו]דות אמת[כ]ה ובחירי עם קודש 2 שמתה לכה בה[ם ו]ספר

שמות כול צבאם במעון קושכה ומ[ספר צד]קים בזבול כבודכה

3 וחסדי ברכו[תיכה] וברית שלומכה חרתה למו בחרט חיים למלוך [...].

בכול מועדי עולמים 4 ולפקוד צב[א]ות ב[ח]יריכה לאלפיהם ולרבואותם

יחד עם קדושיכה [ועם] מלאכיכה לרשות יד 5 במלחמה [ולהכניע [ק]מי

ארץ בריב משפטיכה ועם בחירי שמים נוצ[חים] *vacat* 6 *vacat*

7 ואתה אל נ[ורא] בכבוד מלכותכה ועדת קדושיכה בתוכנו לעזר

עולמי[ם ו]נ[ת]נו בוז למלכים לעג 8 וקלס לגבורים כיא קדוש אדוני ומלך

הכבוד אתנו עם קדושים גבו[ר]ינו ו[צ]בא מלאכים בפקודינו 9 וגבור

המלח[מה] בעדתנו וצבא רוחיו עם צעדינו ופרשינו כ[ע]ננים וכעבי טל

לכסות ארץ 10 וכזרם רביבים להשקות משפט לכול צאצאיה קומה גבור

שבה שביכה איש כבוד ושול 11 שללכה עושי חיל תן ידכה בעורף

אויביכה ורגלכה על במותי חלל מחץ גוים צריכה וחרבכה 12 תואכל בשר

אשמה מלא ארצכה כבוד ונחלתכה ברכה המון מקנה בחלקותיכה כסף וזהב

ואבני 13 חפץ בהיכל[ו]תיכה ציון שמחי מאדה והופיעי ברנות ירושלים

והגלנה כול ערי יהודה פתחי 14 שער[י]ך תמיד להביא אליך חיל גואים

ומלכיהם ישרתוך והשתחוו לך כול מעניך ועפר 15 [רגליך ילחכו בנו]ת

עמי צרחנה בקול רנה עדינה עדי כבוד ורדינה במל[כות ...] 16 [...]

וי[שראל למלוך עולמים *vacat* [...] 17 [...][ל]י[ה]ם גבורי המלחמה

ירושלים [...] 18 [...]ם על השמים אדיני [...]

Col. XIII 1 ואחיו ה[כו]הנים והלויים וכול זקני הסרך עמו וברכו על

עומדם את אל ישראל ואת כול מעשי אמתו וזעמו 2 שם את ב[ל/ל]יעל ואת

כול רוחי גורלו וענו ואמרו ברוך אל ישראל בכול מחשבת קודשו ומעשי

that they know […] *16* […] you shall carry out sentence on Gog and on all his gathering that has ga[th]ered to [him …] *17* […] for you shall wage war against them from the heavens […] *18* […] upon them, for confusion […]

Col. XII   *1* For there is a multitude of holy ones in heaven and hosts of angels in your holy dwelling to [praise] your [truth.] And the chosen ones of the holy nation *2* you have established for yourself among t[hem.] The book of the names of all their armies is with you in your holy dwelling, and the num[ber of the ju]st in your glorious dwelling. *3* [Your] blissful mercies and the covenant of your peace you engraved for them with the chisel of life, in order to rule […] during all times eternal, *4* to muster the arm[ies] of your [ch]osen ones according to its thousands and its myriads, together with your holy ones [and with] your angels, to have the upper hand *5* in the battle [and destroy] the rebels of earth in the lawsuit of your judgments, while the nation of the chosen ones of heaven triu[mphs]. *Blank 6 Blank*

7 You, God, are awe[some] in the splendour of your majesty, and the congregation of your holy ones is amongst us for everlasting assistance. We will [treat] kings with contempt, with jeers *8* and mockery the heroes, for the Lord is holy and the King of glory is with us the nation of his holy ones are [our] he[roes, and] the army of his angels is enlisted with us; *9* the war hero is in our congregation; the army of his spirits is with our steps. Our horsemen are [like] clouds and fogs of dew that cover the earth, *10* like torrential rain that sheds justice on all its sprouts. Get up, Hero, take your prisoners, Man of Glory, *11* collect your spoil, Performer of Valiance! Place your hand on the neck of your enemies and your foot on the piles of slain! Strike the peoples, your foes, and may your sword *12* consume guilty flesh! Fill your land with glory and your inheritance with blessing: may herds of flocks be in your fields, /silver,/ gold, and precious stones *13* in your palaces! Rejoice, Zion, passionately! Shine with jubilation, Jerusalem! Exult, all the cities of Judah! Open *14* your gate[s] continuously so that the wealth of the nations can be brought to you! Their kings shall wait on you, all your oppressors lie prone before you, the dust *15* [of your feet they shall lick. Daughter]s of my nation, shout with jubilant voice! Adorn yourselves with splendid finery! Rule over the king[dom of …] *16* [… and] Israel to reign for ever. *Blank* […] *17* […] their […] the heroes of the war, Jerusalem […] *18* […] above the heavens, Lord […]

Col. XIII (= 4Q495 2)   *1* and his brothers, the [pr]iests and the levites and all the elders of the array with him. And in their positions they shall bless the God of Israel and all the deeds of his truth and they shall damn *2* there Belial and all the spirits of his lot. They shall begin speaking and say: «Blessed be the God of Israel for all his holy plan and for all the deeds of his truth, and blessed be

אמתו וב[ר]וכים   3 כול משרתיו בצדק יודעיו באמונה *vacat*

4 וארור בליעל במחשבת משטמה וזעום הואה במשרת אשמתו וארורים

כול רוחי גורלו במחשבת   *vacat*   5 רשעם וזעומים המה בכול עבודת

טמאתם כיא המה גורל חושך וגורל אל לאור   6 [עולמ]ים *vacat*

7 וא[ת]ה אל אבותינו שמכה נברכה לעולמים ואנו עם [נח]ל[ת]כ[ה]

וברית [כ]רתה לאבותינו ותקימה לזרעם   8 למוע[ד]י עולמים ובכול

תעודות כבודכה היה זכר [חסדי]כה בקרבנו לעזר שארית ומחיה לבריתכה

9 ולס[פר] מעשי אמתכה ומשפטי גבורות פלאכה אתה א[ל פ]דיתנו לכה

עם עולמים ובגורל אור הפלתנו   10 לאמתכה ושר מאור מאז פקדתה

לעזרנו ובי[ד]ו כול מלאכי צד[ק] וכול רוחי אמת בממשלתו ואתה

11 עשיתה בליעל לשחת מלאך משטמה ובחוש[ך] ממשל[ת]ו ובעצתו

להרשיע ולהאשים וכול רוחי   12 גורלו מלאכי חבל בחוקי חושך יתהלכו

ואליו [תש]וקתמה יחד ואנו בגורל אמתכה נשמחה ביד   13 גבורתכה

ונשישה בישועתכה ונגילה בעזר[תכה וב]שלומכה מיא כמוכה בכוח אל

ישראל ועם   14 אביונים יד גבורתכה ומיא מלאך ושר כעזרת פנ[י]כה כי[א

מאז יעדתה לכה יום קרב רב[...].ה.[...]ל[...].ר באמת ולהשמיד   15

באשמה להשפיל חושך ולהגביר אור ול[...]   16 [...]ל למעמד עולמים

לכלות כול בני חושך ושמחה ל[...]ל[...] 17 [...] *vacat* [...] 18 [...] כ[יא

אתה יעדתנו למו[עד ...]

1   Col. XIV   כאש עברתו באלילי מצרים *vacat*

2 ואחר העלותם מעל החללים לבוא המחנה ירננו כולם את תהלת

המשוב ובבוקר יכבסו בגדיהם ורחצו   3 מדם פגרי האשמה ושבו אל מקום

עומדם אשר סדרו שם המערכה לפני נפול חללי האויב וברכו שם   4 כולם

את אל ישראל ורוממו שמו ביחד שמחה וענו ואמרו ברוך אל ישראל

השומר חסד לבריתו ותעודות   5 ישועה לעם פדותו ויקרא כושלים

ל[ג]בורו[ת]ת וקהל גויים אסף לכלה אין שארית ולהריס במשפט   6 לב

נמס ולפתוח פה לנאלמים לרנן בגבור[ות אל וידים]רפות ללמד מלחמה

3 all who serve him in justice, who know him in faith. *Blank 4* Accursed be Belial for his inimical plan, may he be damned for his blameworthy rule. Accursed be all the spirits of his lot for their wicked *5 Blank* plan, may they be damned for their deeds of filthy uncleanness. For they are the lot of darkness but the lot of God is for *6* [everlast]ing light. *Blank 7* Y[o]u, God of our fathers, we bless your name forever. We are the nation of [yo]ur [inhe]rit[ance]. You [est]ablished a covenant with our fathers and ratified it with their offspring *8* for tim[e]s eternal. In all the edicts of your glory there has been a remembrance of your [clemencies] in our midst in order to aid the remnant, the survivors of your covenant *9* and to re[count] the deeds of your truth, and the judgments of your wonderful mighty deeds. You, [God, have re]deemed us to be for you an eternal nation, and you have made us fall into the lot of light *10* in accordance with your truth. From of old you appointed the Prince of light to assist us, and in [his] ha[nd are all the angels of just]ice, and all the spirits of truth are under his dominion. You *11* made Belial for the pit, angel of enmity; in dark[ness] is his [dom]ain, his counsel is to bring about wickedness and guilt. All the spirits *12* of his lot are angels of destruction, they walk in the laws of darkness; towards it goes their only [de]sire. We, instead, in the lot of your truth, rejoice in *13* your mighty hand, we exult in your salvation, we revel in [your] aid [and in] your peace. Who is like you in strength, God of Israel, *14* whose mighty hand is with the poor? And which angel or prince is an aid like [you?] Since ancient time you determined the day of the great battle [...] *15* [...] to [...] because of truth, and destroy because of wickedness, to humiliate darkness and strengthen light, and to [...] *16* [...] for an everlasting stay to exterminate all the sons of darkness and happiness for [...] *17* [...] *Blank* [...] *18* [... f]or you have destined us for the ti[me ...] »

Col. XIV (+ *frag.* 10; = 4Q491 8 - 10)   *1* like the fire of his wrath against the idols of Egypt. *Blank 2* And when they have departed from the slain in order to enter the camp, they shall all sing the hymn of return. In the morning they shall wash their clothes and cleanse themselves *3* of the blood of the guilty corpses. They shall go back to the site of their positions, where they arranged the battle line before the slain of the enemy fell. And there they shall all bless *4* the God of Israel and exalt his name in joyful chorus. They shall begin to speak and say: «Blessed be the God of Israel, the one who keeps mercy for his covenant and pledges of *5* deliverance for the people he has redeemed. He has called those who are tottering to wondrous [exploits], and has gathered the assembly of peoples for destruction with no remnant, in order to raise up in justice *6* the melting heart, and to open the mouth of the dumb to sing [God's] marv[els], and to train feeble [hands] in warfare. Those with knocking knees he gives strength to stand upright, *7* and vigor of loins to broken backs. By the poor in

ונותן לנמוגי ברכים חזוק מעמד   7   ואמוץ מתנים לשכם מכים ובעניי רוח[

...]סם לבב קושי ובתמימי דרך יתמו כול גויי רשעה   8   ולכול גבוריהם אין

מעמד ואנו שאר[י]ת עמכה ברו[ך שמכה אל החסדים השומר ברית

לאבותינו ועם   9   כול דורותינו הפלתה חסדיכה לשאר[י]ת נחלתכה[

בממשלת בליעל ובכול רזי שטמתו לוא הדיחונו[ן]   10   מבריתכה ורוחי

[ח]בלו גערתה ממ[נ]ו ובהתרשע אנ[ש]י ממשלתו שמ[ר]תה נפש פדותכה

ואתה הקימותה   11   נופלים בעוזכה ורמי קומה תגד[ע ל...   ]לכול גבוריהם

אין מציל ולקליהם אין מנוס ולנכבדיהם   12   תשיב לבוז וכול יקום

הבלי[הם יהיה כא]ין ואנו עם קודשכה במעשי אמתכה נהללה שמכה

13   ובגבורותיכה נרוממה תפ[ארתכה בכול]עתים ומועדי תעודות עולמים

עם מ[בו]א יומם ולילה   14   ומוצאי ערב ובוקר כיא גדולה מ[ח]שבת

כבו[ד]כה ורזי נפלאותיכה במרומ[יכה] לה[רי]ם לכה מעפר   15   ולהשפיל

מא[לים *vacat*

16   רומה רומה אל אלים והנשא בעו[ז מלך המלכים ...מעליכה יפו]צו

17   [כו]ל[ב]ני חושך ואור גודלכה י.[...   ]ואנשים ...   אש בוערת במחשכי

אבדונים[18   ]באבדוני ש[אול תוקד לשרפ]ת [...

1   כיא היאה את צרה ליש[ר]אל ועבו[ד]ת מלחמה {על} ²בכול   *Col. xv*

הגויים וגורל אל בפדות עולמים   2   וכלה לכול גוי רשעה וכול ע[ת]ודי

המלחמה ילכו וחנו נגד מלך הכתיים ונגד כול חיל   3   בליעל הנועדים עמו

ליום נ[קם] בחרב אל *vacat*

4   ועמד כוהן הראש ואחיו הכ[הנים]והלויים וכול אנשי הסרך עמו

וקרא באוזניהם   5   את תפלת מועד המלח[מה ככתוב בס]פר סרך עתו עם

כול דברי הודותם וסדר שם   6   את כול המערכות ככת[וב בספר המלח]מה

והתהלך הכוהן החרוץ למועד נקם על פי   7   כול אחיו וחזק את] ידיהם

במלח[מה] וענה ואמר חזקו ואמצו והיו לבני חיל   8   אל תיראו ואל תח[תו

ואל ירך לבבכ]מה ואל תחפזו ואל תערוצו מפניהם ואל   9   תשובו אחור

ואל [תנוסו מפניה]ם כיא המה עדת רשעה ובחושך כול מעשיהם   10   ואליו

תשוקת[ם ...]ל מחסיהם וגבורתם כעשן נמלח וכול קהל   11   [ה]מונם

spirit [...] a hard heart. By the perfect ones of the path all the wicked peoples shall be destroyed. *8* None of their heroes will remain standing. But we are the rem[nant of your people. Bles]sed be your name, God of mercies, who guards the covenant with our fathers, and during *9* all our generations you have wondrously bestowed your mercies to the rem[nant of your inheritance] during the empire of Belial. With all the mysteries of his enmity, they have not separated us *10* from your covenant. You have chased away from [us] his spirits of [de]struction, [when the m]en of his dominion [acted wickedly] you protected the soul of your redeemed ones. You raised *11* the fallen with your strength, but those high in stature, you cut dow[n ...] For none of their heroes there is a saviour, for their swift ones there is no escape; To their notables *12* you return scorn, all [their] useless existence [will turn into noth]ing. We, your holy people, will praise your name for the deeds of your truth, *13* for your mighty deeds we will extol [your] spl[endour, at every] moment and at the times indicated by your eternal edicts, at the on[se]t of day and at night *14* at the fall of evening and at dawn. For great is the p[lan of] your [glo]ry and your marvellous mysteries in [your] height[s], in order to r[ai]se from the dust for yourself *15* and to humble those of the gods. *Blank 16* Rise up, rise up, Oh God of gods, and raise with pow[er, King of kings! ... may scat]ter [from before you] *17* [al]l the [s]ons of darkness, and may your great light [... and men ... a fire burning in the dark places of Abbadon,] *18* [in the places of destruction of She]ol may it burn to consume [...]

Col. xv (+ *frags.* 1, 9)   *1* For this will be a time of suffering for Isra[el and a servi]ce of war /against/ all the nations. For God's lot there will be everlasting redemption *2* and destruction for all the wicked nations. All those who are r[eady for] the war shall go and camp opposite the king of the Kittim and opposite all the army *3* of Belial, assembled with him for the day of ven[geance] by God's sword. *Blank 4* The High Priest will take up position, and his brothers the p[riests] and the levites and all the men of the array with him, and he will say in their hearing *5* the prayer for the time of war, [as it is written in the «Bo]ok of the Rule of his time», with all the words of their thanksgivings. And he will array there *6* all the lines, as is wr[itten in the «Book of Wa]r». And the priest assigned for the time of vengeance according to the decision *7* of all his brothers will step forward, and he will strengthen [their hands for the wa]r. He will begin speaking and say: «Be strong and valiant, become men of valour. *8* Do not be afraid or [tremble, may your hearts not weaken], do not panic, or be terrified by them, do not *9* turn backwards, or [run away from th]em. For they are a wicked congregation and all their deeds are in darkness *10* and to it go [their] desires, [...] their refuge, their power disappears like smoke. All the assembly of *11* their [ho]rdes ... [...] ... will

[...]ממה לוא ימצא וכול יקום היותם מהר ימלו   12 [כצי]ץ בק[ץ]ציר[ק]...
[...] התחזקו למלחמה אל כיא {יום} מוע̇ד מלחמה היום הזה   13 [מ]אל על
כול הג[וים ... מש]פט על כול בשר אל ישראל מרים ידו ב[גבור]ת פלאו
14 [על] כול רוחי רש[עה ... ג]בורי אלים מתאזרים למלחמה וסדר[י]
ק[ד]ושים   15 [מתפ]קדים ליום [...]...[...]...[...   16 ...]אל י]שרא[ל/ל [...
17 להסיר בל[י]על [...   18 באבדונו [...]...[...]

1 *Col.* XVI עד תום כול מקוד[...] אל ישראל קרא חרב על כול הגואים
2 *vacat* ובקדושי עמו יעשה גבורה

3 את כול הסרך הזה יעשו] ביום ה]הואה על עומדם נגד מחני כתיים
ואחר יתקעו להמה הכוהנים בחצוצרות   4 הזכרון ופתחו שערי המ]לחמה
וי]צאו אנשי הבינים ועמדו ראשים בין המערכות ותקעו להם הכוהנים
5 תרועה סדר והראשים [יהיו נפשט]ים לקול החצוצרות עד התיצבם איש
על מעמדו ותקעו להם   6 הכוהנים תרועה שנית] ידי התק]רב ובעומדם ליד
מערכת כתיים כדי הטל ירימו איש ידו בכלי   7 מלחמתו ושש̇ת] הכוהנים
יתקעו בח]צוצרות החללים קול חד טרוד לנצח מלחמה והלוים וכול עם
8 השופרות יריע[ו] תרוע[ת מ]ל[חמה ב]קול גדול ועם צאת הקול יחלו ידם
להפיל בחללי כתיים וכול   9 העם יחשו קול התר[ו]עה [והכוהנ]ים יהיו
10 *vacat* מריעים בחצוצרות החללים והמלחמה מנצחת בכתיים

11 ובהתאזר [בליעל] לעזרת בני חושך וחללי הבינים יחלו לנפול ברזי
אל ולבחון בם כול חרוצי המלחמה   12 והכ[ו]הנים יתק[עו] בחצ[ו]צרות
המקרא לצאת מערכה אחרת חליפה למלחמה ועמדו בין המערכות
13 ולמתקרבי]ם במ]לחמה יתקעו לשוב ונגש כוהן הרואש ועמד לפני
המערכה וחזק את   14 לבבם ב]גבורת א]ל ואת ידיהם במלחמתו *vacat*
15 וענה ואמר [יקום א]ל[ל] ו[ל[ב]ב עמו יבחן במצרף ולוא [...]חלליכם
כיא מאז שמעתם   16 ברזי אל ו]אתם התחזקו ועמדו בפרץ ואל תיראו
[...]... 17 ...]הם ליח̇ל.[...

not be found. All the essence of their being swiftly vanishes *12* [as a flow]er in har[vest] ti[me …] Exert yourselves for God's battle for today is the {day} /time/ of war *13* [by] God against all the p[eoples … judg]ment against all flesh. The God of Israel is raising his hand with his marvellous [powe]r *14* [against] all the wic[ked] spirits [… he]roes of the gods girding themselves for battle, and the formation[s of] the h[o]ly ones *15* [must]ered for the day of […] … […] … *16* God of I[srae]l […] *17* to remove Bel[ial …] *18* at his destruction … […]

Col. XVI (= 4Q491 11 II)   *1* until all … have finished […] The God of Israel has summoned the sword against all the peoples and with the holy ones of his people he will perform a mighty deed».*2* *Blank*

3 They shall act in accordance with all this rule on that [day], when they are positioned opposite the camp of the Kittim. Afterwards, the priests will blow for them the trumpets *4* of memorial, and they shall open the gates of ba[ttle.] The infantrymen [shall go] out and the columns shall take up positions between the lines. The priests will blow for them *5* the call «Formation», and the columns [shall deploy] at the sound of the trumpets until each man is stationed in his position. The priests shall blow for them *6* a second call [for the atta]ck. When they are at the side of the Kittim line, at throwing distance, each man will take up in his hand his weapon *7* of war. The six [priests shall blow the tr]umpets of the slain with a shrill, staccato note to direct the battle. And the levites and all the throng *8* with ram's horns shall blow [the battle call with] a deafening noise. And when the sound goes out, they shall set their hand to cast down the slain of the Kittim. And all *9* the throng will silence the sound of the call, [and the priest]s shall continue blowing the trumpets of the slain, in order that the battle against the Kittim is directed. *10* *Blank*

11 When [Belial] girds himself to assist the sons of darkness, and the slain of the infantry start to fall in accordance with God's mysteries, and all those appointed for battle are tested by them, *12* then the priests shall bl[ow] the trumpets of muster in order that an other relief line goes out to the battle and they shall take up position between the lines. *13* And for those involved in the fight, they shall blow the withdrawal. The High Priest will approach and take up position in front of the line, and will strengthen *14* their hearts [with the power of Go]d, and their hands in their fight. *Blank* *15* And starting to speak he will say: «[Go]d [has risen, and] the h[ea]rt of his people he has tested in the crucible, and not […] your slain, for from ancient times you heard *16* the mysteries of God. [You then, be strong, stand in the breach, and do not fear …] their […] … *17* … […]

Col. xvii 1 ושם שלומם בדלק .[...]. בחוני מצרף ושנן כלי מלחמתה

ולוא יכהו עד [כלות כול גוי] 2 רשע ואתמה זכורו משפטם [נדב ו]אב[י]הוא

בני אהרון אשר התקדש אל במשפטם לעיני [כול העם ואלעזר] 3 ואיתמר

החזיק לו לברית[כהונת]עולמים vacat

4 ואתם התחזקו ואל תיראום [כיא] המה לתהו ולבהו תשוקתם

ומשענתם בלוא ה[...] ולוא [ידעו כיא מאל] 5 ישראל כול הויה ונהיה

ו[...ה][...]ל בכול נהיי עולמים היום מועדו להכניע ולהשפיל שר ממשלת

6 רשעה וישלח עזר עולמים לגורל [ב]ריתו בגבורת מלאך האדיר למשרת

מיכאל באור עולמים 7 להאיר בשמחה ברית ישראל שלום וברכה לגורל

אל להרים באלים משרת מיכאל וממשלת 8 ישראל בכול בשר ישמח צדק

במרומים וכול בני אמתו יגילו בדעת עולמים ואתם בני בריתו 9 התחזקו

במצרף אל עד יניף ידו ומלא מצרפיו רזיו למעמדכם vacat

10 ואחר הדברים האלה יתקעו הכוהנים להם לסדר דגלי המערכה

והראשים נפשטים לקול החצוצרות 11 עד התיצ[בם אי]ש על מעמד[ו]

ותקעו הכוהנים בחצוצרות תרועה שנית ידי התקרב ובהגיע 12 אנשי

[הבינים ליד מע]רכת כתיים כדי הטל ירימו איש ידו בכלי מלחמתו

והכוהנים יריעו בחצוצרות 13 החללים [והלויים וכו]ל עם השופרות

יריעו תרועת מלחמה ואנשי הבינים ישלחו ידם בחיל 14 הכתיים [ועם

צאת קו]ל[הת]רועה יחלו להפיל בחלליהם וכול העם יניח[ו] קול התרועה

והכוהנים 15 יהיו מריעים ב[חצוצרות החללי]ם והמל[חמ]ה מ[תנצח]ת

בכ[תיים וגדודי בליע]ל נגפים לפניהם 16 ובגורל השל[ישי ...] ל[נפ]ול

חללים 17 [...] ...[...] אל ו[...]ל.

Col. xviii 1 [...] ובה[נ]שא יד אל הגדולה על בליעל ועל כול ח[י]ל

ממשלתו במגפת עולמים 2 [...] ותרועת קדושים ברדף אשור ונפלו בני

יפת לאין קום וכתיים יכתו לאין 3 [... ביו]ם משאת יד אל ישראל על כול

המון בליעל בעת ההיאה יריעו הכוהנים 4 [... בחצוצ]רות הזכרון ונאספו

אליהם כול מערכות המלחמה ונחלקו על כול מ[חני הכ]תיים 5 להחרימם

Col. XVII (+ *frag.* 4; = 4Q491 11 II) *1* and he has placed their success in the burning [...] those tested in the crucible; he has whetted her weapons of war and they shall not be blunted until [every] wicked [people is destroyed.] *2* And you, remember the trial [of Nadab and] Ab[i]hu, sons of Aaron; by judging them God showed his holiness to the eyes [of all the people, and Eleazar] *3* and Itamar he confirmed for the covenant of an everlasting [priesthood]. *Blank 4* And you, exert yourselves and do not fear them, [for] their desire goes towards chaos and emptiness, and their support is without [...]. Not [do they know that from the God of] *5* Israel everything is and will be [...] in all that will happen eternally. Today is his appointed time to humiliate and abase the prince of the dominion *6* of evil. He sends everlasting aid to the lot of his [co]venant by the power of the majestic angel for the sway of Michael in everlasting light, *7* to illuminate with joy the covenant of Israel, peace and blessing to God's lot, to exalt the sway of Michael above all the gods, and the dominion of *8* Israel over all flesh. Justice will rejoice in the heights and all the sons of his truth will have enjoyment in everlasting knowledge. And you, sons of his covenant, *9* be strong in God's crucible until he shakes his hand and finishes his testings, his mysteries concerning your existence». *Blank*

10 After these words /the priests/ shall blow for them in order to arrange the battalions of the line: the columns shall deploy at the sound of the trumpets *11* until [each m]an is in [his] position. The priests shall blow a second call on the trumpets, the signal for attack. When *12* [the infantry]men reach [the side of the] Kittim [li]ne, at throwing distance, each man will take his weapon of war in his hand and the priests shall blow the trumpets of *13* the slain. [The levites and al]l the throng with ram's horns shall blow the call for war. The infantrymen will stretch out their hand against the army *14* of the Kittim. [When the soun]d [of the c]all [ends], they shall start to cast down their slain. All the throng will stop with the sound of the call, but the priests *15* shall continue blowing [the trumpets of the slain] and the bat[tl]e against the K[ittim] will be d[irect]ed, [and the troups of Belia]l will be defeated in front of them. *16* In the thi[rd] lot [...] to [fa]ll slain *17* [...] ... God and [...] ...

Col. XVIII   (+ *frags.* 3, 5, 6 + *unpubl. frag.* SHR 3332; + 1Q33 1)   *1* [...] when the mighty hand of God is [r]aised against Belial and against all the a[r]my of his dominion for an everlasting blow *2* [...] and the call of the holy ones when they pursue Assyria; the sons of Japhet shall fall without rising; the Kittim shall be crushed without *3* [... on the da]y when the hand of the God of Israel is raised against the whole horde of Belial. On that moment, the priests shall blow *4* [... the trum]pets of remembrance and all the battle lines shall combine against them and shall divide up against all the c[amps of the Ki]ttim *5* to

141

[... ו]באוץ השמש לבוא ביום ההואה יעמוד כוהן הרואש והכוהנים
והלוי[י]ם אשר 6 אתו ורא[שי ... ואנש]י הסרך וברכו שם את אל ישראל
וענו ואמרו ברוך שמכה אל אלים כיא 7 הגדלתה עם עמכה פל[א להפליא
ובריתכה שמרתה לנו מאז ושערי ישועות פתחתה לנו פעמים רבות
8 למע[ן ב]ריתכה [ותש]א[עניin כטובכה בנו ואתה אל הצדק עשיתה למען
שמכה vacat 9 vacat

10 [...]... הפלתה עמנו הפלא ופלא ומאז לוא נהיתה כמוהה כיא אתה
ידעתה למועדנו והיום הופיע 11 לנו כיא[הרא]תנו יד חסדיכה עמנו
בפדות עולמים להסיר ממ[ש]לת אויב לאין עוד ויד גבורתכה
12 ובמל[חמה ...].[... ע]ל אויבינו למגפח (למגפת) כלה ועתה היום אץ לנו
לרדוף המונם כיא אתה 13 [...]ולב גבורים מגנתה לאין מעמד לכה
הגבורה ובידכה המלחמה ואין 14 [... נפ[ל]או]תיכה ומועדים לרצונכה
וגמול] תשיב [ל]אוי[ב]יכה ותבצור ממדת.[...] 15 [...].[...ים מכול ימ[...]
16 [...] vacat [...]

1 [לעג וקלס לג]בורים כיא קדוש אדירנו ומלך הכבוד אתנו *Col. xix*
וצ[בא רוחיו עם צעדינו ופרשינו] 2 [כעננים וכעבי ט]ל לכסות ארץ
וכזרם רביבים להשקות משפט לכ[ול צאצאיה קומה גבור] 3 [שבה
שביכה איש כבוד וש[ול שללכה עושי חיל תן ידכה בעורף אויביך ורג[ל]ך
על במותי] 4 [חלל מחץ גוים צריכ]ה וחרבך תואכל בשר מלא ארצכה
כבוד ונחלתכה ברכה ה[מון] 5 [מקנה בחלקותיך כסף וזהב]בהיכלותיך
ציון שמחי מואדה והגלנה כול ערי יהו[דה פתחי] 6 [שעריך תמיד להביא
אליך]חיל גוים ומלכיהם ישרתוך והשתחוו לך [כו]ל[מעני]ך 7 [ועפר
רגליך ילחכו]בנות עמי הבענה בקול רנה עדינה עדי כבוד ור[ד]ינה
במלכות 8 [... למחנ]יכה וישראל למלכות עולמים vacat

9 [ואחר יאספו המח]נה [נ]ה [ב]ל[י]לה ההוא למנוח עד הבוקר ובבוקר
יבואו עד מקום המערכה 10 [אשר נפלו שם ג]בורי כתיים והמון אשור

eliminate them. [… And] when the sun travels towards its setting on that day, the High Priest will take up position, likewise the priests and levites who are *6* with him and the ch[iefs of … and the men] of the array. And there they shall bless the God of Israel. They shall begin speaking and say: «Blessed be your name, God of gods, for *7* you have magnified yourself with your nation in order to work wonders. From of old you have kept for us your covenant. You have opened for us many times the gates of salvation. *8* For the sa[ke of] your [co]venant [you have remo]ved our misery in your goodness towards us. You, God of justice, have acted for the sake of your Name. *Blank 9 Blank*

10 […] You have acted wondrously with us, wondrously and wonderfully. From of old there has not been anything similar. /For/ you know our appointed time and today it shines *11* for us, for you [have sho]wed us your merciful hand towards us in everlasting redemption, removing for ever the enemy do[mi]nion and your mighty hand. *12* And in the bat[tle … again]st our enemies for complete extermination. And now there approaches us the day of pursuing their mob, for you *13* […] and the heart of the heroes you have delivered so that they can not hold position. To you belongs the might, and in your hand is the battle, and there is no *14* […] your [wo]n[der]s and the determined moments according to your will, and [you render] retribution to your [enemie]s, and you cut off from the measure […] *15* […] … from all … […] *16* […] *Blank* […]

Col. XIX (+ *frags.* 2, 8; + 1Q33 2 1; = 4Q492 1)   *1* [with jeers and mockery the he]roes. For our Mighty one is holy and the King of glory is with us. The ar[my of his spirits is with our steps. Our horsemen] *2* [are like clouds and fogs of d]ew that cover the earth, like torrential rain that sheds justice on al[l its sprouts. Get up, Hero,] *3* [take your prisoners, Man of Glory, co]llect your spoil, Performer of Valiance! Place your hand on the neck of your enemies and your foo[t on the piles] *4* [of the dead! Strike the peoples, your foes,] and may your sword consume flesh! Fill your land with glory and your inheritance with blessing: [may herds] *5* [of flocks be in your fields, silver and gold] in your palaces! Rejoice, Zion, passionately! Exult, all the cities of Ju[dah! Open] *6* [your gates continuously so that] the wealth of the nations [can be brought to you!] Their kings shall wait on you, [al]l your [oppressors] lie prone before you, *7* [the dust of your feet they shall lick.] Daughters of my people, shout with jubilant voice! Adorn yourselves with splendid finery! R[u]le over the kingdom of *8* [… to] your [camp]s, and Israel to reign for ever. *Blank*

9 [Afterwards they shall gather in the ca]mp on that n[i]ght to rest until the morning. And in the morning they shall go out to the place of the line *10* [where there fell the he]roes of the Kittim, the horde of Assyria and the army of all the

וחיל כול הגוים הנקהלים אם חללים   11 [מתו לאין מקבר אשר]נפלו שם
בחרב אל ונגש שם כוהן הרו[אש ומ]שנהו ו[הכוהנים]   12 [והלוים עם
נשיא ה]מלחמה וכול ראשי המערכות ופקוד[יהם [...]... יחד בעומדם
ע[ל ח]ללי כתי[י]ם וה[ל]לו שם [א]ת אל[ ]ישראל וענו ואמרו[
14 [...]ל[...]

1Q34 + 1Q34bis (1QLitPr) *1QFestival Prayers*

J.T. Milik, *DJD I*, 136 and 152-155, pl. XXXI; J.C. Trever, 'Completion of the
Publication of Some Fragments from Qumran Cave I', *RevQ* 5/18 (1965) 328-
329, 333, pl. II-IV
PAM 40.537

Frags. 1+2   1 [...] מועד שלומ[נו ... כי שמחתנו מיגוננו ואספת
נדחינו[2 למועד ...] ונפ[וצותינו לתקופו]ת ... חסדיך על עדתנו כשעירים
על[3 הארץ במוע[די זרע ו]כרביבים על [עשב במועדי דשא ו... ואנו
נספרה נפלאותיך[4 לדור ודור ברוך אדני אשר שמחנ[ו ...   5 *vacat*
6 תפלה ליום כפורים זכו[ר א]דוני א[ת ...   7 [...]...[...]

Frag. 3 i   1 [...]...[...]   2 [...] . בגורל צד[י]ק ולרשים ג[ו]רל
3 [...]ם בעצמותם חרפה [ל]כל בשר וצדיקים   4 [... להת]דשן בעבי שמים
ותנובת ארץ לד[ע]ת   5 [בין צד]יק לרשע ונתתה רשעים [כ]ופרנו
וב[יש]רים   6 [תעשה]כלה בכל מעינו ואנו נודה לשמך לעולם   7 [ועד
[כי לזאת בראתנו וזה אש[ר נשיב]לך ברוך   8 [...] *vacat*   9 [...]...[...]

Frag. 3 ii   1 [...] [מאור גדו[ל] למועד ה]יום ... 2 [...]ואין לעבור
חוקיהם וכולם [...]   3 [...] וממשלתם בכל תבל ולא הבין זרע האד[ם]בכל
אשר הנחלתו ולא ידעוך   4 [לעשו]ת דברך וירשיעו מכול ולא הבינו
בכוחך הגדול ותמאס בם כי לא תחפץ   5 בעו[ול]ה ורשע לא יכון לפניך

peoples that had gathered together, (to see) whether the slain *11* [had died, without burial, which] had fallen there by God's sword. And the Hi[gh] Priest will approach there, [and] his [se]cond, and [the priests,] *12* [and the levites, together with the princes of the] war and all the chiefs of the lines and [their] enlisted men [...] *13* [... together in their positions ov]er the [sl]ain of the Kitt[im. And] they shall [pr]aise there the God of [Israel and they shall begin speaking and say:] *14* [...] ... [...]

1Q34 + 1Q34bis (1QLitPr) *1QFestival Prayers*

DAJ (frag. 1), Athanasius Samuel (frag. 2, 3)
4Q507, 4Q508, 4Q509+4Q505
Bibliography: J.H. Charlesworth, D.T. Olson, *PTSDSSP 4A*, 50-53

Frags. 1 + 2 (= 4Q509 3)   *1* [...] the time of [our] peace. [... For you console us from our distress, and you gather together our exiles] *2* for the time [...] and our scattered ones (you assemble) for the age of [... your mercies upon our assembly, like drops of water upon] *3* the earth in [seed-]tim[e] like rain upon the [plants in the time of grass ... We will sing of your wonders] *4* from generation to generation. Blessed be the Lord who made [us] rejoice [...] *5* *Blank* [...] *6* Prayer for the day of atonement. Remem[ber, L]ord, [...] *7* [...] ... [...]

Frag. 3 *col.* I (= 4Q508 1)   *1* [...] ... [...] *2* [...] in the lot of the ju[s]t and to the wicked the lot of *3* [...] in their bones a disgrace [for] all flesh. But the just *4* [... in order to flou]rish, thanks to the clouds of the sky and to the produce of the earth, in order to dis[crim]inate *5* [between the ju]st and the wicked. Of the wicked you shall make our [r]ansom, while for the [upri]ght *6* [you will bring about] the destruction of all our enemies. And we, we will celebrate your name for ever *7* [and ever,] for this is why you have created us. And this is wha[t we will answer] you: Blessed *8* [...] *Blank* *9* [...] ... [...]

Frag. 3 *col.* II (= 4Q509 97 - 98)   *1* [...] the gre[at] light for [day]-time, [...] *2* [...] without their laws being broken. And all of them [...] *3* [...] and their dominion over the whole world. But the offspring of ma[n] has not understood all that you have given them as inheritance, and they do not know you, *4* [to d]o your word, and they act more wickedly than anybody. They do not understand your powerful strength. This is why you reject them, because you do not like *5* s[i]n, and the wicked person will not endure before you. How-

ותבחר לך עם בקץ רצונך כי זכרת בריתך   6 ות[תנ]ם להבדל לך לקודש

מכול העמים ותחדש בריתך להם במראת כב[ו]ד ודברי   7 [רוח] קודשך

במעשי ידיך וכתב ימינך להודיעם יסורי כבוד ומעשי עולם   8 [...

והקימותה [ל]ה]ם רועה נאמן [...] ... [...]... עני ור[...]מים

1QHᵃ (1QHᵃ) *1QHodayotᵃ*

E.L. Sukenik, *DSSHU*, cols. i-xviii, frgs. 1-66, pl. 35-58; É. Puech, 'Un Hymne essénien en partie retrouvé et les Béatitudes. 1QH V 12-VI 18 (= col. XII-XIV 7) et 4QBéat', *RevQ* 13/49-52 (1988) 59-66, pl. III (three additional *frags.*) SHR 4236-83, IAA 190.402-441
SHR
1Q35, 4Q427, 4Q428, 4Q429, 4Q430, 4Q431, 4Q432, 4Q471b
Bibliography: A. Dupont-Sommer, 'Le Livre des Hymnes découvert près de la Mer Morte (1QH). Traduction intégrale avec introduction et notes', *Semitica* 7 (1957) 5-120; J. Licht, *The Thanksgiving Scroll* (Jerusalem: Bialik, 1957) [Hebrew]; Günter Morawe, *Aufbau und Abgrenzung der Loblieder von Qumrân* (Ber-

Cols. I-II

Col. III top   1 [...]מרות[...]   2 [...]ע[שוקים   3 ...] ר]חמיו על

אביונ[ים ...   4 [...].[...]. ומי מתכן [...]   5 [...] ומי מתכן גבורת[...]   6 [...].

עולם מי חוש[ב ...   7 [...]. קדומים [...]   8 ...] גב]ורתכה [...]

Col. III bottom   1 [...]...[...]   2 [...]עמדה לכול שני עו]לם [...

3 [...] מי]ך כול חותם [...]   4 [...]... בני איש לפי שכלו [...]...]

5 [...] ... מלכותו מי עשה כול אלה [...]   6 [...]...תם ולך חמד ובצדק

תשימ[ו]...[...]   7 [...] לפניך [...]תהו ויצר ח]מר ... [...]   8 [...] יענה נכבדתה

מכול א]לים ... [...]   9 [...] קודש וכאשר בנפשך [...]...]   10 [...] לשמך

תב[...] בעדת ק]ודשים [...

ever, you have chosen a people in the period of your favour, because you have remembered your covenant. *6* You established them, isolating them for yourself in order to make them holy among all the nations. And you have renewed your covenant with them in the vision of glory, and in the words of *7* your holy [spirit], by the works of your hand. Your right hand has written to let them know the regulations of glory and the everlasting deeds. *8* [... You raised up] a loyal shepherd for them [...] poor and [...] ...

1QHᵃ (1QHᵃ) *1QHodayotᵃ*

lin, 1960); S. Holm-Nielsen, *Hodayot. Psalms from Qumran* (Aarhus, 1960); M. Mansoor, *The Thanksgiving Hymns* (STDJ 3; Leiden: E.J. Brill, 1961); M. Delcor, *Les Hymnes de Qumrân (Hodayot). Texte hébreu, Introduction, Traduction, Commentaire* (Paris, 1962); H. Stegemann, *Rekonstruktion der Hodajot. Ursprüngliche Gestalt und kritisch bearbeiteter Text der Hymnenrolle aus Höhle 1 von Qumran*, Diss. Heidelberg, 1963; B. Kittel, *The Hymns of Qumran* (SBLDS 50; Chico: Scholars Press, 1981). É. Puech, 'Quelques aspects de la Restauration du Rouleau des Hymnes (1QH)', *JJS* 39 (1988) 38-55; E.M. Schuller, L. DiTomasso, 'A Bibliography of the Hodayot 1948-1996', *DSD* 4 (1997) 55-101

Cols. I - II *[Nothing has been preserved]*

Col. III *top* (Sukenik *frag.* 16) *1* [...] ... [...] *2* [... the op]pressed ... [...] *3* [...] his gentleness with the poor [...] *4* [...] And who can measure [...] *5* [...] And who can measure the strength of [...] *6* [...] eternal. Who plots [...] *7* [...] previous [...] *8* [...] your [str]ength [...]

Col. III *bottom* (Sukenik *frag.* 11) *1* [...] ... [...] *2* [...] it has stood for all the years of eternity [...] *3* [...] from your hand every seal ... [...] *4* [...] ... the sons of man according to his intelligence [...] *5* [...] his kingship. Who has made all these things? [...] *6* [...] for you the pleasure. In justice shall you place [...] *7* [...] in your presence [...] and the creature of c[lay ...] *8* [...] he will answer. You are glorified above all the go[ds ...] *9* [...] holiness, and according to what is in your soul ... [...] *10* [...] for your name. You [...] in the congregation of the ho[ly ones ...]

Col. IV 1 [...] ומשפלת מדה מכ[...] 2 [...]מגולה בלוא משפטי[ם]
כי ברוח 3 [...].ת[...] אוכלת בשר[ה]רוגיה בלוא 4 [...].ת ביבושה ומכש[ול
ב]לוא משפט 5 [...] פוגעות פתע פתאו[ם ...] כדונ[ג].[ ] 6 [י]מס מפני אש
[...] משפט מרוח דורשכ[ה ...] יתנשא 7 [...]מתרמה ב[...]ובמצוה *vacat*
מרוח כו[...] 8 [...].ת בנגיעי ב[...] *vacat* [...]

9 [אודך]מנסתרות אש[ר ... א]ש[ר לא השיגום במ[...] 10 [...]
וממשפט קצ.[... מח]שבות רשעה נער.[...] 11 [...]ין וממשפט אח.[...
טהרתה] עבדך מכול פשעיו [בהמון]רחמיך 12 [כאשר ד]ברתה ביד מושה
[לשאת פשע] עוון וחטאה ולכפר בע[ד אשמו]ת ומע[ל 13]ותלהט [מוסדי
הרים ואש [אוכל]ה בשאול תחתיה ואת הנו[...] 14 [שמר]תה
לע[ו]בדיך באמונה [ל]היות זרעם לפניך כול הימים ושם[עולם]הקימותה
15 [לשאת]פשע [ו]להשליך כול עונותם ולהנחילם בכול כבוד אדם [ו]רוב
vacat 16 ימים

17 [אוד]ך מרוחות אשר נתתה בי אמצאה מענה לשון לספר צדקותיך
וארוך אפים 18 [במשפטי]ך ומעשי ימין עוזך [סליח]ות על פשעי
ראשונים ולה[תנפ]ל ולהתחנן על 19 [...] ... מעשי ונעוית לבי כי בנדה
התגוללתי ומסוד [אמת הלכ]תי ולא נלאיתי 20 [...].ם ... לך אתה הצדקה
ולשמך הברכה לעול[ם עשה כ]צדקתך ופדה 21 [את עבדך וי]תמו רשעים
ואני הבינותי כי את אשר בחרתה ה[תישר] דרכו ובשכל 22 [דעתך
תמ]שכהו מחטוא לך ול[הש]יב לו ענותו ביסוריך ובנס[...]תה לבו *vacat*
23 [סוך בעד] עבדך מחטוא לך ומכשול בכול דברי רצונך חזק מ[...]ד
על רוחות 24 [רשעה לה]תהלך בכול אשר אהבתה ולמאוס בכול אשר
שנא[תה ולעשות]הטוב בעיניך [...] 25 [...]לתם בתכמי כי רוח בש[ר]עבדך
vacat

26 [אודך כי] הניפותה רוח קודש[ך] על עבדך [...].[...].[...] לבו
27 [...]ש ואל כול ברית אדם אביט ה[...] 28 [...]ה ימצאוה ...[...]יגיה ואוהביה
[...]עולמי עד

Col. IV (Sukenik *col.* XVII + *frag.* 14)   *1* […] and a low measure … […] *2* […] revealed, without judgment[s,] for by the spirit of *3* […] … which consumes the flesh of its [d]ead without *4* […] in the dry earth and an ob[stacle] without judgment *5* […] striking suddenly, unexpected[ly …] as wa[x] *6* [melts in front of the fire …] judgment by the spirit which seeks y[ou …] will be elevated *7* […] thrust in […] and by the commandment. *Blank* Because of the spirit … […] *8* […] by the blows of […] *Blank* […]

9 [I give you thanks] for the secrets whi[ch … wh]ich have not reached them in […] *10* […] and because of the judgment of … [… th]oughts of wickedness … […] *11* […] and because of the judgment … [… You have purified] your servant from all his offences [by the abundance of] your compassion, *12* [as] you [s]aid through the hand of Moses, [forgiving offence,] iniquity, sin, atoning for [wrongs] and unfaithfulness. *13* [Even though you burn] the foundations of mountains and fire [sears] the base of Sheol, those who … […] in your regulations. *14* You [protect] the ones who serve you loyally, [so that] their posterity is before you all the days. You have raised an [eternal] name, *15* [forgiving] offence, casting away all their iniquities, giving them as a legacy all the glory of Adam [and] abundance of days. *16 Blank*

17 [I give] you [thanks] for the spirits which you placed in me. I want to find a reply on (my) tongue to recount your acts of justice, the patience *18* [of] your [judgments,] the deeds of your mighty right hand, the [pardon]ing of my former offences, to [bow] low and beg favour for *19* … […] of my deeds and the depravity of my heart. Because I defiled myself with impurity, I [separated myself] from the foundation [of truth] and I was not allied with […] *20* […]… To you does justice belong, blessing belongs to your Name for ever! [Act according to] your justice, free *21* [your servant,] the wicked should come to an end! However, I have understood that [you smoothen] the path of the one whom you choose and by the insight *22* [of your knowledge you pre]vent him from sinning against you, you [re]store his humility through your punishments, and by […] you […] his heart. *Blank 23* [Prevent] your servant from sinning against you, from tripping over all the things of your will. Strengthen […] against [fiendish] spirits, *24* [so that] he can walk in all that you love, and loathe all that [you] hate, [so he can do] what is good in your eyes *25* […] in my vitals, for your servant is a spirit of flesh. *Blank*

26 [I give you thanks, because] you have spread [your] holy spirit upon your servant […] … […] his heart *27* […] and I will consider every human treaty […] they shall find it *28* […] … and those who love it […] for ever and ever.

Col. v   1 [מזמור למש]כיל להתנפל לפנ]י אל [...]מעשי אל   2 [...]
ולהבין פ[תאים...]שי עולם   3 [... ד]עת ולהבין אנוש בשר וסוד רוחו[ת
...]ש התהלכו   4 [... ברוך] אתה אדוני כ]י רוח ב]אשר [...]... רוחב [...]
בכוח גבורתך   5 [...].ד עם רוב טוב]ך אורך]אפף וקנאת משפ]טיך ...
בלו]א חקר vacat כול   6 [הבחיר בד]עת כול בינה יב]י]ן ... [ורזי מחשבת
וראשית ... ה]כינותה vacat

7 [כי לך א]תה קודש מקדם ע]ולם ו]לעולמי עד אתה הוא[...] קדושים
8 [...] וברזי פלאך ...[...].[...]וד כבודך ובעומק [...] בינתך לא [...] 9 אתה
גליתה דרכי [אמת] ומעשי רע חוכמה ואולת[...] צדק [...] 10 מעשיהם
אמת ובינה עולה ואולת כול התהלכו[...] [...] 11 ... רח]ם וחסדי עולם לכול
קציהם לשלום ושחת כול מ[...]   12 [...] מש]פטיהם כבוד עולם ו]רוב
עדנים וש]מחת עד למעשה[...]שים למ[עשה 13 [ר]ע vacat

ואלה אשר הכ]ינותה מקדם עולם] לשפוט בם   14 את כול מעשיך
בטרם בראתם עם צבא רוחיך ועדת [קדושיך ע]ם רקיע קודשך ו]כו]ל
15 צבאותיו עם הארץ וכול צאצאיה בימים ובתהומות [כ]כול מחשבותך
לכול קצי עולם   16 ופקודת עד כי אתה הכינותמה מקדם עולם ומעשה
[...]תה בם בעבור   17 יספרו כבודך בכול ממשלתך כי הראיתם את אשר
לא ר[או ... א]שר קדם ולברוא   18 חדשות להפר קימי קדם ול[הק]ים
נהיות עולם כי א[ת]ה ה]כינותם מאז] ואתה תהיה   19 לעולמי עד vacat

וברזי שכלכה פלג]תה] כול אלה להודיע כבודך [ומה אף ה]וא רוח בשר
להבין   20 בכול אלה ולהשכיל בסו]ד פלאך ה]גדול ומה ילוד אשה בכול
מעשיך הנוראים והוא   21 מבנה עפר ומגבל מים א]שר עוון חטא]ה סודו
ערות קלון ומ]קור]נדה ורוח נעוה משלה   22 בו vacat

ואם ירשע והיה [לאות]עולם ומופת דורות דראון [לכול] בשר רק
בטובך   23 יצדק איש וברוב רח]מיך יטהר] בהדרך תפארנו ותמשילה]ו
בר]וב עדנים עם שלום   24 עולם ואורך ימים כי [אמת אתה ו]דברך לא
ישוב אחור vacat

ואני עבדך ידעתי   25 ברוח אשר נתתה בי [...]וצדק כול מעשיך ודברך
לא ישוב אחור וכ]ול]   26 קציך מועד]ים ... ב]רורים לחפציהם ואדע]ה[...]

150

Col. v (Sukenik *col.* XIII + *frags.* 15a + 15b I + 31 + 17 + 20 + 33 + *frag.*
Puech) *1* [Chant for the Ins]tructor to fall down befo[re God ...] God's
deeds *2* [...] and to make the simple understand [...] eternal *3* [...] of knowledge, to make the man of flesh understand, and the council of the spirits [...]
they walked *4* [... Blessed] are you, Lord, bec[ause the spirit of fl]esh [...] ...
breadth [...] with the strength of your power, *5* [...] ... with the abundance of
[your] goodness, [the slowness] of your wrath and the zeal of [your] judgment
[... without] limit. *Blank* Every *6* [one who has been chosen by the know]ledge
of all intelligence will under[stand ...] and the mysteries of the plan and the
begin[ning of ...] you have established. *7* [For to y]ou belongs holiness before
[the centuries and] for ever and ever. You are [...] holy ones *8* [...] And in your
wonderful mysteries ... [...] ... your glory, and in the depth of [...] of your
knowledge (does) not *9* [...] you have revealed the paths of [truth] and the
deeds of evil, wisdom and folly, [...] justice *10* [...] their deeds: truth and
understanding, iniquity and folly. All have walked [...] *11* [... comp]assion
and everlasting favour for all their periods of peace, and ruin for all [...]
12 [...] their [judg]ments. Everlasting glory, and [abundance of delight and]
unending enjoyment for the work of [...] ... for *13* a bad de[ed.] *Blank* These
are those [you] fou[nded before the centuries,] to judge through them *14* all
your works before creating them, together with the host of your spirits and the
assembly of [your holy ones, wi]th your holy vault and [al]l *15* its hosts, with
the earth and all its produce, in the seas and in the deeps, [according to] all
your designs for all the eternal ages *16* and the eternal task. For you have
established them before the centuries, and you have [...] the work of [...] in
them, so that *17* they can recount your glory throughout all your dominion; for
you have shown them what they had never s[een, ...] what was there from of
old and creating *18* new things, demolishing ancient things and [erec]ting
what would exist for ever. For you [have established them long ago] and you
will exist *19* for ever and ever. *Blank* In the mysteries of your insight [you] have
apportioned all these things, to make your glory known. [However, what is]
the spirit of flesh to understand *20* all these matters and to have insight in [your
wondrous] and great counsel? What is someone born of a woman among all
your awesome works? He is *21* a structure of dust fashioned with water, his
counsel is the [iniquity] of sin, shame of dishonor and so[urce of] impurity,
and a depraved spirit rules *22* over him. *Blank* If he acts wickedly, he will be an
eternal [sign,] a portent for generations, shame [for all] flesh. Only by your
goodness *23* is man acquitted, [purified] by the abundance of [your]
compa[ssion.] You embellish him with your splendour, you install [him over
an abun]dance of pleasures, with everlasting peace *24* and length of days. For
[you are the truth, and] your word does not depart. *Blank* And I, your servant,
have known *25* thanks to the spirit you have placed in me [...] and all your
deeds are just, and your word does not depart, and a[ll] *26* your periods are

27 ורשע ש[...]...[...] להתבונן [...] 28 [...]רוחיך ו.[...] 29 [...]...[...]

Col. VI 1 [...] תעודותמ[...] בעמך וח...[...]... 2 [...] גליתה[

אוזננו[... אשרי] אנשי אמת ובחירי צ[דק דורשי] 3 שכל ומבקשי בינה

בו[ני ... או]הבי רחמים וענוי רוח מזוקקי 4 עוני וברורי מצרף [...

מ]תאפקים עד קץ משפטיכה 5 וצופים לישועתך את[ה ...]וחזקתה

חוקיך[בידם] לעשות 6 משפט תבל ולנחיל בכול [...].[...]קודש לדורות עולם

וכול 7 אושי מעשיהם עם תענ[וג ...] אנשי חזונכה *vacat*

vacat 8 [ברוך אתה] אדוני הנותן בלב עבד[ך] בינה 9 [לה]שכ[ל] בכו[ל

אלה ולהת]בונן ...] ולהתאפק על עלילות רשע ולברך 10 [ב]צדק כול

בוחרי רצונך[לאהוב] את כול א[שר אהבתה ולתעב את כול אשר

11 [שנאתה] ותשכל עבדך] ... רוחו]ת אנוש כי לפי רוחות...ולם בין

12 טוב לרשע [ות]כ[ן ...]להוד]עתם פעולתם ואני ידעתי מבינתך 13 כי

ברצונכה בא[נו]ש תגב[רתה גורלו עם] רוח קודשך וכן תגישני לבינתך

ולפי 14 קורבי קנאתי על כול פועלי רשע ואנשי רמיה כי כול קרוביך לא

ימרו פיך 15 וכול יודעיך לא ישנו דבריך כי אתה צדיק ואמת כול בחיריך

וכול עולה 16 [ור]שע תשמיד לעד ונגלתה צדקתך לעיני כול מעשיך *vacat*

17 [וא]ני ידעתי ברוב טובך ובשבועה הקימותי על נפשי לבלתי חטוא

לך 18 [ול]בלתי עשות מכול הרע בעיניך וכן הוגשתי ביחד כול אנשי סודי

לפי 19 [ש]כלו אגישנו וכרוב נחלתו אהבנו ולא אשא פני רע וש[וחד

רשע] לא אכיר 20 [ו]ל[א]אמיר בהון אמתך ובשוחד כול משפטיך כי אם

לפ[י ...]ש 21 [אוה]בנו וכרחקך אותו כן אתעבנו *vacat* ולא אביא בסוד

א[שר לא הח]שבו 22 [בבר]יתך *vacat*

23 [אוד]ך אדוני כגדול כוחך ורוב נפלאותיך מעולם ועד [עולם ואתה

רו]ם וגדול 24 [ורוב חס]דים הסולח לשבי פשע ופוקד עו[ו]ן רשעים

fixed [... pu]rified for their affairs. And I shall know [...] *27* the wicked [...] so that he may realise [...] *28* [...] your spirits and [...] *29* [...] ... [...]

Col. VI (Sukenik *col.* XIV + *frags.* 15b II + 18 + 22 + 44 + 19 + *frag.* Puech)
 1 [...] their instructions [...] in your people [...] ... *2* [... you opened] our ears [... Fortunate,] the men of truth, those chosen by jus[tice, those probing] *3* the mind, those searching for wisdom, those bui[lding ... those who l]ove compassion, the poor in spirit, those refined *4* by poverty and purified in the crucible [... those who keep the]ir nerve until the time of your judgments, *5* those alert for your salvation. You [...] and you have strengthened your precepts [through their hands] to make *6* judgment on the world, to give as an inheritance all [...] holy for everlasting generations. And all *7* foundations of their deeds, with pleas[ure ...] the men of your vision. *Blank*

8 Blank [Blessed are you,] Lord, who puts wisdom in the heart of [your] servant *9* to kn[ow al]l these matters, to unders[tand ...] to restrain oneself when faced with the deeds of wickedness, to bless *10* [in] justic, all the searchers of your will, [to love all th]at you love, and hate all that you *11* [loathe.] You teach your servant [... of the spirit]s of man, for corresponding to the spirits ... them between *12* good and evil, and set over them [... to sho]w them their actions. But I, I know, thanks to your insight *13* that in your kindness towards m[a]n [you] have enlar[ged his share with] the spirit of your holiness. Thus, you make me approach your intelligence, and the more *14* I approach, the more ardently I oppose all those who act wickedly and the men of guile; for all who approach you, do not defy your orders, *15* and all who know you do not change your words. For you are just, and all your chosen ones are truth. All injustice *16* [and wick]edness you obliterate for ever, and your justice is revealed to the eyes of all your creatures. *Blank 17* [But] I, I know, thanks to the abundance of your goodness, and I have enjoined my soul with an oath not to sin against you *18* [and n]ot to do anything which is evil in your eyes. In this way I was brought near in the community of all the men of my counsel. According to *19* his [int]elligence I bring him near, I love him in proportion to the abundance of his inheritance. I do not lift my face to evil, or consider a bri[be]. *20* I do n[ot] exchange your truth for wealth, or for a bribe all your judgments. Quite the reverse, to the deg[ree ...] *21* [I lov]e him, and to the extent that you place him far off, I hate him. *Blank* I will not admit into the council th[ose who are not inclu]ded *22* [in] your [coven]ant. *Blank*

23 [I give] you [thanks,] Lord, according to greatness of your strength and the abundance of your wonders from eternity and for [eternity. You are lof]ty, great, *24* [lavish in fav]ours, forgiving those who turn away from offence, and punishing the iniquity of the wicked. [You love the truth] with a generous

[תאהב אמת] בנדבת   25   [...לב] ...ותשנא עולה לעד ואני עבדך חנותני
ברוח דעה [לאהוב א]מת   26   [וצדק] ולתעב כול דרך עולה ואהבכה נדבה
ובכול לב[...]ך   27   [...] שכליך כי מידך היתה זאת ובלוא ר[צונ]ך ל[וא
יהיה כ]ול   28   [...]כה ימשול בשר [...]ש ות...[...]שב   29   [...]. הוא ותבן
בעזר את [...]   30   [...]רקיע על כנפי רוח וי...[...]

Col. VII   1   [...].[...]   2   [...].[...]...נכה השכלתי[...]   3   ... לפ]לאכה מה
נשיב כי גמלתנו ו[...]הפליא[תה   ...   4   [...] לא יעצרו כוח לדעת בכבוד
[ולספ]ר נפלא[ותיך   ...   5   [...]... לפי שכלם וכפי דעתם ב]כבודכה [...]
6   תחת[...] לאין השבת מקץ לקץ ישמיעו ומו]עד למועד   ...   [...].   7   [...]
ואנחנו ביחד נועדנו ועם ידעים [נוס]רה לכה ונר[ננה   ...   8   רחמי[כה...]ח
עם גבוריכה ובהפלא נספרה יחד בדע]ת אל [ועד   ...   9   בעד]...[...]
וצאצאינו הודע[תה ע]ם בני איש בתוך] בני [אדם   ...   10   כי
...[...ב]הפלא מאדה   *vacat*

11   ברו]ך ...[.]ב *מזמור* למש]כיל ... רנה [גדול אל המפלי]   12   [...]
או]הבי אותך כול הימים וא[...]   13   אמ[...] ואהבכה בנדבה ובכול לב
ובכול נפש בררתי [...]...   14   הק]ימותי לבלתי [סור מכול אשר צויתה
ואחז]קה על רבים מ...[... לבלתי]   15   עזוב מכול חוקיך   *vacat*
ואני ידעתי בבינתך כיא לא ביד בשר [... ולא ל]אדם   16   דרכו ולא
יוכל אנוש להכין צעדו ואדעה כי בידך יצר כול רוח [וכול פעולת]ו
17   הכינותה בטרם בראתו ואיכה יוכל כול להשנות את דבריכה רק אתה
[ברא]תה   18   צדיק ומרחם הכינותו למועד רצון להשמר בבריתך ולתהלך
בכול ולה... עליו   19   בהמון רחמיך ולפתוח כול צרת נפשו לישועת עולם
ושלום עד ואין מחסור ותרם   20   מבשר כבודו   *vacat*
ורשעים בראתה ל[קץ]חרונכה ומרחם הקדשתם ליום הרגה   21   כי
הלכו בדרך לא טוב וימאסו בבריתכ]ה ...[...]ך תעבה נפשם ולא רצו בכול
אשר   22   ציותה ויבחרו באשר שנאתה כול[...]ך הכינותם לעשות בם
שפטים גדולים   23   לעיני כול מעשיך ולהיות לאות ומו]פת לדורות [עולם

154

₂₅ [heart ...] and you hate injustice, for ever. And myself, your servant, you have favoured me with the spirit of knowledge [to love tr]uth ₂₆ [and justice,] and to loathe all the paths of injustice. I love you liberally, and with (my) whole heart [...] you ₂₇ [...] your wisdom, because these things happen at your hand and without your ap[proval] nothing [exists.] ₂₈ [...] flesh will rule it [...] ... [...] ₂₉ [...] him, and he will construct with help, the [...] ₃₀ [...] of the vault upon the wings of the wind and he ... [...]

Col. VII (Sukenik *col.* XV + *frags.* 10 + 32 + 34 + 42; = 4Q427 3 1) ₁ [...] ... [...] ₂ [...] ... I have received intelligence [...] ₃ [... to] your [wo]nder what reply shall we make? For you have dealt [kindly] with us and [... you] have done wonders [...] ₄ [...] they will not gather the strength to know your glory [or to recou]nt [your] wonder[s ...] ₅ [...] ... according to their intelligence. And in accordance with their knowledge [by] your glory [...] ₆ below [...] unceasingly. And from age to age they announce, and from determined [time to determined time ...] ₇ [...] And we are gathered in the Community, and with those who know [we are admoni]shed /by you/ and we shall shout [of joy ...] ₈ [your] compassion [...] the people of your heroes, and wondrously we shall recount together of the knowled[ge of God] and till [...] ₉ for [...] and our offspring [you] have shown [together] with the sons of man among [the sons of] Adam [...] ₁₀ because [...] extremely wondrously. *Blank*

₁₁ Bles[sed [...] /Chant/ for the In[structor ... a loud] cry [for those who magnify (?)] ₁₂ [...] those who [lo]ve you for all days and [...] ₁₃ ... [...] I love you lavishly, with (my) whole heart and with all (my) soul I have purified [...] ₁₄ [I have] imp[osed on myself not] to turn aside from all that you have commanded. I join the Many [... so as not] ₁₅ to desert all your precepts. *Blank* But I, I know, thanks to your intellect, that [...] is not by the hand of flesh, and that a man [can not choose] ₁₆ his way, nor can a human being establish his steps. I know that the impulse of every spirit is in your hand, [and all] its [task] ₁₇ you have established even before creating him. How can anyone change your words? You, you alone, have [created] ₁₈ the just man, and from the womb you determined him for the period of approval, to keep your covenant, and to walk on all (your paths), and to ... on him ₁₉ with the abundance of your compassion, to open all the narrowness of his soul to eternal salvation and endless peace, without want. And you have raised ₂₀ his glory above flesh. *Blank* But the wicked you have created for [the time] of your wrath, from the womb you have predestined them for the day of slaughter. ₂₁ For they walk on a path that is not good, they reject your covenant, their soul loathes your [...], and they take no pleasure in what ₂₂ you command, but choose what you hate. You have established all those [who ...] your [...] to carry out great judgments against them ₂₃ before the eyes of all your creatures, so they

לדעת כול את כבודך ואת כוחך   24   הגדול ומה אף הוא בשר כי ישכיל
[ברזיך] עפר איך יוכל להכין צעדו   *vacat*

25   אתה יצרתה רוח ופעולתה הכינו[תה מקדם עולם] ומאתך דרך כול
חי ואני ידעתי כיא   26   לא ישוה כול הון באמתך ואי[...] ק[ודשך ואדעה
כי בם בחרתה מכול   27   ולעד הם ישרתוך ולא תקב[ל שוחד לעולה]ולא
תקח כופר לעלילות רשעה כיא   28   אמת אתה וכול עולה ת[שמיד
...] לא תהיה לפניך ואני ידעת[י ...   29   [...]...[...] כי לך [...] עשה וא[...
[ל]   30   קודשך [...]   31   כי ב[...]

[...]   1   *Col.* VIII   2   [...]...[...]   שפה הביא במספר
[...]ו[...]ר בשמים ובארץ   4   [...]ות ובידך משפט כולם   5   [...]דך ומה
יחשב ...   6   [...]היו ולא יעשה כול   7   [...] ולעצתך פקד את   8   [...]... עם
...   9   [...] אל[...]   10   ברוח קו[דשך ...]ה...[...]...[...]... ולא יוכ[ל]   11   רוח
קוד[שך ...] מלוא ה[ש]מים והארץ [...כ]בודך מלוא כ[...]   12   ואדעה כי
ברצו[נך] באיש הרביתה.[...].ד אמתך בכול [...]   13   ומעמד צדק ... אשר
הפקדתה בו פן [...]... כשול בכול מ[...]   14   בדעתי בכול אלה אמצאה
מענה לשון להתנפל ולה[תחנן ...   ע]ל פשעי ולבקש רוח [...].
15   ולהתחזק ברוח קו[דשך] ולדבוק באמת בריתך ולעבדך באמת ולב שלם
ולאהוב את [רצונך]

16   ברוך אתה אדוני גדול [הע]צה ור[ב]העלילייה אשר מעשיך הכול
הנה הואלתה לעשו[ת]עם עבדך   17   חסד ותחונני ברוח רחמיך וב[...]וד
כבודך לך אתה הצדקה כי אתה עשיתה את כו[ל אלה]   18   ובדעתי כי אתה
רשמתה רוח צדיק ואני בחרתי להבר כפי כרצו[נך] ונפש עבדך תעבה כול
19   מעשה עולה ואדעה כי לא יצדק איש מבלעדיך ואחלה פניך ברוח אשר
נתתה [בי] להשלים   20   [חס]דיך עם עב[דך ל]ע[ד] לטהרני ברוח קודשך
ולהגישני ברצונך כגדול חסדיך [...].[...]... עמדי   21   [ו]לעשות   [...]
רצו[ונך] אשר בח[ר]תה לאוהביך ולשומרי מ[צו]תיך [...]   22   לפניך
[לעו]לם [...].[...]...[...]... אל [התערב ברוח עבדך ובכול מעשי]ו   23   [...]ו

will be a sign and a por[tent for] eternal [generations,] so that all will know your glory and your great might. *24* What, then, is flesh, to understand [your mysteries?] How can dust direct its steps? *Blank 25* You have fashioned the spirit and have organised its task [before the centuries.] From you comes the path of every living being. But I, I know that *26* no wealth can compare to your truth, and ...[...] your [ho]liness. I know that you have chosen them above all *27* and they will serve you forever. You do not take [bribes for injustice,] or accept a ransom for wicked acts. For *28* you are God of truth and you [destroy] all injustice. [...] will no longer exist in your presence. I know that [...] *29* belongs to you [...] ... and [...] *30* your holiness [...] *31* because [...]

Col. VIII (Sukenik *col.* XVI + *frag.* 13)   *1* [...] all [...] *2* [...] he brings into the number of *3* [...] in heaven and on earth *4* [...] and in your hand is the judg-ment of them all *5* [...] and what will he think ... *6* [...] and nothing is done *7* [...] according to your advice you visited the *8* [...] with ... *9* [...] ... *10* by [your] ho[ly] spirit [...] ... [...] and *11* [your] ho[ly] spirit is unable to [...] the fullness of he[av]en and earth [...] your [gl]ory. The fullness [...] *12* I know that in [your] kind[ness] towards man you have multiplied [...] your truth in all [...] *13* and the service of justice [...] which you have imposed on him lest[...] to stumble in all [...] *14* Since I know all this I want to find a reply of the tongue to prostrate myself and to ask [forgiveness ... fo]r my offence, to look for the spirit [...] *15* to be strengthened by [your] ho[ly] spirit, to adhere to the truth of your covenant, to serve you in truth, with a perfect heart, to love [your will.]

16 Be blessed, Lord, great [in pla]ns and mi[ghty] in acts, everything is your work. You have resolved, in fact, to take pity [on your servant,] *17* to show me favour by the spirit of your compassion and by the [...] of your glory. To you belongs the justice because you have done al[l this.] *18* And since I know that you have recorded the spirit of the just man, I have chosen to purify my hands in ac-cordance with [your] will and your servant's soul detests every *19* work of iniquity. I know that no-one besides you is just. I have appeased your face by the spirit which you have placed [in me,] to lavish *20* your [kind]nesses on [your] serv[ant] for [ever,] to purify me with your holy spirit, to bring me near by your will according to the extent of your kindnesses [...] and to act *21* with me [...] the place of [your] wi[ll] which you have cho[sen] for those who love you, and for those who keep your precep[ts ...] *22* in your presence [for ev]er. [May ... not] associate with the spirit of your servant or with all [his] works [...] *23* [...] May no affliction [come] upon him which would let him fall away

ואל י[היה] לפניו כול נגע מכשול מחוקי בריתך כי[...] 24 פניך ואד[עה כי

אתה אל חנון] ורחום א[רו]ך א[פ]ים ורב חסד ואמת ונושא פשע [...]

25 ונחם על [רעת אוהביך] ושומרי מצו[תי]ך ה[שבים אליך באמונה ולב

שלם [...] 26 לעובדך [ולעשות] טוב בעיניך אל תשב פני עבדך [וא[ל]

תדח] בן אמתך [...] 27 [...]ה ואני על דבריך קרב[תי ...] 28 [...].[...].[...]

Col. IX   1 [...] ... 2 [...].[...].[...]... 3 עולם [...].[...].[...] 4 בם

ומש[פט ...]... כיא[...]. ומקה[...]... 5 ומעין הגב[ורה ...]גדול העצה

[...] אין מספר וקנאתך[ה] [...]... 6 לפני [...]... וארוך אפים במשפ[ט ואתה

צדקתה בכל מעשיכה 7 ובחכמתכ[ה] ה[כינותה ...]עולם ובטרם בראתם

ידעתה {כול} מעשיהם 8 לעולמי עד [מבלעדיכה לא] יעשה כול ולא יודע

בלוא רצונכה אתה יצרתה 9 כול רוח ו.[...] ומשפט לכול מעשיהם vacat

ואתה נטיתה שמים 10 לכבודכה כול [אשר בם ה]כינותה לרצונכה

ורוחות עוז לחוקיהם בטרם 11 היותם למלאכי ק[ודש ...] לרוחות עולם

בממשלותם מאורות לרזיהם 12 כוכבים לנתיבות[ם] וכול רוחות סערה[

למשאם זקים וברקים לעבודתם ואוצרות 13 מחשבת לחפציה[ם ...

לרזיהם vacat

אתה בראתה ארץ בכוחכה 14 ימים ותהומות ...[...].[...]ביהם הכינותה

בחוכמתכה וכ'ל אשר בם 15 תכנתה לרצונכ[ה ...] לרוח אדם אשר יצרת

בתבל לכ'ל ימי עולם 16 ודורות נצח למ[...]ל' ובקציהם פלגתה עבודתם

בכול דוריהם ומש[פ]ט 17 במועדיה לממשל[...]... לדור ודור ופקודת

שלומם עם 18 <עם> כול נגעיהם [...]ה ותפלג'ה' לכול צאצאיהם למספר

דורות עולם 19 ולכול שני נצח .[...]ה ובחכמת דעתכה הכ[י]נותה

תע[ו]דתם בטרם 20 היותם ועל פי רצ[ו]נכה יה[י]ה כול ומבלעדיך לא

יעשה vacat

21 אלה ידעתי מבינתכה כיא גליתה אוזני לרזי פלא ואני יצר החמר

ומגבל המים 22 סוד הערוה ומקור הנדה כור העוון ומבנה החטאה רוח

התועה ונעוה בלא 23 בינה ונבעתה במשפטי צדק מה אדבר בלא נודע

ואשמיעה בלא סופר הכול 24 חקוק לפניכה בחרת זכרון לכול קצי נצח

from the precepts of your covenant! For [...] *24* your face. And I kn[ow that you are a lenient] and compassionate [God,] s[lo]w to a[ng]er, full of kindness and of truth, who forgives offence [...] *25* and has pity on the [evil of those who love you] and keep [your] prec[epts, those] who turn to you with trust and a perfect heart [...] *26* to serve you [and to do what] is good in your eyes. Do not turn your face away from your servant, [do not reject] the son of [your] maidservant! [...] *27* [...] And I, through your words [I] have approached [...] *28* [...] ... [...]

Col. IX (Sukenik *col.* I; = 4Q432 2)   *1-2* ... [...] *3* eternal [...] *4* by them, and the judg[ment ...] for [...] ... *5* source of the po[wer ...] great of counsel [...] without number, and your zeal *6* before [...] and slow to anger in the judgme[nt and you] are just in all your works. *7* In your wisdom [you] es[tablished] eternal [...]; before creating them you know {all} their deeds *8* for ever and ever. [Without you no]thing is done, and nothing is known without your will. You have fashioned *9* every spirit and [...] and the judgment of all their deeds. *Blank* You have stretched out the heavens *10* for your glory. Everything [which it contains] you have [es]tablished according to your will, and powerful spirits, according to their laws, before *11* they became h[oly] angels [...] eternal spirits in their realms: luminaries according to their mysteries, *12* stars according to [their] circuits, [all the stormy winds] according to their roles, lightning and thunder according to their duties and well-designed storehouses *13* according to th[eir] purposes [...] according to their secrets. *Blank* You have created the earth with your strength, *14* seas and deeps [...] you have founded their [...] with your wisdom, everything which is in them *15* you have determined according to your will. [...] for the spirit of man which you created on earth for all days everlasting *16* and unceasing generations, so that [...] and in their seasons. You have shared out their tasks in all their generations and the regulation *17* at its predetermined times to rule [...] generation after generation and the visitation of their retribution with *18* <with> all their afflictions. [...] and you will share it out among all their offspring according to the number of their eternal generations *19* and for all years continuously. [...] And in the wisdom of your knowledge you have determined their course before *20* they came to exist. And in accordance with [your] wi[ll] everything happens, and without you nothing occurs. *Blank* *21* These things I know through your knowledge, for you opened my ears to wondrous mysteries although I am a creature of clay, fashioned with water, *22* a foundation of shame and a source of impurity, an oven of iniquity and a building of sin, a spirit of error and depravity without *23* knowledge, terrified by your just judgments. What can I say which is not known? Or declare which has not been told? Everything *24* has been engraved before you with the stylus of remembrance for all the incessant periods and the cycles of the number of

ותקופות מספר שני עולם בכול מועדיהם   25   ולוא נסתרו ולא נעדרו

מלפניכה ומה יספר אנוש חטאתו ומה יוכיח על עוונותיו   26   ומה ישיב ע'ל

{כו}על משפט הצדק   *vacat*

לכה אתה ⁴⁼ הדעות כול מעשי הצדקה   27   וסוד האמת ולבני האדם

עבודת העוון ומעשי הרמיה   *vacat*

אתה בראתה   28   רוח בלשון ותדע דבריה ותכן פרי שפתים בטרם

היותם ותשם דברים על קו   29   ומבע רוח שפתים במדה ותוצא קוים

לרזיהם ומבעי רוחות לחשבונם להודיע   30   כבודכה ולספר נפלאותיכה

בכול מעשי אמתכה ומ[שפטי צ]דקכה ולהלל שמכה   31   בפה כול וידעוכה

לפי שכלם וברכוכה לעולמי[ם עד]   *vacat*

ואתה ברחמיכה   32   וגדול חסדיכה חזקתה רוח אנוש לפני

נגע...[...]טהרתה מרוב עוון   33   לספר נפלאותיכה לנגד כול מעשיכה

vacat

ו[אגידה בקהל פ]תיים משפטי נגיעי   34   ולבני אנוש כול נפלאותיכה

אשר הגברתה [...] ... *vacat*

שמעו   35   חכמים ושחי דעת ונמהרים והיו ליצר סמוך [...]   הוסיפו

ערמה   36   צדיקים השביתו עולה וכול תמימי דרך החזיק[ו ...]. עני האריכו

37   אפים ואל תמאסו בכו[ל ... ואו]ילי לב לא יבינו   38   אלה [...]...[...]

39   [וער]יצים יחרוק[ו שנים ...]

[...] כול מעשי   3   [...]...[...]   2   [...]...[...]   1   *Col. x*   ... [... ישרתה בלבבי]

עולה ...[...]... בכל [...].   4   ... ו]תשם [אמת נגד עיני ומוכי]חי {אמת}צ̇ד̇ק̇ בכל [...].

5   [...] מחץ מכ[ת]י[ם ...]ומשמיעי שמחה לאבל יג[וני]   6   [מבשר

ש]לום לכול הוות שמוע]ה ... [...] חזקים למוס לבבי ומאמצי [כוח]   7   לפני

[נג]ע ותתן מענה לשון לע[רו]ל] שפתי ותסמוך נפשי בחזוק מותנים

8   ואמוץ כוח ותעמד פעמי בגבול רשעה ואהיה פח לפושעים ומרפא לכול

9   שבי פשע ערמה לפתיים ויצר סמוך לכול נמהרי לב ותשימני חרפה

10   וקלס לבוגדים סוד אמת ובינה לישרי דרך   *vacat*

ואהיה על עון רשעים   11   דבה בשפת עריצים לצים יחרוקו שנים ואני

everlasting years in all their predetermined times, *25* and they will not be hidden, and will not be lacking from before you. How will a man count his sin? How will he defend his iniquities? *26* How will an unjust respond to a just judgment? *Blank* To you, you, God of knowledge, belong all the works of justice *27* and the foundation of truth; but to the sons of Adam belongs the service of iniquity and the deeds of deception. *Blank* You created *28* breath on the tongue, you know its words, you instituted the fruits of the lips, before they came to be; you placed words to the rhythm, *29* and the puff of breath from the lips to the beat; you make the rhythms emerge according to their mysteries and the puffs of breaths by their measures, to show *30* your glory and recount your wonders, in all the deeds of your truth and your just judg[ments], to praise your name *31* through the mouth of all. And they will know you according to their intellect and they will bless you for [everlasting] centuries. *Blank* And you, in your compassion, *32* and in the greatness of your kindness, have strengthened the spirit of man against affliction [...] you have purified from the abundance of iniquity *33* so that he can recount your wonders before all your creatures. *Blank* [I want to report in the assembly of the sim]ple folk the judgments of my afflictions, *34* and to the sons of man, all the wonders which you have made great [...] *Blank* Listen, *35* wise men, and you, meditating on knowledge, and (you) impetuous ones, be of staunch purpose! [...] increase in cleverness! *36* Just men, finish with injustice! And all of you, of perfect way, strengthen [...] the poor! Be slow *37* to anger, and do not despise an[y ... the fool]ish of heart do not understand *38* these matters [...] *39* [and the bru]tal will grind [their teeth ...]

Col. x (Sukenik *col.* ɪɪ; = 4Q428 20; 4Q432 3)   *1-2* [...] ... [...] *3* [... you have straightened in my heart] all the deeds of injustice [...] *4* [... and] you place [truth before my eyes and the reprove]rs {of truth} /of justice/ in all [...] *5* [...] smitten by bl[ows of the comforters ...] who announce joy for [my de]ep sorrow, *6* [proclaiming pe]ace to all disaster [...] the strong, to weaken my heart, and those who gain [strength] *7* before the [afflic]tion. But you give a reply of the tongue to my uncir[cumcised] lips, you support my soul by strengthening my loins *8* and increasing my strength; you made my steps sturdy on the frontier of evil, so that I became a trap for offenders, but a medicine for all *9* who turn away from offence, a wit for simple folk, and a staunch purpose for the timorous at heart. You have set me as a reproach *10* and a mockery of traitors, a foundation of truth and of knowledge for those on the straight path. *Blank* Because of the iniquity of the wicked I have become *11* the target of slander on the lips of violent men, the scoffers ground their teeth. I

הייתי נגינה לפושעים 12 ועלי קהלת רשעים תתרגש ויהמו כנחשולי ימים
בהרגש גליהם רפש 13 וטיט יגרושו ותשימני נס לבחירי צדק ומליץ דעת
ברזי פלא *vacat*

לבחון 14 [אנשי] אמת ולנסות אוהבי מוסר ואהיה איש ריב למליצי
תעות [ובעל] 15 [של]ום לכול חוזי נכוחות ואהיה לרוח קנאה לנגד דורשי
חל[קות] 16 [כול] אנשי רמיה עלי יהמו כקול המון מים רבים ומזמות
בליעל [כול] 17 מ[ה]שבותם ויהפוכו לשוחה חיי גבר אשר הכינותה
בפי(ו) ותלמד{נ}ו בינה 18 שמתה בלבבו לפתוח מקור דעת לכול מבינים
וימירום בערול שפה 19 ולשון אחרת לעם לא בינות להלבט במשגתם
vacat

vacat 20 אודכה אדוני כי שמתה נפשי בצרור החיים 21 ותשוך בעדי
מכול מוקשי שחת כ[י] עריצים בקשו נפשי בתומכי 22 בבריתכה והמה
סוד שוא ועדת בליעל לא ידעו כיא מאתכה מעמדי 23 ובחסדיכה תושיע
נפשי כיא מאתכה מצעדי והמה מ{...}אתכה גרו 24 על נפשי בעבור
הכבדכה במשפט רשעים והגבירכה בי נגד בני 25 אדם כיא בחסדכה עמדי
ואני אמרתי חנו עלי גבורים סביבים בכל 26 כלי מלחמותם ויפרו חצים
לאין מרפא ולהוב חנית באש (כאש) אוכלת עצים 27 וכהמון מים רבים
שאון קולם נפץ זרם להשחית רבים למזורות יבקעו 28 אפעה ושוא
בהתרומם גליהם ואני במוס לבי כמים ותחזק נפשי בבריתך 29 והם רשת
פרשו לי תלכוד רגלם ופחים טמנו לנפשי נפלו בם *vacat* ורגלי עמדה
במישור 30 מקהלם אברכה שמכה *vacat*

31 אודכה אדוני כיא עינכה על[דה] על נפשי ותצילני מקנאת מליצי כזב
32 ומעדת דורשי חלקות פדית[ה] נפש אביון אשר חשבו להתם דמו
33 לשפוך על עבודתכה אפס כי [לא יד]עו כי מאתך מצעדי וישימוני לבוז
34 וחרפה בפי כל דורשי רמיה *vacat* ואתה עזרתה נפש עני ורש
35 מיד חזק ממנו ותפד נפשי מיד אדירים ובגדפותם לא החתיתני

have become a laughing-stock for offenders, *12* and the assembly of the wicked is roused against me; they roar like the breakers of the seas: when their waves beat they spew out slime *13* and mud. But you have set me like a banner for the elect of justice, like a knowledgeable mediator of secret wonders. *Blank* To put to the test *14* [the men of] truth, to refine those who love learning. I have become a man of contention to the mediators of error, [but a man of] *15* [pea]ce to all who view truth. I have turned into an ardent spirit against all the seekers of flat[tering things.] *16* [All] men of deceit mutter against me like the sound of the din of turbulent waters; devilish schemes are [all] *17* their thoughts. They throw into the grave the life of the man in whom's mouth you have established and imparted understanding. *18* You placed in his heart to open the source of knowledge for all those who understand. But they have changed them for an uncircumcised lip *19* and a weird tongue of a people without understanding, and so they will be ruined by their mistake. *Blank*

20 Blank I give you thanks, Lord, because you put me in the bundle of the living *21* and have protected me from all the traps of the pit, for vicious men have sought my soul when I relied *22* on your covenant. They are a council of futility, an assembly of Belial. They do not know that because of you I stand firm *23* and that by your kindness you save my life, because from you come my steps. And they, because of {...} you, they attack *24* my life, so that you will be honoured by the judgment of the wicked, and you will make yourself great through me before the sons of *25* Adam because through your kindness I stand firm. I thought: heroes have set up camp against me, surrounding with all *26* their weapons of war; they loose off arrows without any cure; a spear-head, like fire which consumes trees. *27* Like the din of turbulent water is the roar of their voices, like a hurricane storm which destroys many. Right up to the stars burst *28* emptiness and deceit when their waves heave upwards. But I, even when my heart turned to water, my soul held steadfast to your covenant. *29* But they, the net which they spread for me, entangled their own feet, in the traps they hid for my life, they have fallen. *Blank* «My foot remains on firm ground, *30* from their assembly I shall bless your Name». *Blank*

31 I give you thanks, Lord, for your eye keeps [firm] over me. You have freed me from the zeal of the mediators of deceit, *32* from the congregation of the seekers of flattering things. You have freed the life of the poor person which they thought to finish off by pouring out his blood *33* because he was at your service. But they did [not kn]ow that my steps come from you. They have put me as a mockery *34* and a reproof in the mouth of all who search deceit. *Blank* But you, my God, have freed the soul of the poor and needy *35* from the hand of someone stronger than him; from the hand of the powerful you have saved my

36 לעזוב עבודתכה מפחד הוות רשעים ולהמיר בהולל יצר סמוך אשר

37 ה[...]מו חוקים ובתעודות נתנו לאזנים 38 [...].חת לכול צאצאי[הם]

39 [...] בלמודיכה ...

2-1 [...]...[...] 3 [...]לי האירותה פᵃ..."[...] 4 [...] לכה

בכבוד עולם עם כול [...] 5 [...]. פיכה ותצילני מ[...ומ]

6 *vacat* עתה נפש[י ...].. יחשובוני וישימו נפש[י] כאוניה ב[מ]צולות ים

7 וכעיר מבצר מלפני[אויביה]אהיה בצוקה כמו אשת לדה מבכריה כיא

נהפכו ציריה 8 וחבל נמרץ על משבריה להחיל בכור הריה כיא באו בנים

עד משברי מות 9 והרית גבר הצרה בחבליה כיא במשברי מות תמליט זכר

ובחבלי שאול יגיח 10 מכור הריה פלא יועץ עם גבורתו ויפלט גבר

ממשברים בהריתו החישו כול 11 משברים וחבל<י> (נ)מרץ במולדיהם

ופלצות להורותם ובמולדיו יהפכו כול צירים 12 בכור הריה והרית אפעה

לחבל נמרץ ומשברי שחת לכול מעשי פלצות ויריעו 13 אושי קיר כאוניה

על פני מים ויהמו שחקים בקול המון ויושבי עפר 14 כיורדי ימים נבעתים

מהמון מים וחכמיהᵐ למו כמלחים במצולות כי תתבלע 15 כול חכמתם

בהמות ימים ברתוח תהומות על נבוכי מים ויתרגשו לרום גלים

16 ומשברי מים בהמון קולם ובהתרגשם יפתחו ש[או]ל[ו]א[בד]ון כו]ל

חצי שחת 17 עם מצעדם לתהום ישמיעו קולם ויפתחו שערי [שאול לכול]

מעשי אפעה 18 ויסגרו דלתי שחת בעד הרית עול ובריחי עולם בעד כול

רוחי אפעה *vacat*

19 *vacat* אודכה אדוני כי פדיתה נפשי משחת ומשאול אבדון

20 העליתני לרום עולם ואתהלכה במישור לאין חקר ואדעה כיא יש מקוה

לאשר 21 יצרתה מעפר לסוד עולם ורוח נעוה טהרתה מפשע רב להתיצב

במעמד עם 22 צבא קודשים ולבוא ביחד עם עדת בני שמים ותפל לאיש

גורל עולם עם רוחות 23 דעת להלל שמכה ביחד רנה ולספר נפלאותיכה

soul, and at their taunts you have not let me lose heart *36* so as to desert your
service from fear of destruction by the wicked and exchange a firm purpose
for follies which *37* [...] the precepts, and by attestations given to (their) ears
38 [...] to all [their] offspring *39* [...] among your followers.

Col. XI (Sukenik *col.* III + *frag.* 25; = 4Q428 2 - 3; 4Q432 4 I - III)   *1-2* [...] ...
[...] *3* [...] you have made /my face/ shine [...] *4* [...] to you, with everlasting
glory, together with all [...] *5* [...] your mouth, and you have freed me from
[...] and from [...] *6 Blank* Now, [my] soul [...] they have considered me, and
have set [my] soul like a boat in the [de]pths of the sea, *7* like a fortified city
positioned opposite [its enemies]. I was in distress like a woman giving birth
the first time when her labour-pains come on her *8* and a pang racks the mouth
of her womb to begin the birth in the «crucible» of the pregnant woman. For
children come through the breakers of death *9* and the woman expectant with
a boy is racked by her pangs, for through the breakers of death she gives birth
to a male, and through the pangs of Sheol there emerges, *10* from the «crucible» of the pregnant woman a wonderful counsellor with his strength, and the
boy is freed from the breakers. In the woman expectant with him rush all
11 the contractions and the racking pain at their birth; terror (seizes) those
expectant with them, and at his birth all the labour-pains come suddenly, *12* in
the «crucible» of the pregnant woman. And she who is pregnant with a serpent is with a racking pang; and the breakers of the pit result in all deeds of
terror. *13* The foundations of the wall shake like a ship on the surface of the
sea, and the clouds thunder with a roar. Those who live on the dust, *14* as well
as those who sail upon the sea are terrified by the din of the water. For them
their wise men are like sailors on the deeps, for swallowed up is *15* all their
wisdom by the roar of the seas. When the deeps boil over the springs of water,
they rush forth to form huge waves, *16* and breakers of water, with clamorous
sound. And when they rush forth, Sh[eo]l [and A]bad[don] open; [al]l the
arrows of the pit *17* make their voice heard while going down to the abyss; and
the gates of [Sheol] open [for all] the deeds of the serpent. *18* And the doors of
the pit close upon the one expectant with injustice, and everlasting bolts upon
all the spirits of the serpent. *Blank*

19 Blank I thank you, Lord, because you saved my life from the pit, and from the
Sheol of Abaddon *20* have lifted me up to an everlasting height, so that I can
walk on a boundless plain. And I know that there is hope for someone *21* you
fashioned out of dust for an everlasting community. The depraved spirit you
have purified from great offence so that he can take a place with *22* the host of
the holy ones, and can enter in communion with the congregation of the sons
of heaven. You cast eternal destiny for man with the spirits of *23* knowledge,

לנגד כול מעשיכה ואני יצר 24 החמר מה אני מגבל במים ולמי נחשבתי
ומה כוח לי כיא התיצבתי בגבול רשעה 25 ועם חלכאים בגורל ותגור נפש
אביון עם מהומות רבה והוות מדהבה עם מצעדי 26 בהפתח כל פחי שחת
ויפרשו כול מצודות רשעה ומכמרת חלכאים על פני מים 27 בהתעופף כול
חצי שחת לאין השב ויורו לאין תקוה בנפול קו על משפט וגורל אף 28 על
נעזבים ומתך חמה על נעלמים וקץ חרון לכול בליעל וחבלי מות אפפו לאין
פלט 29 וילכו נחלי בליעל עֲל כול אגפי רום כאש אוכלת בכול שנאביהם
להתם כול עץ לח 30 ויבש מפלגיהם ותשוט בשביבי להוב עד אפס כול
שותיהם באושי חמר תאוכל 31 וברקוע יבשה יסודי הרים לשרפה
ושורשי חלמיש לנחלי זפת ותאוכל עד תהום 32 רבה ויבקעו לאבדון נחלי
בליעל ויהמו מחשבי תהום בהמון גורשי רֶפֶש וארץ 33 תצרח על ההווה
הנהיה בתבל וכול מחשביה ירועו ויתהוללו כול אשר עליה 34 ויתמוגגו
בהווה גד[ו]לה כיא ירעם אל בהמון כוחו ויהם זבול קודשו באמת
35 כבודו וצבא השמים יתנו בקולם [ו]יתמוגגו וירעדו אושי עולם ומלחמת
גבורי 36 שמים תשוט בתבל ולא תש[וב ע]ד כלה ונחרצה לעד ואפס
כמוה *vacat*

vacat 37 אודכה אדוני כיא הייתה לי לחומת עוז 38 [...] כו[ל משחיתים
וכול [...]... תסתירני מהוות מהומה ... 39 [....].[...] ברי]חי ברזל בל יבוא
[...]... 40 [...]... בסביביה פן [...]...

Col. XII 2-1 [...]...[...] 3 [...]על סלע רגלי ...[...] 4 [...] דרך
עולם ו²נתיבות אשר בחרתה ...[...]

vacat 5 אודכה אדוני כיⁱ האירותה פני לבריתכה ומ[...] 6 [...]
אדורשכה וכשחר נכון לאור[תו]ם הופעתה לי והמה עמכה [...]
7 [...]...רים החליקו למו ומליצי רמיה [ה]תעום וילבטו בלא בינה כיא
[עשו] 8 בהולל מעשיהם כי נמאס(ת)י למו ולא יחשבוני בהגבירכה בי כיⁱ

so that he praises your name in the community of jubilation, and tells of your wonders before all your creatures. But I, a creature of *24* clay, what am I? Mixed with water, as whom shall I be considered? What is my strength? For I find myself at the boundary of wickedness *25* and share the lot of the scoundrels. The soul of a poor person lives amongst great turmoil, and the calamities of hardship are with my footsteps. *26* When all the traps of the pit open, all the snares of wickedness are spread and the nets of the scoundrels are upon the surface of the sea. *27* When all the arrows of the pit fly without return and are shot without hope. When the measuring line falls upon judgment, and the lot of anger *28* on the forsaken and the outpouring of wrath against the hypocrites, and the period of anger against any Belial, and the ropes of death enclose with no escape, *29* then the torrents of Belial will overflow all the high banks like a devouring fire in all their watering channels (?), destroying every tree, green *30* or dry, from their canals. It roams with flames of fire until none of those who drink are left. It consumes the foundations of clay *31* and the tract of dry land; the bases of the mountains does he burn and converts the roots of flint rock into streams of lava. It consumes right to the great deep. *32* The torrents of Belial break into Abaddon. The schemers of the deep howl at the din of those extracting mud. The earth *33* cries out at the calamity which overtakes the world, and all its schemers scream, and all who are upon it go crazy, *34* and melt away in the great calamity. For God will thunder with the roar of his strength, and his holy residence echoes with the truth of *35* his glory, and the host of the heavens adds to their noise, [and] the eternal foundations melt and shake, and the battle of heavenly heroes *36* roams unceas[ingly] over the earth, [un]til the determined eternal unparalleled destruction. *Blank*

37 Blank I give you thanks, Lord, for you are a massive rampart for me *38* [... al]l destroyers and all [...] you hide me from the turbulent calamities ... *40* [...] iron [ba]rs. Not shall enter [...] *41* [...] around it, lest ... [...]

Col. XII (Sukenik *col.* IV + *frag.* 43; = 4Q430 1) *1-2* [...] ... [...] *3* [...] my feet upon a rock [...] *4* [...] eternal path, and /on/ the tracks which you have chosen [...]

5 Blank I give you thanks, Lord, because you have lightened my face for your covenant and *6* [...] I have looked for you. Like perfect dawn you have revealed yourself to me with per[fect] light. But they, your people [...] *7* [...] ... they lure them, and mediators of deceit [mis]direct them, so that they come to ruin without perceiving it. For [they carry out] *8* their deeds in folly. For I have been rejected by them, and they do not esteem me when you made yourself

ידיחני מארצי 9 כצפור מקנה וכול רעי ומודעי נדחו ממני ויחשבוני לכלי

אובד והמה מליצי 10 כזב וחוזי רמיה זממו עלי {בי} בליעל להמיר

תורתכה אשר שננתה בלבבי בחלקות 11 לעמכה ויעצורו משקה דעת

מצמאים ולצמאם ישקום חומץ למע(ן) 12 תעותם להתהולל

במועדיהמ להתפש במצודותם כי אתה אל תנאץ כל מחשבת 13 בליעל

ועצתכה היא תקום ומחשבת לבכה תכון לנצח והמה נעלמים זמות בליעל

14 יחשובו וידרשוכה בלב ולב ולא נכונו באמתכה שורש פורה רוש ולענה

במחשבותם 15 ועם שרירות לבם יתורו וידרשוכה בגלולים ומכשול

עוונם שמו לנגד פניהם ויבאו 16 לדורשכה מפי נביאי כזב מפותי תעות

והם [ב]ל[וע]ג שפה ולשון אחרת ידברו לעמך 17 להולל ברמיה

כול מעשיהם כי לא בחרו בדרך] לב]כה ולא האזינו לדברכה כי אמרו

18 לחזון דעת לא נכון ולדרך לבכה לא היאה כי אתה אל תענה להם

לשופטם 19 בגבורתכ]ה כ]גלוליהם וכרוב פשעיהם למען יתפשו

במחשבותם אשר נזורו מבריתכה 20 ותכרת במ[שפ]ט כול אנשי מרמה

וחוזי תעות לא ימצאו עוד כי אין הולל בכול מעשיך 21 ולא רמיה

[ב]מזמת לבכה ואשר כנפשכה יעמודו לפניכה לעד והולכי בדרך לבכה

22 יכונו לנצח [וא]ני בתומכי בכה אתעודדה ואקומה על מנאצי וידי על כול

בוזי כיא 23 לא יחשבוני ע]ד הגבירכה בי ותופע לי בכוחכה לאורתום

ולא טחתה בבושת פני 24 כול הנדרש]ים] לי הנועדים יⁿ לבריתכה

וישומעוני ההולכים בדרך לבכה ויערוכו לכה 25 בסוד קודשים ותוצא

לנצח משפטם ולמישרים אמת ולא תתעם ביד חלכאים 26 כזומם למו

ותתן מוראם על עמכה ומפץ לכול עמי הארצות להכרית במשפט כול

27 עוברי פיכה ובי האירותה פני רבים ותגבר עד לאין מספר כי הודעתני

ברזי 28 פלאכה ובסוד פלאכה הגברתה עמדי והפלא לנגד רבים בעבור

כבודכה ולהודיע 29 לכול החיים גבורותיכה מי בשר כזאת ומה יצר חמר

great through me; for they drive me from my land *9* like a bird from its nest; all my friends and my acquaintances have been driven away from me, and rank me like a broken jug. But they are mediators of *10* fraud and seers of deceit, they have plotted a devilish thing against me { ... } to change your Law, which you engraved in my heart, for flattering teachings *11* for your people; they have denied the drink of knowledge to the thirsty, but for their thirst they have given them vinegar to drink, to consider *12* their mistake, so they may act like fools in their feasts so they will be caught in their nets. But you, O God, abhor every plan of *13* Belial and your counsel remains, and the plan of your heart persists endlessly. But they, hypocrites, plot intrigues of Belial, *14* they search you with a double heart, and are not firmly based in your truth. A root which produces poison and bitterness is in their thoughts, *15* with stubbornness of heart they inquire, they search for you among the idols, place in front of themselves the stumbling-block of their iniquities, they go *16* to search for you in the mouth of prophets of fraud attracted by delusion. They speak to your people [with] stut[ter]ing lip and weird tongue *17* to convert to folly all their deeds with deceit. For they have not chosen the path of your [heart] nor have they listened to your word. For they said *18* of the vision of knowledge: It is not certain! and of the path of your heart: It is not that! But you, O God, will answer them, judging them *19* with your power [according to] their idols and the abundance of their offences, so that in their plans are caught those who deviate from your covenant. *20* At the ju[dgm]ent you will annihilate all the men of deception, seers of delusion will no longer be found. For there is no folly in any of your acts, *21* and there is no deceit [in] the intentions of your heart. Those who are in harmony with you, will stand in your presence always; those who walk on the path of your heart, *22* will be established permanently. [And I,] when I lean on you, I remain resolute and rise above those who scorn me, and my hands succeed against all those who mock me; for *23* they do not esteem me, even though you exhibit your power in me and reveal yourself in me with your strength as perfect light. You have not covered in disgrace the face of *24* all those sought by me, those who unite /together/ for your covenant. Those who walk on the path of your heart have listened to me, they have aligned themselves before you *25* in the council of the holy ones. You will make their right triumph, and truth leading to justice. You will not let them be misled by the hand of scoundrels *26* as they have schemed against them; instead you will put their fear into your people and the scattering of all the peoples of the lands, to destroy, at the judgment, all *27* who violate your word. Through me you have enlightened the face of the Many, you have increased them, so that they are uncountable, for you have shown me your wondrous mysteries. *28* By your wondrous counsel you have strengthened my position and worked wonders in the presence of the Many on account of your glory, and to show *29* your powerful acts to all living things. What is flesh

להגדיל פלאות והוא בעוון   30 מרחם ועד שבה באשמת מעל ואני ידעתי כי
ל'א לאנוש צדקה ול'א לבן אדם תום   31 דרך לאל עליון כול מעשי צדקה
ודרך אנוש ל'א תכון כי אם ברוח יצר אל לו   32 להתם דרך לבני אדם
למען ידעו כול מעשיו בכוח גבורתו ורוב רחמיו על כול בני   33 רצונו ואני
רעד ורתת אחזוני וכול גרמ'י ירועו וימס לבבי כדונג מ{ל}{פ}ני אש וילכו ברכי
34 כמים מוגרים במורד כי זכרתי אשמותי עם מעל אבותי בקום רשעים על
בריתך   35 וחלכאים על דברכה ואני אמרתי בפשעי נעזבתי מבריתכה
ובזוכרי כוח ידכה עם   36 המון רחמיכה התעודדתי ואקומה ורוחי החזיקה
במעמד לפני נגע כי נשען{ת}'   37 בחסדיכה והמון רחמיכה כי תכפר עוון
ולטה{ר] אנוש מאשמה בצדקתכה   38 ולא לאדם [...]...[עשיתה כי
אתה בראתה צדיק ורשע [...]   39 ...[...] אתחזיקה בבריתכה עד[...]
40 [...]יכה כי אמת אתה וצדק כול] מעשיכה [...

Col. XIII   1 ליום עם חד.[...]   2 סליחותיכה והמון [רחמיכה ...
3 ובדעתי אלה נחמ[תי ...]...[...].   4 על פי רצונכה ובי[ד]כה משפט כולם
vacat

5 אודכה אדוני כי לא עזבתני בגורי בעם נכר[י ... ולא]כאשמתי
6 שפטתני ולא עזבתני בזמות יצרי ותעזור משחת חיי ותתן ...[...]... בתוך
7 לביאים מועדים לבני אשמה אריות שוברי עצם אדירים ושותי ד[ם]
גבורים ותשמני   8 במגור עם דיגים רבים פורשי מכמרת על פני מים
וצידים לבני עולה ושם למשפט   9 יסדתני וסוד אמת אמצתה בלבבי ומזה
ברית לדורשיה ותסגור פי כפירים אשר   10 כחרב שניהם ומתלעותם
כחנית חדה חמת תנינים כול מזמותם לחת{ו}{ף} וירבו ולא   11 פצו עלי
פיהם כי אתה אלי סתרתני נגד בני אדם ותורתכה חבתה ב[י ע]ד קץ
12 הגלות ישעכה לי כי בצרת נפשי לא עזבתני ושועתי שמעתה במרורי
נפשי   13 ודנת יגוני הכרתה באנחתי ותצל נפש{י} עני במעון אריות אשר

compared to this? What creature of clay can do wonders? He is in iniquity
30 from his maternal womb, and in guilt of unfaithfulness right to old age. But
I know that justice does not belong to man nor to a son of Adam a perfect
31 path. To God Most High belong all the acts of justice, and the path of man
is not secure except by the spirit which God creates for him *32* to perfect the
path of the sons of Adam so that all his creatures come to know the strength of
his power and the abundance of his compassion with all the sons of *33* his
approval. And I, dread and dismay have gripped me, all /my bones/ have frac-
tured, my heart has melted like wax in front of the fire, my knees give way
34 like water which flows down a slope, for I have remembered my guilty
deeds with the unfaithfulness of my ancestors, when the wicked rose up
against your covenant *35* and the scoundrels against your word - I thought
«For my offences I have been barred from your covenant». But when I remembered the strength of your hand and *36* the abundance of your compassion I remained resolute and stood up; my spirit kept firmly in place in the
face of affliction. For I leaned *37* on your kindnesses and the abundance of
your compassion. For you atone iniquity and cle[anse] man of his guilt
through your justice. *38* It is not for man […] you made […]. For you created
the just and the wicked […] *39* […] I will hold firm to your covenant until […]
40 […] your […] for you are the truth and all [your deeds] are justice.

Col. XIII (Sukenik *col.* V + *frag.* 29; = 4Q428 4; 4Q429 1 I - IV)   *1* to the day with
[…] *2* your pardons and the abundance of [your compassion …] *3* And when I
knew this [I] gained comfort […] … […] *4* in accordance with your will, and
in your ha[nd] is the judgment of them all. *Blank*

5 I give you thanks, Lord, because you did not desert me when I stayed among a
for[eign] people [… and not] according to my guilt *6* did you judge me, nor
did you abandon me to the plottings of my inclination but you saved my life
from the pit. You gave […] among *7* lions, appointed for the sons of guilt, lions
which grind the bones of strong men, and drink the bl[ood] of heroes. You
made my *8* lodging with many fishermen, those who spread the net upon the
surface of the water, those who go hunting the sons of injustice. And there you
established me for the judgment, *9* and strengthened in my heart the foundation of truth. The covenant, therefore, for those searching for it. You closed the
mouth of the lion cubs, whose *10* teeth are like a sword, whose fangs are like a
sharpened spear. Vipers' venom is all their scheming to snatch away. They lay
in wait, but did not *11* open their mouths against me. For you, my God, hid me
from the sons of Adam, concealed your law in [me, un]til the moment of
12 revealing your salvation to me. For in the distress of my soul you did not
desert me, you heard my call in the bitterness of my soul, *13* you paid attention
to the outcry of my pain in my complaint and saved {my} the soul of the poor

שננו כחרב לשונם   14   ואתה אלי סגרתה בעד {ל}ש{ו}נ{מ}יהם פן יטרפו
נפשי} עני ורש ותוסף לשונם   15   כחרב אל תערה בלוא{ כר]תה נפש
עבדכה ולמען הגבירכה ב' לנגד בני אדם הפלתה   16   באביון ותביאהו
במצר]ף כז]הב במעשי אש וככסף מזוקק בכור נופחים לטהר שבעתים
17   וימהרו עלי רשעי עמים במצוקותם וכול היום ידכאו נפשי   *vacat*
18   ואתה אלי תשיב {נפשי} סערה לדממה ונפש אביון פלטתה כ...[...].
טרף מכח   19   אריות   *vacat*

20   {אודכה} ברוך אתה אדוני כי לא עזבתה יתום ולא בזיתה רש כי
גבורתכה [לאין חק]ר וכבודכה   21   לאין מדה וגבורי פלא משר]י{תיכה
ועם ענוים בטאטאי רגלי]כה ...[עם נמהרי   22   צדק להעלות משאון יחד
כול {...} אביוני חסד ואני הייתי על ע]ו{ן מ]דני לריב   23   ומדנים לרעי
קנאה ואף לבאי בריתי ורגן ותלונה לכול נועדי ג]ם או{כלי לחמי   24   עלי
הגדילו עקב ויליזו עלי בשפת עול כול נצמדי סודי ואנשי [עד]תי סוררים
25   ומלינים סביב וברז חבתה בי ילכו רכיל לבני הוות ובעבור הגד[דר]כי
ולמען   26   אשמתם סתרת מעין בינה וסוד אמת והמה הוות לבם יחשובו
וא]נשי ב]ליעל פתחו   27   לשון שקר כחמת תנינים פורחת לקצים וכזוחל[ֿ
עפר יורו לחתו]ף מבלגות} פתנים   28   לאין חבר ותהי לכאיב אנוש ונגע
נמאר בתכמי עבדכה להכשיל [רוח] ולהתם   29   כוח לבלתי החזק מעמד
וישיגוני במצרים לאין מנוס ולא ...   30   בכנור ריבי ובנגינות יחד
תלונתם עם שאה ומשואה זלעופות אחזוני וחבלים כצירי   31   יולדה ויהם
עלי לבי קדרות לבשתי ולשוני לח]כי}ך תדבק וסבבוני בהוות לבם ויצרם
32   הופיע לי למרורים ויחשך מאור פני לאפלה והודי נהפך למשחור   *vacat*
ואת אלי   33   מרחב פתחתה בלבבי ויוספוה לצוקה וישוכו בעדי
בצלמות ואוכלה בלחם אנחה   34   ושקוי בדמעות אין כלה כי עששו מכעס

man in the lair of lions, who sharpen their tongue like swords. *14* And you, my God, you closed {their tongue} their teeth so they would not rip up {my} the soul of the poor and wretched; their tongue has been drawn in *15* like a sword into the scabbard, so that it would not [dest]roy the soul of your servant. And to show your greatness /through me/ before the sons of Adam, you did won-ders *16* with the poor, you placed him [like g]old in the cruci[ble] to be worked by fire, and like purified silver in the furnace of the smiths to be refined seven times. *17* The wicked of the nations hustle me with their trials, and the whole day they crush my soul. *Blank 18* But you, my God, have changed {my soul} the storm to a calm and have freed the soul of the poor like [...] prey from the power of *19* lions. *Blank*

20 {I give you thanks} /Blessed are you,/ Lord, because you did not desert the orphan nor have you slighted the wretch. For your might [is unfathom]able and your glory *21* measureless. Wonderful heroes are your attendants, and with the humble ones in the mud before [your] feet [...] with those apprehen-sive *22* of justice, to raise from desolation the community of all {...} the poor of kindness. But I have been the target of sl[ander for my rivals,] cause for quarrel *23* and argument to my neighbours, for jealousy and anger to those who have joined my covenant, for challenge and grumbling to all my follow-ers. Ev[en those who e]at my bread *24* have raised their heel against me; they have mocked me with an unjust tongue all those who had joined my council; the men of my [congrega]tion are stubborn, *25* and mutter round about. And about the mystery which you have concealed in me they go slandering to the sons of destruction. In order to show my [pa]th and because of *26* their guilt you have concealed the source of understanding and the foundation of truth. They plot evil in their heart, m[en of Be]lial have opened *27* a lying tongue, like vipers' venom that spreads to the extremities, like crawlers in the dust they shoot to gra[b,] serpents' [poison], *28* against which there is no incanta-tion. It has become an incurable pain, a wasting disease in the innards of your servant, which makes [the spirit] stagger and makes an end *29* of strength, so that he is unable to remain firm in his place. They have overtaken me in nar-row places where there is no escape, and not .... They announce *30* the charge against me with the harp, their grumblings with verses in harmony, with demolition and destruction. Resentment has taken hold of me and pangs like the labours of *31* a woman giving birth. My heart is in turmoil within me. I have dressed in black and my tongue sticks to {my} palate, because they sur-round me with the calamity of their heart; and their intention *32* appeared to me in bitterness. The light of my face has become gloomy with deep darkness, my countenance has changed into gloom. *Blank* And you, my God, *33* have opened a broad space in my heart but they have increased the narrowness and have wrapped me in darkness. I am eating the bread of weeping, *34* my drink

עיני ונפשי במרורי יום אנחה ויגון   35 יסובבוני ובושת על פנים ויהפך לי

לחמי לריב ושקוי לבעל מדנים ויבוא[ו] בעצמ[י]   36 להכשיל רוח ולכלות

כוח כרזי פשע משנים מעשי אל באשמתם כי נאסר[תי] בעבותים   37 לאין

נתק וזקים ללוא ישוברו וחומת עו[ז יסבני]ובריחי ברזל ודלתי[נחושת

לאין]   38 [פתוח כ]לאי עם תהום נחשב{ת} לאין [...]   39 [נחלי ב]ל[י]על

[...] אפפו נפשי ל[...]

1 ...[...]   2 לבי בנאצות ...[...]   3 והווה לאין חקר וכלה   *Col.* XIV

לאין ...[... ואתה אלי]   4 גליתה אוזני [למו]סר מוכיחי צדק עם [...]

5 מעדת שוא ומסוד חמס ותביאני בעצת [...].   6 ואדעה כי יש מקוה

לשבי פשע ועוזבי חטאה ב[ה...] ולהתהלך   7 בדרך לבכה לאין עול

ואנחמה על המון עם ועל שאון מ[מ]לכות בהאספם [כי יד]עתי אשר

8 תרים למצער מחיה בעמכה ושארית בנחלתכה ותזקקם להטהר מאשמה

vacat

כיא כול   9 מעשיהם באמתכה ובחסדיך תשפטם בהמון רחמים ורוב

סליחה וכפיכה להורותם   10 וכי[ ]שיר אמתכה להכינם בעצתכה לכבודכה

ולמענכה עשי[תה] ל[גד]ל תורה ו[אמת]ל...   11 אנשי עצתכה בתוך בני

אדם לספר לדורות עולם נפלאותיכה ובגבורות[יכה יש]והו (יש]וחח)

12 לאין השבת וידעו כול גוים אמתכה וכול לאומים כבודכה כי הביאותה

[אמתכה וכ]בודכה   13 לכול אנשי עצתכה ובגורל יחד עם מלאכי פנים

ואין מליץ בנים לק[דושיכה ...]...   14 פריו כי ...[...] והם ישובו בפי

כבודכה ויהיו שריכה בגור[ל קדושיכה שורשם]   15 פרח כצי[ץ שדה ע]ד

עולם לג[ד]ל נצר לעופי מטעת עולם ויצל צל על כול ת[בל וענפי]ו   16 עד

שחקי[ם ו]שרשיו עד תהום וכול נהרות עדן [תשקו את ד]ל[י]ותיו והיה

לימים לאין]   17 חקר ויערו על תבל לאין אפס ועד שאול [שורשיה

ות]היה מעין אור למקור   18 עולם לאין הסר בשביבי נוגהו יבערו כול בנ[י

עולה והיה]לאש בוערת בכול אנשי   19 אשמה עד כלה והמה נצמדי

is tears without end. For my eyes are blinded by the grief and my soul by the bitterness of the day. Agony and pain *35* surround me, shame covers my face, my bread has turned into quarrel and my drink into argument. They have entered in [my] bones *36* to make my spirit stagger and make an end of strength in accordance with the mysteries of offence, they who, by their guilt, have altered the deeds of God. For [I] am tied with ropes *37* which can not be untied, with chains which can not be broken; a str[ong] rampart [surrounds me,] iron bars and [bronze] doors [which can not] *38* [be opened]; my [ga]ol is comparable to the deep without there being [...] *39* [The streams of Be]l[i]al surround my soul [...]

Col. XIV (Sukenik *col.* VI + *frag.* 26; = 4Q428 5; 4Q429 2 I - II)   *1* ... [...] *2* my heart. With scorn [...] *3* and calamity without limit and destruction without [... But you, my God,] *4* have opened my ears [to the instruc]tion of those who rebuke with justice, with [...] *5* from the assembly of futility and from the counsel of violence. You have brought me into the council of [...] [...] guilt. *6* And I know that there is hope for whoever turn from offence and relinquish sin [...] to walk *7* on the path of your heart, without injustice. I will take comfort above the noise of the nation and the uproar of ki[ng]doms, when they join together. [For] I [kn]ow that *8* shortly you will raise a survivor among your people, a remnant in your inheritance. You will purify them to cleanse them of guilt. *Blank* For all *9* their deeds are in your truth and in your kindness you judge them with an abundance of compassion and a multitude of forgiveness. According to your mouth you teach them, *10* and according to the correctness of your truth, to establish them in your council for your glory. For your own sake have [you] done (it), to make the law and [truth gre]at, to [...] *11* the men of your council amongst the sons of Adam, to recount to everlasting generations your wonders, that they may contemplate [your] exploits *12* unceasingly, and all the peoples may know your truth and all the nations your glory. For you have brought [your truth and] your [glo]ry *13* to all the men of your council and in the lot, together with the angels of the face, without there being a mediator between [your holy ones ...]... *14* Its fruit, because [...] They will respond to your glorious commands, and they will be your princes in the lo[t of your holy ones. Their root] *15* will sprout like a flo[wer of the field f]or ever, to make a shoot grow in branches of the everlasting plantation so that it covers all the wo[rld] with its shade, [and] its [crown] *16* (reaches) up to the skie[s, and] its roots down to the abyss. All the streams of Eden [will water] its [bra]n[ch]es and they will be [seas without] *17* limits; and its forest will be over the whole world, endless, and as deep as to Sheol [its roots.] The source of light [will] be an eternal spring, *18* inexhaustible, in its shining flames all the son[s of injustice] will burn [and it will be turned] into a fire that singes all the men of *19* guilt until destruction. But those, followers of my

175

תעודתי פותו במל[יצי שקר ...] 20   בעבודת צדק   ואתה אל צויתם להועיל

מדרכיהם בדרך קו[דשכה אשר ילכו] בה וערל וטמא ופריץ   21   בל

יעוברנה ויתמוטטו מדרך לבכה ובהווה [...] יכמוא ויעץ בליעל   22   עם

לבבם [...]... מחשבת רשעה יתגוללו באשמה [והיי]תי כמלח באוניה בזעף

23   ימים גליהם וכול משבריהם עלי המו רוח עועיים [לאין]דממה להשיב

נפש ואין   24   נתיבת לישר דרך על פני מים ויהם תהום לאנחתי ונ[פ]שי

תגיע] עד שערי מות ואהיה   25   כבא בעיר מצור ונעוז בחומה נ{ש}גבה עד

פלט ואשע[ן]באמתכה אלי כי אתה   26   תשים סוד על סלע וכפיס על קו

משפט ומשקלת א[מ]ת ל[נ]טות אבני בחן לבנות   27   עוז ללוא תתזעזע

וכול באיה בל ימוטו כי לא יבוא זר [שע]ריה דלתי מגן לאין   28   מבוא

ובריחי עוז ללוא ישוברו בל יבוא גדוד בכלי מלחמתו עם תום כול ח[רבות]

29   מלחמות רשעה ואז תחיש חרב אל בקץ משפט וכול בני א[מ]תו יעורו

להתם [בני]   30   רשעה וכול בני אשמה לא יהיו עוד וידרוך גבור קשתו

ויפתח מצור [...]   31   למרחב אין קץ ושערי עולם להוציא כלי מלחמות

ויעצו[מ]ו מקצה עד [קצה]   32   ... ואין פלט ליצר אשמה לכלה ירמוסו ואין

שאר[י]ת ואין] תקוה ברוב ...   33   ולכול גבורי מלח'מ'ת אין מנוס   vacat

כי לאל עליון .[...].[...]   34   ושוכבי עפר הרימו תרן ותולעת מתים נשאו

נס לה.[...].[...]   35   במלחמות זדים ומעביר שוט שוטף בל יבוא במבצר

[... ...] 36   [...]... 37   [...]... 38   אמת ... [...]

_____

vacat [...] 1   _Col. xv_

... אני נאלמתי ...   [...] 2   ... זרו]ע נשברת מקניה

ותטבע <ב>בבץ רגלי שעו עיני מראות   3   רע אוזני משמוע דמים השם

לבבי ממחשבת רוע כי בליעל עם הופע יצר   4   הוותם ויריעו כול אושי

מבניתי ועצמי יתפרדו ותכמי עלו כאוניה בזעף   5   חרישית ויהם לבי לכלה

ורוח עועיים תבלעני מהוות פשעם   vacat

_____

vacat 6   אודכה אדוני כי סמכתני בעוזכה ורוח   7   קודשכה הניפותה בי

בל אמוט ותחזקני לפני מלחמות רשעה ובכול הוותם   8   ל[א] החתתה

176

testimony, have allowed themselves to be enticed by those spread[ing lies] …
in the service of justice, *20* even though you, God, commanded them to seek
fortune far from their paths, [walking] on [your] ho[ly] path, on which the
uncircumcised, the unclean, the vicious, *21* do not travel. They have staggered
off the path of your heart and in […] calamity they languish. Belial is the
counsellor *22* of their heart, […] … schemes of wickedness they wallow in
guilt. I [have become] like a sailor in a ship in the raging *23* seas: their waves
and all their breakers roar over me, a whirlwind [without a] lull for taking
breath, without *24* a track to take a straight path over the surface of the water.
The deep thunders at my sigh, [my] so[ul nears] the gates of death. I have
become *25* like someone who enters a fortified city, and finds shelter on the
high wall until salvation. My God, I le[an] on your truth, for you *26* place the
foundation upon rock, and beams to the correct size, and a t[rue] plumb line to
[str]etch out, tested stones to build *27* a fortress which will not shake. All those
who enter there will not stagger, for a foreigner will not penetrate it; its [ga]tes
are armoured doors which do not permit *28* entry, with unbreakable strong
bars. No band at all with its weapons of war will enter, when all the s[words]
29 of the wicked battles will come to an end. Then the sword of God will
pounce in the era of judgment, and all the sons of his t[ru]th will awaken, to
destroy [the sons of] *30* wickedness, and all the sons of guilt will no longer
exist. The hero will draw his bow and break open the encirclement […] *31* into
an endless broad place. (He will open) the everlasting gates to take out weapons of war, and they will be mig[ht]y from one end to [the other.] *32* … There
will be no salvation for a guilty inclination. They will trample to destruction
without there being a rem[nant. There is no] hope in the multitude of … *33* nor
for all the heroes of war will there be shelter. *Blank* For to God Most High
belongs […] *34* Those who lie in the dust will hoist the flag, and the worm of
the dead will raise the banner to […] *35* in the battles of the insolent. He who
makes an overwhelming whip pass, will not invade the fortress. […] *36* […]
for plaster, and as beams not […] *37* … […] *38* the truth … […]

Col. xv (Sukenik *col.* vii; = 1Q35 1; 4Q428 6 - 7)   *1* […] I remain silent … *2* […]
my [ar]m is broken at the elbow, my feet sink in the mud, my eyes are blind
from having seen *3* evil, my ears, through hearing the shedding of blood, my
heart is horrified at evil schemes, for Belial is present when their destructive
inclination becomes apparent. *4* The foundations of my build have crumbled,
my bones have been disjointed, my entrails heave like a boat in the rage of the
storm, *5* my heart pulsates to destruction, a whirlwind swallows me, due to the
destruction of their offence. *Blank*

6 Blank I give you thanks, Lord, because you have sustained me with your
strength, *7* you have spread your holy spirit over me so that I will not stumble,

מבריתכה ותשימני כמגדל עוז כחומה נשגבה ותכן על סלע 9 מבניתי

ואושי עולם לסודי וכול קירוות לחומת בחן ללוא ת{ד}{ז}עזע 10 ואתה אלי

נתת(ן)י לעפים לעצת קודש ות[...]בבריתכה ולשוני כלמודיך 11 ואין פה

לרוח הוות ולא מענה לשון לכול [ב]ני אשמה כי תאלמנה שפתי

12 <שפתי> שקר כי כול גרי למשפט תרשיע להבדיל בי בין צדיק לרשע

13 כי אתה ידעתה כול יצר מעשה וכול מענה לשון הכרתה ותכן לבי

14 [בל]מודיכה ובאמתכה לישר פעמי לנתיבות צדקה להתהלך לפניך

בגבול 15 [חיי]ם לשביל ֗כבוד {וחיים} ושלום לאין ה[ס]ר ולא[להשבת

לנצח *vacat*

16 ואתה ידעתה יצר עבדכה כי לא .[...]נש[ענתי להרים ל[ב]

17 ולהעיז בכוח ומחסי בשר אין לי [...] אין צדקות להנצל מפ[שע]

18 [בל]וא סליחה ואני נשענתי ברו[ב] רחמיכה ובהמון] הסדכה אוחיל

להציץ 19 [מ]טע ולגדל נצר להעיז בכוח ו.[... ב]צדקתכה העמדתני

20 לבריתכה ואתמוכה באמתכה ואת[...] ותשימני אב לבני חסד

21 וכאומן לאנשי מופת ויפצו פה כיונ[ק שדי אמו]וכשעשע עוליל בח֗[ק

22 אומניו ותרם קרני על כול מנאצי ויתפ[צצו ש]ארית אנשי מלחמתי

ובעלי 23 רבי כמוץ לפני רוח וממשלתי על [...]. אתה א[לי]עזרתה נפשי

ותרם קרני 24 למעלה והופעתי בא[ור]שבעתים בא[ור אשר הכ]ינותה

לכבודכה *vacat*

25 כי אתה לי למאור [עו]לם ותכן רגלי במ[ישור]*vacat*

26 *vacat* אוד[כה אדוני] כי השכלתני באמתכה 27 וברזי פלאכה

הודעתני ובחסדיכה לאיש [...] ברוב רחמיכה לנעוי לב 28 מי כמוכה

באלים אדוני ומי כאמתכה ומי יצדק לפניכה בהשפטו ואין 29 להשיב על

תוכחתכה כול רוח ולא יוכל כול צבא להתיצב לפני ח{ן}מתדה וכול בני

30 אמתכה תב֗יא֗ בסליחות לפניכה ל[ט]הרם מפשעיהם ברוב טובכה ובהמון

ר[ח]מיכה 31 להעמידם לפניכה לעולמי עד *vacat*

כי אל עולם אתה וכול דרכיכה יכונו לנצח 32 [נ]צ[ח]ים] ואין זולתכה

you have fortified me against the wars of wickedness, and in all their calami- ties *8* you have n[ot] discouraged (me) from your covenant. You placed me like a sturdy tower, like a high wall, you founded upon rock, *9* my building and everlasting foundations as my base, all my walls are like a tested un- shakeable wall. *10* And you, my God, you have placed «me» for the down- trodden of the holy council; you have […] in your covenant and my tongue is like your disciples. *11* But there is no word for the spirit of destruction, nor is there a reply of the tongue of all the [so]ns of guilt, for silent will be lips of *12* <lips of> deceit. For, at the judgment you pronounce guilty all those who harass me, separating the just from the wicked through me. *13* For you know the inclination of every creature, and scrutinise every reply of the tongue. You establish my heart *14* [with] your [tea]chings and with your truth, to straighten my steps on the paths of justice, to walk in your presence on the frontier *15* of [lif]e along tracks of glory {and life} and peace without e[nd which will ne]ver stop. *Blank 16* And you, you know the inclination of your servant, that I […] do not [re]ly […] uplifting the he[art] *17* and seeking shelter in strength; I do not have the defences of flesh, […] there are no deeds of justice, to be saved from of[fence,] *18* [with]out forgiveness. And I rely on the multi[tude of your compassion] and hope on the [abundance] of your kindness, to make *19* the [planta]tion thrive, and make the shoot grow; to seek refuge in strength and […in] your justice. You have established me *20* for your covenant and I will cling to your truth, and […] You have made me a father for the sons of kindness, *21* like a wet-nurse to the men of portent; they open their mouth like a chi[ld on the breast of its mother,] like a suckling child in the lap of *22* its wet-nurse. You have exalted my horn above all those who denounce me, and sca[ttered is the rem]nant of those who fight me, and those *23* who bring a complaint, like straw in the wind, and my dominion is over … [… You, my Go]d, have saved my life, and lifted my horn *24* up high. I am radiant with sevenfold li[ght,] in the li[ght which] you prepared for your glory. *Blank 25* For you are my [ever]lasting luminary, and have established my foot on the le[vel ground]. *Blank*

26 Blank I give [you] thanks, [Lord,] because you have taught me your truth, *27* you have made me know your wonderful mysteries, your kindness towards […] man, with the abundance of your compassion with the depraved of heart. *28* Who is like you, Lord, among the gods? Who is like your truth? Who is just before you when he goes to court? No *29* spirit can reply to your reproach, no /host/ can stand up against your anger. All the sons of *30* your truth /you bring/ to forgiveness in your presence, you pu[ri]fy them from their offences by the greatness of your goodness, and by the abundance of your com[pas]sion, *31* to make them stand in your presence, for ever and ever. *Blank* For you are an eternal God and all your paths remain from eternity *32* [to e]ter[nity.] And

vacat ם[י]ל[הגדו] 33   ומה הוא איש תהו ובעל הבל להתבונן במעשי פלאך

34 [אודכ]ה אדוני כי לוא הפלתה גורלי ב‏ᵃדת שו ובסוד נעלמים לא
שמתה חוקי 35 [ותקר]אני לחסדיכה ולסליחו[תיכה הביאותני] ובהמון
רחמיכה לכול משפטי 36 [... הוריתי באשמת מעל ...] עולה ובחיק

[...].ל לא כי לעד תכון צדקתכה 2 [...] [...]...[...] 1   *Col.* XVI
vacat [דרכי ... ‏תה] 3

4 [אוד]כה אדוני [כי נתתני במקור נוזלים ביבשה ומבוע מים בארץ ציה
ומשקי 5 [...] גן [...] ... מטע ברוש ותדהר עם תאשור יחד לכבודכה עצי
6 חיים במעין רז מחובאים בתוך כול עצי מים והיו להפריח נצר למטעת
עולם 7 להשריש טרם יפריחו ושורשיהם ליוב[ל/ל] ישלחו ויפתח למים
חיים <ו>גזעו 8 ויהי למקור עולם ובנצר עליו ירעו כול [חי]ת יער ומרמס
גזועו לכל עוברי 9 דרך ודליתו לכל עוף כנף וירמו עליו כול ע[צי] מים כי
במטעתם יתשגשגו 10 ואל יובל לא ישלחו שורש ומפריח נצר ק[ו]דש
למטעת אמת סותר בלוא 11 נחשב ובלא נודע חותם רזו *vacat*
ואתה] א[ל שכתה בעד פריו ברז גבורי כוח 12 ורוחות קודש ולהט אש
מתהפכת בל י[בוא ב]מעין חיים ועם עצי עולם 13 לא ישתה מי קודש בל
ינובב פריו עם [...]ע שחקים כי ראה בלא הכיר 14 ויחשוב בלא האמין
למקור חיים ויתן י.[...].[...]...ח עולם ואני הייתי ל[ב]זא{ו}י ‏להרות 15 שוטפים
כי גרשו עלי רפשם *vacat*
16 ואתה אלי שמתה בפי כיורה גשם לכול [...] ומבוע מים חיים ולא
יכזב לפתוח 17 השמים לא ימישו ויהיו לנחל שוטף ע[ל ...] מים ולימים
לאין ח[קר] 18 פיתאום יביעו מחובאים בסתר [...] ויהיו למי מ[ן... לכול
עץ] 19 לח ויבש מצולה לכול חיה ו.[... כ]עופרת במים אדירי[ם ...
20 ... אש ו‏יבשו ומטע פרי [...]...[...] עולם לעדן כבוד ופר[ח לעולם]
21 ובידי פתחתה מקורם עם ᵐפלגי[ם ...]ם לפנות על קו נכון ומטע

there is no-one apart from you. What is the man of emptiness, or the owner of futility, to understand your wonderful [great] deeds? *33 Blank*

34 [I give you thanks,] Lord, because you did not /make/ my lot /fall/ in the congregation of deceit, nor have you placed my regulation in the council of hypocrites, *35* [but you have cal]led me to your kindness, to [your] forgiveness [you have brought me], and in the abundance of your compassion, to all the judgments of [...] *36* [... I have been cast in guilt of unfaithfulness ...] injustice, and in the lap

Col. XVI (Sukenik *col.* VIII; = 1Q35 2; 4Q428 7) *1* [...] ... [...] *2* [...] your justice is constant for ever, because not belongs [...] *3* [ways of ...] ... *Blank*

4 I give [you] thanks, [Lord,] because you have set me at the source of streams in a dry land, at the spring of water in a parched land, *5* in a garden watered by channels [...] ... a plantation of cypresses and elms, together with cedars, for your glory. Trees of *6* life in the secret source, hidden among all the trees at the water, which shall make a shoot grow in the everlasting plantation, *7* to take root before they grow. Their roots extend to the gul[ly], and its trunk opens to the living waters *8* to be an everlasting spring. On the shoots of its leaves all [the anima]ls of the wood will feed, its trunk will be pasture for all who cross *9* the path, and its leaves for all winged birds. Above it will rise all the tr[ees] at the water for they will grow in their plantation *10* although they do not extend their root to the gully. However, he who causes the holy shoot to grow in the true plantation hides, not *11* considered, nor known, its sealed mystery. *Blank* But you, [O G]od, you protect its fruit with the mystery of powerful heroes *12* and spirits of holiness, so that the flame of the searing fire [will] not [reach] the spring of life, nor with the everlasting trees *13* will it drink the waters of holiness, nor produce its fruit with [...] of the clouds. For it sees, but does not know, *14* notices, but does not believe, in the spring of life, and gives eternal [...] But I had become the mockery of the raging torrents *15* for they threw their mire over me. *Blank 16* But you, my God, you have placed in my mouth as it were an early rain for all [...] and a spring of living water; *17* the skies will not fail to open, they will not stop, but will become a torrent overflowing in[to ...] of water and into the seas, without e[nd.] *18* They will swell suddenly from secret hiding-places, [...] they will become waters of [... for every tree,] *19* green and dry, a marsh for every animal. [...] like lead in powerful waters,[...] *20* ... of fire and dry up. But the plantation of fruit [...] eternal, for the glorious garden and will bear [fruit always.] *21* By my hand you have opened their spring with channels [of water ...] to turn their [...] to the correctly measured position, and the planting of *22* their trees with the plumb-

22 עציהם על משקלת השמש לא[...]נו לפארת כבוד בהניפי יד לעזוק

23 פלגיו יכו שרשיו בצור חלמיש ו[...]. בארץ גזעם ובעת חום יעצור

24 מעוז ואם אשיב יד יהיה כערע]ר בערבה ו[גזעו כחרלים במלחה ופלגיו

25 יעל קוץ ודרדר לשמיר ושית ו[...]שפתו יהפכו כעצי באושים לפני

26 חום יבול עליו ולא נפתח עם מ' עי[ן ...] מגור עם חוליים ומ[וד]ע לב

27 בנגיעים ואהיה כאיש נעזב ביגונ[י]ם [...] אין מעוז לי כי פרח נגעי

28 למרורים וכאיב אנוש לאין עצור [...]מה עלי כיורדי שאול ועם

29 מתים יחפש רוחי כי הגיעו לשחת ח[י]י בתוכ[י] תתעטף נפשי יומם ולילה

30 לאין מנוח ויפרח כאש בוער עצור בע[צ]מי] עד ימימה תואכל

שלו(ה)בתה   31 להתם כוח לקצים ולכלות בשר עד מועדים ויתעופפו עלי

משברים   32 ונפשי עלי תשתוחה לכלה כי נשבת מעוזי מגויתי וינגר כמים

לבי וימס   33 כדונג בשרי ומעוז מותני היה לבהלה ותשבר זרועי מקניה

[ואי]ן להניף יד   34 [רג]לי נלכדה בכבל וילכו כמים ברכי ואין לשלוח

פעם ולא מצעד לקול רגלי   35   ... זרועי רותקו בזקי מכשול ולשון

הגברתה בפ[י] בלא נאספה ואין להדים   36 קול] לש[ון למודי ... לחיות

רוח כושלים ולעות לעאף דבר נאלם כול שפתי [...]   37 [...].בזקי משפט ...

לבי ...[...]... במרורי [...] לבב ...רים ממשל [...]   38 [...]...[...]. התבל ...

39 [...] נאלמו כאין   40 [...] אנוש לא

1 [...]...[...]   2 [...] תנום בלילה [...]   3 [...] לאין   *Col. XVII*

רחמים באף יעורר קנאה וכלה [... אפפוני]   4 משברי מות ושאול על

יצועי ערשי בקינה תשא [...] בקול אנחה   5 עיני כעש בכבשן ודמעתי

כנחלי מים כלו למנוח עיני ו[...]י עמד לי   6 מרחוק וחיי מצד ואני משאה

{א}למשואה וממכאוב לנגע ומחבלים   7 למשברים תשוחח נפשי

בנפלאותיכה ולא הזנחתני בחסדיכה מקץ   8 לקץ תשת[ע]שע נפשי בהמון

רחמיכה ואשיבה למבלעי דבר   9 ולמשתוחיחי בי תוכחת וארשיעה דיני

ומשפטכה אצדיק כי ידעתי   10 באמתכה ואבחרה במשפטי ובנגיעי רציתי

כי יחלתי לחסדיכה ותתן   11 תחנה בפי עבדכה ולא גערתה חיי ושלומי לא

line of the sun, so that [...] with foliage of glory. When I stretch my hand to dig out *23* its ditches, its roots pierce the rock of silex, [...] their trunk into the earth, and in the time of heat it retains *24* its vitality. But if I remove my hand it will be like the acac[ia in the desert,] its trunk like nettles in salt flats, (in) its furrows *25* thorns and reeds shoot up; to brambles and thistles [...] of its banks will turn into sour vines; because of *26* the heat its leaves wither, they do not open in /the water of/ the spr[ing ... (my)] residence is with the sick, my heart kn[ow]s *27* diseases, and I am like a forsaken man in pai[ns ...,] there is no refuge for me. For my disease has increased *28* to bitterness and an incurable pain which does not stop, [...] over me like those who go down to Sheol, and with *29* the dead my spirit hides, because [my] li[fe] has gone down to the pit. [Within me] my soul languishes day and night, *30* without rest. And it grows like a searing fire enclosed in [my] bo[nes] whose flame consumes for days without end, *31* devouring (my) strength by periods, and destroying (my) flesh by seasons. Breakers rush against me, *32* and my soul within me has weakened right to destruction, for my vitality has left my body, my heart pours out like water, *33* my flesh melts like wax, the vitality of my loins has turned into listlessness, my arm is broken at the elbow [with]out my being able to wave my hand, *34* my [fo]ot has been caught in the snare, my knees slide like water, and it is impossible to move one step forward, there is no sound to the tread of my feet, *35* ... my arms are bound by chains which cause stumbling. But you have made the tongue in [my] mouth strong, it cannot be taken away; it is impossible to silence *36* the voice of [the tong]ue of my instruction ... to give life to the spirit of those who stagger, and to support the fatigued with a word. Silent are all the lips of *37* [...] with chains of judgment [...] my heart ... [...] ... in bitterness [...] ... dominion *38* [...] ... [...] the world *39* [...] have been silenced like nothing *40* [...] man not

Col. XVII (Sukenik *col.* IX) *1* [...] ... [...] *2* [...] sleeps at night ... [...] *3* [...] without compassion. In anger his zeal is aroused, and for destruction [...] *4* The breakers of death [surround me,] Sheol is upon my bed, my couch breaks into a lament, [...] a sighing sound; *5* my eyes are like the smoke in an oven, and my tears like streams of water, my eyes yearn for rest and my [...] stands far away from me, *6* and my life at a distance. As for me, from ruin to annihilation, from sickness to disease, from pangs *7* to labours, my soul reflects on your wonders; you, in your kindness, have not rejected me, from one moment *8* to the next my soul delights in the abundance of your compassion. I can give a reply to who wish to devour me *9* and a rebuke to who wish to cast me down. I have pronounced my own verdict as unjust, but your judgment I have pronounced just, for I know *10* your truth. I have chosen my judgment, I have been pleased with my afflictions, because I hope for your kindness. You have placed *11* a plea in the mouth of your servant, you have not threatened

הזנחתה ולא עזבתה   12   תקוותי ולפני נגע העמדתה רוחי כי אתה יסדתה

רוחי ותדע מזמתי   13   ובצוקותי נחמתני ובסליחות אשתעשע ואנחמה על

פשע ראשון   14   ואדעה כ]י[יש מקוה ב]ח[סדיכה ותוחלה ברוב כוחכה כי

לא יצדק   15   כול במ]שפ[טכה ולא יז]כה ב]ר'[בכה אנוש מאנוש יצדק

וגבר] מרעה[ו   16   ישכיל ובשר מיצר]חמר[יכבר ורוח מרוח תגבר

וכגב]ורת[כה אין   17   בכוח ולכבודכה אין]חקר[לחכמתכה אין מדה

ולאמ]ונתכה אי[ן   ...   18   ולכול הנעזב ממנה]...[*vacat*

ואני בכה הצ]...[19   עמדי ולא ה]...[...[...[...] וכזומם לי ת]...] ואם

לבושת פנים]...[...   21   לי ואתה בר]... ולא]תגבר צרי עלי למכשול

ל]...[22   אנשי מלחמ]ה ... בו]שת פנים וכלמה לנרגני בי *vacat*

23   כי אתה אלי ל]מ]...[תריב ריבי כי ברז חכמתכה הוכחתה בי

24   ותחבא אמת לק]ץ[... ל]מועדו ותהי תוכחתכה לי לשמחה וששון

25   ונגיעי למרפא ע]ולם ו...[ ]נצח ובוז צרי לי לכליל כבוד וכשלוני לגבורת

26   עולם כי כש]...[ובכבודכה הופיע אורי כי מאור מחושך   27   האירותה

ל]י ... מח]ץ מכתי ולמכשולי גבורת פלא ורחוב   28   עולם בצרת נפש]י כי

אתה אל]מנוסי משגבי סלע עוזי ומצודתי בכה   29   אחסיה מכול מ]...[לי

לפלט עד עולם *vacat*

כי אתה מאבי   30   ידעתני ומרחם]...[אמי נמלתה עלי ומשדי ה'רותי

רחמיך   31   עלי ובחיק אומנתי]...[ה ומנעורי הופעתה לי בשכל משפטכה

32   ובאמת נכון סמכתני וברוח קודשכה תשעשעני ועד היום]...[...

33   ותוכחת צדקכה עם ...ותי ומשמר שלומכה לפלט נפשי ועם מצעדי

34   רוב סליחות והמון]רח]מים בהשפטכה בי ועד שיבה אתה תכלכלני כיא

35   אבי לא ידעני ואמי עליכה עזבתני כי אתה אב לכול]בנ]י אמתכה ותגל

36   עליהם כמרחמת על עולה וכאומן בחיק תכלכל לכול מעש]י]כה *vacat*

vacat 37

38   ]אודכה אדוני כי ... הגברתה עד אין מספר   39   ]...[שמכה בהפלא

מ]...[40   ... לא]ין השבת   ]...[.   41   ]...[כלו והלל]...[

my life, nor have you removed my well-being, nor have you deserted *12* my expectation; rather, in the face of the affliction you have upheld my spirit, for you have established my spirit and you know my intentions. *13* In my troubles you comfort me, I delight in forgiveness, I regret my former offence. *14* I know th[at] there is hope, thanks to your [ki]ndness, and trust, thanks to the abundance of your strength, for no-one is pronounced just *15* in your ju[dgme]nt, or inno[cent at] your trial; one man may be more just than another man, a guy wiser [than] his [neighbour], *16* flesh may be respected more than something made from [clay,] one spirit more powerful than another spirit, but compared to your mig[ht], no-one *17* is strong, and there is no [limit] to your glory, and to your wisdom there is no measure, and to your fait[hfulness there is n]o …; *18* and anyone which is excluded from it […] *Blank* But in you I […] *19* my position and not […] … […] *20* and as someone who devises against me […] and when for shame of face […] … […] *21* to me, but you [… that not] grows great my enemy against me to make me stumble […] *22* men of war [… sh]ame of face and disgrace for those who plot against me. *Blank 23* For you, my God, […] you argue my case. For in the mystery of your wisdom you have rebuked me, *24* you have hidden the truth till the period of [… till] its ordained time. Your rebuke has been changed into happiness and joy for me, *25* my diseases into ev[erlasting] healing [and] unending […,] the scoffing of my rival into a crown of glory for me, and my weakness into everlasting strength. *26* For … […] and through your glory, my light becomes visible, for from darkness you make a light *27* shine for [me, … the wou]nd inflicted on me, my weakness to wonderful force, *28* the constriction of [my] soul to everlasting expanse. [For you, o God, are] my refuge, my protection, the rock of my strength, my fortress. In you *29* I will be guarded from every […] salvation for me unto eternity. *Blank* For you have known me since my father, *30* from the womb […, … of] my mother you have rendered good to me, from the breasts of her who conceived me your compassion *31* has been upon me, on the lap of my wet-nurse […] from my youth you have shown yourself to me in the intelligence of your judgment, *32* and with certain truth you have supported me. You have delighted me with your holy spirit, and until this very day […] …. *33* Your just rebuke is with my …, your wholesome watch has saved my soul, with my steps *34* there is an abundance of forgiveness and a multitude of [compas]sion when you judge me, until old age you take care of me. For *35* my father did not know me, and my mother abandoned me to you. Because you are father to all the [son]s of your truth. You rejoice *36* in them, like her who loves her child, and like a wet-nurse you take care of all your creatures on (your) lap. *Blank 37 Blank*

38 [I give you thanks Lord, for …] you have enlarged without number *39* […] your name for doing wonders *40* […] unceasingly […] *41* […] … and praise […]

Col. XVIII‏ 1 ‏...[...] נהיה ...[...]...[מזמת לבכה ...[...]   2 ‏...[...]ל ובלוא

רצונכה לא יהיה ולא יתבונן כול בחוכ[מתכה]   3 ‏...[]יכה לא יביט כול ומה

אפהו אדם ואדמה הוא   vacat

[מחמר]   4 ‏קורץ ולעפר תשובתו כי תשכילנו בנפלאות כאלה ובסוד

אמ[תכה]   5 ‏תודיענו   vacat

ואני עפר ואפר מה אזום בלוא חפצתה ומה אתחשב   6 ‏באין רצונכה מה

אתחזק בלא העמדתני ואיכה אכשיל (אשכיל) בלא יצרתה   7 ‏ומה אדבר

בלא פתחתה פי ואיכה אשיב בלוא השכלתני   vacat

8 ‏הנה אתה שר אלים ומלך נכבדים ואדון לכול רוח ומושל בכל מעשה

9 ‏ומבלעדיכה לא יעשה כול ולא יודע בלוא רצונכה ואין זולתך   10 ‏ואין

עמכה בכוח ואין לנגד כבודכה ולגבורתכה אין מחיר ומי   11 ‏בכול מעשי

פלאכה הגדולים יעצור כוח להתיצב לפני כבודכה   12 ‏ומה אפהוא שב

לעפרו כי יעצור [כ]ח רק לכבודכה עשיתה כול אלה

vacat 13

14 ‏ברוך אתה אדוני אל הרחמים [ורב ה]חסד כי הודעתנ[י בא]ל[ה

[ל]ספר]   15 ‏נפלאותכה ולא להס יומם ול[י]לה ...[...]...[...]   16 ‏לחסדכה

בגדול טובכה ור[ב רחמיכה ...[17   ‏כי נשענתי באמתכה[...

18 ‏מצבמ[ו]תכה ובלא ...[...ובלא]גערתכה אין מכשול[ואין]   19 ‏נגע

בלוא ידעתה ו[...]תכה   vacat

20 ‏ואני לפי דעתי באמ[תכה ...   ‏ובהביטי בכבודכה אספרה

21 ‏נפלאותיכה ובהביני ב[... ה]מון רחמיכה ולסליחותיכה   22 ‏אקוה כי

אתה יצרתה ר[וח עבדכה וכרצ]ונכה הכינותני ולא נתתה   23 ‏משעני על

בצע ובהון[... ל]בי ויצר בשר לא שמתה לי מעוז   24 ‏חיל גבורים על רוב

עדנים[...]רוב דגן תירוש ויצהר   25 ‏ויתרוממו במקנה וקנין [... כעץ

ר]ענן על פלגי מים לשת עלה   26 ‏ולהרבות ענף כי בחר...[...] בני]אדם

ולהדשן כול מארץ   27 ‏ולבני אמתכה נתתה שכל[...] עד ולפי דעתם יכבדו

28 ‏איש מרעהו וכן לבן אמ[תכה ...]... הרביתה נחלתו   29 ‏בדעת אמתכה

Col. xvɪɪɪ (Sukenik *col.* x; = 4Q427 3 1)   *1* […] has become […] the plan of your heart […] *2* […] And without your will it shall not be. And no-one understands [your] wis[dom,] *3* your […], no-one contemplates them. What, then, is man? He is nothing but earth. *Blank* [From clay] *4* he is fashioned and to dust he will return. But you teach him about wonders like these and the foundations of [your] tru[th] *5* you show to him. *Blank* I am dust and ashes, what can I plan if you do not wish it? What can I devise *6* without your will? How can I be strong if you do not make me stand? How can I be learned if you do not mould *7* me? What can I say if you do not open my mouth? And how can I answer if you do not give me insight? *Blank 8* See, you are the prince of gods and the king of the glorious ones, lord of every spirit, ruler of every creature. *9* Apart from you nothing happens, and nothing is known without your will. There is no-one besides you, *10* no-one matches your strength, nothing equals your glory, there is no price on your might. And who *11* among all your wonderful great creatures will have the strength to stand before your glory? *12* And what, then, is someone who returns to his dust, to retain [stren]gth? Only for your glory have you done all this. *13 Blank*

14 Blessed are you, Lord, God of compassion [and of abundant] kindness, because you have made [me] know [these] th[ings] so that [I recount] *15* your marvels, and not keep silent day and ni[ght. […] … […] *16* for your kindness in your great goodness and in the abund[ance of your compassion …] *17* for I have leaned on your truth, […] *18* from your will, and without [… and without] your threat there is no fall, [nor is there] *19* an affliction that you do not know, and […] your […] *Blank 20* And I, in accordance with what I know of [your] tru[th …,] in contemplating your glory I will recount *21* your wonders, and in understanding [… the ab]undance of your compassion, and I hope in your forgiveness. *22* Because you have fashioned the sp[irit of your servant and in accordance with] your [wi]ll you have established me. You have not placed *23* my support in robbery, nor in wealth […] my [hea]rt, nor have you placed the inclination of the flesh as my refuge. *24* The strength of heroes lies in the abundance of luxuries, [… the abund]ance of grain, wine, oil; *25* they take pride in their belongings and possessions, [… like a ve]rdant [tree] at the streams of water to produce foliage *26* and increase leaves, for in … [… the sons of] Adam, and that all shall grow fat from the earth. *27* But to the sons of your truth you have given intelligence, […] everlasting; and to the extent of their knowledge they are honoured, *28* the one more than the other. And so for the son of [your] maid-[servant …] you have increased his legacy *29* in the knowledge of your truth, and according to his insight and … […] The soul of

ולפי דעתו ו...[...]נפש עבדכה תעבה הון   30 ובצע וברום עדנים לא י ...

שש לבי בבריתכה ואמתכ[ה]   31 תשעשע נפשי ואפרחה כ[שו]שנה ולבי

נפתח למקור עולם   32 ומשענתי במעוז מרום ו... עמל ויבול כנץ לפני חם

33 ויתהולל לבי בחלחלה ומותני ברעדה ונהמתי עד תהום תבוא

34 ובחדרי שאול תחפש יחד ואפחדה בשומעי משפטיכה עם גבורי

35 כוח וריבכה עם צבא קדושיכ^ה ב[...]שה   36 ומשפט ב[כ]ול מעשיכה

וצדק ...[...].   39-37 [...]... ...

1 בפחד ...[...]ר עמל מעיני ויגונ[י ...[...]   *Col.* xix   2 בהגו

לבי   *vacat*

3 אודכה אלי כי הפלתה עם עפר וביצר חמר הגברתה מודה ^{מודה} ואני

מה כיא   4 [הו]דעתני בסוד אמתכה ותשכילני במעשי פלאכה ותתן בפי

הודות ובלשוני   5 תהלה ומזל שפתי במכון רנה ואזמרה בחסדיכה

ובגבורתכה אשוחחה כול   6 היום תמיד אברכה שמכה ואספרה כבודכה

בתוך בני אדם וברוב טובכה   7 תשתעשע נפשי ואני ידעתי כי אמת פיכה

ובידכה צדקה ובמחשבתכה   8 כול דעה ובכוחכה כול גבורה וכול כבוד

אתכה הוא באפכה כול משפטי נגע   9 ובטובכה רוב סליחות ורחמיכה לכול

בני רצונכה כי הודעתם בסוד אמתכה   10 וברזי פלאכה השכלתם   *vacat*

ולמען כבודכה טהרתה אנוש מפשע להתקדש   11 לכה מכול תועבות

נדה ואשמת מעל להיחד ע[ם] בני אמתך ובגורל עם   12 קדושיכה להרים

מעפר תולעת מתים לסוד ע[ולם] ומרוח נעוה לבינת[כה]   13 ולהתיצב

במעמד לפניכה עם צבא עד ורוחי[...] להתחדש עם כול   14 נהיה ועם

ידעים ביחד רנה   *vacat*

15 *vacat* אודכה אלי ארוממכה צורי ובהפלא[...[16 [...] כי הודעתני

סוד אמת [...]   17 [נפלא]ותי[כ]ה גליתה לי ואביט [...]י חסד ואדעה

18 [כי] לכה הצדק ובחסדיכה יש[...]ה וכלה בלוא רחמיך   19 ואני נפתח

188

your servant loathes wealth *30* and robbery, and in the affluence of luxuries he
does not …. My heart rejoices in your covenant and in your truth *31* my soul is
delighted. I flourish like a [li]ly, my heart opens to an everlasting spring,
32 my support is in the refuge from up high. And … grief, and wilts like a
flower in the heat. *33* My heart fluttered in anxiety, my loins in alarm, my
groaning reached down to the abyss, *34* even searched through the caverns of
Sheol. I was appalled to hear your verdict against the powerful heroes, *35* your
trial against the host of your holy ones. […] *36* and judgment against [a]ll your
creatures, and justice […] *37 -39* […] …

Col. XIX (Sukenik *col.* XI; = 4Q427 1; 4Q428 8 1)   *1* […] in terror […] grief [has
not been hidd]en from my eyes, and [my] sorrow […] … *2* in the meditation of
my heart. *Blank*

3 I give you thanks, my God, because you have done wonders with dust; with the
creature of mud you have acted in a very, /very/ powerful way. And I, what am
I that *4* you have [ta]ught me the basis of your truth, and have instructed me in
your wonderful works? You have put thanksgiving into my mouth, praise on
my tongue, *5* the utterance of my lips in a place of jubilation. I will chant your
kindness, I will ponder your might the whole *6* day, I will bless your name
continually, I will recount your glory among the sons of Adam, and in your
abundant goodness *7* my soul will delight. I know that truth is your mouth,
and justice in your hand, and in your thoughts *8* all knowledge, and in your
might all strength, and all glory is with you. In your wrath are all punishing
judgments, *9* but in your goodness, abundance of forgiveness; and your compassion for all the sons of your approval, for you have taught them the basis of
your truth, *10* and have instructed them in your wonderful mysteries. *Blank* For
the sake of your glory, you have purified man from offence, so that he can
make himself holy *11* for you from every impure abominations and guilt of
unfaithfulness, to become united wi[th] the sons of your truth and in the lot
with *12* your holy ones, to raise the worms of the dead from the dust, to an
ever[lasting] community and from a depraved spirit, to [your] knowledge,
13 so that he can take his place in your presence with the perpetual host and
the spirits […], to renew him with everything *14* that will exist, and with those
who know in a community of jubilation. *Blank*

15 Blank I give you thanks, my God, I exalt you, my rock, and in your working
wonders […] *16* […] because you have made me know the foundation of
truth. […] *17* you have revealed [yo]ur [wonder]s to me, and I have contem-
plated […] of kindness. And I know *18* [that] the justice belongs to you, and in

לי מקור לאבל מרורים [...]לא נסתר עמל מעיני   20 בדעתי יצרי גבר
ותשובת אנוש [אתבונן ואכירה]לחטאה ויגון   21 אשמה ויבואו בלבבי
ויגעו בעצמי ל[...]ים ולהגות הגו   22 יגון ואנחה בכנור קינה לכול אבל יגו[ן
ומספד מרורים עד כלות עולה וא[...] ואין נגע להחלות ואז   23 אזמרה
בכנור ישועות ונבל שמ[חות ותף גי]לה וחליל תהלה לאין   24 השבת ומי
בכול מעשיכה יוכל לספר [...]כה בפי כולם יהולל   25 שמכה לעולמי עד
יברכוכה בפי שכל[ם יום יום לי]עם ישמיעו יחד   26 בקול רנה ואין יגון ואנחה
ועולה [לא תמצא עוד]   27 לכבוד עד ושלום עולם *vacat*

ברוך את[ה אדוני א]שר נתתה לע[בדכה]   28 שכל דעה להבין
בנפלאותיכה ...[...] ל[ספר ברוב חסדיכה   29 ברוך אתה אל הרחמים
והח̇נינה בגדו[ל]כחכה ורוב אמתכה והמו[ן   30 חסדיכה בכול מעשיכה
שמח נפש עבדכה באמתכה וטהרני   31 בצדקתכה כאשר יחלתי לטובכה
ולחסדיכה אקוה ולסליחות[יכ]ה   32 פתחתה משב̇רי וביגוני נחמתני כיא
נש(ע)נתי ברחמיכה ברוך את[ה]   33 אדוני כי אתה פעלתה אלה ותשם בפי
עבדכה הודות ו[...]   34 ותחנה ומענה לשון והכינותה לי פעול[ות   35 [...]
ואעצו[ר כוח   [...] 36 ואתה]   [...   38-37   [...]...

1 [...]תרחב נפשי[...]   2 [...]ה לבטח במעון קו[דש]בשקט
ושלוה   3 [עם רחות עולם]באהלי כבוד וישועה ואהללה שמכה בתוך
יראיכה

4 [למשכיל ה]ו̇דות ותפלה לה̇תנ̇פ̇ל והתחנן תמיד מקץ לקץ עם מבוא
אור   5 לממש̇ל[תו]בתקופות יום לתכונו לחוקות מאור גדול בפנות ערב
ומוצא   6 אור ברשית ממשלת חושך למועד לילה בתקופתו ל̇פ̇נות בוקר
ובקץ   7 האספו א̇ל מ̇עונתו מפני̇ }{אור למוצא לילה ומבוא יומם תמיד בכול

your kindness there is [...] and destruction without your compassion. *19* As for me, a source of bitter sorrow has opened for me, [...] grief has not been hidden from my eyes, *20* when I knew man's inclinations. [I considered] the response of mankind [and paid attention] to sin and the anguish *21* of guilt. These things have entered my heart, they have penetrated my bones, to [...] and to ponder in meditation *22* of anguish. /I have sighed on the harp of lament for every sorrow of anguish,/ with bitter wailing, until iniquity be destroyed, and [...], and there be no more ravaging diseases. Then *23* will I sing with the harp of salvation, the zither of happi[ness, the tambourine of j]oy and the flute of praise, without *24* cease. And who among your creatures can recount your [...]? In the mouth of them all is your name praised, *25* for ever and ever they bless you, to the extent of [their] knowledge, [day after d]ay they proclaim together, *26* with a joyous voice. There will be neither anguish nor sighing, and injustice [will not be found anymore]. But your truth will be displayed *27* for endless glory and eternal peace. *Blank*

Blessed are yo[u, Lord,] because you have given [your] ser[vant] *28* the insight of knowledge to understand your wonders [... to] recount through the abundance of your kindness. *29* Blessed are you, God of compassion and pity, though your grea[t] power, through the greatness of your truth, and through the abunda[nce of] *30* your kindness towards all your creatures. Gladden the soul of your servant with your truth and purify me *31* with your justice, since I have trusted in your goodness and I have hoped in your kindness. By your forgiveness *32* you have freed (me) from my breakdown, in my distress you comforted me, for I have leaned on your compassion. Blessed are yo[u,] *33* Lord, because you have done these things. You have put into the mouth of your servant thanksgiving and [...,] *34* entreaties and the reply of the tongue. For me you have established action[s ...] *35* I have retain[ed the strength ...] *36* And you [...] *37-38* ... [...]

Col. xx (Sukenik *col.* xii + *frag.* 60; = 4Q427 2, 3 ii, 4; = 4Q428 8 ii) *1* [...] you broaden my soul [...] *2* [...] safely in the ho[ly] residence, in rest and at ease, *3* [with the eternal spirits] in the tents of glory and salvation. Among those who fear you, I will praise your name.

4 [For the Instructor, pr]aises and prayer, to bow down and entreat always, from period to period: when the light comes *5* to [its] domini[on] through the course of the day, according to its regulation, in accordance with the laws of the great luminary; at the return of the evening, at the departure of *6* light, when the dominion of the darkness begins; at the appointed moment of the night; through its course towards the return of dawn, at the moment *7* when it withdraws to its quarter before the light; at the departure of night and the coming

8 מולדי עת יסודי קץ ותקופת מועדים בתכונם באותותם לכול 9 ממשלתם
בתכון נאמנה מפי אל ותעודת הווה והיאה תהיה 10 ואין אפס וזולתה לוא
היה ולוא יהיה עוד כי אל ה{ו}{ד}{ו}עות 11 הכינה ואין אחר עמו *vacat*
ואני משכיל ידעתיכה אלי ברוח 12 אשר נתתה בי ונאמנה שמעתי
לסוד פלאכה ברוח ק֯ודשכה 13 [פ]תחתה לתוכי דעת ברז שכלכה ומעין
גבורת[כה ... 14 ...[...]ה לרוב חסד וקנאת כלה והשב[...]
15 [...]והדר כבודכה לאור עול]ם ... [...]ב֯ 16 [...]פחד רשעה ואין רמיה [...]
17 [...]מועדי שממה כיא אין ע[...] 18 [...]אין עוד מדהבה כיא לפני
אפכ]ה [... 19 ...]וחפזו ואין צדיק עמכה [...]. 20 ו[ל]השכיל בכול
רזיכה ולשיב דבר[...] 21 כתוכחתכה ולטובכה יצפו כיᴬ בחס[דכה ...
22 וידעוכה ובקץ כבודכה יגילו ולפי [...].[...] 23 הגשתם ולפי
ממשלתם ישרתוכה למפלג[י]הם ...[...]ב ממכה 24 ולוא לעבור על דברכה
ואני מעפר לקח[תי ומחמר ק]ו֯רצתי 25 למקור נדה וערות קלון מקוי עפר
ומגבל] מים ...[...]ה ומדור 26 חושך ותשובת עפר ליצר חמר בקץ [...].
בעפר 27 אל אשר לקח משם ומה ישיב עפר ואפ]ר ... ומה [יבין
28 [במ]עשיו ומה יתיצב לפני מוכיח בו ...[...]. ק]ודש 29 [...] עולם ומקוי
כבוד ומקור דעת וגבו]רת פל]א והמה לוא 30 [יוכל]ו לספר כול כבודכה
ול֯י֯תיצב לפני אפכה ואין להשיב 31 על תוכחתכה כיא צדקתה ואין
לנגדכה ומה אפהו שב אל עפרו 32 ואני נאלמתי ומה אדבר על זות כדעתי
דברתי֯ מציר֯וק יצר חמר ומה 33 אדבר כיא אם פתחתה פי ואיכה אבין כיא
אם השכלתני ומה או[מר] 34 בלוא גליתה לבי ואיכה אישר דרך כיא אם
הכינות]ה [צע]ד]י ואיכ֯ה] 35 תעמוד פעמ]י כיא אם ת[חזק בכוח ואיכה
אתקומם [כיא אם ... 36 [... וכול]...[...]. 39-37 [...]

[...] 1 *Col.* XXI *top* 2 [...]...[...] [ש]ע ילוד א[שה] [פ]... 3 צדקתכה [...]
[כ]יא ראיתי זות ... 4 איכ]ה אביט בלוא גליתה עיני ואשמעה 5 [בלוא
פתחתה אוזני ...] השם [ל]ל[בבי כיא לערל אוזן נפתח דבר ולב 6 [...]

of day; continually, at all *8* the births of time, the foundations of the period, and the course of seasons in their order, by their signs for all *9* their dominion, in the order established through God's mouth, and through the witness of what is. And this will be, *10* and nothing more; besides it there is no other, nor will there ever be another. For the God of knowledge *11* has established it and no-one else with him. *Blank* And I, the Instructor, have known you, my God, through the spirit *12* which you gave in me, and I have listened loyally to your wonderful secret through your holy spirit. *13* You have [op]ened within me knowledge of the mystery of your wisdom, and the source of [your] power, [...] ... *14* [...] according to the abundance of kindness, and zeal for annihilation and ... [...] *15* [...] and the majesty of your glory to eter[nal] light [...] *16* [...] fear of wickedness and there will be no deceit [...] *17* [...] times appointed for ruin, for not [...] *18* [...] there will be no more annihilation, because before yo[ur] wrath [...] *19* [...] and they fled away. And there is no-one just with you [...] *20* and [to] understand all your mysteries and to be able to answer [...] *21* according to your reproach, and they will be attentive to your goodness because in [your] kindn[ess ...] *22* and they will know you and in the era of your glory they will rejoice, and in accordance with [...] and to the extent of their intellect *23* you bring them near and in accordance with their domain they will serve you, corresponding to [their] division[s ...] from you *24* so as not to transgress your word. And I, from dust [I] have been gathered, [and from clay] I have been [fo]rmed *25* to be a source of impurity, and of vile filth, a pile of dust, mixed with [water, ...] a lodging of *26* darkness. The creature of clay must return to the dust at the time of ... [...] in the dust, *27* to the place from which he has been taken. What will dust and ash[es] reply? [... How] can it understand *28* his [wo]rks? How will he stand up the one who reproaches him? [... h]oliness *29* [...] eternal, storehouse of glory, spring of knowledge, pow[er of wond]er. They [can] not *30* recount all your glory, or stand up before of your anger. There is no reply *31* to your reproach, for you are just and there is no-one before you. What is he (to do that), he who returns to his dust? *32* I have kept silence, for what can I say about this matter? In accordance with my knowledge /I spoke/, spat saliva, one fashioned from clay. What *33* can I say unless you open my mouth? How can I understand unless you teach me? What can I pro[pose] *34* if you do not open my heart? How can I keep a straight path unless [you steady [my] ste[ps? How] *35* can [my] steps stay secure [unless you] strengthen [me] with strength? And how can I rise [unless ...] *36* and everything [...] ... [...] *37-39* ...[...]

Col. XXI *top* (Sukenik *col.* XVIII *16-33* I; = 4Q427 5; 4Q428 10)   *1* [... the of]fence of one born of a wo[man] *2* [...] ... your justice *3* [...]... For I saw this *4* [... Ho]w can I see if you do not open my eyes, and hear *5* [if you do not open my ears? ...] My [he]art is perturbed, because the word has been disclosed to an

ואדעה כיא לכה עשיתה אלה אלי ומה בשר 7 [...ל]הפליא ובמחשבתכה
להגביר ולהכין כול לכבודכה [...] 8 צבא דעת לספר ל^בשר גבור^ות וחוקי
נכונות לילוד 9 [אשה ... הב]יאותה בברית עמכה ותגלה לב עפר להשמר
10 [...] מפחי משפט לעומת רחמיכה ואני יצר 11 [חמר ... אוז]ן ע[פר ולב
האבן למי נחשבתי עד זות כיא 12 [...] נ]תתה באוזן עפר ונהיות עולם
חקותה בלב 13 [האבן ...] השבתה להביא בברית עמכה ולעמוד
14 [לפניכה ...במכו]ן עולם לאור אורתום עד נצח ואין חושך 15 [...
בל]א סוף וקצי שלום לאין ח[קר ...] 16 [...] ואני יצר העפר [...]...[
17 [...]ה אפתח[...]...[...] 18 [...]

1 *Col.* xxi *bottom* [...]...[...] 2 [...]...[...] ... נפתחה דרך ל[...
להתהלך] 3 [ב]נתיבות שלום ועם בשר להפליא] כאלה כיא [...
4 [...]ופעמי על מט(מ)יני פחיה ומפרשי ר[שת ...] 5 אשמר ביצר עפר
מהתפרר ומתוך דונג ב]המס לפני אש [...] 6 [ו]מקוי אפר איכה אעמוד
לפני רוח סוע]רה ואני יכונני ב...[7 וישמורוהו לרזי חפצו כיא הוא ידע
למ[...] 8 [... ע]ד כלה ופח לפח יטמונו צמי רשעה [...] 9 [...]ו בעול
ותמו כול יצר רמיה כיא לא ...[...] 10 [...]לאין ואפס יצר עולה ומעשי
רמיה [...]

11 *vacat* ואני י]צר ה]חמר [...]...[12 [...]ומה יתחזק לכה אתה אל הדעות]
[... 13 [...] עשיתם ומבלעדיכה לוא יעשה [כול ...] 14 [ואני י]צר העפר
ידעתי ברוח אשר נתתה בי ...[...] 15 [...]...מה]... כו]ל עולה ורמיה יגורו
וחדל זדון] [... 16 [...]מעשי נדה לתחלויים ומשפטי נגע וכלה] [...
17 [...]...[...] לכה חמה וקנאה נו]...[18 [...]יצר הח]מר [...

Col. xxii *top* 1-2 [...] 3 [...] 4 [... קו]דש אשר בשמים 5 [...
ג]דול והואה פלא והם לוא יוכלו 6 [... נפלאו]תיכה ולוא יעצורו לדעת
בכול 7 [... ש]ב אל עפרו ואני איש פשע ומגולל 8 [...]אשמת רשעה
ואני בקצי חרון 9 [... לה]תקומם לפני נגעי ולהשמר 10 [... תוד]יעני
אלה כיא יש מקוה לאיש 11 [... ת]געל ואני יצר החמר נשענתי

uncircumcised ear and a […] heart *6* […] And I know that you, my God, have done these things for yourself. And what is flesh *7* [… to] perform wonderfully, and in your plan to strengthen and establish everything for your glory. *8* […] the host of knowledge to proclaim mighty deeds to flesh and solid precepts to the one born of *9* [a woman …] You have [br]ought him into the covenant with you and you have opened the heart of dust so that he will observe *10* […] from the traps of judgment, by reason of your compassion. And I, I am a creature *11* [of clay …an ear of du]st and heart of stone. With whom will I be reckoned until these things? For *12* […] you have [gi]ven to the ear of dust, and you have inscribed for ever what is to happen in the heart of *13* [stone …] you have made stop, to bring into the covenant with you and so that he will stand *14* [in your presence …] in the everlasting residence, in the light of perfect light for ever, without darkness *15* [… witho]ut end, and eras of peace without li[mits …] *16* […] And I, creature of dust […] *17* […] I will open […] *18* […] … […]

Col. XXI *bottom* (Sukenik *frag.* 3; = 4Q427 6; 4Q428 11)   *1* […] … […] *2* […] … […] … the path is open for [… to walk] *3* [in] the tracks of peace, and with flesh to perform wonders [as those, for…] *4* […] my steps over those who hide its traps and who stretch a n[et …] *5* I preserve the one fashioned from dust from being scattered, and in the midst of wax when [it melts before the fire …] *6* [and a] heap of ash, how can I stand firm before the hurric[ane? But me, he establishes me in …] *7* and he protects him for the mysteries of his pleasure. For he knows […] *8* [… un]til destruction. They have hidden trap upon trap, the snares of wickedness […] *9* […] in injustice. And every deceitful creature will come to an end. For […] not *10* […] And there will be no more inclination of injustice nor works of deception. […] *11* […] *Blank* And I, creature of [clay …] *12* […] And how will it appear strong before you? You are the God of knowledge […] *13* […] You have made them, and without you no[thing] is made […] *14* [And I, cr]eature from dust, I have known by the spirit which you have given in me … […] *15* […] … [al]l injustice and deceit will be driven out, and presumption will end […] *16* […] deeds of impurity (lead) to illnesses and judgments of affliction and destruction […] *17* […] … […] Yours is wrath and zeal […] *18* […] creature of c[lay …]

Col. XXII *top* (Sukenik *col.* XVIII *16-33* II + *frags.* 1 1 + 52 ?)   *1-2* […] *3* […] … *4* [… holi]ness which is in heaven *5* [… gr]eat […,] and it is a wonder, but they cannot *6* […] your [wonder]s but they are not able to know all *7* [… go]es back to its dust. I, I am a man of offence, defiled *8* […] wicked guilt. In the periods of anger I *9* [… to] endure before my diseases and to be preserved from *10* [… you] have [ta]ught me these things. For there is hope for man *11* [… you] loathe. And I, creature of clay, I have leaned *12* … […] my God. I

[...]אלי ואדעה כיא אמת 13 פיכה [ודברכה לא ישוב]אחור ואני בקצי
אתמוכה 14 בברי[תכה ...].מה במעמד העמדתני כיא [...] 15 [...]איש
ותשיבהו ובמה ית[...] 16 [...]...[...] עצמתה [...] 17 [...]בושה ללוא
מקו]ה [...] 18 [...] ואני יצר[...]

1 [...] נשמח [...] 2 ונדיבים לוא [.]...[...] 3 לי   *Col.* XXII *middle* (?)
מאז כוננתי ל]...[...] 4 לוא יבוא כי]...[5 כמבניתי ותכמ]י [...]

1 ...פ]לגתה].[...] 2 [...] אשר [...] 3 ... [ע]רב   *Col.* XXII *bottom*
ובוקר עם [.]...[4 ...]מנגי]עי גבר וממכא]וב ...[5 [...]ורת יצפו ועל
משמרתם] ... [6 [...]תג֯ר בכול שטן משחית ומרצ]ח[7 [...]בה ואתה
גליתה אוזני כי]א [... 8 [...]... אנושו ברית פותו בם ויבוא]ו [...
9 [...]כחות לפניכה ואני פחדתי ממשפטכה] [...] 10 [...]יכה ומי יזכה
במשפטכה ומה אפ]ה[ו ...] 11 [...]אני במשפט ושב אל עפרו מה [...]...[...]
12 [...]... פתחתה לבבי לבינתכה ותגל או]זני[13 [...]להשען על טובכה
ויהם לבי ...[...] 14 [...].ולבבי כדונג ימס על פשע וחטאה [...]תימה
ברוך אתה אל הדעות אשר הכינות]ה[16 [...] ותפגע בעבדכה זות
למענכה כיא ידעתי 17 [...]כה א֯ח֯ל֯ בכול היותי ושמכה אברכה תמיד
18 [...]...[...] 19 [...].דכה אל תעזובני בקצי [...]...[...] וכבודכה וטו]בכה]
20 [...] על [...].

1 אורכה ותעמד מא]ורות ... [2 אורכה לאין השב]ת   *Col.* XXIII *top*
[... 3 כיא אתכה אור ל]...[4 ותגל אוזן עפר]...[...].[...] 5 מזמה אשר
הו]דעתה ... [ותאמנה באו]זני[6 עבדכה עד עולם]... ש]מועות פלאכה
להופיע 7 לעיני כול ש]מעי]...[בימין עוזכה לנהל דל]ים[8 בכוח
גבורתכה]...[לשמכה ויתגבר בכבו]דכה[9 אל תשב ידכה ... ל]היות לו
מתחזק בבריתכה 10 ועומד לפניכה ... מק]ור פתחתה בפי עבדכה
ובלשונו 11 חקקתה על קו]... לה]שמיע ליצר מבינתו ולמליץ באלה
12 לעפר כמוני ותפתח מק]ור [להוכיח ליצר חמר דרכו ואשמות ילוד

know that truth *13* is your mouth, [and you do not go] back [on your word]. And I, in my era, will keep *14* [your] covenant [...] You have kept me in my position, for *15* [...] man, and you have made him turn back. Why ... *16* [...] ... [...] you are strong ... *17* [...] shame without hop[e ...] *18* [...] I, creature of [...]

Col. xxii *middle (?)* (Sukenik *frag.* 47)   *1* [...] will rejoice [...] *2* and the volunteers do not [...] *3* for me since the time when I was established for [...] *4* he will not enter, for [...] *5* like my build, and [my] entrails [...]

Col. xxii *bottom* (Sukenik *frag.* 4)   *1* [...] you have [ap]portioned [...] *2* [...] which [...] *3* [... ev]ening and morning with [...] *4* [... from the disea]ses of man and from sick[ness ...] *5* [...] ... they keep watch and at their turns [...] *6* [...] you threaten every destroying and murder[ous] adversary *7* [...] ... And you, you have opened my ear, for [...] *8* [...] ... the men of the covenant have been seduced by them and have entered [...] *9* [...] ... before you. And I, I was in trembling of your judgment [...] *10* [...] your [...] Who will be innocent in your judgment? And what then [...] *11* [...] I in the judgment? He who goes back to his dust, what ... [...] ? *12* [...] you have opened my heart to your knowledge, and you open my ea[rs] *13* [...] to lean on your goodness. But my heart is disturbed ... [...] *14* [...] and my heart melts like wax on account of offence and sin. *15* [...] ... Blessed are you, God of knowledge, who have established *16* [...] this happens to your servant on your account. Because I have known *17* [...] I hope with all that I am. Always I will bless your name *18* [...] ... [...] Do not desert me in the periods of *19* [...] and your glory and [your] good[ness.] *20* [...] upon [...]

Col. xxiii *top* (Sukenik *col.* xviii *1-16* I + *frag.* 57 I + 1 II; = 4Q428 9) *1* your light, and you have established the lum[inaries ...] *2* your light, without cea[se. ...] *3* Because light is with you to [...] *4* You have opened the ear of dust [...] ... *5* the plan [you] have ta[ught ...] ... and have entrusted to the ea[rs of] *6* your servant for ever. [...] your wonderful [pro]nouncements to show yourself *7* to the eyes of all those who listen [...] by your powerful right (hand), to lead the weak *8* by the strength of your might [...] for your name and to show yourself mighty in [your] glo[ry.] *9* Do not withdraw your hand, [... that he may] be one who holds fast to your covenant *10* and stands up before you! [...] You have opened a [spr]ing in the mouth of your servant, on his tongue *11* you have inscribed according to the measuring cord [... to an]nounce from his knowledge to a creature, to mediate these matters *12* to dust such as me. You

13 אשה כמעשיו ולפתח מ[קו]ר אמתכה ליצר אשר סמכתה בעוזכה

14 ל[היות] כאמתכה מבשר[...]. טובכה לבשר ענוים לרוב רחמיכה

15 ...[...] ממקור [...] דכ]אי רוח ואבלים לשמחת עולם 16 [...]...[...]

Col. xxiii bottom 1-2 [...]...[...] 3 [...] ובארצכה ובבני אלים

ובבנ[י ...]...[...] 4 [...] .לכה ולספר כול כבודכה ואני מה כיא מעפר

לוקחתי וא[ל] 5 [עפר שבתי לכ]בודכה עשיתה כול אלה כרוב חסדיכה תן

משמר צדקכה 6 [...]ה תמיד עד פלט ומליצי דעת עם כול צעודי ומוכיחי

אמת 7 [...] כיא מה עפר בכפ[ם מע]שה אפר בידם לוא הנה ואתה

8 [...]חמר ...[...]רצונכה יעל הבנים תבחנני 9 [...]...[...]...[...]ברי ועל

עפר הניפותה רוח 10 [...]בטיט... ב]ני אלים להחיד עם בני שמים

11 [...] ע]ולם ואין תש`בת חושך כיא 12 [...]ומאור גליתה ולוא להשיב

13 [... רוח ק]ודשכה הניפותה לכפר אשמה 14 [...מ]שרתים עם צבאכה

ומתהלכים 15 [...]בות מלפניכה כיא נכונו באמתכה 16 [...]הפלתה אלה

לכבודכה ומציריק 17 [...]... עול יצר נתעב 18 [... יצ]ר נתעב

Col. xxiv top 1 [...]. 2 ...[...]...[יצר בשר 3 ...[...]...[מ]י יועדכה

4 במשפטו[...]. למלאכי 5 ...[...] ורזי פשע להשנות 6 בשר ב]...

[ויעופפו בה כול 7 מלאכי ...[...].מ כעבותי רוח ותכנע 8 אלים ממכון]

...[יכה במעון כבודכה ואתה 9 אדם על [...] אסיר עד קץ רצונכה

10 ולשלח[ה]... [ר]מות כוח ורוב בשר להרשיע 11 בקצ[...]א להכין בסוד

עמכה 12 [...] ממזרים כול 13 [...]...[...]

Col. xxiv middle (?) 1 [...] צדקה וע[...] 2 [...]עב ל`חת בעת

עווני[ו ...] 3 [...].מ כול שטן ומשחית[ו ...] 4 [...]גרשתם ולשלחם גוי

ב[...] 5 [...]איש זודן במרבי מעל וע[...] 6 [...]בים בבסר כי כול

רוחות[...] 7 [...]הרשיעו בחייהם [...] 8 [...]...[...]

have opened a spr[ing] to rebuke the path of the fashioned from clay, the guilt of the one born of *13* woman according to his deeds, to open the sp[rin]g of your truth to the creature whom you have supported with your power, *14* to [be,] according to your truth, a herald […] of your goodness, to proclaim to the poor the abundance of your compassion, *15* […] … from the spring [… the bro]ken of spirit, and the mourning to everlasting joy. *16* […]…[…]

Col. XXIII *bottom* (Sukenik *frag.* 2 1) *1-2* […] … […] *3* […] and in your land and among the sons of gods and among the son[s of …] … […] *4* […] your […] and to recount all your glory. And I, what am I? For from the dust I have been taken and t[o] *5* [the dust I will return. For] your [gl]ory have you done all this. Give according to the abundance of your kindness the observance of your justice.   *6* […] continually, until salvation. The mediators of knowledge are with all my steps, the reproachers of truth *7* […] For, what is dust in [their] palms? [The wo]rk of ash between their hands? They are nothing. But you *8* […] clay […] your will. Upon stones (?) do you put me as a test *9* […] and upon the dust you stretch out the spirit *10* […] in the mud [… the so]ns of gods, to be in communion with the sons of heaven. *11* [… et]ernal, without return of darkness. For *12* […] and light you have revealed, but not in order to make […] return *13* […] you have stretched out your [h]oly [spirit] to cover up guilt *14* [… at]tendants with your host and those who walk *15* […] … from before your presence, because they have been established in your truth *16* […] you have done these wonders for your glory. And spat saliva *17* […] … the injustice of the abominable creature. *18* […] abominable [crea]ture.

Col. XXIV *top* (Sukenik *col.* XVIII *1-16* II + *frags.* 57 II + 9 + 50; = 4Q428 14)   *1* […] … *2* … […] creature of flesh *3* … […] who will summon you *4* in his judgment […] to the angels *5* … […] the secrets of offence /to change/ *6* flesh into […] and above it will sour all *7* the angels of […] as the cords of the spirit, and you have humbled *8* the gods from the place of […] in the dwelling of your glory. And you, *9* man upon […] I will withdraw until the period of your will, *10* and to send […] heights (?) of power and the abundance of the flesh, to sentence as guilty *11* in the period of […] to establish in council with you *12* […] the bastards, all the *13* […] … […]

Col. XXIV *middle (?)* (Sukenik *frag.* 45)   *1* […] justice and […] *2* […] to the pit in the time of his iniquities […] of every adversary and destroyer […] *4* […] their expropriation and to send them away, a people […] *5* […] the presumptuous man in very many disloyalties and […] *6* […] with contempt. Because all the spirits […] *7* […] (they) will be condemned as guilty during their lives […] *8* […] … […]

Col. xxiv *bottom*   1 [...]... רשע   2 [...]...ם ובמשפטים
3 [...]ממזרים להרשיע בבשר   4 [...]כן רוחם להושיע   5 [...]פלא רזיכה
גליתה   6 לבנ[י ...]אני לבשר ידעתי   7 כי [...]ם עולה בקץ   8 כל[...]יה
ולכול מביט   9 [...]ולוⁿ יחד   10 [...]עבדתה מבני   11 אל ...[...]עולות
עמים   12 לחזקם[...]רבות אשמה   13 בנחלתו [...]עזבתם ביד   14 כול
מב[...]... 15   [...]... 16 על [...]

Col. xxv *top*   1 [... מש]פט צדק ב[...]   2 [...]הפרידם ממעמד [...]...[...]
3 [...]ות עם עדת קדושיכה בהפלא[...]   4 עד ע[ו]לם ורוחות רשעה תבית
מא[...]   5 ולוא יהיו עוד ותשם מקום רש]עה ... [...] כול   6 רוחות עולה אשר
יושדו לאבל [...]   7 ועדן לדורי נצח וברום רשעה למ[...]   8 רבה אנינם
לכלה ונגד כול מעש'כ]ה ... רוב   9 חסדיכה ולדעת כול בכבודכה ולפר[...]
הו]דעתה   10 משפט אמתכה ואוזן בשר גליתה ו[...]יש במזמת   11 לבכה
וקץ תעודה השכלתה לבש[ר ... ת]שפוט במרום   12 ויושבי האדמה על
האדמה וגם[...] מיושבי   13 חושך תריב לאצד[יק צדיק ולהר]שיע רשע
... 14 ולוא להפרד [...]דברכה [...]   15 ל[...]

Col. xxv *bottom*   2-1 [...]... 3 ותרים[...]   4 עצה ו[...]
5 משרתים [...]   6 והכירום [... ורננו]לזמר   7 ולהלל ל[...].דעתי
8 ספרתי וע]...[...] אל   9 הדעות [...]... *vacat*

10 למשכיל מזמ]ור ...[...]   11 כיא[...]... מלכי קדם   12].... רזי
[עורמתו   13 [...] ירוממה

Col. xxvi *top*   6 ... [...] רע לקדושים ולוא]   7 יבוא [בי ... כיא אני עם
אלים מעמד]י   8 וכבוד]י עם בני מלך לוא בפז אכתיר לי וכתם אופרים לוא
שמ[ו   9 בי וה]... לוא יחשב בי זמרו ידידים שירו למלך כבוד[10 שמח]ו
בעדת אל הרנינו באהל ישועה הללו במעון קודש]   11 רוממו [יחד בצבא

Col. xxiv *bottom* (Sukenik *frags.* 6 + 2 ii)   *1* [...] wicked *2* [...] and in the judgments *3* [...] the bastards to condemn the flesh as guilty *4* [...] their spirit to
save *5* [...] you have revealed the wonder of your mysteries *6* to the so[ns of
...] ... to the flesh, I have known *7* that [...] injustice in the time of *8* ... [...]
and for all who look *9* [...] and he will not hide *10* [...] you have worked more
than the sons of *11* God [...] the unjust works of the nations *12* to strengthen
them [...] increasing the guilt *13* in his inheritance [...] you have abandoned
them into the hand of *14* all ... [...] ... *15* ... [...] *16* on [...]

Col. xxv *top* (Sukenik *frags.* 5 + 56 i + 46 i; = 4Q428 12)   *1* [... the judg]ment of
justice against [...] *2* [...] he will scatter them from the position of [...] *3* [...]
with the congregation of the holy ones. Wondrously [...] *4* for ever. You will
make the spirits of wickedness dwell away from [...] *5* and they will no longer
exist. You will destroy the place of wick[edness ...] all *6* the spirits of injustice
who have been oppressed by sorrow [...] *7* and delight for everlasting generations. And when wickedness arises to [...] *8* its oppression has grown right to
destruction. And opposed to all your creatures [...] the abundance of *9* your
kindness, and to know everything in your glory, and to [...] you have made
[kno]wn *10* the judgment of your truth. You have opened the ear of flesh [...]
... in the plan of *11* your heart. And you have made known the time of the
testimony to the fle[sh ... you] judge in the height, *12* and the dwellers of the
land, upon the land. And also [...] from those who dwell in *13* darkness. You
will make a lawsuit to pronounce the ju[st man ju]st and sen[tence the wicked
man ...] *14* and not to scatter [...] your word [...] *15* ... [...]

Col. xxv *bottom* (Sukenik *frags.* 8 + 7 i; = 4Q428 15?)   *1-2* ...[...] *3* you exalt
[...] *4* counsel and [...] *5* those who serve [...] *6* and they acknowledge them
[... and they exult] to sing *7* and to praise [...] my knowledge *8* I have told and
[...] the God of *9* knowledge [...] *Blank*

10 For the Instructor, so[ng ...] ... *11* because [...] kings of old *12* ... [... the
secrets] of his intelligence *13* [...] will exalt

Col. xxvi *top* (Sukenik *frags.* 56 ii, 46 ii, 55 ii; = 4Q427 7 i)   *6* ... [... companion
of the holy ones, and not] *7* shall come [to me ... for I, with the gods is my
position] *8* and [my] glory [is with the sons of the king. I will not crown myself with pure gold, and gold from Ophir they will not place] *9* on me and [...
will not be considered for me. Sing, favoured ones, sing to the king of glory,]
10 rejoice [in the assembly of God, exult in the tent of salvation, praise in the

עולם הבו גדול לאלנו וכבוד למלכנו הקדישו] 12   ש]מו בשפתי עוז ולשון
נצח הרימו לבד קולכמה בכול קצים] 13   השמ]יעו הגידנה הביעו בשמחות
עולמים ואין השבת השחוו] 14   ביחד [קהל *vacat* ברכו המפלי גאות
ומודיע עוז ידו לחתום] 15   רזים ולהגלות נסתרות לה]רים כושלים
ונופליהם להשיב לכת קוי דעות] 16   [ולהש]פיל נועדות רום גאים] עולם
[...

1   עוד [...]...[...]... כיא השפיל גבהות]   *Col.* xxvi *bottom*   2   רוח לאין
שרית ויר]ם מעפר אביון ... ועד שחקים]   3   וגבוה בקומה ועם [אלים
בעדת יחד ... לכלת]   4   עולם וכ'שלי ארץ י]רים לאין מחיר ... מצעדם]
5   ושמחת עולם במכוניה]ם כבוד נצח ואין השבת [...   6   [להודיע גבורה}
ו...[...]   7   בדעתם ברוב חסד [והמון רחמיו לכול בני אמתו ידענוכה]
8   אל הצדק והשכל]נו ...הכבוד כיא ראינו קנאתכה]   9   בכוח גבורה
וה]כרנו ... רחמים והפלא סליחות]   10   מה בשר לאלה ו]מה ... לספר אלה
מקץ לקץ]   11   ולהתיצב במעמד[... בני שמים ואין מלי]ן   12   להשיב דבר
ב]...   13   [...] ל [...]

1Q35 (1QHᵇ) *1QHodayotᵇ*

J.T. Milik, *DJD I*, 136-138, pl. XXXI
PAM 40.451, 40.453
DAJ
1QHª, 4Q427, 4Q428, 4Q429, 4Q430, 4Q431, 4Q432, 4Q471b

1   [...] ברוב רחמיכה]לנעוי   *Frag.* 1 ı   2   [לב מי כמוכה באלים אדוני
ומי כאמתכה ומי יצדק לפני]כה בהשפטכה   3   [ואין להשיב על תוכחתכה
כול רוח ולוא יוכל כול צבא להתיצב]לפני   4   [חמתכה וכול בני אמתכה
תביא בסליחות לפניכה לטהרם מפשעי]הם   5   [ברוב טובכה ובהמון

holy residence,] *11* exalt [together with the eternal host, ascribe greatness to our God and glory to our King; sanctify] *12* [his] na[me with stalwart lips and powerful tongue, raise your voices in unison in all periods,] *13* cause [the sound of the shout] to be hea[rd, rejoice with everlasting happiness, and bow down unceasingly] *14* in the united [assembly. *Blank* Bless the one who does amazing wonders, and shows the might of his hand sealing up] *15* mysteries and revealing hidden things, rais[ing up those who stumble and those of them who fall, changing the behaviour of those who await knowledge] *16* [and low]ering the exalted meetings of the [eternally] proud [...]

Col. xxvi *bottom* (Sukenik *frag.* 7 ii; = 4Q427 7 ii; 4Q431 1)   *1* more. [...] ... [... For he brings down the arrogant] *2* spirit, without even a remnant, and he rai[ses the poor from the dust ... up to the clouds] *3* and high in its elevation, with [the gods in congregation of the community ...] for everlasting [destruction]. *4* And those who fall earth he [lifts up with no price, ... their steps] *5* and eternal enjoyment in their dwellings, [everlasting glory, unceasing ...] *6* {to make known power} ...[...] *7* so that they know the greatness of his kindness [and the abundance of his compassion for all the sons of his truth. We have known you] *8* God of justice and [we] have understood [... the glory for we have seen your zeal] *9* in the strength of might and [we have recognized ... compassion and wonderful forgiveness] *10* What is flesh to these things? And [what ... to recount these things from period to period] *11* and to stand in position [... the sons of the heavens. And there is no mediator] *12* to return a reply [...] *13* ...[...]

1Q35 (1QHᵇ) *1QHodayotᵇ*

Bibliography: É. Puech, 'Restauration d'un texte hymnique à partir de trois manuscrits fragmentaires: 1QHᵃ xv 37-xvi 4 (vii 34-viii 3), 1Q35 (Hᵇ) 1,9-14, 4Q428 (Hᵇ) 7', *RevQ* 16/64 (1995) 543-558

Frag. 1 *col.* i (= 1QHᵃ xv)   *1* [... the abundance of your compassion] with the perverted *2* [of heart. Who is like you, Lord, among the gods? Who is like your truth? Who is just before] you when you go to court? *3* [No spirit can reply to your reproach, and no host can stand up] against *4* [your anger. All the sons of your truth you bring to forgiveness in your presence, you purify them from] their [sins] *5* [by the greatness of your goodness and in the abundance of your compassion, to make them stand in your presence for ever and ever. Fo]r [you

רחמיכה להעמידם לפניכה לעולמי עד כי[א   6   ⌐F   עולם אתה וכול]
דרכיכה יכונו לנצח נצחים ואין זולתכה ומה ה[ו]ה[א   7   איש תהו ובעל הבל]
להתבונן במעשי פל]אכה הגדולים   8   *vacat*   [...]   9   *vacat*   אודכה אדוני]
כיא לוא הפלתה גורלי בעדת שו ובס[וד נעלמים לוא   10   שמתה חוקי]
ותקראני לחסדיכה ולסליחותיכה הביאות[ני ובה[מון   11   רחמיכה לכול]
משפטי [...   הוריתי בא[שמת]   12   מעל ...   עולה ובחיק ...   לרוב נדה]
ו[מנעורי בדמים ועד   13   שיבה ...   ⌐F z   כוננתה רגלי בדר]ך לבכה]
ולשמועת   14   [...   אוזני ולבי להבין באמתכה [...]...[...]

[עם] עצי   2   א]ש מתהפכת בל י[גיד במעין חיים   1   *Frags. 2 + 1 II*
עולם לוא ישתה   3-10(?) *vacat*

1Q36 *1QHymnic Composition*

J.T. Milik, *DJD I*, 138-141, pl. XXXII
PAM 40.538, 40.541

עולם עם   3   [...]   [...]לם תעודות שלום   2   [...]...[...]   1   *Frag. 1*
קדושיכה ובג[ורל ...   4   [...]... הכביר המודיע אלה[...]

...]   3   [...]   א[נשי משמרת לרזיכה   2   [...]...[...]   1   *Frag. 16*
מש]פט אף ונפילי בש[...   פ]לאיכה[...   4   [...   מ]שפטיכה[...]

[...] צדקכה   4   [...   וספ] נו צ[דקכה   3   [...]...   2-1   *Frag. 25 II*
[...] בבני איש   5

1Q37 *1QHymnic Composition (?)*

J.T. Milik, *DJD I*, 141, pl. XXXII
PAM 40.548

are an eternal] God, *6* [and all your paths remain from eternity to eternity. And there is no-one apart from you. What] is *7* [the man of emptiness, owner of futility, to understand] your [wonder]ful great [deeds?] *Blank 8* [...] *Blank 9* [I give you thanks, Lord, because you did not make my lot fall in the congregation of deceit, and in the coun]cil of hypocrites [you have] not *10* [placed my regulation, but you have called me to your grace and to your forgiveness you have brought] me and in [the abundance] *11* [of your compassion, to all the judgments of ...] I have been cast in gu[ilt] *12* [of unfaithfulness ... injustice, and in the lap ... to an abundance of impurity, and] since my youth in bloodshed, and up to *13* [old age ... my God, you have established my feet in the wa]y of your heart and to hear *14* [... my ears and my heart to understand your truth ...] ... [...]

Frags. 2 + 1 col. II (= 1QHᵃ XVI)   *1* [of the searing fire will not] reach the spring of life, *2* [with] the everlasting trees it will not drink *3-10(?) Blank*

1Q36 *1QHymnic Composition*

DAJ

Frag. 1   *1* [...] ... [...] *2* [...] ... the regular times of peace [...] *3* [...] eternal with your holy ones; and in the l[ot ...] *4* [...] ... he has made many, he who makes these things known [...]

Frag. 16   *1* [...] ... [...] *2* [... the m]en who guard your mysteries [...] *3* [... the judg]ment of anger, and the Nephilim of ... [...] your [w]onders [...] *4* [...] your [ju]dgments [...]

Frag. 25 col. II   *1-2* ... [...] *3* and we will tell [your] ri[ghteousness ...] *4* your righteousness [...] *5* amongst the sons of mankind [...]

1Q37 *1QHymnic Composition (?)*

DAJ

Frag. 1 1 [...]עה בו ישרא[ל ...] [...]...[...] 2 [...]יהם אשר גמלו
לנפשם רעה ו[...] 3 [...]בחירי ישראל למל[...] 4 [...].[...]

1Q38 *Hymnic Composition (?)*

J.T. Milik, *DJD I*, 141, pl. XXXIII
PAM 40.480

Frag. 4 1 [...]...[...] 2 [...]כה ומוקדש[י ...] 3 [...]השפלתני
[...]. 4 [... עש]יתה כל אל[ה ...] 5 [...]במוצל[י ...

1Q39 *Hymnic Composition (?)*

J.T. Milik, *DJD I*, 142-143, pl. XXXIII
PAM 40.499

Frag. 1 1-2 [...]...[...] 3 [...] לפניכה כול הימ[ים ...] 4 [...]...
ונכבד [...] 5 [...]...[...] 6 [...]אים ברוח קודשכה [...]

1Q40 *Hymnic Composition (?)*

J.T. Milik, *DJD I*, 143, pl. XXXIII
PAM 40.512, 40.516

Frag. 9 1 [...] במעש[...] 2 [...]עולמים ותש[...] 3 [...]...[...]
ב]ליעל וא[...]

Frag. 1   *1* […] … in him. Israe[l …] *2* […] … who have rewarded their souls with evil and […] *3* […] the chosen of Israel … […] *4* […] … […]

1Q38 *Hymnic Composition (?)*

BNP

Frag. 4   *1* […] … […] *2* […] … and those made holy […] *3* […] you have humiliated me […] *4* […] you [di]d all thi[s …] *5* […] among those saved […]

1Q39 *Hymnic Composition (?)*

BNP

Frag. 1   *1-2* […] … […] *3* […] before you all the day[s …] *4* […] and he will be honoured […] *5* […] … […] *6* […] … by your holy spirit […]

1Q40 *Hymnic Composition (?)*

BNP

Frag. 9   *1* […] in […] work(s) […] *2* […] eternal and you … […] *3* [… Be]lial and […]

1Q41-70, 1Q70bis *1QUnclassified Fragments*

J.T. Milik, *DJD I*, 144-149, 155, pl. XXXIII-XXXVII; J.C. Trever, 'Completion of the Publication of Some Fragments from Qumran Cave I', *RevQ* 5/18 (1965) 334, pl. VII

1Q71 (1QDan^a) *1QDaniel^a*

D. Barthélemy, *DJD I*, 150-151; J.C. Trever, 'Completion of the Publication of Some Fragments from Qumran Cave I', *RevQ* 5/18 (1965) 330, 333, pl. V
Athanasius Samuel
1Q72, 4Q112, 4Q113, 4Q114, 4Q115, 4Q116

| Frag. 1 i | Dan 1:10-17 | Frag. 1 ii | Dan 2:2-6 |

1Q72 (1QDan^b) *1QDaniel^b*

D. Barthélemy, *DJD I*, 151-152; J.C. Trever, 'Completion of the Publication of Some Fragments from Qumran Cave I', *RevQ* 5/18 (1965) 330-331, 334, pl. VI
Athanasius Samuel
1Q71, 4Q112, 4Q113, 4Q114, 4Q115, 4Q116

| Frag. 1 | Dan 3:22-28 | Frag. 2 | Dan 3:27-30 |

2Q1(2QGen) *2QGenesis*

M. Baillet, *DJD III*, 48-49, pl. X
PAM 42.957
ROC 643
1Q1, 4Q1, 4Q2, 4Q3, 4Q4, 4Q5, 4Q6, 4Q7, 4Q8, 4Q8a, 4Q8b, 4Q8c,
4Q9, 4Q10, 4Q11, 4Q12, 4Q576, 6Q1, 8Q1

Frag. 1	Gen 19:27-28	Frag. 2 ii	Gen 35:35-37
Frag. 2 i	Gen 36:6		

2Q2 (2QExod^a) *2QExodus^a*

M. Baillet, *DJD III*, 49-52, pl. X
PAM 42.957
ROC 643
1Q2, 2Q3, 2Q4, 4Q11, 4Q13, 4Q14, 4Q15, 4Q16, 4Q17, 4Q18, 4Q19,
4Q20, 4Q21, 4Q22

Frag. 1	Exod 1:11-14	Frag. 7	Exod 26:11-13
Frag. 2	Exod 7:1-4	Frag. 8	Exod 30:21
Frag. 3	Exod 9:27-29	Frag. 9	Exod 30:23-25
Frag. 4	Exod 11:3-7	Frag. 10	Exod 32:32-34
Frag. 5	Exod 12:32-41	Frag. 11-13	?
Frag. 6	Exod 21:18-20?		

2Q3 (2QExod^b) *2QExodus^b*

M. Baillet, *DJD III*, 52-55, pl. XI
PAM 42.958
ROC 739
1Q2, 2Q2, 2Q4, 4Q11, 4Q13, 4Q14, 4Q15, 4Q16, 4Q17, 4Q18, 4Q19,
4Q20, 4Q21, 4Q22

Frag. 1	Exod 4:31	Frag. 6 ii	Exod 27:11-19
Frag. 2	Exod 12:26-27?	Frag. 7	Exod 31:16-17
Frag. 3	Exod 18:21-22	Frag. 8	Exod 19:9; 34:10
Frag. 4	Exod 21:37 - 22:2	Frag. 9-13	?
Frag. 5	Exod 22:15-19		

2Q4 (2QExod^c) *2QExodus^c*

M. Baillet, *DJD III*, 56, pl. XI
PAM 42.960
ROC 742
1Q2, 2Q2, 2Q3, 4Q11, 4Q13, 4Q14, 4Q15, 4Q16, 4Q17, 4Q18, 4Q19, 4Q20, 4Q21, 4Q22

Frag. 1   Exod 5:3-5

2Q5 (2QpaleoLev) *2QLeviticus*

M. Baillet, *DJD III*, 56-57, pl. XII
PAM 42.960
ROC 742
1Q3, 4Q23, 4Q24, 4Q25, 4Q26, 4Q26a, 4Q26b, 6Q2, 11Q1, 11Q2

Frag. 1   Lev 11:22-29

2Q6 (2QNum^a) *2QNumbers^a*

M. Baillet, *DJD III*, 57-58, pl. XII
PAM 42.960
ROC 742
2Q7, 2Q8, 2Q9, 4Q23, 4Q27

Frag. 1   Num 3:38-41
Frag. 2   Num 3:51 - 4:3

2Q7 (2QNum^b) *2QNumbers^b*

M. Baillet, *DJD III*, 58-59, pl. XII
PAM 42.960
ROC 742
2Q6, 2Q8, 2Q9, 4Q23, 4Q27

Frag. 1   Num 33:47-53

2Q8 (2QNum^c) *2QNumbers^c*

M. Baillet, *DJD III*, 59, pl. XII
PAM 42.960
ROC 742
2Q6, 2Q7, 2Q9, 4Q23, 4Q27

Frag. 1   Num 7:88

2Q9 (2QNum^d) *2QNumbers^d ?*

M. Baillet, *DJD III*, 59-60, pl. XII
PAM 42.960
ROC 742
2Q6, 2Q7, 2Q8, 4Q23, 4Q27

Frag. 1   Num 18:8-9 (or Lev 23:1-3)

2Q10 (2QDeut^a) *2QDeuteronomy^a*

M. Baillet, *DJD III*, 60, pl. XII
PAM 42.960
ROC 742
1Q4, 1Q5, 2Q11, 2Q12, 4Q28, 4Q29, 4Q30, 4Q31, 4Q32, 4Q33, 4Q34,
4Q35, 4Q36, 4Q37, 4Q38, 4Q38a, 4Q39, 4Q40, 4Q41, 4Q42, 4Q43,
4Q44, 4Q45, 4Q46, 5Q1, 6Q3, 11Q3

Frag. 1   Deut 1:7-9

2Q11 (2QDeut^b) *2QDeuteronomy^b*

M. Baillet, *DJD III*, 60-61, pl. XII
PAM 42.960
ROC 742
1Q4, 1Q5, 2Q10, 2Q12, 4Q28, 4Q29, 4Q30, 4Q31, 4Q32, 4Q33, 4Q34,
4Q35, 4Q36, 4Q37, 4Q38, 4Q38a, 4Q39, 4Q40, 4Q41, 4Q42, 4Q43,
4Q44, 4Q45, 4Q46, 5Q1, 6Q3, 11Q3

Frag. 1   Deut 17:12-15

2Q12 (2QDeut^c) *2QDeuteronomy^c*

M. Baillet, *DJD III*, 61-62, pl. XII
PAM 42.960
ROC 742
1Q4, 1Q5, 2Q10, 2Q11, 4Q28, 4Q29, 4Q30, 4Q31, 4Q32, 4Q33, 4Q34,
4Q35, 4Q36, 4Q37, 4Q38, 4Q38a, 4Q39, 4Q40, 4Q41, 4Q42, 4Q43,
4Q44, 4Q45, 4Q46, 5Q1, 6Q3, 11Q3

Frag. 1   Deut 10:8-12

2Q13 (2QJer) *2QJeremiah*

M. Baillet, *DJD III*, 62-69, pl. XIII
PAM 42.952
ROC 741
4Q70, 4Q71, 4Q71a, 4Q71b, 4Q72

Frag. 1	Jer 42:7-11	Frag. 13 i	Jer 48:43-45
Frag. 2	Jer 42:14	Frag. 13 ii	Jer 49:10?
Frag. 3-4	Jer 43:8-11	Frag. 14	Jer 13:22?
Frag. 5	Jer 44:1-3	Frag. 15	Jer 32:24-25?
Frag. 6	Jer 44:12-14	Frag. 16	Jer 48:2-4?
Frag. 7-8	Jer 46:27 - 47:2	Frag. 17	Jer 48:41-42
Frag. 9 i	Jer 48:7	Frag. 18-27	?
Frag. 9 ii-12	Jer 48:25-39		

2Q14 (2QPs) *2QPsalms*

M. Baillet, *DJD III*, 69-71, pl. XIII.
PAM 42.952
ROC 741
1Q10, 1Q11, 1Q12, 3Q2, 4Q83, 4Q84, 4Q85, 4Q86, 4Q87, 4Q88, 4Q89,
4Q90, 4Q91, 4Q92, 4Q93, 4Q94, 4Q95, 4Q96, 4Q97, 4Q98, 4Q98a,
4Q98b, 4Q98c, 4Q98d, 4Q236, 5Q5, 6Q5, 8Q2, 11Q5, 11Q6, 11Q7,
11Q8, 11Q9

Frag. 1	Ps 103:2-11	Frag. 2	Ps 104:6-11

2Q15 (2QJob) *2QJob*

M. Baillet, *DJD III*, 71, pl. XIII
PAM 42.952
ROC 741
4Q99, 4Q100, 4Q101

Frag. 1   Job 33:28-30

2Q16 (2QRuth[a]) *2QRuth[a]*

M. Baillet, *DJD III*, 71-74, pl. XIV
PAM 42.964, 42.965
ROC 62
2Q17, 4Q104, 4Q105

Col. I	Ruth 2:13-14	Col. IV	Ruth 2:22 - 3:3
Col. II	Ruth 2:14-19	Col. V	Ruth 3:4-8
Col. III	Ruth 2:19-22	Frg. 8	Ruth 4:3-4

2Q17 (2QRuth[b]) *2QRuth[b]*

M. Baillet, *DJD III*, 74-75, pl. XV
PAM 42.959
ROC 644
2Q16, 4Q104, 4Q105

Frag. 1	Ruth 3:13-18	Frag. 2	?

2Q18 (2QSir) *2QBen Sira*

M. Baillet, *DJD III*, 75-77, pl. XV
PAM 42.959
ROC 644

Frag. 1	Eccl 6:14-15 (or 1:19-20?)
Frag. 2	Eccl 6:20-31

2Q19 (2QJub^a) *2QJubilees^a*

M. Baillet, *DJD III*, 77-78, pl. XV
PAM 42.959
ROC 644

Frag. 1   1 [... במערת מ[כפלה א[צל ...[2 [...] ארבעים יום כול
אנש[י ...[3 [...] *vacat* [...]   4 [... אבר[הם שלושה יובלים חיה
וארן[בעה ...[5 [...]זקן ושבע ימים [...]

2Q20 (2QJub^b) *2QJubilees^b*

M. Baillet, *DJD III*, 78-79, pl. XV
PAM 42.959
ROC 644

Frag. 1   1 [...] שבו[עי[שנים כ[ול ...[2 [...] כול י[מ[י חיי יוסף
א[שר ...[3 [...] היו נותנים *vacat* כב[ודם ...[4 [...]ב[ן]מאה ו[עשר
[...

2Q21 (2QapMoses?) *2QApocryphon of Moses*

M. Baillet, *DJD III*, 79-81, pl. XV
PAM 42.959

Frag. 1   1 [... נדב ו[אב[י[הוא אלע[זר ואיתמר ...[2 [...] לעשות[
לך משפט באמת ולהוכיח באמו[נ[ה [...]   3 [...] *vacat* [...]   4 [ויצא
מושה אל מחו[ץ למחנה ויתפלל לפני יהוה ויתנפ[ל לפני ...[5 [ויואמר

214

2Q19 (2QJub^a) *2QJubilees^a*

1Q17, 1Q18, 2Q20, 3Q5, 4Q176a, 4Q216, 4Q217, 4Q218, 4Q219, 4Q220, 4Q221, 4Q222, 4Q223-4Q224, 4Q482?, 4Q483?, 11Q12
Bibliography: J.C. VanderKam, *Textual and Historical Studies in the Book of Jubilees* (Missoula, Mont.: Scholars Press, 1977) 65-70

Frag. 1 (= *Jub* 23:7-8; 3Q5 3)   *1* [... And Isaac and Ishmael his sons buried him in the cave of Ma]chpelah ne[xt to Sara, his wife.] *2* [And for him wept] for forty days all the me[n of his household, and Isaac and Ishmael and all their sons and all the sons of Qetura] *3* [in their places.] *Blank* [And the mourning ended,] *4* [the lament for Abra]ham. He had lived for three jubilees and fo[ur weeks of years, one hundred and seventy-five years and he ended] *5* [the days of his life] old and replete with days. [...]

2Q20 (2QJub^b) *2QJubilees^b*

1Q17, 1Q18, 2Q19, 3Q5, 4Q176a,b, 4Q216, 4Q217, 4Q218, 4Q219, 4Q220, 4Q221, 4Q222, 4Q223-4Q224, 4Q482?, 4Q483?, 11Q12
Bibliography: J.C. VanderKam, *Textual and Historical Studies in the Book of Jubilees* (Missoula, Mont.: Scholars Press, 1977) 88-91

Frag. 1 (= *Jub* 46:1-3)   [... And they were very fruitful] *1* [and multiplied greatly during ten] wee[ks of] years, a[ll the days of Joseph's life.] *2* [And he had neither rival nor any evil] all the d[ay]s of Joseph's life wh[ich he lived after] *3* [his father Jacob, for all Egypt] paid *Blank* hono[ur to Jacob's sons] *4* [all the days of Joseph's life. And Joseph died at the] ag[e of] one hundred and [ten years]

2Q21 (2QapMoses?) *2QApocryphon of Moses*

ROC 644

Frag. 1 *1* [... Nadab and] Ab[i]hu, Elea[zar and Itamar ...] *2* [... in order to do] you justice in truth, and in order to reprove with faith[ful]ness [...] *3* [...] *Blank* [...] *4* [And Moses went outsi]de the camp and pleaded with YHWH and bowed do[wn before ...] *5* [And he said: YHWH Go]d, how can I look at you,

2QapMoses?, 2QapDavid?, 2QapProph

יהוה אלוהי]ם מה אביט אליך ואיך אש]א[פני]אליך ... [6]...[ל]...[עם
אחד ב]מ[עשיך] ... [7]...[לה]...[

2Q22 (2QapDavid?) *2QApocryphon of David?*

M. Baillet, *DJD III*, 81-82, pl. XV
PAM 42.959
ROC 644
4Q373, 4Q371?, 4Q372?

Col. I   1]... ולא שניתי כי שברו י]הוה אלוהינ]ו ל]פי]חרב[2]...
ועשיתי ק]לעי המזור עם קשתות ולא   3]... כי ... מ]לחמה לתפש ערי
מבצרים ולחריד   4]...[ל]...[ל]...[.תה

Col. II   1 .].[ ]שרים כי ידעת]י ... [2 כי רחמיו על ישרא]ל ...
3 הוא בכל דרכיו דבר]י[ולא]...[4 יתנם למשפט וכל]...[

2Q23 (2QapProph) *2QApocryphal Prophecy*

M. Baillet, *DJD III*, 82-84, pl. XV
PAM 42.959

Frag. 1   1]...[יושב]...[2]... [ ]והוי עליכה והוי]על]
3]...צר הרבה אכלתמה   4]...[... תעשו כל]5]...[בחרב וחנית
6]...[תדוחו]ן[מאבן פנת   7]...[.ות המלאה שעירים   8]... לא]תתהללו
בעצביכם   9]...[ינו הנה ממזרח ומצפון   10]... יכ]שלון ברכים וש]...[ן
11]... [חללים רבים]...[

Frag. 6   1]... מכ]מרם יתמל]א ...   2]...[כל מסלות]...[
3]...[משול בכל]...[4]...[חם בדר]...[5]...[לעשות]...[

216

and how can I li[ft] my face [towards you…] *6* […] one nation by your d[e]eds […] *7* […] … […]

2Q22 (2QapDavid?) *2QApocryphon of David?*

Bibliography: E. Schuller, 'A Preliminary Study of 4Q373 and Some Related (?) Fragments', in J. Trebolle Barrera, L. Vegas Montaner (eds.), *The Madrid Qumran Congress on the Dead Sea Scrolls 18-21 March 1991. Vol. II* (STDJ 11; Leiden, E.J. Brill, 1993) 515-525

Col. I (= 4Q373 1 + 2)   *1* [… and I did not do it again, because Y]HWH our God [struck him with] the edge of [the sword.] *2* [… and I made] deadly [ca]tapults with bows and not *3* [… because … ba]ttle to seize fortified cities and to terrify *4* […] …

Col. II   *1* … because [I] knew […] *2* for his kindness (is) towards Israe[l …] *3* he in all his paths /his words/ and not […] *4* he will deliver them to judgment. And all[…]

2Q23 (2QapProph) *2QApocryphal Prophecy*

ROC 644

Frag. 1 *1* […] dwelling […] *2* […] and woe to you, and woe [to] *3* […] much … you have eaten *4* […] … you shall make all *5* […] by the sword and the spear *6* […] you will be pushed away from the cornerstone of *7* […] … which is full of demons *8* […] you will [not] boast about your idols *9* […] … behold, from the East and from the North […] *10* […] the knees [will tr]emble and […] *11* […] many slain […]

Frag. 6 *1* […] their [n]et will be fil[led …] *2* […] all the paths […] *3* […] reign over all […] *4* […] … […] *5* […] to do […]

2Q24 (2QNJ ar) *2QNew Jerusalem ar*

M. Baillet, *DJD III*, 84-89, pl. XVI
PAM 42.948
ROC 645
1Q32, 4Q554, 4Q554a, 4Q555, 5Q15, 11Q18
Bibliography: M. Baillet, 'Fragments araméens de Qumrân 2. Description de la

Frag. 1   1 [פרזיתא בריתא אורכא   [ואעלני לגוא קרית ומשח   ...]
סחור אמין תלת   2 [חמשין וחד ב]חמשין וחד מרבעה סחור]   ופותיא קנין חמשין וחד ב
לפרזיתא ברית שוק   3 [מאה וחמשין ושבע לכול רו]ח ושבק סחור סח]ור]
פרזיתא בין   4 [כול משחת   קנין תלתא אמין עשרין וחדא] וכדן אח]זי]נ]י
ארבעין ותרתין   פרזא לפרזא שוק פתה קנין שתא אמין]

Frag. 3   1 [...]חד[...]...[...]   2 [... ומ]שח עד תרע ספי]רא ...]
3 [... פתו]רא די קודמוהי ל]מרא [...   4 [...]..כתול ת]...]

Frag. 4   1 בשרהון [...]   2 לקורבן רעוא [...]   3 [וי]עלון להיכלא]
[...   4 תמנא סאין סול]תא [...   5 ויטלון לחמא [...]   6 מן] לקדמין על
מד]בחא ... תרי]   7 סדרין על פת]ורא [...   8 תרי סדרי לח]מא ... כול
ימין   9 [... לחמא ויסבון לחמ]א לברא מן היכלא
לימין   10 מערבה ויתפלג]ון [...   11 וחזית עד די פל]ג לתמנין וארבעה
כהנין [...   12 ר]שמתא מ]...]ע.[... מן כול שבעת פלוגת פתורי [...
13 שביא די בהון וארבעת עשר כה]נין [...   14 כהניא *vacat* תרתי לחמא
די הו]ת לבונתא עליהון ... חזי]   15 הוית עד חדא מן תרתי לחמא יהיבת
[...   16 עמה ואחריתא] י]היבת לתנינה די קאם פנבד]   ל[כ]הנא רבא ...
17 [...]...[...] *vacat*   חזי הוית עד די יהיב לכ]ול כהניא [...   18 [...]ל די
[...   19 [...]ל[...]   [עד עדן די יתבו [...   איל ען חד לכול גבר וגבר] ...
20 [... ח]ד בכול [...]   21 [...]ל[...]

Frag. 8   1 [...].[...]   2 [... ע]שרא שורא ארב]עא [...   3 [...]

2Q24 (2QNJ ar) *2QNew Jerusalem ar*

Jérusalem Nouvelle', *RB* 62 (1955) 225-245, pls. II-III; J.A. Fitzmyer, D.J. Harrington, *MPAT*, 50-54; K. Beyer, *ATTM*, 214-222; F. García Martínez, *Qumran and Apocalyptic. Studies on the Aramaic Texts from Qumran* (STDJ 9; Leiden: E.J. Brill, 1992) 180-213

Frag. 1   (= 4Q554 1 ɪɪ; 5Q15 1)   [... And he led me to the interior of the city and measured each] *1* [block, length and width: fifty-one rods by] fifty-on[e in a square,] *2* [three hundred and fifty-seven cubits on each si]de. And a peristyle arou[nd] *3* [the block, the portico of the street: three rods, twenty-one cubits.] Also he sho[wed me] all the measurements *4* [of the blocks. Between one block and another there is the street, six rods wide: cubits,] forty-two.

Frag. 3 *1* [...] one [...] *2* [... and] he measured up to the sapph[ire] door [...] *3* [...] the [tab]le which is before [the Lord ...] *4* [...] the wall [...]

Frag. 4 (= 11Q18 20)   *1* their flesh [...] *2* as a pleasant offering [...] *3* [and] they [shall] go into the temple [...] *4* eight sheahs of finest fl[our ...] *5* and they shall lift the bread [...] *6* first upon [the] alt[ar ... two] *7* rows upon [the] ta[ble ...] *8* two rows of loa[ves ... every seventh day before God, a memorial offering ...] *9* the bread. And they shall take [the] bread [outside the temple, to the right of] *10* its west side, and it shall be shar[ed ...] *11* And while I was watching it was distri[buted to the eighty-four priests ...] *12* the list (?) [... with everything was satiated the division of the tables of ...] *13* the eldest among them and fourteen pri[ests ...] *14* the priests. *Blank* The two loaves [upon] which wa[s the incense ... And] *15* while I was [watching] one of the two loaves was given [to the high] p[riest ...] *16* with him. And the other was [g]iven to the deputy who was standing close to him [...] *17* [...] ... [...] *Blank* And while I was watching [one of the two breads] was given to a[ll the priests ...] *18* [...] of the ram of the flock to each person [...] *19* [...] until the moment when they sat down [...] *20* [... on]e in all [...] *21* [...] ... [...]

Frag. 8   *1* [...] ... [...] *2* [... t]en. The fou[rth] row [...] *3* [...] the{ir} walls of

כותלי}{הן}א אבן חו]ר [... ‏ ‏ 4 ‏ [...]ה אחרניא מן בר עשר]י[ן...]

5 [...]...[...] ולהיון מכפרין בה עלו]הי ... ‏ ‏ 6 ‏ [...] ולא יתכלא עוד כול

יומ] ויו]ם[...] ‏ ‏ 7 ‏ [...]עזרתא ‏ ו]אחזינ]י ‏[...].[...]אוחרי בר מן[...] ‏ ‏ 8 ‏ [...]

מאה ועשר]...[

2Q25 *2QJuridical text*

M. Baillet, *DJD III*, 90, pl. XVII
PAM 42.954

Frag. 1 ‏ 1 [... ימ]לא פיהם[...] ‏ ‏ 2 [...].י האסרים האלה[...]

3 [... כי]כן כתוב בספר מוש]ה ...[

2Q26 (2QEnGiants ar) *2QBook of Giants ar*

M. Baillet, *DJD III*, 90-91, pl. XVII
PAM 42.954
ROC 740
1Q23, 1Q24, 4Q203, 4Q530, 4Q531, 4Q532, 4Q533?, 4Q556, 6Q8

Frag. 1 ‏ 1 [... ו]הדיחו לוחא לממ]חק [... ‏ ‏ 2 [...] וסלקו מיא עלא מן

לו]חא [...] ‏ ‏ 3 [...]א ונטלו לוחא מן מיא לוחא די] ... [... ‏ ‏ 4 [...]...[...]

להן כול.[...]

2Q27 *2QUnidentified text*

M. Baillet, *DJD III*, 91, pl. XVII
PAM 42.954

whi[te] stone [...] *4* [...] the others, on the outer side, twenty [...] *5* [...] ... [...] and they shall make atonement with it for [him ...] *6* [...] and it will not be ended any more. Each day [...] *7* [...] the courtyard. [And] he showed [me ...] another [...] outside [...] *8* [...] one hundred and ten [...]

2Q25 *2QJuridical text*

ROC 740
Bibliography: J.H. Charlesworth, *PTSDSSP 2*, 218-219

Frag. 1   *1* [...] their mouth [is fu]ll [...] *2* [...] these obligations [...] *3* [... for] this is what is written in the book of Mos[es ...]

2Q26 (2QEnGiants ar) *2QBook of Giants ar*

Bibliography: J.T. Milik, *The Books of Enoch. Aramaic Fragments of Qumrân Cave 4* (Oxford: Clarendon, 1976) 334: L.T. Stuckenbruck, *The Book of Giants from Qumran* (TSAJ 63: Tübingen: Mohr Siebeck, 1997) 63-66

Frag. 1   *1* [... and] they washed the tablet to er[ase ...] *2* [...] and the water rose above the [tab]let [...] *3* [...] and they lifted the tablet from the water, the tablet which [...] *4* [...] ... [...] to them all [...]

2Q27 *2QUnidentified text*

ROC 740

1 [...].‏יהם מב[...]   2 [...]ם ולו יומ[רו ...   3 [...]נם ויקח

את[...]   4 [...] ולו יבינו מוע[...]   5 [...]מי אנחנו ה[...]ל[...]

2Q28 *2QUnidentified text*

M. Baillet, *DJD III*, 91-92, pl. XVII
PAM 42.954

Frag. 2 1 [...]...[...]   2 [...]ש מעמו דין לרתוק ב[...]   3 [...]

[תולא]ים ...[...]   4 [...]שרירות {ליש} לבם[...]

2Q29-33 *2QUnclassified fragments*

M. Baillet, *DJD III*, 92-93, pl. XVII
PAM 42.954

1 [...] their ... [...] *2* [...] and they will not s[ay ...] *3* [...] their [...] ... and he took [...] *4* [...] and they will not understand ... [...] *5* [...] who are we ... [...]

2Q28 *2QUnidentified text*

ROC 740
Bibliography: J.H. Charlesworth, *PTSDSSP* 2, 221-223

Frag. 2   *1* [...] ... [...] *2* [...] from him a verdict to bind with [...] *3* [...] hanged [...] *4* [...] stubbornness {...} of their heart [...]

3Q1 (3QEzek) *3QEzekiel*

M. Baillet, *DJD III*, 94, pl. XVIII
PAM 42.955
ROC 648
1Q9, 4Q73, 4Q74, 4Q75, 11Q4

Frag. 1   Ezek 16:31-33

3Q2 (3QPs) *3QPsalms*

M. Baillet, *DJD III*, 94, pl. XVIII
PAM 42.955
ROC 648
1Q10, 1Q11, 1Q12, 2Q14, 4Q83, 4Q84, 4Q85, 4Q86, 4Q87, 4Q88, 4Q89,
4Q90, 4Q91, 4Q92, 4Q93, 4Q94, 4Q95, 4Q96, 4Q97, 4Q98, 4Q98a, 4Q98b,
4Q98c, 4Q98d, 4Q236, 5Q5, 6Q5, 8Q2, 11Q5, 11Q6, 11Q7, 11Q8, 11Q9

Frag. 1   Ps 2:6-7

3Q3 (3QLam) *3QLamentations*

M. Baillet, *DJD III*, 95, pl. XVIII
PAM 42.955
ROC 648
4Q111, 5Q6, 5Q7

Frag. 1   Lam 1:10-12
Frag. 2   Lam 3:53-62

3Q4(3QpIsa) *3QIsaiah Pesher*

M. Baillet, *DJD III*, 95-96, pl. XVIII
PAM 42.955

1 חזון ישעיה בן א[מוץ אשר חזה על יהודה וירושלים בימי עזיה]
2 ויותם אחז וי[חזקיה מלכי יהודה ...]   3 [י]שע[יה]נבא על[...]
4 ל[...] מלך יהו[דה] שמעו שמים והאזיני ארץ כיא יהוה דבר[...] 5
[...] *vacat*   6 [י]ום המשפ[ט ...]   7 [...]...[...]

3Q5 (3QJub) *3QJubilees*

M. Baillet, *DJD III*, 96-98, pl. XVIII
PAM 42.955
ROC 648
1Q17, 1Q18, 2Q19, 2Q20, 4Q176a,b, 4Q216, 4Q217, 4Q218, 4Q219,
4Q220, 4Q221, 4Q222, 4Q223-4Q224, 4Q482?, 4Q483?, 11Q12

Frag. 3 1 [...] נשמע ב[בית ...]   2 ... ו]יבוא אל א[ברהם ...]
3 [... אנ[שי בית א[ברהם ...]   4 [...]במערת מכ[פלה אצל ...]

Frag. 1 1 [... יאמר]ו עליו הרבה לחיות[...]   2 [... וצ]רה ואין
שלום כיא מכה על מכה ומה[ומה ...]   3 [... וצר]ה על צרה ושמועה רעה
על שמועה] רעה [...]

3Q6 *3QHymn*

M. Baillet, *DJD III*, 98, pl. XVIII
PAM 42.955

3Q4(3QpIsa) *3QIsaiah Pesher*

ROC 648
4Q161, 4Q162, 4Q163, 4Q164, 4Q165

1 Is 1:1 Vision of Isaiah, son of A[moz, concerning Judah and Jerusalem in the period of Uzziah] *2* and of Jotham, of Achaz and of [Hezekiah, kings of Judah. ...] *3* [I]sa[iah] prophesied concer[ning ...] *4* to [...] king of Ju[dah *Is 1:2* Listen, heavens; pay attention, earth; for the Lord speaks.] *5* [...] *Blank* [...] *6* [the] [d]ay of judgm[ent ...] *7* [...] ... [...]

3Q5 (3QJub) *3QJubilees*

Bibliography: A. Rofé, 'Further Manuscript Fragments of the Jubilees in the Third Cave of Qumran', *Tarbiz* 34 (1965) 333-336; R. Deichgräber, 'Fragmente einer Jubiläen-Handschrift aus Höhle 3 von Qumran', *RevQ* 5/19 (1965) 415-422; J.C. VanderKam, *Textual and Historical Studies in the Book of Jubilees* (Missoula, Mont.: Scholars Press, 1977) 70-75; 99-101

Frag. 3 (= *Jub* 23:6-7; 2Q19)   *1* [... and this] was heard in [Abraham's house. *Blank*] *2* [And Ishmael his son got up and] went to A[braham his father. And he wept for Abraham] *3* [his father, he and all the me]n of the house(hold) of A[braham; they wept a great deal. And] *4* [Isaac and Ishmael his sons buried him] in the cave of Mach[pelah next to Sara, his wife.]

Frag. 1 (= *Jub* 23:12-13)   *1* [...] they [will say] about him: «He has lived long, [but most of his days were pain] *2* [labour, and dis]tress without peace, for blow upon blow, confu[sion upon confusion,] *3* [distre]ss upon distress, and bad news upon [bad] news [...]

3Q6 *3QHymn*

ROC 648

Frag. 1 1 [...]כול אשר ישמחו] בכה [...   2 [...] ושירם יערב
על]יכה [... 3 [...] ל[עולם יהללוכ]ה [...

3Q7 (3QTJuda?) *3QTestament of Judah* (?)

M. Baillet, *DJD III*, 99, pl. XVIII
PAM 42.955
ROC 648
4Q484

Frag. 5 1 [...]ש[...]   2 [... שמעון החמ]ישי יש[שכר הששי [...
3 [...]מלאך הפנים [...]   4 [...]ש[...].[...].מ[...]...[...]

3Q8 *3QUnidentified text*

M. Baillet, *DJD III*, 100, pl. XIX
PAM 42.956

Frag. 1 1 [...]מכות [...]   2 [...]מלאך שלו]ם [...

3Q9 *3QSectarian text* (?)

M. Baillet, *DJD III*, 100-101, pl. XIX
PAM 42.956

Frag. 3 1 [...].[...]   2 [... אש]מת פשע[...]   3 [...] אלה פת[...]
4 [...]ובעדתנו *vacat* [...]

Frag. 1   *1* […] all those who rejoice [in you …] *2* […] and their song will please [you …] *3* […] they will praise yo[u for] ever […]

3Q7 (3QTJuda?) *3QTestament of Judah* (?)

Bibliography: J. T. Milik, 'Écrits préesséniens de Qumrân: d'Hénoch à Amram', in M. Delcor (ed.), *Qumrân: Sa piété, sa théologie et son milieu* (BETL 46; Paris-Gembloux: Duculot, 1978) 98

Frag. 5   (> *Test. Judah* 25:1-2 ?)   *1* […] … […] *2* [… Simeon the fi]fth, Is[sachar the sixth …] *3* […] the angel of the presence […] *4* […] … […]

3Q8 *3QUnidentified text*

ROC 745

Frag. 1   *1* […] blows […] *2* […] angel of pea[ce …]

3Q9 *3QSectarian text* (?)

ROC 745

Frag. 3   *1* […] … […] *2* [… the gui]lt of iniquity […] *3* […] these … […] *4* […] and in our congregation. *Blank* […]

3Q10 *3QUnclassified fragments*

M. Baillet, *DJD III*, 101, pl. XIX
PAM 42.956

Frag. 1   1 [...]תם[...]   2 [...] ע]ל פני כו]ל [...

3Q11 *3QUnclassified fragments*

M. Baillet, *DJD III*, 101, pl. XIX
PAM 42.956

Frag. 2   1 [...] לעשות מ[...]   2 [...]...[...]   3 [...].[...]. ואין פלי]טה
                4 [...].[...]   [...

3Q12 *3QUnclassified fragments ar*

M. Baillet, *DJD III*, 101, pl. XIX
PAM 42.956

Frag. 1   1 ...[...]יומ[...]   2 בת ולמחרת]...[3 שמיא וארע]א ...[
                4 [...].[...]

3Q13 *3QUnclassified fragments ar*

M. Baillet, *DJD III*, 102, pl. XIX
PAM 42.956

3Q10 *3QUnclassified fragments*

ROC 745

Frag. 1   *1* […] their […] *2* [… o]n the surface of al[l …]

3Q11 *3QUnclassified fragments*

ROC 745

Frag. 2   *1* […] to make *2* […] … […] *3* […] and there is no esc[ape …] *4* […] …
[…]

3Q12 *3QUnclassified fragments ar*

ROC 745

Frag. 1   *1* … […] day […] *2* … and the next day […] *3* heaven and earth […]
4 […] … […]

3Q13 *3QUnclassified fragments ar*

ROC 745

3Q14 *3QUnclassified fragments*

M. Baillet, *DJD III*, 101, pl. XIX
PAM 42.956

Frag. 6   1 [...] סתרין [...]   2 [...] ס[תרין א.[...]   3 [...] *vacat* [...]

3Q15 *3QCopper Scroll*

J.T. Milik, *DJD III*, 211-302, pl. XLVIII-LXXI
PAM 40.096-40.111; 42.977-43.000
DAJ
Bibliography: J.M. Allegro, *The Treasure of the Copper Scroll* (London: Routledge & Keegan, 1960); B.Z. Luria, *The Copper Scroll from the Desert of Judah*, (Jerusalem, 1963) [Hebrew]; B. Pixner, 'Unravelling the Copper Scroll Code: A Study on the Topography of 3Q15', *RevQ* 11/43 (1983) 323-366; A. Wolters, 'Notes on the Copper Scroll (3Q15)', *RevQ* 12/48 (1987) 589-596; P. Kyle McCarter, 'The Mystery of the Copper Scroll', in H. Shanks *et al.* (eds.), *The Dead Sea*

Col. I   1 בחריבה שבעמק עכור תחת   2 המעלות הבואת למזרח אמות
3 אריח ארבעין שדת כסף וכליה   4 משקל ככרין שבעשרה KEN   5 בנפש
בן דבך השלשי עשתות   6 זהב 100 בבור הגדול שבחצר   7 הפרסטלין
בירך קרקעו סתום בחליא   8 נגד הפתח העליון ככרין תשע מאת   9 בתל
של כחלת כלי דמע בלגין ואפודת   10 הכל של הדמע והאצר השבעי מעסר
11 שני מפוגל פתחו בשולי האמא מן הצפון   12 אמות שש עד מיקרת
הטבילה XAΓ   13 בשיאח מעבא של מנס בירדא לסמל   14 גבה מן הקרקע
אמות שלוש [כ]סף ארבעין *vacat*   15 *vacat* [כ]כר

Col. II   1 בבור המלח שתחת המעלות   2 ככרין 42 *vacat* HN *vacat*
3 במערת בית המדח הישן ברובד   4 הש^לשי עשתות זהב ששין וחמש ΘE
5 בצריח שבחצר מתיה עצין ובתכו   6 בור ב(ו) כלין וכסף ככרין שבעין
7 בבור שנגד השער המזרחי   8 רחוק אמות ח(מ)ש עסרא בו כלין

3Q14 *3QUnclassified fragments ar*

ROC 745

Frag. 6   *1* […] secrets […] *2* […se]crets […] *3* […] *Blank* […]

3Q15 *3QCopper Scroll*

Scrolls after Forty Years (Washington, D.C.: Biblical Archaeology Society, 1991) 41-54; J. Lefkovits, *The Copper Scroll: 3Q15, a New Reading, Translation, and Commentary* (diss. New York University, 1993); A. Wolters, 'History and the Copper Scroll', in M.O. Wise (ed.), *Methods of Investigation of the Dead Sea Scrolls and the Khirbet Qumran Site: Present Realities and Future Prospects* (New York: Academy of Sciences, 1994) 285-298; A. Wolters, *The Copper Scroll. Overview, Text and Translation* (Sheffield: Sheffield Academic Press, 1996); É. Puech, 'Quelques résultats d'un nouvel examen du Rouleau de Cuivre (3Q15)', *RevQ* 18/70 (1997) 163-190

Col. I   *1* In the ruin which is in the valley of Acor, under *2* the steps leading to the East, *3* forty long cubits: a chest of silver and its vessels *4* with a weight of seventeen talents. *KEN 5* In the sepulchral monument, in the third course: *6* one hundred gold ingots. In the great cistern of the courtyard *7* of the peristyle, in a hollow in the floor covered with sediment, *8* in front of the upper opening: nine hundred talents. *9* In the hill of Kohlit, tithe-vessels, flasks and sacred vestments; *10* the total of the tithes and of the treasure is a seventh of a *11* second tithe made unclean. Its opening lies on the edges of the channel from the North, *12* six cubits in the direction of the cave of the ablutions, *XAΓ 13* In the plastered cistern of Manos, going down to the left, *14* at a height of three cubits from the bottom: silver, forty *15 Blank* talents. *Blank*

Col. II   *1* In the salt pit which is underneath the steps: *2* forty-two talents. *Blank HN Blank 3* In the cave of the old carpeted house, in the *4* {sixth} third platform, sixty-five gold ingots. *θE 5* In the cellar which is in Matia's courtyard there is wood and in the middle of it *6* a cistern; in i[t] there are vessels and seventy talents of silver. *7* In the cistern which is in front of the Eastern Gate, *8* at a distance of fifteen cubits, there are vessels. *9* And in the gutter which is

9 ובמזקא שבו ככריו עסר ΔI   10 בבור שתחת החומא מן המזרח   11 בשן

הסלע בדין של כסף שש   12 ביאתו תחת הסף הגדול   13 בברכא שבבמזרח

כחלת במקצע   14 הצפני חפור אמות {...מת}   15 ארבע ככרין 22 *vacat*

Col. III   1 בחצ]ר...[יאט תחת הפנא הדרו-   2 מית אמות תשע כלי כסף

וזהב של   3 דמע מזרקות כוסות מנקיאות   4 קסאות כל שש מאות ותשעה

5 תחת הפנא האחרת המזרח-   6 ית חפר אמות שש עסרה כסף   7 כך 40

8 *vacat* TP *vacat*   9 כלי דמע לבושי ביאתא

10 תחת הפנא המערבית   11 בקבר שבבמלחם מזרחי   12 בצפון אמות תחת

המ-   13 דף שלוש *vacat* כך *vacat* 13

Col. IV   1 בבור הגדול שב[...] כ]חלת בעמוד   2 בצפונו ככ[...]   14 ΣK

3 *vacat* באמא הבא]ה ל...[4 אמות ארבע]ין ואח]ת כסף   5 כך

6 בין שני הבינין שבעמק עכון   7 באמצען חפור אמות שלוש   *vacat* 55

8 שם שני דודין מלאין כסף   9 בשית האדמא שבשולי העצ-   10 לא כסף

כך מאתין   11 *vacat* בשית המזרחית שבצפון כח-   12 לת כסף כך שבעין

13 בירג של גי הסככא חפור   14 אמת כסף כך 12 *vacat*

Col. V   1 ברוש אמת המים [...]   2 סככא מן הצפון תח]ת האבן]

3 הגדולא חפור אמ]ות של-[4 ש כסף *vacat* כך 7 [*vacat*]   5 בסדק

שבסככא מזר]ח[6 אשיח שלומו כאלין של   7 דמע וכתכן אצלם *vacat*

8 מעל החריץ של שלומ-   9 ו עד הרגב הגדול   10 אמות ששין חפור אמות

11 שלוש כסף *vacat* כך 23   12 בקבר שבנחל הכפא   13 בביאה מירחו

לסככא   14 חפור אמות שבע כך 32

Col. VI   1 [ב]מערת העמוד של שני   2 [ה]פתחין צופא מזרח

3 [ב]פתח הצפוני חפור   4 [א]מות שלוש שם קלל   5 בו ספר אחד תחתו

6 *vacat* כך 42 *vacat*   7 במערא של הכנא   8 של הרגב הצופא

9 למזרח חפר בפתה   10 אמות תשע כך 21   11 במשכן המלכא בצד

12 המערבי חפר אמות   13 שתים עסרה כך 27   14 ביגר שבבמגזת הכוהן

234

in it: ten talents. *ΔI 10* In the cistern which is underneath the East wall, *11* in a spur of the rock: six silver bars. *12* Its entrance is underneath the large threshold. *13* In the pool to the East of Koḥlit, in the *14* North corner dig for {...} four cubits: *15 Blank* twenty-two talents. *Blank*

Col. III *1* In the courtyard of [...], underneath the South corner, *2* at nine cubits: gold and silver *3* tithe-vessels, goblets, cups, jars, *4* vases; total: six hundred and nine. *5* Beneath the other, eastern corner, *6* dig for sixteen cubits: *7* forty talents of silver. *Blank TP Blank 8* In the tunnel which is in Milcham, to the North: *9* tithe-vessels (and) sacred garments. Its entrance is *10* beneath the western corner. *11* In the tomb which is in Milcham, to the North-*12* east, three cubits below the stone- *13* slab: *Blank* thirteen *Blank* talents.

Col. IV *1* In the large cistern which is in [... of Ko]ḥlit in the pillar *2* of its north side [...] fourteen talents. *ΣK 3* In the channel which goes [up to ...,] when you go forward *4* fort[y-o]ne cubits: *5* fifty-five talents of silver. *Blank 6* Between the two buildings which are in the valley of Akon, *7* at their midpoint, dig for three cubits: *8* there are there two pots filled with silver. *9* In the earth trench which is on the edge of the Asla: *10* two hundred talents of silver. *Blank 11* In the eastern trench which is to the North of Koḥlit: *12* seventy talents of silver. *13* In the (burial-)mound of the ravine of Sekaka, dig *14* for a cubit: twelve talents of silver. *Blank*

Col. V *1* At the start of the water conduit [...] *2* Sekaka, from the North, bene[ath the] *3* large [stone,] dig for [thre]e cubi[ts:] *4* seven talents *Blank* of silver. [*Blank*] *5* In the fissure which is in Sekaka, to the Eas[t of] *6* Solomon's cistern: tithe-vessels. *7* And their document is next to them. *Blank 8* Above Solomon's channel, *9* sixty cubits up to the big clod of earth, *10* dig for three cubits: *11* twenty-three talents of silver. *12* In the tomb which is in the ha-Kippa stream, *13* in the approach from Jericho to Sekaka, *14* dig for seven cubits: thirty-two talents.

Col. VI *1* In the cave of the column with two *2* entrances, facing East, *3* in the northen entrance, dig for *4* three cubits: there is an amphora there, *5* in it a book, under it *6 Blank* forty-two talents. *Blank 7* In the cavity at the base of *8* the clod of earth, facing *9* East, dig in the entrance *10* for nine cubits: twenty-one talents. *11* In the Queen's residence, on the *12* West side dig for twelve *13* cubits: twenty-seven talents. *14* In the burial-mound of the ford of the High

Col. VII 1 הגדול חפור [אמות] 2 תשע ככ...] 22 3 באמא של ק[...]

4 האשיח הצפו[ני הגד]ול 5 בארבע רוח[ות ... 6 משח אמות עסרין

[ואר]בע 7 ככרין ארבע מאות vacat 8 במערא שאצל המקר[ה] של-

9 בית הקק הפור אמות שש 10 בדין של כסף שש vacat 11 בדוק תחת

פנת המשמרה 12 המזרחית חפור אמות שבע 13 vacat כב 22 vacat

14 על פי יציאת המים של הכוז- 15 בא חפור שלוש אמות עד הטור

16 כב 60 זהב ככרין שתים

Col. VIII 1 [בא]מא שבדרך מזרח בית 2 אוצר שמזרח אחיה

3 כלי דמע וספרין אל תדקם 4 בגי החיצונא בתך הדר 5 על האבן חפור

אמות שבע 6 עסרא תחתיה כסף vacat 7 vacat וזהב כב 17 vacat

8 ביגר של פי צוק הקדרון 9 חפור אמות שלוש כב 7 10 בשלף של השוא

הצופא 11 מערב בדרום בצריח 12 הצופא צפון חפור אמות

13 עשרין וארבע כב 66 14 ברוי של השוא בציה שבא חפור 15 אמות

אחת עסרה vacat 16 vacat כסף כב 70

Col. IX 1 בשובך שבשולי הנטף משח משולו 2 אמות שלוש (עש)רא

שתין חפור וגב שעת שבע 3 בדין אסתרין ארבע vacat 4 בחבלת השניג

(בחבלה השנית) בצריח הצופא 5 מזרח חפור אמות שמונא 6 vacat

ומחצא כב 23.5 7 בצריחי החורון ברוח הצופא ים 8 בזרב חפור אמות שש

עסרה 9 vacat כב 22 vacat 10 בקומעה כסף מנחה רב 11 בקילח (ה)מים

הקרובין לכף הביב 12 מ(ז)רח כלפנהם חפור אמות 13 vacat שבע כב 9

14 בשית שיבצפון פי הצוק של בית 15 תמר בצחיאת גר פלע

16 vacat כל שבה חרם vacat 17 בשובך שבמצד נאבתה[...]

Col. X 1 דרום בעליאה השנית ירידתו 2 מלמעלא כב 9 vacat

3 בבור גר מזקות שרוו מהנחל 4 הגדול בקרקעו כב 12 5 באשיח שיבית

הכרם בבואך 6 לסמול אמות עסר כסף vacat 7 vacat ככרין ששין ושנין

8 בים של גי זוך בצדו המערבי 9 אבן שחורא אמות שתין vacat

10 הו הפתח ככרין שלש מאות 11 vacat זהב vacat וכלין כופרין עסרין

Col. VII *1* Priest, dig *2* for nine [cubits]: twenty-two talents. In the channel of Qi[…] *4* in the North cistern [which is lar]ge *5* on the four si[des …] *6* measure twenty-four cubits: *7* four hundred talents. *Blank 8* In the cavity which is next, the one called of *9* the family of Hakkoz, dig for six cubits: *10* six silver bars. *Blank 11* In Doq, under the East corner of the citadel, *12* dig for seven cubits: *13 Blank* twenty-two talents *Blank 14* Above the mouth of the water outlet of Koziba *15* dig for three cubits towards the parapet: *16* sixty talents (of silver), two talents of gold.

Col. VIII *1* [In the chan]nel which is on the road of the house of *2* the treasure, to the East of Aḥiyah: *3* tithe-vessels and books, do not crush them! *4* In the outer valley, in the middle of the sheepfold, *5* by the stone, dig for seven- *6* teen cubits under it: silver *Blank 7 Blank* and gold, seventeen talents. *Blank 8* In the burial-mound which is at the entrance to the narrow pass of the Qidron, *9* dig for three cubits: seven talents. *10* In the ploughed land which is in ha-Shave', facing the *11* West, in the southern part, in the cellar *12* facing North, dig *13* for twenty-four cubits: sixty-six talents. *14* In the irrigated land which is in ha-Shave', in the burial mark which is there, dig for *15* eleven cubits: *Blank 16 Blank* seventy talents of silver.

Col. IX *1* In the dovecote which is on the edge of Nataf, measure from its edge *2* thirteen cubits, dig for two, and under seven slabs: *3* four bars of steryn (coins?). *Blank 4* <In the second estate,> under the cellar facing *5* to the East, dig for eight cubits: *6 Blank* and a half: twenty-three and a half talents. *7* In the cellars of Choron, in the side facing the sea, *8* in the basin dig for sixteen cubits: *9 Blank* twenty-two talents. *Blank 10* In the fosse: much silver of offering. *11* In the waterfalls near the edge of the conduit, *12* to the East of their outlet, dig *13 Blank* for seven cubits: nine talents. *14* In the cistern which is to the North of the mouth of the narrow pass of Beth *15* Tamar, in the rocky ground of Ger Pela, *16 Blank* everything which is there is a sacred offering. *Blank 17* In the dovecote of the fortress of Nabata […]

Col. X *1* to the South, on the second floor when going down *2* from above: nine talents. *Blank 3* In the lime-plastered cistern of the irrigation ditches fed by the *4* great stream, at its bottom: twelve talents. *5* In the cistern which is in Beth ha-Keren, as you go in, *6* to the left ten cubits: *Blank 7 Blank* sixty-two talents of silver. *Blank 8* In the water tank of the valley of Zok (?) on the West side, *9* there is a black stone, two cubits: *10* it is the entrance: three hundred talents *11 Blank* of gold *Blank* and twenty atonement vessels. *12* Under Absalom's memorial,

12 תחת יד אבשלום מן הצד   13 המערבי חפור אמות שתין עסרה
14 *vacat* כב 80 *vacat*   15 בי^ם בית המים של רחיל תחת   16 השקת *vacat*
17 כב   17 בגנת צדוק בארבעת

Col. XI   1 מקצועות זהב כלי דמע כתכן אצלם   2 מתחת פנה האסתאן
הדרומית   3 בקבר צדוק תחת עמוד האכסדרן   4 כלי דמע סוח דמע סנה
ותכן אצלם   5 בהכסה ראש הסלע הצופא מערב   6 נגד גנת צדוק תחת
המסמא ה-   7 גדולא שבשילוחו חרם {ב}   8 בקבר שתחת הסכין כב 40
9 בקבר בני העבט הירחו   10 בו כלי דמע אז דמע סוח   11 כתכן אצלן
12 בבית האשוחין באשיח   13 בביאתך לימומית *vacat*   14 שלו כלי דמ(ע)
לאה דמע סירא   15 כתכן אצלן *vacat*   16 במבא רוח בית חמשכב המערבי
17 טיף על מ[... כסף כב]תשע מאות

Col. XII   1 זהב כב 5 ככרין ששין ביאתו מן המ(ע)רב   2 תחת האבן
השחורא בידן תחת סף *vacat*   3 הכוך ככרין 42 *vacat*   4 בהר גריזין תחת
המעלהא של השיח (השית) העליונא   5 שדא אחת וכל כליה וכסף כב *vacat*
60 *vacat*   6 בפי המבוע של בית שם כל(י) כסף וכלי זהב   7 של דמע וכסף
הכל ככרין *vacat* שש מאות   8 בביבא הגדולא של הכוך כלבית הכוך
9 הכל משקל *vacat* ככרין 71 מנין עסרין   10 בשית שבינה בצפון כחלת
פתחא צפון   11 וקברין על פיה משנא הכתב הזא   12 ופרושה ומשחותיהם
ופרוט כל   13 *vacat* אחד ואח[ד] *vacat*

238

on the *13* West side dig for twelve cubits: *14 Blank* eighty talents. *Blank 15* In the basin of the water reserve of Rachel, beneath the *16* water outlet: *Blank* seventeen talents. *17* In Zadok's courtyard, at the four

Col. XI *1* corners, gold, tithe-vessels. Their document is next to them. *2* Underneath the South corner of the Portico, *3* in Zadok's tomb, underneath the column of the exedra: *4* tithe-vessels *swḥ* (?), tithe *snh* (?). And very near there, *5* in the 'throne' at the tip of the rock, towards the West, *6* opposite Zadok's courtyard, under the large *7* slab which covers its water outlet: (a) sacred offering. *8* In the grave which is underneath the 'knife': forty talents. *9* In the grave of the sons of 'Abeṭ of Jericho, *10* there are in it tithe-vessels *'z* (?), tithe *swḥ* (?). *11 Blank* Their document is next to them. *12* In Beth ha-Ashuḥin, in the cistern *13* at the entrance to the *ymwmyt* (smallest water basin ?) *Blank 14* of it, tithe-vessels of *l'h*, tithe of *syr'*. *15* Their document is next to them. *Blank 16* At the side entrance of the sepulchre room, *17* a platform over [...] nine-hundred [talents of silver,]

Col. XII *1* five talents of gold. Sixty talents in its West entrance, *2* under the black stone. At its side, underneath the *3 Blank* threshold of the burial-chamber: forty-two talents. *Blank 4* On Mount Garizim, underneath the staircase of the upper tunnel: *5* a chest and all its vessels, and sixty talents of silver. *6 Blank* In the mouth of the spring of Beth-Sham: silver vessels and gold vessels *7* for the tithes; in total: *Blank* six hundred talents. *Blank 8* In the large conduit of the crypt up to Beth-Hakuk: *9* the total of its weight: *Blank* seventy-one talents, twenty minas. *10* In the tunnel which is in *ynḥ*, to the North of Koḥlit, which opens towards the North *11* and has graves in its entrance: a copy of this text *12* and its explanation and their measurements and the inventory of everything, *13 Blank* item by item.

4Q1 (4QGen-Exodᵃ) *4QGenesis-Exodusᵃ*

J.R. Davila, *DJD XII*, 7-30, pl. I-V
PAM 43.006, 43.009, 43.010, 43.157
ROC 169, 397, 391
1Q1, 2Q1, 4Q2, 4Q3, 4Q4, 4Q5, 4Q6, 4Q7, 4Q8, 4Q8a, 4Q8b, 4Q8c, 4Q9,
4Q10, 4Q11, 4Q12, 4Q576, 6Q1, 8Q1
1Q2, 2Q2, 2Q3, 2Q4, 4Q1, 4Q11, 4Q13, 4Q14, 4Q15, 4Q16, 4Q17, 4Q18,
4Q19, 4Q20, 4Q21, 4Q22
Bibliography: J.R. Davila, *Unpublished Pentateuchal Manuscripts from Qumran Cave IV: 4QGenExᵃ, 4QGenᵇ⁻ʰ,ʲ⁻ᵏ* (Diss. Harvard 1988); .- 'The Name of God at Moriah: An Unpublished Fragment from 4QGen-Exodᵃ', *JBL* 110 (1991) 577-582; .- 'Text-Type and Terminology: Genesis and Exodus as Text Cases', *RevQ* 16/61 (1993) 3-37; .- 'New Qumran Readings from the Joseph Story (Genesis 37-50)', in J. Trebolle Barrera, L. Vegas Montaner (eds.), *The Madrid Qumran Congress. Proceedings of the International Congress on the Dead Sea Scrolls 18-21 March 1991. Vol. I* (STDJ 11; Leiden: E.J. Brill, 1993) 167-175

Frag. 1	Gen 22:14	Frag. 19 i	Exod 1:22 - 2:5
Frag. 2	Gen 27:38-39	Frag. 19 ii	Exod 3:8-16
Frag. 3	Gen 27:42-43	Frag. 20	Exod 3:18-21
Frag. 4	Gen 34:17-21	Frag. 21-22 i	Exod 4:4-7
Frag. 5	Gen 35:17 - 36:13	Frag. 23	Exod 4:8-9
Frag. 6	Gen 36:19-27	Frag. 24-25 i	Exod 4:26 - 5:1
Frag. 7	Gen 37:5-6	Frag. 22 ii, 26	Exod 5:3-14
Frag. 8	Gen 37:22-27	Frag. 27	Exod 5:14-17
Frag. 9	Gen 39:11 - 40:1	Frag. 25 ii, 28-31	Exod 6:4-21
Frag. 10	Gen 45:23	Frag. 32	Exod 6:25
Frag. 11	Gen 47:13-14	Frag. 33	Exod 7:5-13
Frag. 12	Gen 48:2-4	Frag. 34-35	Exod 7:15-20
Frag. 13	Gen 48:15-17	Frag. 36	Exod 8:20-22
Frag. 14	Gen 48:18-22	Frag. 37	Exod 9:8 ?
Frag. 15-16	Gen 49:1-5	Frag. 38-61	?
Frag. 17-18	Exod 1:3-17		

4Q2 (4QGenᵇ) *4QGenesisᵇ*

J.R. Davila, *DJD XII*, 31-38, pl. VI-VIII
PAM 42.703, 42.704, 43.004
ROC 215

1Q1, 2Q1, 4Q1, 4Q3, 4Q4, 4Q5, 4Q6, 4Q7, 4Q8, 4Q8a, 4Q8b, 4Q8c, 4Q9, 4Q10, 4Q11, 4Q12, 4Q576, 6Q1, 8Q1

Frag. 1 i	Gen 1:1-25	Frag. 3 i	Gen 4:2-11
Frag. 2	Gen 1:25-28	Frag. 3 ii	Gen 5:13 ?
Frag. 1 ii	Gen 2:14-19	Frag. 4	?

4Q3 (4QGen*c*) *4QGenesis*c

J.R. Davila, *DJD XII*, 39-42, pl. IX
PAM 42.154, 43.698, 44.016
ROC 393
1Q1, 2Q1, 4Q1, 4Q2, 4Q4, 4Q5, 4Q6, 4Q7, 4Q8, 4Q8a, 4Q8b, 4Q8c, 4Q9, 4Q10, 4Q11, 4Q12, 4Q576, 6Q1, 8Q1

Frag. 1 i	Gen 40:12-13	Frag. 1 ii	Gen 40:18 - 41:11

4Q4 (4QGen*d*) *4QGenesis*d

J.R. Davila, *DJD XII*, 43-45, pl. IX
PAM 42.155, 42.725
ROC 1071
1Q1, 2Q1, 4Q1, 4Q2, 4Q3, 4Q5, 4Q6, 4Q7, 4Q8, 4Q8a, 4Q8b, 4Q8c, 4Q9, 4Q10, 4Q11, 4Q12, 4Q576, 6Q1, 8Q1

Frag. 1	Gen 1:18-27

4Q5 (4QGen*e*) *4QGenesis*e

J.R. Davila, *DJD XII*, 47-52, pl. X
PAM 42.740, 43.005
ROC 420
1Q1, 2Q1, 4Q1, 4Q2, 4Q3, 4Q4, 4Q6, 4Q7, 4Q8, 4Q8a, 4Q8b, 4Q8c, 4Q9, 4Q10, 4Q11, 4Q12, 4Q576, 6Q1, 8Q1

Frag. 1	Gen 36:43 - 37:2	Frag. 7	Gen 42:17-19
Frag. 2-3	Gen 37:27-30	Frag. 8	Gen 43:8-14
Frag. 4 i-5	Gen 40:18 - 41:8	Frag. 9	Gen 49:6-8
Frag. 4 ii, 6	Gen 41:35-44	Frag. 10	?

4Q6 (4QGen^f) *4QGenesis^f*

J.R. Davila, *DJD XII*, 53-55, pl. XI
PAM 42.152, 42.727
ROC 273
1Q1, 2Q1, 4Q1, 4Q2, 4Q3, 4Q4, 4Q5, 4Q7, 4Q8, 4Q8a, 4Q8b, 4Q8c, 4Q9, 4Q10, 4Q11, 4Q12, 4Q576, 6Q1, 8Q1

Frag. 1   Gen 48:1-11

4Q7 (4QGen^g) *4QGenesis^g*

J.R. Davila, *DJD XII*, 57-60, pl. XII
PAM 42.153, 42.723
ROC 275
1Q1, 2Q1, 4Q1, 4Q2, 4Q3, 4Q4, 4Q5, 4Q6, 4Q8, 4Q8a, 4Q8b, 4Q8c, 4Q9, 4Q10, 4Q11, 4Q12, 4Q576, 6Q1, 8Q1

Frag. 1   Gen 1:1-11   Frag. 3   Gen 3:6-7?
Frag. 2   Gen 1:13-22

4Q8 (4QGen^h1) *4QGenesis^h1*

J.R. Davila, *DJD XII*, 61-62, pl. XII
PAM 42.723
ROC 275
1Q1, 2Q1, 4Q1, 4Q2, 4Q3, 4Q4, 4Q5, 4Q6, 4Q7, 4Q8a, 4Q8b, 4Q8c, 4Q9, 4Q10, 4Q11, 4Q12, 4Q576, 6Q1, 8Q1

Frag. 1   Gen 1:8-10

4Q8a (4QGen^h2) *4QGenesis^h2*

J.R. Davia, *DJD XII*, 62, pl. XII
PAM 43.352
ROC 275
1Q1, 2Q1, 4Q1, 4Q2, 4Q3, 4Q4, 4Q5, 4Q6, 4Q7, 4Q8, 4Q8b, 4Q8c, 4Q9, 4Q10, 4Q11, 4Q12, 4Q576, 6Q1, 8Q1

Frag. 1   Gen 2:17-18

4Q8b (4QGen^h-para^) *4QGenesis^h-para^*

J.R. Davila, *DJD XII*, 62-63, pl. XII
PAM 41.996
ROC 275

Frag. 1   A paraphrase of Gen 12:4-5

4Q8c (4QGen^h-title^) *4QGenesis^h-title^*

J.R. Davila, *DJD XII*, 63-64, pl. XII
PAM 43.157
ROC 1073
The title of a Genesis manuscript written on the recto of a *page de garde*

4Q9 (4QGen^j^) *4QGenesis^j^*

J.R. Davila, *DJD XII*, 65-73, pl. XIII
PAM 43.007, 43.157
ROC 1072
1Q1, 2Q1, 4Q1, 4Q2, 4Q3, 4Q4, 4Q5, 4Q6, 4Q7, 4Q8, 4Q8a, 4Q8b, 4Q8c, 4Q10, 4Q11, 4Q12, 4Q576, 6Q1, 8Q1

Frag. 1	Gen 41:15-18	Frag. 6	Gen 43:38 - 43:2
Frag. 2 i	Gen 41:23-27	Frag. 7-8	Gen 43:5-8
Frag. 3-4	Gen 41:29-36	Frag. 9 i-10	Gen 45:14-22
Frag. 2 ii	Gen 41:38-43	Frag. 9 ii	Gen 45:26-28
Frag. 5	Gen 42:15-22	Frag. 11-13	?

4Q10 (4QGen^k^) *4QGenesis^k^*

J.R. Davila, *DJD XII*, 75-78, pl. XIII
PAM 43.008
ROC 393
1Q1, 2Q1, 4Q1, 4Q2, 4Q3, 4Q4, 4Q5, 4Q6, 4Q7, 4Q8, 4Q8a, 4Q8b, 4Q8c, 4Q9, 4Q11, 4Q12, 4Q576, 6Q1, 8Q1

Frag. 1	Gen 1:9	Frag. 4	Gen 2:1-3
Frag. 2	Gen 1:14-16	Frag. 5	Gen 3:1-2
Frag. 3	Gen 1:27-28		

4Q11 (4QpaleoGen-Exod¹) *4QpaleoGenesis-Exodusˡ*

P.W. Skehan, E. Ulrich, J.E. Sanderson, *DJD IX*, 17-50, pl. I-VI
PAM 41,387, 41.388, 41.404, 41.639, 42.011, 42.802, 42.803, 42.976, 44.100
ROC 395, 398, 402, 422
1Q1, 2Q1, 4Q1, 4Q2, 4Q3, 4Q4, 4Q5, 4Q6, 4Q7, 4Q8, 4Q8a, 4Q8b, 4Q8c, 4Q9, 4Q10, 4Q12, 4Q576, 6Q1, 8Q1
1Q2, 2Q2, 2Q3, 2Q4, 4Q1, 4Q13, 4Q14, 4Q15, 4Q16, 4Q17, 4Q18, 4Q19, 4Q20, 4Q21, 4Q22
Bibliography: P. Skehan, 'The Biblical Scrolls from Qumran and the Text of the Old Testament', *BA* 28 (1965) 88. 99; M.D. McLean, *The Use and Development of the Palaeo-Hebrew in the Hellenistic and Roman Periods* (Diss. Harvard 1982) 66-71, pl. 3; E. Ulrich, 'The Palaeo-Hebrew Biblical Manuscripts from Qumran Cave 4', in D. Dimant, L.H. Schiffman (eds.), *Time to Prepare the Way in the Wilderness: Papers on the Qumran Scrolls by Fellows of the Institute for Advanced Studies of the Hebrew University, Jerusalem (1989-1990)* (STDJ 16; Leiden: E. J. Brill, 1995) 103-129

Frag. 1	Gen 50:26; Exod 1:1-5	Frag. 15	Exod 16:23-25
Frag. 2 i	Exod 2:10	Frag. 16	Exod 16:26-31
Frag. 3-4	Exod 2:22 - 3:4	Frag. 17-18	Exod 16:33 - 17:3
Frag. 2 ii	Exod 3:17-21	Frag. 19	Exod 17:5-11
Frag. 5 i	Exod 8:13-15	Frag. 20	Exod 18:17-24
Frag. 6	Exod 8:19-21	Frag. 21	Exod 19:24 - 20:2
Frag. 5 ii	Exod 9:25-29	Frag. 22	Exod 22:23-24
Frag. 7 i-8	Exod 9:33 - 10:5	Frag. 23	Exod 23:5-16
Frag. 7 ii	Exod 11:4 - 12:12	Frag. 24-29, 30 i	Exod 25:7-20
Frag. 9	Exod 12:42-46	Frag. 30 ii, 31-34	Exod 26:29 - 27:1
Frag. 10 ii	Exod 14:15-24	Frag. 35	Exod 27:6-14
Frag. 11	Exod 16:2-6	Frag. 36	Exod 28:33-35
Frag. 12	Exod 16:7	Frag. 37	Exod 28:40-42
Frag. 13	Exod 16:13-14	Frag. 38	Exod 36:34-36
Frag. 14	Exod 16:18-20	Frag. 39-64	?

4Q12 (4QpaleoGen^m) *4QGenesis^m*

P.W.Skehan, E. Ulrich, J.E. Sanderson, *DJD IX*, 51-52, pl. VI
PAM 41.387
ROC 1125

1Q1, 2Q1, 4Q1, 4Q2, 4Q3, 4Q4, 4Q5, 4Q6, 4Q7, 4Q8, 4Q8a, 4Q8b, 4Q8c,
4Q9, 4Q10, 4Q11, 4Q576, 6Q1, 8Q1

Frag. 1   Gen 26:21-28

4QGen^n cf. **4Q576**

Frag. 1   Gen 34:7-10   Frag. 2   Gen 50:3

4Q13 (4QExod^b) *4QExodus^b*

F.M. Cross, *DJD XII*, 79-95, pl. XIV-XV
PAM 42.157, 42.728
ROC 659
1Q2, 2Q2, 2Q3, 2Q4, 4Q1, 4Q11, 4Q14, 4Q15, 4Q16, 4Q17, 4Q18, 4Q19,
4Q20, 4Q21, 4Q22

Frag. 1	Exod 1:1-6	Frag. 3 ii, 5-6 i	Exod 3:13 - 4:8
Frag. 2	Exod 1:16-21	Frag. 6 ii	Exod 5:3-14
Frag. 3 i-4	Exod 2:2-18		

4Q14 (4QExod^c) *4QExodus^c*

J.E. Sanderson, *DJD XII*, 97-125, pl. XVI-XX
PAM 42.734, 42.735, 42.739, 43.011, 43.013
ROC 1074, 1075, 1076
1Q2, 2Q2, 2Q3, 2Q4, 4Q1, 4Q11, 4Q13, 4Q15, 4Q16, 4Q17, 4Q18, 4Q19,
4Q20, 4Q21, 4Q22

Frag. 1	Exod 7:17-19	Frag. 8-9	Exod 8:16-18
Frag. 2-3	Exod 7:20-23	Frag. 10	Exod 8:22
Frag. 4	Exod 7:26 - 8:1	Frag. 11	Exod 9:10-11
Frag. 5-7	Exod 8:5-14	Frag. 12-15	Exod 9:15-20

Frag. 16	Exod 9:22-25	Frag. 31	Exod 12:12-16
Frag. 17-19	Exod 9:27-35	Frag. 32 i	Exod 12:31-48
Frag. 20-21	Exod 10:1-5	Frag. 33 i	Exod 13:18 - 14:3
Frag. 22-23	Exod 10:7-9	Frag. 32 ii, 34	Exod 14:3-13
Frag. 24-28	Exod 10:12-19	Frag. 35-36	Exod 17:1 - 18:12
Frag. 29	Exod 10:23-24	Frag. 37-45	?
Frag. 30	Exod 11:9-10		

4Q15 (4QExod^d) *4QExodus^d*

J.E. Sanderson, *DJD XII*, 127-128, pl. XXI
PAM 43.012
ROC 242
1Q2, 2Q2, 2Q3, 2Q4, 4Q1, 4Q11, 4Q13, 4Q14, 4Q16, 4Q17, 4Q18, 4Q19, 4Q20, 4Q21, 4Q22

Frag. 1	Exod 13:15-16 followed directly by Exod 15:1

4Q16 (4QExod^e) *4QExodus^e*

J.E. Sanderson, *DJD XII*, 129-131, pl. XXI
PAM 43.012
ROC 396
1Q2, 2Q2, 2Q3, 2Q4, 4Q1, 4Q11, 4Q13, 4Q14, 4Q15, 4Q17, 4Q18, 4Q19, 4Q20, 4Q21, 4Q22

Frag. 1	Exod 13:3-5

4Q17 (4QExod-Lev^f) *4QExodus-Leviticus^f*

F.M. Cross, *DJD XII*, 133-144, pl. XXII
PAM 42.266, 42.267, 42.586
ROC 1002
1Q2, 2Q2, 2Q3, 2Q4, 4Q1, 4Q11, 4Q13, 4Q14, 4Q15, 4Q16, 4Q18, 4Q19, 4Q20, 4Q21, 4Q22
1Q3, 2Q5, 4Q23, 4Q24, 4Q25, 4Q26, 4Q26a, 4Q26b, 6Q2, 11Q1, 11Q2

Frag. 1 i	Exod 38:18-22	Frag. 1 ii	Exod 39:20-24
Frag. 2 i	Exod 39:3-19	Frag. 2 ii	Exod 40:8-27

Frag. 3	Lev 1:13-15	Frag. 5	?
Frag. 4	Lev 1:17 - 2:1		

4Q18 (4QExod^g) *4QExodus^g*

J.E. Sanderson, *DJD XII*, 145-146, pl. XXI
PAM 43.012
ROC 1075
1Q2, 2Q2, 2Q3, 2Q4, 4Q1, 4Q11, 4Q13, 4Q14, 4Q15, 4Q16, 4Q17, 4Q19, 4Q20, 4Q21, 4Q22

Frag. 1   Exod 14:21-27

4Q19 (4QExod^h) *4QExodus^h*

J.E. Sanderson, *DJD XII*, 147, pl. XXI
PAM 43.012
ROC 201
1Q2, 2Q2, 2Q3, 2Q4, 4Q1, 4Q11, 4Q13, 4Q14, 4Q15, 4Q16, 4Q17, 4Q18, 4Q20, 4Q21, 4Q22

Frag. 1   Exod 6:3-6

4Q20 (4QExod^j) *4QExodus^j*

J.E. Sanderson, *DJD XII*, 149-150, pl. XXI
PAM 42.603
ROC 201
1Q2, 2Q2, 2Q3, 2Q4, 4Q1, 4Q11, 4Q13, 4Q14, 4Q15, 4Q16, 4Q17, 4Q18, 4Q19, 4Q21, 4Q22

Frag. 1-2	Exod 7:29 - 8:1	Frag. 3-7	?

4Q21 (4QExod^k) *4QExodus^k*

J.E. Sanderson, *DJD XII*, 151, pl. XXI
PAM 43.012
ROC 201

1Q2, 2Q2, 2Q3, 2Q4, 4Q1, 4Q11, 4Q13, 4Q14, 4Q15, 4Q16, 4Q17, 4Q18, 4Q19, 4Q20, 4Q22

Frag. 1   Exod 36:9-10

4Q22 (4QpaleoExod^m) *4QpaleoExodus^m*

P.W. Skehan, E. Ulrich, J.E. Sanderson, *DJD IX*, 53-130, pls. VII-XXXII
PAM 42.012, 42.012-42.020, 42.582, 42.645-42.649
ROC 661, 1005, 1126-1137, 1154-1163
DAJ
1Q2, 2Q2, 2Q3, 2Q4, 4Q1, 4Q11, 4Q13, 4Q14, 4Q15, 4Q16, 4Q17, 4Q18, 4Q19, 4Q20, 4Q21
Bibliography: P.W. Skehan, 'Exodus in the Samaritan Recension from Qumran', *JBL* 74 (1955) 182-187; .- 'The Biblical Scrolls from Qumran and the Text of the Old Testament', *BA* 28 (1965) 87-100; .- *SDB* 51 (1979) 887-890; M. Baillet, 'Le texte samaritain de l'Exode dans les manuscrits de Qumrân', in A. Caquot, M. Philonenko (eds.), *Hommages à André Dupont-Sommer* (Paris: Adrien-Maisonneuve, 1971) 363-381; J.E. Sanderson, *An Exodus Scroll from Qumran; 4QpaleoExod^m and the Samaritan Tradition* (HSS 30; Atlanta: Scholars Press, 1986)

Col. I	Exod 6:25 - 7:16
Col. II	Exod 7:16-19
Col. III	Exod 7:29 - 8:1; 12-18
Col. IV	Exod 8:19-22
Col. V	Exod 9:5-16; 19-21
Col. VI	Exod 9:35 - 10:1; 2-5
Col. VII	Exod 10:5-12; 19-24
Col. VIII	Exod 10:25-28; 11:8 - 12:2
Col. IX	Exod 12:6-8; 13-15; 17-22
Col. X	Exod 12:31-32; 34-39
Col. XI	Exod 13:3-7; 12-13
Col. XII	Exod 14:3-5; 8-9
Col. XIII	Exod 14:25-26
Col. XV	Exod 15:23 - 16:1; 4-5; 7-8
Col. XVI	Exod 16:31-32
Col. XVII	Exod 16:32 - 17:16
Col. XVIII	Exod 17:16 - 18:21
Col. XIX	Exod 18:21 - 19:1
Col. XX	Exod 19:7-17; 19:23 - 20:1

Col. **XXI**	Exod 20:18-19
Col. **XXII**	Exod 21:5-6
Col. **XXIII**	Exod 21:13-14; 22-32
Col. **XXIV**	Exod 22:3-4; 6-7; 11-12; 16-19
Col. **XXV**	Exod 22:20-30; 23:15-16
Col. **XXVI**	Exod 23:29-31; 24:1-4; 6-11
Col. **XXVII**	Exod 25:11-12; 20-22
Col. **XXVIII**	Exod 25:22-29; 31-34
Col. **XXIX**	Exod 26:8-15; 21-30
Col. **XXX**	Exod 30:10; 27:1-3; 9-14
Col. **XXXI**	Exod 27:18-19; 28:3-4; 8-12
Col. **XXXII**	Exod 28:22-24; 26-28; 30-39
Col. **XXXIII**	Exod 28:39 - 29:5
Col. **XXXIV**	Exod 29:20.22-25; 31-34
Col. **XXXV**	Exod 29:34-41; 30:12-18
Col. **XXXVI**	Exod 30:29-31; 30:34 - 31:7
Col. **XXXVII**	Exod 31:7-8; 13-15; 32:2-9
Col. **XXXVIII**	Exod 32:10-19; 25-30
Col. **XXXIX**	Exod 33:12-15
Col. **XL**	Exod 33:16 - 34:3; 10-13
Col. **XLI**	Exod 34:15-18; 20-24; 27-28
Col. **XLII**	Exod 35:1
Col. **XLIV**	Exod 36:21-24
Col. **XLV**	Exod 37:9-16
Frag. 1-447	?

4Q23 (4QLev-Num^a) *4QLeviticus-Numbers^a*

E. Ulrich, *DJD XII*, 153-176, pl. **XXIII-XXX**
PAM 42.744, 42.747, 43.034, 43.035, 43.039, 43.050
ROC 271, 272, 399, 401, 418, 419
1Q3, 2Q5, 4Q17, 4Q24, 4Q25, 4Q26, 4Q26a, 4Q26b, 6Q2, 11Q1, 11Q2
2Q6, 2Q7, 2Q8, 2Q9, 4Q27

Frag. 1	Lev 13:32-33	Frag. 14 ii, 15	Lev 18:16-21
Frag. 2-3	Lev 14:22-34	Frag. 16-19	Lev 19:3-8
Frag. 4	Lev 14:40-50	Frag. 20	Lev 24:11-12
Frag. 5	Lev 14:51-54	Frag. 21 i	Lev 26:26-33
Frag. 6	Lev 15:10-11	Frag. 21 ii, 22-23	Lev 27:5-13
Frag. 7	Lev 15:19-24	Frag. 24-26	Lev 27:14-22
Frag. 8-14 i	Lev 16:15-29	Frag. 27	Num 1:1-5

Frag. 28	Num 1:21-22	Frag. 60-61	Num 12:3-11
Frag. 29	Num 1:36-40	Frag. 62	Num 13:21
Frag. 30	Num 2:18-20	Frag. 63	Num 22:5-6
Frag. 31, 32 i, 33	Num 2:31-32,	Frag. 64	Num 22:22-24
	3:3-19	Frag. 65	Num 26:5-7
Frag. 32 ii, 34 i-43	Num 3:51 - 4:12	Frag. 66	Num 30:3?
Frag. 34 ii, 44-50	Num 4:40 - 5:9	Frag. 67	Num 30:7?
Frag. 51	Num 8:7-12	Frag. 68 i	Num 32:8-15
Frag. 52	Num 8:21-22	Frag. 69	Num 32:23-42
Frag. 53-54	Num 9:3-10	Frag. 70-71	Num 35:5-9
Frag. 55	Num 9:19-20	Frag. 68 ii	Num 33:22-34
Frag. 56	Num 10:13-23	Frag. 72-74	Num 33:52-54
Frag. 57	Num 11:4-5	Frag. 74	Num 35:4-5
Frag. 58-59	Num 11:16-22	Frag. 75-104	?

4Q24 (4QLev^b^) *4QLeviticus^b^*

E. Ulrich, *DJD XII*, 177-187, pl. XXXI-XXXIV
PAM 43.038, 43.042, 43.043, 43.157
ROC 1077, 1078, 1079
1Q3, 2Q5, 4Q17, 4Q23, 4Q25, 4Q26, 4Q26a, 4Q26b, 6Q2, 11Q1, 11Q2

Frag. 1-7	Lev 1:11 - 3:1	Frag. 21	Lev 23:40
Frag. 8	Lev 3:8-14	Frag. 20 ii, 22-25	Lev 24:2-23
Frag. 9 i, 10-17	Lev 21:17-20;	Frag. 26	Lev 25:28-29
	21:24 - 23:1	Frag. 27-28	Lev 25:45-49.51-52
Frag. 9 ii, 11 ii,		Frag. 29-30	?
18-20 i	Lev 23:2-25		

4Q25 (4QLev^c^) *4QLeviticus^c^*

E. Tov, *DJD XII*, 189-192, pl. XXXV; P.W. Skehan, E. Ulrich, *DJD XV*, 74, pl. XII
PAM 43.041, 43.157, 43.437
ROC 316
1Q3, 2Q5, 4Q17, 4Q23, 4Q24, 4Q26, 4Q26a, 4Q26b, 6Q2, 11Q1, 11Q2

Frag. 1 i	Lev 1:1-7	Frag. 2	Lev 3:16 - 4:6
Frag. 1 ii	?	Frag. 3	Lev 4:12-14

Frag. 4	Lev 4:23-28
Frag. 5	Lev 5:12-13
Frag. 6	Lev 8:26-28
Frag. 7-9	?

4Q26 (4QLev^d^) *4QLeviticus^d^*

E. Tov, *DJD XII*, 193-195, pl. XXXVI
PAM 43.040
ROC 198
1Q3, 2Q5, 4Q17, 4Q23, 4Q24, 4Q25, 4Q26a, 4Q26b, 6Q2, 11Q1, 11Q2

Frag. 1	Lev 14:27-29	Frag. 4	Lev 17:2-11
Frag. 2	Lev 14:33-36	Frag. 5-11	?
Frag. 3	Lev 15:20-24		

4Q26a (4QLev^e^) *4QLeviticus^e^*

E. Tov, *DJD XII*, 197-201, pl. XXXVII
PAM 43.036
ROC 197
1Q3, 2Q5, 4Q17, 4Q23, 4Q24, 4Q25, 4Q26, 4Q26b, 6Q2, 11Q1, 11Q2

Frag. 1	Lev 3:2-4	Frag. 6	Lev 21:9-12
Frag. 2	Lev 3:5-8	Frag. 7	Lev 21:21-24
Frag. 3	Lev 19:34-37	Frag. 8	Lev 22:4-6
Frag. 4	Lev 20:1-3	Frag. 9	Lev 22:11-17
Frag. 5	Lev 20:27 - 21:4		

4Q26b (4QLev^g^) *4QLeviticus^g^*

E. Tov, *DJD XII*, 203-204, pl. XXXVIII
PAM 43.036
ROC 197
1Q3, 2Q5, 4Q17, 4Q23, 4Q24, 4Q25, 4Q26, 4Q26a, 6Q2, 11Q1, 11Q2

Frag. 1	Lev 7:19-26

4Q27 (4QNum^b) *4QNumbers^b*

N. Jastram, *DJD XII*, 205-267, pl. XXXVIII-XLIX
PAM 43.037, 43.045-43.049, 43.166, 43.221, 43.554, 43.661, 43.693
ROC 1080-1086, 1088
2Q6, 2Q7, 2Q8, 2Q9, 4Q23
Bibliography: N. Jastram, *The Book of Numbers from Qumrân Cave IV (4QNum^b)*
(Diss. Harvard 1990); .- 'The Text of 4QNum^b', *The Madrid Qumran Congress*,
I, 177-198

Col. I	Num 11:31 - 12:11
Col. II	Num 13:7-24
Col. VI	Num 15:41 - 16:11; 14-16
Col. VIII	Num 17:12-17
Col. X	Num 18:25 - 19:6
Col. XI	Num 20:12-13
Col. XII	Num 20:16 - 21:2
Col. XIII	Num 21:12-13; 20-21
Col. XIV	Num 22:5-7
Col. XV	Num 22:7-21; 31-34
Col. XVI	Num 22:37-38; 22:41 - 23:6; 13-15
Col. XVII	Num 23:21-22; 23:27 - 24:10
Col. XVIII	Num 25:4-8; 25:16 - 26:3
Col. XIX	Num 26:4-34
Col. XX	Num 26:62-64
Col. XXI	Num 26:64 - 27:10; 18-19; 21-23
Col. XXII	Num 28:13-17
Col. XXIII	Num 28:28-31; 29:10-13; 16-18
Col. XXIV	Num 29:26-30; 30:1-3; 5-9
Col. XXV	Num 30:15 - 31:6
Col. XXVI	Num 31:21-25; 30-38; 43-47
Col. XXVII	Num 31:48-32:1; 4-10; 13-19
Col. XXVIII	Num 32:21-30; 35-39; 32:41 - 33:4
Col. XXIX	Num 33:23-31; 45-48; 50-52
Col. XXX	Num 34:4-9; 19-23; 35:3-5
Col. XXXI	Num 35:11-15; 18-25; 27-28; 35:33 - 36:2
Col. XXXII	Num 36:4-7
Frag. 85-109	?

4Q28 (4QDeut^a) *4QDeuteronomy^a*

S.A. White Crawford, *DJD XIV*, 7-8, pl. I
PAM 43.102
ROC 256
1Q4, 1Q5, 2Q10, 2Q11, 2Q12, 4Q29, 4Q30, 4Q31, 4Q32, 4Q33, 4Q34,
4Q35, 4Q36, 4Q37, 4Q38, 4Q38a, 4Q38b, 4Q39, 4Q40, 4Q41, 4Q42, 4Q43,
4Q44, 4Q45, 4Q46, 5Q1, 6Q3?, 11Q3
Bibliography: S.A. White, *A Critical Edition of Seven Manuscripts of Deuteronomy:
4QDt^a, 4QDt^c, 4QDt^d, 4QDt^f, 4QDt^g, 4QDtⁱ, 4QDtⁿ* (Diss. Harvard 1988); .-
'Three Deuteronomic Manuscripts from Cave 4, Qumran', *JBL* 112 (1993)
23-42; .- 'Special Features of Four Biblical Manuscripts from Cave IV,
Qumran: 4QDt^a, 4QDt^c, 4QDt^d, and 4QDt^g', *RevQ* 15/57-58 (1991) 157-167

Frag. 1	Deut 23:26 - 24:8

4Q29 (4QDeut^b) *4QDeuteronomy^b*

J.A. Duncan, *DJD XIV*, 9-14, pl. II
PAM 43.064
ROC 1089
1Q4, 1Q5, 2Q10, 2Q11, 2Q12, 4Q28, 4Q30, 4Q31, 4Q32, 4Q33, 4Q34,
4Q35, 4Q36, 4Q37, 4Q38, 4Q38a, 4Q38b, 4Q39, 4Q40, 4Q41, 4Q42, 4Q43,
4Q44, 4Q45, 4Q46, 5Q1, 6Q3?, 11Q3
Bibliography: J.A. Duncan, *A Critical Edition of Deuteronomy Manuscripts from
Qumran, Cave IV: 4QDt^b,4QDt^e, 4QDt^h, 4QDt^j, 4QDt^k, 4QDt^l* (Diss. Harvard
1989)

Frag. 1	Deut 29:24-27	Frag. 2 ii, 4	Deut 31:9-17
Frag. 2 i, 3	Deut 30:3-14	Frag. 5-8	Deut 31:24 - 32:3

4Q30 (4QDeut^c) *4QDeuteronomy^c*

S.A. White Crawford, *DJD XIV*, 15-34, pl. III-IX
PAM 43.065, 43.067, 43.069, 44.016
ROC 237, 238, 243
1Q4, 1Q5, 2Q10, 2Q11, 2Q12, 4Q28, 4Q29, 4Q31, 4Q32, 4Q33, 4Q34,
4Q35, 4Q36, 4Q37, 4Q38, 4Q38a, 4Q38b, 4Q39, 4Q40, 4Q41, 4Q42, 4Q43,
4Q44, 4Q45, 4Q46, 5Q1, 6Q3?, 11Q3

Frag. 1	Deut 3:25-26	Frag. 26-17	Deut 15:1-4
Frag. 2,3 i	Deut 4:13-17	Frag. 28-30	Deut 15:15-19
Frag. 3 ii	Deut 4:31-32	Frag. 31	Deut 16:2-3
Frag. 4	Deut 7:3-4	Frag. 32 i, 33	Deut 16:6-11
Frag. 5	Deut 8:1-5	Frag. 32 ii, 34	Deut 16:21 - 17:5
Frag. 6	Deut 9:11-12	Frag. 35	Deut 17:7
Frag. 7-8	Deut 9:17-19	Frag. 36-41	Deut 17:15 - 18:1
Frag. 9	Deut 9:29 - 10:2	Frag. 42	Deut 26:19 - 27:2
Frag. 10	Deut 10:5-8	Frag. 43-45 i	Deut 27:24 - 28:7
Frag. 11	Deut 11:3	Frag. 46-47	Deut 28:8-11
Frag. 12-15	Deut 11:9-13	Frag. 48	Deut 28:12-14
Frag. 16	Deut 11:18	Frag. 49	Deut 28:20
Frag. 17-18	Deut 12:18-19	Frag. 50	Deut 28:29-30
Frag. 19	Deut 12:26	Frag. 51	Deut 28:48-50
Frag. 20	Deut 12:31	Frag. 52	Deut 28:61
Frag. 21	Deut 13:5	Frag. 53	Deut 29:17-19
Frag. 22-23	Deut 13:7	Frag. 54 i-55	Deut 31:16-19
Frag. 24	Deut 13:11-12	Frag. 54 ii	Deut 32:3
Frag. 25 i	Deut 13:16	Frag. 56-66	?

4Q31 (4QDeut^d) *4QDeuteronomy^d*

S.A. White Crawford, *DJD XIV*, 35-38, pl. X
PAM 43.221
ROC 323
1Q4, 1Q5, 2Q10, 2Q11, 2Q12, 4Q28, 4Q29, 4Q30, 4Q32, 4Q33, 4Q34,
4Q35, 4Q36, 4Q37, 4Q38, 4Q38a, 4Q38b, 4Q39, 4Q40, 4Q41, 4Q42, 4Q43,
4Q44, 4Q45, 4Q46, 5Q1, 6Q3?, 11Q3

Frag. 1 i	Deut 2:24-26	Frag. 1 ii	Deut 3:14 - 4:1

4Q32 (4QDeut^e) *4QDeuteronomy^e*

J.A. Duncan, *DJD XIV*, 39-44, pl. XI
PAM 43.068
ROC 233
1Q4, 1Q5, 2Q10, 2Q11, 2Q12, 4Q28, 4Q29, 4Q30, 4Q31, 4Q33, 4Q34,
4Q35, 4Q36, 4Q37, 4Q38, 4Q38a, 4Q38b, 4Q39, 4Q40, 4Q41, 4Q42, 4Q43,
4Q44, 4Q45, 4Q46, 5Q1, 6Q3?, 11Q3

Frag. 1	Deut 3:24	Frag. 3 ii, 5	Deut 8:5-7; 10-11; 15-16
Frag. 2 i	Deut 7:12-16		
Frag. 2 ii, 3 i, 4	Deut 7:21 - 8:4	Frag. 6-8	?

4Q33 (4QDeut^f) *4QDeuteronomy^f*

S.A. White Crawford, *DJD XIV*, 45-54, pl. XII-XV
PAM 43.058, 43.062
ROC 317, 322
1Q4, 1Q5, 2Q10, 2Q11, 2Q12, 4Q28, 4Q29, 4Q30, 4Q31, 4Q32, 4Q34, 4Q35, 4Q36, 4Q37, 4Q38, 4Q38a, 4Q38b, 4Q39, 4Q40, 4Q41, 4Q42, 4Q43, 4Q44, 4Q45, 4Q46, 5Q1, 6Q3?, 11Q3

Frag. 1	Deut 4:24-26	Frag. 17-19	Deut 21:4-12
Frag. 2-3	Deut 7:22-25	Frag. 20-23	Deut 22:12-19
Frag. 4-6	Deut 8:2-14	Frag. 24-25	Deut 23:2-26
Frag. 7	Deut 9:6-7	Frag. 26-28	Deut 24:2-7
Frag. 8	Deut 17:17-18	Frag. 29-31	Deut 25:3-9
Frag. 9	Deut 18:6-10	Frag. 32-35	Deut 26:18 - 27:10
Frag. 10-12	Deut 18:18-22	Frag. 36-40	?
Frag. 13-16	Deut 19:17 - 20:6		

4Q34 (4QDeut^g) *4QDeuteronomy^g*

S.A. White Crawford, *DJD XIV*, 55-59, pl. XVI
PAM 43.063
ROC 400
1Q4, 1Q5, 2Q10, 2Q11, 2Q12, 4Q28, 4Q29, 4Q30, 4Q31, 4Q32, 4Q33, 4Q35, 4Q36, 4Q37, 4Q38, 4Q38a, 4Q38b, 4Q39, 4Q40, 4Q41, 4Q42, 4Q43, 4Q44, 4Q45, 4Q46, 5Q1, 6Q3?, 11Q3

Frag. 1	Deut 9:12-14	Frag. 6-9	Deut 25:14 - 26:5
Frag. 2	Deut 23:18-20	Frag. 10	Deut 28:21-25
Frag. 3	Deut 24:16-22	Frag. 11	Deut 28:27-29
Frag. 4-5	Deut 24:1-5		

4Q35 (4QDeut^h) *4QDeuteronomy^h*

J.A. Duncan, *DJD XIV*, 60-70, pl. XVII-XVIII
PAM 42.711, 43.357

ROC 389

1Q4, 1Q5, 2Q10, 2Q11, 2Q12, 4Q28, 4Q29, 4Q30, 4Q31, 4Q32, 4Q33, 4Q34, 4Q36, 4Q37, 4Q38, 4Q38a, 4Q38b, 4Q39, 4Q40, 4Q41, 4Q42, 4Q43, 4Q44, 4Q45, 4Q46, *4Q122*, 5Q1, 6Q3?, 11Q3

Bibliography: E. Eshel, M. Stone, 'A New Fragment of 4QDeut[h]', *JBL* 112 (1993) 487-489

Frag. 1	Deut 1:1-17	Frag. 8	Deut 4:31-34
Frag. 2-4	Deut 1:22-24; 29-39	Frag. 9	Deut 19:21?
Frag. 5-6	Deut 1:41; 1:43 - 2:6	Frag. 10	Deut 31:9-11
Frag. 7	Deut 2:28-30	Frag. 11-15	Deut 33:18-22

4Q36 (4QDeut[i]) *4QDeuteronomy[i]*

S.A. White Crawford, *DJD XIV*, 71-74, pl. XIX
PAM 42.006, 43.066
ROC 323
1Q4, 1Q5, 2Q10, 2Q11, 2Q12, 4Q28, 4Q29, 4Q30, 4Q31, 4Q32, 4Q33, 4Q34, 4Q35, 4Q37, 4Q38, 4Q38a, 4Q38b, 4Q39, 4Q40, 4Q41, 4Q42, 4Q43, 4Q44, 4Q45, 4Q46, 5Q1, 6Q3?, 11Q3

Frag. 1-2 i	Deut 20:9-13	Frag. 6	Deut 23:23 - 24:1
Frag. 3 i, 4, 5 i	Deut 21:23 - 22:9	Frag. 7-8	?
Frag. 3 ii, 5 ii	Deut 23:6-8; 12-16		

4Q37 (4QDeut[j]) *4QDeuteronomy[j]*

J.A. Duncan, *DJD XIV*, 75-91, pl. XX-XXIII
PAM 43.051, 43.053, 43.054
ROC 170, 171, 172
1Q4, 1Q5, 2Q10, 2Q11, 2Q12, 4Q28, 4Q29, 4Q30, 4Q31, 4Q32, 4Q33, 4Q34, 4Q35, 4Q36, 4Q38, 4Q38a, 4Q38b, 4Q39, 4Q40, 4Q41, 4Q42, 4Q43, 4Q44, 4Q45, 4Q46, 5Q1, 6Q3?, 11Q3
Bibliography: J.A. Duncan, 'Considerations of 4QDt[j] in Light of the 'All Souls Deuteronomy' and Cave 4 Phylactery Texts', in *The Madrid Qumran Congress I*, 199-215, pls. 356-361

Col. I	Deut 5:1-11	Col. IV	Deut 5:29-33
Col. II	Deut 5:13-15; 21	Col. V	Deut 8:5-10
Col. III	Deut 5:22-28	Col. VIII	Deut 11:6-13

Col. IX	Deut 11:21?;	Col. XII	Deut 32:7-8
	Exod 12:43-44		
Col. X	Exod 12:46 - 13:5	Frag. 35-47	?

4Q38 (4QDeut^{k1}) *4QDeuteronomy^{k1}*

J.A. Duncan, *DJD XIV*, 93-98, pl. XXIV
PAM 43.056
ROC 1090
1Q4, 1Q5, 2Q10, 2Q11, 2Q12, 4Q28, 4Q29, 4Q30, 4Q31, 4Q32, 4Q33,
4Q34, 4Q35, 4Q36, 4Q37, 4Q38a, 4Q38b, 4Q39, 4Q40, 4Q41, 4Q42, 4Q43,
4Q44, 4Q45, 4Q46, 5Q1, 6Q3?, 11Q3

Frag. 1	Deut 5:28-32	Frag. 4	Deut 32:22-23
Frag. 2	Deut 11:6-13	Frag. 5	Deut 32:25-27
Frag. 3	Deut 32:17-18		

4Q38a (4QDeut^{k2}) *4QDeuteronomy^{k2}*

J.A. Duncan, *DJD XIV*, 99-105, pl. XXV
PAM 43.056
ROC 1090
1Q4, 1Q5, 2Q10, 2Q11, 2Q12, 4Q28, 4Q29, 4Q30, 4Q31, 4Q32, 4Q33,
4Q34, 4Q35, 4Q36, 4Q37, 4Q38, 4Q38b, 4Q39, 4Q40, 4Q41, 4Q42, 4Q43,
4Q44, 4Q45, 4Q46, 5Q1, 6Q3?, 11Q3

Frag. 1	Deut 19:8-16	Frag. 5	Deut 25:19 - 26:5
Frag. 2-3	Deut 20:6-19	Frag. 6-7	Deut 26:18 - 27:1?
Frag. 4	Deut 23:22 - 24:3	Frag. 8-13	?

4Q38b (4QDeut^{k3}) *4QDeuteronomy^{k3}*

J.A. Duncan, *DJD XIV*, 107, pl. XXV
PAM 43.054
ROC 172
1Q4, 1Q5, 2Q10, 2Q11, 2Q12, 4Q28, 4Q29, 4Q30, 4Q31, 4Q32, 4Q33,
4Q34, 4Q35, 4Q36, 4Q37, 4Q38, 4Q38a, 4Q39, 4Q40, 4Q41, 4Q42, 4Q43,
4Q44, 4Q45, 4Q46, 5Q1, 6Q3?, 11Q3

| Frag. 1 | Deut 30:16-18 |

4Q39 (4QDeutⁱ) *4QDeuteronomyⁱ*

J.A. Duncan, *DJD XIV*, 109-112, pl. XXVI
PAM 43.052
ROC 390
1Q4, 1Q5, 2Q10, 2Q11, 2Q12, 4Q28, 4Q29, 4Q30, 4Q31, 4Q32, 4Q33,
4Q34, 4Q35, 4Q36, 4Q37, 4Q38, 4Q38a, 4Q38b, 4Q40, 4Q41, 4Q42, 4Q43,
4Q44, 4Q45, 4Q46, 5Q1, 6Q3?, 11Q3

Frag. 1-2	Deut 10:12-15	Frag. 8-9	Deut 33:1-2
Frag. 3	Deut 28:67-68	Frag. 10	Deut 34:4-6
Frag. 4-5	Deut 29:2-5	Frag. 11	?
Frag. 6-7	Deut 31:12		

4Q40 (4QDeut^m) *4QDeuteronomy^m*

J.A. Duncan, *DJD XIV*, 113-116, pl. XXVII
PAM 42.714
ROC 255
1Q4, 1Q5, 2Q10, 2Q11, 2Q12, 4Q28, 4Q29, 4Q30, 4Q31, 4Q32, 4Q33,
4Q34, 4Q35, 4Q36, 4Q37, 4Q38, 4Q38a, 4Q38b, 4Q39, 4Q41, 4Q42, 4Q43,
4Q44, 4Q45, 4Q46, 5Q1, 6Q3?, 11Q3
Bibliography: F. García Martínez, 'Les manuscrits du désert de Juda et le
Deutéronome', in F. García Martínez *et al.* (eds.), *Studies in Deuteronomy* (SVT
53; Leiden: E.J. Brill, 1994) 66-69.

Frag. 1-3	Deut 3:18-22	Frag. 5	Deut 7:18-22
Frag. 4	Deut 4:32-33		

4Q41 (4QDeutⁿ) *4QDeuteronomyⁿ*

S. A. White, *DJD XIV*, 117-128, pl. XXVIII-XXIX.
PAM 42.642
ROC 981
1Q4, 1Q5, 2Q10, 2Q11, 2Q12, 4Q28, 4Q29, 4Q30, 4Q31, 4Q32, 4Q33,
4Q34, 4Q35, 4Q36, 4Q37, 4Q38, 4Q38a, 4Q38b, 4Q39, 4Q40, 4Q42, 4Q43,
4Q44, 4Q45, 4Q46, 5Q1, 6Q3?, 11Q3
Bibliography: S.A. White, '4QDtⁿ: Biblical Manuscript or Excerpted Text?', in

H. Attridge *et al.* (eds.), *Of Scribes and Scrolls. Studies on the Hebrew Bible, Intertestamental Judaism, and Christian Origins, Presented to John Strugnell on the Occasion of His Sixtieth Birthday* (Lanham, Md.: University Press of America, 1990) 13-20; E. Eshel, '4QDeut^n - A Text That Has Undergone Harmonistic Editing', *HUCA* 62 (1991) 117-154

Col. I	Deut 8:5-10	Col. IV	Deut 5:14-21
Col. II	Deut 5:1-6	Col. V	Deut 5:22-28
Col. III	Deut 5:6-14	Col. VI	Deut 5:28 - 6:1

4Q42 (4QDeut^o) *4QDeuteronomy^o*

S. A. White, *DJD XIV*, 129-133, pl. XXX
PAM 43.055
ROC 1091
1Q4, 1Q5, 2Q10, 2Q11, 2Q12, 4Q28, 4Q29, 4Q30, 4Q31, 4Q32, 4Q33, 4Q34, 4Q35, 4Q36, 4Q37, 4Q38, 4Q38a, 4Q38b, 4Q39, 4Q40, 4Q41, 4Q43, 4Q44, 4Q45, 4Q46, 5Q1, 6Q3?, 11Q3

Frag. 1	Deut 2:8	Frag. 9-11	Deut 28:33-36
Frag. 2-4	Deut 4:30-34	Frag. 12-14	Deut 28:47-52;
Frag. 5	Deut 5:1-5		28:58-62
Frag. 6-7	Deut 5:8-9	Frag. 15	Deut 29:22-25
Frag. 8	Deut 28:15-18		

4Q43 (4QDeut^p) *4QDeuteronomy^p*

S. A. White, *DJD XIV*, 135-36, pl. XXXI
PAM 43.055
ROC 1091
1Q4, 1Q5, 2Q10, 2Q11, 2Q12, 4Q28, 4Q29, 4Q30, 4Q31, 4Q32, 4Q33, 4Q34, 4Q35, 4Q36, 4Q37, 4Q38, 4Q38a, 4Q38b, 4Q39, 4Q40, 4Q41, 4Q42, 4Q44, 4Q45, 4Q46, 5Q1, 6Q3?, 11Q3
Bibliography: F. García Martínez, 'Les manuscrits du désert de Juda et le Deutéronome', in F. García Martínez *et al.* (eds.), *Studies in Deuteronomy* (SVT 53; Leiden: E.J. Brill, 1994) 66-69

Frag. 1, 2 i, 3	Deut 6:4-11	Frag. 2 ii	?

4Q44 (4QDeut^q) *4QDeuteronomy^q*

P.W. Skehan, E.Ulrich, *DJD XIV*, 137-142, pl. XXXI
PAM 41.350, 42.164
ROC 676
1Q4, 1Q5, 2Q10, 2Q11, 2Q12, 4Q28, 4Q29, 4Q30, 4Q31, 4Q32, 4Q33,
4Q34, 4Q35, 4Q36, 4Q37, 4Q38, 4Q38a, 4Q38b, 4Q39, 4Q40, 4Q41, 4Q42,
4Q43, 4Q45, 4Q46, 5Q1, 6Q3?, 11Q3

Frag. 1	Deut 32:9-10?	Frag. 5 ii	Deut 32:41-43
Frag. 2-5 i	Deut 32:37-41		

4Q45 (4QpaleoDeut^r) *4QpaleoDeuteronomy^r*

P.W. Skehan, E. Ulrich, J. Sanderson, *DJD IX*, 131-152, pl. XXXIV-XXXVI
PAM 41.640, 41.645
ROC 1138, 1139
1Q4, 1Q5, 2Q10, 2Q11, 2Q12, 4Q28, 4Q29, 4Q30, 4Q31, 4Q32, 4Q33,
4Q34, 4Q35, 4Q36, 4Q37, 4Q38, 4Q38a, 4Q38b, 4Q39, 4Q40, 4Q41, 4Q42,
4Q43, 4Q44, 4Q46, 5Q1, 6Q3?, 11Q3

Frag. 1	Deut 1:8?	Frag. 25	Deut 15:5-6
Frag. 2	Deut 7:2-5	Frag. 21 ii	Deut 15:8-10
Frag. 3-4	Deut 7:6-7	Frag. 26	Deut 19:2-3
Frag. 5-6	Deut 7:16-21	Frag. 27-29	Deut 22:3-6
Frag. 7-10	Deut 7:21-25	Frag. 30	Deut 23:7
Frag. 11	Deut 10:11-12	Frag. 31-32	Deut 23:12-15
Frag. 12	Deut 11:28	Frag. 33	Deut 28:15-18.20
Frag. 13-14	Deut 11:30 - 12:1	Frag. 34	Deut 31:29
Frag. 15-16	Deut 12:2-5	Frag. 35	Deut 32:6-8
Frag. 17	Deut 12:11-12	Frag. 36-37	Deut 32:10-11
Frag. 18	Deut 12:22	Frag. 38-40	Deut 32:13-14
Frag. 19	Deut 13:19 - 14:1	Frag. 41	Deut 32:33-35
Frag. 20	Deut 14:2-4	Frag. 42-43	Deut 33:2-8
Frag. 21 i, 22	Deut 14:19-22	Frag. 44	Deut 33:29 - 34:1
Frag. 23-24	Deut 14:26-29	Frag. 45-65	?

4Q46 (4QpaleoDeut^s) *4QpaleoDeuteronomy^s*

P.W. Skehan, E. Ulrich, J. Sanderson, *DJD IX*, 153-154, pl. XXXVII

PAM 41.387
ROC 1139
1Q4, 1Q5, 2Q10, 2Q11, 2Q12, 4Q28, 4Q29, 4Q30, 4Q31, 4Q32, 4Q33, 4Q34, 4Q35, 4Q36, 4Q37, 4Q38, 4Q38a, 4Q38b, 4Q39, 4Q40, 4Q41, 4Q42, 4Q43, 4Q44, 4Q45, 5Q1, 6Q3?, 11Q3

Frag. 1   Deut 26:14-15

4Q47 (4QJosh^a) *4QJoshua^a*

E. Ulrich, *DJD XIV*, 143-152, pl. XXXII-XXXIV
PAM 43.057, 43.060
ROC 1092, 1093
4Q48
Bibliography: A. Rofé, 'The Editing of the Book of Joshua in the Light of 4QJosh^a', in G.J. Brooke, F. García Martínez (eds.), *New Qumran Texts and Studies. Proceedings of the First Meeting of the International Organization for Qumran Studies, Paris 1992* (STDJ 15; Leiden: E.J. Brill, 1994) 73-88; E. Ulrich, '4QJoshua^a and Joshua's First Altar in the Promised Land', in *New Qumran Texts and Studies*, 89-104, Pl. 4-6; K. Bieberstein, *Lukian und Theodotion im Josuabuch. Mit einem Beitrag zu dem Josuarollen von Hirbet Qumrân* (Biblische Notizen Beihefte 7; München, 1994)

Frag. 1-2	Josh 8:34-35; 5:2-7	Frag. 9 ii, 13-16	Josh 8:3-14, 18?
Frag. 3-8	Josh 6:5-10	Frag. 17-18	Josh 10:2-5
Frag. 9 i-12	Josh 7:12-17	Frag. 19-22	Josh 10:8-11

4Q48 (4QJosh^b) *4QJoshua^b*

E. Tov, *DJD XIV*, 153-160, pl. XXXV
PAM 43.061
ROC 392
4Q47
Bibliography: E. Tov, '4QJosh^b', in Z.J. Kapera (ed.), *Intertestamental Essays in Honour of Józef Tadeusz Milik* (Qumranica Mogilanensia 6; Kraków, 1992) 205-212; K. Bieberstein, *Lukian und Theodotion im Josuabuch. Mit einem Beitrag zu dem Josuarollen von Hirbet Qumrân* (Biblische Notizen Beihefte 7; München, 1994)

Frag. 1	Josh 2:11-12	Frag. 5	Josh 17:11-15
Frag. 2-3	Josh 3:15 - 4:3	Frag. 6 i-ii	?
Frag. 4	Josh 17:1-5		

4Q49 (4QJudg^a) *4QJudges^a*

J. Trebolle Barrera, *DJD XIV*, 161-164, pl. XXXVI
PAM 43.059
ROC 305
1Q6, 4Q50
Bibliography: J. Trebolle Barrera, 'Textual Variants in 4QJudg^a and the Textual and Editorial History of the Book of Judges', *RevQ* 14/54 (1989) 229-245

| Frag. 1 | Judg 6:2-6.11-13 |

4Q50 (4QJudg^b) *4QJudges^b*

J. Trebolle Barrera, *DJD XIV*, 165-169, pl. XXXVI
PAM 43.059, 43.157
ROC 1123
1Q6, 4Q49
Bibliography: J. Trebolle Barrera, 'Edition préliminaire de 4QJudges^b. Contribution des manuscrits qumrâniens des Juges à l'étude textuelle et littéraire de ce livre', *RevQ* 15/57-58 (1991) 79-100

| Frag. 1 | Judg 19:5-7 | Frag. 2-3 | Judg 21:12-25 |

4Q51 (4QSam^a) *4QSamuel^a*

F.M. Cross, 'A New Qumran Biblical Fragment Related to the Original Hebrew Underlying the Septuagint', *BASOR* 132 (1953) 15-26; .- 'The Oldest Manuscript from Qumran', *JBL* 74 (1955) 165, n. 40; .- 'The Ammonite Oppression of the Tribes of Gad and Reuben: Missing verses from 1 Sam 11 Found in 4QSamuel^a, in E. Tov (ed.), *The Hebrew and Greek Texts of Samuel. 1980 Proceedings IOSCS* (Jerusalem, 1980) 105-116
PAM 43.107-43.109, 43.111, 43.113-43.117, 43.119-120, 43.122-43.125
ROC 998, 1094-1107
1Q7, 4Q52, 4Q53
Bibliography: E. Ulrich, *The Qumran Text of Samuel and Josephus* (HSM 19;

Chico: Scholars Press, 1978); E.D. Herbert, *Reconstructing Biblical Dead Sea Scrolls. A New Method Applied to the Reconstruction of 4QSam^a* (STDJ XXII; Leiden: E.J. Brill, 1997); D.W. Parry, '4QSam^a (4Q51): A Preliminary Edition of 1 Samuel 25:3-31:4', in *Provo Conference*, 58-71; A. Rofé, '4QMidrash Samuel? - Observations Concerning the Character of 4QSam^a', *Textus* 19 (1998) 63-74

1 Sam 1:11-13, 22-28	2 Sam 2:5-16, 25-27
1 Sam 2:1-6, 8-10, 16-36	2 Sam 2:29-32
1 Sam 3:1-3, 18-20	2 Sam 3:1-8, 23-21
1 Sam 4:9-12	2 Sam 4:1-4, 9-12
1 Sam 5:8-12	2 Sam 5:1-16 (5:4-5 omitted)
1 Sam 6:1-7, 12-13, 16-18, 20-21	2 Sam 6:2-9, 12-18
1 Sam 7:1	2 Sam 7:23-29
1 Sam 8:9-20	2 Sam 8:2-8
1 Sam 9:6-8, 11-12, 16-24	2 Sam 10:4-7, 18-19
1 Sam 10:3-18, 25-27	2 Sam 11:2-12, 16-20
1 Sam 11:1, 7-12	2 Sam 12:4-5, 8-9, 13-20, 30-31
1 Sam 12:7-8, 14-19	2 Sam 13:1-6, 13-34, 36-39
1 Sam 14:24-25, 28-34, 47-51	2 Sam 14:1-3, 18-19
1 Sam 15:24-32	2 Sam 15:1-6, 27-31
1 Sam 17:3-6	2 Sam 16:1-2, 11-13, 17-18, 21-23
1 Sam 24:4-5, 8-9, 14-23	2 Sam 18:2-7, 9-11
1 Sam 25:3-12, 20-21, 25-26, 39-40	2 Sam 19:7-12
1 Sam 26:10-12, 21-24	2 Sam 20:2-3, 9-14, 23-26
1 Sam 27:8-12	2 Sam 21:1-2, 4-6, 15-17
1 Sam 28:1-3, 22-25	2 Sam 22:30-51
1 Sam 30:27-31	2 Sam 23:1-6
1 Sam 31:2-4	2 Sam 24:16-20

4Q52 (4QSam^b) *4QSamuel^b*

F.M. Cross, 'The oldest Manuscript from Qumran',*JBL* 74 (1955) 147-172, pl. 6; .- *The Ancient Library of Qumran*, pl. 18
PAM 43.072, 43.076
ROC 195, 206
1Q7, 4Q51, 4Q53
Bibliography: F.I. Anderson, 'Another Look at 4QSam^b', *RevQ* 14/53 (1989) 7-29

Frag. 1	1 Sam 16:1-11	Frag. 3-4	1 Sam 21:3-10
Frag. 2	1 Sam 19:10-17	Frag. 5-6	1 Sam 23:9-17

4Q53 (4QSam^c) *4QSamuel^c*

E. Ulrich, '4QSamuel^c: A Fragmentary Manuscript of 2 Samuel 14-15 from the
Scribe of the Serek Hay-yaḥad (1QS)', *BASOR* 235 (1979) 1-25, pls. 4-5
PAM 43.071, 43.077
ROC 405, 406
1Q7, 4Q51, 4Q52

Frag. 1	1 Sam 25:30-32	Frag. 7-11	2 Sam 15:4-15
Frag. 2-5	2 Sam 14:7-21	Frag. 12	?
Frag. 5-7	2 Sam 14:22 - 15:4		

4Q54 (4QKgs) *4QKings*

J. Trebolle Barrera, *DJD XIV*, 165-169, pl. XXXVI
PAM 43.079
ROC 1108
5Q2, 6Q4
Bibliography: J. Trebolle Barrera, 'A Preliminary Edition of 4QKings (4Q54)',
The Madrid Qumran Congress I, 229-246, pl. 362

Frag. 1	1 Kings 7:20-21	Frag. 6	1 Kings 7:51 - 8:9
Frag. 2 i	1 Kings 7:25-27	Frag. 7	1 Kings 8:16-18
Frag. 3-4	1 Kings 7:29-31	Frag. 8	?
Frag. 5	1 Kings 7:31-42		

4Q55 (4QIsa^a) *4QIsaiah^a*

P.W. Skehan, E. Ulrich, *DJD XV*, 7-18, pls. I-II
PAM 43.015
ROC 266, 660
1QIsa^a, 1QIsa^b (+ 1Q8), 4Q56, 4Q57, 4Q58, 4Q59, 4Q60, 4Q61, 4Q62,
4Q62a, 4Q63, 4Q64, 4Q65, 4Q66, 4Q67, 4Q68, 4Q69, 4Q69a, 4Q69b, 5Q3
Bibliography: J. Muilenberg, 'Fragments of Another Qumran Isaiah Scroll',
BASOR 135 (1954) 28-32; P.W. Skehan, *SDB* 51, 811; F.J. Morrow, *The Text
of Isaiah at Qumran* (Diss. The Catholic University of America, 1973)

Frag. 1	Isa 1:1-3	Frag. 6	Isa 6:4-8
Frag. 2-3	Isa 2:7-10	Frag. 7	Isa 11:11-15
Frag. 4-5	Isa 4:5 - 5:1	Frag. 8	Isa 12:4 - 13:16

Frag. 9	Isa 17:9-14	Frag. 16, 18	unidentified
Frag. 10, 11 i, 12-14	Isa 19:24 - 21:16	Frag. 17	Isa 33:16-17 (?)
Frag. 11 ii	Isa 22:13 - 23:12		

4Q56 (4QIsa[b]) *4QIsaiah[b]*

P.W. Skehan, E. Ulrich, *DJD XV*, 19-43, pls. III-VI
PAM 43.017, 43.031
ROC 1140, 1141
1QIsa[a], 1QIsa[b] (+ 1Q8), 4Q55, 4Q57, 4Q58, 4Q59, 4Q60, 4Q61, 4Q62,
4Q62a, 4Q63, 4Q64, 4Q65, 4Q66, 4Q67, 4Q68, 4Q69, 4Q69a, 4Q69b, 5Q3

Frag. 1	Isa 1:1-6	Frag. 26	Isa 40:22-26
Frag. 2	Isa 2:3-16	Frag. 27	Isa 41:8-11
Frag. 3 i	Isa 3:14-22	Frag. 28-30	Isa 42:2-7.9-12
Frag. 3 ii	Isa 5:15-28	Frag. 31 i	Isa 43:12-15
Frag. 4	Isa 9:10-11	Frag. 31 ii	Isa 44:19-28
Frag. 5	Isa 11:7-9	Frag. 32, 33 i	Isa 45:20 - 46:3
Frag. 6	Isa 12:2	Frag. 33 ii	Isa 48:6-8
Frag. 7	Isa 13:3-18	Frag. 34	Isa 49:21-23
Frag. 8-9	Isa 17:8 - 18:1	Frag. 35	Isa 51:1-2
Frag. 10-13	Isa 18:5 - 20:4	Frag. 36	Isa 51:14-16
Frag. 14	Isa 21:11-14	Frag. 37	Isa 52:2
Frag. 15	Isa 22:24-25	Frag. 38	Isa 52:7
Frag. 16 i	Isa 24:2, 4	Frag. 39	Isa 53:11-12
Frag. 16 ii, 17-20	Isa 26:1-5.7-19	Frag. 40	Isa 61:1-3
Frag. 21	Isa 35:9 - 36:2	Frag. 41	Isa 64:5 - 65:1
Frag. 22-23	Isa 37:29-32	Frag. 42	Isa 66:24
Frag. 24-25	Isa 39:1 - 40:4	Frag. 43-47	unidentified

4Q57 (4QIsa[c]) *4QIsaiah[c]*

P.W. Skehan, E. Ulrich, *DJD XV*, 45-74, pls. VII-XII
PAM 43.020, 43.022, 43.029
ROC 363, 382, 387
1QIsa[a], 1QIsa[b] (+ 1Q8), 4Q55, 4Q56, 4Q58, 4Q59, 4Q60, 4Q61, 4Q62,
4Q62a, 4Q63, 4Q64, 4Q65, 4Q66, 4Q67, 4Q68, 4Q69, 4Q69a, 4Q69b, 5Q3
Bibliography: P.W. Skehan, 'The Text of Isaiah at Qumran', *CBQ* 17 (1955)
158-163

Frag. 1-2	Isa 9:3-12	Frag. 6	Isa 11:4-11
Frag. 3-5	Isa 10:23-33	Frag. 7	Isa 11:14 - 12:1

Frag. 8	Isa 14:1-5	Frag. 28	Isa 48:10-11
Frag. 51	Isa 14:13?	Frag. 29	Isa 48:12-13
Frag. 9 i	Isa 22:10-14	Frag. 30	Isa 48:14-15
Frag. 10	Isa 22:23	Frag. 31	Isa 48:17-19
Frag. 9 ii, 11, 12 i, 52	Isa 23:8 - 24:15	Frag. 32	Isa 49:22
Frag. 13	Isa 24:19 - 25:2	Frag. 33-35,	
Frag. 12 ii, 14-15, 53	Isa 25:8 - 26:9	55-57	Isa 51:8-16
Frag. 16-17	Isa 28:6-14	Frag. 36-38	Isa 52:10 - 53:3
Frag. 18-20	Isa 30:8-17	Frag. 39	Isa 53:6-8
Frag. 21-22	Isa 33:2-8	Frag. 40	Isa 54:3-5
Frag. 23	Isa 33:16-23	Frag. 41	Isa 54:7-8
Frag. 24	Isa 44:3-7	Frag. 43	Isa 54:9
Frag. 54	Isa 44:23	Frag. 44-47	Isa 54:9 - 55:7
Frag. 25-26	Isa 45:1-4.6-8	Frag. 48	Isa 66:20-24
Frag. 27	Isa 45:8-13	Frag. 58-77	unidentified

4Q58 (4QIsa^d) *4QIsaiah^d*

P.W. Skehan, E. Ulrich, *DJD XV*, 75-88, pls. XIII-XV
PAM 43.0118, 43.019
ROC 236, 250
1QIsa^a, 1QIsa^b (+ 1Q8), 4Q55, 4Q56, 4Q57, 4Q59, 4Q60, 4Q61, 4Q62, 4Q62a, 4Q63, 4Q64, 4Q65, 4Q66, 4Q67, 4Q68, 4Q69, 4Q69a, 4Q69b, 5Q3

Col. I	Isa 45:20	Col. VIII	Isa 53:8 - 54:2
Col. II	Isa 46:10 - 47:6	Col. IX	Isa 54:2-11
Col. III	Isa 47:8-9; 48:8-16	Col. XI	Isa 57:9-17
Col. IV	Isa 48:17 - 49:15	Col. XII	Isa 57:18 - 58:3.5-7
Col. VII	Isa 52:4-7	Frag. 16	unidentified

4Q59 (4QIsa^e) *4QIsaiah^e*

P.W. Skehan, E. Ulrich, *DJD XV*, 89-97, pls. XVI-XVII
PAM 43.025
ROC 262
1QIsa^a, 1QIsa^b (+ 1Q8), 4Q55, 4Q56, 4Q57, 4Q58, 4Q60, 4Q61, 4Q62, 4Q62a, 4Q63, 4Q64, 4Q65, 4Q66, 4Q67, 4Q68, 4Q69, 4Q69a, 4Q69b, 5Q3
Bibliography: E. Ulrich, P.W. Skehan, 'An Edition of 4QIsa^e, Including the Former 4QIsa^l', *RevQ* 17/65-68 (1996) 23-36

Frag. 1	Isa 2:1-4	Frag. 2-3	Isa 7:17-20

Frag. 4-10	Isa 8:2-14	Frag. 20-22	Isa 14:1-13
Frag. 7 ii, 11-16 i	Isa 9:17 - 10:10 (11?)	Frag. 18 ii, 23-24	Isa 14:20-24
Frag. 16 ii	Isa 11:14-15	Frag. 25	Isa 59:15-16
Frag. 17, 18 i, 19	Isa 12:1 - 13:4		

4Q60 (4QIsa^f) *4QIsaiah^f*

P.W. Skehan, E. Ulrich, *DJD XV*, 99-111, pls. XVIII-XX
PAM 43.024
ROC 324
1QIsa^a, 1QIsa^b (+ 1Q8), 4Q55, 4Q56, 4Q57, 4Q58, 4Q59, 4Q61, 4Q62, 4Q62a, 4Q63, 4Q64, 4Q65, 4Q66, 4Q67, 4Q68, 4Q69, 4Q69a, 4Q69b, 5Q3

Frag. 1-2	Isa 1:10-16	Frag. 19-20	Isa 24:1-3
Frag. 3-6	Isa 1:18 - 2:3	Frag. 21	Isa 27:1
Frag. 7	Isa 5:13-14	Frag. 22	Isa 27:5-6
Frag. 8	Isa 5:25	Frag. 23-24	Isa 27:8-10
Frag. 9-10	Isa 6:3-8	Frag. 25	Isa 27:11-12
Frag. 11	Isa 6:10-13	Frag. 26	Isa 28:6-9
Frag. 12 i	Isa 7:16-18	Frag. 27	Isa 28:16-17 (?)
Frag. 13	Isa 7:23 - 8:1	Frag. 28	Isa 28:18?
Frag. 12 ii, 14, 15	Isa 8:4-11	Frag. 29	Isa 28:22
Frag. 16	Isa 20:4-6	Frag. 30	Isa 28:24?
Frag. 17	Isa 22:14-22	Frag. 31	Isa 29:8?
Frag. 18	Isa 22:25	Frag. 32-34	unidentified

4Q61 (4QIsa^g) *4QIsaiah^g*

P.W. Skehan, E. Ulrich, *DJD XV*, 113-115, pl. XXI
PAM 43.162
ROC 175
1QIsa^a, 1QIsa^b (+ 1Q8), 4Q55, 4Q56, 4Q57, 4Q58, 4Q59, 4Q60, 4Q62, 4Q62a, 4Q63, 4Q64, 4Q65, 4Q66, 4Q67, 4Q68, 4Q69, 4Q69a, 4Q69b, 5Q3

Frag. 1-8	Isa 42:14 - 43:4.16-24

4Q62 (4QIsa^h) *4QIsaiah^h*

P.W. Skehan, E. Ulrich, *DJD XV*, 117-119, pl. XXI
PAM 43.014

ROC 261

1QIsaᵃ, 1QIsaᵇ (+ 1Q8), 4Q55, 4Q56, 4Q57, 4Q58, 4Q59, 4Q60, 4Q61, 4Q62a, 4Q63, 4Q64, 4Q65, 4Q66, 4Q67, 4Q68, 4Q69, 4Q69a, 4Q69b, 5Q3

Frag. 1-2   Isa 42:2.4-11

4Q62a (4QIsaⁱ) *4QIsaiahⁱ*

P.W. Skehan, E. Ulrich, *DJD XV*, 121-122, pl. XXI
PAM 43.014
ROC 261
1QIsaᵃ, 1QIsaᵇ (+ 1Q8), 4Q55, 4Q56, 4Q57, 4Q58, 4Q59, 4Q60, 4Q61, 4Q62, 4Q63, 4Q64, 4Q65, 4Q66, 4Q67, 4Q68, 4Q69, 4Q69a, 4Q69b, 5Q3

Frag. 1   Isa 56:7-8   Frag. 2   Isa 57:5-8

4Q63 (4QIsaʲ) *4QIsaiahʲ*

P.W. Skehan, E. Ulrich, *DJD XV*, 123, pl. XXII
PAM 43.029
ROC 1142
1QIsaᵃ, 1QIsaᵇ (+ 1Q8), 4Q55, 4Q56, 4Q57, 4Q58, 4Q59, 4Q60, 4Q61, 4Q62, 4Q62a, 4Q64, 4Q65, 4Q66, 4Q67, 4Q68, 4Q69, 4Q69a, 4Q69b, 5Q3

Isa 1:1-6

4Q64 (4QIsaᵏ) *4QIsaiahᵏ*

P.W. Skehan, E. Ulrich, *DJD XV*, 125-127, pl. XXII
PAM 43.019
ROC 250
1QIsaᵃ, 1QIsaᵇ (+ 1Q8), 4Q55, 4Q56, 4Q57, 4Q58, 4Q59, 4Q60, 4Q61, 4Q62, 4Q62a, 4Q63, 4Q65, 4Q66, 4Q67, 4Q68, 4Q69, 4Q69a, 4Q69b, 5Q3

Frag. 1-5   Isa 28:26 - 29:9

4Q65 (4QIsa^l) *4QIsaiah^l*

P.W. Skehan, E. Ulrich, *DJD XV*, 129-130
PAM 42.043, 43.014
ROC 261
1QIsa^a, 1QIsa^b (+ 1Q8), 4Q55, 4Q56, 4Q57, 4Q58, 4Q59, 4Q60, 4Q61, 4Q62, 4Q62a, 4Q63, 4Q64, 4Q66, 4Q67, 4Q68, 4Q69, 4Q69a, 4Q69b, 5Q3

| Frag. 1 | Isa 7:14-15 | Frag. 2 | Isa 8:11-14 |

4Q66 (4QIsa^m) *4QIsaiah^m*

P.W. Skehan, E. Ulrich, *DJD XV*, 131-132, pl. XXII
PAM 43.014
ROC 261
1QIsa^a, 1QIsa^b (+ 1Q8), 4Q55, 4Q56, 4Q57, 4Q58, 4Q59, 4Q60, 4Q61, 4Q62, 4Q62a, 4Q63, 4Q64, 4Q65, 4Q67, 4Q68, 4Q69, 4Q69a, 4Q69b, 5Q3

| Frag. 1-3 | Isa 60:20 - 61:1 | Frag. 4-6 | Isa 61:3-6 |

4Q67 (4QIsa^n) *4QIsaiah^n*

P.W. Skehan, E. Ulrich, *DJD XV*, 133-134, pl. XXIII
PAM 43.014
ROC 261
1QIsa^a, 1QIsa^b (+ 1Q8), 4Q55, 4Q56, 4Q57, 4Q58, 4Q59, 4Q60, 4Q61, 4Q62, 4Q62a, 4Q63, 4Q64, 4Q65, 4Q66, 4Q68, 4Q69, 4Q69a, 4Q69b, 5Q3

Isa 58:13-14

4Q68 (4QIsa^o) *4QIsaiah^o*

P.W. Skehan, E. Ulrich, *DJD XV*, 135-137, pl. XXIII
PAM 43.014
ROC 261
1QIsa^a, 1QIsa^b (+ 1Q8), 4Q55, 4Q56, 4Q57, 4Q58, 4Q59, 4Q60, 4Q61, 4Q62, 4Q62a, 4Q63, 4Q64, 4Q65, 4Q66, 4Q67, 4Q69, 4Q69a, 4Q69b, 5Q3

| Frag. 1 | Isa 14:28 - 15:2 | Frag. 2 | unidentified |

4Q69 (pap4QIsa^p) *4QIsaiah^p*

P.W. Skehan, E. Ulrich, *DJD XV*, 139, pl. XXIII
PAM 43.014
ROC 261
1QIsa^a, 1QIsa^b (+ 1Q8), 4Q55, 4Q56, 4Q57, 4Q58, 4Q59, 4Q60, 4Q61, 4Q62, 4Q62a, 4Q63, 4Q64, 4Q65, 4Q66, 4Q67, 4Q68, 4Q69a, 4Q69b, 5Q3

Frag. 1-2   Isa 5:28-30

4Q69a (4QIsa^q) *4QIsaiah^q*

P.W. Skehan, E. Ulrich, *DJD XV*, 141, pl. XXIII
PAM 43.018
ROC 261
1QIsa^a, 1QIsa^b (+ 1Q8), 4Q55, 4Q56, 4Q57, 4Q58, 4Q59, 4Q60, 4Q61, 4Q62, 4Q62a, 4Q63, 4Q64, 4Q65, 4Q66, 4Q67, 4Q68, 4Q69, 4Q69b, 5Q3

Isa 54:10-13

4Q69b (4QIsa^r) *4QIsaiah^r*

P.W. Skehan, E. Ulrich, *DJD XV*, 143, pl. XXIII
PAM 43.018
ROC 261
1QIsa^a, 1QIsa^b (+ 1Q8), 4Q55, 4Q56, 4Q57, 4Q58, 4Q59, 4Q60, 4Q61, 4Q62, 4Q62a, 4Q63, 4Q64, 4Q65, 4Q66, 4Q67, 4Q68, 4Q69, 4Q69a, 5Q3

Isa 30:23

4Q70 (4QJer^a) *4QJeremiah^a*

E. Tov, *DJD XV*, 145-170, pls. XXIV-XXIX
PAM 43.073, 43.074, 43.075, 43.216
ROC 1109, 1110, 1111
2Q13, 4Q71, 4Q72, 4Q72a, 4Q72b
Bibliography: J.G. Janzen, *Studies in the Text of Jeremiah* (HSM 6; Harvard University, Cambridge, 1973) 173-184; E. Tov, 'The Jeremiah Scrolls from Cave

4', *RevQ* 14/54 (1989) 189-206; .- '4QJer^a - A Preliminary Edition', *Textus* 17 (1994) 1-41, pls. i-vii

Col. I	Jer 7:1-2	Col. IX	Jer 13:27; 14:4-7
Col. II	Jer 7:15-19	Col. X	Jer 15:1-2
Col. III	Jer 7:28 - 9:2	Col. XI	Jer 17:8-26
Col. IV	Jer 9:7-15	Col. XII	Jer 18:15 - 19:1
Col. V	Jer 10:9-14; 23	Col. XIII	Jer 20:14-18; 21:1?
Col. VI	Jer 11:3-6; 19-20	Col. XIV	Jer 22:3-16
Col. VII	Jer 12:3-7; 13-16	Col. XV	Jer 26:10?
Col. VIII	Jer 12:17 - 13:7; 22?	Frag. 37-50	unidentified

4Q71 (4QJer^b) *4QJeremiah^b*

E. Tov, *DJD XV*, 171-176, pl. XXIX
PAM 43.078
ROC 152
2Q13, 4Q70, 4Q72, 4Q72a, 4Q72b
Bibliography: E. Tov, 'Three Fragments of Jeremiah from Qumran Cave 4', *RevQ* 15/60 (1992) 531-537

Jer 9:22 - 10:21

4Q72 (4QJer^c) *4QJeremiah^c*

E. Tov, *DJD XV*, 177-201, pls. XXX-XXXVI
PAM 43.101, 43.103-43.106
ROC 232, 244-346, 671
2Q13, 4Q70, 4Q71, 4Q72a, 4Q72b
Bibliography: E. Tov, '4QJer^c (4Q72)', in G.J. Norton, S. Pisano (eds.), *Tradition of the Text. Studies Offered to Dominique Barthélemy in Celebration of His 70th Birthday* (OBO 109; Freiburg/Göttingen, 1991) 248-276, pls. I-VII

Col. I	Jer 4:5	Col. VIII	Jer 20:7-9
Col. II	Jer 4:13-16	Col. IX	Jer 20:13-15
Col. III	Jer 8:1-3	Col. X	Jer 21:7-10
Col. IV	Jer 8:21 - 9:5	Col. XI	Jer 22:4-6
Col. V	Jer 10:12-13	Col. XII	Jer 22:10-17
Col. VI	Jer 19:8-9	Col. XIII	Jer 22:17-28
Col. VII	Jer 20:2-5	Col. XIV	Jer 25:7-8

Col. XV	Jer 25:15-17	Col. XX	Jer 30:6-9
Col. XVI	Jer 25:24-26	Col. XXI	Jer 30:17 - 31:4
Col. XVII	Jer 26:10-13	Col. XXII	Jer 31:4-14
Col. XVIII	Jer 27:1-3	Col. XXIII	Jer 31:19-26
Col. XIX	Jer 27:13-15	Col. XXV	Jer 33:16-20

4Q72a (4QJer[d]) *4QJeremiah[d]*

E. Tov, *DJD XV*, 203-205, pl. XXXVII
PAM 43.078
ROC 152
2Q13, 4Q70, 4Q71, 4Q72, 4Q72b
Bibliography: E. Tov, 'Three Fragments of Jeremiah from Qumran Cave 4', *RevQ* 15/60 (1992) 538-540

Jer 43:2-10

4Q72b (4QJer[e]) *4QJeremiah[e]*

E. Tov, *DJD XV*, 207, pl. XXXVII
PAM 43.078
ROC 152
2Q13, 4Q70, 4Q71, 4Q72, 4Q72a
Bibliography: E. Tov, 'Three Fragments of Jeremiah from Qumran Cave 4', *RevQ* 15/60 (1992) 540-541

Jer 50:4-6

4Q73 (4QEzek[a]) *4QEzekiel[a]*

J.E. Sanderson, *DJD XV*, 209-214, pl. XXXVIII
PAM 43.082
ROC 1112
1Q9, 3Q1, 4Q74, 4Q75, 11Q4
Bibliography: J. Lust, 'Ezekiel Manuscripts in Qumran', in J. Lust (ed.), *Ezekiel and his Book: Textual and Literary Criticism and their Interrelation* (BETL 74; Leuven, 1986) 90-100; L.A. Sinclair, 'A Qumran Biblical Fragment: 4QEz[a] (Ezek 10,17-11,1)', *RevQ* 14/53 (1989) 99-105; É. Puech, '4QEz[a]: Note additionnelle', *RevQ* 14/53 (1989) 107-108

Frag. 1	Ezek 10:6-16	Frag. 3 ii	Ezek 23:44-47
Frag. 2	Ezek 10:17 - 11:11	Frag. 4	Ezek 41:3-6
Frag. 3 i	Ezek 23:14-15, 17-18		

4Q74 (4QEzek[b]) *4QEzekiel[b]*

J.E. Sanderson, *DJD XV*, 215-218, pl. XXXIX
PAM 43.088
ROC 207
1Q9, 3Q1, 4Q73, 4Q75, 11Q4

Frag. 1-4	Ezek 1:10-13	Frag. 6 ii	Ezek 1:20-24
Frag. 5-6 i	Ezek 1:16-17, 19		

4Q75 (4QEzek[c]) *4QEzekiel[c]*

J.E. Sanderson, *DJD XV*, 219-220, pl. XXXIX
PAM 43.088
ROC 207
1Q9, 3Q1, 4Q73, 4Q74, 11Q4

Ezek 24:2-3

4Q76 (4QXII[a]) *4QMinor Prophets[a]*

R.E. Fuller, *DJD XV*, 221-232, pls. XL-XLII
PAM 43.099, 43.100, 43.220
ROC 296, 314, 1114
4Q77, 4Q78, 4Q79, 4Q80, 4Q81, 4Q82, 5Q4
Bibliography: R.E. Fuller, *The Minor Prophets Manuscripts from Qumrân, Cave 4* (Diss. Harvard, 1988) 5-38; R. Fuller, 'Text-Critical Problems in Malachi 2:10-16', *JBL* 110 (1991) 47-57

Frag. 1	Zech 14:18	Col. V	Jon 1:1-5, 7-8
Col. I	Mal 2:10-14	Col. VI	Jon 1:9 - 2:1
Col. II	Mal 2:15 - 3:4	Frag. 21	Jon 2:7
Col. III	Mal 3:5-14	Frag. 22	Jon 3:2
Col. IV	Mal 3:14-24	Frag. 23	unidentified

4Q77 (4QXII^b) *4QMinor Prophets^b*

R.E. Fuller, *DJD XV*, 233-236, pl. XLIII
PAM 43.087
ROC 1113
4Q76, 4Q78, 4Q79, 4Q80, 4Q81, 4Q82, 5Q4
Bibliography: R.E. Fuller, *The Minor Prophets Manuscripts from Qumrân*, 39-53

Frag. 1	Zeph 1:2	Frag. 4-5	Hag 2:2-4
Frag. 2	Zeph 2:13-15	Frag. 6	unidentified
Frag. 3	Zeph 3:19 - Hag 1:2		

4Q78 (4QXII^c) *4QMinor Prophets^c*

R.E. Fuller, *DJD XV*, 237-251, pls. XLIV-XLVI
PAM 43.112, 43.118
ROC 161, 162
4Q76, 4Q77, 4Q79, 4Q80, 4Q81, 4Q82, 5Q4
Bibliography: M. Testuz, 'Deux fragments inédits des manuscrits de la Mer Morte', *Semitica* 5 (1955) 37-38; R.E. Fuller, *The Minor Prophets Manuscripts from Qumrân*, 55-104

Frag. 1-2	Hos 2:13-15	Frag. 18-20	Joel 4:6-21
Frag. 3	Hos 3:2-4	Frag. 21-23	Amos 2:11 - 3:7
Frag. 4-7	Hos 4:1 - 5:1	Frag. 24-29, 48	Amos 3:8 - 4:2
Frag. 44	Hos 7:12-13	Frag. 30-33	Amos 6:13 - 7:16
Frag. 8	Hos 13:3-10	Frag. 34	Zeph 2:15 - 3:2
Frag. 9	Hos 13:15 - 14:6	Frag. 35	Mal 3:6-7?
Frag. 10-12	Joel 1:10 - 2:1	Frag. 36-37, 39-43,	
Frag. 13	Joel 2:8-10	45-47, 49-52	unidentified
Frag. 14-17	Joel 2:10-23	Frag. 38	4Q83 Ps 38:4-6

4Q79 (4QXII^d) *4QMinor Prophets^d*

R.E. Fuller, *DJD XV*, 253-256, pl. XLVI
PAM 43.091
ROC 410
4Q76, 4Q77, 4Q78, 4Q80, 4Q81, 4Q82, 5Q4
Bibliography: L.A. Sinclair, 'A Qumran Biblical Fragment: Hosea 4QXII^d (Hos

1:7-2:5)', *BASOR* 239 (1980) 61-65; R.E. Fuller, *The Minor Prophets Manuscripts from Qumrân*, 105-115

Frag. 1-2   Hos 1:7 - 2:5

4Q80 (4QXII°) *4QMinor Prophets°*

R.E. Fuller, *DJD XV*, 257-265, pl. XLVII
PAM 43.110, 43.220
ROC 258
4Q76, 4Q77, 4Q78, 4Q79, 4Q81, 4Q82, 5Q4
Bibliography: R.E. Fuller, *The Minor Prophets Manuscripts from Qumrân*, 116-140

Frag. 1	Hag 2:18-19	Frag. 14-15	Zech 5:8 - 6:5
Frag. 2	Hag 2:20-21	Frag. 16	Zech 8:2-4
Frag. 3	Zech 1:4-6	Frag. 17	Zech 8:6-7
Frag. 4-5	Zech 1:9-10, 13-14	Frag. 18	Zech 12:7-12
Frag. 6-7	Zech 2:10-14	Frag. 19-25	unidentified
Frag. 8-13	Zech 3:2 - 4:4		

4Q81 (4QXII^f) *4QMinor Prophets^f*

R.E. Fuller, *DJD XV*, 267-270, pl. XLVIII
PAM 43.091
ROC 410
4Q76, 4Q77, 4Q78, 4Q79, 4Q80, 4Q82, 5Q4
Bibliography: R.E. Fuller, *The Minor Prophets Manuscripts from Qumrân*, 141-150

Col. I	Jon 1:6-8	Frag. 5	Mic 5:1-2
Col. II	Jon 1:10-16		

4Q82 (4QXII^g) *4QMinor Prophets^g*

R.E. Fuller, *DJD XV*, 271-318, pls. XLIX-LXIV
PAM 41.519, 41.967, 41.976, 41.980, 41.998, 42.023. 42.975
ROC 1143-1147, 1164-1171
4Q76, 4Q77, 4Q78, 4Q79, 4Q80, 4Q81, 5Q4

Frag. 1-2 verso, 3 i, 4 i	Hos 2:1-5
Frag. 3 ii, 4 ii, 5-7	Hos 2:14-19, 22 - 4:1
Frag. 8b-9	Hos 4:10-11, 13-14
Frag. 10	Hos 6:3-4
Frag. 11 verso	Hos 6:8 - 7:1
Frag. 12	Hos 7:12-13
Frag. 13	Hos 7:13 - 8:1
Frag. 14	Hos 9:1-4
Frag. 15-16a, 17-19a, 20 recto-26	Hos 9:9 - 10:14; 11:2-5
Frag. 19b, 27-30a, 31 verso-32	Hos 11:6 - 13:1
Frag. 33	Hos 13:6-8(?)
Frag. 16b	Hos 13:11-13
Frag. 8a	Hos 14:9-10
Frag. 34-35	Joel 1:12-14
Frag. 30b, 31a recto, 36-37	Joel 2:2-13
Frag. 31b recto, 38-40a	Joel 4:4-9, 11-14, 17, 19-20
Frag. 30g, 40b-43b, 44	Amos 1:3 - 2:1
Frag. 43a	Amos 2:7-9
Frag. 45-46	Amos 2:15 - 3:2
Frag. 47a i-48	Amos 4:4-9
Frag. 49	Amos 5:1-2
Frag. 47a ii, 50	Amos 5:9-18
Frag. 47b, 51-52a, 53a-54a, 55-56a, 57-58	Amos 6:1-4, 6 - 7:1
Frag. 52b, 53b, 54b, 56b, 59-60 verso, 61 verso-64	Amos 7:7-12, 14 - 8:5
Frag. 65-68	Amos 8:11 - 9:1
Frag. 69	Amos 9:6
Frag. 70-75	Amos 9:14 - Obad 1-5, 8-12, 14-15
Frag. 76-78 i, 79-81	Jon 1:1-9
Frag. 78 ii, 82-87	Jon 2:3 - 3:3
Frag. 88-91 i	Jon 4:5-11
Frag. 92	Mic 1:7
Frag. 91 ii, 93-94 i	Mic 1:12-15; 2:3-4
Frag. 94 ii	Mic 3:12 - 4:2
Frag. 95	Mic 5:6-7
Frag. 96	Mic 7:2-3
Frag. 97 verso	Mic 7:20
Frag. 98	Nah 1:7-9
Frag. 97 recto, 99	Nah 2:9-11
Frag. 100	Nah 3:1-3
Frag. 101	Nah 3:17
Frag. 102	Hab 2:4?

Frag. 103	Zeph 3:3-5
Frag. 104	Zech 10:11 - 11:2
Frag. 105	Zech 12:1-3
Frag. 106-258	unidentified

4Q83 (4QPsᵃ) *4QPsalmsᵃ*

P.W. Skehan, E. Ulrich, P. Flint, *DJD XVI* (in press); R.E. Fuller, *DJD XV*, 251, pl. XLVI
PAM 43.027
ROC 1148
1Q10, 1Q11, 1Q12, 2Q14, 3Q2, 4Q84, 4Q85, 4Q86, 4Q87, 4Q88, 4Q89, 4Q90, 4Q91, 4Q92, 4Q93, 4Q94, 4Q95, 4Q96, 4Q97, 4Q98, 4Q98a, 4Q98b, 4Q98c, 4Q98d, 4Q236, 5Q5, 6Q5, 8Q2, 11Q5, 11Q6, 11Q7, 11Q8, 11Q9
Bibliography: P.W. Skehan, 'The Qumran Manuscripts and Textual Criticism', 218; .- SDB 51, 813-817; .- 'Qumran and Old Testament Criticism', in M. Delcor (ed.), *Qumrân. Sa piété, sa théologie et son milieu* (BETL 46; Paris-Leuven, 1988) 173-182; G.H. Wilson, *The Editing of the Hebrew Psalter* (SBLDS 76; Chico, 1985) 96-98; P.W Flint, *The Dead Sea Psalms Scrolls and the Book of Psalms* (Diss. Notre Dame 1993); .- 'The Psalms Scrolls from the Judaean Desert: Relationships and Textual Affiliations', in G.J. Brooke, F. García Martínez (eds.), *New Qumran Texts and Studies*, 31-52; E. Ulrich, 'The Oldest Psalms Manuscript: 4QPsᵃ (4Q83)', in *Provo Conference*, 72-92, pls. 1-4

Frag. 1	Ps 5:9 - 6:4	Frag. 9	Ps 38:16-23;
Frag. 2	Ps 25:8-12		71:1-14
Frag. 3	Ps 25:15	Frag. 10	Ps 47:2
Frag. 4 i	Ps 31:23-25; 33:1-12	Frag. 11-12	Ps 53:2 - 54:6
Frag. 5	Ps 34:21 - 35:2	Frag. 13	Ps 56:4
Frag. 6	Ps 35:13-20	Frag. 14 i-15	Ps 62:13 - 63:4
Frag. 4 ii	Ps 35:26 - 36:9	Frag. 14 ii-19 i	Ps 66:16 - 67:8
Frag. 7-8	Ps 38:2-12.	Frag. 19 ii-20	Ps 69:1-19

4Q84 (4QPsᵇ) *4QPsalmsᵇ*

P.W. Skehan, E. Ulrich, P. Flint, *DJD XVI* (in press)
PAM 42.023, 42.025, 42.026, 43.032
ROC 360, 383, 999
1Q10, 1Q11, 1Q12, 2Q14, 3Q2, 4Q83, 4Q85, 4Q86, 4Q87, 4Q88, 4Q89, 4Q90, 4Q91, 4Q92, 4Q93, 4Q94, 4Q95, 4Q96, 4Q97, 4Q98, 4Q98a, 4Q98b, 4Q98c, 4Q98d, 4Q236, 5Q5, 6Q5, 8Q2, 11Q5, 11Q6, 11Q7, 11Q8, 11Q9

Bibliography: P.W. Skehan, 'A Psalm Manuscript from Qumran (4QPsᵇ)', *CBQ* 26 (1964) 313-322

Col. I	Ps 91:5-8	Col. XXI	Ps 102:18-25
Col. II	Ps 91:12-15	Col. XXII	Ps 102:26-103:3
Col. III	Ps 92:4-8	Col. XXIII	Ps 103:4-6.9-11
Col. IV	Ps 92:13-15	Col. XXIV	Ps 103:11-14
Col. VI	Ps 94:1-4.8-9	Col. XXV	Ps 103:20-21
Col. VII	Ps 94:10-14.17-18	Col. XXXI	Ps 112:4-5
Col. VIII	Ps 94:21-22	Col. XXXIIII	Ps 116:17-19
Col. XV	Ps 99:5-6	Col. XXXIV	Ps 118:1-3.6-11
Col. XVI	Ps 100:1-2	Col. XXXV	Ps 118:18-20. 23-26
Col. XX	Ps 102:10-17		

4Q85 (4QPsᶜ) *4QPsalmsᶜ*

P.W. Skehan, E. Ulrich, P. Flint, *DJD XVI* (in press)
PAM 43.023, 43.156
ROC 312
1Q10, 1Q11, 1Q12, 2Q14, 3Q2, 4Q83, 4Q84, 4Q86, 4Q87, 4Q88, 4Q89, 4Q90, 4Q91, 4Q92, 4Q93, 4Q94, 4Q95, 4Q96, 4Q96, 4Q98, 4Q98a, 4Q98b, 4Q98c, 4Q98d, 4Q236, 5Q5, 6Q5, 8Q2, 11Q5, 11Q6, 11Q7, 11Q8, 11Q9
Bibliography: P.W. Skehan, E. Ulrich, P. Flint, 'The Preliminary Edition of 4QPsᶜ (4Q85)', *RevQ* 18/71 (1998) 343-357. pls. 1-4

Frag. 1	Ps 16:7-9	Frag. 9	Ps 42:5
Frag. 2	Ps 17:1?	Frag. 10	Ps 44:8-9?
Frag. 3 i	Ps 18:3-14	Frag. 11	Ps 45:8-11
Frag. 4	Ps 18:16-17	Frag. 12-14 i	Ps 48:15 - 49:17
Frag. 3 ii	Ps 18:32-36, 39-41	Frag. 14 ii - 15	Ps 50:13 - 51:5
Frag. 5	Ps 27:12-28:3	Frag. 14 iii - 16	Ps 52:5 - 53:1
Frag. 6	Ps 28:4	Frag. 17-19	unidentified
Frag. 7	Ps 35:27-28	Frag. 20	?
Frag. 8	Ps 37:18-19		

4Q86 (4QPsᵈ) *4QPsalmsᵈ*

P.W. Skehan, E. Ulrich, P. Flint, *DJD XVI* (in press)
PAM 43.021
ROC 225

1Q10, 1Q11, 1Q12, 2Q14, 3Q2, 4Q83, 4Q84, 4Q85, 4Q87, 4Q88, 4Q89, 4Q90, 4Q91, 4Q92, 4Q93, 4Q94, 4Q95, 4Q96, 4Q97, 4Q98, 4Q98a, 4Q98b, 4Q98c, 4Q98d, 4Q236, 5Q5, 6Q5, 8Q2, 11Q5, 11Q6, 11Q7, 11Q8, 11Q9
Bibliography: P.W. Flint, 'A Preliminary Edition of 4QPs^d (4Q86)', in *Provo Conference*, 93-105, pls. 1-2

Col. I	Ps 106:48?; 147:1-4
Col. II	Ps 147:13-17, 20; 104:1-5
Col. III	Ps 104:8-11. 14-15
Col. IV	Ps 104:22-25
Col. V	Ps 104:33-35

4Q87 (4QPs^e) *4QPsalms^e*

P.W. Skehan, E. Ulrich, P. Flint, *DJD XVI* (in press)
PAM 43.028
ROC 263
1Q10, 1Q11, 1Q12, 2Q14, 3Q2, 4Q83, 4Q84, 4Q85, 4Q86, 4Q88, 4Q89, 4Q90, 4Q91, 4Q92, 4Q93, 4Q94, 4Q95, 4Q96, 4Q97, 4Q98, 4Q98a, 4Q98b, 4Q98c, 4Q98d, 4Q236, 5Q5, 6Q5, 8Q2, 11Q5, 11Q6, 11Q7, 11Q8, 11Q9
Bibliography: P.W. Flint, 'The "11QPs^a-Psalter" in the Dead Sea Scrolls, Including the Preliminary Edition of 4QPs^e', in C.A. Evans, S. Talmon (eds.), *The Quest for Context and Meaning. Studies in Biblical Intertextuality in Honor of James A. Sanders* (Biblical Interpretation Series 28; Leiden: Brill, 1997) 173-196, pls. 1-3

Frag. 1	Ps 76:10-12; 77:1	Frag. 13	Ps 105:23-25
Frag. 2 i	Ps 78:6-7	Frag. 14-16 ii,	Ps 105:36-45;
Frag. 2 ii	Ps 78:31-33	17-19	146:1?
Frag. 3	Ps 81:2-3	Frag. 20	Ps 109:1?
Frag. 4	Ps 86:10-11	Frag. 21	Ps 109:8?
Frag. 5	Ps 88:1-5	Frag. 22	Ps 109:13
Frag. 6-7	Ps 89:44-48	Frag. 23	Ps 114:5?
Frag. 8	Ps 89:50-53	Frag. 24	Ps 115:15 - 116:3
Frag. 9	Ps 118:29?; 104:1-3	Frag. 25	Ps 120:6-7
Frag. 10-11	Ps 104:20-22	Frag. 26 i	Ps 125:2 - 126:5
Frag. 12, 16 i	Ps 105:1-3	Frag. 26 ii	Ps 129:8 - 130:6

4Q88 (4QPsf) *4QPsalmsf*

P.W. Skehan, E. Ulrich, P. Flint, *DJD XVI* (in press)
PAM 43.026, 43.603
ROC 436, 1149
1Q10, 1Q11, 1Q12, 2Q14, 3Q2, 4Q83, 4Q84, 4Q85, 4Q86, 4Q87,
4Q89,4Q90, 4Q91, 4Q92, 4Q93, 4Q94, 4Q95, 4Q96, 4Q97, 4Q98, 4Q98a,
4Q98b, 4Q98c, 4Q98d, 4Q236, 5Q5, 6Q5, 8Q2, 11Q5, 11Q6, 11Q7, 11Q8,
11Q9
Bibliography: J. Starcky, 'Psaumes apocryphes de la grotte 4 de Qumrân (4QPsf
VII-X)', *RB* 73 (1966) 350-371, pl. XVIII; P.W. Skehan, E. Ulrich, P.W. Flint,

[מודי א]ני   15   [ציון בכול]   אז]כרך לברכה   14   *vacat*]   Col. VII

[ושלום   17   [זכרך ג]דולה תק[ותך ציון]   16   אהבתי]ך ברוך לעולמים
ותו]חל[ת ישועתך לבוא]

הו]א   [ולוא תשכח תוחלתך מי   2   [לוא תובד תקותך ציון]   1   Col. VIII
אנוש   5   בעולו נבחן אד]ם כדרכו   מלט]   4   [הוא זנה   [זנה אבד צדק או מי   3
מסנאיך כול   התפזרו   7   סביב נכרתו צריך ציון   6   *vacat*   שתלם   כמ]עשיו י[
אזכרך   רבות   פעמים   כול   תבל   *vacat*   9   באף תשבוחתך ציון מעל כול   8   ערבה
...   12   [אה]בתיך צדק עולמים תסיגי   11   [לברכ]ה ציון בכול מודי אני   10
נבי[א]ים   14   [נ]אמר עליכי חלמת   קחי חזון   13   ברכות נכבדים תקבלי
נפשי   [תשמח   16   [ציון שבחי ע]ל[י]ון פודך]   15   תתבעך רומי ורחבי
בכבודך]

[כ]י בא   שם יהוה   5   ויהללו את   [...]   רבים   4   [...]   3-1 ...   Col. IX
[עולה לוא   מן הארץ   [בני   7   כל מע[ש]ה להשבית רשעים   6   לשפט את
פריה   10   ואין שח[ת בגבו]ליהם והארץ   9   יתנו] שמ[י]ם טלם   8   ימצאו
גפניהם ולוא   פרי ב.. 12   תכחש [תבו]אותיה עצי   11   תתן [בעתה ולוא
[...]   15   [י]ראי יהוה   ענוים וישבעו   14   יוכלו   *vacat*   13   יכזב]ו עינו]תיה

כל   יחד יהללו נא   6   אז יהללו שמים וארץ   ...   5   [...]   4-3 ...   Col. X
וגילה גילך   שמחה שמחתכה   8   שמחה יהודה שמחתכה   7   כוכבי נשף

4Q88 (4QPs^f) *4QPsalms^f*

'A Scroll Containing "Biblical" and "Apocryphal" Psalms: A Preliminary Edition of 4QPs^f (4Q88)', *CBQ* 60 (1998) 267-282; *PTSDSSP 4A*, 202-211

Frag. 1-2	Ps 22:15-17	Col. VII	Ps 109:24-28;
Col. I	Ps 107:2-5		Apostrophe to Zion
Col. II	Ps 107:8-16	Col. VIII	Apostrophe to Zion
Col. III	Ps 107:18-19, 22-30	Col. IX	Eschatological Hymn
Col. IV	Ps 107:35-42	Col. X	Apostrophe to Judah
Col. VI	Ps 109:4-6	Frag. 3	unidentified

Col. VII (= 11Q5 XXII)   *14* [*Blank* I rem]ember you, [Zion] for blessing; [with all] *15* [my strength] I have loved [you. May your memory be blessed for ever!] *16* [Gr]eat is [your] ho[pe, O Zion;] *17* [peace will come and the expect]ation [of your salvation.]

Col. VIII (= 11Q5 XXII)   *1* [The hope for you does not perish, O Zion] *2* [nor is the expectation of you forgotten. Who i]s *3* [the one that died being just or who] is the one *4* who has been saved [in his iniquity? Ma]n [is examined] according to his path, *5* each one [is] rewarded according to [his] de[eds.] *Blank 6* All round you, O Zion, your enemies are quelled *7* and all those who hate you are scattered. It is pleasant *8* to hear your praise, O Zion, throughout the whole *9* world. *Blank* Many times I remember you *10* [for blessi]ng, Zion; with all my strength I *11* [lo]ve you. May you receive everlasting justice *12* ... the blessings of the glorious ones may you obtain! *13* Accept a vision [sp]oken in your regard, a dream *14* of prophets, requested for you! Be glorified and magnified, *15* [O Zion! Praise the Mos]t H[igh, your Saviour!] *16* [May my soul be happy in your glory!]

Col. IX   *1-3* ...[...] *4* many [...] and may they praise the *5* name of YHWH. [Bec]ause he comes to judge *6* every cre[at]ure, to obliterate evil-doers *7* from the earth, [the sons] of wickedness will not *8* be found. The heavens [will give] their dew, *9* and there will be no corru[pt dealing in] their [terri]tories. The earth *10* [will give] its fruit in its season, and *11* its [pro]duce will not fail. The fruit-trees *12* [...] of their grape-vines, and *13* their [spring]s will not deceive. *Blank 14* The poor will eat and those who [f]ear YHWH will be replete. *15* [...] ...

Col. X   *3-4* [...] ... *5* ... Then the heavens and earth will exult *6* together. Let all the stars of dusk, then, exult. *7* Be happy, Judah, be happy! *8* Be happy and

9 חג חגיך נדריך שלם כי אין   10 בקרבך בליעל תרם ידך   11 תגבר ימינך
הנא אואבים   12 יובדו ויתפרדו כול [פוע]לי   13 און ואתה יהוה לעו[לם]
14 תהיה כבודכה לועל[ם וע]ד   15 [ה]ללו ...[...]

4Q89 (4QPsᵍ) *4QPsalmsᵍ*

P.W. Skehan, E. Ulrich, P. Flint, *DJD XVI* (in press)
PAM 43.026
ROC 1150
1Q10, 1Q11, 1Q12, 2Q14, 3Q2, 4Q83, 4Q84, 4Q85, 4Q86, 4Q87, 4Q88,
4Q90, 4Q91, 4Q92, 4Q93, 4Q94, 4Q95, 4Q96, 4Q97, 4Q98, 4Q98a, 4Q98b,
4Q98c, 4Q98d, 4Q236, 5Q5, 6Q5, 8Q2, 11Q5, 11Q6, 11Q7, 11Q8, 11Q9
Bibliography: P.W. Skehan, E. Ulrich, P.W. Flint, 'Two Manuscripts of Psalm
119 from Qumran Cave 4', *RevQ* 16/64 (1995) 477-486

Frag. 1	Ps 119:37-43	Frag. 4	Ps 119:73-74
Frag. 2	Ps 119:44-46	Frag. 5	Ps 119:81-83
Frag. 3	Ps 119:49-50	Frag. 6	Ps 119:89-92

4Q90 (4QPsʰ) *4QPsalmsʰ*

P.W. Skehan, E. Ulrich, P. Flint, *DJD XVI* (in press)
PAM 43.026
ROC 1150
1Q10, 1Q11, 1Q12, 2Q14, 3Q2, 4Q83, 4Q84, 4Q85, 4Q86, 4Q87, 4Q88,
4Q89, 4Q91, 4Q92, 4Q93, 4Q94, 4Q95, 4Q96, 4Q97, 4Q98, 4Q98a, 4Q98b,
4Q98c, 4Q98d, 4Q236, 5Q5, 6Q5, 8Q2, 11Q5, 11Q6, 11Q7, 11Q8, 11Q9
Bibliography: P.W. Skehan, E. Ulrich, P.W. Flint, 'Two Manuscripts of Psalm
119 from Qumran Cave 4', *RevQ* 16/64 (1995) 477-486

Frag. 1-2   Ps 119:10-21

4Q91 (4QPsⁱ) *4QPsalmsⁱ*

P.W. Skehan, E. Ulrich, P. Flint, *DJD XVI* (in press)

burst with joy! *9* Celebrate your feasts, fulfil your vows because *10* within you there is no Belial. Lift up your hand, *11* strengthen your right hand! See, the enemies *12* will perish and all who [wor]k evil will be scattered. *13* And you, YHWH, are for ev[er!] *14* Your glory shall be for ev[er and ev]er! *15* [Ex]ult …
[…]

PAM 43.030
ROC 1151
1Q10, 1Q11, 1Q12, 2Q14, 3Q2, 4Q83, 4Q84, 4Q85, 4Q86, 4Q87, 4Q88, 4Q89, 4Q90, 4Q92, 4Q93, 4Q94, 4Q95, 4Q96, 4Q97, 4Q98, 4Q98a, 4Q98b, 4Q98c, 4Q98d, 4Q236, 5Q5, 6Q5, 8Q2, 11Q5, 11Q6, 11Q7, 11Q8, 11Q9
Bibliography: P. Flint, E. Ulrich, P.W. Skehan, 'A Preliminary Edition of 4QPsʲ (4Q91)', *IBR* 8 (1998) 89-96

| Frag. 1 | Ps 48:1-9 | Frag. 3-7 | Ps 49:9-12, 15, 17 |
| Frag. 2 | Ps 49:6? | Frag. 8 | Ps 51:2-5 |

4Q92 (4QPsᵏ) *4QPsalmsᵏ*

P.W. Skehan, E. Ulrich, P. Flint, *DJD XVI* (in press)
PAM 43.030
ROC 1151
1Q10, 1Q11, 1Q12, 2Q14, 3Q2, 4Q83, 4Q84, 4Q85, 4Q86, 4Q87, 4Q88, 4Q89, 4Q90, 4Q91, 4Q93, 4Q94, 4Q95, 4Q96, 4Q97, 4Q98, 4Q98a, 4Q98b, 4Q98c, 4Q98d, 4Q236, 5Q5, 6Q5, 8Q2, 11Q5, 11Q6, 11Q7, 11Q8, 11Q9
Bibliography: P. Flint, E. Ulrich, P. Skehan, 'A Preliminary Edition of 4QPsᵏ (4Q92)', *JSS* 43 (1998) 259-263, pl. 1

| Col. I | Ps 135:6-16 | Col. II | Ps 99:1-5 |

4Q93 (4QPsˡ) *4QPsalmsˡ*

P.W. Skehan, E. Ulrich, P. Flint, *DJD XVI* (in press)
PAM 43.030
ROC 1151
1Q10, 1Q11, 1Q12, 2Q14, 3Q2, 4Q83, 4Q84, 4Q85, 4Q86, 4Q87, 4Q88, 4Q89, 4Q90, 4Q91, 4Q92, 4Q94, 4Q95, 4Q96, 4Q97, 4Q98, 4Q98a, 4Q98b, 4Q98c, 4Q98d, 4Q236, 5Q5, 6Q5, 8Q2, 11Q5, 11Q6, 11Q7, 11Q8, 11Q9

Ps 104:3-5   Ps 104:11-12

4Q94 (4QPs^m) *4QPsalms^m*

P.W. Skehan, E. Ulrich, P. Flint, *DJD XVI* (in press)
PAM 43.030
ROC 1151
1Q10, 1Q11, 1Q12, 2Q14, 3Q2, 4Q83, 4Q84, 4Q85, 4Q86, 4Q87, 4Q88,
4Q89, 4Q90, 4Q91, 4Q92, 4Q93, 4Q95, 4Q96, 4Q97, 4Q98, 4Q98a, 4Q98b,
4Q98c, 4Q98d, 4Q236, 5Q5, 6Q5, 8Q2, 11Q5, 11Q6, 11Q7, 11Q8, 11Q9

Ps 93:3-5   Ps 97:6-9
Ps 95:3-6   Ps 98:4-8

4Q95 (4QPs^n) *4QPsalms^n*

P.W. Skehan, E. Ulrich, P. Flint, *DJD XVI* (in press)
PAM 43.030
ROC 1151
1Q10, 1Q11, 1Q12, 2Q14, 3Q2, 4Q83, 4Q84, 4Q85, 4Q86, 4Q87, 4Q88,
4Q89, 4Q90, 4Q91, 4Q92, 4Q93, 4Q94, 4Q96, 4Q97, 4Q98, 4Q98a, 4Q98b,
4Q98c, 4Q98d, 4Q236, 5Q5, 6Q5, 8Q2, 11Q5, 11Q6, 11Q7, 11Q8, 11Q9

Ps 135:6-8   Ps 136:23
Ps 135:11-12

4Q96 (4QPs^o) *4QPsalms^o*

P.W. Skehan, E. Ulrich, P. Flint, *DJD XVI* (in press)
PAM 43.030
ROC 1151
1Q10, 1Q11, 1Q12, 2Q14, 3Q2, 4Q83, 4Q84, 4Q85, 4Q86, 4Q87, 4Q88,
4Q89, 4Q90, 4Q91, 4Q92, 4Q93, 4Q94, 4Q95, 4Q97, 4Q98, 4Q98a, 4Q98b,
4Q98c, 4Q98d, 4Q236, 5Q5, 6Q5, 8Q2, 11Q5, 11Q6, 11Q7, 11Q8, 11Q9

Ps 114:7-8   Ps 116:5-10
Ps 115:1-4

4Q97 (4QPs^p^) *4QPsalms^p^*

P.W. Skehan, E. Ulrich, P. Flint, *DJD XVI* (in press)
PAM 43.030
ROC 1151
1Q10, 1Q11, 1Q12, 2Q14, 3Q2, 4Q83, 4Q84, 4Q85, 4Q86, 4Q87, 4Q88,
4Q89, 4Q90, 4Q91, 4Q92, 4Q93, 4Q94, 4Q95, 4Q96, 4Q98, 4Q98a, 4Q98b,
4Q98c, 4Q98d, 4Q236, 5Q5, 6Q5, 8Q2, 11Q5, 11Q6, 11Q7, 11Q8, 11Q9

Ps 143:6-8

4Q98 (4QPs^q^) *4QPsalms^q^*

P.W. Skehan, E. Ulrich, P. Flint, *DJD XVI* (in press)
Inst. Cathol. Paris
1Q10, 1Q11, 1Q12, 2Q14, 3Q2, 4Q83, 4Q84, 4Q85, 4Q86, 4Q87, 4Q88,
4Q89, 4Q90, 4Q91, 4Q92, 4Q93, 4Q94, 4Q95, 4Q96, 4Q97, 4Q98a, 4Q98b,
4Q98c, 4Q98d, 4Q236, 5Q5, 6Q5, 8Q2, 11Q5, 11Q6, 11Q7, 11Q8, 11Q9
Bibliography: J.T. Milik, 'Deux documents inédits du Désert de Juda', *Biblica*
38 (1957) 245-255, pl. I

Ps 31:25 + 33:1-18   Ps 35:4-20

4Q98a (4QPs^r^) *4QPsalms^r^*

P.W. Skehan, E. Ulrich, P. Flint, *DJD XVI* (in press)
PAM 43.030
ROC 1151
1Q10, 1Q11, 1Q12, 2Q14, 3Q2, 4Q83, 4Q84, 4Q85, 4Q86, 4Q87, 4Q88,
4Q89, 4Q90, 4Q91, 4Q92, 4Q93, 4Q94, 4Q95, 4Q96, 4Q97, 4Q98, 4Q98b,
4Q98c, 4Q98d, 4Q236, 5Q5, 6Q5, 8Q2, 11Q5, 11Q6, 11Q7, 11Q8, 11Q9

Ps 26:7-12   Ps 30:9-13
Ps 27:1

4Q98b (4QPs^s) *4QPsalms^s*

P.W. Skehan, E. Ulrich, P. Flint, *DJD XVI* (in press)
PAM 43.028, 43.029
ROC ?
1Q10, 1Q11, 1Q12, 2Q14, 3Q2, 4Q83, 4Q84, 4Q85, 4Q86, 4Q87, 4Q88,
4Q89, 4Q90, 4Q91, 4Q92, 4Q93, 4Q94, 4Q95, 4Q96, 4Q97, 4Q98, 4Q98a,
4Q98c, 4Q98d, 4Q236, 5Q5, 6Q5, 8Q2, 11Q5, 11Q6, 11Q7, 11Q8, 11Q9
Bibliography: P.W. Skehan, 'Gleanings from Psalm Texts from Qumran', in A.
Caquot, M. Delcor (eds.), *Mélanges bibliques et orientaux en l'honneur de M.
Henri Cazelles* (AOAT 212; Kevelaer/Neukirchen-Vluyn, 1981) 445-448

Ps 5:8 - 6:1   Ps 88:15-17

4Q98c (4QPs^t) *4QPsalms^t*

P.W. Skehan, E. Ulrich, P. Flint, *DJD XVI* (in press)
PAM 42.081
ROC 1151
1Q10, 1Q11, 1Q12, 2Q14, 3Q2, 4Q83, 4Q84, 4Q85, 4Q86, 4Q87, 4Q88,
4Q89, 4Q90, 4Q91, 4Q92, 4Q93, 4Q94, 4Q95, 4Q96, 4Q97, 4Q98, 4Q98a,
4Q98b, 4Q98d, 4Q236, 5Q5, 6Q5, 8Q2, 11Q5, 11Q6, 11Q7, 11Q8, 11Q9
Bibliography: E. Ulrich, 'The Biblical Manuscripts from Cave 4', 226

Psalm 42:5

4Q98d (4QPs^u) *4QPsalms^u*

P.W. Skehan, E. Ulrich, P. Flint, *DJD XVI* (in press)
PAM 43.021
ROC 1151
1Q10, 1Q11, 1Q12, 2Q14, 3Q2, 4Q83, 4Q84, 4Q85, 4Q86, 4Q87, 4Q88,
4Q89, 4Q90, 4Q91, 4Q92, 4Q93, 4Q94, 4Q95, 4Q96, 4Q97, 4Q98, 4Q98a,
4Q98b, 4Q98c, 4Q236, 5Q5, 6Q5, 8Q2, 11Q5, 11Q6, 11Q7, 11Q8, 11Q9
Bibliography: E. Ulrich, 'The Biblical Manuscripts from Cave 4', 226

Psalm 88:12   Psalm 99:1

See also: **4QPs89 (4Q236)** *4QPsalm 89* and **4QPs122 (4Q522)** *4QPsalm 122*

4Q99 (4QJob^a^) *4QJob^a^*

E. Ulrich, *DJD XVI* (in press)
PAM 43.096
ROC 1116
2Q15, 4Q100, 4Q101
Bibliography: G.W. Nebe, 'Qumranica I: Zu unveröffentlichten Handschriften aus Höhle 4 von Qumran', *ZAW* 106 (1994) 307-322 [307-308]

Job 7:11-13	Job 32:3-4
Job 31:14-19	Job 33:23.25-30

4Q100 (4QJob^b^) *4QJob^b^*

E. Ulrich, *DJD XVI* (in press)
PAM 43.094
ROC 1117
2Q15, 4Q99, 4Q101
Bibliography: G.W. Nebe, 'Qumranica I', 308

Job 8:15?	Job 14:4-6
Job 13:14	Job 31:21

4Q101 (4QpaleoJob^c^) *4QpaleoJob^c^*

P.W. Skehan, E. Ulrich, J. Sanderson, *DJD IX*, 155-157, pl. XXXVII
PAM 43.033
ROC 1152
2Q15, 4Q100, 4Q101

Frag. 1-2	Job 13:18-20; 23-27	Frag. 3	Job 14:13-18

4Q102 (4QProv^a^) *4QProverbs^a^*

E. Ulrich, *DJD XVI* (in press)
PAM 43.563
ROC 1153
4Q103
Bibliography: G.W. Nebe, 'Qumranica I', 308; J. de Waard, '4QProv and Textual Criticism', *Textus* 19 (1998) 87-96

Prov 1:27 - 2:1

4Q103 ((4QProv^b) *4QProverbs^b*

E. Ulrich, *DJD XVI* (in press)
PAM 43.563
ROC 1153
4Q102
Bibliography: G.W. Nebe, 'Qumranica I', 308-309; J. de Waard, '4QProv and Textual Criticism', *Textus* 19 (1998) 87-96

Prov 9:16   Prov 14:31 - 15:8
Prov 13:6-9   Prov 15:11-12; 19-31
Prov 14:6-10; 12-13 ?

4Q104 (4QRuth^a) *4QRuth^a*

E. Ulrich, *DJD XVI* (in press)
PAM 43.090
ROC 410
2Q16, 2Q17, 4Q105
Bibliography: G.W. Nebe, 'Qumranica I', 309

Ruth 1:1-12

4Q105 (4QRuth^b) *4QRuth^b*

E. Ulrich, *DJD XVI* (in press)
PAM 43.090, 43.161
ROC 1117
2Q16, 2Q17, 4Q104
Bibliography: G.W. Nebe, 'Qumranica I', 309

Frag. 1   Ruth 1:1-5   Frag. 2   Ruth 1:13-15

4Q106 ((4QCant^a) *4QCanticles^a*

E. Tov, *DJD XVI* (in press)
PAM 43.097

ROC 1118
4Q107, 4Q108, 6Q6
Bibliography: G.W. Nebe, 'Qumranica I', 309-310; E. Tov, 'Three Manuscripts (Abbreviated Texts?) of Canticles from Qumran Cave 4', *JJS* 46 (1995) 88-111 [91-97]

Col. I	Cant 3:7 - 4:6	Col. II	Cant 4:7; 6:12 - 7:7

4Q107 (4QCant^b) *4QCanticles^b*

E. Tov, *DJD XVI* (in press)
PAM 43.093
ROC 1119
4Q106, 4Q108, 6Q6
Bibliography: G.W. Nebe, 'Qumranica I', 310-312; E. Tov, 'Three Manuscripts (Abbreviated Texts?) of Canticles from Qumran Cave 4', *JJS* 46 (1995) 97-110

Frag. 1	Cant 2:9 - 3:2	Frag. 2 ii	Cant 4:1-3.8-11
Frag. 2 i	Cant 3:4-5.9-11	Frag. 3	Cant 4:14 - 5:1

4Q108 (4QCant^c) *4QCanticles^c*

E. Tov, *DJD XVI* (in press)
PAM 43.097
ROC 1118
4Q106, 4Q107, 6Q6
Bibliography: G.W. Nebe, 'Qumranica I', 312; E. Tov, 'Three Manuscripts (Abbreviated Texts?) of Canticles from Qumran Cave 4', *JJS* 46 (1995) 110-111

Cant 3:7-8

4Q109 (4QQoh^a) *4QQohelet^a*

E. Ulrich, *DJD XVI* (in press)
PAM 43.092
DAJ
4Q110
Bibliography: J. Muilenburg, 'A Qohelet Scroll from Qumran, *BASOR* 135 (1954) 20-28; E. Ulrich, 'Ezra and Qohelet Manuscripts from Qumran

(4QEzra, 4QQoh[a,b])', in E. Ulrich *et al.* (eds.), *Priest, Prophets and Scribes. Essays on the Formation and Heritage of Second Temple Judaism in Honour of Joseph Blenkinsopp* (JSOTS 149; Sheffield, 1992) 142-147, pl. 2; G.W. Nebe, 'Qumranica I', 312-313

Col. I	Qoh 5:13-17	Col. II	Qoh 6:3-8. 12-7:6
Frag. 2	Qoh 6:1 ?	Col. III	Qoh 7:7-10. 19-20

4Q110 (4QQoh[b]) *4QQohelet[b]*

E. Ulrich, *DJD XVI* (in press)
PAM 43.090
ROC 1117
4Q109
Bibliography: E. Ulrich, 'Ezra and Qohelet Manuscripts from Qumran', 148, pl. 1; G.W. Nebe, 'Qumranica I', 313

Frag. 1	Qoh 1:10-13	Frag. 2	Qoh 1:13-14

4Q111 (4QLam) *4QLamentations*

F.M. Cross, *DJD XVI* (in press)
PAM 43.161, 43.220
ROC 667
3Q3, 5Q6, 5Q7
Bibliography: F.M. Cross, 'Studies in the Structure of Hebrew Verse: The Prosody of Lamentations 1:1-22', in C.L. Meyers and M. O'Connor (eds.), *The Word of the Lord Shall Go Forth* (Winona Lake, 1983) 129-155; G.W. Nebe, 'Qumranica I', 313-315

Frag. 1 i	Lam 1:1-6	Frag. 2	Lam 2:5
Frag. 1 ii	Lam 1:6-10	Frag. 3	Lam ?
Frag. 1 iii	Lam 1:10-16		

4Q112 (4QDan[a]) *4QDaniel[a]*

E. Ulrich, *DJD XVI* (in press)
PAM 43.080, 43.437
ROC 388, 394

1Q71, 1Q72, 4Q113, 4Q114, 4Q115, 4Q116, 6Q7
Bibliography: E. Ulrich, 'Daniel Manuscripts from Qumran. Part 1: A Preliminary Edition of 4QDanᵃ', *BASOR* 268 (1987) 17-37; .- 'Orthography and Text in Danᵃ and Danᵇ and in the Related Masoretic Texts', in H. Attridge *et al.* (eds.), *Of Scribes and Scrolls* (Lanham, Md, 1990) 29-42

Frag. 1 i-2	Dan 1:16-20	Frag. 11	Dan 5:13-14
Frag. 1 ii	Dan 2:9-11	Frag. 12	Dan 5:16-19
Frag. 3 i	Dan 2:19-33	Frag. 13	Dan 7:5-7
Frag. 3 ii -4-6	Dan 2:33-46	Frag. 14	Dan 7:25 - 8:5
Frag. 7	Dan 2:47 - 3:2	Frag. 15	Dan 10:16-20
Frag. 8	Dan 4:29-30	Frag. 16	Dan 11:13-16
Frag. 9	Dan 5:5-7	Frag. 17	Dan 12:27-28?
Frag. 10	Dan 5:12-13	Frag. 18	?

4Q113 (4QDanᵇ) *4QDanielᵇ*

E. Ulrich, *DJD XVI* (in press)
PAM 43.085, 43.086
ROC 1120, 1121
1Q71, 1Q72, 4Q112, 4Q114, 4Q115, 4Q116, 6Q7
Bibliography: E. Ulrich, 'Daniel Manuscripts from Qumran. Part 2: Preliminary Editions of 4QDanᵇ and 4QDanᶜ', *BASOR* 274 (1989) 3-26

Frag. 1-4	Dan 5:10-12. 14-16	Frag. 14	Dan 7:11?
Frag. 5-6	Dan 5:19-22	Frag. 15	Dan 7:26-28
Frag. 7 i	Dan 6:8-13	Frag. 16, 17, 18 i, 19	Dan 8:1-8
Frag. 7 ii, 8	Dan 6:13-22	Frag. 18 ii	Dan 8:13-16
Frag. 9-11	Dan 6:27 - 7:4	Frag. 20	?
Frag. 12-14	Dan 7:5-6		

4Q114 (4QDanᶜ) *4QDanielᶜ*

E. Ulrich, *DJD XVI* (in press)
PAM 43.081
ROC 224
1Q71, 1Q72, 4Q112, 4Q113, 4Q115, 4Q116, 6Q7
Bibliography: E. Ulrich, 'Daniel Manuscripts from Qumran. Part 2: Preliminary Editions of 4QDanᵇ and 4QDanᶜ', *BASOR* 274 (1989) 3-26

Col. I	Dan 10:5-9. 11-13	Col. III	Dan 11:13-17
Col. II	Dan 10:13-16.21; 11:1-2	Col. IV	Dan 11:25-29

4Q115 (4QDan^d) *4QDaniel^d*

E. Ulrich, *DJD XVI* (in press)
PAM 43.084
ROC 1122
1Q71, 1Q72, 4Q112, 4Q113, 4Q114, 4Q116, 6Q7
Bibliography: S. Pfann, '4QDan^d (4Q115): A Preliminary Edition with Critical Notes', *RevQ* 17/65-68 (1996) 37-72

Col. V	Dan 3:5-8	Col. VII	Dan 4:12-16
Col. VI	Dan 3:23-25. 4:5-9	Col. XII	Dan 7:15-23

4Q116 (4QDan^e) *4QDaniel^e*

E. Ulrich, *DJD XVI* (in press)
PAM 43.094
ROC 153
1Q71, 1Q72, 4Q112, 4Q113, 4Q114, 4Q115, 6Q7

Frag. 1-5	Dan 9 ?

4Q117 (4QEzra) *4QEzra*

E. Ulrich, *DJD XVI* (in press)
PAM 43.089
ROC 1124
Bibliography: E. Ulrich *et al.* (eds.), *Priest, Prophets and Scribes. Essays on the Formation and Heritage of Second Temple Judaism in Honour of Joseph Blenkinsopp* (JSOTS 149; Sheffield, 1992) 140-143, pl. 1

Frag. 1	Ezra 4:2-6	Frag. 3	Ezra 5:17 - 6:5
Frag. 2	Ezra 4:9-11		

4Q118 (4QChr) *4QChronicles*

J. Trebolle Barrera, *DJD XVI* (in press)

PAM 43.089
ROC 1124
Bibliography: J. Trebolle Barrera, 'Edition préliminaire de 4QChroniques', *RevQ* 15/60 (1992) 523-529

Frag. 1 i   ?
Frag. 1 ii   2 Chron 28:27 - 29:3

4Q119 (4QLXXLev^a) *4QSeptuagint Leviticus^a*

P.W. Skehan, E. Ulrich, J.E. Sanderson, *DJD IX*, 161-165, pl. XXXVIII
PAM 42.583
ROC 1004
4Q120
Bibliography: P.W. Skehan, 'The Qumran Manuscripts and Textual Criticism', *Volume du congrès, Strasbourg 1956* (VTS 4; Leiden: E.J. Brill, 1957) 157-160

Lev 26:2-16

4Q120 (4QpapLXXLev^b) *4QSeptuagint Leviticus^b*

P.W. Skehan, E. Ulrich, J.E. Sanderson, *DJD IX*, 167-186, pl. XXXIX-XLI
PAM 43.558, 43.559, 43.561
ROC 376, 378, 379
4Q119
Bibliography: E. Ulrich, 'The Greek Manuscripts of the Pentateuch from Qumrân, including newly-identified fragments of Deuteronomy (4QLXXDeut)', in A. Pietersma, C. Cox (eds.), *The Septuagint. Studies in Honour of John William Wevers on his sixty-fifth birthday* (Mississauga, Benben, 1984) 71-82

Frag. 1	Lev 1:11	Frag. 16	Lev 4:10-11
Frag. 2	Lev 2:3-5	Frag. 17-18	Lev 4:18-19
Frag. 3	Lev 2:7-8?	Frag. 19	Lev 4:26
Frag. 4	Lev 3:4	Frag. 20-21	Lev 4:26-28
Frag. 5	Lev 3:7	Frag. 22	Lev 4:30
Frag. 6-7	Lev 3:9-13	Frag. 23	Lev 5:6
Frag. 8	Lev 3:13-14	Frag. 24-25	Lev 5:8-10
Frag. 9	Lev 4:3-4	Frag. 26	Lev 5:16-17
Frag. 10-11	Lev 4:4	Frag. 27-31	Lev 5:18 - 6:5
Frag. 12-15	Lev 4:6-8	Frag. 32-97	?

4Q121 (4QLXXNum) *4QSeptuagint Numbers*

P.W. Skehan, E. Ulrich, J.E. Sanderson, *DJD IX*, 187-194, pl. XLII-XLIII
PAM 43.291
ROC 265
Bibliography: P.W. Skehan, 'The Qumran Manuscripts and Textual Criticism',
155-157; .- '4QLXXNum: A Pre-Christian Reworking of the Septuagint', *HTR*
70 (1977) 39-50; E. Ulrich, 'The Greek Manuscripts of the Pentateuch from
Qumrân', 80-81

Col. I	Num 3:40-43	Frag. 6	Num 3:50-51?
Col. II	Num 4:1?; 5-9	Frag. 23	Num 3:29?
Col. III	Num 4:11-16		

4Q122 (4QLXXDeut) *4QSeptuagint Deuteronomy*

P.W. Skehan, E. Ulrich, J.E. Sanderson, *DJD IX*, 195-197, pl. XLIII
PAM 43.291, 41.933
ROC 265
Bibliography: E. Ulrich, 'The Greek Manuscripts of the Pentateuch from Qum-
rân', 72-77

Frag. 1	Deut 11:4	Frag. 2-5	?

4Q123 (4QpaleoParaJosh) *4QParaphrase of Joshua*

P.W. Skehan, E. Ulrich, J.E. Sanderson, *DJD IX*, 201-203, pl. XLVI
PAM 43.033
ROC 1152
Four fragments, inscribed in a formal Palaeo-Hebrew hand of the last half of the
second century BCE, 'reminiscent of, but not identical with, the received form
of Joshua 21'

4Q124 (4QpaleoUnid[1]) *4Qunidentified paleo-Hebrew text 1*

P.W. Skehan, E. Ulrich, J.E. Sanderson, *DJD IX*, 205-214, pl. XLIV-XLV.
PAM 43.033
ROC 1152
Thirty-six fragments, inscribed in a formal, but uneven and inconsistent,

Palaeo-Hebrew hand, of the first half of the first century BCE, of an unidentified text

4Q125 (4QpaleoUnid[2]) *4Qunidentified paleo-Hebrew text 2*

P.W. Skehan, E. Ulrich, J.E. Sanderson, *DJD IX*, 215, pl. XLVI
PAM 43.676
ROC 1152
One fragment of an unidentified text, written with a mixture of formal and cursive styles

4Q126 (4QUnid gr) *4Qunidentified text gr*

P.W. Skehan, E. Ulrich, J.E. Sanderson, *DJD IX*, 219-221, pl. XLVI
PAM 43.291, 41.933
ROC 265

4Q127 (pap4QParaExod gr) *4QParaphrase of Exodus*

P.W. Skehan, E. Ulrich, J.E. Sanderson, *DJD IX*, 223-242, pl. XLVII
PAM 43.560
ROC 374, 375
Bibliography: E. Ulrich, 'A Greek Paraphrase of Exodus on Papyrus from Qumran Cave 4', in D. Fraenkel *et al.* (eds.), *Studien zur Septuagint-Robert Hanhart zu Ehren* (Mitteilungen des Septuaginta-Unternehmens 20; Göttingen: Vandenhoeck & Ruprecht, 1990) 287-298; D. Dimant, '4Q127: An Unknown Jewish Apocryphal Work?', in D.P. Wright *et al.* (eds.), *Pomegranates and Golden Bells. Studies in Biblical, Jewish, and Near Eastern Ritual, Law, and Literature in Honor of Jacob Milgrom* (Winona Lake: Eisenbrauns, 1995) 805-813

4Q128 (4QPhyl A) *4QPhylactery A*

J.T. Milik, *DJD VI*, 48-51, pls. VII-VIII
PAM 43.454-43.457
ROC 1003
Heidelberg
Bibliography: K.G. Kuhn, *Phylakterien aus Höhle 4 von Qumran* (Heidelberg, 1957) 15-16, pls. 9-10

Recto: Deut 5:1-14; 5:27 - 6:3; 10:12 - 11:17
Verso: Deut 11:18-21; Exod 12:43 - 13:7

4Q129 (4QPhyl B) *4QPhylactery B*

J.T. Milik, *DJD VI*, 51-53, pl. IX
PAM 43.454, 43.455
ROC 211
Heidelberg
Bibliography: K.G. Kuhn, *Phylakterien aus Höhle 4 von Qumran*, 11-15, pls. 1-4

Recto: Deut 5:1 - 6:2
Verso: Exod 13:9-16

4Q130 (4QPhyl C) *4QPhylactery C*

J.T. Milik, *DJD VI*, 53-55, pls. X-XI
PAM 43.450, 43.451
ROC 211

Exod 13:1-16; Deut 6:4-9; 11:13-21

4Q131 (4QPhyl D) *4QPhylactery D*

J.T. Milik, *DJD VI*, 55-56, pl. XII
PAM 43.458, 43.459
ROC 173

Frag. 1-2 recto	Deut 11:13	Frag. 3 recto	Deut 11:19
Frag. 2 verso	Deut 11:14	Frag. 1 recto	Deut 11:21
Frag. 1 recto	Deut 11:16-17	Frag. 4-6	?

4Q132 (4QPhyl E) *4QPhylactery E*

J.T. Milik, *DJD VI*, 56-57, pl. XIII
PAM 43.458, 43.459
ROC 173

Frag. 1 recto	Exod 13:1-2	Frag. 1 verso,	
Frag. 3 recto	Exod 13:5-6	5,6 recto	Exod 13:8-9
Frag. 4 recto	Exod 13:6-7	Frag. 7-13	?

4Q133 (4QPhyl F) *4QPhylactery F*

J.T. Milik, *DJD VI*, 57, pl. XIV
PAM 43.458, 43.459
ROC 173

| Frag. 1 | Exod 13:11-18 | Frag. 2-4 | ? |

4Q134 (4QPhyl G) *4QPhylactery G*

J.T. Milik, *DJD VI*, 58-60, pl. XV
PAM 43.452, 43.453
ROC 809

| Frag. 1 recto | Deut 5:1-21 | Frag. 1 verso | Exod 13:11-12 |

4Q135 (4QPhyl H) *4QPhylactery H*

J.T. Milik, *DJD VI*, 60-62, pl. XVI
PAM 43.450, 43.451
ROC 212
Heidelberg
Bibliography: K.G. Kuhn, *Phylakterien aus Höhle 4 von Qumran*, 16-20, pls. 11, 14

| Frag. 1 recto | Deut 5:22 - 6:5 | Frag. 1 verso | Exod 13:14-16 |

4Q136 (4QPhyl I) *4QPhylactery I*

J.T. Milik, *DJD VI*, 62-63, pl. XVII
PAM 43.452, 43.453
ROC 809
Bibliography: J.T. Milik, 'Fragment d'une source du Psautier', *RB* 73 (1966) 105-106, pl. IIb

| Frag. 1 recto | Deut 11:13-21; Exod 12:43 - 13:10 |
| Frag. 1 verso | Deut 6:6-7 (?) |

4Q137 (4QPhyl J) *4QPhylactery J*

J.T. Milik, *DJD VI*, 64-67, pls. XVIII-XIX
Heidelberg
Bibliography: K.G. Kuhn, *Phylakterien aus Höhle 4 von Qumran*, 5-11, pls. 5-8

| Frag. 1 recto | Deut 5:1-24 |
| Frag. 1 verso | Deut 5:24-32; 6:2-3 |

4Q138 (4QPhyl K) *4QPhylactery K*

J.T. Milik, *DJD VI*, 67-69, pl. XX
PAM 43.452, 43.453
ROC 809

| Frag. 1 recto | Deut 10:12 - 11:7 | Frag. 1 verso | Deut 11:7-12 |

4Q139 (4QPhyl L) *4QPhylactery L*

J.T. Milik, *DJD VI*, 70, pl. XXII
PAM 43.454, 43.455
ROC 211

| Frag. 1 | Deut 5:7-24 |

4Q140 (4QPhyl M) *4QPhylactery M*

J.T. Milik, *DJD VI*, 71-72, pl. XXI
PAM 43.450, 43.451
ROC 1003

| Frag. 1 recto | Exod 12:44 - 13:10 | Frag. 1 verso | Deut 5:33 - 6:5 |

4Q141 (4QPhyl N) *4QPhylactery N*

J.T. Milik, *DJD VI*, 72-74, pl. XXII

PAM 43.456, 43,457
ROC 212

Frag. 1   Deut 32:14-20.32-33

4Q142 (4QPhyl O) *4QPhylactery O*

J.T. Milik, *DJD VI*, 74-75, pl. XXII
PAM 43.454, 43.455
ROC 211

Frag. 1 recto   Deut 5:1-16   Frag. 1 verso   Deut 6:7-9

4Q143 (4QPhyl P) *4QPhylactery P*

J.T. Milik, *DJD VI*, 75-76, pl. XXII
PAM 43.452, 43.453
ROC 809

Frag. 1 recto   Deut 10:22 - 11:3   Frag. 1 verso   Deut 11:18-21

4Q144 (4QPhyl Q) *4QPhylactery Q*

J.T. Milik, *DJD VI*, 76, pl. XXIII
PAM 43.456, 43.457
ROC 212

Frag. 1 recto   Deut 11:4-8   Frag. 1 verso   Exod 13:4-9

4Q145 (4QPhyl R) *4QPhylactery R*

J.T. Milik, *DJD VI*, 77-78, pl. XXIII
PAM 43.456, 43.457
ROC 212

Frag. 1 recto   Exod 13:1-7   Frag. 1 verso   Exod 13:7-10

4Q146 (4QPhyl S) *4QPhylactery S*

J.T. Milik, *DJD VI*, 78, pl. XIII
PAM 43.461
ROC 212

Frag. 1   Deut 11:19-21

4Q147-148 (4QPhyl T, U) *4QPhylacteries T,U*

J.T. Milik, *DJD VI*, 79, pls. XXIV-XXV
PAM 43.456, 43.457
ROC 813

4Q149 (4QMez A) *4QMezuzah A*

J.T. Milik, *DJD VI*, 80-81, pl. XXVI
PAM 43.461
ROC 813

Frag. 1   Exod 20:7-12

4Q150 (4QMez B) *4QMezuzah B*

J.T. Milik, *DJD VI*, 81, pl. XXVI
PAM 43.461
ROC 210

Frag. 1   Deut 6:5-6; 10:14 - 11:2

4Q151 (4QMez C) *4QMezuzah C*

J.T. Milik, *DJD VI*, 82-83, pl. XXVII
PAM 43.460
ROC 174

Frag. 1   Deut 5:27 - 6:9; 10:12-20

4Q152 (4QMez D) *4QMezuzah D*

J.T. Milik, *DJD VI*, 83, pl. XXVI
PAM 43.460
ROC 174

Frag. 1   Deut 6:5-7

4Q153 (4QMez E) *4QMezuzah E*

J.T. Milik, *DJD VI*, 83, pl. XXVI
PAM 43.460
ROC 174

Frag. 1   Deut 11:17-18

4Q154 (4QMez F) *4QMezuzah F*

J.T. Milik, *DJD VI*, 83-84, pl. XXVI
PAM 43.461
ROC 813

Frag. 1   Exod 13:1-4

4Q155 (4QMez G) *4QMezuzah G*

J.T. Milik, *DJD VI*, 84-85, pl. XXV
PAM 43.459
ROC 173

Frag. 1   Exod 13:11-18

4Q156 (4QtgLev) *4QTargum of Leviticus*

J.T. Milik, *DJD VI*, 86-89, pl. XXVIII
PAM 43.449
ROC 299
Bibliography: M.M. Kasher, *DJD VI*, 92-93; J.A. Fitzmyer, 'The Targum of
Leviticus from Qumran Cave 4', *Maarav* 1 (1978) 5-21; K. Beyer, *ATTM*,

Frag. 1 1 [...] גמ[רי...]   2 [יהוה ומלא] הפנוה[י] כש[ת ...]
3 [ויעל מן גוא לפ]רכתא: וישוה[כשתא על נורא] 4 [לקדם יהוה ו]יכסה
ענ נה [...].[...]   5 [על שהדותא ו]לא ימות[:] ויסב מן [דם תורא] 6 [וידה
באצבעתה ע]ל כסיא: וקדם כסיא למדנחא   7 [ידה שבעה זמנין]מן דמא
באצבעתה: ויכס

Frag. 2 1 [... עלו]הי: ו[יס]ב] מן דם תורא ומן דם צפירא]   2 [וישוה
על] קרנ[י] מ[ד]ב[ח]א סח[ור סחור: וידה עלוהי מן דמא]   3 [באצבעתה
ש]בעה [זמנין ויד]כנה ויקדשנה [מן ט]מאת[הו]ן[די בני]   4 [ישראל:] כד]י
...[ה על בית קדשא [ועל] משכן זמנא ו[על]   5 [מדבחא: ויקרב] צפיר[א]
חיא: ויסמך אהרן ת]רתין ידו]ה[י ע]ל   6 [ראשא די צ]פיר[א ח]יא [ויהוד]א
עלוהי כל[...]   7 [...].[...]לכ]ל הטאי[הו]ן [...]

4Q157 (4QtgJob) *4QTargum of Job*

J.T. Milik, *DJD VI*, 90, pl. XXVII
PAM 43.449
ROC 130
11Q10

Frag. 1 1 [...] 2 ...[עלו]הי עננה   3 [... ביו]מי שנה 4-5 [...]

4Q156 (4QtgLev) *4QTargum of Leviticus*

278-280; A. Angerstorfer, 'Überlegungen zu Sprache und Sitz im Leben des Toratargums 4QtgLev (4Q156), sein Verhältnis zu Targum Onkelos', *BN* 55 (1990) 18-35; L.T. Stuckenbruck, 'Bibliography on 4QTgLev (4Q156)', *JSP* 10 (1992) 53-55

Frag. 1 (= *Lev* 16:12-15)   *1* [... And he shall take an incense-burner full of] coals [of fire from the surface of the altar which is before] *2* [YHWH and he shall fill] his two fists with in[cense (?) ...] *3* [and shall place them within] the veil. And he shall place [the incense on top of the fire] *4* [before YHWH, and] the cloud shall cover [...] *5* [above the testimony, and] he will not die. [...] And he shall take some of the [blood of the bullock] *6* [and he shall sprinkle with his finger ov]er the cover. And in front of the cover, towards the East, *7* [he shall sprinkle] the blood [seven times] with his finger. And he shall slaughter

Frag. 2 (= *Lev* 16:18-21)   *1* [... for] him. [He shall ta]ke [some of the blood of the bullock and some of the blood of the he-goat] *2* [and shall put it on] the horn[s of] the a[l]t[a]r, ar[ound. And he shall sprinkle upon it some of the blood] *3* [with his finger se]ven [times and he shall cle]anse it and make it holy [from the im]purities [of the sons of] *4* [Israel.] Whe[n he has finished aton]ing for the holy house, [for] the tent of meeting and [for] *5* [the altar, he shall bring near the] living he-goat. Aaron shall lay his t[wo hands up]on *6* [the head of the] live [he]-goat. And he shall confess over it all [...] *7* [...] for al[l] their [sins ...]

4Q157 (4QtgJob) *4QTargum of Job*

Bibliography: R.I. Vasholz, '4QTargum Job versus 11QTargum Job', *RevQ* 11/41 (1982) 109; E. Kutsch, 'Die Textgliederung im hebräischen Hiobbuch sowie in 4QtgJob und in 11QtgJob', *BZ* 27 (1983) 221-228; K. Beyer, *ATTM*, 294

Frag. 1 *col.* I (= *Job* 3:5- ?)   *1* [...] *2* [... may] a cloud [cover] him *3* [... among the d]ays of the year *4-5* [...] ...

[...] ובמלאכו]הי 3   [...] האנש מא]לה 2   [...]אנ[1   *Frag.* 1 ɪɪ

[...] ימותון ולא ב]חכ[מ]ה 6   [...] ומן בלי מני]ן 5   [...] דבעפרא 4

[...]... ואנה חזית דרשע 8   [... הלא סכל יק]טל *vacat* תבקה 7

9 ...[...]...[...]   10 [...]...[...]

4Q158 (4QRPᵃ) *4QReworked Pentateuchᵃ*

J.M. Allegro, *DJD V*, 1-6, pl. I; J. Strugnell, 'Notes en marge du volume V des "Discoveries in the Judaean Desert of Jordan"', *RevQ* 7/26 (1970) 168-76, pl. I
PAM 43.424, 43.343, 44.180, 44.191
ROC 138
4Q364, 4Q365 + 4Q365a, 4Q366, 4Q367
Bibliography: E. Tov, '4QReworked Pentateuch: A Synopsis of Its Contents, *RevQ* 16/64 (1995) 647-653; .- 'The Relation between 4Q364-7 and 4Q158', *DJD XIII*, 189-191

Frag. 1-2   Gen 32:25-33; Exod 4:27-28

וי]ותר [...] 3   [...]שרית ופ[...] 2   [...]ץ[למען] [...] 1   *Frags.* 1-2

[ו]יאחזהו [...] יעקו]ב בהאבקו עמו ... 4   [...] י]עקו]וב ל]בדו שמה ויאבק[...]

...[6   [...] לו[ן ויאמר] לו מה שמכה[אלי ויאמר לו מה [...].[...] 5   [...] אל]יו ויאמ]ר[

[ויבר]ך 7   [...] מ]ה לי ד נᴬ[ו]יאמ]ר הגי]ד [ע]קוב וי]אנשים ותוכל ויש²ᵃל י

ויצילכה וירב]כה [...] יה]וה פרכה לו יאמר שם אותו 8   [ד]עת ובינה

לדרכו וילך 10   [...] הזה ועד דורות עולמ]ים עד היום 9   [...ו] המס מכול

[... פנוא]ל עבר את כאשר השמש לו 11   [...] וי]קרא שם אותו בברכו

ה]יום עד הירך כפות שתי על 13   [...] אל תוא]כל ויאמר ההואה ביום 12

שלחו אשר יהוה דברי 15   [...] לקרא]ת לך לאמור אהרון אל 14   [...] הזה

Frag. 1 *col.* II (= *Job* 4 : 16 - 5 : 4)   *1* ... [...] *2* [Can] a man before G[od be just? ...] *3* and with h[is] angels [...] *4* which [have their foundations] in dust [...] *5* and without number [...] *6* they die, but without w[is]do[m ...] *7* will you consider? *Blank* Does not the stupid k[ill ...] *8* But I have seen that the wicked person ... [...] *9* ... [...] *10* [...] ... [...]

4Q158 (4QRP^a) *4QReworked Pentateuch^a*

Frag. 3	Gen 32:31 ?
Frag. 4	Exod 3:12; 24:4-6
Frag. 5	Exod 19:17-23
Frag. 6	Exod 20:19-21 (Samaritan)
Frag. 7-8	Exod 20:12-17; Deut 5:30-31; Exod 20:22-26; 21:1-10
Frag. 9	Exod 21:15-25
Frag. 10-12	Exod 21:32-37; 22:1-13
Frag. 13	Exod 30:32.34
Frag. 15	?

Frags. 1 - 2   *1* [...] in order that [...] *2* [...] you shall fight and [...] *3* [...] *Gen 32:25-30* And [J]ac[ob remain]ed [al]one there, and [a man] struggled [with him until first light. Since he saw that he could not prevail against him, he seized him in the thigh joint] *4* [and Jaco]b['s thigh joint was dislocated] while he struggled with him. [And] he caught hold of him, and sai[d] to [him: Let me walk, for dawn is breaking. But Jacob replied: I shall not let you walk] *5* [unless you have blessed] me. He asked him: What is your name? [And he told] him: [Jacob. He said to him: Now you will no longer be called Jacob, but Israel, for you have fought] *6* [with God and with] men and you have won. And J[a]cob asked him [and] sai[d: Tel]l me wh[at is your name] /please/! [And he said to him: Why do you ask me my name?] *7* [And he bless]ed him right there. And he said to him: May YH[WH] make you fertile and [make] you [numerous. ... May he fill you with] *8* [know]ledge and intelligence; may he free you from all violence and [...] *9* until this day and for everlasting genera-tions [...] *10* And he walked on his way after having blessed him there. *Gen 32:31-33* And [Jacob name]d [the place Penu'el: Because I saw God face to face and in spite of that my life has remained safe. And there rose] *11* the sun as he passed Penu'e[l and he went on with a lame thigh ...] *12* on that day. And he said to him: You shall not ea[t ...] *13* above the two joints of the thigh until the [present day ... *Exod 4:27-28* ...] *14* to Aaron saying: Go towar[ds Moses in

ואת כול] האותות [... 16 יהוה לי לאמור בהוציאכה את] ... [17 ללכת
עבדים והנה המה שלושי]ם [... 18 יהוה אלוהים] ... [19 נשל]...[

Frag. 3 1 ויקרא יעקוב [...] 2 בארץ הזות מן] ... [3 אבותי לבוא
אל] ...[

Frag. 4 II 1 [...] צוה לכה] ... [2 העם ממצרים תעבד]ון [...
3 למספר שנים עשר שבטי] ישראל [... 4 ויעל את העולה על המזב]ח [...
5 באגונות וחצ]י ה]דם זרק על ה]מזבח [... 6 אשר היראתי אל אברהם
ואל ... [...] 7 אתם להיו]ת להמה ולזרעם לאלוהים [...]. 8 [ע]ד עולם
[...]...[...]. יהוה [...].

Frags. 7-8 1 [את אבי]כה ואת אמכה] [...] 2 [ברע]כה עד שקר לוא
תחמוד אשת ר]עכה [... 3 ויאמר יהוה אל מושה לך אמור להמה שובו
ל]כמה [... 4 ואת המשפטים אשר תלמדם ועשו בארץ אשר] ...[
5 וישובו העם איש לאהליו ויעמוד מושה לפני [...] 6 ראיתמה כי מן
השמים דברתי עמכמה לוא תעשו]ן [... 7 עליו את עולותכ]ה ואת
שלמיכ]ה את צואניכ]ה [...] 8 תעשה לי לוא תבנה אתהנה גזית כי
חרבכה [...] 9 עליו *vacat* אלה המשפטים [אשר] תשי]ם [... 10 ...] אם[

the desert! He went, then, and coming across him on God's mountain he kissed him. Moses repeated to Aaron all] *15* the words of YHWH which he had transmitted to him, and all [the signs which he had commanded ...] *16* YHWH to me, saying: When you bring out [...] *17* in order to go (like) slaves. And see, these are the thi[rty ...] *18* YHWH God [...] *19* ... [...]

Frag. 3   *1* And Jacob called [...] *2* in this land from [...] *3* my fathers, in order to enter [...]

Frag. 4 *col.* II   *1* [...] he commanded you [...] *2* the people from Egypt: you shall serve [...] *3* according to the number of the twelve tribes of [Israel ...] *4* and he offered the holocaust on the alta[r ... *Exod 24:6* And Moses took half the blood and put it] *5* in earthenware bowls and the (other) hal[f of the] blood he poured over the [altar ...] *6* as I showed Abraham and ... [...] *7* with them, so that he would be God for them and for their descendants [...] *8* [f]or eve[r ...] YHWH [...]

Frags. 7 - 8   *1* *Exod 20:12-17* your [father] and your mother [so that your days on the soil which YHWH your God gives you are lengthened. You shall not kill. You shall not commit adultery. You shall not rob. You shall not give] *2* false evidence [against] your [neigh]bour. You shall not covet the wife of [your] neigh[bour, or his house, or his servant, or his maid, or his ass, or anything of what belongs to your neighbour.] *3* And YHWH said to Moses: *Deut 5:30-31* Go and tell them: Go back to [your tents! You, however, stay here with me, for I am going to explain to you all the commandments, the laws] *4* and the statutes, which you shall teach them, so that they shall do (them) in the land which [I give them so that they can possess it ...] *5* And the people did return, each man to his tent. But Moses remained in the presence [of YHWH ...] *6* *Exod 20:22-26* You have seen that I have spoken with you from the heavens. You shall not make [alongside me gods of silver or gods of gold, do not make them! You shall construct for me an earthen altar, and sacrifice] *7* on it your holocausts and your peace-offerings, your flocks [and your cattle. In any place where I make you commemorate my name, I shall come to you and bless you. If] *8* you construct [an altar of stone] for me, you are not to chisel it in the manner of blocks of stone, for by [passing] your chisel [over each one of them you will desecrate it. Nor are you to climb to my altar by steps, in case you reveal your nakedness] *9* on it. *Blank Exod 21:1-10* These are the statutes [which] you are to pro[pound to them. When you purchase a Hebrew slave he will serve for six years, but on the seventh he shall go away free] *10* [for nothing. If] he came in alone he will go away alone; i[f he was married, his wife will go with him.

בגפיו בא בגפיו יצא א[ם ...] 11   [...]ל[א]דונו והוא[...]   12 וה]גישו [...
13 אזנו במרצע] ...]   14 [וה]פדה לע[ם ...]   15 [...] ל[וא ...

[...] לברכה   3 [...] כול ב]שר וכול הרֹחות ...] 2   ה[...] 1   *Frag.* 14 I
[...].ו [...] 5 תהי צרה ו.[...] הגויים] ...] זה ובארץ מצרים   4 [...]...[...] להארץ
אברא בק...[...] עול יֹד]מצרים וגאלתים   6 מידם ועשיתי לי לעם עד דור[ות
עולמים ...]ל ממצרים ואת [זר]ע   7 בניכה א[ו]שיב לבטח ל[...] ואת
מצרים השלכתי ב]לבב ים במצו[ל]ות   8 תהום [...] אשר יישבו   9 בה]...[
ג]בולות

4Q159 (4QOrdᵃ) *4QOrdinancesᵃ*

J.M. Allegro, *DJD V*, 6-9, pl. II; J. Strugnell, 'Notes', 175-179
PAM 43.347, 43.426
ROC 474
4Q513, 4Q514 (?)
Bibliography: J.M. Allegro, 'An Unpublished Fragment of Essene Halakah (4QOrdinances)', *JSS* 6 (1961) 71-73; J. Liver, 'The Half-Shekel Offering in Biblical and Post-Biblical Literature', *HTR* 56 (1963) 173-98; Y. Yadin, 'A Note on 4Q159 (Ordinances)', *IEJ* 18 (1968) 250-252; F.D. Weinert, '4Q159:

ישר]אל את ...] 2   [...]נחל לי[...]   [...]הו אל [...]. 1   *Frags.* 1 II + 9
ע]ון]ותיו ולכפר לכול פשעיה[ם ...]   3 [...] ואם י]עשה איש ממנה גורן וגת
הבא לגור[ן] ולגת [...]   4 אשר בישראל אשר אין לו יאוכלנה וכנס לו
ולב]יתו לוא יכנס]   5 השדה יאכל בפיהו ואל ביתו לוא יביא להניחו[...]
6 ע[ל] הכופר [כסף הערכים אשר נתנו איש ᶜפר נפשו מחצית] השקל]
7 רק פ]עם] אחת יתננו כול ימיו עשרים גרה השקל ב]שקל הקודש]

If his master gave him a wife and she bore him sons or daughters] *11* [the wife and her children will be] for his [m]aster and he [will go away alone. But if the slave should say clearly: I love my master, my wife and my children; I do not wish to go away free,] *12* [his master] will [lead him before God, place him near the door or the jambs … His master will pierce] *13* his ear with an awl, [and he will serve him for ever. When a man sells his daughter as a slave-girl, she is not to leave as the slaves leave. If she turns out to be unpleasant in the eyes of her master, who had intended her for himself, he shall allow her to be] *14* redeemed; [he cannot sell her] to a [foreign] peo[ple, …] *15* […] n[ot …]

Frag. 14 *col.* I   *1* […] … *2* [… all fl]esh and all the spirits *3* […] for blessing for the land *4* […] … […] the peoples […] this, and in the land of Egypt *5* there shall be oppression […] I will create in … […] the yoke of /the hand/ of Egypt, and I shall free them *6* from their hands and I shall make them a people for myself for [eternal] gener[ations …] from Egypt. And the [see]d *7* of your sons I shall [cause to live in the la]nd in security [… And Egypt I shall hurl into] the middle of the sea, into the depths *8* of the abyss […] who dwell *9* in it [… the fro]ntiers (?)

4Q159 (4QOrd^a) *4QOrdinances^a*

Legislation for an Essene Community Outside of Qumran?', *JSJ* 5 (1974) 179-207; .- 'A Note on 4Q159 and a New Theory of Essene Origins', *RevQ* 9/34 (1977) 223-230; L.H. Schiffman, *Sectarian Law in the Dead Sea Scrolls* (BJS 33; Chico: Scholars Press, 1983) 55-65; J.H. Tigay, 'Examination of the Accused Bride in 4Q159: Forensic Medicine at Qumran', *JANES* 22 (1993) 129-34; L.H. Schiffman, 'Ordinances and Rules (4Q159 = 4QOrd^a, 4Q513 = 4QOrd^b)', *PTSDSSP 1*, 145-175

Frags. 1 *col.* II + 9 (= 4Q513 1 - 2 I ?)   *1* […] Not […] … […] *2* [… Isra]el its ini[quiti]es and to atone for all th[eir] sins. […] *3* [… And if] someone [ma]kes it into a threshing floor or a press, whoever comes to the threshing floor [or to the press, …] *4* whoever in Israel owns nothing, that person can eat some and gather for himself; but for [his] house[hold he is not to gather.] *5* (In) the field he may eat it himself, but is not to bring it to his house to store it […] *6* [Concer]ning [the ransom:] the money of valuation which one gives as ransom for his own person will be half [a shekel,] *7* only on[ce] will he give it in all his days. The shekel comprises twenty geras in the she[kel of the temple.]

8 לשש מא[ו]ת האלף מאת ככר לשלישית מחצית הככר] [... 9 ולחמשים
מחצית המ[נ]ה עשרים [ו]חמשה שקל הכול [...] 10 המנה ש[...] של[וש
לעשרת המנים] [... 11 ...] חמ[שה [כ]סף מעשר ה[מנה ...] 12 [...]
שקל הקודש מחצ[ית [... 13 ...] [הא'פה והבת תכון א[חד [... 14 ...]
ש[לושת העשרונים ...]. [...] vacat [...] 15 [...] 16 ...] ע[ל העם ועל
ב[ג]די[הם [... 17 ...] י[שראל שרף מוש]ה [...

1 ואם ...] ל[גר או לעוקר משפח]ת גר ... [... *Frags. 2-4* 2 לעיני
יש[ראל לו]א יעבודו הגויים בזר[... מארץ] 3 מצרים ויצו עלי<הי>הם
לבלתי ימכר ממכרת עבד ו.[... עשר]ה אנשים 4 וכוהנים שנים ונשפטו
לפני שנים העשר האלה .[... וכול] 5 דבר בישראל על נפש על פיהם
ישאלו ואשר ימרה [...] 6 יומת אשר עשה ביד רמה אל יהיו כלי גבר על
אשה כול [איש ... ואל] 7 יכס בשלמות אשה ואל ילבש כתונת אשה כיא
[ת]ועבה היא [...] vacat [...] 8 כי יוצי איש שם רע על בתולת ישראל
אם ב[עת] קחתו אותה יואמר ובקרוה 9 נאמנות ואם לוא כחש עליה
והומתה ואם בש[קר] ענה בה ונענש שני מנים [ולוא] 10 ישלח כול ימיו
כול [...] [אשר] [...] לעשות את [...].

1 ...] לפ[ני אל וימותו פשר] [... *Frag. 5* 2 [...] vacat בני לו[י ...]
3 [...]במשפט ואשר אמ[ר...] 4 [...] בקחת מושה את [...] 5 [...]יצאו
שמה פשר הדבר [...] 6 ... לד[רוש התורה בצוקה ו.[...] 7 ... אש[ר
דבר מושה] [... 8 ...] כול[...]

4Q160 (4QVisSam) *4QVision of Samuel*

J.M. Allegro, *DJD V*, 9-11, pl. III; J. Strugnell, 'Notes', 179-183, pl. I
PAM 43.434, 44.191

1 ... כ[י]א נשב[עתי ל]בית [עלי אם יתכפר עוון בית עלי *Frag. 1*
בזבח] 2 [ובמנחה עד עלם וי]שמע שמוא[ל א]ת דב[רי... [...] 3 [...]שמואל

8 For the six hundred thousand: one hundred talents; for the third, half a talent, […] *9* and for the fifty, half a mina, twenty-five shekels. The total […] *10* the mina. [… t]hree for ten minas […] *11* [… fi]ve (shekels) of silver (make) the tenth part of [a mina …] *12* [… the she]kel of the temple; ha[lf a shekel …] *13* […] the ephah and the bath are of the s[ame] size […] *14* [… t]hree tenths […] *15* […] *Blank* […] *16* [… u]pon the people, and upon [their] g[ar]ments […] *17* [… I]srael, Mos[es] burnt […]

Frags. 2 - 4   *1* And if [… to a] foreigner or the descendant of a [foreign] fam[ily …] *2* in the presence of Is[rael.] They are [no]t to serve gentiles; with … [… from the land of] *3* Egypt and commanded them not be sold for the price of a slave. And [… te]n men *4* and two priests, and they shall be judged by these twelve. [… In every] *5* capital offence in Israel their authority should be consulted, and whoever disobeys […] *6* he will be executed, for he acted presumptuously. A woman is not to wear the clothes of a male; every[one … and he is not] *7* to put on a woman's cloak, and he is not to dress in a woman's tunic, for it is an [ab]omination. […] *Blank* […] *8* In the case where a man slanders a maiden of Israel, if he says it at the [moment] of taking her, they shall examine her *9* regarding (her) trustworthiness. If he has not lied about her, she shall be put to death; but if he has testified [false]ly against her, they are to fine him two minas [and he is not] *10* to divorce her for all the days (of his life). Anyone who […] to do … […]

Frag. 5 *1* [… be]fore God, and they died. The interpretation of […] *2* […] *Blank* The sons of Lev[i …] *3* […] in judgment. And what he sa[ys …] *4* […] when Moses took the […] *5* […] they will go out there. Interpretation of the matter: […] *6* [… to ex]pound the Law in distress and […] *7* [… a]s Moses said […] *8* […] all […]

4Q160 (4QVisSam) *4QVision of Samuel*

ROC 137

Frag. 1   *1* [… *1 Sam 3:14-15* F]or [I] swo[re to] the House of [Eli that the sin of the House of Eli would not be atoned for, either by sacrifices] *2* [or by offerings,

שוכב לפני עלי ויקום ויפתח את ד[לתות ...]   4   [...ל[ה]ל]גיד את המשא
לעלי ויען עלי ב[...]   5   [... הו]דיעני את מראה האלוהים אלנ]א תכחד
ממני כה יעשה לכה]   6   [אלוהים וכה יוסיף] אם תכחד ממני ד]בר מכול
הדבר אשר דבר אליכה]   7   [...]שמואל [...].

Frags. 3-5 ɪɪ   1   [...]עבדכה לוא עצרתי כוח עד זואת כיא   2   [... י]קוו
אלוהי לעמכה ועזרתה היה לו והעלהו   3   [... ו]מטיט יון [הצל רג]ל]ם
ו]העמד להמה סלע למרואש כיא תהלתכה   4   [על כול לא]ומים היאה]
בביתכה י]עוז עמכה ומ[...]דש. ובזעם שונאי עמכה תגביר תפארת
5   [ו]בארצוא ובימים [... ו]יראתכה על כול [...] וממלכה וידעו כול עמי
ארצותיכה] כיא   6   אתה בראתה [אותם ... י]בינו רבים כיא עמכה הואה]
[...   7   ...[...] קדו]שיכה אשר הקדשת]ה [...

Frag. 7   1   [...]פני יהי ע[...]   2   הגרתי עמו מועדי ונלויתי לֹו מ[...]
לוא]   3   יחלתי פניה רכוש והון ומחיר[...]   4   אדוני ובחרתי לשכוב לפני
יצוע[...]

4Q161 (4QpIsaᵃ) *4QIsaiah Pesher*ᵃ

J.M. Allegro, *DJD V*, 11-15, pls. IV-V; J. Strugnell, 'Notes', 183-186, pl. I
PAM 43.431, 43.433
ROC 583, 585
3Q4, 4Q162, 4Q163, 4Q164, 4Q165, 4Q515
Bibliography: J.M. Allegro, 'Further Messianic References in Qumran Litera-
ture', *JBL* 75 (1956) 177-182, pls. II-III; J.D. Amoussine, 'A propos de
l'interprétation de 4Q161 (fragments 5-6 et 8)', *RevQ* 8/31 (1974) 381-392;
J.D. Amoussine, 'The Reflection of Historical Events of the First Century B.C.

Frag. 1   20   [והיה ביום ההואה לוא יוסיף עוד שאר ישראל ופליטת
יעקוב]   21   [להשען על מכהו ונשען על 7ד7 קדוש ישראל באמת]
22   [שאר ישוב שאר יע[קו]ב] אל א]ל גבור [*vacat*   23   [פשרו שאר

for ever.] Samue[l h]eard the wor[ds of ...] *3* [...] Samuel was lying down before Eli, and he arose and opened the do[ors ...] *4* [...] to explain the oracle to Eli. But Eli answered: [...] *5* [... *1 Sam 3:17* Le]t me know the vision of God! Do not [hide it from me, please! May] *6* [God do this to you, and this to you in addition] if you hide from me one w[ord of all the words which he told you] *7* [...] Samuel [...]

Frags. 3 - 5 col. II *1* [...] your servant. I did not control my strength before this, because *2* [... may they be re]united, my God, with your people; be assistance for him and raise him up *3* [... free their fee]t from the muddy swamp [and] establish for them a rock from of old, for your praise *4* is [above all the na]tions. Your people [will] take shelter [in your house] and [...] ... and in the anger of those who hate your people you shall exalt your splendour *5* [and] over the lands and the seas [... and] your fear will be over every [...] and kingdom. And all the peoples of your lands will know [that] *6* you created [them ...] multitudes [will] understand that this is your people [...] *7* ... [...] your [hol]y ones whom you made holy [...]

Frag. 7 *1* [...] ... will be [...] *2* I dwelt with him my feasts and joined /him/ from [... Not] *3* did I solicit her favour with estates, riches or merchandise [...] *4* my lord, and I chose to lie down in front of the bed of [...]

4Q161 (4QpIsaᵃ) *4QIsaiah Pesherᵃ*

in Qumran Commentaries (4Q161, 4Q169, 4Q166)', *HUCA* 48 (1977) 123-152; J.M. Rosenthal, 'Biblical Exegesis of 4QpIs', *JQR* 60 (1969-70) 27-36; M.P. Horgan, *Pesharim: Qumran Interpretations of Biblical Books* (CBQMS 8; Washington, D.C.: Catholic Biblical Association, 1979) 70-89; M.G. Abegg, 'The Messiah at Qumran: Are We Still Seeing Double?', *DSD* 2 (1995) 125-144; R. Bauckham, 'The Messianic Interpretation of Isa 10:34 in the Dead Sea Scrolls: 2 Baruch and the Preaching of John the Baptist', *DSD* 2 (1995) 202-216

Frag. 1 (*col.* I) (cf. 4Q163 4 - 6 II) *20 Isa 10:20* [On that day, the remnant of Israel, the survivors of Jacob, will cease to lean] *21* [on their assailant but will lean loyally on YHWH, the Holy One of Israel.] *22* [*Isa 10:21* A remnant will return, a remnant of Ja]c[ob to] G[od the warrior. *Blank*] *23* [Its interpretation: the

י[שראל הואה] עדת בחירו [...]   24   [...]לו אנשי חילו ופו[...] ושאר יעקוב

הואה [...]   25   [...]. הכוהנים כיא הוא[ה ...]

Frags. 2-6   1   [כיא אם יהיה עמכה ישראל כחול הים שאר ישוב בו

כליון חרוץ]   2   [ושוטף צדקה כיא כלה ונחרצה אדוני ⁷⁶ᴴᴵ צבאות עושה

בקרב כול הארץ]   3   [פשרו על ...   [כיא]...   [בי בני]ן...   4   [...] עמו[]

וא[שר אמר אם הי]ה עמכה ישראל כחול הים]   5   [שאר ישוב בו] כ[ליון

חר]וץ ושוטף צד]קה *vacat* פשרו על]   6   [...   לכ]לות ביו[ם הר]גה ורבים

יוב]דו [...   7   [...   והם ימ]לטו למטו[עם ב]ארץ באמת   [...].   8   [...] *vacat*

לכן כ]וה אמ]ר אד]וני ⁷⁶ᴴᴵ צבאות אל תירא עמי]   9   [יוש]ב ציו]ן מאשור

בש]בט] יככה ומטהו ישא עליכה בדרך מצרים]   10   [כיא]עוד מע]ט מזער

וכלה זעם ואפי על תבלית]ם ויע]י]ר עליו]   11   [⁷⁶ᴴᴵ] צבאות שוט כמכת

מדין בצור עו]רב ומט]הו על הים ונשאו]   12   [בדרך מצרים והיה ביום

ההואה] יסור סב]לו מעל שכמכה ועולו]   13   [מעל צוארכה *vacat* פשר

הדבר על [...]...[...]   14   [...]   [בשובם ממדבר העם]מי]ם   [... ב]...   15   [...]

[נשיא העדה ואחר יס]ו]ר מעלי]הם   16   [...] *vacat* [...]   17   [...] בא אל

עיתה עבר [במגרון]למכמ]ש   18   [יפקיד כליו עברו]מעברה גבע מלון

למו חר]דה הרמה גבעת]   19   [שאול נסה צהלי]קולכי בת גלים הקשיב]י

לישה עניה ענתות]   20   [נדדה]מדמנה י]ושבי הגבים]ה]עיזו עוד] היום

בנוב לעמוד]   21   [ינופף]ידו הר בת ציון גבעת ירושלים [*vacat*]

22   [פשר ה]פתגם לאחרית הימים לבוא. [...].   23   [...]רה בעלותו מבקעת

עכו ללחם בפל]שת   24   [...]דה ואין כמוה ובכול ערי המ]...[25   ועד

גבול ירושלים] [...

Frags. 8-10   1   [הנה האדון ⁷⁶ᴴᴵ צבאות מסעף פארה במערצה ורמי

הקו]מה [גדו]ע]ים   2   [והגבוהים ישפלו וינקפו] סובכי [היער] בברזל

ולבנון באדיר   3   [יפול *vacat*]פשרו על ה]כתאים אשר]ינת]נו] ביד

ישראל ועני   4   [ארץ ...   [כול הגואים וגבורים יחתו ונמס ל]בם   5   [...

ואשר אמר ורמי]הקומה גדועים המה גבורי כת]יאים   6   [אשר...]ר

remnant of I]srael is [the assembly of his chosen one ...] *24* [...] the men of his army and ... [... and the remnant of Jacob is] *25* [...] the priests, since [...]

Frags. 2 - 6 (*col.* II) (cf. 4Q163 4 - 6 II)   *1* [*Isa 10:22* Even if your people, Israel were like the sand of the sea, only a remnant will return; extermination is decreed,] *2* [but justice will overflow. For it is decided and decreed: the Lord, YHWH of Hosts, will execute it in the midst of the whole earth.] *3* [Its interpretation concerns ...] since [...] the sons of [...] *4* [...] of his people. [And a]s for what he says: *Isa 10:22* Even if [your people, Israel were like the sand of the sea,] *5* [only a remnant will return;] ex[termination is decr]eed, but just[ice] will overflow. [*Blank* Its interpretation concerns] *6* [... to des]troy on the da[y of slaugh]ter; and many will per[ish ...] *7* [... but they will be s]aved, surely, by their plan[ting] in the land [...] *8* [...] *Blank Isa 10:24-27* This is why the Lo[rd YHWH of Hosts] says: [Do not fear, my people] *9* [who liv]e in Zio[n, of Assyria: it will hit you with a st]ick [and lift its rod against you in the fashion of Egypt;] *10* [for] very shortly [my anger will end and my wrath will destroy] them. [YHWH of Hosts] will la[sh against them] *11* [the flail as in the destruction of Midian, on the rock of Ho]reb, and he will lift his rod [against the sea] *12* [in the fashion of Egypt. And on that day it will happen] that [his] loa[d] will be removed [from your shoulder, and his yoke] *13* [from your neck. *Blank* The interpretation of the word concerns] ... [...] *14* [...] when they returned from the wilderness of the pe[op]le]s [...] *15* [...] the Prince of the Congregation, and after it will be rem[o]ved from [them] *16* [...] *Blank* [...] *17* [*Isa 10:28-32* ...] come up to Aiath; cross [Migron;] at Michma[sh] *18* [leave the baggage-train; traverse] the gorge; spend the night in Geba; fea[rful is Ramah; Gibeah of] *19* [Saul deserts. Raise] your voice, Bat-Gallim; pay attention, [Laishah; answer, Anathoth.] *20* [Retreat,] Madmenah, the [r]esidents of Gebiom flee; this very day [he makes a stopover in Nob,] *21* [already he stretches] his hand towards the mount of the daughter of Zion, towards the hill of Jerusalem. [*Blank*] *22* [The interpretation of the] word concerns the final days, when the [...] comes [...] *23* [...] from his climb from the plain of Akko to do battle against Pale[stine ...] *24* [...] and there is none like her, and in all the cities of the [...] *25* and up to the boundary of Jerusalem. [...]

Frags. 8 - 10 (col. III)   *1* [*Isa 10:33-34* See! The Lord YHWH of Hosts will rip off the branches at one wrench; the] tall[est trunks] will be felled, *2* [the loftiest chopped.] The thickest [of the wood will be cut] with iron and Lebanon, with its grandeur, *3* [will fall. *Blank* Its interpretation concerns the] Kittim, wh[o] will be pla[ced] in the hands of Israel, and the meek *4* [of the earth ...] all the peoples and soldiers will weaken and [their] he[art] will melt *5* [... and what it says: «The] tallest [trunks] will be destroyed», they are the soldiers of the

ונ'קפו סובכי [ה]יער בברזל *vacat* ה[מה] ה[מה] 7 [...].ם למלחמת כתיאים
vacat ולבנון בא[דיר] 8 [יפול המה מושלי ה]כתיאים אשר ינת[נו] ביד
גדולי [...] *vacat* [...] 10 [...].ים בברחו מלפ[ני יש[ראל] 9 [...].
11 [ויצא חוטר מגז]ע ישי ונצר משו[רשיו יפרה ונח]ה עלו ר[וח]
12 רוח יהוה [חוכמה ובינה רוח עצ]ה וגבורה] רוח דע[ת] 13 [ויראת
יהוה והריחו ביראת [יהוה] לוא [למראה [עיניו] 14 [ישפוט ולוא
למשמע אוזניו יוכי]ח ושפט[בצדק דלים והוכיח] 15 [במישור לעוני ארץ
והכה ארץ בשפט פיו וברוח שפתיו] 16 [ימית רשע והיה צדק אזור מ]תניו
וא[מונה אזור הלציו] 17 [...] *vacat* [...] 18 [פשר הדבר על צמ]ח דויד
העומד באח[רית הימים אשר] 19 [ברוח שפתיו ימית או]יבו ואל יסומכנו
ב[רוח ג]בורה [...] 20 [... כ]סא כבוד נזר ק[דוש]ובגדי ריקמו[ת]
21 [...]ן בידו ובכול הג[ואי]ם ימשול ומגוג 22 [... כו]ל העמים תשפוט
חרבו ואשר אמר לוא 23 [למראה עיניו ישפוט]ולוא למשמע אוזניו יוכיח
פשרו אשר 24 [...] וכאשר יורוהו כן ישפוט ועל פיהם 25 [...] עמו יצא
אחד מכוהני השם ובידו בגדי

4Q162 (4QpIsaᵇ) *4QIsaiah Pesherᵇ*

J.M. Allegro, *DJD V*, 15-17, pl. VI; J. Strugnell, 'Notes', 186-188
PAM 41.311, 41.802
DAJ
3Q4, 4Q161, 4Q163, 4Q164, 4Q165, 4Q515

Col. I 1 [... הסר משוכתו ויהי לבער פר]ץ גדרו ויהי למרמס אשר
2 [אשיתהו בתה לא יזמר ולא יעדר ועלה שמיר ושי]ת פשר הדבר אשר
עזבם 3 [...]ד ואשר אמר ועלה שמיר 4 [ושית פשרו ...]עת ואשר
{אשר'} 5 [אמר ... .נת דרך [...]עיניהם 6

Kit[tim] *6* [since …] «and the thickest of [the] wood will be cut with iron» *Blank* Th[ey are] *7* […] for the war of the Kittim. *Blank* «And Lebanon, with its gran[deur], *8* [will fall». They are the commanders of the] Kittim, who will be pla[ced] in the hand of the great of […] *9* […] in his flight befo[re Is]rael. […] *10* […] *Blank* […] *11* [*Isa 11:1-5* A shoot will issue from the stu]mp of Jesse and [a bud] will sprout from [its] ro[ots.] Upon him [will be placed] the spi[rit of] *12* [YHWH; the spirit] of discretion and wisdom, the spirit of ad[vice and courage,] the spirit of knowl[edge] *13* [and of respect for YHWH, and his delight will be in respecting] YHWH. [He will not judge] by appearances *14* [or give verdi]cts [on hearsay alone;] he will judge [the poor with justice and decide] *15* [with honesty for the humble of the earth. He will destroy the land with the rod of his mouth and with the breath of his lips] *16* [he will execute the evil. Justice will be the belt of] his [l]oins and lo[yalty the belt of his hips.] *17* […] *Blank* […] *18* [The interpretation of the word concerns the shoot] of David which will sprout in the fi[nal days, since] *19* [with the breath of his lips he will execute] his [ene]my and God will support him with [the spirit of c]ourage […] *20* [… thro]ne of glory, h[oly] crown and multi-colour[ed] vestments *21* […] in his hand. He will rule over all the pe[ople]s and Magog *22* […] his sword will judge [al]l the peoples. And as for what he says: «He will not *23* [judge by appearances] or give verdicts on hearsay», its interpretation: which *24* […] and according to what they teach him, he will judge, and upon their authority *25* […] with him will go out one of the priests of renown, holding in his hand clothes (of)

4Q162 (4QpIsa^b) *4QIsaiah Pesher^b*

Bibliography: J.M. Allegro, 'More Isaiah Commentaries from Qumran's Fourth Cave', *JBL* 77 (1958) 215-218, pl. 1; W.R. Lane, 'Pesher Style as a Reconstruction Tool in 4QPesher Isaiah B', *RevQ* 2/6 (1960) 281-283; M.P. Horgan, *Pesharim: Qumran Interpretations of Biblical Books*, 86-93

Col. I *1* [*Isa 5:5* … remove its fence so that it can be used for pasture, destr]oy its wall so that you trample it. *Is 5:6* For *2* [I will leave it flattened; they shall not prune it or weed it, brambles and thist]les [will grow.] The interpretation of the word: that he has deserted them *3* […] and as for what he says: *Isa 5:6* «Brambles will grow, *4* [and thistles»: its interpretation concerns …] and what *5* [it says: …] of the path *6* […] their eyes

Col. II   1 פשר הדבר לאחרית הימים לחובת הארץ מפני החרב והרעב
2 בעת פקדת הארץ הוי משכימי בבקר שכר ירדפו מאחרי בנשף יין   והיה
3 ידלקם והיה כנור ונבל ותוף וחליל יין משתיהם ואת פעל יהוה   4 לא
הביטו ומעשי ידו לא ראו לכן גלה עמי מבלי דעת וכבדו מתי רעב   5 והמנו
צחי צמא לכן הרחיבה שאול נפשה ופערה פיה לבלי חוק   6 וירד הדרה
והמנה ושאנה עליז בא vacat אלה הם אנשי הלצון   7 אשר בירושלים הם
אשר מאסו את תורת יהוה ואת אמרת קדוש   8 ישראל נאצו על כן חרה אף
יהוה בעמו ויט ידו עליו ויכהו וירגזו   9 ההרים ותהי נבלתם כסחה בקרב
החוצות בכל זאת לא שב   10 [אפו ועוד ידו נטויה] היא עדת אנשי הלצון
אשר בירושלים   11 [...] ל[...]

Col. III   1 ואין מצ[יל וינהם עליו ביום ההוא]   2 כנהמ[ת ים ונבט
לארץ והנה חשך צר ואור חשך]   3 בער[י]פיה ...[4 הוא [...]
5 האלה[...]   6 הבאי[ם ...   7 אמר .[...]   8 ראו [...]   9 תבי.[...]

4Q163 (4Qpap pIsaᶜ) *4QIsaiah Pesherᶜ*

J.M. Allegro, *DJD V*, 17-27, pl. V; J. Strugnell, 'Notes', 188-195
PAM 42.067, 42.455, 42.456, 43.415, 43.416, 43.466
ROC 584, 599
3Q4, 4Q161, 4Q162, 4Q164, 4Q165, 4Q515

Frag. 1   1 [...]...[...]   2 [...] כי]א הואה [...]   3 [...]ובלע דרך .[...]
4 [... כאשר כ]תוב על[יו] ביר[מיה ...   5 [...]ו [...]   6 [...] יה[...]

Frag. 2   1 [ולכן הנה אדני מ]עלה עליה[ם] את מי הנהר ה[עצומים
והרבים את מלך אשור]   2 [ואת כל כבודו ועלה] על כל אפיקו והלך על כל
גדו[תו וחלף ביהודה שטף ועבר]   3 [עד צואר יגיע וה]יו מטות כנפו מלא

318

Col. II *1* The interpretation of the word concerns the last days, laying waste the land through drought and hunger. This will happen *2* at the time of the visitation of the land. *Isa 5:11-14* Woe to those who rise early in search of intoxicants and carry on until by twilight the wine *3* excites them and with zithers, harps, tambourines and flutes they feast their drunkenness, but they pay no attention to the action of YHWH *4* or notice the works of his hands! For this, my people will be exiled because of their lack of knowledge, their nobles will die of hunger *5* and the ordinary folk have a raging thirst. For this, the abyss distends its jaws and enlarges its mouth immeasurably; *6* down go its nobility and its ordinary people and its revelling throng enters. *Blank* These are the arrogant men *7* who are in Jerusalem. They are the ones who *Isa 5:24* «Have rejected the law of YHWH and mocked the word of the Holy One of *8* Israel. *Isa 5:25* For this the wrath of YHWH has been kindled against his people and he has stretched out his hand against them and wounded them. *9* The mountains quake, their corpses lie like dung in the middle of the streets. In spite of this *10* [his anger] is not appeased [and his hand continues to be stretched out]». This is the Congregation of the arrogant men who are in Jerusalem. *11* [...] ... [...]

Col. III *1* *Isa 5:29-30* with no-one to sa[ve it. On that day he will roar against him] *2* like the roa[r of the sea. It will be seen by the earth. See, deep darkness, even the light is obscured] *3* by [her] clo[uds ...] *4* He is [...] *5* these [...] *6* who com[e ...] *7* he has said [...] *8* they have seen [...] *9* ... [...]

4Q163 (4Qpap pIsaᶜ) *4QIsaiah Pesherᶜ*

Bibliography: J.M. Allegro, 'More Isaiah Commentaries from Qumran's Fourth Cave', *JBL* 77 (1958) 218-220, pl. 2; M.P. Horgan, *Pesharim: Qumran Interpretations of Biblical Books*, 94-124

Frag. 1 *1* [...] ... [...] *2* [... becau]se he is [...] *3* [...] and he has confused the path of [...] *4* [... for it is] written concerning him in Jere[miah ...] *5* [...] ... [...] *6* [...] ... [...]

Frag. 2 *1* [*Isa 8:7-8* For this, behold, the Lord will bri]ng up against th[em] the [torrential and violent] waters of the river, [the king of Assyria] *2* [and all his pomp. He will come up] through all its channels and overflow all [its] bank[s. He will invade Judah, he will flood, he will brim over] *3* [and will reach right up to the neck.] The opening of his wings [wi]ll cover the breadth of yo[ur]

רחב ארצכ]ה עמנואל פשר הדבר על [... 4 [...ע]...[ם התרה הוא רצין

ובן] רמליהו [... 5 ... כאשר כ]תוב ב]...[. [...] 6 [...]ה ולא[...]

Frags. 4-6 ו [...] 1 ... [2 [כאשר] כתוב 3 [...].[...]ע[...]ליהמה

4 [ארם מקדם ופלשתים מאחור ויואכלו א[ת] י] שראל בכול 5 [פה בכול

זאת לוא שב אפו פשרו ...]ור והואה [... 6 ... ויכרת יהוה מישראל רואש

וזנב כפה ואג]מון ביום אחד זקן 7 [ונשוא פנים הואה הרואש ונביא מורה

שקר]הואה הזנב 8 [ויהיו מאשרי העם הזה מתעים ומאשריו מב]לעים על

כן 9 [על בחורו לוא ישמח אדוני ואת יתמו ואת אל]מנותו לוא ירחם

10 [פשרו ... 11vacat? [...] 12 [...]שה. vacat? [...] 13 [...] vacat

14 [... כיא בערה כאש רשע]ה שמיר [ושית תו]אכל ותצית 15 [בסבכי

היער ויתאבכו גוא]ות עשן [בעברת יהוה צ]באות [נת]עם 16 [ארץ ויהי

העם כמאכולת אש] איש אל אחי]ו ל]וא 17 [יחמולו ויגזור על ימין ורעב

ויאכל על]שמאול ולוא ישב[ע]ו 18 [איש בשר זרועו יואכלו מנשה א]ת

אפרים ואפרי]ם[את 19 [מנש]ה יחדיו [המה על יהודה בכול זאת לוא

שב אפו]

Frags. 4-6 וו 1 [יהיו ונע]ר יכת[בם ...] 2 פשר הדבר על חק

בבל]...[3 חקות עמים ה...[...].[...] 4 [ל]בגוד רבים הוא]ה [... 5 ישראל

ואשר אמר] ושאר עץ יערו מספר יהיו ונער יכתבם] 6 פשרו למעוט

האדם] [... vacat 7 [...] 8 והיה ביום ההואה] לוא יוסיף עוד שאר ישראל

ופליטת] 9 בית יעקוב להש[ע]ן על מכהו ונשען על יהוה קדוש]

10 [יש]רא]ל באמת ש[א]ר] ישוב שאר יעקוב אל אל גבור] 11 כי אם יהיה

עמכה י]שראל כחול הים שאר ישוב בו] 12 פשר הדבר לאחרית ה]ימים

[... 13 ילכו בש]בי ... וא]שר] 14 אמר] כי אם יהיה עמכה ישראל כחול

הים שאר ישוב בו] 15 פשרו למועט[...]16 כאשר כתוב [כליון חרוץ

שוטף צדקה כיא כלה ונחרצה] 17 אדוני יהוה צ]באות עושה בקרב כול

הארץ [... 18 vacat [...] 19 לכן כוה אמר אדוני י]הוה צבאות אל תירא

עמי יושב ציון]

land, [O Emmanuel! The interpretation of the word concerns ...] *4* [...] ... the law; he is Rezin and the son of [Romeliah ...] *5* [... as it is wr]itten in [...] *6* [...] and not [...]

Frags. 4 - 6 *col.* I   *1* [...] *2* [... as it is] written *3* [... concer]ning them *4* [*Isa 9:11* Aram from the East and the Philistines from the West, and they have devoured I]srael in one *5* [mouthful. For all this, his anger is not turned away. Its interpretation ...] ... and he *6* [... *Isa 9:13-16* And YHWH has cut off from Israel head and tail, reed and ru]sh in one day. The old *7* and of radiant face, he is the head; and the prophet, the Teacher of Lies,] he is the tail. *8* [Those who lead this people lead (them) astray, and those who are lead by him are swa]llowed up. Therefore *9* [the Lord does not rejoice over his young men, and with his orphans and] his [wi]dows he has no compassion. *10* [Its interpretation: ...] *Blank?* *11* [...] *Blank?* *12* [...] ... *13* [...] *Blank* *14* [... *Isa 9:17-20* Because evi]l [is burning like a fire which] consumes thistles [and brambles;] it catches fire *15* [in the dense wood and the height] of the smoke [coils upwards. By the wrath of YHWH of H]osts [the land is devas]tated *16* [and the people have become like fuel for the fire. N]o-one [forgives his] brother, *17* [he destroys to the right and remains hungry, he consumes] to the left and is not satia[ted;] *18* [a man eats the flesh of his arm. Manasseh again]st Ephraim and Ephrai[m] against *19* [Mana]sseh; [the two] together [against Judah. And with all this] his wrath is not mollified.

Frags. 4 - 6 *col.* II (cf. 4Q161 1; 2 - 6)   *1* [*Isa 10:19* will be, and a young ma]n will cou[nt them.» *Blank* ...] *2* The interpretation of the word concerns the edict of Babylon [...] *3* the edicts of the peoples [...] *4* [to] betray many. He [...] *5* Israel. And what it says: [*Isa 10:19* «The remainder of the trees of the wood will be a small number and a young man will count them».] *6* Its interpretation concerns the reduction of men [...] *7* *Blank* [...] *8* *Isa 10:20-22* On that day it will happen [that the remainder of the House of Israel and the survivors] *9* of the House of Jacob [will cease] to le[an on their assailant but will lean] loyally [on YHWH, the Holy One] *10* [of Is]rael. A re[mna]nt [will return, a remnant of Jacob, to God the warrior.] *11* Even if your people, I[srael] were [like the sand of the sea, only a remnant will return.] *12* The interpretation of the word concerns the final [days ...] *13* they will go into cap[tivity ... And what] *14* it says: *Isa 10:21* [«Even if your people, [Israel] were like the sand of the sea, only a remnant will return.»] *15* Its interpretation concerns the reduction [...] *16* Since it is written: [*Isa 10:22-23* «Extermination is decreed but justice will overflow. Because destruction is decreed] *17* the Lord YHWH of H[osts will execute it in the midst of the whole earth»] *18* *Blank* [...] *19* *Isa 10:24* Therefore, the Lord Y[HWH of Hosts says: Do not fear, my people who live in Zion]

Frags. 8-10   1   [פשר הדב]ר על מלך בבל [אשר ... כאשר כתוב גם
ברושים]   2   [שמחו ל]כה ארזי לבנון מאז [שכבת לוא יעלה]   3   [הכורת]
עלימו הברושים וארז]י לבנון המה [... ...[...]   4   [... ואשר אמר זא]ת העצה
היעוצה על]   5   [כול] הארץ וזאת היד [הנטויה על כול הגואים]   6   [כיא
יהו]ה צבאות יע]ץ ומי יפר וידו הנטויה]   7   [ומי יש]יבנה הואה מז[...]
8   [כאשר כת]וב בספר זכריה מפ]תח פתחה נאום יהו]ה   9   [צבאות] vacat
[...]   10   [...] vacat   11   [בשנת מו]ת היה המלך אח]ז היה המשא הזה אל
ת]שמחי[י]   12   [פלשת כו]לך כיא נשבר שבט] מכך כיא משורש [נחש
יצ]א[13   [צפע ופריו שרף]מעופף ו]רעו בכורי דלים]ואביונים
14   [לבטח ירבצו והמתי ברעב שורשך וש]ארית]ך יהרוג[

Frag. 11 I   1   [...[ב]...] 2   [...]ה עובדי   3   [...]המה   4   [...]הציחים
5   [...] הזאת

Frag. 11 II   1   [ואורגים] חורי והיו שתותיה מדכאים כול עושי]   2   שכר
אגמ]י נפש אך אולים שרי צוען חכמי יועצי]   3   פרעוה עצ]ה נבערה איך
תואמרו אל פרעוה בני חכמים]   4   אנו בני מל]כי קדם אים אפוא חכמיכה
ויגידו נא]   5   לכה] וידעו מה יעץ יהוה צבאות על מצרים]

Frags. 15-16   1   [עליכ]מה יהוה [רוח ת]רדמה ויעצם את] עיניכמה את
הנביאים]   2   [ואת ר]אשיכמה הה]וזים [כסה ותהי לכמה ח]זות הכול
כדברי]   3   [הספר הח]תום אשר [יתנו אל יודע ספר לא]מור קרא נא
זה]   4   [ואמר לוא אוכל כ]יא ח]תום הוא] ונתן הספ]ר על אשר לוא ידע
ספר]

Frags. 18-19   1   [דברי ספר] ומאופל ומח]ושך עיני עורים תראינה
ויספו ענוים ביהוה]   2   [שמחה ואב]יוני אדם בקד]וש ישראל יגילו כיא
אפס עריץ וכלה לץ]   3   [ונכרתו כו]ל שוקדי און מ]חטיאי אדם בדבר
ולמוכיח בשער יקושון]   4   [ויטו בתוהו צדיק]לכן כוה א]מר יהוה אל בית
יעקוב אשר פדה את]   5   [אברהם לוא עתה יבו]ש יעקוב] ולוא עתה פניו

322

Frags. 8 - 10   *1* [The interpretation of the wor]d concerns the king of Babylon, [since ... as it is written: *Isa 14:8* «The very cypresses] *2* [laugh at] you, and the cedars of Lebanon. Since [you lie down, the hewer] *3* [does not come up] against them». The cypresses and the cedar[s of Lebanon are ...] *4* [...] ... And what it says: *Isa 14:26-27* «Thi[s is the strategy decided for] *5* [all] the earth and this is the hand [stretched out against all the peoples.] *6* [For YHW]H of Hosts has dec[ided, who will thwart him? His hand is stretched out,] *7* [who] will push it aside?». This is ... [...] *8* [as it is writ]ten in the book of Zechariah: *Zech 3:9* [See, I will] en[grave its inscription, oracle of YHWH] *9* [of Hosts.] *Blank* [...] *10* [...] *Blank* [...] *11* [*Isa 14:28-30* In the year of the deat]h of king Acha[z this oracle was uttered: Do not] rejoice, *12* [al]l [Philistia,] that the rod [which injured you] is shattered, [because from the root of the] snake shall [come] *13* [a viper and its fruit will be a] flying [asp. The most destitute] will be fed and the poor *14* [will lie down in safety. I will make your root die of hunger and he will kill your re]mnant.

Frag. 11 *col.* I   *1* [...] ... *2* [...] servants of *3* [...] they are *4* [...] the insults (?) *5* [...] this

Frag. 11 *col.* II   *1* *Isa 19:9-12* those who weave [white cloths. Their masters will be dismayed, all their] *2* labourers knocked [down. How deranged the princes of Zoan; the wise advise] *3* Pharaoh with [inane] advice. [How can you say to Pharaoh: We are sons of wise men,] *4* we are sons of [ancient] kin[gs? Where are your wise men? Let them announce] *5* you, [so that they know, what YHWH of Hosts is planning against Egypt.]

Frags. 15 - 16   *Isa 29:10-12* [For] *1* YHWH has poured [upon] you [a spirit of de]ep stupor and he has closed [your eyes - the prophets - and] *2* he has covered your [h]eads - the seers - . For you the vi[sion of this all] has become [like the words of a] *3* [sea]led [book,] which one [gives] to someone who can read, te[lling him: Please read this,] *4* [and he answers: I cannot be]cause [it is] se[aled;] and when one gives the boo[k to someone who cannot read]

Frags. 18 - 19   *1* *Isa 29:18-23* [words of a book;] without darkness or glo[om the eyes of the blind will see. The oppressed will rejoice even more in YHWH] *2* [and the poor]est of men [will delight] in the Ho[ly One of Israel. Because the tyrant is destroyed, the sceptic finished off] *3* [and al]l those alert for evil [will be obliterated,] those [who are going to seize another in speaking and the one who defends in the gate with snares and, for nothing, engulf] *4* [the inno-cent.] Therefore, so says [YHWH to the House of Jacob, he who ransomed]

יחזרו כיא בראותו ילדיו] 6 [מעשה ידי בקרבו]יקדיש[ו ש[מי וה]קדישו
את קדוש יעקוב]

Frag. 21 1 [...] הל[וא עוד מעט מזער ושב] 2 [לבנון לכרמל ליער]
יחשב הל[ב]נון ה[מה] 3 [...]ל לכרמל ושבו ה[...]. בחרב ואשר]
אמר [... 5 [...].מ.[...]...[...] 6 [...]...[...] מורה] ... כאשר כתוב] 7 [ותופר
ביום ההואה וידע]ו כן עני הצואן ה[שומרים] 8 [אותי כיא דבר יהוה
הואה *vacat* [...] 9 [הוי בנים סוררים נאום] יהוה לעשות עצ]ה ולוא]
10 [מני ולנסוך מסכה]ולוא רוחי למען ס[פות חטאת] 11 [על חטאת
ההולכים לר]דת מצרים ופי ל[וא שאלו לעוז] 12 [במעוז פרעוה ולחס]ות
בצל מצ]רים והיה לכם מעוז] 13 [פרעוה לבושת והחסו]ת בצל מצרי]ם
לכלמה כיא היו] 14 [בצוען שריו ומלאכיו כ]חנס יגיעו כ]ול הובאיש על עם
לוא] 15 [יועילו למו לוא לעז]ר ולוא [להועיל]

Frag. 22 1 [...]פשר הדבר[...] 2 [...]ם אשר דרך[...] 3 [...] בני
צדוק [...] 4 [... ואש]ר אמר לחם תב[ואת האדמה והיה דשן ...
5 [...].אם ההואה[...] 6 [...]...[...]

Frag. 23 ii 1 [...]ם והמה ה[...] 2 [...].ה כול [...]. *vacat* [...]
3 [כי]א כ[ו]ה אמר יהוה קדוש ישראל בשובה ונ[חת תושעון] 4 [בה]שקט
ובטח תהיה גבורתכמה ולוא אביתמה ות[אמרו] 5 לוא כיא על סוס ננוס
על כן תנוסון ועל קל נרכב על כן 6 יקלו רודפיכמה אלף אחד [מ]פני גערת
אחד מפני גערת 7 חמשה תנוסון עד אם נותרתמה כתון על רואש הר
8 וכנס על גבעה לכן יחכה אדוני לחנ[נכ]מה ולכן ירום 9 לרחמכמה כיא
אלוהי משפט יהוה אשרי כול חוכי לו 10 פשר הדבר לאחרית הימים על
ד[ורשי] החלקות 11 אשר בירושלים... [...] 12 בתורה ולוא
יה[...]...[...] 13 לב כיא לדוש[...] 14 כיחכה איש גדו]דים חבר כוהנים]
התורה מאסו [...] 15 [כ]יא עם בציון [ישב בירושלים בכו לוא תבכה חנון
יחנכה לקול[ו] 16 זועקכה כשמע]עתו ענכה ונתן לכמה אדוני לחם צר ומים

5 [Abraham: No longer will] Jacob [be asham]ed, [no longer will his face grow pale. For when his sons see] *6* [the work of my hands in his midst, t]he[y] shall hallow my [na]me, and keep [the Holy One of Jacob in awe.]

Frag. 21   *1* [...] *Isa 29:17* Per[haps, in a very little while,] *2* [will the Lebanon turn into] an orchard, and will the orchard] seem like [a wood?] The Le[b]anon a[re] *3* [...] into an orchard and they will turn into [...] *4* [...] by the sword. And what [it says ...] *5* [...] ... [...] *6* [...] ... [...] the Teacher of [... as it is written:] *7* *Zech 11:11* [It was annulled on that day, and] thus the most helpless of the flock which [were watching me knew] *8* [that] it [was in fact the word of YHWH.] *Blank* [...] *9* *Isa 30:1-5* [Woe to the rebellious sons - oracle of] YHWH - who make pla[ns without counting] *10* [on me; who sign deals,] but without my spirit, to a[dd sin] *11* [to sin; who proceed to go do]wn to Egypt [without conferring with me, to seek protection] *12* [in the refuge of the Pharaoh and shel]ter in the shadow of Eg[ypt! Their disgrace will be] *13* [the refuge of the Pharaoh, and the she]lter of the shadow of Egyp[t, their shame. For though] *14* [their princes were in Zoan, and their messengers] reached Hanes, [they are] a[ll ashamed of a] *15* [powerless people which could neither hel]p nor [oblige ...]

Frag. 22   *1* [...] The interpretation of the word [...] *2* [...] who walks [...] *3* [...] the sons of Zadok [...] *4* [... And wha]t he says: *Isa 30:23* Grain, the pro[duce of the earth, and it will be fat ...] *5* [...] ... he [...] *6* [...] ... [...]

Frag. 23 col. ꞇꞇ   *1* [...] and they [...] all [...] ... [...] *2* [...] ... [...] *Blank* [...] *3* *Isa 30:15-18* [For] th[u]s says YHWH, the Holy One of Israel: By turning back and being pla[cid will you be saved;] *4* your courage will comprise [com]posure and trust. But you did not wish and [said:] *5* No, let us flee on horseback — Well, then, you need to flee — and: We will run at a gallop — Well, then *6* those chasing you will run faster. A thousand (shall flee) [be]fore the menace of one, before the menace *7* of five shall you flee, until you end up like a flagpole on the peak of a mountain, *8* like a standard upon a hill. This is why the Lord waits to take pit[y on y]ou, this is why he rises *9* to be lenient with you. For YHWH is a God of justice. Happy are all those waiting for him. *10* The interpretation of the word, for the last days, concerns the congregation of those l[ooking] for easy interpretations *11* who are in Jerusalem [...] *12* in the law and not [...] *13* heart, for in order to crush [...] *14* /*Hos 6:9* As bandits lie in wait, [the priests scheme]./ They have rejected the law [...] *15* *Isa 30:19-21* [F]or (you) a people [living] in Zion, [in Jerusalem, will no longer need to weep; he will have pity on you at the sound of] *16* your cry; when he hea[rs it, he will

לחץ[17   ולוא יכניף ע]וד מוריכה והיו עיניכה רואות את מוריכה]
18 ואוזניכה תש[מענה דבר מאחריכה לאמור זה הדרך לכו בו]   19 כיא
תימ]ינו וכיא תשמאילו פשר הדבר לאחרית הימים]   20 על עון ע]...[

Frag. 25   1]...[מלך בבל]...[2]...[בתופים ובכנו]רות ...[3]...
נפץ ו]זרם כלי מלחמה המה]...[4]...[*vacat*]...[5]הוי היורדים
מצרים על סוסים]ישענו ויבטחו על רכב]   6]כ]יא רב ועל פרשים כיא
עצמ]ו מאוד ולוא שעו על] 7]קד]וש ישראל ואת יה]וה לוא דרשו]*vacat*
8]פשרו ה]מה העם אשר יב]טחו ...[

4Q164 (4QpIsa^d^) *4QIsaiah Pesher^d^*

J.M. Allegro, *DJD V*, 27-28, pl. IX; J. Strugnell, 'Notes', 195-196
PAM 43.349, 43.436
ROC 291
3Q4, 4Q161, 4Q162, 4Q163, 4Q165, 4Q515
Bibliography: J.M. Allegro, 'More Isaiah Commentaries from Qumran's Fourth

Frag. 1   1]יער]ך כול ישראל כפוך בעין ויסדתיך בספי]רים פשרו]
2]אש]ר יסדו את עצת היחד] ה]כוהנים והע]ם ...[3] עדת בחירו כאבן
הספיר בתוך האבנים] ושמתי כדכוד]   4 כול שמשותיך פשרו על שנים
עשר]ראשי הכוהנים אשר]   5 מאירים במשפט האורים והתומים]...
ולוא] 6 הנעדרות מהמה כשמש{ל} בכול אורו וכו]ל שעריך לאבני אקדח]
7 פשרו על ראשי שבטי ישראל לא]חרית הימים ...[8 גורלו מעמדי]...[.

4Q165 (4QpIsa^e^) *4QIsaiah Pesher^e^*

J.M. Allegro, *DJD V*, 28-30, pl. IX; J. Strugnell, 'Notes', 197-199, pl. I
PAM 43.345, 43.436, 44.191
ROC 587

answer you. Even though the Lord has given you measured bread and rationed water,] *17* no lo[nger] will he hide [your Teacher, and your eyes will see your Teacher.] *18* Your ears will h[ear a word behind you which says: This is the path, walk on it,] *19* when you need to go to the rig[ht or to the left. The interpretation of the word, for the last days,] *29* concerns the sin of [...]

Frag. 25   *1* [...] the king of Babylon [...] *2* [...] with tambourines and zith[ers ...] *3* [... downpour and] hailstorm, implements of war, they are [...] *4* [...] *Blank* [...] *5* [*Isa 31:1* Woe to those who go down to] Egypt! In horses [they trust and they rely on chariots] *6* [beca]use they are numerous, and on cavalry, because they are [very] strong, [without regard for] *7* [the Ho]ly One of Israel or [consulting] YH[WH. *Blank*] *8* [Its interpretation: th]ey are the people who re[ly ...]

4Q164 (4QpIsa^d) *4QIsaiah Pesher^d*

Cave', *JBL* 77 (1958) 220-221, pl. 3; D. Flusser, 'The Pesher of Isaiah and the Twelve Apostles', *Eretz Israel* 8 (1967) 52-62 [Hebrew]; J.M. Baumgarten, 'The Duodecimal Courts of Qumran, Revelation, and the Sanhedrin', *JBL* 95 (1976) 59-78; M.P. Horgan, *Pesharim: Qumran Interpretations of Biblical Books*, 125-131

Frag. 1   *1* [he will mak]e all Israel like eye-paint around the eye. *Isa 54:11* And I will found you in sapphi[res. Its interpretation:] *2* they will found the council of the Community, [the] priests and the peo[ple ...] *3* the assembly of their elect, like a sapphire stone in the midst of stones. [*Isa 54:12* I will make] *4* all your battlements [of rubies]. Its interpretation concerns the twelve [chiefs of the priests who] *5* illuminate with the judgment of the Urim and the Thummim [... without] *6* any from among them missing, like the sun in all its light. *Isa 54:12* And a[ll your gates of glittering stones.] *7* Its interpretation concerns the chiefs of the tribes of Israel in the l[ast days ... of] *8* its lot, the posts of [...]

4Q165 (4QpIsa^e) *4QIsaiah Pesher^e*

3Q4, 4Q161, 4Q162, 4Q163, 4Q164, 4Q515
Bibliography: M.P. Horgan, *Pesharim: Qumran Interpretations of Biblical Books*, 131-138

ואשר vacat ד[... וירושלם] 2   [...]...[...]...[...]הנ[1   *Frags. 1-2*
כתוב] ובחיקוה ישא עולות ינהל] 3   פשר הדבר] על מורה הצדק אשר]
גלה את תורה הצ]דק ... מי מדד בשועלו מים] 4   ושמים ב]זרת תכן וכול
בשלש עפר]הארץ שקל] בפלס הרים וגבעות במואזנים]

[וכל פסילי אלהיה שבר] לאר]ץ מדשתי ובן גרני אשר 1   *Frag. 5*
שמעתי מאת יהוה צבאות אלוהי[2   ]ישראל הגדתי לכמ]ה vacat פשר
הדבר ע]ל [...   3   ]משא דומה אלי קור]א משעיר שומר מה מ]לילה שומר
מה מליל אמר שומר אתה בוקר וגם לילה אם תבעיון בעיו[4   ]שובו אתיו
משא בערב]ביער בערב תלינו]אורחות דדנים לקראת צמא התיו מים
יושבי ארץ תימא בלחמו]   vacat   5   ]קדמו נודד כי]מפ]ני חרבות נדד מפני
]חרב נטושה מפני] קשת דרוכה] מפ]ני כובד מלחמה פשר הדבר על] 6   [...]
העמים והלחם[...]   7   [...]שודד ע[...]

[...]ב]חירי ישראל א[...]   2   [...]עולם ואשר כ]תוב לא 1   *Frag. 6*
יקרא עוד לנבל נדיב]   3   ]ולכילי]לא יאמר שוע כי נ]בל נבלה ידבר ולבו
יעשה און לעשות חנף[4   ]ולדבר א]ל vacat (יהוה) תועה ולהכ]ות נ]פש
רעב ומשקה צמא יחסיר וכלי[5   ]כליו ר]שע]ים ו]הואה זמות יעץ] לחבל
ענוים באמרי שקר ובדבר]   6   ]אביון מ]שפט vacat פשרו על]...[.]...[7
[...].את התורה]...[שר.]...[

4Q166 (4QpHos^a) *4QHosea Pesher^a*

J.M. Allegro, *DJD V*, 31-32, pl. X; J. Strugnell, 'Notes', 199-201
PAM 42.181, 42.457
ROC 675
4Q167
Bibliography: J.M. Allegro, 'A Recently Discovered Fragment of a Commentary on Hosea from Qumran's Fourth Cave', *JBL* 78 (1959) 142-147; J.D.

Frags. 1 - 2 *1* ... [...] ... *2* and Jerusalem [...] *Blank* And what is written: [*Isa 40:11*
«He carries them on his chest and leads the sucklings».] *3* The interpretation
of the word [concerns the Teacher of Righteousness who] reveals j[ust] teaching [... *Isa 40:12* Who has measured the sea in fistfuls,] *4* or [charted] the sky in
[palm-breadths, or seized the dust] of the earth [in bushels,] weighed [the
mountains on the balance or the hills in the scales?]

Frag. 5 *1* *Isa 21:9-10* [and all the statues of her gods has he smashed] to the
grou[nd. My (people,) trodden and winnowed on the threshing floor, what I
have heard from YHWH of Hosts, God] *2* [of Israel, I have told yo]u. *Blank* The
interpretation of the word con[cerns ...] *3* [*Isa 21:11-15* Oracle against Dumah:
Someone shou]ts [to me] from Seir: Watchman, what is left of the [night?
Watchman, what is left of the night? The Watchman replies: Morning will
come and also the night. If you wish to ask, ask,] *4* [come back, return. Oracle
against Arabia:] In the scrub of the steppe shall you spend the night, [caravans
of Dedan; take out water to meet the thirsty, dwellers in the land of Teman,
take bread] *5* [to the refugee, for] /he flees [fr]om of the swords,/ from the
unsheathed sword /from [the taut bow,]/ fr[om the fierce fighting. The interpretation of the word concerns] *6* [...] the peoples and the bread [...] *7* [...]
lays waste [...]

Frag. 6 *1* [... the ch]osen ones of Israel [...] *2* [...] eternal. And what is wr[itten:
Isa 32:5-7 No longer will the fool be called noble,] *3* [or the rogue] thought to be
superior. For the f[ool says foolish things and his heart produces evil, to commit wicked deeds] *4* [and to speak] absurdities [agai]nst *Blank* ‹YHWH›; to
destr[oy the] s[oul of the hungry person and refuse water to the thirsty. As for
the rogue] *5* [his roguish deeds are e]vil [and] he hatches plots [to destroy the
poor with lies,] *6* [even when the helpless defends his r]ights. *Blank* Its interpretation concerns [...] *7* [...] ... the law [...] ... [...]

4Q166 (4QpHos³) *4QHosea Pesher*

Amoussine, "Observatiunculae qumraneae", *RevQ* 7/28 (1971) 533-552; M.P.
Horgan, *Pesharim: Qumran Interpretations of Biblical Books*, 138-148; D.C.
Carson, 'An Alternative Reading of 4QpHos³ II 3-6', *RevQ* 11/43 (1983) 417-
421; M.J. Bernstein, "Walking in the Festivals of the Gentiles': 4QpHosea³
2:15-17 and Jubilees 6:34-38', *JSP* 9 (1991) 21-31

Col. I   6 [...] וילוזו   5 [...]   4 וירצו [...]   3 [...]יצור[...]   2-1 [...]

vacat   7 [... לכן הנני שך את דרכ]ה בסירים ונתיבותיה   8 [לוא תמצא
פשרו אשר בשגעון]ובעורון ובתמהון   9 [לבב הכם ...]. וקץ מועלם לוא
10 [... כיא] הם דור הפקודה   11 [...]מן מ[חזי]קי ה[ב]רית   12 [... נ]אסף
בקצי חרון כיא   13-14 [...] vacat

15 [ואמרה אלכה ואשובה אל אישי הרא]ישון כיא   16 [טוב לי אז
מעתה פשרו אשר ...] בשוב שבי   17 [...]טהורים   18-19 [...]

Col. II   1 [לוא ידעה כיא] אנוכי נתתי לה הדגן [והתירוש]   2 [והיצהר
וכסף]הרביתי וזהב{...} עשו[ן] לבעל פשרו]   3 אשר אכל[ו וי]שבעו וישכחו
את אל המש[פט ואת כול]   4 מצוותיו השליכו אחרי גום אשר שלח אליהם
[בפי]   5 עבדיו הנביאים ולמתעיהם שמעו ויכבדום   6 וכאלים יפחדו מהם
בעורונם vacat   7 vacat

8 לכן אשוב ולקחתי דגני בעתו ותירושי[ן] במועדו]   9 והצלתי צמרי
ופושתי מלכסות את] ערותה]   10 ועתה אגלה את נבלותה לעיני מאה]ביה
ואיש[11 לוא יצילנה מידי vacat

12 פשרו אשר הכם ברעב ובערום להיות לקלו[ן]   13 וחרפה לעיני
הגואים אשר נשענו עליהם והמה   14 לוא יושיעום מצרותיהם והשבתי כול
משושה   15 ח[גה חד]שה ושבתה וכול מועדיה פשרו אשר   16 [כול
המו]עדות יוליכו במועדי הגואים vacat וכ[ול]   17 [שמחה]נהפכה להם
לאבל והשמותי [גפנה]   18 [ותאנתה] אשר אמרה אתנם הם לי [אשר נתנו]
19 [לי מאהב]י ושמתים ליער ואכלתם ח[ית השדה]

4Q167 (4QpHos^b) *4QHosea Pesher^b*

J.M. Allegro, *DJD V*, 32-36, pls. X-XI; J. Strugnell, 'Notes', 201-203, pl. III
PAM 43.419, 43.429, 44.184, 44.189
ROC 354
4Q166

Col. I *1-2* [...] *3* [...] he will show his hostility *4* [...] and they shall beg *5* [...] and get lost *6* [...] *Blank 7* [*Hos 2:8* Therefore, I will block] her [road] with brambles, and her footpaths *8* [she will not find. Its interpretation: with madness,] blindness and confusion *9* [of heart he has stricken them ...] and the era of their disloyalty not *10* [... for] they are the generation of the visitation *11* [...] from those who [upho]ld the [cov]enant. *12* [... has be] taken away in the ages of wrath, because *13-14* [...] *Blank 15* [*Hos 2:9* And he will say: I shall go and return to my fir]st [husband] because *16* [I was better off then than now. Its interpretation: ...] at the return of the captives of *17* [...] pure *18-19* [...]

Col. II *1* [*Hos 2:10* she does not know that] it was I who gave her wheat, [wine] *2* [and oil.] I increased [the silver] and the gold (which) they used [for Ba'al. Its interpretation:] *3* they at[e and] became replete and forgot the God of [justice, and] *4* cast behind their back [all] his precepts which he had sent to them [through] *5* his servants, the prophets. But they listened to those who misdirected them and they acclaimed them, *6* and feared them in their blindness like gods. *Blank 7 Blank 8 Hos 2:11-12* Because of this I will collect back my wheat in its time and my wine [in its season,] *9* I will reclaim my wool and my flax so that she cannot cover [her nakedness.] *10* Now I will uncover her disgrace in the sight of [her] love[rs and] no [one] *11* will free her from my hand. *Blank* [...] *12* Its interpretation: he has punished them with hunger and with nakedness so they will be sham[e] *13* and disgrace in the eyes of the nations on whom they relied. But they *14* will not save them from their sufferings. *Hos 2:13* I will make an end to her joys, *15* her fea[st, her new] moon and her sabbath and all her celebrations. Its interpretation: *16* they fix [all cele]brations in agreement with the celebrations of the nations, but a[ll] *17* [joy] will be changed into mourning for them. *Hos 2:14* I will devastate [her vine] *18* [and her fig tree] about which she said: they are their gifts for me [which] *19* my [lovers gave me;] I will turn them into thickets and the [wild be]asts will eat them.

4Q167 (4QpHos^b) *4QHosea Pesher^b*

Bibliography: J.M. Allegro, 'Further Light on the History of the Qumran Sect', *JBL* 75 (1956) 93, pl. 2; M.P. Horgan, *Pesharim: Qumran Interpretations of Biblical Books*, 148-158

Frag. 2 1 [ולוא יגהה מכ]ם מזור *vacat* פ[שר ...] 2 [...].‏ כפיר
החרון כי אנוכי כשח]ל לא[פ]רי[ם] וככפיר לבית] 3 [יהודה פשרו ע]ל
כוהן האחרון אשר ישלח ידו להכות באפרים   4 [... י]דו *vacat* 5 [אלך
אשובה א]ל[מקומי ע]ד אשר [י]אשמו ובקשו פני בצר 6 [להם ישחרנני
פשרו אשר יסתי]ר אל את פניו מן הא[ר]ץ [...]   7 [...]הו ולוא שמעו[...]

Frags. 5-6 1 [...]אנשי [...]   2 [...].‏ מוריהם[...] 3 [... על]‏[...]‏ מה
א[עשה לכה] אפרים [מה] אעשה לכה יהודה [...]

Frags. 7-8 1 [והמה כאדם]עברו ברית *vacat* פשר[ו ...]   2 [...]עזבו
את אל ו[י]לכו בחוקות[...]לים [א]ותם בכול[...]

Frags. 10+26 1 ואשר זמה [עשו בבית ישראל ראיתי שערוריה שם
זנות לאפרים נטמא] 2 ישראל פש[רו ...]   3 [ר]שעי הגואי[ם ...]   4 כול
מכ[...].‏[.] 5 [...]ל[.]

Frags. 10a+4+18+24 1 [... גם יהודה שת ק]ציר לכה   2 [בשובי
שבות עמי פשרו ...] ביום   3 [...]ם לנו [...]   4 *vacat* 5 [...]תו ואשר
6 [אמר בשובי שבות עמי ... פשרו א]שר ישוב 7 [...]יהם וה[...]

Frags. 11-13 1 [...]הת לס[...]   2 [...] בן ..[...]   3 [...] והו]א חרש
עשה]ו ולוא אלוהים הוא [...]   4 [... פ]שר[ו א]שר היו בעמים[...]   5 [...]
[כי שו]בבי]ם היה ע[ג]ל שומרון פשרו [...]   6 [ישר]אל[כי]רוח יזרעו
סופות] יקצורו קמה אין לו צמח בלי יעשה]   7 [קמח אולי יעשה זרים
יבלעוהו]ו נבלע ישראל עתה היו בגואים ככלי] 8 [אין חפץ בו] *vacat* [...]
9 פשר[ו ... הס]‏[...]   10 הב[...]

Frags. 15+16+33 II 1 [ישו]בו וישכ]ח ישראל את עושהו ויבן היכלות
ויהודה]   2 הרבה ערי[ם בצורות ושלחתי אש בעריו ואכלה ארמנותיה]

332

Frag. 2   *1* [*Hos 5:13* but he cannot heal] your sores. *Blank* The interpre[tation ...]
2 [...] raging lion. *Hos 5:14* For I will be like a lio[n [to E]phrai]m [and like a
lion cub to the House of] *3* [Judah. Its interpretation con]cerns the last priest
who will stretch out his hand to strike Ephraim *4* [...] his ha[nd.] *Blank 5 Hos
5:15* [I will go and return t]o [my position un]til they acknowledge their crime
and seek my face; in [their] distress *6* [they will get up early in search of me.
Its interpretation:] God [will hid]e his face fr[om the l]an[d ...] *7* [...] ... and
they did not listen [...]

Frags. 5 - 6   *1* [...] the men of [...] *2* [...] their teachers [...] upon [...] *3* [*Hos 6:4*
What] shall I do with you, [Ephraim;] what [shall I do with you Judah? ...]

Frags. 7 - 8   *1* [*Hos 6:7* But they, like Adam,] broke the covenant. *Blank* [Its] interpretation: [...] *2* [...] they deserted God and followed the laws of [...] ... them
in all [...]

Frags. 10 + 26   *1* And concerning: [*Hos 6:9-10* «They commit] evils. [In the
House of Israel I have seen something horrifying: there Ephraim prostitutes
himself,] *2* Israel [degrades herself». Its] interpreta[tion: ...] *3* [the evil]doers
of the nations [...] *4* all the ... [...] *5* ... [...]

Frags. 10a + 4 + 18 + 24   *1* [... *Hos 6:11* Judah, also] a harvest [is ready] for you,
2 [when I will change the bondage of my people. The interpretation concerns
...] on the day of *3* [...] for us *4* [...] *Blank 5* [...] and what *6* [it says: *Hos 7:1*
«When I will change the bondage of my people ...», its interpretation:] He
will bring back *7* [...] their [...] and ... [...]

Frags. 11 - 13   *1-2* [...] ... [...] *3* [...] (*Hos 8:6*) A sculptor made [i]t [and it is not
God ...] *4* [... Its inter]pretation: they were among the peoples [...] *5* [...] *Hos
8:6* For shat[tered to piec]es was the ca[lf of Samaria. Its interpretation: ...]
6 [Isra]el. *Hos 8:7-8* [For] they sow wind and [reap] storms. [It will not have
shoots; the stalk will not have fruit;] *7* [if it di]d [have any,] foreigners would
eat i[t. Israel has been devoured. Now they are among the nations like a ves-
sel] *8* [which no-one wants] *Blank* [...] *9* [Its] interpretation [...] ... [...] *10* ...
[...]

Frags. 15 + 16 + 33 *col.* II   *1* they [shall ret]urn. *Hos 8:14* And [Israel] forg[ot his
Maker and built palaces. And Judah] *2* increased her [fortified] citie[s. But I
shall send fire against his cities and it will consume her palaces.] *3 Blank* [...]

3 vacat [...] פ[שרו אשר] [...] 4 להיו[ת ... ו]יתפושו איש [...] 5 לפנ[י
... [א]ל ל[וא]ר[צה ...]

4Q168 (4QpMic?) *4QMicah Pesher (?)*

J.M. Allegro, *DJD V*, 36, pl. XII; J. Strugnell, 'Notes', 204, pls. II, III
PAM 43.419, 43.429, 44.179, 44.192
ROC 326
1Q14

Frags. 1+3 1 [לבת ירוש[ל]י[ם] עתה למה תריעי רע המלך אין בך
אם יועצך אבד] 2 כי ה[ח]זיקכה] חיל כיולדה חולי וגחי בת ציון כיולדה
כי] 3 עתה תצאי מקר[י]ה ושכנת בשדה ובאת עד בבל שם תנצלי שם]
4 [יגא[לך] י]הוה מ[כף אויביך ועתה נאספו עליך גואים רבים]
5 [האו]מרים ת[חנף ותחז בציון עינינו והמה לוא ידעו מחשבות] 6 [יהוה
ולוא הבינו [עצתו...]

4Q169 (4QpNah) *4QNahum Pesher*

J.M. Allegro, *DJD V*, 37-42, pls. XII-XIV; J. Strugnell, 'Notes', 204-210
PAM 43.350, 43.351, 43.429
ROC 980
Bibliography: J.M. Allegro, 'Further Light on the History of the Qumran Sect',
90-93, pl. 1; .- 'More Unpublished Pieces of a Qumran Commentary on
Nahum (4QpNah)', *JSS* 7 (1962) 304-308; J. Maier, 'Weitere Stücke zum
Nahumkommentar aus der Höhle 4 vom Qumran', *Judaica* 18 (1962) 215-250;
A. Dupont-Sommer, 'Le Commentaire de Nahum découvert près de la Mer
Morte (4Q p Nah): Traduction et notes', *Semitica* 13 (1963) 55-88; .- 'Obser-
vations sur le Commentaire de Nahum découvert près de la Mer Morte', *Jour-
nal des Savants* (1963) 201-227; D. Flusser, 'Pharisees, Sadducees and Essenes
in the Pesher Nahum', in *Essays in Jewish History and Philology. In Memory of
Gedaliahu Alon* (Tel Aviv: Hakibbutz Hameuchad, 1970) 133-168

Its [inter]pretation: [...] *4* to be [... and] each will be captured [...] *5* in front [of ...] God does n[ot] want [...]

4Q168 (4QpMic?) *4QMicah Pesher (?)*

Bibliography: M.P. Horgan, *Pesharim: Qumran Interpretations of Biblical Books*, 261-63; L.A. Sinclair, 'Hebrew Text of the Qumran Micah Pesher and Textual Traditions of the Minor Prophets', *RevQ* 11/42 (1983) 253-263

Frags. 1 + 3   *1* [*Mic 4:8-12* of the daughter of Jerusa]lem. [Now, why do you yell, complaining? Have you no king? Are you lacking a counsellor,] *2* that [pain] has gripped you [like a woman giving birth? Have pain and push (it) out, daughter of Zion, like a woman giving birth, because] *3* now shall you leave the ci[ty and live on waste ground and go right to Babylon. There you shall be redeemed. There,] *4* [Y]HWH will deliver you from [the hand of your enemies. Now many nations collaborate against you] *5* [sa]ying: [Let her be defiled and let us fix our gaze on Zion. They do not know the thoughts] *6* [of YHWH, nor understand] his plan. [...]

4Q169 (4QpNah) *4QNahum Pesher*

[Hebrew]; Y. Yadin, 'Pesher Nahum (4QpNah) Reconsidered', *IEJ* 21 (1971) 1-12; F. García Martínez, '4QpNah y la crucifixión: Nueva hipótesis de reconstrucción de 4Q169 3-4 I 4-8', *Estudios Bíblicos* 38 (1978-79) 221-235; L.I. Rabinowitz, 'The Meaning of the Key ('Demetrius') Passage of the Qumran Nahum-Pesher', *JAOS* 98 (1978) 394-399; M.P. Horgan, *Pesharim: Qumran Interpretations of Biblical Books*, 158-191; A. Palumbo, 'A New Interpretation of the Nahum Commentary', *FO* 29 (1992-93) 153-162; L.H. Schiffman, 'Pharisees and Sadducees in *Pesher Nahum*', in M. Brettler, M. Fishbane (eds.), *Minhah Le-Nahum* (Sheffield: JSOT, 1993) 272-290; I. Tantevskij, 'The Reflection of the Political Situation in Judaea in 88 B.C.E. in the Qumran Commentary of Nahum (4QpNah, Columns 1-4)', *St. Petersburg Journal of Oriental Studies* 6 (1994) 221-231

Frags. 1-2   1   [...] בסופה ובשערה דרכו ו]ענן א[בק רגליו פשרו ...]

2 ה]סופה והשערו]ת ר]קי]עי שמיו וארצו אשר בר[א ...   3 גוע]ר]בים

ויוב]ישהו פ]שרו הים הם כל הכ]תיים ...[4 לעשׂ]ות]בהם משפט

ולכלותם מעל פני [הארץ וכל הנהרות החריב פשרו על הכתיים]   5 עם] כל

מו]שליהם אשר תתם ממשלתם   5 [אמלל בשן]וכרמל ופרח לבנן אמלל vacat

פ]שרו ...[6 [יאב]דו בו רבים רום רשעה כי הב]שׁן היא הכתיים ולמלכו

קרא]   7 [כר]מל ולמושׁליו לבנן ופרח ל[ב]נון היא[...   8 [ובני עצ]תם

ואבדו מלפני[עדת] בחירו]י ...[9 ...]כו]ל יושבי תבל vacat הר]ים רעשו

ממנו והגבעות יתמוגגו]   10 [ותשא]הארץ ממנו ומלפני]ו תבל וכו]ל]

יושבי בה לפני זעמו מי יעמוד ומי]   11 [יקום]בחרון אפו פ]שרו ...]

Frags. 3-4 i   1 [...] מדור לרשעי גוים אשר הלך ארי לבוא שם גור

ארי   2 [ואין מחריד vacat פשרו על דמי]טרוס מלך יון אשר בקש לבוא

ירושלים בעצת דורשי החלקות   3 [ולוא בוא כי לוא נתן אל את ירושלים

]ביד מלכי יון מאנתיכוס עד עמוד מושלי כתיים ואחר תרמס [...]   4 vacat

ארי טורף בדי גוריו [ו]מחנק ללביותיו טרף   5 [וימלא טרף חורה ומעונתו

טרפה פשר הדבר] על כפיר החרון אשר יכה בגדוליו ואנשי עצתו   6 [את

פתאי אפרים ואשר אמר וימלא טרף]חורה ומעונתו טרפה vacat פשרו על

כפיר החרון   7 [אשר ימלא חורה רוב פגרי לעשות נק]מות בדורשי

החלקות אשר יתלה אנשים חיים   8 [על העץ לפעול תועבה אשר לוא

יעשה] בישראל מלפנים כי לתלוי חי על העץ [י]קרא הנני אלי[כה]   9 נא[ם

יהוה צבאות והבערתי בעשן רובכ]ה וכפיריכה תאכל חרב והכר]תי מארץ

ט]רפה vacat   10 ולא י]שמע עוד קול מלאכיכה vacat פש]רו רובכה הם

גדודי חילו א]...[ם וכפריו הם   11 גדוליו] ואנשי עצתו ...]וטרפו הוא

ההון אשר קב]צו כוה]ני ירושלים אשר   12 [י]תנוהו ע]... א]פרים ינתן

ישראל [...] vacat

Frags. 1 + 2   *1* [*Nah 1:3* … His path is in the hurricane and in the storm, and] a cloud is the du[st of his feet. Its interpretation: …] *2* the [storms and the hurricane]s, v[aul]ts of his skies and his earth which he cr[eated …] *3 Nah 1:4* He roa[rs] against the sea and dri[es it up.] Its [inter]pretation: the sea are all the Ki[ttim …] *4* to car[ry out] judgment against them and to eliminate them from the face of [the earth. *Nah 1:4* And dries up all the rivers. /Its interpretation concerns the Kittim/] *5* /with [all their chi]efs, whose rule will end./ [*Nah 1:4* Bashan and] Carmel [wither] and the bloom of Lebanon withers. *Blank* [Its] inter[pretation …] *6* many [will per]ish because of it at the height of wickedness. For [the Kittim] are Bas[han, and his king is called:] *7* [Car]mel and his chiefs: Lebanon; and the bloom of Lebanon is […] *8* [and the sons of] their [coun]sel, and they will perish in front of [the assembly of] the chosen [of …] *9* [… al]l the inhabitants of the world. *Blank Nah 1:5-6* The mou[ntains quake in front of him and the hillocks shake,] *10* the earth [rises] in front of him and before [him the world and al]l [that lives in it. Before his wrath who can endure? And who] *11* [can tolerate] the fire of his anger? [Its] inter[pretation …]

Frags. 3 + 4 *col.* I   *1* […] residence for the wicked of the nations. *Nah 2:12* Where a lion went to go into it, a lion cub *2* [without anyone confining him. *Blank* Its interpretation concerns Deme]trius, king of Yavan, who wanted to enter Jerusalem on the advice of the those looking for easy interpretations, *3* [but he did not enter, for God had not given Jerusalem] into the hand of the kings of Yavan from Antiochus up to the appearance of the chiefs of the Kittim. But later, it will be trampled *4* […] *Blank Nah 2:13* The lion catches enough for his cubs [and] strangles prey for his lionesses, *5* [and fills his cave with prey, and his den with spoil. The interpretation of the word] concerns the Angry Lion who struck (together) with his nobles and the men of his counsel *6* [the simple folk of Ephraim. And concerning what he says: *Nah 2:13* «he fills] his cave [with prey] and his den with spoils», *Blank* Its interpretation concerns the Angry Lion *7* [who filled his cave with a mass of corpses, carrying out rev]enge against those looking for easy interpretations, who hanged living men *8* [from the tree, committing an atrocity which had not been committed] in Israel since ancient times, for it is [hor]rible for the one hanged alive from the tree. *Nah 2:14* See, I am against [you]! *9* Orac[le of YHWH of Hosts. I shall burn yo]ur [throng in the fire] and the sword will consume your cubs. [I will] eradica[te the sp]oils [from the earth], *Blank 10* and no [longer] will [the voice of your messengers be heard. *Blank*] Its [interpre]tation: «Your throng» are his gangs of soldiers […]; «his cubs» are *11* his nobles [and the members of his council, …] and «his spoils» is the wealth which [the pries]ts of Jerusalem accu[mulated] which *12* they will deliver [… E]phraim, will be given Israel […] *Blank*

Frags. 3-4 II   1 ומלאכיו הם צירו אשר לא ישמע קולם עוד בגוים
הוי עיר הדמים כולה] כחש פר]ק מלאה   2 פשרו היא עיר אפרים vacat
דורשי החלקות לאחרית הימים אשר בכחש ושקר]ים י]תהלכו vacat   3 לא
ימוש טרף וקול שוט וקול רעש אופן וסוס דהר ומרכבה מרקדה פרש מעלה
להוב (חרב)   4 וברק חנית ורוב חלל וכבוד פגר ואין קץ לגויה וכשלו
וגויתם (בגויתם) vacat   פשרו על ממשלת דורשי החלקות   5 אשר לא
ימוש מקרב עדתם חרב גוים שבי ובז וחרחור בינותם וגלות מפחד אויב
ורוב   6 פגרי אשמה יפולו בימיהם ואין קץ לכלל חלליהם ואף בגוית
בשרם יכשולו בעצת אשמתם   7 מרוב זנוני זונה טובת חן בעלת כשפים
הממכרת גוים בזנותה ומשפחות ב]כש]פיה vacat   8 פשר]ו ע]ל מתעי
אפרים אשר בתלמוד שקרם ולשון כזביהם ושפת מרמה יתעו רבים
9 מלכים שרים כוהנים ועם עם גר נלום ערים ומשפחות יובדו בעצתם
נ]כ]בדים ומוש]לים]   10 יפולו [מז]עם לשונם vacat הנני אליך נאם יהוה
צ]בא]ו]ת וגלית   11 שולי]ך]על פניך והרא]י]ת גוים מער]ך] וממלכות {...}
קלונך vacat פשרו .[...].   12   ...[...]]ערי המזרח כי השולי]י]ם [...]

Frags. 3-4 III   1 הגוים בנדתם [ובש]קוצי תועבותיהם והשלכתי עליך
שקוצים [ונ]בלתיך ושמתיך   2 כאורה והיה כול רואיך ידודו ממך vacat
3 פשרו על דורשי החלקות אשר באחרית הקץ יגלו מעשיהם הרעים לכול
ישראל   4 ורבים יבינו בעוונם ושנאום וכארום על זדון אשמתם ובה]ג]לות
כבוד יהודה   5 ידודו פתאי אפרים מתוך קהלם ועזבו את מתעיהם ונלוו על
[רו]ב]ן י]שראל   6 שודדה נינוה מי ינוד לה מאין אבקשה מנחמים לך
vacat פשרו] על]דורשי   7 החלקות אשר תובד עצתם ונפרדה כנסתם ולא
יוסיפו עוד לתעות] ה]קהל ופת]אים]   8 לא יחזקו עוד את עצתם vacat
התיטיבי מני אמ]ון היושבה ב]יארים vacat   9 פשרו אמון הם מנשה
והיארים הם גד]ו]לי מנשה נכבדי ה]עם הסוב]בים את מ]נשה   10 מים

Frags. 3 - 4 col. II *1* And his messengers are his emissaries, whose voice will no longer be heard among the nations. *Blank Nah 3:1* Alas the bloody city, all of it [treachery,] stuffed with [loo]t! *2* Its interpretation: it is the city of Ephraim, those looking for easy interpretations, in the final days, since they walk in treachery and lie[s.] *Blank 3 Nah 3:1-3* Spoils will not be lacking, nor the noise of the whip nor the din of colliding wheels. Horses at the gallop, chariots bouncing, horsemen lunging, flashing ‹of swords› *4* and flickering of spears! Masses of wounded and heaps of corpses! Endless corpses, they trip ‹over› their corpses! *Blank* Its interpretation concerns the rule of those looking for easy interpretations, *5* from whose assembly the sword of the gentiles will not be lacking, nor captivity or looting, nor fire among them, nor exile for fear of the enemy; a mass *6* of guilty corpses will fall in their days; there will be no end to the tally of their wounded and they will even trip over their bodies of flesh because of their guilty counsel. *7 Nah 3:4* On account of the many fornications of the prostitute, full of elegance and mistress of enchantment, who misled nations with her fornications and clans with her [enchant]ment. *Blank 8* [Its] interpretation [con]cerns those who misdirect Ephraim, who with their fraudulent teaching and lying tongue and perfidious lip misdirect many; *9* kings, princes, priests and people together with the proselyte attached to them. Cities and clans will perish through their advice, n[o]bles and lea[ders] *10* will fall [due to the fero]city of their tongues. *Blank Nah 3:5* See, I am against you! - oracle of YHWH of H[ost]s - You shall hoist *11* [your] skirts up to your face and show the nations [your] nudity and kings {…} your shame. *Blank* Its interpretation […] … *12* […] the cities of (the) East, because «the skirts» […]

Frags. 3 - 4 *col*. III *1* The nations with their uncleanness [and with] their detestable abominations. *Nah 3:6* I will throw refuse on top of you, [af]front you and make you *2* repulsive. *Nah 3:7* And what will happen is that all those who see you will run away from you. *Blank 3* Its interpretation concerns those looking for easy interpretations, whose evil deeds will be exposed to all Israel in the final time; *4* many will fathom their sin, they will hate them and loathes them for their reprehensible arrogance. And when the glory of Judah is re[ve]aled *5* the simple people of Ephraim will flee from among their assembly and desert the ones who misdirected them and will join the [majori]ty [of I]srael. *Nah 3:7* They shall say: *6* Nineveh is laid waste, who will be sorry for her? Where shall I find comforters for you? *Blank* Its interpretation [concerns] those looking for *7* easy interpretations, whose council will die and whose society will be disbanded; they shall not continue misdirecting [the] assembly and simple [folk] *8* shall no longer support their council. *Blank Nah 3:8* Do you act better than Am[mon, seated between] the streams of the Nile? *Blank 9* Its interpretation: Amon is Manasseh and the streams of the Nile are the nob[l]es of Manasseh, the honorable of the [people who surround] Ma[nasseh] *10 Nah 3:8*

339

סביב לה אשר חילה ים ומים ח{ו}מותיה   *vacat*   11 [פ]שרו הם אנשי
[ח]ילה גבור[י מ]לחמתה {ע} כוש עוצמה] ומצרים ואין קץ]   12 [פשרו
[...]...[...]...[...].המד[...]..מ[... פ]וט וה]לובים היו בעזרתה]

Frags. 3-4 iv   1 פשרו הם רשע]י יהוד]ה בית פלג הנלוים על מנשה גם
היא בגולה ה]לכה בשבי גם]   2 עילוליה ירוטשו בראש כל חוצות ועל
נכבדיה יורו גורל וכול ג]דו]ל[י]ה רותקו]   3 בזקים פשר' על מנשה לקץ
האחרון אשר תשפל מלכותו ביש]ראל [...   4 נשיו עילוליו וטפו ילכו
בשבי גבוריו ונכבדיו בחרב [יובדו גם את תשכרי]   5 ותהי נעלמה   *vacat*
פשרו על רשעי א]פרים [...   6 אשר תבוא כוסם אחר מנשה]... גם את
תבקשי]   7 מעוז בעיר מאויב   *vacat*   פש]רו ע]ל[[...   8 אויביהם בעיר] ...
כל מבצריך]   9 תאנים ע]ם בכורים [...   10 .[...]   11 [...]   12 [...]

Frag. 5   1 [הנה עמך נ]שים ב]קרבך לאיביך פתוח נפתחו שערי ארצך
אכלה אש בריחיך]   2 [פשרו כ]ול גבל ישרא]ל] לים] ... מי מצור שאבי
לך]   3 [חזקי מבצ]ריך באי בטיט] ורמסי בחמר ...

4Q170 (4QpZeph) *4QZephaniah Pesher*

J.M. Allegro, *DJD V*, 42, pl. XIV; J. Strugnell, 'Notes', 210-211
PAM 43.429, 43.514
ROC 600

Frags. 1+2   1 [לוא ייט]יב יהוה ולוא ירע והיה] חילם למשוסה
ובתיהם לשממה פשרו [...   2 [...]...[...] לוא יוכל]ו [...   3 [ואשר אמר
והיה חילם למ]שוסה [...]   4 ... [פשרו] ע]ל] [...

Water surrounds the one whose rampart was the sea, and the water her walls. *Blank 11* Its interpretation: they are her men [at a]rms, her [m]ighty warrior[s]. *Nah 3:9* {.} Ethiopia was her strength [and Egypt, without end.] *12* [Its interpretation:] … […] … […] *Nah 3:9* Put and [Libya were her guards]

Frags. 3 - 4 *col.* IV *1* Its interpretation: they are the wick[ed ones of Juda]h, the house of Peleg, which consorted with Manasseh. *Nah 3:10* She, too, is in exile, we[nt into captivity, also] *2* her children were dashed to pieces at every crossroad, for their honoured ones they cast lots, and all [their] nobles [were bound] *3* with chains. Its interpretation concerns Manasseh, in the last time, in which his dominion over Is[rael] will weaken […] *4* his women, his children and his babies will go into captivity, his warriors and his honoured ones [will perish] by the sword. [*Nah 3:11* You, too, will get drunk] *5* and hide away. *Blank* Its interpretation concerns the wicked of E[phraim who …] *6* whose cup will come after Manasseh [… *Nah 3:11* You, too, will seek] *7* a refuge in the city from the enemy. *Blank* [Its] interpre[tation con]cerns […] *8* their enemies in the city, [… *Nah 3:12* All your fortresses] *9* are fig-trees wi[th young fruits …]

Frag. 5 *1* [*Nah 3:13* Look, your people are wo]men a[mong you. The gates of your land stand open to your enemy, fire has devoured your bars.] *2* [Its interpretation …] the whole region of Israel to the sea [… *Nah 3:14* Draw yourself water for the siege;] *3* [reinforce] your [fortifica]tions; tread mud [and stamp on clay, …]

4Q170 (4QpZeph) *4QZephaniah Pesher*

1Q15
Bibliography: M.P. Horgan, *Pesharim: Qumran Interpretations of Biblical Books*, 191-192

Frags. 1 + 2 *1 Zeph 1:12-13* YHWH [does not do go]od and does not do evil. [Their wealth will be plundered and their houses flattened. Its interpretation …] *2* [… t]he[y] shall not eat […] *3* [And what it says: Their wealth will be pl]undered, […] *4* […] Its interpretation [conc]erns […]

4Q171 (4QpPs^a) *4QPsalms Pesher^a*

J.M. Allegro, *DJD V*, 42-51, pls. XIV-XVII; J. Strugnell, 'Notes', 211-218, pl. III

PAM 42.623, 42.627, 42.628, 42.640, 43.341, 43.417, 43.418, 43.421, 44.184

ROC 600, 672

1Q16, 4Q173, 4Q173a

Bibliography: J.M. Allegro, 'A Newly Discovered Fragment of a Commentary

Col. I   13-19 [...]   20 [...] והוציא כאור צדקכה ומשפטכה

כצ[הרים   21 [פשרו על עדת האביונים המתנדבים לעשות א]ת רצון

22 [אל ...]ת הוללים בחרו [... 23 ...א]והבי פרע ומתעים   24 [...]רשעה
ביד אפ[רי]ם vacat

25 [דו]ם ל[י]הוה ⁊וₒ⁊⁊ ו]התחולל לו ואל תחר במצליח דרכו באיש

26 [עוש]ה מזמות [פשר]ו על איש הכזב אשר התעה רבים באמרי

27 שקר כיא בחרו בקלות ולוא שמ[עו]למליץ דעת למען

Col. II   1 יובדו בחרב וברעב ובדבר חרף מאף ועזוב חמה ואל

2 תחר אך להרע כיא מרעים יכרתו פשרו על כול השבים   3 לתורה אשר

לוא ימאנו לשוב מרעתם כיא כול הממרים   4 לשוב מעונם יכרתו וקואי

⁊וₒ⁊⁊ המה ירשו ארץ פשרו   5 המה עדת בחירו עושי רצונו ועוד מעט ואין

רשע   6 vacat

7 ואתבוננה על מקומו ואיננו פשרו על כול הרשעה לסוף

8 ארבעים השנה אשר יתמו ולוא ימצא בארץ כול איש   9 [ר]שע וענוים

ירשו ארץ והתענגו על רוב שלום פשרו על   10 עדת האביונים אשר

יקבלו את מועד התענית ונצלו מכול פחי   11 בליעל ואחר יתענגו כול

יו[ר]שי הארץ והתדשנו בכול תענ[וג]   12 בשר vacat

13 זומם רשע לצדיק וחורק ע]ליו שניו ⁊וₒ⁊⁊ ישחק לו כיא ראה

14 כיא בא יומו פשרו על עריצי הברית אשר בבית יהודה אשר15יזומו

לכלות את עושי התורה אשר בעצת היחד ואל לוא יעזבם   16 בידם חרב

פתחו רשעים וידרוכו קשתם לפיל עני ואביון   17 ולטבוח ישרי דרך חרבם

342

4Q171 (4QpPs^a) *4QPsalms Pesher^a*

on Psalms XXXVII', *PEQ* 86 (1954) 69-75; .- 'Further Light on the History of the Qumran Sect', 94-95, pl. 4; H. Stegemann, 'Weitere Stücke von 4QpPsalm 37', *RevQ* 6/22 (1967) 193-210, pl. 1; M.P. Horgan, *Pesharim: Qumran Interpretations of Biblical Books*, 192-226; D. Pardee, 'A Restudy of the Commentary on Psalm 37 from Qumran Cave 4', *RevQ* 13/49-52 (1973) 163-194; R.B. Coote, 'MW'D HT'NYT in 4Q171 (*Pesher Psalm 37*) fragments 1-2, col. II, line 9', *RevQ* 8/29 (1972) 81-85

Col. I (*frag.* 1 I)   *13-19* […] … *20* [*Ps 37:6* … He will make your justice come out like the dawn and your rights like mi]dday. *21* [Its interpretation concerns the congregation of the poor who are ready to do] the will of *22* [God …] the arrogant ones choose *23* [… who l]ove slovenliness and misdirect *24* […] wickedness at the hands of E[phra]im. *Blank 25* [*Ps 37:7* Be si]lent before [YHWH and] wait for him, do not be annoyed with one who has success, with someone *26* [who hatch]es plots. Its [interpretation] concerns the Man of Lies who misdirected many with *27* deceptive words, for they have chosen worthless things and did not lis[ten] to the Interpreter of Knowledge. This is why

Col. II (*frags.* 1 II + 2 + 4Q183 3)   *1* they will die by the sword, by hunger and by plague. *Ps 37:8-9* Curb anger and control temper and do not get *2* irritated - it only leads to evil. For those doing evil will be cut off. Its interpretation concerns all who converted *3* to the law, who do not refuse to convert from their wickedness, for all those who resist *4* to convert from their sin will be cut off. *Ps 37:9* But they who hope in YHWH will possess the land. Its interpretation: *5* they are the congregation of his chosen ones who carry out his will. *Ps 37:10* A little while, and the wicked will be no more. *6 Blank 7 Ps 37:10* I will stare at his place and he will no longer be there. Its interpretation concerns all the wickedness at the end *8* of the forty years, for they will be completed and upon the earth no [wic]ked person will be found. *9 Ps 37:11* And the poor shall possess the land and enjoy peace in plenty. Its interpretation concerns *10* the congregation of the poor who will tough out the period of distress and will be rescued from all the snares of *11* Belial. Afterwards, all who shall po[sse]ss the land will enjoy and grow fat with everything enjoy[able to] *12* the flesh. *Blank 13 Ps 37:12-13* The wicked plots against the just person, grinding [his teeth] aga[inst him;] YHWH laughs at him because he sees *14* that his day is coming. Its interpretation alludes to the ruthless ones of the covenant who are in the House of Judah, who *15* plot to destroy those who observe the law, who are in the Community Council. But God will not surrender them *16* into their hands. *Ps 37:14-15* The evildoers unsheathe the sword and string their bows to

תבוא בלבם וקשתותיהם תשברנה 18 פשרו על רשעי אפרים ומנשה אשר
יבקשו לשלוח יד 19 בכוהן ובאנשי עצתו בעת המצרף הבאה עליהם ואל
יפדם 20 מידם ואחר כן ינתנו ביד עריצי גואים למשפט *vacat 21 vacat*
22 טוב מעט לצדיק מהמון רשעים רבי[ם פשרו על כול] 23 עושה
התורה אשר לוא י.[...]ה 24 לרעות כיא אזרוע]ות רשעים תשברנה וסומך
צדיקים [ק]ד[ו]ק 25 [...] 26 רצונ]ו [...] 27 ל[ו]א י[בושו ב]עת רעה פשרו
על [...]

1 *Col.* iii שבי המדבר אשר יחיו אלף דור בישו[ע]ה ולהם כול נחלת
2 אדם ולזרעם עד עולם ובימי רעב יש[בע]ו כיא רשעים 3 יובדו פשרו
א]שר י]חים ברעב במועד ה[תע]נית ורבים 4 יובדו ברעב ובדבר כול אשר
לוא יצא[ו משם [להיות] ע[ם 5 עדת בחירו ואוהבי יהוה כיקר כורים פשר]ו על
[...] אשר יהיו רשים ושרים ע[ל כול העדה כרועי] 6 צון בתוך עדריהם
vacat
7 כלו כעשן כולו פשר(ו) על שרי הר[ש]עה אשר הונו את עם
8 קודשו אשר יובדו כעשן האוב]ד ברו[ח לוה רשע ולוא ישלם 9 וצדיק
חונן ונותן כיא מבורכ]ו יר[שו ארץ ומקֹ]ללו יכ]רתו 10 פשרו על עדת
האביונים א]שר לה[ם נחלת כול ה...].[...] 11 ירשו את הר מרום ישר[אל
ובה[ר קודשו יתענגו ו]מקול]לו 12 יכרתו המה עריצי הב[רית ר]שעי
ישראל אשר יכרתו ונשמד[ו] *vacat* 13 לעולם
14 כיא מ[ו]ק מצעדי גבר [כונ]נו וד]רכו יחפץ כיא י[פו]ל] לוא[
15 יוטל כיא ק[ו]ק סומך ידו [פשרו על הכוהן מורה ה]צדק אשר[
16 [ב]חר בו אל לעמוד .[...] [הכינו לבנות לו עדת] בחירו באמת[
17 [ודר]כו ישר לאמת [נער היי]תי וגם זקנתי ולוא] ראיתי צדיק] 18 נעזב
וזרעו מבקש לח[ם כול היום] חונן ומלוה וזר[עו לברכה פשר] 19 הדבר
על מו]רה הצדק אשר [...] אל מ[...] 20 ואת [...] 26-21 [...] 27 [...] כיא
ק[ו]ק אוהב[

bring down the poor and humble, *17* to slaughter those on the correct path. Their swords shall pierce their own hearts and their bows shall break. *18* Its interpretation concerns the wicked of Ephraim and Manasseh who will attempt to lay hands *19* on the Priest and the members of his council in the period of testing which will come upon to them. However, God will save them *20* from their hands and after they will be delivered into the hands of ruthless nations for judgment. *Blank 21 Blank 22 Ps 37:16* Better is the little for the just man than the wealth of many wicked. [Its interpretation concerns all] *23* who observe the law, who does not [...] ... *24* for evil things. *Ps 37:17-18* For the arms [of the wicked will be broken, but *25* YH[WH supports the just ...] *26* [his] will [...] *27* [*Ps 37:19* They shall] n[ot] be ashamed in [the evil time. Its interpretation concerns ...]

Col. III (*frags.* 1 III + 3 I + 4) *1* those who have returned from the wilderness, who will live for a thousand generations, in salva[tio]n; for them there is all the inheritance of *2* Adam, and for their descendants for ever. *Ps 37:19-20* And in the days of famine they shall be re[plete]; but the wicked *3* shall perish. Its interpretation: he will keep them alive during the famine of the time of [dis]tress, but many *4* will perish because of famine and plague: all who did not leave [from there] with *5* the congregation of his chosen ones. /*Ps 37:20* Whoever loves YHWH will be like precious lambs. [Its] interpretation [concerns ...]/ who will be chiefs and princes over [the whole congregation, like shepherds] *6* of ewes in among their flocks. *Blank* [...] *7 Ps 37:20* Like smoke they all vanish. ‹Its› interpretation concerns the wi[ck]ed princes who oppress his holy people, *8* who will perish like smoke which disapp[ears in the win]d. *Ps 37:21-22* The wicked borrows but does not pay back, *9* while the just man is sympathetic and gives. For those who are blessed [by him shall pos]sess the land, but those who are cursed by him [shall be c]ut off. *10* Its interpretation concerns the congregation of the poor [to whom is] the inheritance of the whole ... [...] *11* They will inherit the high mountain of Isra[el and] delight [in his] holy [mou]ntain. «But those who are [curs]ed by him *12* will be cut off». These are the ruthless ones of the co[venant, the wi]cked men of Israel who will be cut off and exterminated *13* for ever. *Blank 14 Ps 37:23-24* For by YHW[H the steps of a man] are secure; he delights in his [pa]th: even though he stumbles he will not *13* fall, for Y[HWH supports his hand]. Its interpretation concerns the Priest, the Teacher of [Righteousness, whom] *16* God [ch]ose to stand [...] he installed him to found the congregation [of his chosen ones of the truth] for him, *17* [and] straightened out his [pa]th, in truth. *Ps 37:25-26* I have [been young] and am old now; yet [I have] not [seen a just person] *18* deserted or his offspring begging for bre[ad. Daily] he has compassion and lends, and [his] off[spring is blessed. The interpretation] *19* of the word concerns the Teac[her of Righteousness who ...] ... [...] *20* and [...] *21-26* [...] *27* [... For YHWH loves]

Col. IV   1   מש[פט ולוא יעזוב את חסידיו לעו]לם נשמדו וזרע ר[שעים

נכרת פשרו]המה עריצי   2   [הברית אשר ...]התורה צדיק[ים ירשו ארץ

וישכנו ל]עד עליה   3   פשרו ... ירשו את הארץ] בא[לף] דור פי צדיק יהגה

ח]וכמה ולשונו תדבר   4   [משפט תורת אלוהיו בלבו לוא תעמוד אשוריו

פשרו על ...]האמת אשר דבר   5   [משפט ...] אליהם הגיד *vacat*

vacat [*vacat*]   6

7   צופה רשע לצדיק ומבקש] להמיתו ⸀יו⸀[ה] לוא יעזבנו בידו ו[ל]וא

י]רשיענו {ו}בהשפטו   8   פשרו על [הכו]הן הרשע אשר צ[ופ]ה הצד]יק

ומבקש ל]המיתו [...]ן והתורה   9   אשר שלח אליו ואל לוא יע[זבנו]ולוא

ירשיענו ב]השפטו ול]ו י]שלם] אל את]גמולו לתתו   10   ביד עריצי גואים

לעשות בו [נקמות קוה אל ⸀יוה] ושמור דרכו וירוממכה לרשת   11   ארץ

בהכרת רשעים תר]אה פשרו על עדת האביונים [אשר יראו במשפט רשעה

ועם   12   בחירו ישמחו בנחלת אמת [...]. *vacat*

13   [ראי]תי רשע עריץ ומתע]רה כאזרח רענן ו[אעבור על מ[קו]מו

וה]נה אינ]נו וא[בקשהו] ולוא   14   [נמצא פשרו] על [א]יש הכזב] אשר

[...]...[...]...[...] על בח]יר]י אל] ויב]קש לשבית את   15   [...]...[...] לעשות]

מ]ננו משפט [...]הזיד ביד רמה   16   [...]...[...] שמור תם וראה [ישר] כיא

אח]ר]ית לאי]ש שלום פשרו על] שלו[ם]ת[...]...[...]   17   ]ת שלו[ם] ופושעים

18   נשמדו יחד ואחר]ית] ר[שעים נכרתה פשרו על ... אשר]יובדו ונכרתו

19   מתוך עדת היחד ות]שועת צדיקים מ⸀יו⸀ה מעוזם בעת צרה ויעזרם

20   וימלטם ויפלטם מרשעים ויושיעם כיא חסו בו פשרו [... ⸀יו⸀ה]

21   יושיעם אל ו[י]צילם מיד ר[שעי   22   [... *vacat*

23   למנצח על] שושנ]ים [לבני קורח משכיל שיר ידידות פשרו ה]מה

שבע מחלקות   24   שבי יש[ראל אשר ... רח[ש ל]ב]י דבר טוב   25   או]מר

אני מעשי למלך פשרו [...].. קודש כיא   26   [...]ספרי[...] ולשוני עט

27   [סופר מהיר פשרו]על מורה] הצדק אשר ... ל]פני אל במעני לשון

Col. IV (*frags.* 3 II, 5 - 10)   *1 Ps 37:28* jus[tice and does not desert his devout ones. For e]ver they shall be annihilated and the offspring of the wi[cked will be cut off. Its interpretation:] they are the ruthless ones *2* [of the covenant who …] the law. *Ps 37:29* The just [will possess the earth and live] on it [for] ever. *3* [Its interpretation … they shall possess the earth] over a thousand [generations. *Ps 37:30-31* The mouth of the just man utters wi]sdom and his tongue speaks *4* [justice; the law of his God is in his heart; his steps will not falter. Its interpretation concerns …] of the truth, who speaks *5* [justice …] announces them. *Blank 6* [*Blank*] *Blank 7 Ps 37:32-33* The wicked person spies on the just person and tries [to kill him. YH]WH [will not relinquish him into his hand,] n[or] let him be condemned {and} when he is judged. *8* Its interpretation concerns the Wicked [Pri]est, who sp[ie]s on the ju[st man and wants to] kill him […] and the law *9* which he sent him; but God will not re[linquish him] nor [let him be condemned when] he is judged. But [God will] pay [him] his reward, delivering him *10* into the hands of ruthless nations so that they can carry out [vengeance] upon him. [*Ps 37:34* Wait for Y]HWH and observe his path and he will raise you, so that you possess *11* the land; and you shall s[ee] the destruction of the wicked. [Its interpretation concerns the community of the poor] who will see the judgment of wickedness, and with *12* his chosen one will rejoice in the true inheritance. *Blank 13 Ps 37:35-36* I [saw] a ruthless wicked man, who displ[ayed] himself [like a leafy tree.] I passed by his p[la]ce and he [no longer existed;] I [looked for him] but he could not *14* [be found. Its interpretation] concerns the [M]an of Lies [who …] … […] against God's cho[sen and tr]ied to end *15* […] … […] to carry out … judgment [ag]ainst him […] he acted impertinently with an arrogant hand *16* […] … [*Ps 37:37* Observe the perfect man and watch] the upright man, [for there is a fu]t[ure for the ma]n of peace. Its interpretation conc[erns *17* […] … […] pea[ce.] *Ps 37:38* But the rebels *18* will be obliterated together, and the futu[re] of the wi[cked will be cut off. Its interpretation concerns … who] will perish and be cut off *19* from among the congregation of the Community. *Ps 37:39* The sal[vation of just men comes from YHWH. He is their refuge in the moment of danger. YHWH assists them] *20* and rescues them, he delivers them from the wicked [and saves them, because they take refuge in him. Its interpretation …] *21* God will save them and free them from the hand of the wi[cked …] *22 Blank 23 Ps 45:1* To the choirmaster. According to the [Lili]es. [For the sons of Korah. A wisdom-song: a love-song. Its interpretation: Th]ey are the seven divisions of *24* the converts of Is[rael who …] [*Ps 45:2*] My he[art] [over]flows with a good theme, *25* [I] re[cite my verses to the king. Its interpretation …] holy …, for *26* […] books […] *Blank Ps 45:2* And my tongue is the pen of *27* [a skilled scribe. Its interpretation] concerns the Teach[er of Righteousness … befo]re God with the reply of the tongue

Col. v   1 [... ו]בשפת ע[וז ...] לשוב יחד לתורה ב[כול לב ...]
2 [...] בחיר[י] ישראל [...]...[...]

Frag. 13   1 [...].[...]   2 [...] vacat   3 ...[אלו]הים דבר [בקדשו
אעלזה אחלקה שכם]   4 [ועמק סכ]ות אמדדה לי [גלעד ולי מנשה ואפרים
מעוז ראשי]   5 [פשרו על גלע]ד וחצי שבט [מנשה ...]   6 [...]ונקבצו[
[...

4Q172 (4QpUnid) 4QUnidentified Pesher Fragments

J.M. Allegro, DJD V, 50-51, pl. XVIII; J. Strugnell, 'Notes', 218-219
PAM 43.421
ROC 600

Frag. 1   1 [... א]מר כול[...]   2 [...]בעת רעב ואשר] אמר ...[
3 [...]... ו היאה [...]   4 [... יא]ספו את צ.[...]   5 [...]

Frag. 2   1 [...]... אשר האו.[...]   2 [...]תוכן כבגד על הא[...]
3 [...]...[...]

Frag. 3   1 [...]כ[ות ביד]   2 [...]תרבות מלכותו[...]   3 [...]
[...] vacat

Frag. 4   1 [...]כן ויזנו עמם]   2 [...]וכול אנשי [העול ברחו]
3 [...]פחז עמורה[...]   4 [...]בוערת וגם כ.[...]   5 [...]לבבם vacat [...]
6 [...]..יתי ב.[...]

348

Col. v (*frags.* 11 + 12)   *1* [... and] with influe[ntial] mouth [...] to return together to the law with [all one's heart ...] *2* [...] ... [...] the chose[n ones of] Israel [...] ... [...]

Frag. 13   *1* [...] ... [...] *2* [...] *Blank* [...] *3* [... *Ps 60:8-9 = Ps 108:8-9* G]od spoke [in his sanctuary: I will exult, I will divide up Shechem,] *4* parcel out [the Valley of Succ]oth; mine is [Gilead and mine Manasseh, and Ephraim is the helmet of my head.] *5* [Its interpretation concerns Gilea]d and half the tribe [of Manasseh ...] *6* [...] and they will be gathered [...]

4Q172 (4QpUnid) *4QUnidentified Pesher Fragments*

Bibliography: M.P. Horgan, *Pesharim: Qumran Interpretations of Biblical Books*, 263-266

Frag. 1   *1* [...] he s]aid: «All [...] *2* [...] in the time of hunger, and what [he says ...] *3* [...] ... it is ... [...] *4* [...] they [will ga]ther ... [...] *5* [...] ... [...]

Frag. 2   *1* [...] what ... [...] *2* [...] fastened like a garment upon the [...] *3* [...] ... [...]

Frag. 3   *1* [...] ... in the hand of [...] *2* [...] the increase of his kingdom [...] *3* [...] *Blank* [...]

Frag. 4   *1* [...] ... and they will feed with them [...] *2* [... all the men of] iniquity have fled [...] *3* [...] lasciviousness of Gomorrah [...] *4* [...] burning, and also ... [...] *5* [...] their heart. *Blank* [...] *6* [...] ... [...]

4Q173 (4QpPs^b) *4QPsalms Pesher^b*

J.M. Allegro, *DJD V*, 51-52, pl. XVIII; J. Strugnell, 'Notes', 219-220
PAM 41.817, 43.440
ROC 290

Frag. 1   1 [...].[...]   2 [...]א לכ.[...]   3 [...]א[שר יבקשו]...[

4 [...] תרות מורה הצדק]...[5 [... כו]הן לאחרית הק]ץ [...]6 [...]

[...]*vacat* [...] 7]ורשף הנחלה]...[

Frag. 2   1 [...] *vacat* פשר הפת]גם ...[2 [... מ]ורה הצד]ק ...[

Frag. 3   1 [...]א[שרי הגבר]...[2 [...] אשר יהיו ק]...[3 [...]לוא
יבושו כ]י ...[

Frag. 4   1 [...]שלוא]מלא כפו קוצר ו]חצנו מעמר ולוא אמרו
העוברים[2]ברכת י]הוה על]יכ]ם בר]כנו אתכם בשם יהוה ...[
3 [...]רשע]...[ל]...[

4Q173a (= 4Q173 *frag. 5*)

J.M. Allegro, *DJD V*, 52-53, pl. XVIII; J. Strugnell, 'Notes', 220
PAM 41.817, 43.440

1 [...]ע]ברו מ..[...]   2 [...]בית מכשול]...[3 [... עד קרנ]ות המזבח
י.[...]   4 [... זה] השער לאל צדי]קים יבואו בו ...[5 [... מר]חיבי שמות
וחריב]ות ...[6 [...]ל ליעקוב] ...[

350

4Q173, 4Q173a

4Q173 (4QpPs^b) *4QPsalms Pesher^b*

1Q16, 4Q171, 4Q173a
Bibliography: M.P. Horgan, *Pesharim: Qumran Interpretations of Biblical Books*, 226-228

Frag. 1   *1-2* [...] ... [...] *3* [... w]ho looked for [...] *4* [...] the warnings (?) of the Teacher of Righteousness [...] *5* [... pri]est in the final e[ra ...] *6* [...] *Blank* [...] *7* [...] and fever; the inheritance [...]

Frag. 2   *1* [...] *Blank* The interpretation of the wo[rd ...] *2* [... the Te]acher of Right[eousness ...]

Frag. 3   *1* [... *Ps 127:5* Bl]essed the man [...] *2* [...] who will be ... [...] *3* [...] they shall not be ashamed wh[en ...]

Frag. 4   *1* [... *Ps 129:7-8* which does not] fill the hand of the reaper or [the armful of the one who binds, nor do those who pass by say to him:] *2* [«May the blessing of Y]HWH be up[on y]ou, [we] ble[ss you in the name of YHWH ...] *3* [...] the wicked [...] ... [...]

4Q173a (= 4Q173 *frag.* 5)

ROC 234
1Q16, 4Q171, 4Q173

1 [...] they [we]nt over from ... [...] *2* [...] the house of stumbling [...] *3* [... *Ps 118: 27* to the horn]s of the altar ... [...] *4* [... *Ps 118:20* This is] the gate of God (*written in cryptic letters*); the right[eous ones shall enter through it ...] *5* [... those who wi]den the waste places and the desolate [places ...] *6* [...] to Jacob [...]

4Q174 (4QFlor) *4QFlorilegium*

J.M. Allegro, *DJD V*, 53-57, pls. XIX-XX; J. Strugnell, 'Notes', 220-225
PAM 43.423, 43.440
ROC 281, 286
Bibliography: J.M. Allegro, 'Further Messianic References', *JBL* 75 (1956) 176-
177, pl. 1; .- 'Fragments of a Qumran Scroll of Eschatological Midrashim', *JBL*
77 (1958) 350-354; J.M. Baumgarten, 'The Exclusion of 'Netinim' and Pros-
elytes in 4QFlorilegium', *RevQ* 8/29 (1972) 87-96; D.R. Schwartz, 'The Three
Temples of 4QFlorilegium', *RevQ* 10/37 (1979) 83-91; G.J. Brooke, *Exegesis at
Qumran. 4QFlorilegium in its Jewish Context* (JSOTS 29; Sheffield: JSOT Press,

Frags. 1 i, 21, 2   1 [לוא] [ישׂיא בוא ע]וד אויב] ולוא יוסי]ף בן עולה
2 [צויתי שופטים [על עמי   [לענות]ו כאשר בראישונה ולמן היום אשר
3 [מושה מקדש] יהוה כ]ו]ננו ידיכה יהוה ימלוך עולם ועד הואה הבית אשר   ישׂראל הואה הבית אשר [יכין] ל[וא]באחרית הימים כאשר כתוב בספר
4 [...] עד [עולם ועמוני ומואבי וממזר ובן נכר וגר עד עולם   לוא יבוא שׂמה
5 י]הו]ה [ימלוך ל[עולם תמיד עליו יראה ולוא ישׂמוהו   כיא קדושׂו שׂם
6 את מקד[שׂ י]שׂראל בחטאתמה   עוד זרים כאשׂר השׂמו בראישונה
7 לפניו מעשׂי   ויואמר לבנות לוא מקדשׂ אדם להיות מקטירים בוא לוא
8 בני בליעל המכשׂילים אותמה לכלותמ]ה בעונ]מה כאשׂר באו   תודה ואשׂר אמר לדויד ו[הניחו]תי לכה מכול אויביכה אשׂר יניח להמה מכ]ול]
9 או]ר]ולחשׂוב עליהמה מחשׂבות און   במחשׂבת [ב]ל]י]על להכשׂיל ב[ני]
10 [וה]גיד לכה יהוה כיא   למ]ען ית]פשׂו לבליעל במשׂגת א]שׂ]מה   *vacat*
11 [לעו]לם אני אהיה לוא לאב והוא יהיה לי לבן הואה צמח דויד העומד   בית יבנה לכה והקימותי את זרעכה אחריכה והכינותי את כסא ממלכתו
12 [יקים] בצי]ון בא]חרית הימים כאשׂר כתוב   עם דורשׂ התורה אשׂר
13 דויד הנופל]ת א]שׂר   והקימותי את סוכת דויד הנופלת היאה סוכת
14 מדרשׂ מאשׂרי] ה]איש אשׂר לוא הלך   יעמיד להושׂיע את ישׂראל   *vacat*
15 אשׂר כתוב   בעצת רשׂעים פשׂר הדב]ר המ]ה] סרי מדרך] הרשׂעים]
בספר ישׂעיה הנביא לאחרית [ה]ימים ויהי כחזקת] היד ויסרני מלכת בדרך]

4Q174 (4QFlor) *4QFlorilegium*

1985); D. Dimant, '4QFlorilegium and the Idea of the Community as Temple', in A. Caquot *et al.* (eds.), *Hellenica et Judaica. Hommage à V. Nikiprovetzky* (Leuven-Paris: Peeters, 1986) 165-189; M.O Wise, '4QFlorilegium and the Temple of Adam', *RevQ* 15/57-58 (1991) 103-132; È. Puech, *Croyance des Esséniens*, 547-587; A. Steudel, *Der Midrasch zur Eschatologie aus der Qumrangemeinde (4QMidrEschat^{a,b}). Materielle Rekonstruktion, Textbestand, Gattung und traditionsgeschichtliche Einordnung des durch 4Q174 ('Florilegium') und 4Q177 ('Catena A') repräsentierten Werkes aus den Qumranfunden* (STDJ 13; Leiden: E.J. Brill, 1994)

Frags. 1 *col.* I, 21, 2 [*Ps 89:23* «Not] *1* [will] an enemy [strike him any]more, *2 Sam 7:10* [nor will] a son of iniquity [afflict] him [aga]in as in the past. From the day on which *2* [I appointed judges] over my people, Israel». This (refers to) the house which [he will establish] for [him] in the last days, as is written in the book of *3* [Moses: *Exod 15:17-18* «The temple of] YHWH your hands will est[a]blish. YHWH shall reign for ever and ever». This (refers to) the house into which shall not enter *4* [... for] ever either an Ammonite, or a Moabite, or a bastard, or a foreigner, or a proselyte, never, because his holy ones are there. *5* «Y[HW]H [shall reign for] ever». He will appear over it for ever; foreigners shall not again lay it waste as they laid waste, in the past, *6* the tem[ple of I]srael on account of their sins. And he commanded to build for himself a temple of man, to offer him in it, *7* before him, the works of thanksgiving. And as for what he said to David: *2 Sam 7:11* «I [shall obtain] for you [rest] from all your enemies»: (it refers to this,) that he will obtain for them rest from a[ll] *8* the sons of Belial, those who make them fall, to destroy th[em on account of] their [sins,] when they come with the plan of [B]el[i]al to make the s[ons of] *9* lig[ht] fall, and to plot against them wicked plans so th[at] they [are] trapped by Belial because of their gui[l]ty error. *Blank 10* [And] YHWH [de]clares to you that *2 Sam 7:12-14* «he will build you a house. I will raise up your seed after you and establish the throne of his kingdom *11* [for ev]er. I will be a father to him and he will be a son to me.» This (refers to the) «branch of David», who will arise with the Interpreter of the law who *12* [will rise up] in Zi[on in] the [l]ast days, as it is written: *Amos 9:11* «I will raise up the hut of David which has fallen», This (refers to) «the hut of *13* David which has fall[en», w]hich he will raise upto save Israel. *Blank 14* Midrash of *Ps 1:1* «Blessed [the] man who does not walk in the counsel of the wicked». The interpretation of this wor[d: they are] those who turn aside from the path of [the wicked,] *15* as it is written in the book of Isaiah, the prophet, for [the] last days: *Isa 8:11* «And it happened that with a strong [hand he turned me aside from walking on the path of]

16 העם הזה והמה אשר כתוב עליהמה בספר יחזקאל הנביא אשר לו[א

יטמאו עוד בכול] 17 [ג]ל[ו]ליהמה המה בני צדוק וא[נ]שי עצת[מ]ה

רוד[פי צ]דק מאחריהמה לעצת היחד 18 [למה רגש]ו גויים ולאומים יהג]ו

ריק ית]יצבו [מלכי ארץ ור]וזנים נוסדו ביחד על יהוה ועל 19 [משיחו

פ]שר הדבר] אשר ירגשו מלכי הגו]יים וה]גו ריק על] בחירי ישראל

באחרית הימים

1 *Frags.* 1 II, 3, 24, 5 היאה עת המצרף הב]אה ... י]הודה להתם[...]

2 בליעל ונשאר ש]אר ...]ם [לג]ורל ועשו את כול התורה] [...] 3 מושה

היאה ה]... כאש]ר כתוב בספר דניאל הנביא להרשי]ע רשעים [...]

4a וצדיקים ...]. יתלב]נו ויצטרפו ועם יודעי אלוה יחזיקו המ]ה [...]

4 ...]...]אחרי המצרף אשר אליהמה יו.]...]   5 [...]ה ברדתו מ]...]

6 [רש]עה כאשר ה.]...]...[...]   7 [י]שראל ואהרון [...]   8 [י]דע כיא

הואה מ.]...]   9 [...].[...] בכול החוזים [...]   10 [...]ל .[...]   11 מ.]...]

1 [...]המבלעים את צאצאי   2 ... נ]וטרים להמה בקנאתמה   *Frag. 4*

3 [...]היאה העת אשר יפתח בליעל   4 ... ע]ל בית יהודה קשות לשוטמם

5 [...]ובקש בכול כוחו לבזרמה   6 ... אש]ר הביאמה להיות

7 [...יה]ודה ואל י]שר]אל י.[...]

4Q175 (4QTest) *4QTestimonia*

J.M. Allegro, *DJD V*, 57-60, pl. XXI; J. Strugnell, 'Notes', 225-229
PAM 41.796
DAJ
4Q378, 4Q379
Bibliography: J.M. Allegro, 'Further Messianic References', 182-187, pl. 4; J.A. Fitzmyer, '4QTestimonia and the New Testament', in *Essays on the Semitic Background of the New Testament* (London: Chapman, 1971) 59-89; C. Newsom, 'The 'Psalms of Joshua' from Qumran Cave 4', *JJS* 39 (1988) 56-73; H. Burgmann, *Der 'Sitz im Leben' in den Josuafluch-Texten in 4Q397 22 II und*

16 this people». And (this refers to) those about whom it is written in the book of Ezekiel, the prophet, that *Ez 44:10* «[they should] no[t defile themselves any more with all] *17* their [i]d[o]ls». This (refers to) the sons of Zadok and (to) the m[e]n of [the]ir council, those who see[k jus]tice eagerly, who have come after them to the council of the community. *18 Ps 2:1* [«Why ar]e the nations [in turmoil] and hatch the peoples [idle plots? The kings of the earth t]ake up [their posts and the ru]lers conspire together against YHWH and against *19* [his anointed one». Inter]pretation of the saying: [the kings of the na]tions [are in turmoil] and ha[tch idle plots against] the elect ones of Israel in the last days.

Frags. 1 col. II, 3, 24, 5   *1* It is the time of trial which co[mes ... J]udah to complete [...] *2* Belial, and a rem[nant] will remain [... for the l]ot, and they shall put into practice all the law [...] *3* Moses; it is [... a]s is written in the book of Daniel, the prophet: *Dan 12:10. 11:32* «[The wicked] act wicked[ly ...] *4a* and the just [... shall be whi]tened and refined and a people knowing God will remain strong». Th[ey ...] *4* ... [...] after the trial which is for them ... [...] *5* [...] when he descends [...] *6* [wic]kedness when [...] ... [...] *7* [I]srael and Aaron [...] *8* [k]now that he [...] *9* [...] among all the seers [...] *10* [...] ... [...] *11* ... [...]

Frag. 4   *1* [...] those who devour the offspring of *2* [... fu]rious against them in their zeal *3* [...] This (refers) to the time when Belial will open *4* [... up]on the house of Judah difficulties to persecute them *5* [...] and he will seek with all his might to scatter them *6* [... w]ho will bring them to be *7* [... Ju]dah and to I[sra]el ... [...]

4Q175 (4QTest) *4QTestimonia*

4QTestimonia (Cracow: Offenburg 1990); H. Eshel, 'The Historical Background of the Pesher Interpreting Joshua's Curse on the Rebuilder of Jericho', *RevQ* 15/59 (1992) 409-420; T. Lim, 'The 'Psalms of Joshua' (4Q379 fr. 22 col. 2): A Reconsideration of Its Text', *JJS* 44 (1993) 309-312; C.A. Newsom, '4Q378 and 4Q379: An Apocryphon of Joshua', in H.J. Fabry *et al.* (eds.), *Qumranstudien: Vorträge und Beiträge der Teilnehmer des Qumranseminars auf dem internationalen Treffen der Society of Biblical Literature, Münster, 25.-26. Juli 1993* (Göttingen: Vandenhoeck & Ruprecht, 1996) 35-85

1 וידבר **** אל מושה לאמור שמעת את קול דברי   2 העם הזה
אשר דברו אליכה היטיבו כול אשר דברו   3 מי ינתן ויהיה לבבם זה
להם}ה{ לירא אותי ולשמור את כול   4 מצותי כול }יו{ ה-ימים למען יטב
להם ולבניהם לעולם   5 נבי אקים לאהמה מקרב אחיהמה כמוכה ונתתי
דברי   6 בפיהו וידבר אליהמה את כול אשר אצונו והיה ⁿהאיש   7 אשר לוא
ישמע }ע{אל דברי אשר ידבר הנבי בשמי אנוכי   8 אדרוש מעמו   vacat
9 ויש}ה{א משלו ויאמר נאום בלעם בנבעור ונאם הגבר   10 שהתם
העין נואם שומע אמרי אל וידע דעת עליון אשר   11 מחזה שדי יחזה נופל
וגלו עין אראנו ולוא עתהא   12 אשורנו ולוא קרוב דרך כוכב מיעקוב ויקום
שבט מישראל ומחץ   13 פאתי מואב וקרקר את כול בני שית   vacat
14 וללוי אמר הבו ללוי תמיך ואורך לאיש חסידך אשר   15 נסיתי
במסה ותרבהי על מי מריבה ⁿהאמר לאביו }לוא{   16 }...{ ולאמו לא
דⁿתיכהי ואת אחיו לוא הכיר ואת בנו לוא   17 ידע כי שמר אמרתכה
ובריתך ינצר ⁿיאירו משפטיך ליעקוב   18 תורתכה לישראל יש'מו קטורה
באפך וכל'ל על מזבחך   19 ברך **** חילו ופעל ידו תרצה מחץ מתנים קמו
ומשנאו
20 בל יקומו   vacat

vacat 21   בעת אשר כלה ישוע להלל ולהודות בתהלותוהי   22 ויאמר
ארור ה(א)יש אשר יבנה את העיר הזות בבכורו   23 יוסדנה ובצעירו יציב
דלתיה ואנה ⁿאיש ארור אחד בליעל   24 עומד להיות פ]ח י[קוש לעמו
ומחתה לכול שכניו ועמד   25 [...].מ.[...] לה[י]ות שניהמה כלי חמס ושבו
ובנו את   26 [העיר הזות ויצ]יבו לה חומה ומגדלים לעשות לעוז רשע
27 [בארץ ורעה גדולה] בישראל ושערוריה באפרים וביהודה   28 [...
וע]שו חנופה בארץ ונ(א)צה גדולה בבני   29 [יעקוב ושפכו ד]ם כמים על
חל בת ציון ובחוק }ב[ירשלם   vacat 30

4Q176 (4QTanḥ) *4QTanḥûmîm*

J.M. Allegro, DJD V, 60-67, pls. XXII-XXIII; J. Strugnell, 'Notes', 229-236, pl. II (cf. 4Q379 22 II)   *1* And **** spoke to Moses saying: *Deut 5:28-29* «You have heard the sound of the words of *2* this people, what they said to you: all they have said is right. *3* If (only) it were given (that) they had /this/ heart to fear me and keep all *4* my precepts all the days, so that it might go well with them and their sons for ever!» *5 Deut 18:18-19* «I would raise up for them a prophet from among their brothers, like you, and place my words *6* in his mouth, and he would tell them all that I command him. And it will happen that /the/ man *7* who does not listen to my words which the prophet will speak in my name, I *8* shall require a reckoning from him.» *Blank 9* And he uttered his poem and said: *Num 24:15-17* «Oracle of Balaam, son of Beor, and oracle of the man *10* of penetrating eye, oracle of him who listens to the words of God and knows the knowledge of the Most High, who *11* sees the vision of Shaddai, lying down and with an open eye. I see him, but not now, *12* I espy him, but not close up. A star has departed from Jacob, and a sceptre /has arisen/ from Israel. He shall crush *13* the temples of Moab, and cut to pieces all the sons of Sheth.» *Blank 14* And about Levi he says: *Deut 33:8-11* «Give to Levi your Thummim and your Urim, to your pious man, whom *15* I tested at Massah, and with whom I quarrelled about the waters of Meribah, /he who/ said to his father {not} *16* {...} and to his mother 'I have not known you', and did not acknowledge his brothers, and his sons he did not *17* want to know. For he observed your word and kept your covenant. /They have made/ your judgments /shine/ for Jacob, *18* your law for Israel, they have placed incense in your nose and a whole-offering upon your altar. *19* Bless, ****, his courage and accept with pleasure the work of his hand! Crush /the loins/ of his adversaries, and those who hate him, *20* may they not rise!» *Blank 21 Blank* At the moment when Joshua finished praising and giving thanks with his psalms, *22* he said *Jos 6:26* «Cursed be the man who rebuilds this city! Upon his first- born *33* will he found it, and upon his youngest son will he erect its gates!» And now an accursed /man/, one of Belial, *24* will arise to be a [fo]wler's tr[ap] for his people and ruin for all his neighbours. And *25* [...] will arise [to b]e the two instruments of violence. And they will rebuild *26* [this city and ere]ct for it a rampart and towers, to make it into a fortress of wickedness *27* [in the country and a great evil] in Israel, and a horror in Ephraim and Judah. *28* [... And they will com]mit a profanation in the land and a great blasphemy among the sons of *29* [Jacob. And they will shed blo]od like water upon the ramparts of the daughter of Zion and in the precincts of *30 Blank* {in} Jerusalem.

4Q176 (4QTanḥ) *4QTanḥûmîm*

PAM 43.427, 43.435, 44.192
ROC 285, 293

Bibliography: C.D. Stanley, 'The Importance of 4QTanhumim (4Q176)', *RevQ*

Frags. 1-2 i 1 ועשה פלאכה והצדק בעמכה והז.[...] 2 מקדשכה
וריבה עם ממלכות על דם[...] 3 ירושלים וראה נבלת כ[ו]הניכה [...]
4 ואין קובר ומן ספר ישעיה תנחומים[... נחמו נחמו עמי] 5 יומר
אלוהיכם דברו על לב ירושלים וקר[או אליה] כ[יא מלאה צבא]ה כיא
6 נרצה עוונה כיא לקחה מיד **** כפלים בכול הטותיהא קול קורה
7 במדבר פנו דרך **** ישרו] בערבה [מסלה לאלוהינ[ו] כול גיא ינשא
8 [וכול הר וגב]עה ישפלו והיה העקוב ל[מי]שור] והרכסים ל[ב]קעה
9 [ונגלה כ]בוד **** ואתה ישראל עב[די י]עקו[ב] אשר ב[חרת]י[כה
10 [זרע אבר]הם אהבי אשר ʰחזקתיכה] מקצו[ות ה[א]רץ ומאצילʰʰ[א
11 [קראתיכה ואמר] לכה עבדי אתה [בחרתיכה ולוא מאסת]יך

Frags. 1-2 ii 4 [**** אשר נ]אמן קדוש יש[ראל ויבחרכה רנו שמים
וגילי ארץ] 5 פצחו הרים כיא נחם אלה]ים עמו ועניו ירחם ותאמר ציון]
6 עזבני **** [ואדני שכחני התשכח אשה עולה מרחם בן בטנה] 7 גם אלה
תשכח]נה ואנכי לוא אשכחך הן על כפים חקותיך] 8 וחומותיך נג]די תמיד
מהרו בניך מהרסיך ומחרביך] 9 ממך יצ]או [...

Frags. 8-11 1 ...[...]... כאר]ץ [...].ירים *vacat* 2 עורי] עורי לבשי עזך
[ציון לב]שי בגדי תפארתך י]רושלים עיר הקודש כיא 3 [לוא יוסיף יבוא
בך עוד ערל וטמא התנערי מעפר קומ]י שובי ירושלם התפתחי 4 [מוסרי
צוארך ש[ביה] בה ציון כיא כה] אמר [**** חנם נמכרתם ולוא]בכסף
תגאלו 5 *vacat* [*vacat?*] אל תיר]אי כיא [לוא {פ} תבושין] ואל תכלמי כי]א
לא תחפירי כיא בשת 6 [עלומי]כי תשכחין וח]רפת ארמלותך לוא [תזכרי
עוד]כבעלך עושיך **** 7 [צבאות] שמו וגאליכי קדוש יש[רא]ל[ל]
א[ל]והי כול ה]ארץ יקרא כיא כאשה עזובה 8 [ועצובת]רוח קראך ****
ואשת נעורים כיא ת[מאס אמר **** אלוהיך 9 [ברגע] קטנה עזבתיך

15/60 (1992) 569-82

Frags. 1 - 2 *col.* I *1* Perform your marvel, do your people justice and … […] *2* your temple. Argue with kingdoms over the blood of […] *3* Jerusalem. See the corpses of your priests […] *4* there is no-one to bury them. And from the book of Isaiah: Words of consolation. [*Is 40:1-5* … Be consoled, consoled, my people!] *5* says your God; speak to the heart of Jerusalem and sho[ut to her] t[hat] her [service is done,] that *6* her fault has been forgiven, that from the hand of **** she has received double for all her sins. A voice shouts: *7* in the wilderness clear the path of ****, straighten out a roadway for o[ur] God [in the steppe]. Every valley is to be raised, *8* [and every mountain and hi]ll to be flattened; the rough terrain is to be made into a [pl]ain, [and the peaks] into a [pl]ateau. *9* [And the gl]ory of **** [will be revealed.] *Is 48:1-9* But you, Israel, are [my] serv[ant, J]ac[o]b, [whom I ch]ose, *10* [seed of Abra]ham, my favour-ite, whom I took [from the end]s of the [ea]rth, and [whom I called] from faraway lands; *11* [and I said] to you: You are my servant, [I chose you and did not reject] you!

Frags. 1 - 2 *col.* II *4* [**** who is l]oyal, the Holy One of Is[rael, and he has chosen you. *Is 49:13-17* Celebrate, heavens; rejoice, earth;] *5* erupt with ap-plause, mountains! For Go[d] has consoled [his people, and has compassion on his poor. But Zion said:] *6* **** has deserted me [and the Lord has forgot-ten me. Does a woman, perhaps, forget her suckling child, stop having com-passion for the fruit of her womb?] *7* Even should she forge[t, I will not forget you! See, I have inscribed you on the palms of my hand,] *8* your ramparts [are always] be[fore me. Your rebuilders are in a hurry, your wreckers and your destroyers] *9* de[part] from you. […]

Frags. 8 - 11 *1* […] … […] like a lan[d …] … *Blank 2 Is 52:1-3* Wake up, [wake up, put on your strength,] Zion; put [on your party clothes, Je]rusalem, holy city, for *3* [no longer will either uncircumcised or unclean enter you! Shake the dust from yourself, get u]p, be seated, Jerusalem, undo *4* [the fetters from your neck, pri]soner, [daughter of Zion! For so] says [****: For nothing have you been sold, and without] money will you be ransomed. *Blank 5* [*Blank?*] *Is 54:4-10* Do not fe[ar, for] you will { } not be ashamed, [do not be confounded, fo]r you will not be insulted. Because the indignity of *6* your [youth] you are to forget [and the hu]miliation of your widowhood you are not [to remember any more] when your maker marries you, **** *7* [of Hosts] is his name, and your re-deemer is the Holy One of Is[rae]l, [G]o[d of all the] earth he will be called. Because, as a woman, abandoned *8* [and troubled in] spirit has **** called you; and (as) a wife of youth, when [she] was discarded, says **** your God. *9* [A] short [moment] I deserted you, but with great compassion I will take you

וברחמים גדולים אקבצך בשצף קצף הש[תרתי פני]   10   [רגע מ]מך

ובחסדי עולם רחמתיכה אמר גואלך **** כימי נוח זות לי אשר

11   [נשבעתי מ]עב[ור מי] נוח אל ארץ כן נשבעתי מקצוף עליך ע[ו]ד

ו^מלגעור בך   12   [כיא ההר]ים ימושו והגבעות תמוטטנה וחסדי מאתיכי

לוא ימוש[...]   13   [...] נ[וא]ש עד דברי תנחומים וכבוד רב כתוב [...]

14   [...] [באוהב]י ... [...] אין עוד מעת[...] vacat   15   [...] בלי[על לענות

את עבדיו בו[...]...[...]   16   [...]י ישמח [...] ארים יושבת[...

17   [...].בת[...]תמע[...].

Frags. 16, 17, 18, 22, 23, 33, 51, 53   1   [...].וי   vacat   [...] וגם אף ב^מ[קדוש]

...[נחלת ידו כי לוא יצדק [איש]   2   מל[פניו ...] כיא הוא ברא את כול] רוח

דור[ו]ת עולמים ו[הכין כ]משפטו דרכי כולם והאר[ץ]   3   בר[א בימי]נו טרם

היותם ובעוד] אינם פק[ד על כול א]שר בה וב[רזו הפיל גורל לאיש לתת[

[... 4   ל[...]ל[...]ול אם ל[...] במלאך פד[...]ות קודש ולתת פעולת איש

ל[פי]   5   [...]...[...] שמונה ש.[...]עד על אוהבו ועל שומרי מצ[ותיו

6   ... ה]ופע לנו מפר[...] [שכח את בריתו   vacat   ול.[...]   7   [...]שו התורה

ו[...]. שנאתה להיות ל[...]   8   [...] התורה [...] כלותם ל.[...]

9   [...]...[...]

4Q176a,b (= 4Q176 frags. 19-21) (4QJub^{i,f?}) *4QJubilees^{i,f?}*

J.M. Allegro, *DJD V*, 60-65, pl. XXIII
PAM 43.435
ROC 293
1Q17, 1Q18, 2Q19, 2Q20, 3Q5, 4Q216, 4Q217, 4Q218, 4Q219, 4Q220, 4Q221, 4Q222, 4Q223-4Q224, 4Q482?, 4Q483?, 11Q12

Frags. 19-20   1   [...] ובשם הגדול יזכירו לוא באמ[ת ולוא בצדקה

2   [ויטמאו את קודש הקודשים בטמ]א בח[בל תועבותיהמה]ויהי קצף גדול

על מעשי הדור   3   [ההואה מלפני אדוני ויתן אות]ם בחרב ולמשפט

back. In a fit of anger [I] h[id my face] *10* [fr]om you [for a moment,] but with everlasting tenderness I took pity on you, says your redeemer, ****. As in (the) days of Noah will this be for me; as *11* [I swore that the waters of] Noah [would not] flo[od] the earth, so have I sworn not to become angry with you ag[a]in or threaten you. *12* Should [even the mountain]s move or the hills wobble, my compassion will not move from you [...] *13* [... des]perate (?) until the words of comfort and of great glory. It is written [...] *14* [...] among those who love [...] no more since the time of [...] *Blank* [...] *15* [... Beli]al to oppress his servants by [...] ... [...] *16* [...] will rejoice [...] I will raise her who sits [...] *17* [...] ... [...] ... [...]

Frags. 16, 17, 18, 22, 23, 33, 51, 53 *1* and [...] *Blank* And how much more in the temple [...] the possession of his hand, for [man] is not vindicated *2* bef[ore him ...] Because he created every [spirit] of the eternal [generation]s, and [according to] his judgment [he established] the paths of them all. The ear[th] *3* he cre[ated with] his [rig]ht (hand) before they existed, and he con[tinually superv]ises everything th[ere is in it. And in] his mystery he causes the lot to fall on man in order to give [...] *4* [...] ... [...] with the angel of ... [...] holy, and in order to give man's reward ac[cording] *5* [...] ... [...] eight [...] over those who love him and over those who keep [his] comm[andments.] *6* [...] he showed himself to us since ... [...] forget his covenant. *Blank* And to [...] *7* [...] ... the Law and [...] you have despised, in order to be [...] *8* [...] the Law [...] their end ... [...] *9* [...] ... [...]

4Q176a (= 4Q176 frags. 19-21) (4QJub?) *4QJubilees*?

Bibliography: M. Kister, 'Newly-identified Fragments of the Book of Jubilees: Jub. 23:21-23, 30-31', *RevQ* 12/48 (1987) 529-536; G.W. Nebe, 'Ergänzende Bemerkungen zu 4Q176, Jubiläen 23:21', *RevQ* 14/53 (1989) 129-130; J.C. VanderKam, *The Book of Jubilees Translated* (CSSO 511; Louvain: E. Peeters, 1989) viii-ix

Frags. 19 - 20 (= *Jub* 23:21-23) *1* [... and they will invoke the great name, (but) not in trut]h nor in justice; *2* [and they will defile the Holy of Holies with impu]rity, with the cor[ruption of their contaminations.] And there will be great anger against the deeds of [that] generation *3* [on the part of the Lord.

ו[לשביה]ולבז ולאוכולה [ו]יער עליהום   4   [רשעי גואים אשר אין בהם
חסד ור]חמים עליהמה ו[אשר פנ]י כ[ו]ל [איש] ל[וא י]שאו לואו

Frag. 21   1   וראו ש[ונאיהם את כול משפטם]   2   בכול קללת[ם וינוחו
עצמותיהם בארץ]   3   ורוחותיהם י[רבו שמחה וידעו כיא]   4   יש אל עושה
[משפט ועושה חסד]   5   ל[אלפי]ם ולר[בבות לכול אוהביו]

4Q177 (4QCatena A) *4QCatena A*

J.M. Allegro, *DJD V*, 67-74, pls. XXIV-XXV; J. Strugnell, 'Notes', 236-248, pls. IV-V
PAM 43.420, 43.422

Col. I   1   [...]ה ההוללים אשר י[... ...במצרף ה]בא על אנשי הי[חד]
2   [כאשר כתוב בספר ישעיה הנ]ביא אכול השנה שפ[יח ובשנה השנית
שחיס *vacat* ואשר אמ[ר השפיח הו]אה]   3   [...]רה עד עת המצ]רף הבאה
על ... ו]אחרי כן יעמוד[...   4   [...]כיא כולם ילדים[...]אמרו ההוללי]ם
[...   5   ...] כאשר כתוב] עליהם בספר י[שעיה הנביא ... כ]יא תורת
ההו[...]   6   [...]קרא להם כאשר] כתוב עליהם בספר ישעיה הנביא הוא
ז]מות יעץ לח[בל ענוים]   7   [באמרי שקר ... איש]הלצון את ישרא]ל ...
למנצח] לדויד ביהוה] חסיתי]   8   [כיא הנה הרשעים ידרכון קשת]ויכינו
חצים ע]ל יתר לרות במו אפל לישרי לב פשרו א[שר ינודו אנ]שי [...
9   [... כצ]פור ממקומו וגל]ה מארצו *vacat* והמה אשר כתוב עליה]ם בספר
ה[...]   10   [כעבור טמאה תחבל וחבל נמר]ץ לה איש הולך רו]ח ושקר כזב
... והיה מ[טף העם הזה ...   11   ...] כ]אשר כתוב עליהם בספר] [...חד
ערומי .[...].   12   [...]ך {ראו} *vacat* למנצח על ה]שמינית ... כיא לוא עם
ב]ינות [...   13   [הוא ...]המה העונה השמינית [...]סף חסד ספו[...]   14   [...]
וא[ין שלום אשר המה ד.[...]   15   [כאשר כתוב בספר ישעיה הנביא]הרוג

And he will deliver the]m to the sword, to judgment, [to captivity,] to pillage and to be devoured. [And] he will rouse against them *4* [the sinners of the nations, who have neither mercy nor com]passion towards them, and [who h]ave n[o] regard for a[n]y person, nor

Frag. 21 (= *Jub* 23 : 30 - 31; *belongs to* 4Q221 *?*)   *1* And [those who] h[ate them] will see [all their judgment] *2* in all [their] curse. [And their bones will rest in the earth] *3* and their spirits will [rejoice exceedingly and they will know that] *4* there is a God who performs [judgment and shows mercy] *5* to [thousand]s and to t[ens of thousands, to all that love him]

4Q177 (4QCatena A) *4QCatena A*

ROC 277, 289

Bibliography: A. Steudel, *Der Midrasch zur Eschatologie aus der Qumrangemeinde (4QMidrEschat*^{a,b}*)* (STDJ 13; Leiden: E.J. Brill, 1994)

Col. I (*frags.* 5 + 6 + 8)   *1* [...] the braggarts who [... in the trial to] come upon the men of the Com[munity,] *2* [as it is written in the book of Isaiah the pro]phet: *Isa 37:30* «This year what gro[ws of itself] will be eaten, [and the following year the self-seeded yield.» *Blank* And what it sa]ys: «what grows of itself», i[s] *3* [...] ... until the period of the tri[al which comes upon ...] After this [...] will arise *4* [...] for all of them are children [...] The braggarts said [...] *5* [... as is written] about them in the book of I[saiah the prophet: ... f]or the law of [...] *6* [...] calls them, as [is written about them in the book of Isaiah the prophet: *Isa 32:7* He] hatches [p]lots to des[troy the poor] *7* [with cunning words ... the] Insolent One to Israe[l ... *Ps 11:1* For the choirmaster.] Of David. In YHWH [I trust.] *8* [For, see, the wicked draw the bow,] notch arrows t[o the string, to aim in the darkness at those with an honest heart. Its interpretation:] the me[n of ...] will flee *9* [... like a b]ird from its spot and will be exi[led from his land. *Blank* And this is what is written about th]em in the book of [...] *10* [*Mic 2:10-11* On account of uncleanness he will ravage you with a dread]ful [destruction.] If a man should run after the win[d and invent untruths: ... he would be a pre]acher for this people. [...] *11* [... a]s is written about them in the book of [...] ... the experts of [...] *12* [...] {...} *Blank Ps 12* For the choirmaster. On the [eighth ...] for [it is] a people without kn[owledge] *13* [...] they are the eighth division [...] ... compassion ... [...] *14* [... and] there is [n]o peace, for they are ... [...] *15* [as is written in the book of Isaiah, the prophet:] *Isa 22:13* Sacrifice of oxen and slaughter of flocks,

בקר ושחוט צואן א[כול בשר ושתות יין ...] 16 [...].ת התורה עושי היחד
[...].ס

Col. II   1 [אמרות יהוה אמרות טהרות כסף צרוף בעליל לארץ מזק]ק
שבעתים כאשר כתוב 2 [בספר זכריה הנביא על אבן אחת שבעה עינים
הנני מפ[תח פתוחה נאם יהוה אשר 3 [... כא]שר עליהם כתוב ורפאתי
את 4 [... כ]ול אנשי בליעל וכול האספוף 5 [...]המה דורש התורה כיא
אין 6 [...]איש על מצורו בעומדם 7 [...]המכשילים את בני האור
8 [... עד אנה יהו]ה תשכח[ני נצח עד אנה תס]תיר פניכה ממני עד אנה
אשיתה 9 [עצות] בנפשי [יגון בלבבי יומ]ם עד אנה [ירום אויבי עלי פ]שר
הדבר [ע]ל נצח לב אנשי 10 [היחד [...]...]ה באחרית הימים כיא[...
[לבוחנם ולצורפם 11 [...]יהם ברוח וברורים ומזוקק[ים ... ואשר א]מר
פן יאמר אויב vacat 12 [יכלתו]המה עדת דורשי ה[חל]קות המ.[...] אשר
יבקשו לחבל 13 [אנשי היחד...]בקנאתמה ובמשטמ[תמה ...ל פש]...
כאש]ר כתוב בספר יחזקאל הנ[בי]א [14 [בית ישראל]ויהודה ככול
העמי[ם [פשר הדהר לאחרית]הימים אשר יקבצו עליה[מ] 15 [...] [עם
צדיק ורשע אויל ופת]י ...[ני האנשים אשר עבדו אל].[...] 16 [... הס]ירו
ערלות ל[ב ב]שרם בדור הא[חרון ... וכו]ל אשר להמה טמא ול[וא]

Col. III   1 [... כו]ל דבריהמ] ... ת]שבחות הכבוד אשר יואמ]ר [...
2 [... והסיר יהוה] ממכה כול חלי לקד[ושים אשר [בא]רץ ה]מה ואדי[ר]י
כול חפצי [בם ...] 3 [...]... נהיה כמוהו] ... ו]פיק [ב]רכים וחלחלה בכול
מתנ[ים ...] 4 [...]...[...]ל.תמה שמעה] יהוה צדק] הקשיבה רנתי האזינה
ל[תפלתי ...] 5 [...]ו באחרית הימים בעת אשר יבקש ...[...]ר את עצה
היחד והוא ה[...] 6 [...]. פשר הדבר אשר יעמוד איש מבי[ת ...]הרי
[...]...[...] 7 [...]היו כאש לכול תבל והמה אשר כתוב עליהם באחרית]
הימים [...]...ה פוח[...] 8 [...]מ[ו]ש]ל בג[ורל אור אשר היה מתאבל
בממשלת בל[י]על ומושל בגורל חושך] אשר היה מתאבל[...] 9 [...]בה

364

e[ating meat and drinking wine ...] *16* [...] ... the Law, those who make up the Community ... [...]

Col. II (*frags.* 11 + 10 + 26 + 9 + 20 + 7)   *1* [*Ps 12:7* The words of YHWH are pure words, silver purified in a clay crucible, refin]ed seven times. As is written *2* [in the book of the prophet Zechariah: *Zech 3:9* Upon one single stone there are seven eyes; see, I will en]grave its inscription, oracle of YHWH. What *3* [... a]s is written about them: «I shall cure the *4* [... a]ll the men of Belial and all the rabble *5* [...] them, the Interpreter of the Law, because there is no *6* [...] each one upon his wall when they stand firm *7* [...] those who make the sons of light stumble *8* [... *Ps 13:2-3* How long, YHW]H? Are you going to forget [me for ever? How long will you hi]de your face [from me?] How long am I to churn over *9* [worries] in my soul, [anxieties in my heart each da]y? How long [is my enemy to lord it over me? The inter]pretation of the word [con]cerns the purification of the heart of the men of *10* [the Community] ... [...] in the last days, because [...] to test them and refine them *11* [...] their [...] by the spirit, and the spotless and purified [ones ... What it s]ays: «Lest an enemy say *12* [I have overthrown him» *Blank*] These are the congregation of those looking for [easy inter]pretations, who [...] who seek to destroy *13* [the members of the Community ...] by their fervour and [their] animosity [...] ... [... a]s is written in the book of Ezekiel, the pro[phet] *14* [*Ez 25:8* The house of Israel] and of Judah is like all the peoples. [The interpretation of the word concerns the last] days when against th[em] will rally *15* [...] a just people, but the wicked, the demented and the simple[ton ...] ... the men who serve God [...] *16* [... who have cir]cumcised the foreskin of their he[art in] the l[ast] generation [... and al]l that belongs to them, he will pronounce unclean and n[ot]

Col. III (*frags.* 2 + 24 + 14 + 3 + 4 + 1 + 31)   *1* [... al]l their words [...] glorious [pr]aises, as [...] sa[ys] *2* [... *Deut 7:15* YHWH will remove] all illness from you. *Ps 16:3* As for the ho[ly ones who are] in the la[nd,] and the power[ful] ones [in whom] I fully delight [...] *3* [...] will be like him [... *Nah 2:11* and] shaking of [kn]ees and trembling in all loin[s ...] *4* [...] ... [...] ... *Ps 17:1* Listen, [YHWH, to a just case,] take notice of my shout, give ear to [my plaint ...] *5* [...] in the last days, at the time when [...] will seek the advice of the Community. He is [...] *6* [...] The interpretation of the word: A man of the ho[use of ...] will arise ... [...] *7* [...] they will be like fire for the whole world. And these are ones about whom it is written for the last [days ...] ... [...] *8* [...] r[u]le[s over the l]ot of the light which is in mourning during the reign of Bel[ial, and the one who rules over the lot of darkness,] which is in mourning [...] *9* [...] ... of

ממנו ו[...]לראשי אבל שוב ..[...] א[לוהי הרחמים ואל ישרא]ל [...מול
[...].. 10 [...]אשר ה[ת]גוללו ברוח[י ב]ליעל ונסלו להם לעולם וברכם[
...]עוד {מיד} לעולם יברכם[...]לאי קציה[ם] 11 [...]ת אבותם במספר
שמות[ם] מפורשים בשמות לאיש ואיש ה[... ש]נותיהם וקץ מעמדם ו[...]ו
לשונם 12 [...]א את צא[צ]אי יהודה[ו]עתה הנה הכול כתוב בלוחות
אשר [...]אל וידיעהו את מספר [כול דורו]ת וינח[י]ל[ה]ו 13 [...].. .[...]ל[ו]ל[
ולזרעו [עד] עולם ויקום משמה ללכת מן ארם [...]תקעו שופר בגבעה
השופר הואה ספר 14 [...]הו[אה ספר התורה שנית אשר מאסו כ]ול א[נשי
עצתו וידברו עליו סרה וישלח 15 [...]או[תות {ע} גדולות על ה]ל[...].
ויעקוב עומד על הגתות ושמח על רדת 16 [...]ת בחרב אפ.[...] לאנשי
עצתו המה החרב ואשר אמר

[...]ה[...]. ..[...]. ל[אה ...]. כיא לוא תואבד [תורה מכ]והן ועצה מחכם Col. IV 6
ודבר] מנביא [...] 7 [... לאחרית ה[י]מים אשר אמר דויד יה[ו]ה אל באפכה
תו]כיחני חונני יהוה כי[א אמלל אני ...] 8 [...]ונפשי נבהלה מאדה ועתה יהוה
עד מתי חונני חלצה נפ[שי ...]מים על 9 [... ב]ליעל להאבידמה בחרונו
אשר לוא יותיר ל[... לוא]יניח לבליעל 10 [... אב]רהם עד עשרה צדיקים
בעיר כיא רוח אמת ה.[... כי]א אין [ ] 11 [...].מה ואחיהמה במחשבל
(במחשבת) בליעל ויחזק עליה[ם ...ם ל...]ל[...] 12 [...]מלאך אמתו יעזור
לכול בני אור מיד בליעל[...] 13 ידיהם[...].המה...[...]]ולפזר[ם] בארץ
ציה ושממה היא עת ענות המו.[...]. כיא ה[...]. תמד ידוד הצ[ד]י[ק ויד
אל הגדולה עמהמה לעוזרם מכול רוח[ין בליעל ...] 15 [... וי]ראי אל
יקדישו שמו ובאו ציון בסמחה וירושלים[...] 16 [...ב]ל[י]ע[ל וכול אנשי
גורלו ה]תמו [לעד ונאספו כול בני א]ור [...

[...ה..ר 4 Col. V [...]. 5 בליעל [...]. 6 לאחרית] הימים [... 7 שופר
ב.[...] 8 [...... 9 אל את [...] 10 בליע[ל ...] 11 אנשי[...] 12 [...]..

him [...] to the chiefs of mourning a return ... [... G]od of compassion and God of Israe[l ...] ... [...] *10* [...] who have rebelled against the spirit[s of Be]lial and they will be forgiven for ever, and [...] will bless them again {by the hand of} for ever, and [...] will bless them [...] ... the[ir] periods *11* [...] of their fathers, according to the number of [their] names, according to the precise list of their names, of each man individually, [...] their [y]ears and the period of their service and [...] their tongues *12* [...] the des[cen]dants of Judah. [And] now, see, everything has been written on the tablets which [...] ... and made him known the number of [all the generation]s, and gave [him] in inher[itance] *13* [...] ... [...] to [him] and to his seed [for]ever. And he lifted him from there to walk from Aram [...] *Hos 5:8* Sound the horn in Gibeah. The horn is the book of *14* [... i]s the book of the Second Law which a[ll the m]en of his council have spurned and they have spoken revolt against him. And he sent *15* [...] great [si]gns {...} over [...] And Jacob will stand at the winepresses and will rejoice over the flow of *16* [...] by the sword ... [...] to the men of his council. They are the sword. And as for what he says:

Col. IV (*frags.* 12 + 13 I + 15; *frag. 19, which was previously placed in lines 1-6 of this column, is now numbered 4Q525 frag. 22*) *6* [...] ... [... *Jer 18:18* For] the Law [is not to disappear] from the pr[iest, nor advice from the sage, nor a word] from the prophet *7* [...] for the last [d]ays, as David said: *Ps 6:2-3* YH[W]H, do not sc[old me] in anger. [Take pity on me YHWH, fo]r I am collapsing. *8* [...] *Ps 6:4-5* My soul is very troubled; and now, YHWH, how long? Take pity on me, save [my] li[fe ...] ... over *9* [... Be]lial, to destroy them in his anger, for there will no longer be [... he will not] give rest to Belial *10* [... Ab]raham, until there are ten just men in the city, for the spirit of truth [... fo]r there are no *11* [...] ... and their brothers through the ‹scheming› of Belial, and he will triumph over th[em ...] ... [...] *12* [...] the angel of his truth will rescue all the sons of light from the power of Belial [...] *13* their hands [...] their [...] to scatter [them] in a dry and bleak land. This is the period of distress ... [...] *14* because [...] continually (?) the j[us]t man will flee and God's great hand will be with them to rescue them from all the spirits of [Belial ...] *15* [... those who f]ear God will sanctify his name and enter Zion with joy, and Jerusalem [...] *16* [... Be]l[ia]l and all the men of his lot will be fin[ished] for ever, and all the sons of li[ght] will be reunited [...]

Col. V (*frag.* 13 II) *1-3* [...] *4* ... [...] *5* Belial [...] *6* for the last [days ...] *7* horn [...] *8* ... [...] *9* God [...] *10* Belia[l ...] *11* the men (of) [...] *12* ... [...]

4Q178 *4QUnclassified fragments*

J.M. Allegro, *DJD* V, 74-75, pl. XXV: J. Strugnell, 'Notes', 248-249, pl. I
PAM 43.420, 44.180, 44.191
ROC 160

Frag. 1   1 [...] ל[שרתם ולע[מ]וד לפני .[...]   2 [...] אשר צוה בצר
למו בא[...] 3 [...].דת הארץ ונ[...] 4 [...]בקש הי.[...] 5 [...] [השלום
ו[...] 6 [...]הרוח [...]

Frag. 3   1 [...]שאו[...].[...].   2 [...] כאשר כתוב [...]   3 [...].ם
ושבי יש[ו]ראל [... 4 ...] אחרי]ת הימי]ם [... 5 [...].דם] ...]

4Q179 (4QapocrLam A) *4QApocryphal Lamentations A*

J.M. Allegro, *DJD* V, 75-77, pl. XXVI; J. Strugnell, 'Notes', 250-252
PAM 43.425
ROC 235
Bibliography: M.P. Horgan, '4Q179 A Lament over Jerusalem', *JSS* 18 (1973)

Frag. 1 i   1 [...].[...] 2 [...]..ר כל עוונותינו ואין לאל ידנו כי לוא
שמע[נו] 3 [... בקץ]הפקודה לקרותנו כל אלה ברוע 4 [...]. את בריתו
vacat אוי לנו 5 [...] היה לשרפת אש והפכה 6 [...]ר תפארתנו וניחוח
אין בו במז[בח] 7 [...]חצרות קודשנו היו 8 [...].[...]...[...]...תים ירושלים
עיר 9 [... מרב]ץ לחיה ואין .[...] ורחובותיה 10 [...]ן הוי כל
ארמונותיה שממו 11 [...].[...]. ובאי מועד אין בם כל ערי 12 [...]נחלתנו
היתה כמדבר ארץ לוא 13 [...]קו]ל שמ[ח]ה לוא נשמ{ש}עה בה ודורש
14 [...]לאנוש {ל}{מכ}{אוב}ˣ'נו כול חובינו 15 [...].פ[שעינו ומ]...
חטאותינו]

4Q178 *4QUnclassified fragments*

Bibliography: A. Steudel, *Der Midrasch zur Eschatologie aus der Qumrangemeinde (4QMidrEschat^{a,b})* (STDJ 13; Leiden: E.J. Brill, 1994) 154-155

Frag. 1 *1* [… to] serve them and to st[a]nd before […] *2* […] which he ordered in their hardship in … […] *3* […] … the land and … […] *4* […] seek … […] *5* […] the peace, and […] *6* […] the spirit […]

Frag. 3 *1* […] … […] *2* […] as it is written […] *3* […] … and the returned of Is[rael …] *4* [… the las]t days […] *5* […] … […]

4Q179 (4QapocrLam A) *4QApocryphal Lamentations A*

222-234; H. Pabst, 'Eine Sammlung von Klagen in den Qumranfunden (4Q179)', in M. Delcor (ed.), *Qumrân: Sa piété, sa théologie et son milieu* (Paris: Duculot, 1978) 137-149

Frag. 1 *col.* I *1* […] … […] *2* […] … all our sins. And it is not in the power of our hands, because [we] have not listened *3* [… at the time of] the visitation, so that all these things will happen to us because of the evil of *4* […] his covenant. *Blank* Woe to us! *5* […] It has been burned by fire and ravaged *6* […] our honour, and in it there is no pleasing odour; upon the al[tar] *7* […] our holy courtyards were *8* […] … […] … Jerusalem, city *9* [… a la]ir of animals, and there is no […] And her squares *10* […] … Alas! All her palaces are desolate *11* […] and those who used to come to the festival are not in them. All the cities of *12* […] Our inheritance has been turned into a desert, land which does not *13* [… the soun]d of j[o]y is not heard in her. And he who is looking for *14* […] for our incurable {pain} wounds. All our debts *15* […] our [trans]gressions and … […] our sins

369

Frag. 1 II   3 אוי לנו כי אף אל עלינ[ו ...]   4 ונגוללה עם המתים .[...]

5 כמשונאה יש.[...]   6 לעוליהן ובת עמי אכזריה]...[7 עלומיה שוממו

בני ע[מי ...]   8 מלפני חורף בדל ידיהן]   9 אשפתות מדור ביתו[...]

10 שאלו מים ואין מגיר[...]   11 המסלאים [ב]פז וכתם] ...[12 וחפץ

אין בו ^האמונים עלי תול[ע ...]   13 וכתם טוב עדים נושאי{ם} הלבו[ש ...]

14 ומשי תכלת ורוקמה מ.[...]   15 בנו^ת ציון {היקרים} הרכות .מע.[...]

Frag. 2   2-1 [...]...[...]   3 [...]...[...]ע באהל[ך]   4 [איכה ישבה]

בדד העיר[הג]דול[ה ירוש]לים ר[בתי]   5 [הע]מים שרתי כל לאומ[ים

[שוממה כעזובה וכל [בנ]ותיה עזוב[ות]   6 [כ]אשה ער[י]ריה כעצובה

וכעזובת [אישה]כל ארמונתיה ורחו[בותיה]   7 כעקרה וכמסככה כול

אורחו[ת]י[ה ו..]ה ו...]ה ^כאשת מרורים   8 וכל בנותיה כאבלות על <על>

בע[ו]ליהן ...].יה כמשכלות   9 ליחידיהן בכו תבכה ירו[שלים דמעות ירד]ו

על לחיה על בניה   10 [...]...[...]ל. והגתה

4Q180 (4QAgesCreat A?) *4QAges of Creation A*

J.M. Allegro, *DJD V*, 77-79, pl. XXVII; J. Strugnell, 'Notes', 252-254, pl. VI
PAM 43.425, 44.183, 44.193
ROC 468
Bibliography: J.M. Allegro, 'Some Unpublished Fragments of Pseudepigraphi-
cal Literature from Qumran's Fourth Cave', *ALUOS* 4 (1962-63) 3-4; J.T.
Milik, 'Milkî-ṣedeq et Milkî-reša' dans les anciens écrits juifs et chrétiens', *JJS*

Frag. 1   1 פשר על הקצים אשר עשה ^{ל+} קץ להתם] כול הויה]

2 ונהיה בטרם בראם הכין פעולות]יהם בכול סרך הקצים]   3 קץ לקצו

והוא חרות על לחות] השמים לבני אדם]   4 [ל]^כ[ול קצי ממשלותם זה סרך

בנ[י נוח משם לאברהם]   5 [ע]ד הוליד ישחק את עשרה ה]תולדות ...[

6 [...] *vacat* [...]   7 [ו]פשר על עזזאל והמלאכים אש]ר באו אל בנות

Frag. 1 *col.* II *3* Woe to us, because the wrath of God against u[s ...] *4* and we have been defiled with the dead [...] *5* like a detested woman ... [...] *6* for their sucklings. The daughter of my people is cruel [...] *7* her youth. The sons of [my] peo[ple] are desolate [...] *8* due to the winter, when their hands are weak [...] *9* dunghills are the lodging where they spend the night [...] *10* they ask for water and there is no-one to pour it [...] *11* those weighed [against] gold and pure gold [...] *12* and there is no delight in him. Those brought up in scarl[et ...] *13* and jewellery of pure gold; those who wear clot[hes ...] *14* and silk, purple and multi-coloured ... [...] *15* The {valuable} tender daughters of Sion ... [...]

Frag. 2 *1-2* [...] ... [...] *3* [...] ... [...] in your tent [...] *4* [How] solitary [lies] the [l]arg[e] city [Jerusa]lem (once) f[ull] *5* [of pe]ople; the princess of all the nation[s] has become desolate like an abandoned woman; all her [daug]hters have been aban[doned,] *6* [like] a woman without sons, like a distressed and abandoned [woman.] All her palaces and [her] squa[res] *7* are like a barren woman, and all [her] paths like an imprisoned woman, [and] her [...] /like/ a bitter woman. *8* And all her daughters like those mourning for <for> [their] hu[sbands ...] her [...] like those bereft *9* of their only sons. How Jeru[salem] must weep, [the tears will flow] down her cheek for her sons *10* [...] ... and her sigh

---

4Q180 (4QAgesCreat A) *4QAges of Creation A*

23 (1972) 109-126; .- *The Books of Enoch*, 248-252; D. Dimant, 'The 'Pesher on the Periods' (4Q180) and 4Q181', *Israel Oriental Studies* 9 (1979) 77-102; R.V. Huggins, 'A Canonical 'Book of the Periods' at Qumran?', *RevQ* 15/59 (1992) 421-436; A. Lange, 'Eine neue Lesart zu 4Q180: *kllh* vice *klh*', *ZAH* 9 (1993) 232-234; J.J.M. Roberts, 'Wicked and Holy (4Q180-181)', in *PTSDSSP* 2, 204-213

Frag. 1 *1* Interpretation concerning the ages which God has made: An age to conclude [all that there is] *2* and all that will be. Before creating them he determined [their] operations [according to the precise sequence of the ages,] *3* one age after another age. And this is engraved on the [heavenly] tablets [for the sons of men,] *4* [for] /[a]ll/ the ages of their dominion. This is the sequence of the son[s of Noah, from Shem to Abraham,] *5* [unt]il he sired Isaac; the ten [generations ...] *6* [...] *Blank* [...] *7* [And] interpretation concerning 'Azaz'el and the angels wh[o came to the daughters of man] *8* [and s]ired themselves

האדם] 8 [וי]לדו להם גברים ועל עזזאל [כתוב ...] 9 [לאהבת] עולה
ולהנחיל רשעה כל ק[צו ...] 10 [...]. משפטים ומשפט סוד[...].[...]

1 [... הר צי]ון הוא אשר שכן [...] *Frags. 2-4* ıı 2 אשר א[רץ
זא[ת יפה אל לוט לרשת...] *vacat* 3 ארץ מ[...] שלושת האנשי[ם אשר]
4 יראו[אל אברה]ם באלוני ממרה מלאכים המה] ואשר 5 [אמר זע]קת
סודם ועמורה כי ר[בה]והטאתמה כי 6 כבדה מאדה ארדה נא ואראה
הזעקתמה הבאה 7 [אלי ע]שה כלה ואם לא אדע[ה פשר] הדבר [על כול]
8 בש[ר] אשר[... ו]על כול[פה] 9 דובר[...] ואראה כיא הכול [חקוק
לק[ץ] 10 תע[ו]דתו כי] בטרם בראם ידע מחשב[ותיהם]

1 [...] לעו[לם *vacat* [...] 2 [...] ואשר כ]תוב על הארץ] *Frags. 5-6*
[... 3 [...] דרך שני ימים [...] 4 [...] הו[א הר ציון ירושלי]ם [...] 5 [...
ואש]ר כתוב על פרעה] [... 6 [...].[...]

4Q181 (4QAgesCreat B) *4QAges of Creation B*

J.M. Allegro, *DJD V*, 79-80, pl. XVIII; J. Strugnell, 'Notes', 254-255
PAM 43.346, 43.421

1 לאשמה ביחד עם סו[ד] עמ[ו ו]ל[ה]תג[ו]ל[ל] בחטאת בני *Frag. 1* ıı
אדם ולמשפטים גדולים ומחלים רעים 2 בבשר לפי גבורות אל ולעומת
רשעם לפי {סוד נדתם} טמ^אתם מסיר בני ש[מים] וארץ ליחד רשעה עד
3 קצה לעומת רחמי אל לפי טובו והפלא כבודו הגיש מבני תבל *vacat*
להתחשב עמו בי[חד] 4 [א]לים לעדת קודש במעמד לחיי עולם ובגורל עם
קדושיו כ[...] 5 [רזי פ]לאו איש לפי גורלו אשר הפ[י]ל ל[ו ...] 6 [...
[לחיי ע[ו]ל[ם ...

giants. And concerning 'Azaz'el [is written …] *9* [to love] injustice and to let him inherit evil for all [his] ag[e …] *10* […] (of the) judgments and the judgment of the council of […]

Frags. 2 - 4 *col.* II   *1* […] is [Mount Zi]on on which resides […] … *2* because [thi]s l[and] is attractive for Lot (?), to inherit […] *3* a land […] *Blank* The three men [who] *4* appear[ed to Abraha]m in the oak wood of Mambre are angels. [And what it] *5* [says: *Gen 18:20-21* «The sh]out of Sodom and Gomorrah is l[oud] and their sin is *6* very serious. I am going down to see: (if it corresponds to) their shout which comes *7* [right to me, I will wre]ak destruction, and if not, I will know [it.» The interpretation of] the word [concerns all] *8* fle[sh] which [… and] to every [mouth] *9* which speaks […] and I will check it, for everything [is inscribed in conformity with the age of] *10* [its] tes[timony, since] before creating them he knew [their] thou[ghts.]

Frags. 5 - 6   *1* [… for e]ver. *Blank* […] *2* [… And what is wr]itten concerning the land […] *3* […] two days' journey […] *4* [… is] Mount Zion, Jerusale[m …] *5* [… and wh]at is written concerning Pharaoh […] *6* […] … […]

4Q181 (4QAgesCreat B) *4QAges of Creation B*

ROC 473
Bibliography: See 4Q180

Frag. 1 *col.* II   *1* for guilt in the community with the coun[sel of his] people, [and] to [be] defiled with the sin of the sons of man, and for great judgments and vile maladies *2* in the flesh. According to the powerful deeds of God and in line with their evil, according to {the foundation of their impurity} their impurity, he delivered the sons of the he[avens] and the earth to a wicked community until *3* its end. In accordance with God's compassion and in accordance with his goodness and the wonder of his glory he approaches some from among the sons of the world *Blank* so that they can be considered with him in the com[munity of] *4* [the g]ods to be a holy congregation in the position of eternal life and in the lot with his holy ones […] *5* his [wonder]ful [mysteries], each man according to his lot which he as[sig]ned to [him …] *6* […] for et[e]rn[al] life […]

Frag. 2   1   [לאברה]ם [עד הולי]ד ישחק [את עשרה התולדות ...]

2   [בנות]האדם וילד[ו] להמה גבור[ים ...]   3   [א]ת ישראל בשבעים

השבוע ל[...]   4   ואוהבי עולה ומנחילי אשמה .[...]   5   לעיני כול יודעיו

...ש[...]   6   ולטובו אין חקר[...]   7   אלה נפלאי מדע[ו ...]   8   תכנם

באמתו ו[...]   9   בכול קצותם[...]   10   בריאותיה[ם ...]

4Q182 (4QCatena B) *4QCatena B*

J.M. Allegro, *DJD V*, 80-81, pl. XXVII; J. Strugnell, 'Notes', 256
PAM 43.428
ROC 160

Frag. 1   1   [...] פשרו לא[א]חרית הימים על {ע.}   2   [...]ה אשר יקשו את

עורפם   3   [...]ויפרעו ביד רמה להחל   4   [... כאשר כ]תוב עליהם {מ}

בספר ירמ[יה]   5   [הנביא אי לזאת אסלוח לך בני]כה עזבוני [...]

Frag. 2   1   [...]שא לאחרית הימי[ם ...]   2   [...]ה.[...] להכותם .[...]

3   [...]ל[...]

4Q183 *4QHistorical Work*

J.M. Allegro, *DJD V*, 81-82, pl. XXVI; J. Strugnell, 'Notes', 256, 263, pl. III
PAM 43.428
ROC 139

Frag. 1 ii   1   אויביהם ויטמאו את מקדשם[...]   2   מהם ויקימו

למלחמות איש[לרעהו ...]   3   בבריתו הושיע ⌐⌐ וימלט[...]   4   רצון ויתן

להם לב אחד ללכ[ת ...]   5   כול הון רשעה וינזרו מדר[ך ...]   6   תועי רוח

ובלשון האמת .[...]   7   וירצו את עוונם בנגיעי[הם ...]   8   עוונם *vacat* [...]

9   ואשר אמר ר.[...]   10   [...]...[...]

Frag. 2   *1* [to Abraha]m [until he sire]d Isaac; [the ten generations …] *2* [the daughters of] man and sired giant[s] for themselves […] *3* to Israel in the seventieth week to […] *4* And those who love injustice and inherit evil […] *5* for the eyes of all those who know him … […] *6* and his goodness is unfathomable […] *7* these are the wonders of [his] knowledge […] *8* he has established them in his truth and […] *9* in all their ages […] *10* the[ir] creatures […]

4Q182 (4QCatena B) *4QCatena B*

Bibliography: A. Steudel, *Der Midrasch zur Eschatologie aus der Qumrangemeinde (4QMidrEschat*^{a,b}*)* (STDJ 13; Leiden: E.J. Brill, 1994) 152-154

Frag. 1   *1* [… Its interpretation for] the [l]ast days concerns {.} *2* […] who stiffened their necks *3* […] and without restraint, with arrogant hand, they defiled *4* [… as is wr]itten about them in the book of [the prophet] Jere[miah:] *5* [*Jer* *5:7* Why should I have to forgive you?] Your [sons] have deserted me […]

Frag. 2   *1* […] … for the last days […] *2* […] to destroy them […] *3* […] … […]

4Q183 *4QHistorical Work*

Bibliography: A. Steudel, *Der Midrasch zur Eschatologie aus der Qumrangemeinde (4QMidrEschat*^{a,b}*)* (STDJ 13; Leiden: E.J. Brill, 1994) 155-157

Frag. 1 *col.* II *1* their enemies. And they defiled their temple […] *2* of them, and they raised for wars, one man [against the other …] *3* in his covenant, God saved and set free […] *4* favour, and gave them one heart to wal[k …] *5* any wicked wealth. And they went away from the pat[h of …] *6* those with misguided spirit, and with the language of the truth […] *7* and they expiated their iniquities through [their] sufferings […] *8* their iniquities. *Blank* […] *9* As for what he says: … […] *10* […] … […]

4Q184 4QWiles of the Wicked Woman

J.M. Allegro, *DJD V*, 82-85, pl. XXVIII; J. Strugnell, 'Notes', 263-268
PAM 43.432
ROC 287; frag. 2, Oriental Institute of the University of Chicago
Bibliography: J.M. Allegro, 'The Wiles of the Wicked Woman: A Sapiential
Work from Qumran's Fourth Cave', *PEQ* 96 (1964) 53-55; J. Carmignac,
'Poème allégorique sur la secte rivale', *RevQ* 5/19 (1965) 361-374; A.M.
Gazov-Ginzberg, 'Double-Meaning in a Qumran Work: The Wiles of the

Frag. 1   1 [...]ה תוציא הבל ובו[...]א תועות תשחר תמיד [וי]שנן
דבר[י פיה ...] 2 וקלס תחל[י]ק ולהליץ יחד בש[וא תו]עיל לבה יכין פחין
וכליותיה מק[שות עיניה] 3 בעול נגעלו ידיה תמכו שוח רגליה להרשיע
ירדו וללכת באשמות[...] 4 מוסדי חושך ורוב פשעים בכנפיה [...]ה
תועפות לילה ומלבשיה [...] 5 מכסיה אפלות נשף ועדיה נגועי שחת
ערשיה {יצועיה} יצועי שחת[...] 6 מעמקי בור מלונותיה משכבי חושך
ובאישני ליל[ה]אשלותיה ממוסדי אפלות 7 תאהל שבת ותשכון באהלי
דומה בתוך מוקדי עולם ואין נחלתה בתוך בכול 8 מאירי {.} נוגה והיאה
ראשית כול דרכי עול הוי הוה לכול נוחליה ושדדה לכ[ול] 9 תומכי בה
כיא דרכיה דרכי מות ואורחותיה שבילי חטאת מעגלותיה משגות 10 עול
ונתיבו[תי]ה אשמות פשע שעריה שערי מות בפתח ביתה תצעד שאו[ל]
11 כ[ו]ל[ ] באיה בל [י]שובון וכול נוחליה ירדו שחת וה[י]א במסתרים
תארוב. [...] 12 כו[ל ...]ברחובות עיר תתעלף ובשערי קריות תתיצב ואין
להרג[י]עה] 13 מה[זנו]ת תמיד עיניה הנה והנה ישכילו ועפעפיה בפחז
תרים לראו[ת ל]אי[ש] 14 צדיק ותשיגהו ואיש[ע]צום ותכשילהו ישרים
להטות דרך ולבחירי צדק 15 מנצור מצוה סמוכי ה[לב] להביל בפחז
והולכי ישר להשנות ח[ו]ק להפשיע 16 ענוים מאל ולהטות פעמיהם
מדרכי צדק להביא זד[ו]ן ב[לב]במה בל ידרוכו 17 במעגלי יושר להשגות
אנוש בדרכי שוחה ולפתות בחלקות בני איש

4Q184 *4QWiles of the Wicked Woman*

Wicked Woman', *RevQ* 6/22 (1967) 279-285; H. Burgmann, 'The Wicked Woman: Der Makkabäer Simon?', *RevQ* 8/31 (1974) 323-359; R.D. Moore, 'Personification of the Seduction of Evil: 'The Wiles of the Wicked Women'', *RevQ* 10/40 (1981) 505-519; J.M. Baumgarten, 'On the Nature of the Seductress in 4Q184', *RevQ* 15/57-58 (1991) 133-143; Y. Zur, 'Parallels between Acts of Thomas 6-7 and 4Q184', *RevQ* 16/61 (1993) 103-107

Frag. 1 *1* She [...] utters futility and in [...]. She is always looking for depravities, [and] whets the word[s of her mouth, ...] *2* and implies insult, and is [bu]sy leading the community astray with non[sense.] Her heart weaves traps, her kidneys n[ets. Her eyes] *3* have been defiled with evil, her hands grasp the pit, her feet descend to act wickedly and to walk in crimes. [...] *4* (are) foundations of darkness, and there are plenty of sins in her wings. Her [...] (are) night gloom and her clothes [(are) ...] *5* Her veils are shadows of the twilight and her adornments diseases of the pit. Her beds {her couches} are couches of the pit, [...] *6* (are) deep ditches. Her lodgings are couches of darkness and in the heart of the nigh[t] are her tents. In the foundations of gloom *7* she sets up her dwelling, and camps in the tents of silence, in the midst of eternal fire. She has no inheritance among all *8* those who shine {.} brightly. She is the start of all the ways of wickedness. Alas! She is the ruination of all who inherit her, and the calamity of a[ll] *9* who grasp her. For her paths are paths of death, and her roads are tracks to sin. Her trails lead astray *10* towards wickedness, and her pathways to the guilt of transgression. Her gates are the gates of death, in the entrance to her house Sheo[l] proceeds. *11* A[l]l [those who go to her will not] come back, and all those who inherit her will descend to the pit. S[h]e hides in ambush in secret places, [...] *12* al[l ...] In the city squares she veils herself, and in the gates of the village she stations herself, and there is no-one who can ke[ep her] *13* from (her) incessant [fornicat]ing. Her eyes scan hither and thither, and she raises her eyebrows impudently, to spot a *14* just ma[n] and overtake him, and a [no]ble man, to trip him up; the upright to turn (from) the path, the righteous chosen ones *15* from keeping the precept, to make those with a steady [mind] ridiculous with recklessness, and those who walk uprightly to alter the ordi[na]nce. To make *16* the simple rebel against God, to turn their steps off the paths of justice, to bring presumpt[uous]ness into their [hea]rt, so that they do not walk *17* in the paths of uprightness. To sidetrack man into the ways of the pit, and seduce the sons of men with smooth words.

4Q185 *4QSapiential Work*

J.M. Allegro, *DJD V*, 85-87, pls. XXIX-XXX; J. Strugnell, 'Notes', 269-273
PAM 43.439, 43.514
ROC 801
Bibliography: H. Lichtenberger, 'Eine weisheitliche Mahnrede in den Qumran-
funden (4Q185)', in M. Delcor (ed.), *Qumrân: Sa piété, sa théologie et son milieu*

Frags. 1-2 i 3 [...].[...] 4 [...]טהור וקדוש[...] 5 [...]מתו

וכחמתו [...] 6 [...]ש ועד עשר פעמים [...] 7 [...] ואין כח לעמוד לפניה

ואין מקוה 8 לזעם] אף אלהינו[ומי יכלכל לעמוד לפני מלאכיו כי באש

9 להבה ישפט[...]. רוחתיו ואתם בני אדם א[וי לכם]כי הנה 10 כחציר

יצמח מארצו ופרח כציץ חסדו נשב[ה בו] רוחו 11 ויבש עגזו וציצו תשא

רוח עד אי'קום לעמ]דו מל[בד vacat 12 ולא ימצא כי רוח יבקשוהו ולא

ימצאהו ואין מקוה 13 והוא כצל ימיו על הא[רץ] ועתה שמעו נא עמי

והשכילו 14 לי פתאים וחכמו מן [ג]בורת אלהינו וזכרו נפלאות עשה

15 במצרים ומופתיו ב[ארץ חם]ויערץ לבבכם מפני פחדו

Frags. 1-2 ii 1 ועשו רצ[ו]נו ... נ]פשכם כחסדיו הטבים חקרו לכם

דרך 2 לחיים ומסלה] ...]לשארית לבניכם אחריכם ולמה תתנו

3]נפש[כם לשוא] ו... מ]שפט שמעוני בני ואל תמרו דברי יהוה 4 [ו]אל

תצעדו [... ודרך אשר צוה לי]עקב ונתיבה חקק לישחק הלוא ט'ב יום

5 אחד] בבי[תו מעשר]ו [...]. יראתו ולא לעתת מפחד ומפה יקוש 6 [...]

ולהבדיל מן מלאכיו כי אין חשך 7 [...].[...]...ה הוא ...[...ר]צונו ודעתו

ואתמה 8 מה תת[...].[...] לפניו תצא רעה לכל עם אשרי אדם נתנה לו

9 בן אד[ם ...עים ואל יתהלל[ו] רשעים לאמור לא נתנה 10 לי ולא [...

אלהים נתנה]לישראל וכזבד[ט]וב זבדה וכל עמו גאל 11 והרג שנאי]

ח[כמ]תו [... יאמר המתכבד בה ישאנה י[רו]שה 12 ומצאה וח[ז]ק בה

ונחלה ועמה] ארך י]מים ודשן עצם ושמחת לבב עש[ר וכבוד] 13 וחסדיו

4Q185 *4QSapiential Work*

(BETL 46; Paris: Duculot, 1978) 151-162; T.H. Tobin, '4Q185 and Jewish Wisdom Literature', in H.W. Attridge *et al.* (eds.), *Of Scribes and Scrolls*, 145-152; D.J. Verseput, 'Wisdom, 4Q185, and the Epistle of James', *JBL* 117 (1998) 691-707

Frags. 1 - 2 *col.* I (cf. 4Q370 II 5 - 9) *3* […] … […] *4* […] pure and holy […] *5* […] … and according to his anger […] *6* […] and up to ten times […] *7* […] And there is no strength to stand before her nor there is hope *8* for the fury of [the anger of our God,] and who can endure to stand before his angels? For with *9* burning fire will he judge […] his spirits. But you, O sons of man, w[oe to you!] For see, *10* (man) sprouts like grass from the earth and his loveliness blooms like a flower. (But then) his wind blows [over him], *11* his root shrivels, the wind scatters his leaves, until hardly anything remains in [its] pla[ce], *12* and nothing but wind is found. *Blank* They will look for him and not find him, and no hope remains; *13* as for him, his days are like a shadow on the ea[rth.] And now, please, hear me, my people! Pay attention *14* to me, simpletons! Draw wisdom from the [p]ower of our God, remember the miracles he performed *15* in Egypt, his portents in [the land of Ham]. And may your heart tremble because his terror

Frags. 1 - 2 *col.* II *1* and do [his] wi[ll …] your [s]ouls according to his good favours. Look for a path *2* towards life, a road […,] a remnant for your sons after you. Why do you give *3* your [soul] to futility [and (your) … (of) jud]gment? Listen to me, my sons, and do not defy the words of YHWH *4* [and] do not walk [… but the way which he commanded to J]acob and the path which he decreed to Isaac. Is one day [in his hou]se not better *5* than riches […] … to fear him, and not be afflicted (?) by terror and the net of the hunter. *6* […] … and to be separated from his angels, for there is no darkness *7* … […] … he … […] his [w]ill and his knowledge. And you, *8* what […] … […] before him shall the evil go out to all people. Blessed is the man to whom she has been given, *9* the son of ma[n …] … The wicked persons should not brag, saying: She has not been given *10* to me and not [… God has given her] to Israel, and like a [g]ood gift, gives her. He has saved all his people, *11* but has destroyed those who hate [his wi]sdo[m …] Whoever glories in her should say: one should take her as po[ssess]ion *12* and find her and ho[ld] fast to her and get her as an inheritance; with her [there are long d]ays, and greasy bones, and a happy heart, rich[es and honour.] *13* His mercies are her youth, and [his]

עלמיה וישועות[יו ...]... אשרי אדם יעשנה ולא רגל על[יה וברו]ח
14 מרמה לא יבקשנה ובחלקות לא יחזיקנה כן תתן לאבתיו כן ירשה[
וחזק] בה   15 בכל עוז כחו ובכל [מא]דו לאין חקר וירישנה לצאצאיו
ידעתי לעמ[ל לט]וב

Frags. 1-3 III   1 אליה כי טו[ב ...   2 וממגרות ית.[...]   3 ומ.[...]
vacat 6-4   7 ...[...]...[...]   8 ...]... אל[ה]ים יבחן כל מזמ[ו]ת [...
9 והוא]... עשה דברי ברי[תו ...   10 ולא ע[ש]ה א[להים] מש[פט
במסורר]ים ...   11 הלא א[ל]הי[ם] עשה לבות ויד[ע מזמותם אלהים יביט]
12 אל כל חדרי בטן ויחפש כליתו [אל[ה]ים עשה]   13 לשון וידע דברה
אלהים עשה ידים] וידע פעולתיה[ן]   14 ... אם]טוב ואם רע]...[15 ...]
[במחש]בות [...

4Q186 *4QHoroscope*

J.M. Allegro, *DJD V*, 88-91, pl. XXXI; J. Strugnell, 'Notes', 274-276
PAM 43.344, 43.438
ROC 109
Bibliography: J.M. Allegro, 'An Astrological Cryptic Document from Qumran',
JSS 9 (1964), 291-294; J. Carmignac, 'Les Horoscopes de Qumrân', *RevQ*
5/18 (1965) 199-227; M. Delcor, 'Recherches sur un horoscope en langue

Frag. 1 I   4 ...[...]   5 ה[...]   6 vacat   7 ואיש אשר יהיה ק[...]
9 רחבים סגלגלים [...]   9 מעורבים ולוא שאר רוש[ו ...]

Frag. 1 II   1 [...]ג טמא   2 [אבן צונם ...]   3 [...]איש עי[...]
4 [...]...ות וה[נ]ה נצר[ו]ת   5 ושוקיו ארוכות ודקות ואצבעות רגליו
6 דקות וארוכות והואה מן העמוד השני   7 רוח לו בבית האור שש ושלוש
בבית   8 החושך וזה הואה המולד אשר הואה ילוד עליו   9 ברגל השור עני
יהיה וזה בהמתו שור

salvation [...] ... Blessed the man who does her, does not deceive her, does not slander against [her,] does not [with a] *14* fraudulent [spir]it seek her, nor holds fast to her with flatteries. As she was given to his fathers so will he inherit her [and hold fast] to her *15* with all force of his strength and with all his [vig]our without restriction. And he will give her in inheritance to his descendants. I know the strug[gle it takes to do go]od

Frags. 1 - 3 *col.* III *1* to her, for go[od ...] *2* and from the horrors (?) ... [...] *3* and ... [...] *4-6 Blank 7* ... [...] ... [...] *8* ... [... Go]d tests all the pla[ns ...] *9* and he [...] fulfills the words of [his] covena[nt ...] *10* And [G]od does not per[form judg]ment upon those that turn away [...] *11* Did not [Go]d make the hearts, and does he kno[w their thoughts? God sees] *12* all the inmost being, and puts its kidneys to the test. [God made] *13* the tongue, and knows its word. God made hands, [and knows their deeds.] *14* [... whether] good or evil [...] *15* [...] with thoug[hts ...]

4Q186 *4QHoroscope*

hébraïque provenant de Qoumrân', *RevQ* 5/20 (1966) 521-542; A. Dupont-Sommer, 'Deux documents horoscopiques esséniens découverts à Qoumrân', *CRAI* 1966, 239-253; M. Philonenko, 'Deux horoscopes qoumrâniens: identification des personnages', *RHPR* 65 (1985) 61-66; F. Schmidt, 'Astronomie juive ancienne: Essai d'interprétation de 4QCryptique (1Q186)', *RevQ* 18/69 (1997) 125-141

Frag. 1 *col.* I *4-5* ... [...] *6 Blank* [...] *7* And a man who will be [...] *8* wide, circular [...] *9* pleasant and not the flesh of [his] head [...]

Frag. 1 *col.* II *1* [...] impure *2* [...] a granite stone *3* [...] a man of ... [...] *4* [...] ... and s[e]e: secrets. *5* And his thighs are long and slender, and his toes are *6* slender and long. And he is in the second column. *7* His spirit has six (parts) in the house of light and three in the house of *8* darkness. And this is the sign in which he was born: *9* the period of Taurus. He will be poor. And his animal is the bull.

Frag. 1 III 1 ואבה[...] 2 וראושו[...] 3 מיראות [...]ושניו רומות
לאבר ואצבעות 4 ידיו (ע)בות ושוקיו עבות ומלאות [ש]ער לאחת
5 ואצבעות רגליו עבות וקצרות ורוח לו בבית 6 [החושך ש]מונה ואחד
מבית האור ו..ש

Frag. 1 IV 6 [...]שמה אלה 7 [...]יהיה תוך 8 [...] ל

Frag. 2 I 1 סרכמ[ה וע]יניו בין שחורות וב[ין] מגמריות וזקנו 2 ממ.
[...] והיאה תרגל ובת קולו עניה ושניו 3 דקות ויושבות על סרכמה והואה
לוא ארוך 4 ולוא קצר והואה ממולדו אצבעות ידיו דקות 5 וארו[כ]ות
ושוקיו חלקות וכפות רגליו 6 [...]ל[...] ו[י]ושבות על סרכמה ורוח ל[ו]
7 [בבית האור מן ה]עמוד השני שמונה וא[חת] 8 [בבית החושך]מולדו
ילוד הו[א]ה עליו] 9 [...] ה[ו]אה בהמתו ...[...] 10 [...].גי זות[...]
11 [...]...[...]

4Q187-195

No manuscripts have been assigned to these numbers

4Q196 (4QpapTob^a ar) *4QpapTobit^a ar*

J. Fitzmyer, *DJD XIX*, 7-39, pls. I-V
PAM 43.175-43.179
ROC 666, 808, 822, 851, 852
4Q197, 4Q198, 4Q199, 4Q200

Frag. 1 1 [...]שורא די נינו[ה ...]

Frag. 2 1 [חד מ]ן ב^י נינוה והחוי למלכ[א ... ד]י אנה קב[ר אנון
ו]אחוית וכדי ידעת [די] ידע בי 2 [ולי בעה למקט]ל ודחלת וערקת[... כ]ל

Frag. 1 *col.* III   *1* and he will consent [...] *2* and his head [...] *3* terrifying [...]. And his teeth are of differing lengths (?). His fingers *4* are ‹stumpy›. His thighs are stumpy and each one covered in [h]air, *5* and his toes are stumpy and short. His spirit has *6* [ei]ght (parts) in the house [of darkness] and one in the house of light. And ...

Frag. 1 *col.* IV   *6* [...] there. These *7* [...] (he) will be in the middle of *8* [...] ...

Frag. 2 *col.* I   *1* (on) their order. His [ey]es are of a colour between black and striped. His beard is *2* ... [...] and curly. The sound of his voice is simple. His teeth *3* are sharp and regular. He is neither tall *4* nor short, and like that from his conception. His fingers are slender *5* and long. His thighs are smooth and the soles of his feet *6* are [... and] regular. [His] spirit *7* has eight (parts) [in the house of light, in the] second column, and o[ne] *8* [in the house of darkness.] And the sign in which he was born is *9* [...] his animal is [...] *10* [...] ... this [...] *11* [...] ... [...]

4Q196 (4QpapTob^a ar) *4QpapTobit^a ar*

Bibliography: K. Beyer, *ATTME*, 134-147; M. Wise, 'A Note on 4Q196 (Paptob AR^a) and Tobit i 22', *VT* 43 (1993) 566-569; J.A. Fitzmyer, 'Preliminary Publication of pap4QTob^a ar', *Biblica* 75 (1994) 220-224; P. Grelot, 'Les noms de parenté dans le livre de Tobie', *RevQ* 17/65-68 (1996) 327-337

Frag. 1 (= *Tob* 1:17)   *1* [...] the wall of Nineveh [...]

Frag. 2 (= *Tob* 1:19 - 2:2)   *1* [And one o]f the Ninevites [went] and informed [the] king [... th]at I was bur[ying them, but] I found out. And when I knew

ד]י]הוה לי ולא שביק {פ} לי כל מנד[עם]   3   [...]ל[...] חנ]ה אנתתי וטוביה

ברי ולא הוה יומין א[רבעין]   4   [וק]טלוהי תרי בנ]והי ואנון ערקו לטורי

אררט ומלך {ומ]לך} אסרחדו[ן   5   ]ברה בתרה והוא]אשלט לאחיקר בר

ענאל אחי על כל ש[יזפנות]   6   [מלכותה ... ולה הוה ש]לטן על[ ]כ]ל

המרכלות מלכא ובעה אחיקר עלי   7   [ותבת לנינוה ארי ואחי]קר אחי הוה

רב שקה ורב עזקן והמרכל   8   [ו]שיזפן קדם אסרחריב מלך אתור ואשלטה

אסרחדון תנין לה ארי   9   בר אחי הוה ומן בית אבי ומן משפחתי וביומי

אסרחדון [מל]כא כדי תבת   10   לביתי ואתבת לי חנה אנתתי וטוביה ברי

ביום חג שבו[עיא הות] ל[י]   11   שרי טבה ורבעת ל[מאכ]ל ואקרבו

פת[ו]רא לקודמי וחזית נפתניא די קרבו   12   עלוהי שגיאין ואמר]ת

לטו]ביה ברי ברי אזל דבר לכל מן [די ת]השכח בא[חינא]   13   [...] ברי

אזל דבר ואתהייתה ויכל [...]...

[...]   1   *Frag. 6*   [...] אזלי [בתרהון ול[א] נחזי לכי בר [...]   2   [...] ובכת

וסלק[ת לעלית בית [אבוה ...]   3-4   [...]   5   [...] ולא אשמע ח]סד עוד בחיי

ו[...]   6   [...]לק[ב]ל[...]   7   [...] ובריך [שמך קדישא] וי]קירא לכל ע]למין

ויברכ]ונך כל עובדיך]   8   [וכען פנית ע]ליך אנפי ועינ]י נ]טלת וא^מר

לאפטרותני מן ע]ל ארעא]   9   [... אנתה **** י]דע ד]י]דכיה אנה בגרמי

מ]ן כל טמאת גבר]   10   [ולא ג]עלת ש]מי ושם אב]י בכל ארעת שבינא]

יחי]דא אנה] לאבי]   11   [ולא]בר לה אחרן די ירתנ]ה [ואח לה] ו]ק]ריב

לא איתי] ל]ה די]   12   [אנטר נ]פשי לבר ד]י אהו]ה לה אנתה כבר אב]דו

[מני שבע]ת גברין]

[...]   4   [...]...[...]   5   [... שד] קטל להן   6   [... יחידא אני   1   *Frag. 14*

לאבי ולאמי ... חי]י אבי ואמי   7   [... ובר אחרן לא איתי להון]די יקבר

8   [אנון ... לפק]ודי אבוך די פקדך   9   [... וכע]ן שמע לי אחי אל

[that] he knew about me 2 [and sought to ki]ll [me] I took fright and fled. [And a]ll th[at] I had [was seized], and I was left with noth[ing] 3 [... except Ann]a, my wife, and Tobias, my son. However, f[orty] days had not [passed] 4 [when] his [two sons killed him.] And they fled to the mountains of Ararat and [Esarhaddo]n, [his son] ruled {ru[led]} 5 [after him]. And to Ahikar, son of my brother Anael, he gave power over all the t[reasures] 6 [of his kingdom ... so that he held con]trol over [a]ll the king's finances. And Ahikar interceded for me 7 [so that I could return to Nineveh. Now Ahi]kar, my brother, had been the chief of the cupbearers and the keeper of the seals and the treasurer 8 [and] the administrator under Asharcharib, king of Assyria, and Esarhaddon made him his second-in-command. See, 9 he was my brother's son and from my father's house and from my family. And in the days of [ki]ng Esarhaddon, when I had returned 10 to my home and Anna, my wife, had been returned to me, and Tobias, my son, on the day of the Feast of Wee[ks, they] prepared for [me] 11 a good banquet, and I reclined to [ea]t. They brought the table near, in front of me, and I saw that the dishes that they placed 12 upon it were many. And [I] said [to To]bias, my son: « My son, go and fetch all those [you] find from among [our] brot[hers] 13 [...] ... My son, go and fetch them, so they may come and eat [...] ...

Frag. 6 (= *Tob* 3:9-15; cf. 4Q200 1 II)   1 [... Go] after them; may we ne[ver] see a son [...] of yours». 2 [... and she wept and went up] to the upstairs room of [her father's] house [...] 3-4 [...] 5 [... and may I not hear a re]proach again in my lifetime. 6 [And then she spread her hands] tow[ar]ds [the window and prayed] 7 [saying: «Blessed be you, merciful God, and blessed (be)] your holy [and gl]orious name for e[ver, and] may [all your works] bless [you.] 8 [And now, t]o you [I have turned] my face and I have [li]fted [my] eyes: and /say/ that I may be freed from [the earth] 9 [and not return to hear reproaches. You, ****, kn]ow th[at] I am clean in my bones fr[om every impurity of a male,] 10 [that] I [have not def]iled [my] na[me or] my [father's name] in all the land of our deportation; I am [my father's only daugh]ter, 11 he has [no] other son to be [his] heir, nor has he a brother [or a] re[lative for whom] 12 [I should keep] my [so]ul, a son, for who[m I shall b]e a wife. Already seven [husbands] have peri[shed] on me

Frag. 14 *col.* I (= *Tob* 6:14-17; 4Q197 4 II)   4 [...] ... [...] 5 [... And I have heard that the people said that a demon] killed them. 6 [And now I am afraid to die. I am my parents' only daughter, and I am afraid that sorrow for me will bring to the grave the li]fe of my father and of my mother. 7 [... And they have no other son] who could bury 8 [them». And he said to him: «Do you not remem-ber the prec]epts of your father who commanded you 9 [to take a wife from your father's house? No]w, listen to me, my brother, do not 10 [fear this de-

10 [תדחל מן שדא דן וסבה ... בלי]ליא דן   11 [... ס]ב מן לבב   12 [נונא

... ויר]ח שדא וי[ערק]   13 [...] ל[...]

Frag. 14 ii   4 שגיא ר[חמה ולבה דבק בה לחדא וכדי עלו לגוא אחמתא

אמר לה טוביה]   5 עזריה אח]י דברני קשיטא לבית רעואל אחונא ודברה

ואזלו לבית רעואל]   6 וה[ש]כחו לרעואל יתב ק[דם תרע] דרת[ה דרתא]ה ושאלו

שלמה לקדמין ואמר]   7 להון לשלם אתיתון ועל[ו ב]שלם] אחי ואעל אנון

לביתה ואמר לעדנא אנתתה]   8 כמה ד[מה עלימא דן לטובי] ושאל[ת אנון

עדנא ואמרת להון מנאן אנתון אחי]   9 ואמר[ו לה מן בני נפתלי] די שבי[ן

בנינוה ואמרא להון ידעין אנתון לטובי אחונא]   10 וא[מרין לה די די]ידעין

אנח[נא לה השלם הוא ואמרו לה שלם]   11 [ואמר טוביה די] אבי הוא

וש[ור רעואל [...

Frag. 17 ii   1 לבכון ו[בכל נ]פשכון ל[מעבד קושטא אדין י[תפנה

עליכון   2 ולא [יסתר אנפוה]י מנכון ע[וד ... והודו]לה בכל פמכון

3 ובר[כו למרה [קושטא ור]וממו לה אנה בארעת] שביא מהודה לה

4 ומח[וה אנה לג]בורתה ורבו[תה קדם עם חט]אין על לבבכון   5 קו[שטא

עבדו [קדמוה]י מן[יד]ע הן תהוה ס]ליחא] לכון ולאלהי]   6 [מרומם אנה

ונ[פשי למ]לך שמיא ... [כל יומ]י חיי]   7 [... יש]ב[חו רבותה ימללין

בתהלין[[...   8 [... ירושלם [קרית קדשא י[כת]שנכ[י ...]   9 [...]

בקו[שתא הוד]י [...   10 [... יתבנ]ה לכ]י ... [...] 13-11 [...]   14 [...] מן

ד[רין לדרין ינתנון בכי[...   15 [ו]שם רב] יהוה לד]רי עלמא ארין רין כ]ל[

[דין ביזין ו[כ]ל די עלי[כי]   16 [ו]אריררין כ[ל שנאי]כי ו[ל] ממ[ל]ל[ין ע]ליכי

אריר[ין [...

Frag. 18   1 [... שורי]כי וכל ממגרין]ן מגדליכי [...   2 [... אדין [חדי

ובועי בב]ני קשיטיא [...   3 [... טובי כ]ל רחמיכי וטוב]י כל [...   4 [... ע]ל

[כ]ל מכתשיכי ד]י [...   5 [... ברכי ל****] למלכא רבא ד]י [...   6 [...]

שארי]תא מן זרעי ל]מחזה [...   7 [תרעי ירושלם ברקת ו]ספיר תתבנין

mon and take her … in] this [ni]ght *11*[she will be given to you as a wife. And when you enter the bridal chamber, ta]ke some of the heart *12* [of the fish and (some) of its liver, place it upon the embers of the incense and the smell will come out,] the demon [will sme]ll (it), and will [flee] *13* […] … […]

Frag. 14 *col.* II (= *Tob* 6:19 - 7:3; 4Q197 4 III) *4* he lo[ved her] very [much, and his heart clung to her. And when they arrived within Ecbatana, Tobias said to him:] *5* «Azarias, [my] brother, [take me straight to the house of Raguel, our brother». And he took him and they entered the house of Raguel.] *6* And they f[o]und Raguel seated in [front of the door of the] courtyard, [and first they wished him peace. And he said] *7* to them: «In peace you came and [in] peace shall you go, [my brothers». And he made them enter his house. And he said to Edna, his wife:] *8* «How [like Tobit, my uncle's son, is this young man!» And Edna] asked [them and said: «Where are you from, brothers?»] *9* And [they] said [to her: «From the sons of Naphtali,] who are exile[s in Nineveh». And she said to them: «Do you know Tobit, our brother?»] *10* [They] sa[id to her:] «We know [him». «Is he well?» They said to her: «He is well».] *11* [And Tobias [said:] «He is my father». [Raguel] jum[ped up …]

Frag. 17 *col.* II (= *Tob* 13:6-12) *1* your heart and [with all] your [s]oul to [act justly. Then, he] will turn to you *2* and no lo[nger hide his face] from you. [And now, consider what he has done for you and give] him [thanks] with your whole mouth, *3* and ble[ss the Lord of] justice and ex[alt him. I, in the land of] exile, give him thanks *4* and dec[lare] his [p]ower and his great[ness to a nation of sin]ners. According to your heart *5* [act] just[ly] before hi[m. Who] kno[ws whether pa]rdon [will befall you. My God] *6* [I exalt, and] my [s]oul the k[ing of heaven …] all the day[s of my life] *7* [… will pra]ise his greatness. Let them chant psalms […] *8* [… Jerusalem] the holy city, he will [pun]ish you […] *9* [… on] the [ju]st. Give thanks […] *10* [… shall be bui]lt for you […] *11-13* […] *14* [… ge]nerations upon generations will give in you […] *15* [and] a great name [it will be for] eternal [ge]nerations. Curs[ed be al]l [those who] say harsh things and all those who are against [you] *16* [and] cursed be al[l who hate] you and all who [speak again]st you. Cursed […]

Frag. 18   (= *Tob* 13:12 - 14:3; 4Q198 1; cf. 4Q200 7 II) *1* […] your [walls] and all those who make [your towers] fall […] *2* [… Then] be happy and rejoice in the so[ns of the righteous …] *3* [… Blessed are al]l those who love you and bles[sed are all …] *4* [… a]t [a]ll your sufferings whi[ch …] *5* [… Bless ****,] the great king wh[o …] *6* […] the [remna]nt of my descendants to [see …] *7* [The gates of Jerusalem] will be built of [beryl and] sapphire […] *8* [… The

[...] 8 [...] מגדלי ירושלם ד[הב תתבנין ועע]יתא [...] 9 [...]ין ובאבן די
י[...] 10 [...] י]מ[ל]לו להל]לויה [...] 11 [...] בריך עד עלם]עלמיא דביכי
יברכון ש]מה קדישא עד עלם עלמיא[12 [וספו מלי תודת טו]בי ומית
בשלם ב]ר שנין מאה תרתי עשרה וקביר[13 [... והוא בר]שנין חמשין
ותמנ[ה הוה [...] 14 [...] חזות ע]ינוהי חי בטב ובכ]ל עבד ... צדקה[
15 [והוסף למדחל ל]****** ולהודיה רב]ותה ... וקרא] 16 [לטוביה ברה
ושבע]ת בנוהי ובקדה (ופקדה) ואמ]ר לה [...

4Q197 (4QTob^b ar) *4QTobit^b ar*

J. Fitzmyer, *DJD XIX*, 41-56, pls. VI-VII
PAM 43.180, 43.181
ROC 132, 133

Frag. 2   1 [...]ח[יי מסכניא] [...] 2 [...] לכלהון [...]

Frag. 3   1 [... צ]ריך לך] [...] 2 [...]למנדע [...]... 3 [...] אנה[
עזר]יה [... 4 [...] ואמר לה] [...] 5 [...] למנדע בק]ושתא [...

Frag. 4 I   1 [...]אל ידבק [בכס]ף ברי וכא...]...[2 [... ו]אמר לה אל
תדחלי בשלם יהך ברי   3 [...] בש]לם אל תדחלי ואל תצפי לה אחתי
4 [...]ה אר]חה ... ושתק]ה עוד ולא בכה *vacat* 5 [... ומלא]כא עמה
ו]ה]ך] כלבא ... ואזלו [כחדא וסדר להון 6 [... ע]ד דלקת ונחת עלימ]א ...
ושור נו]ן חד רב מן 7 [מיא למב]לע רגל עלימ]א ... א]תקף נ]ונא וג]בר
עלימא   8 [לנונא ואנפק]ה ליבשא ו]אמר לה מלאכא פר]קהי ואנפק]
למררתא ולבב]ה   9 [וכבדה שים ב]ידך ומעוה]י טרד סם הוא מררתא

towers of Jerusalem] will be built [of go]ld and wo[od …] *9* […] and stone of
[…] *10* [… let] them s[a]y: Halle[lujah …] *11* [… Blessed be he for ever] and
ever, for in you they will bless [his holy] na[me for ever and ever».] *12* [And
To]bit's [words of thanksgiving ended], and he died in peace at the a[ge of one
hundred and twelve, and he was buried] *13* [… And he was] fifty-eig[ht] years
[old when …] *14* [… the vision of] his [e]yes. He lived well and in every[thing
he did … justice.] *15* [And he continued to fear] **** and to praise [his]
great[ness … And he called] *16* [Tobias his son and] his [seven] sons and he
commanded him, and sai[d to him …]

4Q197 (4QTob^b ar) *4QTobit^b ar*

4Q196, 4Q198, 4Q199, 4Q200
Bibliography: K. Beyer, *ATTME*, 134-147

Frag. 2 (= *Tob* 4:21 - 5:1) *1* [… the l]ife of the poor […] *2* […] for them all […]

Frag. 3 (= *Tob* 5:12-14) *1* [… ne]cessary for you[…] *2* […] to know … […]
3 […] I am Azar[ias …] *4* […] and he said to him […] *5* […] to know in tr[uth
…]

Frag. 4 col. I (= *Tob* 5:19 - 6:12) *1* [… May] my son not cling [to mon]ey! And
… […] *2* [… and] he said to him: «Do not fear, my son will leave in peace
3 [and he will return to us in peace. Your eyes will see him on the day when he
returns to you in pea]ce. Do not fear and do not be worried for him, my sister,
4 [for a good angel will go with] him, [his] pa[th will be successful and he will
return in peace». And she was silent] and wept no more. *Blank* *5* [The young
man left and] the [ang]el [went] with him; [the dog le]ft [with them, and the
two walked] together. And he arranged for them *6* [… t]o Diqlat (the Tigris).
And [the] young [man] went down [to the river Tigris to bathe his feet, and] a
great [fis]h [leapt] from *7* [the water which tried to swal]low the young man's
foot. [The young man shouted, but the angel said to him: «Catch and] grasp
[the] fi[sh». And] the young man [ca]ught *8* [the fish and grasped it and
brought] it out on dry land. And [the angel said to him: «Spli]t it and remove
[its gall,] its [heart] *9* [and its liver, and keep them in] your hand, but [throw
away] its guts, [for its gall,] its [heart] and its liver [are a good medicine».]

ולבב]ה וכבדה ו[...] 10 [מררתא ול]בבה ו[כבדה ... מן נ]ונא ואכל ואף[
לארחא שוה מליחא] 11 [שארית]א אזלין תריה[ו]ן [כ]חדא [עד] ק[רבו
ל]הון למדי *vacat* [...] 12 [וא]מר לה עזריה אחי מה סם בלבב נונא
ובכ[בדה ובמררתה ... הך] 13 [ת]אתנה קדם גבר או אנתא נגיעי שד או
רוח[באישא ...] 14 [לא]יסחרון סחרתהו[ן] לעלם ומררתא למכחל עי[ני
...] 15 [...]חרריא ויחין וכ[די] עלו לגו מדי וכבר הוא מ[דבק לאחמתא
אמר רפאל] 16 [לעלי]מא ט[ו]ביה אחי ואמר לה הא אנה ואמר לה אבית[
רעואל נבית] 17 [וג]ברא מן בית אבונא הוא ואיתי לה ברא שפירה [...
ואחרן] 18 [לא] איתי לה לה[ן] שרה[... ב]ל[חודי]ה ואנתה ק[רי]ב לה
[על כל אנש למירתה] 19 [וכל די לאבוה סבה]לך ל[אנת]א[ו]דינא ל[ך
... ועלימתא]

Frag. 4 II 1 [דא היא חכימא ותקיפ]א ושפירא לחדא ואבוה רחם] לה
וכל די לה יהב לה] 2 [ול]ך[גזיר למירת ל]אבוהא ועליך דין קשטא גזר
למ[סבה וכען שמע לי] 3 [אחי]תמלל בעל[ימ]תא דא בליליא דן תקימנה
ותסבנה לך לאנת[ה ...] 4 [נעבד לה]משתותא וידע אנה די לא יכול
רעואל למכליה מנך בדיל די הוא ידע 5 [...]ולמסב ברתה מן כל אנ[ש
ארי ה]וא ידע די הן ינתננה לגבר 6 [אחרן ... ספר]מושה וכען[נמלל
בעלי]מת[א]דא ליליא דן ונקימנה 7 [לך ... אדין ענה טוביה ואמר
לרפ]אל עזריה אחי שמעת 8 [... ומיתו כד]י עללין עליה הוו 9 [... ד]חל
אנה [מ]ן שדא די 10 [רחם לה ... שד קטל להן ... לא]בי ולאמי 11 [...י
אבי ואמי... וברא א]חרן לא 12 [איתי להון די יקבר אנון ... לפקודי אבוך
]די פקדך 13 [... וכען שמע לי אחי אל תדחל מן ש]דא דן וסבה

And [the young man split the fish and removed] *10* [the gall,] its [he]art and [its liver. The young man cooked part of] the [fi]sh and ate it, and also [for the journey he prepared with salt] *11* the [rest.] The two of them walked together [until they] ap[proached] Media. *Blank* [The young man questioned the angel *12* [and s]aid to him: «Azarias, my brother, what good medicine is there in the heart of the fish and in [its] liv[er and in its gall?» And he said to him: «If] *13* [you] smoke it before a man or a woman attacked by a demon or by an [evil] spirit [they will flee from them; the attack will cease and not will] *14* their encounters occur ever again. As for the gall, it is to anoint the ey[es of the man on whom burns had been caused,] *15* the scales [shall fall away from him] and they shall be cured». And wh[en] they came within Media and were ap[proaching Ecbatana, Raphael said] *16* [to the young] man: «T[o]bias, my brother». And he answered him: «Here I am». And he said to him: [«We are going to spend the night in Raguel's] house *17* [and] he is a [m]an from our father's house and has a beautiful daughter [whose name is Sarah.] *18* [And] he has [no other son or daughter] exc[ept] Sarah [...] and you are the closest re[lati]ve to her [from all men to inherit her] *19* [and all that belongs to her father. Take her] for yourself as a [wife, and you] have the right [to inherit all the property of her father. This young woman]

Frag. 4 *col.* II (= *Tob* 6:12-19; 4Q196 14 I)   *1* [is sensible, and vivaci]ous and very beautiful, and her father loves [her and all he has he gives to her,] *2* [and the inheritance of] her father [is determined for] you. And as for you, a lawful right has decided [that you] t[ake her. And now, listen to me,] *3* [my brother.] Tonight you will speak about this you[ng] woman, you will engage her and take her for a wif[e, and when we return from Rages] *4* [we will organize] the nuptial feast [for her.] I know that Raguel will not be able to deny her to you because he knows *5* [that it pertains to you to secure] and take his daughter more than to any other ma[n, for h]e knows that if he gives her to [another] man *6* [he deserves death according to the sentence of the book of] Moses. And now, [we shall speak about] this [young] woman tonight, we shall engage her *7* [for you». ... Then Tobias answered and said to Rapha]el: «Azarias, my brother, I have heard *8* [that she has already been given to seven men who died in her bridal chamber. They died whe]n they went in to her. *9* [And I have heard that the people said it was a demon who killed them. And now,] I am [af]raid [o]f the demon who *10* [loves her, for the demon kills those who try to approach her. I am an only son for] my [fa]ther and for my mother *11* [and I am afraid of dying and that sorrow for me might bring to the grave the life of my father and of my mother. And they have] no [ot]her [son] *12* [who could bury them». And he said to him: «Do you not remember the precepts of your fa-ther] who commanded you *13* [to take a wife from your father's house? Now,] listen to me, my brother, do not fear] this [de]mon and take her. *14* [I know that

14-15 [...] 16 [...] למהוה ע[מה עו]רו מן [... 17 [...] וא[ל תדחל] די ל[ך
היא חליקא ולך] דינא גזר למסכה] 18 [...]תשזב]ה ... ו]מדמה אנה די
להוון לך] מנה בנין ול]הוון 19 [... לך כאחין וכדי ש]מע טוביה מלי
רפא]ל די היא ל]ה אחא ומן

Frag. 4 III 1 [זרע בית אבוהי ש]גיא רחמה ולבה (דבק) בה [לחד]א
וכדי עלו לגוא אחמ]תא אמר] 2 לה טוביה עז]ריה אחי ד]ברני קשיטא
לבית רעואל אחונא ודברה ואזל]ו לבית] 3 רעואל ואשכח]ו לר]עוא]ל
י]תב קדם תרע ^דרתה ושאלו שלמה לקדמין ואמר להון 4 לשלם אתיתון
ועלו בשל[ם] אחי ואעל אנון לביתה ואמר לעדנא אנתתה כמא 5 דמה
עלימא דן לטובי בר דדי ושאלת אנון עדנא ואמרת להון מנאן אנתון אחי
6 ואמרו לה מן בני נפתלי [די] שבין בנינוה ואמרא להון ידעין אנתון לטובי
אחונ[א] 7 ואמרין לה די ידעין אנ[ח]נא לה השלם הוא ואמרו לה של[ם
ואמ]ר [טו]ביה 8 די אבי הוא ושור רעואל נשקה ובכ]ה [... 9 טבא על]יך
ברי אנתה] ב]ר [גברא קשיט]א [... 10 צור טוביה] בר אחוהי ובכה [...
11 דכר די ען טב]ח [... 12 למאכל ולמשתה] ... עזריה אחי אמר לרעואל
די ינתן לי שרה] 13 אחתי ושמע [רעואל [...

Frag 5 6 [...] א[ו]יל עמך לבית א]בוך [... 7 [...] ברי אנה אבוך
ועדנא א]מך [... 8 א]ל ת]דחל ברי *vacat* [...] 9 [ואמר ל]ה עזריה אחי
דבר עמך מן תנא אר]בעת עבדין ... [... 10 ו]תאתה בי(ת) גב[א]ל והב
לה כתב וס]ב כספא ... אנתה] 11 [ידע די מנה]להון]ה אבי יו[מיא והן] [...
12 [...]...[...]

in this night she will be given to you as a wife. And when you enter her bridal chamber, take some of the heart of the fish and of its liver,] *15* [place it upon the embers of the incense and the smell will come out, the demon will smell it, flee and will not return to appear near her ever again.] *16* [And when you go to be wi]th her, [first] sta[nd up from ..., both of you, to pray; ask the Lord of heaven that upon you may come mercy] *17* [and salvation. And do n]ot fear, [for] she has been set apart [for] you and [it has been rightfully determined] that you [should take her] *18* [... And] you will save [her and she will walk with you; and] I am sure that for you there will be [sons from her, and] that they will be *19* [like brothers for you». And when] Tobias [he]ard the words of Rapha[el that she was] his sister and from

Frag. 4 *col.* III (= *Tob* 6:19 - 7:10; 4Q196 14 II)   *1* [the descendants of his father's house] he loved her [m]uch and his heart ⟨grew⟩ [extreme]ly fond of her. And when they arrived within Ecba[tana,] *2* Tobias [said] to him: «Az[arias, my brother, t]ake me straight to the house of Raguel, our brother». And he took him and [they] entered [the house] *3* of Raguel. And [they] found [Ra]gue[l sea]ted in front of the door of the courtyard, and first they wished him peace. And he said to them: *4* «In peace you came and in pea[ce] shall you go, my brothers». And he made them enter his house. And he said to Edna, his wife: «How *5* like Tobit, my uncle's son, is this young man!» And Edna asked them and said: «Where are you from, brothers?» *6* And they said to her: «From the sons of Naphtali, [who] are exiles in Nineveh». And she said to them: «Do you know Tobit, o[ur] brother?» *7* They said to her: «We know him». «Is he well?» They said to her: «He is we[ll». And To]bias [sai]d: *8* «He is my father». Raguel jumped up, kissed him and wep[t. And he answered him and said to him:] *9* «Blessings upon [you, my son. You are the] so[n of] a just man!» [... And he fell upon] *10* the neck of Tobias [his brother's son and wept. And Edna his wife and Sarah his daughter also wept for him.] *11* And he slaugh[tered] a ram of the flock [...] *12* to eat and to drink [... «Azarias, my brother, tell Raguel that he should give me Sarah,] *13* my sister». And [Raguel] heard [...]

Frag. 5 (= *Tob* 8:21 - 9:4)   *6* [...] you shall t[ak]e her with you to [your fa[ther's] house [...] *7* [...] my son, I am your father and Edna [is your] mo[ther ...] *8* [do not] fear, my son». *Blank* [Then Tobias called Raphael] *9* [and said to] him: «Azarias, my brother, take with you from here fo[ur servants and two camels and go to Rages] *10* [... and] go to the ⟨house of⟩ Gaba[e]l, give him the document, and re[ceive the money, and take it with you for the wedding, for you] *11* [know that my father] is [counting] the [da]ys, and if [...] *12* [...] ... [...]

4Q198 (4QTob^c ar) *4QTobit^c ar*

J. Fitzmyer, *DJD XIX*, 57-60, pl. VIII
PAM 43.182
ROC 231

Frag. 1   1 צדקה והוסף למדחל לאלהא ולה]ודיה רבותה וקרא לטוביה
[... בנינוה די מל]ל אלהא 3   [... ל]ה ואמר ופקדה בנוהי 2   [ברה ושבעת]
בכל 6   [... לזמ]ניהון יתעבד כלא 5   [... ישראל נביאי ל]לו מ]ל]וה די נינ]ה 4
כלהו]ן ישראל בארע יתבין 7   [ואחינא ... יתאיית]א כל[א אלה]א אמר די
אלהא ורחמין ב]ית יתיב די עדנא 9   [עד ... ושמ]רין צויה [י]שראל[...] 8
בי]קר [לירושלם] [ויבנון 11   [... די] עדנא [עד כקד]ם ל]א [ו]   10   [... אנון
אליל]יהן כל [וירמון בקושטא 13   [... ישראל י]אן[נב] [מללו]...] 12   [...
[...]...[...] 14   [...

Frag. 2   1 לא [...] 2 אנפין ל[...] 3 ...[...] ונדן[4 נפל בפח]מותא
[...]... 5   [...

4Q199 (4QTob^d ar) *4QTobit^d ar*

J. Fitzmyer, *DJD XIX*, 61-62, pl. VIII
PAM 43.182
ROC 231

Frag. 1   1 ...[ואמר טו]ביה די לא אכול תנא ול]א ... [2 [...]...[...]

4Q200 (4QTob^e) *4QTobit^e*

J. Fitzmyer, *DJD XIX*, 63-76, pls. IX-X
PAM 43.183, 43.184
ROC 848, 850

4Q198 (4QTob^c ar) *4QTobit^c ar*

4Q196, 4Q197, 4Q199, 4Q200
Bibliography: K. Beyer, *ATTME*, 134-147

Frag. 1 (= *Tob* 14:2-6; 4Q196 18)   *1* justice. And he continued to fear God and to pr[aise his greatness. And he called Tobias his son and] his [seven] *2* sons and he commanded him and said to [him: ... because he trusted in the word of] *3* God who spo[ke about Nineveh ...] *4* Nine[veh. What the prophets of Israel spo[ke ...] *5* all will happen in [its] tim[e ...] *6* in all that God has said, [everyth]ing will occur [... And our brothers] *7* who dwell in the land of Israel, all of them [will be deported ... And all the land of] *8* [I]srael will be deserted and Sama[ria ... until] *9* the time when [God] will bring [them] back in [mercy ...] *10* [and] not like the first time, [until] the time [that ...] *11* [and they will rebuild] Jerusalem with gl[ory ...] *12* [... as the pro]phet[s of Israel] have spoken [...] *13* [in truth,] and they shall cast away all [their] idol[s ...] *14* [...] ... [...]

Frag. 2 (= *Tob* 14:10 ?)   *1* not [...] *2* face to [...] *3* ... [... and Nadin] *4* fell into the trap of [death ...] *5* ... [...]

4Q199 (4QTob^d ar) *4QTobit^d ar*

4Q196, 4Q197, 4Q198, 4Q200
Bibliography: K. Beyer, *ATTME*, 134-147

Frag. 1 (= *Tob* 7:12 ?)   *1* [... And To]bias [said:] «I shall not eat anything here and no[t ... »]

4Q200 (4QTob^e) *4QTobit^e*

4Q196, 4Q197, 4Q198, 4Q199
Bibliography: Wacholder-Abegg 3, 1-5

Frag. 1 i   1 [...] ...[...]   2 [...] ... עפר   3 [... מאש]ר לחיות כי חרפות
4 [שקר שמעתי ... ועצבת]רבה עמי אמור להרויח   5 [...] ...

Frag. 1 ii   1 יחרפו א[ת אבי ...   2 חיה לכה] ב[ת י]חידה [...
3 עלי אין כשר לה[תלות ... לוא עוד]   4 אשמע ולוא ישמע] אבי [...
5 [הח]לון ות[ת]חנן] [...

Frag. 2   1 [...]...[...]   2 [...] וסבול אותכה במעי]ה [...
3 [...] vacat וכול ימיכה בני לאלהים הי]ה ז[כר]...[...]   4 [...]מאמרו vacat
אמת היה] עושה כ]ול ימי ח[ייכה ואל תלך]   5 [בדרכ]י שקר כי בעשות
ה[אמת מצלחת יה]יה עמך ...[...]   6 [...ו]כאורך ידכה בני היה] עושה
בחסד]צדקות ואל תס[תר פניכה מן]   7 [כול ע]נו אף ממכה לוא יס[תרו
פני אלהי]ם אם יהיה לכה בנ[י רוב כרוב היה]   8 [עוש]ה ממנו צד[קו]ת
[vacat] אם יהיה לך מעט כמעט] היה]   9 [עושה ממנו צדקות בעש]ותך
צדקה שימה טובה [...]

Frag. 4   1 [וכאשר] שלמו להמה ארבע[ת] עשר ימי [החתנה]   2 אשר
נשבע רעואל לעשות לשרה בתו בא [אליו]   3 טו[ב]יה ואמור לו שלחני
כבר אני יודע אשר] אבי איננו]   4 [מאמין ו]אף אמי איננה מאמנת אשר
תראנ[י] עוד ^{ועתה} מבקש   5 [אני אות]כה אבי אשר תשלחני והלכתי אל
אבי כבר   6 ספרתי לך א[י]ככה עזבתים ויומר רעואל לטוביה בני   7 חך
אתי ואני אשלח מלאכים אל טובי אב[יכ]ה וה[מה]   8 [...]...[...]

Frag. 5   1 [... ל[ק]רת בנו עד ...[...]   2 [...] ומר]ורת הדג בידו ונפוץ
[...]   3 [...] ויומר]לו אל תירא אבי [...]   4 [... ע]ל עיניו וחרוק [...]
5 [...]... עיניו וירא את] בנו [... [...]...[...]   6 בני] [...

Frag. 6   1 [...] [המעשה הזה והעלהו vacat?] [...]   2 [...] א[ו]תו והיו
המה {ותומהים} מברכים ו[...]   3 [... מע]שו הגדול ותומהים איכה נראה]
[...]   4 [...] בכן דבר טובי וכתוב תהלה בתשבוחת וא[מור]   5 [ברוך אל

Frag. 1 col. I (= *Tob* 3:6) *1* ... [...] *2* [... and may I return to the] dust; *3* [for it is better for me to die tha]n to live, for [false] reproaches *4* [I have heard ... and there is] much [sorrow] with me. Command that I be freed *5* [from this conflict ...] ...

Frag. 1 *col.* II (= *Tob* 3:10-11; cf. 4Q196 6) *1* Let them [not] reproach [my father ...] *2* You had o[ne living daught]er [...] *3* concerning me. It is not right to [hang myself ... no longer] *4* may I hear, nor may [my father] hear [...] *5* [the wi]ndow and be[g]ged [...]

Frag. 2 (= *Tob* 4:3-9) *1* [...] ... [...] *2* [...] and she carried you in [her] womb [...] *3* [...] *Blank* And all your days /my son/ [re]member God [...] *4* his command. *Blank* [Act] truthfully [a]ll the days of [your] li[fe and do not walk] *5* [on path]s of deceit, for by acting [truthfully success will b]e with you. ... [...] *6* [...] According to the size of your hands, my son, be [generous in doing] just deeds (alms), and do not wit[hdraw your face from] *7* [any po]or person, so that from you [the face of God does] not with[draw.] If, [my] son, you have [much, according to the abundance] *8* [do] ju[st] deeds with it. [*Blank*] If you have little, according to the lit[tle] *9* [do just deeds with it. By] your [do]ing just deeds, a [good] store [...]

Frag. 4 (= *Tob* 10:7-9) *1* [When] the fourteen days of [the wedding feast] ended *2* which Raguel had sworn to have for Sarah, his daughter, To[b]ias came [to him] *3* and said to him: «Allow me to leave, for I know that [my father does not] *4* [believe and] my mother also does not believe that they are going to see [me] again. /And now/ [I] beg *5* you, my father, that you allow me to leave and I will go to my father. Already *6* I have told you how I left them». And Raguel said to Tobias: «My son, *7* stay with me and I will send messengers to Tobit, [yo]ur father and t[hey] *8* [...] ... [...]

Frag. 5 (= *Tob* 11:10-12) *1* [... to] approach his son until ... [...] *2* [... and the ga]ll of the fish in his hand, and he scattered [...] *3* [... and he said] to him: «Do not fear, my father». [...] *4* [... o]n his eyes, and it stinged (?) [...] *5* [...] ... his eyes, and he saw [his son ...] *6* [...] ... my son [...]

Frag. 6 (= *Tob* 12:20 - 13:4) *1* [...] this event. And he ascended. *Blank?* [...] *2* [...] him. And they {were astonished} blessed and [...] *3* [...] his great [de]ed, and they were astonished that there had appeared [...] *4* [...] Thus spoke Tobit and wrote a hymn with praise and s[aid:] *5* [«Blessed be the]

[חי אשר לכול העולמים היאה מלכותו אשר הואה] מכה] 6 [... והוא]ה
מרחם מוריד עד שאול{ה} תחתיה והואה מעלה מתהו[ם] 7 [רבה וג]דול]ה[
ומה אשר יפצה מידו vacat הודו לו בני ישר[אל] 8 [לפני הגוים] אשר
אתמה נדחים בהמה ושמה ספר]ו את גודלו[9 [ורוממו אותו לפני כו]ל חי
כיא הוא אד]יניכ[מה] והוא אלה]יכמה [... 10 [...]...[...]

Frag. 7 i   1 [...]אז שמחי ורוצי   2 [...]וברך את   3 [...] כול
4 [...]...

Frag. 7 ii   1 ירושלם תהלת]ן [... 2 האלהים אש]ר [... 3 אשר] בכי
יברכו את שמו הק]דוש ל]עולם [... 4 ותמ]ו דברי תודה טובי וימ]ות
בשלום בן] [... 5 [...]והו]א בן שמונה וחמש]ים [... 6 [... מ]ראה] ו]אחר
אר]בע וחמשים חיה [...

4Q201 (4QEn[a] ar) *4QEnoch[a] ar*

J.T. Milik, *The Books of Enoch. Aramaic Fragments from Qumrân Cave 4* (Oxford:
Clarendon, 1976) 139-163, 340-343, pls. I-V
PAM 43.197, 43.198
ROC 821, 904
4Q202, 4Q204, 4Q205, 4Q206, 4Q207, 4Q212

Col. i   1 [... בה]ן חנך לבח]ירין [... 2 [...] מתלוה]י וא]מר[[...
3 [...] ומן מלי [עירין] וקדישין כלה] [... 4 [... להד]ן דרה להן לד]ור
ר]חיק אנה אמ]לל [... vacat] 5 [...] ינפק קדיש]ה ר]בה מן מ]דורה [... 6 [...]

living [God], whose kingdom is for all the centuries;   he is the one who [punishes] *6* [... and he is the one who] has pity, he brings down to the deepest Sheol and brings up from the abyss *7* [immense and gr]eat. And who can grab from his hand? *Blank* Give him thanks, children of Isra[el,] *8* [before the nations,] amongst whom you are scattered, and there tell [his greatness,] *9* [and exalt him before eve]ry living creature, for he is yo[ur] Lord, and he is [your] Go[d ...] *10* [...] ... [...]

Frag. 7 *col.* I (= *Tob* 13:13-14)   *1* [...] Then be happy and rejoice *2* [...] and bless the *3* [...] all *4* [...] ...

Frag. 7 *col.* II (= *Tob* 13:18 - 14:2; cf. 4Q196 18)   *1* Jerusalem a hymn [...] *2* the God who [...] *3* because [in you they will bless his h]oly [name] for[ever ...»] *4* And [Tobit's words of thanksgiving] ended [and he di]ed in peace in the age of [...] *5* [... and h]e was fif[ty]-eight years old [...] *6* [...] his [si]ght [and] afterwards [he lived fifty-]fo[ur years ...]

4Q201 (4QEnª ar) *4QEnochª ar*

Full bibliography until 1989: F. García Martínez, E.J.C. Tigchelaar, '*1 Enoch* and the Figure of Enoch. A Bibliography of Studies 1970-1988', *RevQ* 14/53 (1989) 149-174; *Full bibliography until 1996:* E. Larson, *The Translation of Enoch from Aramaic into Greek* (JSJS 53; Leiden: Brill, *forthcoming*)

Col. I (= *1 Enoch* 1:1-6)   *1* [Words of blessing with whi]ch Enoch [blessed] the chos[en just ones, who will be present on the day of distress to eliminate all the enemies and wicked people,] *2* [while the just will be saved. Enoch, a just man to whom a vision of the Holy One and of heaven was revealed, announced] his oracles [and sa]id: [«The vision of the Holy One of heaven] *3* [was revealed to me, and I heard] it all from the words of [the Watchers] and the Holy Ones [and because I heard it from them, I knew and understood everything] *4* [not for thi]s generation but for a [fu]ture genera[tion I shall sp[eak. Now I speak about the chosen, concerning them I declare my oracle, saying:] *5* [*Blank*] The [Gr]eat Holy One shall leave [his] dw[elling and the eternal God will descend upon the earth and will walk to Mount Sinai and will

ר]בה ויופע ב[תקף] גבור[תה ...] 7 [... קצו]ת ארעה ויזו[עון כ]ל קצו]ת

[...] 8 [...] רמן וי[...] 9-15 [...]

Col. II   1 [...]ן ולא מעב[רין [בסרכן ח]זו] לארעה וא[תבו]ננו בעבד[ה

2 [מן קדמיה לא[חרנה דמ[נ]ד[עם לא ל[אשניה וכל מתח[ז]א [לכן] חזו

לדגלי   3 [קיטה ...]... עליה ובדגלי שתוא ד[כל]ארעא   4 [תתמלא מין

ו]עננה מטרה שפכין חזו דכל איל[ניה] כלהן מיבישין   5 [... ברא [מן

ארבעת עסר אילני[ן] דעליהן מתקימי⌐ ⌐   6 [... עד]דתרתין ותלת שנין

[יעברן] חזו לכן לדגלי   7 [קיטה די שמשה בהן כוי]ה ושלקה ואנתן טלל

ומסתרין בעין מן קדמיה   8 [על אנפי ארעא כויתה ולמ]דרך על עפרה

ו]ע]ל [כפ]יה לא תשכחון מן   9 [... בכל א[ילניה כלהן יתניצ[ון] עליהן בהן

ירוקין וחפין   10 [... לה]דר תשבחה [הל]ל]לו ו]אתבוננו בכל עבדיה אלין

11 [...]הוא לעלם דעלמין עבד כל עבדיה אלין שנה   12 [...] ו]כלהן עבדין

ממרה ואנתן שניתן עבדכן   13 [... ותע]ברון עלוהי רברבן וקשין ביום

(בפום) טמתכן   14 [... לב]בן לת שלם לכן אדין יומיכן תלוט[ון ו]שני

15 [... ושנ]י אבדנכן יסגין בל[וט ע]ל[מין ורח]מין   16 [... שמהתכ]ן ללוט

עלם ל]כל [...]   17 [...] ו]לכל[ל [...] 18-27 [...]

Col. III   1 ואמרו לה כלהן נמ]א [...]   2 נתוב כלנה מן מלכה ד]ן [...]

3 כלהן כחדה ואחרמ]ו [...]   4 ביומי ירד על [ראש חרמון [...]   5 די ימו

ואחר]מו חד לחד ב[ה ואלין [שמהת רביניהן [vacat]   6 שמיחזה ד]י הוה

ראשהן ארעתק]ף תנין לה רמט[אל תליתי]   7 לה כוכבא]ל רביעי לה ...אל

חמ]ישי לה רעמ א]ל שתיתי לה]   8 דניאל שבי]עי לה זיקיאל תמי]ני לה

appear] *6* [with his gr]eat [army] and will appear in [the strength of his] might [from the height of the heavens. All the Watchers will shake and will be punished in secret places] *7* [in all the end]s of the earth; [a]ll the ends [of the earth] will spl[it and they will be seized with shuddering and fear as far as the edges of the earth. They will split and fall] *8* [and] the heights [will dissolve] and [the high mountains] will [be made low …] *9-15* […]

Col. ii (= *1 Enoch* 2:1 - 5:6; 4Q204 1)   *1* [they appear in thei]r [constellations] and [they] do not transgr[ess] their order. Ob[serve] the earth and con[sid]er /its/ works *2* [from the first to] the [l]ast, how [n]one changes and everything is vis[ib]le [to you.] Observe the signs of *3* [the summer: …] … above it. And the signs of winter: how [all] the earth *4* [is filled with water and] the clouds pour rain. Observe how all [the] tre[es] wither altogether *5* [and lose all their leaves, apart] from fourteen trees whose leaves remain, *6* [and do not renew their leaves until] two or three years [go by]. Observe for yourselves the signs of *7* [summer: how then (in it) the sun burns] and warms and you look for shade and relief from it *8* [upon the scorching face of the earth] without finding a way of walking on the dust or [o]n the [sto]nes because of *9* [the heat. Observe and understand all the t]rees; on all of them their leaves sprout, turn green, and cover *10* [the trees, and all their fruits are for spl]endid praise. [Pra]is[e and consider all these works *11* [and realise that God, who lives] for everlasting eternity, has made all these works. Year *12* [after year his works do not change, instead] they all carry out his word. However, you have changed your works *13* [and do not carry out his word, instead you tres]passed against him with great and harsh (words) with your unclean ‹mouth› *14* [against his greatness. Hard-hea]rted ones, there will be no peace for you! This is why you will curse your days [and] the years of *15* [your life will perish … The year]s of your destruction will increase with an [ever]la[sting] cu[rse. There will be no mer]cy *16* [or peace for you. This is why yo]ur [name will be] (an) everlasting curse for [all the just ones and through you will be cursed] *17* [all the accursed; and all the sinners and evil ones will swear by you,] and to all [the sinners …] *18-27* […]

Col. iii (= *1 Enoch* 6:4 - 8:1; 4Q202 ii; 4Q204 ii)   *1* And all of them said to him: «We will take [an oath and swear, all under oath, one to another not to] *2* go back, any of us, on th[is] enterprise [until we have completed this work». Then they took an oath] *3* all of them together and they swore under oath [with each other. They were two hundred, all who went down] *4* in the days of Yared upon [the peak of Mount Hermon. They called the mountain «Hermon»] *5* because they took an oath and swore under oa[th with each other upon] it. These are [the names of their chiefs: *Blank*] *6* Shemihazah, wh[o was their chief; 'Ar'teqo]f, second to him; Ramt['el, third] *7* to him; Kokab'e[l, fourth to him; …-'el, fi]fth to him; Ra'ma'e[l, sixth to him;] *8* Dani'el, sev[enth to

ברקאל תשיע]י לה[9   עסאל עסירי]ן לה חרמוני חדעסר]א לה מטר אל

תריעסר]ר לה[10   עננאל תלתת עסר]לה סתואל אר]בעת {א}עׄסר לה

שמשי]אל חמשת[11   עסר לה שהריאל]ש]תת עסר לה תמיאל שבעת]

עסר לה[12   טוריאל תמנית עס]ר[לה ימי]א]ל תשעת (עסר) לה]יהדיאל

עסרין לה[13   אלין אנון רבני רבׄנׄיׄ עס]ר]תא אנׄון ור]בניהן[כלהן נסבו

להן[14   נשין מן כל די בחרו ו]שריו ...[15   ולאלפה אנין חרשה ו]כשפה

...[16   ] והויה בטנן מנהן ויל]דה ...[17   הוו מתילדין על ארעה] כילדותהן

ומתרבין כרביותהן ודי הוו אכלין]   18   עמל כל בני אנשא ולא י]כילו אנשא

לאספקה להן ...[19   קשרין לקטלה לאנשא ו]... מן[

20   קובל כל כנף ו]חיו]ת ארעה]ת ורחשיה ...[21   וב]שמיה ונני ימה ולמכל

בשר]הן ...[23-22]...[...]... 27-24]...[

1   שמי חזה אלף חבר]ו ... חרמוני אלף למשרא[2   כ]שפו   *Col.* iv

וחרטמו ותוש]ין ברקאל אלף נחשי ברקין כוכבאל אלף]   3   נ]חשי כוכבין

זי{כׄ}אׄ]ל אלף נחשי זיקין ארעתקף אלף נחשי ארע]   4   שמ]שיאל אלף

נחשי שמ]ש שהריאל אלף נחשי] שה]ר וכלהן שריו]   5   לגלי]ה רזין

לנשיהן ולקבל מעבד ד]ן אבדו אנשא] מן ארעא וק]להן[6   סלק ק]דם

שמיה אדין] אדיק מיכאל] ושריאל ו]רפאל וגבריא]ל [7   מן קד]שי שמיה

על ארעא וחז]ו דם סגי שפ]יך על ארע]א וכל] ארעא[8   אתמלית ר]שעה

ו]המסה די]את]חטי עליה] ...[9   ואמרו קדמ]יהן ד]קלה וז]עק]תה

בח]רבות בני ארעא סלקין עד]   10   תרעי שמי]ה ואמרו לקדי]שי ש]מיה

...[11   די קבל]ן נפשת ... וא]מרן ...[18-12   ]... 22-19]...[...]

]... 27-23[

1   ]...[.]...[2   ]...[3   ...]ה ק]שטט]ה...]לנצ]ללה[4   ]ולמפלט   *Col.* v

עד]עלמה ו]מנה] ... על]מ]י]ה   5   ]ולרפאל אמ]ר א]זל ...]יתה   *vacat*

ל]השוכה] ...[27-6[

him; Zeq'el, eigh]th to him; Baraq'el, nint[h to him;] *9* 'Asa'el, tenth [to him;
Hermoni, elevent]h to him; Matar'el, twelf[th to him;] *10* 'Anan'el, thirteenth
[to him; Sato'el, fo]urteenth to him; Shamshi['el, fif-] *11* teenth to him;
Sahari'el, [si]xteenth to him; Tumi'el, seven[teenth to him;] *12* Turi'el,
eighteen[th] to him; Yomi['e]l, nine‹teenth› to him; [Yehadi'el, twentieth to
him.] *13* These are the chiefs of the /chi[ef]-of-/te[n]s. Th[ey and th]eir
[ch]iefs [all took for themselves] *14* women, from all they chose, and [they
began to penetrate them, to be defiled by them] *15* and to teach them sorcery,
[incantations and the cutting of roots and to explain herbs.] *16* They became
pregnant by them and gave [birth to giants, some three thousand cubits tall,
who] *17* were born upon the earth [in keeping with their infancy and grew at
the rate of their growth and consumed] *18* the work of all the sons of men, but
not were [the men able to supply them. The giants] *19* plotted to kill the men
and [to consume them. They began to sin and to …] *20* against all the birds and
[animal]s of [the] earth [and (against) the reptiles who move upon the earth
and in the waters] *21* [and in] the sky /and the fish of the sea/, and to consume
the flesh [of one another and drink the blood. Then] *22-23* […] … […]
24-27 […]

Col. IV (= *I Enoch* 8:3 - 9: 3. 6-8; 4Q202 III)   *1* Shemihazah taught incantations
[and (how) to cut roots; Hermoni taught (how) to undo magic,] *2* [sor]cery,
magic and skill[s; Baraq'el taught the signs of the shafts; Kokab'el taught]
3 the [si]gns of the stars; Zeq'e[l taught the signs of the lightning; 'Ar'teqof
taught the signs of the earth;] *4* [Sham]shi'el taught the signs of the su[n;
Sahari'el taught the signs of] the mo[on. And all began] *5* [to reveal] secrets to
their wives, and because of th[is] doing [men expired] from the earth, and
[the] out[cry] *6* went rig[ht up to the heaven. Then] Michael, [Sariel,]
Raphael, Gabri[el] gazed *7* from the sanc[tuaries of the heavens to the earth
and saw] much blood pour[ed upon] the [earth] and all [the earth] *8* was filled
with wi[ckedness and] violence [perpe]trated upon it. [Hearing this the four
of them went] *9* and said to [themselves that] the outcry and the w[ai]l for the
de[struction of the sons of the earth went right up to] *10* the gates of heaven.
[And they said to the hol]y ones of he[aven: «It is now to you, holy ones of
heaven] *11* to whom [the souls of the sons of men] appeal sa[ying:] *12-18* […]
19-22 […] … […] *23-27* […]

Col. V (= *I Enoch* 10:3-4)   *1-2* […] *3* [… Teach the j]ust man [what he had to do
and the son of Lamech] to sav[e his soul for life] *4* [and to escape] for [ever.
And] from him [a plant will be planted and all the generations of the wo]r[ld]s
[will be founded.] *Blank* *5* [He sa]id [to Raphael;] «G[o, then, Raphael and
bind Azael hand and foot and hurl] him into [darkness».] *6-27* […]

[...]ות[ת]רמי[...] 4   [...]...י[תקשטון ו] 3   [...]...[...] 2-1   *Col.* VI

[...] 13-7 [... א[פתח ובאדי]ן ...[6   [...] אש[גר אנה ...] 5

[...] 27-18 [...]...[...] 17-14

4Q202 (4QEnᵇ ar) *4QEnochᵇ ar*

J.T. Milik, *The Books of Enoch*, 164-178, 344-346, pls. VI-IX
PAM 43.203
ROC 380

[טבן ו]שפירן 3   [...] והוא כד[י ... 2   [...]ומי [חייהון 1   *Col.* II [כו]ל[י]

[...]נמא 7   [...]ואמר[ו לה כולהון 6   [...] 5   [...]ואתמ[ללו 4   [...]

שתות עשרי לה 15   [...] נעבד[... 9-14   [...]לכא ד[ן עד די מ]

שתת שתריאל עשרי לה [...] 16   חמ[שת ל]ה עשר[י ארבעת שתועל

עשרי תמנית[17   [טו]ריאל[ו]{י}מאל[לה עשר[י שב[ע]ת ת[מיאל לה

אלין עש[רתא רבני אנו]ן לה עש[ל עד]יא]ל יהד[י עשר[י תשעת ימאל לה

[... 19   ושריו די בחר]ן נשין מן כו[ל נסבו להון כולהון ורבניהון אנון[18

על מתילדין הווא ...[21   [...] 20   [...]פתא שתא ולכש]ולאלפה אנין לחר[

בני כול עמל[אכלין הו]וא[ד]י ומתרבין כרביותהון כי]לדות[הון וארעה

כול] קובל מן [... 23   להון[לאשפ]קה אנשא יכילו ולא אנשא

בשרהון ולמכל כול] על רשיעין אדין קבלת ארעא דמ]א[שתין [ו]חשי[א ... 25   [כנף וחיות ארעא ור]חשי[א ... 24

מתעבד בה מא [כול] על רשיעין על ארעא קבלת אדין דמ]א [שתין והווא לאלין אלין

ד[י ושר[ינין] פרזל די חרבן ל[מעבד [לאנשא א]ל[ף אל[ל] עש]א[ל 26   *vacat*

404

Col. vi (= *1 Enoch* 10:21 - 11:1)   *1-2* [...] ... [...] *3* [And all the sons of men will be]come just and [all of them will worship me; every nation] *4* [will bless me] and prostrate [itself. The whole earth will be cleansed of all defilement and all] *5* [impurity. And] I [shall not again s]end [upon them either anger or punishment for all the generations] *6* [of the world. And the]n I [will open ...] *7-13* [...] *14-17* [...] ... [...] *18-27* [...]

4Q202 (4QEn^b ar) *4QEnoch^b ar*

4Q201, 4Q204, 4Q205, 4Q206, 4Q207, 4Q212
Bibliography: Cf. 4Q201

Col. ii (= *1 Enoch* 5:9 - 6:4 + 6:7 - 8:1; 4Q201 iii; 4Q204 ii)   *1* [al]l the [d]ays [of their life ...] *2* It happened that wh[en in those days the sons of men increased,] *3* pretty and [attractive daughters were born to them. The Watchers, sons of the sky, saw them and lusted for them] *4* and sa[id to each other: «Let's go and choose out women from among the daughters of men and sire for ourselves] *5* [sons». However, Shemihazah, who was their chief, said to them: «I am afraid you do not want to carry out] *6* [this deed and I alone will be guilty of a great sin». They replied] and [all] said [to him:] *7* «Let us [all] take an oath [and all swear under oath to each other not to go back on] th[is cou]nsel [until] *8* we have performed [this deed» ...] *9-14* [...] *15* ['Anan'el, thirteenth to him; Sato'el, fourteent]h to him; [Shamshi'el, fi]f- *16* [teenth to him; Shahari'el, sixteenth to him; Tu]mi'el, sev[en]teen[th to him; {Yo}]{mi'el} /[Tu]ri'e[l]/, *17* [eighteenth to him; Yomi'el, nineteen]th to him; Yehadi['el, tw]entieth [to him. /The]y are the chiefs of te[ns.]/ Those *18* [and their chiefs all took for themselves] women, choosing from al[l they chose,] and they began *19* [to penetrate them and be defiled by them and teach them sor]cery, incanta[tions and the cutting of roots] *20* [and to explain herbs. They became pregnant by them and gave birth to giants, some three] *21* [thousand cubits tall, who were born upon the earth in keeping with their in]fancy [and grew at the rate of their growth and] consumed *22* [the labour of all the sons of men, without the men being able to sup]ply [them. The giants] *23* [plotted to kill the men and to consume them and they began to sin and to ... against all] *24* [the birds and animals of the earth and the re]ptiles [which move upon the earth and in the sea] *25* [and in the skies and the fish of the sea /and for some to consume the flesh of the others and] drink [the] blood. [Then the earth denounced the wicked for all] that/ had been done on it. *Blank* *26* 'Asa'e[l] ta[ug]ht [men to] manufacture swords of iron and breast-[plates o]f copp[er

נ]ח[ש ואחזיא   27   להון מא ית]חפר והיך מא י]עבדון ד]הבא למ]עבדה מכונא

ו[ו]על כספא למעבדה לצמידין]...[28   ]לנשיא אחזיא הו]א על כוחלא ועל

צדיד]א]...[29   ]...[vacat

Col. III   1   ]...[והוו]א פח]זין ... שמיחז]ה אל]ף חברו]ן]... 2   ]...[חרמוני

א]לף חרש למ]שרא כשפו וחרתמו ותושין ברקאל]אל]ף נחשי]   3   ]ברקין

כוכבאל א]לף נחשי כוכב]ין זיקיאל אלף נחשי זיקין]...[4   ]... ארע]תקף

אלף נחשי]י]ארע] שמשיאל אלף נחשי שמש שהריאל]   5   ]אלף נחשי

שהר] וכולהון שריו לגליה]רזין לנשיהון ולקובל מעבד דן]   6   ]אבדו

אנשא מן אר]עא וקלא]סלק קודם ש]מיא [vacat]   7   ]אדין אדיק]מיכאל

ושריא]ל ורפאל וג]ברי]אל מן קודשי שמיא על ארעא]   8   ]וחזוא דם סגיא

שפי]ך]ע]ל ארעא] וכול ארעא אתמלאת רשעא וחמסא די אתחטא]

9   ]עליהא ... ואמרו קודמיהון די קלא וזעקתא]   10   ]בחרב]ות בני]י אר]עא

סלק]ין עד תרעי שמיא ואמרו לקדישי שמיא]...[11   ]... שמ]יא]... די

קב]לן נפש]ת]...[12   ]...[13   ]... ר]פאל ומיכ]אל]...[14   ]...[מרנא

רבא]הו]א מרא עלמא]...[15   ]כורס]א יקרך לל}ל{לכל דר דריא די מן

עלמ]א]...[16   ]...[...]...[28-17]...[

Col. IV   1-4]...[5   ]... עו]ית]א ... מ]ריא אז]ל]...[6   ]בנ]י עיריא]

... וב]קרב אבדן]...[ו]ארו]כת]...[7   ]כול בעו]ל]א ... למח]יא חיי]ן]...[

8   ]... ו]אוד]ע]   9   ]ל]שמ]יחז]א ולכ]ול חברו]הי די אתחברו לנשיא]...[

10   יבדון בניהון ויח]זון לאבד]ן]...[ד]...[שבעין ד]רין]...[

11   ארעא עד יומא רבא]   12-28]...[

and showed] *27* them what is [dug up and how] /they could work [the] go[ld to fashion it/ rea]dy; /and as for/ silver, /to fashion it/ for bracelets [and other jewellery for women.] *28* [To the women he showed] about antimony and eye-shadow [and all the precious stones] *29* [and about dyes …] *Blank*

Col. III (= *1 Enoch* 8:2 - 9:4; 4Q201 IV)   *1* [wickedness became great and they] stray[ed in all their paths. Shemihaza]h taug[ht incantations] *2* [and (how) to cut roots; Hermoni ta]ught (how) to u[ndo] magic, [sorcery, magic and skills; Baraq'el] taught [the signs of] *3* [the shafts; Kokab'el ta]ught the signs of the star[s; Zeq'el taught the signs of the lightning; …'el taught] *4* [the signs of …; 'Ar']teqof taught the sign[s of the] earth; [Shamshi'el taught the signs of the sun; Sahari'el] *5* [taught the signs of the moon.] And all began to reveal [se-crets to their wives. And because of this doing] *6* [men expired from] the [ear]th, and the outcry [went right up to the he]aven. [*Blank*] *7* [Then] Michael, Sarie[l, Raphael and Ga]bri[el gazed from the sanctuaries of the heavens to the earth] *8* [and saw much blood pou]red [up]on the earth; [and all the earth was filled with wickedness and violence perpetrated] *9* [upon it. Hearing this the four of them went and said to themselves that the outcry and the wail] *10* [for the destruct]ion of /the s[ons of]/ [the] ear[th went] right [up] to the gate[s of heaven. And they said to the holy ones of heaven: «It is now to you,] *11* [holy ones of hea]ven [to whom] the sou[ls of the sons of men ap]peal [saying: Take our case in front of the Most High] *12* [and our destruction in front of the Majestic Glory and in front of the Lord of all the lords in respect of majesty».] *13* [Ra]phael and Micha[el, Sariel and Gabriel went and said in front of the Lord of the world:] *14* [«You are] our great Lord, [you are] the Lord of the world; [you are the King of kings. The heavens are] *15* the [throne] of your glory /for all/ the generations which exist since eternity [and all the earth is the footstool in front of you for all of eternity»] *16* […] … […] *17-28* […]

Col. IV (= *1 Enoch* 10:8-12)   *1-4* […] *5* [all si]ns. [And to Gabriel] the [Lo]rd [said]: «G[o to the bastards and the sons of whoring and exterminate] *6* [the son]s of the Watchers [from among the sons of men; and send them in] a war of attrition [for there will not be] lo[ng days for them.] *7* [Absolutely] n[o request in their favour will be granted to their fathers; for they hope to li]ve an [everlasting] life [or that] *8* [each one of them will live five hundred years». And to Michael the Lord said: «Go, Michael and] tel[l] *9* Shem[ihaza]h and a[ll] his [friends] who associated with [women to be defiled by them in their uncleanness that] *10* their sons will expire and they will s[ee the extermi-nat]ion [of their loved ones; chain them up for] seventy ge[nerations in the valleys of] *11* the earth until the great day [of their judgment» …] *12-28* […]

Col. VI 4-1 [...] 5 [... ודי]ן לה[וא ... 6 [... לא תת]ובון ו]לא
[...] 7 [... די]ן גז]יר למאסרכו]ן [עד כול יומי עלמא] 8 [...] די לאבד]נא
[...] 9 [ב]ניהון]וב]קנינ]יא די חביביכון ...] 10 [... ו]ק]ודמיכו]ן [יפ]לון
על] חרב אבד]ן [...] 28-11

4Q203 (4QEnGiantsᵃ ar) 4QBook of Giantsᵃ ar

J.T. Milik, *The Books of Enoch*, 310-317, pls. XXX-XXXII
PAM 42.436, 43.201, 43.202
ROC 188, 189, 906
1Q23, 1Q24, 2Q26, 4Q530, 4Q531, 4Q532, 4Q533?, 4Q556, 6Q8
Bibliography: J.T. Milik, 'Turfan et Qumrân. Livre des Géants juif et manichéen', in G. Jeremias, H.-W. Kuhn, H. Stegemann (eds.), *Tradition und Glaube* (Göttingen: Vandenhoeck & Ruprecht, 1971) 117-127; J.A. Fitzmyer,

Frag. 1 1 כדי אקו]ם ... 2 ברקאל]... 3 אנפי עוד]... 4 אנה
קא]ם ...]

Frag. 2 1 עליהון]... 2 vacat [...] 3 [וע]נ]ה מהו]י ...]

Frag. 3 1 [...]ה[...] 2 חברוה]י ... 3 חובבש ואדכו]... 4 ומה
תתנונני לק]טלה ...]

Frag. 4 1 [...] בהון .[...] 2 vacat [...] 3 [באדי]ן אמר אוהיה
לה]היה אחוהי ... 4 [...].[...] מן עלוי ארעא וש.[...] 5 ... אר]עא vacat
כ]די ... 6 [...]שויו ובכו קוד]ם חנוך ... 7 [...]ל]ל...]

Frag. 5 1 [...]...[...] 2 [...]חמס אנו]שא ... 3 [...]קטילו]...]

Col. vi (= *1 Enoch* 14:4-6; 4Q204 vi)   *1-4* [… may your request] *5* [not be granted to you for all the days of eternity, and the verdi]ct [against you] be [decided and pronounced;] *6* [right from now may you not re]turn [to heaven] and [not ascend for all] *7* [eternity; verdi]ct is pron[ounced to shackle yo]u [for all the days of eternity;] *8* [before this may you see] that for destruct[ion are all your loved ones and all] *9* their [so]ns [and] the belongings [of your loved ones and their sons, you will not enjoy] *10* [they /will f]all/ be[fore you] on [a destructive sword …] *11-28* […]

4Q203 (4QEnGiantsª ar) *4QBook of Giantsª ar*

D. Harrington, *MPAT*, 72-75; K. Beyer, *ATTME*, 119-124; J.C. Reeves, *Jewish Lore in Manichaean Cosmogony: Studies in the Book of Giants Traditions* (Cincinnati: Hebrew Union College, 1991); F. García Martínez, 'The Book of Giants', in *Qumran and Apocalyptic. Studies on the Aramaic Texts from Qumran* (STDJ 9; Leiden: E.J. Brill, 1992) 97-115; L.T. Stuckenbruck, *The Book of Giants from Qumran* (TSAJ 63; Tübingen: Mohr Siebeck, 1997) 66-100

Frag. 1   *1* When I ar[ise …] *2* Baraq'el […] *3* my face still […] *4* I arise […]

Frag. 2   *1* over them […] *2* *Blank* […] *3* [And] Mahaw[ai replie]d […]

Frag. 3   *1* […] *2* his friends […] *3* Hobabes and ADKW […] *4* What will you give me to ki[ll …?]

Frag. 4   *1* […] in them […] *2* […] *Blank* […] *3* [The]n 'Ohyah said to Ha[hyah, his brother …] *4* […] on top of the earth and … […] *5* […] the [ear]th. *Blank* W[hen …] *6* […] they bowed down and wept in front [of Enoch …] *7* […]

Frag. 5   *1* […] … […] *2* […] violence done to me[n …] *3* […] they were killed […]

באד]ין 5   *vacat* 4   [...] ותוקפ[כ]ה 3   [...]...[...] 2-1   *Frag. 7* i
אמר] אוהיה לההי[ה אחוהי ...[אדין עני ולוא 6 לנא [אל]ה לעזא[ז]ל ועבד
ל[ה ... בני] עירין 7 גבריא ול[ו]א יתנשון כול חב[י]ביהון [.... לה עגננא
ותקף לכ]ה]

ותנינא 7   [...] לתרי לוחיא 6   [... לכה מה]וי 5   [...] 4-1   *Frag. 7* ii
עד כען לא קרי]ן [...

ספ]ר 1   *Frag. 8*   [... ר]   *vacat* 2   [...] פרשגן לוחא תני[נ]א די 3
אי]גרתא [...   4 בכתב די חנוך ספר פרשא[...]   5 וקדישא לשמיחזה
ולכול ח[ברוהי ...]   6 ידיע להוא לכון ד[י]ל[א ...]   7 ועובדכון ודי נשיכון
[...]   8 אנון [ו]בני[הו]ן ונשיא ד[י בניהון ...]   9 בזנות[כ]ון ב[א]רעא והוה
ע]ליכו[ן ...]   10 וקבלה עליכון ועל עובד בניכון [...]   11 חבלא די
חבלתון בה   *vacat* [...]   12 עד רפאל מטה ארו אבד[נ]א [...   13 ודי
במדבריא וד[י] בימיא ופשר צבור[א ...   14 עליכון לבאיש וכען שרוא
אסורכון מח[ב]ל [...   15 וצלו *vacat* [...]

[... הדר יק]רך [*Frag. 9*   1 [...]...[...]   2 [...] וכול [...]   ע]לין מן קודם
[... תקפתכה]   3 [...יק]רך די כול רזיא יד[ע אנתה ...   4 [...]וכול צבו לא
[... עלמיא]   5 [... ק]ודמיכה *vacat* וכען ק[...]   6 [...]מלכות רבותכה לש[ני
[...]   7 [...]ו.ם[...] *vacat*   8 [...]י[ן...

תצבא[...]   3 [...]...[...]   2 [... שגית ו.[...]   *Frag. 10*   1 [...] ו[כען מרא]י
[...].[...]   4 [...]וכ]

[... וכפו]רא 2   [...]   *Frag. 11* ii   1

[...]אמר לה[...]   2 [באד]ין [... ק]ו[ד]ם חנוך [...   *Frag. 13*   1 [ושו]לי ו מן
[...]   3 [די לא] איתי לכה ש[לם [...   4 [...]למהוה] [...

410

Frag. 7 *col.* I   *1-2* […] … […] *3* and [yo]ur power […] *4 Blank 5* Th[en] 'Ohyah [said] to Hahy[ah, his brother …] Then he punished, and not *6* us, [bu]t Aza[ze]l and made [him … the sons of] Watchers, *7* the Giants; and n[o]ne of [their] be[loved] will be forgiven […] … he has imprisoned us and has captured yo[u]

Frag. 7 *col.* II   *1-4* […] *5* […] to you, Maha[wai …] *6* the two tablets […] *7* and the second has not been read up till now […]

Frag. 8   *1* scri[be …] *2 Blank* […] *3* Copy of the seco[n]d tablet of [the] le[tter …] *4* by the hand of Enoch, the distinguished scribe […] *5* and holy (one), to Shemihazah and to all [his] com[panions …] *6* You should know th[at] no[t …] *7* and your deeds and those of your wives […] *8* they [and the]ir sons and the wives o[f their sons …] *9* for [yo]ur prostitution in the [l]and. It will happen [t]o yo[u …] *10* and lodges a complaint against you and against the deeds of your sons […] *11* the corruption with which you have corrupted it. *Blank* […] *12* has reached Raphael. Behold, destruction […] *13* and which are in the deserts and whi[ch] are in the seas. And tear loose [the] totality [of …] *14* upon you for evil. Now, then, unfasten your chains which ti[e (you) …] *15* and pray. *Blank* […]

Frag. 9   *1* […] … and all […] *2* […] … before the splendour of [your] glo[ry …] *3* […] your [glo]ry, for [you] kn[ow] all the mysteries […] *4* […] and nothing is stronger than you […] *5* [… be]fore you. *Blank* Now, then, […] *6* […] your glorious rule for the [everlasting] y[ears …] *7* […] … *Blank* […] *8* […] … […]

Frag. 10   *1* [… And] now, [my] Lord […] *2* […] you have multiplied and … […] *3* […] you wish and … […] *4* […]

Frag. 11 *col.* II   *1* […] *2* the dew and [the] fro[st …]

Frag. 13   *1* [And] they [prostra]ted themselves [be]fo[re Enoch …] *2* [Th]en he said to him: [« …] *3* [That] you will have [no] pe[ace …] *4* […] to be […]

4Q204 (4QEnᶜ ar) *4QEnochᶜ ar*

J.T. Milik, *The Books of Enoch*, 178-217, 346-353, pls. IX-XV
PAM 43.199-43.202
ROC 188, 189, 191, 199, 200
4Q201, 4Q202, 4Q205, 4Q206, 4Q207, 4Q212

Col. I   14-1 […]   15 […] רבו[את קדישו]הי […]   16 […] ב[שרא על
עובד]י […]   17 […] רברבן וקשין […]   18 בכול עו[בד וחז]וא לכון
לעובד ש]מיא […]   19 במסורת [נה]וריהון די כולה[ו]ו[ן] ד[נ]חין [...
20 חזוא לכון ל[א]רעא ואתבוננא בעובד]ה מן קדמיא לאחרנא די מנדעם]
21 [לא ל[ל]אשניה ו]כול מתחזא ל[כ]ו[ן] חזוא לכון לדגלי קיטא ואתבוננא]
22 [בדגלי שתו]א די כו[ל ארעא תתמלא מין וענניא מטרא שפכין]
23 [...]   24 […] עלי[הון ברא מן ארבע{א}ת [עשר אילינן] די   25 [עליהן
מתקימין ע[ד דתרתʰין ודתלת שנין [יעברן חזוא לכו]ן   26 [לדגלי קיטא די
שמש]א בהון כוייה ושלקה [ואנתון טלל ומסתרין בע]ין   27 [מן קדמיה על
אנפי אר]עא כויתא ולמדרך ע[ל עפרא ועל כפיא מן חמת]א   28 [לא
תשכחון …]בכול איליניא כולהון יתנ]יצון עליהון וב]הון   29 [ירוקין …
ל[ה]דר תשבחה הל[לוא ואתבוננוא בכול עובדי]א   30 [אלן … חי]א די
לכול עלם […]

Col. II   23-1 […]   24 [ו]אלן שמהת [רבניהו]ן ש[מיחזה די הוה
ראשהון ארעתקף תנין לה *vacat* רמאאל]   25 תליתי לה כוכבאל רביעי לה
[*vacat* …א]ל חמישי לה *vacat* רעמאל שתיתי לה]   26 [ד]ני[אל] ש[ביעי
לה] זיקיאל תמיני [לה ברקאל תשי]עי לה *vacat* עשא]ל עשירי לה]
27 וחרמני [חד] עשר לה מטר]אל תרי עשר לה *vacat* [ענ]נאל תלתת עשר
לה *vacat* סתוא]ל[ ]   28 ארבעת] עשר לה] *vacat* שמשי]אל חמשת עשר לה
[שהריאל שתת עש]ר [ל]ה *vacat*   29 ת]מיאל שבעת עשר לה *vacat*
טוריאל תמנית עשר לה *vacat* ימא]ל[ ] תשעת עשר לה]   30 […]

4Q204 (4QEn^c ar) *4QEnoch^c ar*

Bibliography: J.T. Milik, 'Hénoch au pays des aromates (ch. XXVII à XXXII): Fragments araméens de la grotte 4 de Qumrân', *RB* 65 (1958) 70-77, pl. I; Cf. 4Q201

Col. I (= *1 Enoch* 1:9 - 5:1; 4Q201 II)   *1-14* […] *15* [when he comes with the myri]ads of [his] holy ones [to carry out the sentence against everyone; and he will destroy all the wicked] *16* [and he will accuse all fl]esh for [all their wicked] deed[s which they have committed by word and by deed] *17* [and for all their] arrogant and wicked [words which wicked sinners have directed against him. Observe] *18* all the dee[ds and obse]rve the work of [the] he[avens and the luminaries which do not alter their courses] *19* in the locations of their [lig]hts; how they all [r]i[se and set, each one of them in its turn.] *20* Observe the [ea]rth and consider [its] works, [from the first to the last; how] *21* [none changes and] everything is visible to [y]ou. [Observe the signs of summer and consider] *22* [the signs of winter] that al[l the earth is filled with water and clouds pour down rain] *23* […] *24* [… upon] them apart from four[teen trees] whose *25* [leaves survive un]til two or three years [go by. Observe] *26* [the signs of summer: how (in it)] the [sun] burns and warms [and you look for shade and relief] *27* [from it upon the] scorching [face of] the [ear]th without finding a way of walking o[n the dust or on the stones because of] the [heat.] *28* […] all the trees; on all of them green [leaves] spr[out and on] them *29* [they become green, and all their fruits] are for [dec]oration and show. Exa[lt and consider all these works] *30* [and realise that the living God,] who [lives] for all the everlasting [centuries has made everything.]

Col. II (= *1 Enoch* 6:7; 4Q201 III; 4Q202 II)   *1-23* […] *24* These are the names of [their chiefs:] She[mihazah, who was their chief; 'Ar'teqof, second to him; *Blank* Rama'el,] *25* third to him; Kokab'el, fourth to him; *Blank* […-'el, fifth to him; *Blank* Ra'ma'el, sixth to him;] *26* [Da]ni['el,] se[venth to him;] Zeq'el, eighth [to him; Baraq'el, nin]th to him; *Blank* 'Asa'e[l, tenth to him;] *27* and Hermoni, [el]eventh to him; Matra['el, twelfth to him; *Blank*] 'Anan'el, thirteenth to him; *Blank* Sato'e[l,] *28* four[teenth to him;] *Blank* Shamshi['el, fifteenth to him; *Blank*] Sahari'el, sixteen[th] to [him;] *29* Tu[mi'el, seventeenth to him; *Blank* Turi'el, eighteenth to him; *Blank* Yomi'e]l, [nineteenth to him;] *30* […]

Col. v 1 ‏[ולע]יקא ול[...] ע]למא וכול די חר]יר [...] 2 ‏[דרה]ון ובקץ]

‏... [אדין יאבדון לכו]ל [...] 3 ‏[...] ואכרת עולה מן] 4 ‏[...] נ]צבת

‏קושטא ותהו]א ... יתנצבו]ן 5 ‏[... קש]יטין יפלטון ולהון [... אל]פין וכול

‏יומי 6 ‏[... ו]שיבתכון בשלם ית]מליון 7 ‏[... *vacat*] בקושט וכולה

‏תתנצ]ב [...] ברכה וכול אילנין 8 ‏[...] תתנצב בה 9 ‏[...א]לף 10-18 [...]

‏19 ‏[... ו]ארו ע]י]רא 20-30 [...]

Col. vi 1 ‏עמ] כול תחנ]ניהון על כול נ]פשת]הון לכול חד וחד [...]

2 ‏[...ו] *vacat* וה]וית אז]ל[... חרמונ]ין די למ]ערבהון] 3 ‏[...] תחנניה]ון

‏...נפל]ו עד ד]י [...] 4 ‏לשכני עיני לתרעי ה]יכל [...] 5 ‏וחזית חזיון דרגוז

‏או]כחה [...] 6 ‏עליהון וכולהון כנישין כחדה ויתבין ואב]לין [...] 7 *vacat*

‏וממלת קודמיהון כול] [...] 8 ‏במלי קושטא וחזיה ומוכח לעירי שמ]יא

[*vacat?*

9 *vacat* ‏ספר מלי קושט]א [...] 10 ‏[... רב]א בחלמא די אנה]

11 ‏[ד]י יה]ב]רבא לבני [אנשא]למל]לה [...] 12 ‏[מלי] מנדע ליא חלק

‏ועבד וברא לא]וכחה [...] 13 ‏ובחזיה לי] את]חזית כלקובל די בעו]תכון [...]

Col. v (= *1 Enoch* 10:13-19 + 12:3)   *1* [and to tor]ture and to [confinement in the ev]erlasting [prison]. And everyone who is cond[emned will be lost right from now; he will be shackled with them until the destruction of] *2* [th]eir [generation.] And at the moment of [the judgment by which] I shall judge they will perish for al[l generations. Exterminate all the spirits of the bastards and of the sons of] *3* [the Watchers, because they have caused evil to be done to men.] Exterminate injustice from [the face of the earth, make every evil deed disappear] *4* [and make the p]lant of justice [appear;] it will be [a blessing, and the deeds of justice will be planted in enjoyment for ever.] *5* [At that time all the ju]st will escape and they will [live until they sire thou]sands. All the days of *6* [your youth] and of your old age will be [completed] in peace [... *Blank*] *7* [Then all the earth will be tilled] in justice and it will all be plan[ted with trees and filled with] blessing. All the trees *8* [of the earth which they wish for will be planted in it and in it they will plant vines and each vine which] will be planted in it *9* [will yield a thousand amphoras of wine and each seed sown in it will yield a thou]sand *10* [seahs for every seah ...] *11-18* [...] *19* [I, Enoch, was starting to bless the Lord of Majesty, the King of the Centuries, when] behold, the Wa[tc]her *20-30* [...]

Col. vi (= *1 Enoch* 13:6 - 14:16; 4Q202 vi)   *1* with [all] their [req]uest for their s[ouls] for each and all of [their deeds and for all those who asked: for them there might be] *2* [forgiveness and long life.] *Blank* [I] we[nt and sat next to the waters of Dan, in the country of Dan, which is to the south of Hermo]nim at [its] We[stern side,] *3* [and I was reading the book of records] of th[eir] requests [until I fell asleep. Behold, dreams came to me and visions fell upon me] so th[at I lifted] *4* my eyelids to the portals of the pa[lace of heaven ...] *5* And I saw a vision of the severity of [the] pun[ishment. And a voice came and said to me: «Speak to the sons of heaven to admonish them». When I woke up I went] *6* to them. They were all assembled together and seated and wee[ping in Abel-Maya (The Spring of Weeping) which is between the Lebanon and Senir, with covered faces.] *7* *Blank* In front of them I related all [the visions which I had seen in dreams and I began to speak] *8* with words of justice and of vision and to admonish the heav[enly] Watchers. [*Blank?*]

9 *Blank* Book of the words of truth [and of the admonishing of the Watchers who had always existed, according to the command of] *10* [the Great Holy One] in the dream which I [dreamt. In that vision I saw in my dream what I now speak with a tongue of flesh, with the breath of my mouth,] *11* [wh]ich the Great One ga[ve] the sons of [men] so they can spe[ak with it and so they can understand in (their) heart. So just as God has intended and created the sons of men so they can understand] *12* [the words of] knowledge, he has intended and made and created me to adm[onish the Watchers, the sons of heaven. I wrote down your request, Watchers,] *13* and in a vision [was] revealed to me that [your]

14 ובגזירוא] עלי]כון די עוד מן כ]ען ... דין] 15 [גזיר למאסר]כון עד כול

יומי ע]למא ... [16 בניהון ובק]ניאניא]די חביביכ]ון ... יפלון על חרב]

17 אבדן כלקובל די ב]עותכ]ון על]יהון [... 18 אנתון בעין ומתח]נניין [...

19 מן כתבא די אנה כתבת] [... 20 לי זעקין וזיקין וב]רקין [... 21 לעלא

ואובלוני ואע]לו]ני ב]שמיא [... 22 [ולשנ]י נור סחרין סחור סח]ור [...

23 [עד ד]י אדבקת לביא ר]ב [... 24]...[ד]י תלג אש]ן [... 25]... ל]כול

כתליהו]ן [... 26]...[כ]תלגא וכול] [... 27]... ורע]ד ונפלת [...]

28 [...]מן דן רב וכולה]...[29]... א]כל לאדמה לכו]ן [...] 30 [...]

Col. VIII 26-1 [...] 27 כרסא א]יתי ... [28 ותמן אשת]יציו [...

29 בה עמוד]י [... 30 מן דן נ]קרא [...

Col. XII 22-1 [...] 23]... ולהל]א מנהון ארחקת 24 [... דב]ה

קניא טביא די בשמא די [... 25]... חזי]ת קונם בשמא *vacat* ולהלא מן

נחל]י]א 26 [...] אחרנין ואף בהון חזית אילנין די נפק 27 [...]וחלבנ]ה

416

reque[st will not be granted to you for all the days of eternity and that there will be a verdict against] you [by decision] *14* and pronouncement; that right from n[ow you will not return to heaven or ascend for all the ages; and that the verdict] *15* [has been pronounced to shackle] you for all the days of et[ernity; but that before you will see that all your loved ones will go to destruction with all] *16* their sons; and [you will not enjoy use of the] pos[sessions of] yo[ur] loved ones [and of their sons; they will fall in your presence on the sword of] *17* destruction, for [you]r re[quest] for [them will not be granted you just as it is not granted to yourselves.] You [will carry on] *18* asking and entr[eating … You are not to utter even one word] *19* of the writing which I have written. [This was revealed to me in the vision: Behold, in the vision, the clouds were calling me, the mists] *20* shouted to me and the thunders and li[ghtnings urged me and … In the vision, the winds caused me to fly, they lifted me up] *21* on high, they took me and pla[ced] me in [the heavens. I entered them until I reached the wall of a building made of hailstones] *22* and encircled, so as to be completely surrounded by [tongue]s of fire [which began to alarm me and to … I entered through these tongues of fire] *23* [unti]l I reached a hu[ge] house [made of hailstones; the walls of this house were like stone planks; they were all] *24* [of snow and the] floo[r was made o]f snow. [The roof was like thunders and lightnings and between them, cherubim of fire; and its sky was of water.] *25* [A burning fire surrounded] all their walls [encircling them completely. And the doors were of burning fire. I entered this house which was as hot] *26* [as fire and as cold as] snow; [in it were none of the pleasures of life. Fear shrouded me and trembling clutched me.] *27* [I was shivering and sha]king and I fell [on my face and a vision was revealed to me: Behold I saw another door which opened] *28* [in front of me and another house which] was larger than this, all of it [made of tongues of fire. All of it was so much better than the other in grandeur, glory] *29* [and majesty that I] can[not] describe to you [its grandeur and majesty. Its floor was of fire,] *30* […]

Col. VIII (= *1 Enoch* 18:8-12)   *1-26* [… the top] *27* of the throne w[as of sapphire. I saw a burning fire; beyond those mountains there is a place on the other side of the great earth,] *28* and there [the heavens] e[nd. Then I was shown a great abyss between pillars of heavenly fire and I saw] *29* in it pillar[s of fire which go down to the bottom: its height and its depth were immeasurable. And beyond] *30* this a[byss …]

Col. XII (= *1 Enoch* 30:1 - 32:1; 4Q206 3)   *1-22* […] *23* [… and beyo]nd them I went away far, *24* [to the east, and I saw another huge place with valleys with abundant water in] which there were sweet-smelling reeds *25* [comparable to the mastic; and on the sides of these valleys] I [saw] the aromatic cinnamon. *Blank* And beyond [these] valley[s] *26* [I went on far to the East. I was shown]

[ול]הלא מן טוריא אלן אחזיאת *vacat* טור   28   [... ו]כול אילניא ד[בה
מ]ל[י]ן ... והוא דמא לקלפי ל[וז]   29   [... בש]ם ריח כדי מדקין קליפיא
vacat אלן   30   [... כ]לצפון מדנחה[ו]ן אחזיאת טו[ר]ין

Col. XIII   22-1 [...]   23 תרעין פתי[חין ...]   24 חשבוניהון *vacat*
[...]באד[ין   25 מן תמן אובלת לדרום ס[יאפי ...]   26 לרוח דרומא לטל
[...]ומט[ר   27 אחזית תרעין תל[תתהון ...]   28 שמ[י]א [נפקין ...]
29 *vacat* [*vacat*]   30 באדין ...[...]

Frag. 4   1 [...] וכולהון הווא ד[ח]ל[י]ן [...]   2 [... די הוה ביניהון
לא יכלין אנחנא למק[ם] לקובל [...]   3 [... ב]תנינא וסלק לראש כפא דן
וענא שריוא לאתס[מיה]   4 [... ל]הון ואמרא לא ידע בהון ומרא ענא רגז
על [...]   5 [...]דן ואתה על ענא ואשכח כול שגאהון מת[סמין]   6 [...
ק]ודמוהי ולמה[וא]צבין למ[ת]ב לדירהון   7 [... ע]ל ענא וש[ח]ט[ו כול
טעיתא ושריו למר[עד]   8 [...]אתיב אמרא דן לכול ענא טעיתא לדיריה[ון]
9 [...]דן לא[י ל]בגלא ולבגעה ולאעקה ימא ע[ל]   10 [... א]מר[א]דן
אתהפך והוא אנוש ועבד מ[שכן]   11 [...]...

Frag. 5 ı   19-1 [...]   20 [...]ו[י]שמחון כ[ול]   21 [...]בבני ארע[א]
22 [... אנ]תון תהוון   23 [... ל]כון *vacat* [...]   24 כול *vacat* [...]   25 [*vacat*]
vacat

418

other [mountains] and in those, too, I saw trees from which issued *27* [the resin called styrax and galban]um. [And be]yond these mountains I was shown *Blank* [another] mountain *28* [to the East of the limits of the earth, and] all the trees [in it were f]ul[l] of ..., which is comparable to the bark of the al[mond tree]. *29* [When ... in these trees there comes from them a] fragrant [aro]ma; when these barks are ground, *Blank* *30* [they are superior to any fragrance. Beyond these mountains,] towards the North-east of them, I was shown mount[ain]s

Col. xiii (= *1 Enoch* 35 (?) + 36:1-4)   *1-22* [...] *23* doors ope[n ...] *24* their number. *Blank* Th[en ...] *25* From there I was conveyed to the South of the e[nds of the earth, and there I was shown their three open doors] *26* for the South wind, for the dew and the rai[n and for ... From there I was conveyed to the East of the ends of the earth and there] *27* I was shown [their] th[ree] doors, [open to the East ...] *28* of the heav[en, going out ...] *29 Blank* [*Blank*] *30* Then ... [...]

Frag. 4 (= *1 Enoch* 89:31-36; 4Q205 2 ii)   *1* [...] And they were all af[ra]id [and shaking in front of him.] *2* [And they shouted to the lamb, which was its second,] which was in their midst: «We are unable to sta[nd] in front [of the Lord».] *3* [Then the lamb who led them] climbed [again, for] a second time, to the top of that rock. But the flock began to go bli[nd] *4* [and move off the path which he had indicated to] them without the lamb knowing these matters. The Lord of the flock grew [extremely] angry against [the flock] *5* [and the lamb knew it and came down from the top of] that [rock] and came to the flock and found the complete majority of them b[lind] *6* [and astray. When they saw him they began to get alarmed in fr]ont of him, trying to re[tu]rn to their pen. *7* [The lamb took other lambs with him and came t]o the flock. They but[ch]ered all the strays and they began to tr[emble] *8* [in front of him ... Then] this lamb made all the stray flock return to th[eir] pens. *9* [When the stray flock had returned to their pens,] this [lamb] busied himself [with] scolding, killing and punishing whoever had sworn b[y] *10* [... I continued seeing this dream until] this [l]amb had changed and become a man, and made a Ta[bernacle] *11* [...] ...

Frag. 5 *col.* i (= *1 Enoch* 104:13 - 106:2)   *1-19* [...] *20* [... They shall believe in them and exult in them;] a[ll the just] will exult *21* [in learning from them all the paths of justice. In those days the Lord counted them] among the sons of [the] earth *22* [to read to them and to give them witness concerning their wisdom, saying: Show it to him since y]ou will be *23* [their guides and you will be rewarded among all the sons of the earth.] You [shall have] *Blank* all *24* [reward. Exult, then, sons of justice ...] *Blank* *25* [*Blank*] *Blank*

[...] 26 [שמה למ]ך 27 [...] אנ[תה והיא 28 ...] ו[שמוק 29-30 [...]

Frag. 5 ii 16-1 [...] 17 בל יח[דת ... [ביומי ירד א]בי] 18 עברו
[... חטי]ין ועב]רין ...ה]ון שניו למע]ל[ל 19 [...] 20 [ולהו]א [... אר]עא
[... רב]א [...] 21 די יליד [לכו]ן [... בנו]ה]י יפ]לטון ... [ארעא *vacat* [...]
22 [ותתד]כא ארעא] מן חבלא [ר]בא [...] *vacat* [...]ן בקשוט [...] 23 [עלי]מא
[די י]לי]ד ונוח קר]י שמה [...] 24 [...]י]פלט הוא] [... 25 [...]להוא
ביומ]והי וב[את]רהון יא]תה רש]ע[א תקיפ]ן [... 26 בי[ו]מי]הון בד]י ידע
אנה ברזי [מריא די [קדישין אחויוני ואחזיוני]ודי בלוחת[27 שמיא קרית
וחזית כתיב בהון די]ד]ר מן דר יבאש בכדן ובאש להוא] עד די יקומון]
28 דרי קושטא ובאישתה ורשעה יסוף וחמסא יכלא מן ארעא וע]ד די ...[
29 עליהון *vacat* וכען אזל נא ע]ד]למך [בר]ך [...] 30 די עלימא דן ברה
הואה בקשוט ולא ב[ק]דבין [...]

4Q205 (4QEnᵈ ar) *4QEnochᵈ ar*

J.T. Milik, *The Books of Enoch*, 217-225, 353-355, pls. XVI-XVII
PAM 43.206
ROC 142

Frag. 1 i 1 [...]ן לא יתנזקון ביום דינא מן ... יתקימו]ן מן תנה

26 [After a time, I, Enoch, took a woman for Methuselah, my son and she bore him a son to whom I gave] the name Lame[ch] *27* [saying: « Surely justice has been demeaned until this day». When he reached adulthood, Methuselah took a wo]man [for him] and she *28* [became pregnant by him and gave birth to a son for him. When the child was born his flesh was whiter than snow and] redder *29-30* [...]

Frag. 5 col. II (= *1 Enoch* 106:13 - 107:2)   *1-15* [...] *16* [... Then I, Enoch, replied saying:] *17* Surely [the Lord] will re[new his law upon the earth, according to what I saw and related to you, my son.] In the days of Yared, [my] fa[ther,] *18* they transgressed [the word of the Lord ... they si]nned and trans[gressed ... and] they changed [th]eir [nature] to g[o] *19* [unto women and sin with them; they married some of them who gave birth to creatures not like the spirits but made of flesh.] *20* [There will b]e [great anger and flood over] the [ear]th [and there will be gre]at [devastation for a year. But this boy] *21* born [to yo]u [and hi]s [three sons] will be sa[ved when those die that are above] the earth. *Blank* [Then will rest] *22* the earth, [and it will be cle]ansed [from] the [gr]eat corruption. *Blank* [Now say to Lamech: He is your son] truly [and ... this] *23* [bo]y [who was b]or[n. He is to be ca]lled [Noah, for he will be your repose when you repose in him;] *24* [and he will be your deliverance, for] he [and his sons] will be delivered [from the depravity of the earth - caused by the actions of all sinners] *25* [and by the wicked of the earth - which] will occur in [his] days. [And af]ter[wards there will c]ome worse wicked[ness than that which will have taken place] *26* in [their] d[a]ys. [Fo]r I know the mysteries of [the Lord which] the Holy Ones have told me and have shown me [and which] *27* I read [in the tablets of] heaven. In them I saw written that [gene]ration after generation will perpetrate evil in this way and there will be evil [until there arise] *28* generations of justice, and wickedness and corruption come to an end, and violence vanishes from the earth, and un[til goodness comes to the earth] *29* above them. *Blank* Now, go t[o] Lamech, your [son, and say to him] *30* that this boy is truly, and without lies, his son [...]

4Q205 (4QEn^d ar) *4QEnoch^d ar*

4Q201, 4Q202, 4Q204, 4Q206, 4Q207, 4Q212
Bibliography: Cf. 4Q201

Frag. 1 *col.* I (= *1 Enoch* 22:13 - 24:1)   *1* [...] they will be not be afflicted on the day of judgment away [from there and they will not be removed] away from

2 [... רבות]א ואמרת להוה בריך דין קושט]א ... רבותא   3 [...] ומן תמן
אובלת לאתר א]חרן ... וא]תח]זית]   4 [...] ולא ישרי בדב]רונה ... כח]דה
לבך   5 [... לא אי]תי לה כל שליאו]ן ... ד]גלה ונורא הוא   6 [...ש]מיא ...
ד]לק אשן בינת]הו]ן [...] 30-7

1 [...] Frag. 1 ii   [...]לקובלה די מכ]ין ... ו]אל]ן [...]   2 [... למ]ציע
א]רעא ... [די]בה] איל]ני]ן [...]   3 [...] ונפקי]ן מן תחותוהי [...]   4 [...]
vacat [...]   5 [...] מנה וביניהון חלה ע]מיקה [...]   6 [...] לה]ט]ור או]חרן
[...]   7 [...] ו]בינתהון וח]לה [...]   8 [...] ות]מהת על טור]יא [...]   9 [...]
מת]ברכה]וכ]ול]ה [...] 30-10

Frag. 2 i   1-22 [...]   23 [...]...[...]   24 [...]ו]למדבר אל]ן
25 [לאל]ן ... כח]דה וערדי]ן   26 [...]חזי]ר אכום ודכר די ע]ן   27 [...]תרי
עשר[vacat   28 [...]מ]נהון לערדיא וערדיא   29 [יהבו ... ודבר דכרא
ל]ח]ד עשר אמריא כולהון   30 [...]...[...]

Frag. 2 ii   1-26 [...]   27 [...]סלק לראש כף]חד ראם ו]מרא [...]
28 [...] vacat [...]   29 [...]לקוב]ל ענא וחזיה תקיף ורב וד]חיל [...]

there. *2* [Then I blessed the Lord of Majest]y and said: Blessed be the judgment of justice [and blessed be the Lord of] Majesty *3* [and Justice, who is the
Lord of the World.] From there I was conveyed to an[other] place, [to the
West of the ends of the earth and I wa]s sh[own] *4* [a fire which flows without
resting] or interrupting [its] fl[ow either by day or by night,] remaining steady
at the same time. *5* [I asked, saying: «What is that wh]ich [ha]s [no] rest at
all?» [Ra'u'el answered me: This is] its [pur]pose: that fire *6* [which flows
towards the West directs the luminaries of] he[aven. And he showed me
mountains:] the ground between [them was of bu]rning [fire] *7-30* [...]

Frag. 1 *col.* II (= *1 Enoch* 25:7 - 27:1)   *1* [he gets up] in front of him, who
prepa[res such things for men, for the just ones.] These thin[gs he has created
and has promised to give them. From there] *2* [I was conveyed to the ce]ntre of
[the] ea[rth and saw a blessed place in] which there were tre[es whose
branches blossomed continuously.] *3* [There I was shown a holy mountain;
and there was water coming out] from underneath [the mountain, from the
East, and going down towards the South.] *4* [...] *Blank* [...] *5* [And I saw in the
East another mountain, much higher] than this and between them a d[eep]
ravine [which had no breadth, through which flowed] *6* [the water which came
from underneath the mountain. And to] its [West] ano[ther mo]untain [much
lower than this, with no height,] *7* [and a deep, dry ravine beneath it and]
between them, and [there was another] ra[vine between the three mountains.
All the ravines were deep] *8* [and of hard rock and there were no trees planted
in them.] I was [am]azed at [the] mountain[s and I was amazed at the ravines,
I was absolutely amazed.] *9* [Then I said: «Why is this land] blessed [and
com]plete[ly covered with trees ...?»] *10-30* [...]

Frag. 2 *col.* I (= *1 Enoch* 89:11-14; 4Q206 5 II)   *1-23* [...] *24* [... and they began
to bite and] chase one *25* [another. The white bull which had been born in their
midst sired a wild ass and a white bullock as] well. And the wild asses
26 [increased in number. The white bullock, which had been sired by the white
bull, sired] a black [wild bo]ar and a [white] ram of the flock. *27* [The wild
boar sired several wild boars and the ram sired twe]lve [ewes.] *Blank 28* [When
these twelve ewes had grown, they gave one ewe fr]om among them to the
wild asses and the wild asses *29* [gave this lamb to the wolves. And the ewe
grew up among wolves. The ram brought] all the [el]even ewes *30* [...] ... [...]

Frag. 2 *col.* II (= *1 Enoch* 89:29-31; 4Q206 5 III; 4Q204 4)   *1-26* [...] *27* [and then
the lamb climbed to the top] of a high [rock] and [the Lord of the flock sent
him in the middle of the flock;] *28* [and they all kept their distance.] *Blank* [...]
29 [Then I looked and behold the Lord of the flock got up in fro]nt of the flock:
his appearance was mighty, great and dread[ful, and all] *30* [the flock saw him

30 [... רע]דין ודחל]ין [...

Frag. 2 III   1-26 [...]   27 בקרנוהי [...]   28 חזירין שגיא]ן [...

29 לדכרא די ענ]א [... 30 בארח vacat [...]

4Q206 (4QEn^e ar) *4QEnoch^e ar*

J.T. Milik, *The Books of Enoch*, 225-244, 355-359, pls. XVIII-XXI
PAM 43.204, 43.205
ROC 358, 359, 386

Frag. 2 II   1 [נפש]ת כל בני אנשא והא אלן אנון פחתיא לבית עגנון
2 לכדן עב]יד]ו עד יום די יתד]י]נן ועד זמן יום קצא ד]י[3 דינא רבא די
מנהון יתעבד vacat תמן חזית רוח   4 אנש מת קבלה ו]אנינה ע]ד[שמיא
סלק ומזעק וקב]ל[5 [... לרפא]ל לעירא וקדישא ד]י [...   6 [...]א דמן
היא דכד]ן [...   7 [...] לי א]מר [... 8-21 [...]

Frag. 3   1-2 [...]   3 [...] חד [...].   4 [...] אזלת באת]ר [...
5 [...]ל]מדנ]ח פא]תא [... 6 [...] מד]מעי]ן [...] 7-13 [...] 14 [... דב]ה
מ]לאין [...   15 [...].ו באיל]ניא [...   16 [ריח כדי]מדקק קלפוהי א]נון
[... מן   17 [טוריא] אלן כלצפון מדנחהו]ן[אחז]ית טורין אחרנין
18 [מלאין נ]רד טב וצפר וקרדמן [וף]לפלין vacat ומן תמן הובלת
19 [למד]נח כל טוריא אלן רחוק מנהון למדנח ארעא ואחלפ]ת[20]על]א

and became afraid before him. They were all trem]bling and frightened [before him]

Frag. 2 *col.* III (= *1 Enoch* 89:43-44)   *1-25* [...] *26* [... and this ram began to butt] *27* with his horns [and to chase with his horns, to hit the foxes and then the wild boars; and he destroyed] *28* many wild boars [and then set the dogs free. The ewe, whose eyes had opened, gazed] *29* at this ram of the flock [until he abandoned his path, and began to strike the flock and throw them to the ground and he began to walk off] *30* the path. *Blank* [...]

4Q206 (4QEn^e ar) *4QEnoch^e ar*

4Q201, 4Q202, 4Q204, 4Q205, 4Q207, 4Q212
Bibliography: J.T. Milik, 'Hénoch au pays des aromates', 70-77, pl. I; L.T. Stuckenbruck, *The Book of Giants from Qumran*, 191-196; Cf. 4Q201

Frag. 2 *col.* II (= *1 Enoch* 22:3-7)   *1* [the soul]s of all the sons of men. Thus, then, these are the pits which function as a prison for them. *2* They are ma[de] in this way up to the day on which they will be ju[dg]ed, up to the time of the day of the end, o[f] *3* the great judgment which will be passed on them. *Blank* There I saw the spirit *4* of a dead man, lodging complaints; [and] his lament rose up t[o] heaven, crying and lodging [complaints.] *5* [Then I asked Raphae]l, the Watcher and Holy One wh[o was with me] *6* [and said to him:] «Whose is [this spirit which is lodging complaints, whose groan] in th[is] fashion *7* [rises up to heaven, crying and lodging complaints?» He answered] me sa[ying: ...] *8-21*

Frag. 3 (= *1 Enoch* 28:3 - 29:2 + 31:2 - 32:3; 4Q204 XII)   *1-2* [...] *3* [...] one [... which flowed towards the North-east, taking the water and the dew to every section.] *4* [From there] I went to [another] pla[ce in the desert and I moved away] *5* [a great deal] to the [Ea]st [of this] locat[ion. There I saw uncultivated trees which] *6* gave off [an aroma of incense and myrrh ...] *7-13* [...] *14* [... in] it, f[ull of resin and it is like the bark] *15* [of the almond tree. When ...] ... in [these] tre[es there comes from them a fragrant] *16* [aroma. When] their bark is ground i[t is superior to any fragrance. Beyo]nd *17* these [mountains] towards the North-east of them, I was [sho]wn (still) other mountains *18* [full of] choice [na]rd, mastic, cardamum [and pe]pper. *Blank* From there I went on *19* [to the Ea]st of all those mountains, far from them, to the East of the land;

מן י]מא [שמוקא וארחקת שגיא מנה ואעברת על[א]   21   [מ]ן חשוכא
רח]ו[ק מנה ואחלפת ליד פרדס קשט[א]

Frag. 4   1 ואחזית מ]ן [...   2 שנין [...]   3 ו]שפיר [... 4-9 [...]
10 [ו]אמך רבתא ויד]עו [...   11 די ערטליין מ]...[12-17 [...]
18 [...].[...]   19 [...] עירין וא]חויני[20 [...]בהדמיה למזמ°י]הון[
21 [...]ואחזית עבדין °בר]בין[

Frag. 5 i   1-10 [...] מ[ן   11 [...] כו]כביא שגיאיא   12 [...] ל]כלהון
ידין ורגלין ורמא   13 [... ארב]עתא על על חד מן תוריא   14 [...] וע]בד לה
ערב חדה ויתב בגוה   15 [...]ו עמה לערבא וערבא חפית וכסית
16 [...] חזה והא מרזבין שבעה שפכין   17 [...] והא חדרין פתיחו בגוא
ארעא ושריו   18 [...] ו]אנה הוית חזה עד ארעא חפית מין   19 [...] קאמין[
עליה ותוריא שקעין וטבעין   20 [...] וערבה פרחה עלא מן מיא וכל תוריא
21 [...] ופיליא ירו מי]ן[*vacat*

Frag. 5 ii   1 [... בחל]מי עד מ]רזביא [...]   2 [...]חדריא שכירו ו]...[
3 ונחתין בגוהון עד ספון [...]   4 תקנת [ע]ל[ארעא [...] 5-9 [...]
10 למצ]יעהון ... ולמדבר אלן]   11 לאלן [...]   12 ועגלא]... חזיר אכום
ודכר]   13 זי ע]ן [...   14 אמר]י[ן ת]רי עשר ...[15 וערדיא יהב]ו ...[

426

[I] passed on *20* [above] the Red S[ea] and I moved very far from it; I crossed ov[er] *21* the darkness, far from it, and passed on the Paradise of Justice.

Frag. 4 (= *1 Enoch* 32:3-6 + 33:3 - 34:1)   *1* And I was shown fr[om afar, trees in it, over-abundantly numerous and huge trees] *2* differing [from each other. There I saw a tree which was different from all the others, very large] *3* and [beautiful and splendid ...] *4-9* [... « ...] *10* [and] your mother of old, and they lea[rned wisdom and their eyes opened and they understood] *11* that they were naked». [...] *12-18* [...] *19* [... Uriel, one of] the Watchers. And he s[howed me] *20* [and wrote down everything for me; he even wrote down their names for me,] in accordance with [their] times. *21* [From there I was conveyed to the North of the edges of the earth] and I was shown gre[at] works.

Frag. 5 *col.* I (= *1 Enoch* 88:3 - 89:6)   *1-9* [...] *10* [... I continued watching in my dream, when, behold one o]f *11* [the four who had left received a command from heaven and he took all] the numerous [s]tars *12* [whose sexual organs were like those of horses, and he bound] them all hand and feet and hurled *13* [them into an abyss in the earth. One of the fo]ur went to one of the [white] bulls *14* [and instructed him. He bu]ilt for himself a boat, and dwelt inside it. *15* [And the three bulls went] with him in the boat, and the boat was covered and roofed *16* [above them. I was] watching and behold, seven sluices pouring out *17* [abundant water over the earth.] And behold, chambers in the interior of the earth were opened and (waters) began *18* [to spout and come on it.] I continued to watch until the earth was covered by the water *19* [and by darkness and mists (?) which] stood on it. The bulls were submerging and drowning *20* [and perishing by that water.] The boat floated above the water and all the bulls, *21* [the wild asses, the camels] and the elephants sank in the wat[er].
Blank

Frag. 5 *col.* II (= *1 Enoch* 89:7-16; 4Q205 2 I)   *1* [Once again I watched in] my [dre]am, until [those] s[luices were shut off from that elevated roof] *2* [and the fissures of] the chambers were stopped and [other chambers opened. The water began] *3* to sink to their interior, until [the water] were vanished [from the surface of the land, and it emerged, and the boat] *4* settled [up]on the land; [darkness withdrew and there was light.] *5-8* [...] *9* [... and there was born] *10* in the mid[st of them a white bull. And they began to bite and chase one] *11* another. [The white bull sired a wild ass and also a white bullock. And the wild asses increased in number.] *12* The [white] bullock, [which had been sired by the white bull, sired a black wild boar and a white ram] *13* of the fl[ock; the wild boar sired several wild boars and the ram sired] *14* t[welve] ewes. [When they had grown, they gave one from among those ewes to the

16 ודבר דכרא ל]חד עשר אמריא כולהון [... 17 לות דביא והת]שגאו [...
18 שריו למלחץ לענ]א [... 19 [די י]שקע מין [...] 20 [...] אמר נת]ר
[... 21 [...] תקיפ]ית עד נחת מ]רא [...

Frag. 5 III 12-1 [...] 13 [...]מיא[...] 14 [...]ד[ביא רדפין לענ]א
[... 15 [...] ו]מיא חפו עליהון וע]נא [... 16 [...]ו צדיותא אתר זי [...]
17 [...]ן ועיניהון התפתח]ו [... 18 [...]להון ויהב לה]ון [מיא [למש]ת]א[
19 [...]ס]לק לר]אש כ]ף חד רם ומ]רא] 20 [...]וכלהון ק]מו מן [...
21 [...]

4Q207 (4QEnᶠ ar) *4QEnochᶠ ar*

J.T. Milik, *The Books of Enoch*, 244-245, 359, pl. XXI
PAM 43.214
ROC 143

Frag. 1 1 [...] מן עלה [והא] כוכב ח]ד [...]2 [...] ביניהון הא באדין
חזי]ת [... 3 [...]ן ודיריהון [וע]גל]י]ה]ון [...]4 [...]והא כוכבין שגיא]ין
[... 5 [...] תו]ריא במצ]יע [...

428

wild asses,] *15* and the wild asses gave [that lamb to the wolves. And that ewe grew up among the wolves.] *16* The ram took [all eleven ewes to live and graze with him] *17* among the wolves; and they in[creased in number and changed into a flock with many ewes. And the wolves] *18* began to harass [the] flock [even causing their kids to die and to hurl their kids into a great stream] *19* [to] sink them in the water. [Then the ewes began to shriek for their young and to wail] *20* [before their Lord. One] lam, which had been sav[ed from the wolves, fled and went to the wild asses. And I watched while] *21* [the flock groaned and shrieked horrib]ly until the Lo[rd of the flock] came down […]

Frag. 5 *col.* III (= *1 Enoch* 89:27-30; 4Q205 2 II)   *1-12* […] *13* […] water […] *14* [I continued watching until all the w]olves who went on chasing [that] flock [died] *15* [sinking and drowning, and] the water covered them. [The] fl[ock moved away from] *16* [that water and went to] a barren place [in] which [there was no] *17* [water or grass] and their eyes were opened [and they saw. I watched] *18* [until the Lord of the flock fed] them and gave th[em] water [to dri]n[k] *19* [and grass to eat, and the lamb cli]mbed to the t[op of] a high [ro]ck and [the] L[ord] *20* [of the flock sent him in the middle of the flock and they all st]ood from [a distance. …] *21* […]

4Q207 (4QEn^f ar) *4QEnoch^f ar*

4Q201, 4Q202, 4Q204, 4Q205, 4Q206, 4Q212
Bibliography: Cf. 4Q201

Frag. 1 (= *1 Enoch* 86:1-3)   [… Again I was] *1* [lifting my eyes in the dream and I saw the heaven] above [and behold] a star [fell from heaven in the midst] *2* [of the great bulls and ate and grazed] in the midst of them. Behold, then [I] saw [those bulls, large] *3* [and black; all of them exchanged their feeds,] their pens and th[eir bu]llock[s and began to live with each other.] *4* [I looked again in my dream and watched the sky] and behold many stars [came down and fell from the sky] *5* [in the middle of the first star and were turned into bu]lls in the mid[st of those bullocks and grazed with them and among them]

4Q208 (4QEnastr^a ar) *4QAstronomical Enoch^a ar*

PAM 43.210, 43.211
ROC 814, 823

Frag. 15   1 [... ופ]לג ובליליא] ... בה כסה]   2 [שביעין ... ופלג
וב]ציר מן נהורה לש]ביעין ...]   3 [ובאדין נפק מן תר]עא תליתיא ואניר]
בשאר ליליא דן]   4 [שביעין ... ופלג]וקוי בימימה ד]ן שביעין [...
5 [ובאדין ערב ועל וכסה]שאר יממ]א דן [...   6 [ובליליא ... ב]ה כס]ה ...]

4Q209 (4QEnastr^b ar) *4QAstronomical Enoch^b ar*

J.T. Milik, *The Books of Enoch*, 278-284, 288-296, pls. XXV-XXVII, XXX
PAM 43.208, 43.209, 43.235
ROC 846, 847, 856, 857
4Q208, 4Q210, 4Q211
Bibliography: J.T. Milik, 'Hénoch au pays des aromates', 76; .- 'Problèmes de la littérature hénochique à la lumière des fragments araméens de Qumrân', *HTR* 64 (1971) 338-343; J.C. VanderKam, *Enoch and the Growth of an Apocalyptic Tradition* (CBQMS 36; Washington, 1984) 76-109; O. Neugebauer, 'The 'As-

Frag. 1   1 [...] וב]אדין ער]ב ועל לתרעא רביעיא]   2 [וקבל שאר
ליליא דן שביעין ארבעה וקוי ביממא דן שביעין תלתה ופלג ושוי בה]נהור
שביעין תלת]ה ופל]ג   3 [ובאדין נפק מן תרעא רביעיא ושלט בשאר יממא
דן שביעין תלתה ופלג ואניר [בליליא] ש]בעה בה שביעין תלתה ופלג
4 [ובאדין ערב ועללתרעא תליתיא וקבל שאר ליליא דן שביעין תלתה ופלג
וקו]י ביממא דן שביעין ארבעה ושוי בה   5 [נהור שביעין ארבעה ובאדין
נפק מן תרעא תליתיא ושלט בשאר יממא דן שביעין תלתה] *vacat* ואניר
בליליא תמניה בה שביעין   6 [ארבעה ובאדין ערב ועל וקבל שאר ליליא דן
שביעין תלתה וקוי ביממא דן שבי]עין ארבעה ופלג ושוי בה נהור
7 [שביעין ארבעה ופלג ובאדין נפק ושלט בשאר יממא דן שביעין תרין
ופלג *vacat* ו]אניר בליליא תשעה בה שביעין   8 [ארבעה ופלג ובאדין ערב

4Q208 (4QEnastrᵃ ar) *4QAstronomical Enochᵃ ar*

4Q209, 4Q210, 4Q211
Bibliography: J.T. Milik, *The Books of Enoch*, 273; Cf. 4Q209

Frag. 15 *1* [… and a h]alf. And during [the …] night [of it (i.e. that month), it (i.e. the moon) is covered …] *2* [sevenths and a half, and it la]cks up to […] se[venths] of its light […] *3* [Next it rises from] the third [ga]te and shines [during the rest of that night] *4* [… sevenths and a half.] And it waxes during th[is] day [… sevenths.] *5* [Next it sets and enters and is covered] the rest of [this] day […] *6* [And during night … of] it, it is cove[red …]

4Q209 (4QEnastrᵇ ar) *4QAstronomical Enochᵇ ar*

tronomical' Chapters of the Ethiopic Book of Enoch (72-82)', in M. Black, *The Book of Enoch or 1 Enoch. A New English Edition* (SVTP 7; Leiden: E.J. Brill, 1985) 386-419; U. Gleßmer, 'Das astronomische Henoch-Buch als Studienobjekt', *BN* 36 (1987) 69-129; F. García Martínez, 'Aramaic Enoch and the Books of Enoch', in *Qumran and Apocalyptic. Studies on the Aramaic Texts from Qumran* (STDJ 9; Leiden: E.J. Brill, 1992) 97-115; M. Albani, *Astronomie und Schöpfungsglaube: Untersuchungen zum astronomischen Henochbuch* (WMANT 68; Neukirchen-Vluyn: Neukirchener, 1994)

Frag. 1 *1* [… N]ext, it (i.e. the moon) se[ts and enters the fourth gate.] *2* [And it wanes during the rest of this night by four sevenths. And during this day it waxes up to three and a half sevenths; and its] light [is equivalent to] three [and a ha]lf sevenths. *3* [And then it emerges from the fourth gate and reigns over the rest of this day three and a half sevenths. And it shines] during the [se]venth night of it (i.e. that month) with three and a half sevenths. *4* [Next, it sets and enters the third gate and it wanes three and a half sevenths during the rest of this night. And it wax]es during this day up to four sevenths; and its [light] is equivalent *5* [to four sevenths. Then it emerges from the third gate and reigns over the rest of this day three sevenths.] *Blank* And it shines during the eighth night of this month with [four] sevenths. *6* [And then it sets and enters and it wanes during the rest of this night by three sevenths. And it waxes during this day] up to four and a half [sev]enths; and its light is equivalent *7* [to four and a half sevenths. Then it emerges and reigns over the rest of this day for two and a half sevenths. *Blank* And] it shines during the ninth night of this month *8* [with four and a half] sevenths. [Next, it sets and enters the

ועל לתרעא תנינא וקבל שאר ליליא דן שביעין תרין ופלג וקוי ביממא [דן

שביעין חמשה 9-10 [...] 11 [... ואניר בליל]א חד עשר בה] שביעין

חמשה] 12 [ופלג ובאדין ערב ועל וקבל שאר ליליא דן שביע חד ופלג וקוי

ביממא דן שביע]ין שתה ושוי בה נהור ש[ביעין]

Frag. 2   1 [...].[...] 2 [vacat ואניר בלילא [תר' עשר בה ש]בי[עין

שתה ובאדין ערב ועל וקבל שאר ליליא דן שביע חד] 3 [וקוי בימ]מא דן

שביעין שתה ופלג ושוי ב[ה נהור שביעין שתה ופלג ובאדין נפק ושלט

בשאר יממא דן] 4 [פלג ש]ביע vacat ואניר בלילא תלת]ת עשר בה

שביעין שתה ופלג ובאדין ערב ועל וקבל שאר] 5 [ליליא] דן פלג שביע

וקוי כל יממא דן כלה [...] 6 [vacat ואניר בלילא ארבעת עשר בה כל

לי]ליא דן כלה [...] 7 [ו]בל[י]ל[א חמשת עשר בה כסה פלג שביע ובצ]יר

מנהורה פלג שביע ובאדין נפק ואניר] 8 שאר ל[י]ל[י]א ד[ן שביעין שתה

ופלג וקוי ביממא] דן שביע חד ובאדין ערב ועל וכסה שאר] 9 יממא דן

שביעין שתה <ופלג> vacat ובל[י]לא שתת עשר בה כסה שביע חד ובציר

מנהורה] 10 [ש]ביע חד ובאדין נפק ואניר [ש]אר ליליא ד]ן שביעין שתה

וקוי ביממא דן שביע חד ופלג ובאדין] 11 [ערב ו]על וכסה שאר יממא דן

שבי]עין חמשה ופלג 12 [...].[...]

Frag. 5   1 [שביעין חמ]שה ופלג] ובלילא תמנת עשר בה כסה שביעין

תרין ובציר מנהורה] 2 [שביעי]ן תרין ובאדין [נפק ואניר שאר ליליא דן

שביעין חמשה ופלג וקוי ביממא] 3 דן שביעין תרין ובאדין ע]רב ועל

וכסה שאר ליליא דן שביעין חמשה [vacat 4 ובלילא תשעת עשר בה כ]סה

שביעין תרין ובציר מנהורה שביעין תרין ובאדין] 5 נפק ואניר שאר

ליליא דן שביעין [חמשה וקוי ביממא דן שביעין תרין ופלג ובאדין]

6 [ערב וע]ל] וכסה ש]אר יממא דן שביע]ין ארבעה ופלג ובלילא עשרין בה

כסה שביעין] 7 [תרין ופלג ובציר מנה]ורה שביעין] תרין ופלג [...

Frag. 6   1 [... ואניר בשאר ליליא דן שביע חד ופ]לג וקוי ביממא דן

432

second gate, and it wanes during the rest [of this night by two sevenths and a half. And it waxes during this day] up to five sevenths; *9-10* […] *11* [… And it shines during] the eleventh [night] of this month [with five and a half sevenths.] *12* [And then it sets and enters and it wanes during the rest of that night by one and a half sevenths. And it waxes during this day] up to six [seven]ths; its light is equivalent [to (six) sevenths.]

Frag. 2 *1* […] *2* [*Blank* And it shines during the] twelfth [night] of this month [with six se]ven[ths. Next it sets and enters and it is dark during the rest of this night by one seventh.] *3* [And it waxes during] this [d]ay up to six and a half sevenths; [and its light] is equivalent [to six and a half sevenths. Then it emerges and reigns over the rest of this day] *4* [half a se]venth. *Blank* And it shines during the th[irteenth] night [of this month with six and a half sevenths. Next, it sets and enters and is dark during the rest of] *5* this [night] by a half seventh. And it waxes this entire day (till it is) full. […] *6* [*Blank*] And it shines during the fourteenth night of this month, [this] entire nig[ht fully …] *7* [And] at (the beginning of) the fifteenth ni[ght] of this month it is covered to half a seventh; and there is subtrac[ted from its light half a seventh. Then it emerges and shines] *8* during the rest of [th]is ni[ght] with six and a half sevenths. And it waxes during [this] day [up to one seventh. And then it sets and enters and is covered during the rest of] *9* this day to six <and a half> sevenths. *Blank* And at the [sixteenth] nig[ht of this month it is covered up to one seventh. And there is subtracted from its light] *10* one [se]venth. Then it emerges and shines during the rest of th[is] night with six sevenths. [And it waxes during this day up to one seventh and a half. And then] *11* [it sets and] enters and is covered the rest of this day up to [five and a half] sev[enths …] *12* […] … […]

Frag. 5 *1* [fi]ve and a half [sevenths. And at night eighteen of this month it is covered to two sevenths. And there is subtracted from its light] *2* two [sevenths.] Then [it emerges and shines during the rest of this night with five sevenths and a half. And it waxes during] *3* this [day] up to two sevenths. Next it se[ts and enters and is covered during the rest of this day up to five sevenths. *Blank*] *4* And at the nineteenth night of this month it is [to two sevenths] co[vered; and two sevenths from its light are subtracted. And then] *5* it emerges and shines during the rest of this night with [five] sevenths. [And it waxes during this day up to two and a half sevenths. Next] *6* [it sets and ent]ers [and is to four and a half sevenths covered during the r]est of that day. [And at the twentieth night of this month it is covered to] *7* [two and a half sevenths covered; and there is subtracted from] its [lig]ht [two and a half] sevenths […]

Frag. 6 *1* [… and shines during the rest of this night with one and a h]alf [sev-

שביעי]ן שתה ובאדי]ן   2 [ערב ועל וכסה שאר יממא דן שביע חד ובליל]א
שבעה ועשר]ין בה כסה שביעין שתה ו[בצ]יר מנ[ה]ורה   3 [שביעין שתה
ובאדין נפק ואניר שאר ליליא דן שביע חד וקוי בימ]מא דן שביעין שתה
ופלג ובאדין ער]ב[4 [ועל וכסה שאר יממא דן פלג שביע חד ובליל]א
תמניה ועשרין בה כסה שביעין שתה ופלג ובציר מנה[ורה]   5 [שביעין
שתה ופלג ובאדין נפק ואניר]שאר ליליא דן פלג שביע חד וקוי ביממא דן
כלה ובאדין ערב ועל   6 [לתרעא ...]יא וכסה שאר ימ]מא דן כלה ולקיח כל
שאר נהורה ונפק גלגלה ריקן מן כל נהור מטמר עם ש[משא]
7 [...]...[...]...[...]

1 [... *Frag.* 7 ii   ... ואניר בשאר ליליא דן שביעין תלתא]   2 [וקוי
ביממא דן שביעין ארבעה ופלג ובאדין ערב ועל וכסה שאר]יממא דן
שביעין   3 [תרין ופלג ובליל]א ארבעה ועשרי]ן בה כסה שביעין *vacat*
ארבעה ופלג ובציר מנהורה   4 [שביעין ארבעה ופלג וב]אדין נפק ואניר
בשאר ליליא דן שביעין תרין ופלג וקוי   5 [בי]ממא דן שביעין חמשה
ובאדין ערב ועל וכסה שאר יממא דן שביעין תרין *vacat*   6 ובלילא חמשה
ועשרין בה כסה שביעין חמשה ובציר מנהורה שביעין חמשה   7 ובאדין
נפק ואניר בשאר ליליא דן שביעין תרין וקוי ביממא דן שביעין חמשה ופלג
8 ובאדין ערב [ו]על לתרעא תנינא וכסה שאר יממא דן שביע חד ופלג
vacat   9 ובלילא שתה ועשרין בה כסה שביעין חמשה ופלג ובציר מנהורה
שביעין חמשה   10 ופלג ובאדין נפק מן תרעא תנינא ואניר בשאר ליליא דן
שביע חד ופלג וקוי ביממא   11 דן שביעין שתה ובאדין ערב ועל וכסה
שאר יממא דן שביע חד *vacat* ובלילא שבעה   12 [ועש]רין בה כסה
שביעין שתה ובציר מ[נ]הורה שב[י]עין שתה ובאדין נפק ואניר]
13 [בשא]ר ליליא דן שביע חד וקוי ביממא דן [שביעין שתה ופלג ובאדין
ערב ועל]

1 [... *Frag.* 7 iii   ... ואניר בלילא תמינה ב]ה [ש]ב[ע]ין] ארבעה ובאדין
ערב ועל בלילא דן אשל[מת]   2 שמשא למהך כל חרתיה די בתרעא
קדמיא ומשרה למתב למתה ולמפק בחרתיה [ובאדין שהרא]   3 ערב ועל

enth;] and it waxes during this day up to [six] seven[ths. And then] *2* [it sets and enters and is one seventh covered during the rest of this day. And at the twen]ty-[seventh night] of it, it is six sevenths covered; and there is sub[tracted] from its li[g]ht *3* [six sevenths. And then it emerges and shines during the rest of this night with one seventh, and it waxes during] this [d]ay up to six and a half sevenths. And then it se[ts] *4* [and enters and it is covered during the rest of this day up to a half of a seventh. And at the] twenty-eighth [night] of it, it is six and half sevenths covered; and there is subtracted from [its] li[ght] *5* [six and a half sevenths. And then it emerges and shines] during the rest of this night with a half of one seventh and it waxes during this day to its entirety. And then it sets and enters *6* [the … gate, and it is covered during the rest of] this [d]ay in its entirety. And all the rest of its light is taken away, and its disc emerges, devoid of all light, hidden by [the] s[un.] *7* […] … […] … […]

Frag. 7 col. II   *1* [… and it shines during the rest of this night with three sevenths.] *2* [During this day it waxes up to four and a half sevenths. Next it sets and enters and it is covered the rest of] this day [two and a half] sevenths. *3* [*Blank* During the twent]y[-fourth night] of it, it is covered up to four and a half sevenths], and there is subtracted from its light *4* [four and a half sevenths. And t]hen it rises and shines during the rest of this night with two and a half sevenths. And it waxes *5* [during] this [d]ay up to five sevenths. And then it sets and enters and is covered the rest of this day with two sevenths. *Blank* *6* And in the twenty-fifth night of it, it is covered up to five sevenths; there is subtracted from its light five sevenths. *7* And then it rises and shines during the rest of this night with two sevenths and waxes during this day up to five and a half sevenths. *8* And then it sets [and] enters the second gate and is covered the rest of this day with one a half sevenths. *Blank* *9* During the twenty-sixth night of it, it is five and half sevenths covered; and there is subtracted from its light five sevenths *10* and a half. And then it rises from the second gate and shines during the rest of this night with one and a half sevenths; and it waxes during this day *11* up to six sevenths. And then it sets and enters and is one seventh covered the rest of this day. *Blank* During the [twe]nty-seventh *12* night of it, it is six sevenths covered; and there is subtracted from its [l]ight [six] sev[enths. And then it rises and shines] *13* [during the res]t of this night with one seventh; and it waxes during this day [up to six and a half sevenths. Next it sets and enters]

Frag. 7 col. III   *1* [… And shines during the eighth night of] it with four [se]v-e[nths.] And then it sets and enters. During this night *2* the sun comple[tes] its passage through all its sections of the first gate and again begins to enter and rise through its sections. [And then the moon] *3* sets and enters and wanes

וקבל שאר ליליא דן שביעין תלתה וקוי ביממא דן שביעין ארבעה ו|פלג

ובאדין   4   נפק ושלט בשאר יממא דן שביעין תרין ופ|ל]ג vacat ואניר

בליליא תשעה ב]ה שביעין[5   ארבעה ופלג ובאדין ערב ועל בליליא דן

שרי שמשא למתב ולמתא בחרת]יה ולמערב]   6   בהון ובאדין [שה]רא ערב

ועל לתרעא חמישיא וקבל שאר ליליא דן שבי[עין תרין]   7   ופלג וקוי

ביממא ד]ן שביעין[חמשה ושוי בה נהו]ר[שביעין חמשה שלם [ובאדין

נפק]   8   מן תרעא [ח]מי[שיא ושלט בשאר יממא דן שביעין תרין vacat

ואניר בליליא עשרה בה]   9   [שביעין חמשה ובאדין ערב ועל וקבל שאר

ליליא דן שביעין תרין וקוי ביממא דן]   10   שב[יעין חמשה ופלג ...]

[...] 13-11

    Frag. 23   1   [... יבש וא]בדן [ו]מות ו[חמימו וחרבן ושלמו]   2   [תרי

עשר תרעי ארבע רוחי [שמיא שלמהון ופרשהון אח]זית לך ברי מתושלח]

3   [וקרין לקדימא קדים בדי הוא [קדמיה וקרין לדרומא דרום בדיל לתמן

דאר רבא וב]ה]   4   דאר [...]. עלמא vacat ולרוחא רבא רוח {מא}מערבא

בדי תמן   5   את]ין כו]כבי שמיא מאין ערבין ומאין עללין וכלהון כוכבין

ובדכן קרין מערבא   6   [ולצפונא צפון] בדי בה צפנין ומתכנסין וסחרין כל

ערבי שמיא ואזלין למדנחי שמיא   7   [ולמדנחא מד]נח בדי מן תמן דנחין

מאני שמיא ואף מזרח בדי מא]י]ן זרחין vacat   8   [וחזית תלת ...]ת ארעא

חד מנהון למדבר בה בני אנשא וחד מנהון [לכל ימין]   9   [ולנהרין וחד

מנהון [למדברין ולש]בע ולפרד]ס קושטא vacat   10   [וחזית שבעת טוריא

רמין מן כ]ל ט]ורין די על תבלא ון]חת עליהון תלגא[...]

    Frag. 25   1   [...]שניא ל[.]ל.   2   [...] vacat [...]   3   [... ח]שבון אחרן

אחזית לה די אזל ו[...]   4   [...] ל[... ח]דשין ע[...]

    Frag. 26   1   [...].[...]   2   [...] [בתרעא שתיתיא בה] אשלם נהורה

[...]   3   [... שבעין חמש ועשרין וי]ומין תרין ומחסר מן דבר שמשא [...]

[...].[...]   4   ... בה כדמות חזו דמי כדי נהורה בה האח]ר [... 5   [בליליא מן [קצת

three sevenths the rest of this night. And during this day it waxes up to four
and [a half] sevenths. [And then] *4* it rises and reigns the rest of this day two
and a h[a]lf sevenths. *Blank* During the ninth night of [it], it shines with *5* four
and a half [sevenths]. And then it sets and enters. During this night the sun
again begins to pass through [its] section[s and to set] *6* through them. And
then the [mo]on sets and enters the fifth gate, and wanes the rest of this night
[two] seven[ths] *7* and a half. And during th[is] day it waxes up to five [sev-
enths;] its ligh[t] is equivalent to five sevenths completely. [And then it rises]
8 through the [f]i[fth] gate [and reigns during the rest of this day, two sevenths. *Blank* During the tenth night of it, it shines with] *9* [five sevenths. And
then it sets and enters and wanes two sevenths the rest of this night. And it
waxes during this day] *10* [up to five and a half] seve[nths ...] *11-13* [...]

Frag. 23 (cf. *1 Enoch* 76:13 - 77:4)   *1* [... drought and de]struction [and] death
and [violence and desolation. And completely (described) are] *2* [the twelve
gates of the four quarters of] the heaven. [I] have sho[wn you] their totality
and their explanation, [Methuselah, my son.] *3* [The East they call East, because it is] the first. The South they call South, because the Great One sojourns there, and in [it] *4* sojourns [...] eternally. *Blank* The great quarter they
call the West quarter, because *5* the [st]ars of the heaven go there; there they
set and there they rise, all the stars; that is why they call it the West. *6* [The
North (they call) North] because all the bodies of the heaven hide and gather
in it and return to it and head towards the East of the heaven. *7* [And the Orient
(they call) Ori]ent, because the bodies of heaven ascend from there; also they
call it the Levant because they arise from there. *Blank 8* [And I saw three sec-
tions] of the earth: one for the sons of men to live in it; another [for all the
seas] *9* [and the rivers, and another] for the deserts, for «The Se[ven», and for
the Paradi]se of Justice. *Blank 10* [And I saw seven mountains higher than a]ll
mo[untains which are upon the earth;] snow [co]vers them [...]

Frag. 25 (cf. *1 Enoch* 74:1-2 *or* 78:9-12 ?)   *1* [...] years for [...] *2* [...] *Blank* [...]
3 [...] another [com]putation I was shown for it, that it goes [...] *4* [... n]ew
moons, ... [...]

Frag. 26 (cf. *1 Enoch* 79:2-5)   *1* [...] ... [...] *2* [...] through the sixth gate,
through it [its light is completed ...] *3* [... twenty-five weeks and] two [d]ays.
And it falls short from the move of the sun [...] *4* [...] in it. It seems like the
image of a vision. When its light lags be[hind] in it [...] *5* [In the night] that

דמי חזוא דן כדמות אנש וביממא מן] קצת דמי חזוא דן כדמות שמש בשמיא
[... 6]להן נהור]ה בלחודהי וכען מחוה אנה לך ברי [...] 7 [...]חשבון
אחרן[...]

Frag. 28   1 [... ל]מעדיהון לחדשיהון לדגליהון ו]אלן שמהת [...
2 [... וכש]לטנהון לכל מסרתהון אר]בעת [... 3 ...]ן ראשין ד]א[ל]פין
[... 4 ...] מפ]רשין בי]ומין [... 5 ...] וא]לן שמהת [...]

4Q210 (4QEnastr^c ar) *4QAstronomical Enoch^c ar*

J.T. Milik, *The Books of Enoch*, 284-288, pls. XXVIII, XXX
PAM 41.370, 43.213
ROC 229

Frag. 1 ii   1 ותלתת די בתריהון על שמאל *vacat*]ותלתת די בתריהון
על מערב *vacat* ובארבעא מנהון נפקן רוחיא די] 2 להין לרפי]ה{י}א ארעא
ולאחיתה *vacat* ו]בתמניא מנהון נפקן רוחי נזקא כדי שליחו להין למבד כל
ארעא] 3 ומיא וכל מה די בהן די רבין וצמחין ורחש]ין במיא ועל יבשתא
וכל די דברין בה *vacat* ולקדמין] 4 בתרעא קדמיא נפקא רוח קדים די
ב]מדנחא ופנה לדרומא ונפק מנה אבדן ויבש וחמימו וחרבן [*vacat*
5 ובתרעא תנינא נפקא רוח קדים קד]ימה די במצעתהון מטר ופרי ואחיא
וטל *vacat* ובתרעא תליתיא נפקא רוח] 6 קדים גרבה די קריב לרוח
גרי]בי קרירו ויבש *vacat* ובתריהון מן תלתת תרעיא די על דרום שמיא]
7 נפק לקדמין בתרעא קדמיא] רוח דרום די בדרומא ופנה למדנחא שרב
vacat ובתרעא תנינא נפק רוח דרום] 8 די קרין לה נגבה טל] ומטר ושלם
ואחיא *vacat* ובתרעא תליתיא נפק רוח דרום מערבה טל ומטר וקמץ ואבדן
[*vacat* 9]ו]בתרה נפק רוחא ג]ריביתא [... 13-10 ...] 14 וחרבן ושלמו
תרי עשר תרעי ארבע רוחי שמ]יא שלמהון ופרשוהון אחזית לך ברי
מתושלח וקרין לקדמא קדים] 15 בדי הוא קדמיא וקרין לדרומא דרום
בד]י לתמן דאר רבא ובה דאר ... עלמא ולרוחא רבא רוח מערבא בדי תמן

438

vision seems to be [in] part the image of a man, and in the day [it seems] in [part the image of the sun in the sky; and there is nothing in it,] *6* [except] only its [light.] And now, my son, I will show you […] *7* […] another computation […]

Frag. 28 (cf. *1 Enoch* 82:9-13) *1* [… in relation to] their constellations, their new moons, their signs. And [these are the names …] *2* [… and according to] their [auth]ority in relation to all their stations. Fo[ur …] *3* […] chiefs of [th]ou[sands …] *4* [… sepa]rating the d[ays …] *5* [… and th]ese are the names […]

4Q210 (4QEnastr^c ar) *4QAstronomical Enoch^c ar*

4Q208, 4Q209, 4Q211
Bibliography: Cf. 4Q209

Frag. 1 *col.* II (cf. *1 Enoch* 76:3-10) *1* and the following three, to the North. *Blank* [And the following three, to the West. *Blank* And from four of them the winds depart which] *2* are for the healing of the earth and its revitalization. *Blank* And [from eight of them depart the harmful winds; when they are sent, they destroy all the earth] *3* and the waters and all there is in them, what grows and flowers and creeps, [both in the waters as on dry land and all that lives in it. *Blank* First,] *4* the wind from the East goes out through the first gate which is in [the East and veers to the South. From it depart destruction, drought, heat and desolation. *Blank*] *5* From the second gate, (the middle one), departs the wind from the East-by-Ea[st: rain, fruits, renewal of life and dew. *Blank* From the third departs the wind] *6* from the North-east, which is close to the wind from the Nor[th: cold and aridity. *Blank* After them, from three gates which are towards the south of the heaven] *7* depart, first, through the first gate, [a wind from the South, which is in the South and veers to the East: a hot wind. *Blank* From the second gate departs a wind from the South] *8* which they call the Negeb: dew, [rain, well-being and renewal of life. *Blank* And from the third gate departs a wind from the South-east: dew, rain, locust and destruction. *Blank*] *9* [And] after it a wind from the N[orth] departs […] *10-13* […] *14* and desolation. The twelve gates of the four quarters of [the] hea[ven are completed. I have shown you their totality and their explanation, Methuselah, my son. The East they call East] *15* because it is the first; the South they call South becau[se the Great One sojourns there, and in it he sojourns … eternity. The

אתין כוכבי] 16   שמיא מא}ני{א'ן ערבין ומנאן על]לין כולהון]כוכביא
בדיל כ]ן קרין מערבא וקרין לצפונא צפון בדי בה צפנין]   17   ומתכ(נ)סין
וסחרין {ו}]כל ערבי]ן שמיא ואזלין]למדנח שמיא ו]למדנחא מדנח בדי מן
תמן דנחין מאני שמיא ואף מזרח בדיל]   18   די מ'אין דרחין ירחין
ב}א{השת]מותהון בכל יום וי]ום לאתחזיא על ארעא ...[19   ]וחזית תלת
...ת ארעה חד מנהן למדבר בה בני אנשא] vacat וחד מנהן [...]   20   [...
[... וחזית שב]עת ט]וריא ...]

[...] 2-1   *Frag.* 1 III   3   [...] ... ובמדנח שהרא פלג שביע חד די נהורה
אנ]יר בשמיא לאתח]זיא על ארעה]   4   [... ומשל]מין בכל יום "יום עד יום
ארבעת עשר ומש]למין]   5   [בה כל נהורה וקוי נהורה הד מן חמשת
עשיריא ומשלמין בכול יום ויום עד יום] חמשת עשר ומשלמין בה בכל
נהורה   6   [... ו]דבר ירחיא בפלגי שביעין   vacat   7   [ובמכסיה בציר שהרא
מן נהורה   vacat   ביומא קדמיא חד מן ארבעת עשי]ריא וביומא תנינא חד מן
תל]תת]   8   [עשיריא   vacat   וביומא תליתיא חד מן תרין עשיריא   vacat
וביומא רב]יעיא חד מן חד עש]ירא [vacat]   9   [...]...[...]

4Q211 (4QEnastr^d ar) *4QAstronomical Enoch^d ar*

J.T. Milik, *The Books of Enoch*, 296-297, pl. XXIX
PAM 43.212
ROC 369

[...] 1   *Frag.* 1 I   2   [... טל]ומטר מחתין [ע]ל ארעא וזרע
[...]עשב ארעא יעא ונפק ועל   3   [שמשא ...]ת ושתוא הוה ועלי כל
אילניא   5   [מתיבשין ומתנפלין ברא מן ארבעת]עשר אילנין די לא חזה
להון   6   [...]...[...] ע]ל]יהו]ן מתקימין

[...] 1   *Frag.* 1 II   2   דן מן משחתה .[...]   3   מעשר תשיע ח]ד ...]
4   תשיע חד וכוכ]בין] נזחו ב]תרעי] שמיא קד]מיא ובאדין]נפקו   5   ביומא

440

great quarter (they call) the West because the stars] *16* of the heaven [go there; all] the stars set there and ris[e] there; that is why [they call it the West. The North they call North, because] *17* all the bodies of [the heaven hide,] ‹gather together› and turn back in it, [and head] towards the East of the heaven. [The Orient (they call) Orient because from there the heavenly bodies rise. Also (they call it) the Levant because] *18* the moons arise from there becoming fu[ller day by d]ay to appear abo[ve the earth …] *19* [I saw three sections of the earth: one for the sons of men to live in;] *Blank* another […] *20* [… And I saw sev]en moun[tains …]

Frag. 1 *col.* III (cf. *1 Enoch* 78:6-8) *1-2* […] *3* [… When the moon rises, half of one seventh of its light shi]nes in the heaven to ap[pear above the earth] *4* [… and it becomes com]plete from day /to day/ until day fourteen, when *5* [all its light] is comp[lete in it. Its light waxes by fifteenths and becomes complete, day by day, until day] fifteen, on which all its light is complete. *6* […] and achieves its phases in halves of sevenths. *Blank 7* [In its waning (?) phase the moon decreases from its light. *Blank* The first day, one from the fourtee]nth; the second day, one from the th[ir-] *8* [teenth; *Blank* the third day, one from the twelfth; *Blank* the fou]rth [day] one from the elev[enth; *Blank*] *9* […] … […]

4Q211 (4QEnastr^d ar) *4QAstronomical Enoch^d ar*

4Q208, 4Q209, 4Q210
Bibliography: Cf. 4Q209

Frag. 1 *col.* I   *1* […] … *2* [… dew] and rain falling upon the earth, and seed *3* […] grass of the earth sprouted. [The sun] rises and sets *4* […] and it is winter; the leaves of all the trees *5* [wither and fall, except for the four]teen trees in which does not appear *6* […] … [… thei]r [lea]v[es] remain.

Frag. 1 *col.* II   *1* […] *2* this one, of its measure […] *3* a tenth of o[ne] ninth (part) […] *4* o[ne] ninth (part). The sta[rs] move through [the] fir[st gates] of the heaven. [And then] they go out *5* in the first days, [one] tenth of one [six]th;

קדמיא [חד] מעשר[בשתי]ת חד ותנינ'א חד מן חמשת 6 עשר בשתית ח[ד
ו]תלתיא ח[ד מ]ן תלתין בשתית חד *vacat* 7 [...][...]...[...]

Frag. 1 III 3-1 [...] 4 ב[יום חמ[שת ע[שר ...] ובאותה בימ[מא ...]
5 אך[ב]ליליא דן מן ל[... ת[לת תשיע וחמש]ת [... 6 ומעשר תשיע *vacat*
[...] 7 [...]...[...]

4Q212 (4QEn^g ar) *4QEnoch^g ar*

J.T. Milik, *The Books of Enoch*, 245-272, 360-362, pls. XXI-XXIV
PAM 43.214, 43.215
ROC 227, 228

Col. II 13-1 [...] 14 [...]ה והלכ]ה [... 15 ולה תשב]חה [...
16 ותנוח אר[עא ... [...] 17 כל דרי עלמי]ן [... 18 ארחת קשט]א [...
19 די תדעון מה[ן יתע]ב[ד ... [20 קושטא למהך בהון ו[...] 21 [ע]ל די
אבד לסוף אבדנא[... [22 [די כת]ב ויהב למת[ושלח ... [23 [וח]כים
אנושא ובחי[ר [בני [...] 24 בנו]הי ו[לדריא אחריא לכול י[תבי ...
25 [... אל תה[ון בבהשתא את[ון ... [26 [...]יהב[...

Col. III 14-1 [...] 15 [...].[...] 16 [... בח]שוכא [... 17 מ[ן יומא
18 ד[ן ... ח]נוך מתלה 19 אמר[...]ו מן נצבת 20 יצבתא[... ב]ני אנה
הוא 21 חנוך אחזי]ת ... [ממר עירין וקדשין 22 אנה כלא ידעת [... כל]א
קר]ית ואתבוננ[ת ות]ב[23 נסב חנוך מתלה ואמר א]נה [...]שביע

the second (days), one fif- *6* teenth of o[ne] sixth; the third (days), o[ne] thirti-
eth [o]f one sixth. *Blank 7* [...] ... [...]

Frag. 1 *col.* III   *1-3* [...] *4* On [day fi]ft[een ...] and on [the] same da[y ...] *5* only
[in] this night, of [... a thi]rd of a ninth, and a fif[th ...] *6* and a tenth of a ninth.
Blank [...] *7* [...] ... [...]

4Q212 (4QEn^g ar) *4QEnoch^g ar*

4Q201, 4Q202, 4Q204, 4Q205, 4Q206, 4Q207
Bibliography: Cf. 4Q201

Col. II (= 1 Enoch 91:18 - 92:2)   *1-13* [...] *14* [...] and he will go [...] *15* [... they
will give] him prai[se ...] *16* and [the] ear[th] shall rest [...] *17* all eternal
generations. [And now I am going to speak to you, my sons and show you all]
18 the paths of justice [and all the paths of violence and again I shall show you
them so] *19* you know what [is going to ha]pp[en. Now, then, my sons, listen
to me and choose the tracks of] *20* justice in order to walk on them and [...]
21 [be]cause [everyone] is going to utter destruction [who walks on the path of
injustice.] *22* [What he wro]te and gave to Meth[uselah, his son, and to all his
brothers, Enoch, the celebrated scribe] *23* [and the wis]est of men, the chos[en
one of] the sons of [the earth to judge their deeds. He wrote to the sons of]
24 h[is] sons [and] to future generations, to all who dw[ell on dry land so that
they will do good] *25* [and peace: «Do not b]e upset, yo[u and your spirits, on
account of the times] *26* [because the Great Holy One] has given [times for
everything ...]

Col. III (= *1 Enoch* 92:5 - 93:4)   *1-15* [...] *16* [... in da]rkness *17* [... fr]om th[is]
day *18* [... When he was delivering his letter E]noch [resumed] his speech
19 saying: [«With regard to the sons of justice and about the chosen of the
world who have risen] from a plant *20* of truth [and justice, behold I will
speak, and I will make it known to you,] my [so]ns. I *21* Enoch, [I] have been
shown [everything in a vision of heaven, and from] the word of the Watchers
and holy ones *22* I have come to know everything, [and from the tablets of
heaven I] have rea[d every]thing [and understood».] And aga[in] *23* Enoch
resumed his speech and said: «I, [Enoch,] w[as born] the seventh, [in the] first

א[תילדת ...]   24 קדמי ועד עלי קשטא כב[ר ...]   25 תנין {ז}[ז]די בה שקרא
וחמסא יצמח[...]

Col. IV   1-10 [...]   11 [...] עבד[והי בט]עותא[א]   12 [ועם סופה
י[תבחרון ב]חירי[ן לשהד[ה}י קשט מן נ[צבת]   13 קשט על[מ]א די שבעה
פ[עמי]ן חכמה ומדע תתיה[ב להון]   14 ולהון עקרין אשי חמסא וע[ל}[בד
שקרא בה למעבד] דין[15 ומן בתרה יקום שביע תמיני קשוט דבה
תתיה[ב חרב]   16 לכול קשיטין למעבד {דינא} דין קשוט מן כול רשיעין
17 ויתיהבון בידהון ועם סופה יקנון נכסין בקשוט   18 ויתבנא היכל
[מ]ל[כ]ות רבא ברבות זוה לכול דרי עלמין   19 ומן בתרה שבוע תשעי
וק[שוט ו]ד[י]ן קשוט בה]יתגלא   20 לכול בני ארעא כלה וכול עב[די
רשיעיא יעברו]ן מן כול   21 ארעא כולה וירמון לבור] ... [כלהון   22 לארח
קשט עלמא ומן]... דבשבי]עה   23 דין עלמא וקץ דינא רבא] ... [ושמין
24 קדמין בה יעברון ושמ]ין [...] שמיא   25 צ[הר]ין ודנחין לכול עלמי]ן ...
ש[בעין שגי   26 [די לא]איתי סוף לכול מ[נינהון ... וקש]טא יעבדון

Col. V   1-14 [...]   15 [די יכ]ל ינדע מה בטעם]...[16 [ד]י יכל
ישמע [מ]לי קדשא]   17 [... או מנו הוא כול אנוש די]...[18 זויא די
אנ]ון [ע]ליהו]ן יתנח[ון]...[19 למתב למת]ניה ...[20 או מנו הוא [מן
כול בני א[נוש די יכל] ...[21 אורכה ופתיה די ארעא כולה או] ...[
22 וצרתה ומנו הוא כול אנוש די יכ]ל [...]   23 הוא רומהון והיכה אנון
סמכי]ן [...]   24 וכען לכון אנה אמר בני] ...[25 ארחת קשטא] ...
26 א[נושא ...]

[week] *24* and until my time justice [was] stil[l strong. After me will come the] *25* second [week] in which deceit and violence will spring up [...]

Col. IV (= *1 Enoch* 93:9-10 + 91:11-17)   *1-10* [...] *11* [...] his [deeds] will be in er[ror.] *12* [At its close] the ch[osen one]s [will] be chosen as witnesses to justice from the p[lant] *13* of ever[last]ing justice; sevenf[old] wisdom and knowledge shall be giv[en to them]. *14* They shall uproot the foundations of violence and the work of deceit in it in order to carry out [judgment.] *15* After this, the eighth week will come, the one of justice, in which [a sword] will be giv[en] *16* to all the just, for them to carry out {the judgment} just judgment against the wicked *17* and they will be delivered into their hands. At its close, they will gain riches in justice *18* and there will be built the temple of the [k]in[g]ship of The Great One, in his glorious greatness, for all eternal generations. *19* And after that, the ninth week. [In it] will be revealed jus[tice and just] ju[dgment] *20* to all the sons of the whole earth. All those who ac[t wickedly will vanish] completely from the entire *21* earth and they shall be hurled into the [eternal] pit. All [men will see] *22* the just eternal path. And after [that, the tenth week. In] its [seve]nth (part) *23* there will be eternal judgment and the moment of the great judgment [and he will carry out revenge in the midst of the holy ones.] *24* In it, the first heaven will pass away and [there will appear a new] hea[ven and all the forces of] heaven *25* will ri[se] and shine throughout all eternity, [seven times more. After that there will be] many [w]eeks *26* [the number of which will not] have an end [ever, in which] they shall practice [goodness and just]ice

Col. V (= *1 Enoch* 93:11 - 94:2)   *1-13* [...] *14* [... Who, among all men] *15* [ca]n understand what is the command of [God, or who among all the sons of men] *16* can hear the [wo]rds of the Holy One [without being upset or can think his thoughts?] *17* Or which man at all [can consider all the works of the heavens or the] *18* angular [columns] up[on] which it rests; [or who sees a soul or a spirit and can] *19* go back to tel[l about it? Or go up and see their whole community and think or act like them?] *20* Or who [among all the sons of m]en can [know and measure what is] *21* the length and breadth of the entire earth? Or [to whom has been shown all its ...] *22* and its shape? And which man at all ca[n know what the extent of the heavens is, and what] *23* their height is, or how they are supported, [or how large is the number of the stars?] *24* Now I tell you, my sons: [«Love justice and walk in it, because] *25* the paths of justice [are worthy of being approved, but the paths of injustice will be destroyed and will vanish. To the sons of] *26* m[en ...]

4Q213 (4QLevi^a ar) *4QAramaic Levi^a*

M.E. Stone, J.C. Greenfield, *DJD XXII*, 1-24, pl. I
PAM 43.241
ROC 817
CTL, 1Q21, 4Q213a, 4Q213b, 4Q214, 4Q214a, 4Q214b, 4Q540, 4Q541
Bibliography: A. Hultgård, *L'eschatologie des Testaments des Douze Patriarches. II. Composition de l'ouvrage, textes et traductions* (Acta Universitatis Upsaliensis. Historia Religionum 7; Uppsala: Almqvist, 1982) 92-122; M. de Jonge, 'The

Frag. 1 i 1 [...] *vacat* 2 [ובשנת מאה ותמני עשרה לחיי היא שתא
די מ]ית בה 3 [יוסף אחי קרית לבני ולבניהון ושרית לפקדה]אנון 4 [ית
כל די הוא עם לבבי ענית ואמרת]לבני 5 [שמעו למאמר לוי אבוכן ואציתו
לפקודי ידיד אלה ו]אנה לכן 6 [מפקד בני ואנה קשטא לכן מחוה חביבי
רא]ש כל עבדכן 7 [יהוה קשטא ועד עלם יהוה עמ]כן קא[ם] צדקתא
וקשטא 8 [... תטלון עללה ברי]כה דזרע טב טב מעל 9 [ודזרע ביש
עלוהי תאב זר]עה *vacat* וכען ספר ומוסר וחכמה 10 [אלפו לבניכן ותהוה
חכמתא עמכן]ליקר עלם די אלף חכמה יקר 11 [הוא לה ודי שאט חכמתא
לב]סרון ולשיטו מתיהב חזו לכן בני 12 [ליוסף אחי די מאלף הוא ספר
ומוס]ר חכמה ליקר ולרבו ולמלכין 13 [...] א[ל תמחלו חכמתא למאלף
14 [...כ]ל ... גבר די אלף חכמה כל 15 [יומוהי אריכין וסגא לה שמעה
...]א לכל מת ומדינה די יהך לה 16 [אח איתי בה ולא הוא מתנכ]ר בה ולא
דמא בה לנכרי ולא 17 [דמא בה לכילי מן די כלהון י]הבין לה בה יקר בדי
כלא צבין 18 [למאלף חכמתה רחמו]הי שגיאין ושאלי שלמה רברבין
19 [ועל כרסי די יקר לה מותבי]ן למשמע מלי הכמתה 20 [עותר רב די
יקר היא חכמתה ל]ידעיה ושימה טבה 21 [לכל קניה הן יאתון מלכין
תקיפ]י]ן ועם [רב] 22-23 [...]

Frags. 1 ii + 2 1 מטמוריה ולא יעלון תרעיה ולא [...] ולא[
2 ישכחון למכבש שוריה *vacat* ולא [...] ולא[3 יחזון שימתה שימתה
.[...].[...]. 4 ולא איתי כל מחיר נגדה [...]. 5 בעא חכמת]ה וחכ]מתה
י[...].[...].[...] 6 מטמרה מנה[...].[...].[...] 7 ולא חס[י]ו]ר[...]ן כל בעי]ה[

4Q213 (4QLevi[a] ar) *4QAramaic Levi[a]*

Testament of Levi and Aramaic Levi', *RevQ* 13/49-52 (1988) 367-388; M.E.
Stone, J.C. Greenfield, 'The First Manuscript of *Aramaic Levi Document* from
Qumran (4QLevi[a] aram)', *Le Muséon* 107 (1994) 257-281; R.A. Kugler, *From
Patriarch to Priest. The Levi-Priestly Tradition from Aramaic Levi to Testament of
Levi* (SBL Early Judaism and Its Literature 9; Atlanta: Scholars Press, 1996); .-
'Some Further Evidence for the Samaritan Provenance of Aramaic Levi
(1QTestLevi; 4QTestLevi), *RevQ* 17/65-68 (1996) 351-358

Frag. 1 *col.* I (= CTL Cambridge *cols.* e - f)   *1* [...] *Blank 2* [And in the year one
hundred and eighteen of my life, the year] in which [my brother Joseph] died,
3 [I summoned my sons and their sons, and I began to instruct] them *4* [all that
there was in my heart. I began speaking and said] to my sons: *5* [«Listen to the
word of Levi, your father, and pay attention to the precepts of the beloved of
God.] I, to you *6* [my sons, give orders, and to you I show the truth, my beloved ones. The prin]ciple of all your deeds *7* [should be the truth, and let]
justice and truth [stay with] you [for ever,] *8* [... you will bring in a bles]sed
[harvest.] Whoever sows goodness, harvests good, *9* [and whoever sows evil,
against him] his [see]d [turns.] *Blank* But now, reading and instruction and
wisdom *10* [teach them to your sons, and wisdom will be with you] for eternal
honour. He who teaches wisdom will be honoured *11* [by it, but he who despises wisdom] will be given [to in]sult and scorn. See then, my sons, *12* [my
brother Joseph who taught reading, and instruct]ion of wisdom for honour
and for greatness, and for kings *13* [...] Do not neglect wisdom to teach *14* [...
Ev]ery ... man who teaches wisdom, all *15* [his days will be lengthened and
multiplied will be his renown ...] In each region and province to which he
goes, *16* [there will be a brother, and he will not be considered a foreig]ner in
it, and will not be like a stranger in it, nor *17* [be like a scoundrel in it. Instead,
all] shall give him glory in it, for all desire *18* [to learn his wisdom.] His
[friends] are many, and numerous those who wish him well. *19* [And they shall
seat him upon a throne of glory,] to listen to the words of his wisdom. *20* [A
great richness of glory is wisdom for] whoever knows it, and a treasure *21* [for
all who acquire it. If] powerful [kings come and a [great] people *22-23* [...]

Frags. 1 *col.* II + 2 (= CTL Cambridge *col.* f; cf. 4Q214a 2 - 3 II)   *1* its secrets,
nor enter its gates, nor [... nor] *2* will they be able to conquer its ramparts.
Blank And not [... nor] *3* will they see the treasure, the treasure [...] ... [...]
4 and there is no price at all compared to her [...] *5* seek wisdom, [and
wis]dom ... [...] *6* which has hidden itself from it [...] ... [...] *7* and there is no

8 וקשט]...[ספר ומוסר   9 ח]כמ[ה ^{די}]...[אלפ]ו ...[תרתון אנון
10]...[רבה תתנון   11]... י[קר vacat
12]...[אף בספריא   13 קר] ... תהו]ון ראשין ושפטין   14 ודע]...[ב
ועבדין   15]...[אף כהנין ומלכין   16]...[ן מלכותכן   17 תהוא]...[ר
ולא איתי סוף   18 ל]...[לא]תעבר מנכן עד כל   19 ד]ריא ...[. ביקר רב

Frags. 3 + 4   1]...[... כל עממיא   2]... וש]הרא וכוכביא   3]...[מן
4]...[לשהרא   5]...[כן תחשכון]...[6]...[א הלא קבל] ח[נוך ...
7]...[נא ועל מן תהוא חובתא   8]...[הלא עלי ועליכן בני ארו ידעונה
9]...א[רחת קש^טא תשבק]ו[ן וכל שבילי]...[תמחלון ותהכון בחשוכה
11 ...   ]...[... ח]ש[וכה תתא עליכן ...]ותתי]ה[בון   12]...[...]...[...
זמ]ן די] תהוון לשכלין   13]...[...]...[...]...[...

4Q213a (4QLevi^b ar) *4QAramaic Levi^b*

M.E. Stone, J.C. Greenfield, *DJD XXII*, 25-36, pl. II
PAM 43.242, 43.243
ROC 249
CTL, 1Q21, 4Q213, 4Q213b, 4Q214, 4Q214a, 4Q214b, 4Q540, 4Q541
Bibliography: J.T. Milik 'Le Testament de Lévi en araméen: Fragment de la

Frag. 1 i   4-1]...[5]...[ד]   6]...[אנה   7]... את]רחע[ת וכל
8]... נ[טלת לשמיא   9]... ו[אצבעת כפי וידי   10]... ו[אמרת מרי אנתה
11]...א[נתה בלחודיך ידע   12]... [ארחת קשט ארחק   13]...[באיש^א
וזנותא דחא   14]... ח]כמה ומנדע וגבורה   15]...א[ל שכחה רחמיך
קדמיך   16]... [דשפיר ודטב קדמיך   17]... ו[אל תשלט בי כל שטן

la[c]k […] all those who seek [it] *8* and truth […] reading and the instruction of *9* wi[sd]om /of […]/, teac[h …] you will instruct them *10* … […] great. You shall give *11* [… glo]ry. *Blank 12* … […] also in the books *13* read (?) [… you sh]all be chiefs and judges *14* and … […] and servants *15* […] also priests and kings *16* … […] your kingdom *17* will be […] and will have no end *18* … […] will [not] pass from you until all *19* ge[nerations …] with great glory

Frags. 3 + 4   *1* […] … all the nations *2* [… the m]oon and the stars *3* […] of *4* […] the moon *5* […] … you will become dark […] *6* Did not [E]noch accuse … *7* […] … And upon whom will the blame fall, *8* […] except upon me and upon you, my sons? Know then *9* […] you will forsake the [pa]ths of justice and all the ways of *10* […] you will neglect and you will walk in darkness … *11* […] … da[rk]ness will come upon you, and you will be h[an]ded over *12* […] … […] wh[en] you shall become understanding *13* […] … […] … […]

4Q213a (4QLevi[b] ar) *4QAramaic Levi[b]*

grotte 4 de Qumrân', *RB* 62 (1955) 398-406, pl. IV; .- *RB* 73 (1966) 95, n. 2; J.A. Fitzmyer, D. Harrington, *MPAT*, 88-91; M.E. Stone, J.C. Greenfield, 'The Prayer of Levi', *JBL* 112 (1993) 247-266; .- 'The Second Manuscript of *Aramaic Levi Document* from Qumran (4QLevi[b] aram)', *Le Muséon* 109 (1996) 1-15; Cf. 4Q213

Frag. 1 col. I (cf. Test. Levi additions Mt. Athos MS to 2:3)   *1-4* […] *5* […] … *6* [… And then] I *7* [washed my clothes and I purified them with pure water, and] I [washed myself completely in living water] and all *8* [my paths I made straight. And then] I lifted [my eyes and my face] to heaven *9* [And I opened my mouth and began to speak,] and the fingers of my hands and my arms *10* [I stretched out in the right way, towards the holy ones, and I prayed and] said: «My Lord, you *11* [know all hearts, and all thoughts of minds y]ou alone know. *12* [Now, then, my children are with me. Grant me all the] paths of truth; remove far *13* [from me, Lord, the spirit of injustice and] evil [thought] and fornication; turn away *14* [pride from me. Show me the holy spirit, counsel, wi]sdom, intelligence and [grant me] strength *15* [to do your will, to] find your compassion before you, *16* [to praise your deeds towards me, and to do] what is beautiful and good before you *17* [… and] may no adversary rule over me

18 ...] ע]לי מרי וקרבני למהוא לכה

Frag. 1 II   4-1 [...]   5 לע]ו[...]   6 מרי ב]רכת ...[7 זרע דק]שט ...[

8 צלות עב]דך ...[9 דין קשט לכ]ל ...[10 לבר עבדך מן ק]דמיך ...[

11 באדין נגדת ב]...[12 על אבי יעקוב וכד]י ...[13 מן אבל מין אדין]

14   [...] שכבת ויתבת אנה ע]ל ...[15 *vacat*   אדין חזיון אחזית] ...[

16 בחזית חזויא וחזית שמ]יא ...[17 תחותי רם עד דבק לשמי]א ...[

18 לי תרעי שמיא ומלאך חד] ...[

Frag. 2   1 [...]...[...]   2 ...] [אשבען ו]...[...]...[3 ...] ה]...[ה גבריא ...[

[אנתה ותחלל שמה ושם אבוה   4 [...]...[...]... בהתא וכל 5 ...] בתו]לה

זי חבלת שמה ושם אבהתה ואבהתת לכל אחיה   6 [...]אבוה ולא מתמחא

שם חסיא מן כול עמה}א{ לעלם   7 [...]ל]י]ט לכל דרי עלמא ומ]...[...]

קדישין מן עמא די   8 [...]...[...]מעשר קודש קרבן לאל מן

4Q213b (4QLevi^c ar) *4QAramaic Levi^c*

M.E. Stone, J.C. Greenfield, *DJD XXII*, 37-41, pl. III
PAM 43.242
ROC 816
CTL, 1Q21, 4Q213, 4Q213a, 4Q214, 4Q214a, 4Q214b, 4Q540, 4Q541
Bibliography: J.T. Milik, *The Books of Enoch*, 23-24; R. Eisenman, M. Wise,

1 [...]כה רעיתך מן כל בשר]א[2 ...] ונגדו שבעתין מן לותי ו]אנה

אתעירת מן שנתי אדין   3 [אמרת חזוה הוא דן וכדן אנה מתמה די יהוה לה

כל חזוה וטמר]ת אף בלבבי ולכל אנש לא   4 [גליתה ועלנא על אבי יצחק

ואף הוא כדן ברכני אדין כ]די הוה יעקוב אבי מעשר   5 [כל מה די הוה לה

18 [to lead me astray from your path. Have compassion wi]th me, my Lord, and bring me near to be to you

Frag. 1 *col.* II (cf. Test. Levi additions Mt. Athos MS to 2:3) *1-4* [a servant ...] *5* ... [... You,] *6* my Lord, have ble[ssed my father Abram and my mother Sarah, and you have said to give them] *7* a ju[st] offspring [which will be blessed for ever. Listen then to] *8* the prayer of [your] serv[ant Levi, to be near to you. Let him share in your words to pass] *9* just judgment for a[ll the centuries, me and my sons for all eternal generations. And do not remove] *10* the son of your servant from be[fore you, all the days of eternity». And I became silent, when I was still praying ...] *11* Then I went to [...] *12* to my father Jacob and whe[n ...] *13* from Abel-Mayin. Then, [...] *14* I lay down and settled up[on ...] *15* *Blank* Then I saw visions [...] *16* in the appearance of this vision, I saw [the] heav[en opened, and I saw a mountain] *17* underneath me, high, reaching up to heaven [...] *18* to me the gates of heaven, and an angel [said to me: «Enter Levi» ...]

Frag. 2 *1* [...] ... [...] *2* [...] he adjured us and [...] ... [...] the men *3* [...] a woman and she will defile her name and her father's name *4* [...] ... [...] ... shame, and all *5* [... young wo]man who has profaned her name and of the name of her fathers, and has brought shame upon all her brothers *6* [...] her father, and her disgraceful name will not be wiped out from all her people for ever *7* [...] it will be cu[rs]ed for all eternal generations and [...] ... the holy ones of the people who *8* [...] ... [...] holy tithe, an offering for God from

---

4Q213b (4QLevi^c ar) *4QAramaic Levi^c*

DSSU, 136-141; K. Beyer, *ATTME*, 71-78; M.E. Stone, J.C. Greenfield, 'The Third and Fourth Manuscripts of *Aramaic Levi Document* from Qumran (4QLevi^c aram and 4QLevi^d aram)', *Le Muséon* 109 (1996) 245-259; Cf. 4Q213

(= CTL Bodleian *col.* a) *1* [...] ... I have preferred you above all flesh *2* [... and those seven departed from me, and] I awoke from my dream. Then *3* [I thought: «This vision is like the other one. I am amazed that the whole vision is to come». And] I [hid] (this vision) too, in my heart and to no-one *4* [did I reveal it. And we went to my father Isaac, and he also blessed me likewise. Then, w]hen my father Jacob tithed *5* [everything he had, according to his

כנדרה וכען הוית קדמי בראש כהנות]ה ולי מן בנוהי יהב 6 [קרבן ... לאל
ואלבשני לבוש כהנותה ומלי ידי והוית כהן לא]ל עלמיא] ...[

4Q214 (4QLevi^d ar) *4QAramaic Levi^d*

M.E. Stone, J.C. Greenfield, *DJD XXII*, 43-51, pl. III
PAM 43.243
ROC 370

Frag. 2 1 [למזר]ק [דמא על כותלי מדבחא ועוד רחע] 2 [ידיך
ור]גליך מ]ן דמא ושרי לאסקה אבריא] 3 [מליח]ין ראשא [לקדמין הוי
מסק ועלוהי] 4 [חפי תרב]א ואל יתחזי [לה דם נכסת תורא ובתרוהי]
5 [צואר]א ובתרהן ידיא] ובתרהן ניעא עם בן דפנא] 6 [ובת]רהן ירכתא
ושדרת] חרצא ובתר ירכתא רגלין] 7 [רחי]ען עם קרביא וכלה]ן מליחין
במלח כדי חזי] 8 [לה]ן [כ]מסתן *vacat* וב]תר דנא נשפא בליל במשחא]
9 [ו]בתר כלא חמר [נסך והקטר עליהן לבונה] 10 [ו]הוא עבדך בס]רך
וכל קרבניך ...[

4Q214a (4QLevi^c ar) *4QAramaic Levi^e*

M.E. Stone - J.C. Greenfield, *DJD XXII*, 53-60, pl. IV
PAM 43.260
ROC 370

Frags. 2-3 ı 1 [...] 2 כדי [...] 3 ...]]עלוהי[. בשנת ארבעין לחיי
ילידת בירחא רב]יעא 4 [ועוד אוספת והוית עמה והרת ויילדת לי ברת]א
ושוית 5 [שמה יוכבד אמרת ילידת לי ליקר לישראל]בשנת 6]שתין
וארבע לי לחיי ויילדת בחד בחודשא שב]יעי

452

vow, then I served for the first time at the head of] the [priesthood,] and to me, among his sons, he gave *6* [the offering … to God, and he clothed me with the clothing of the priesthood and filled my hand, and I became a priest for Go]d of eternity […]

4Q214 (4QLevi^d ar) *4QAramaic Levi^d*

CTL, 1Q21, 4Q213, 4Q213a, 4Q213b, 4Q214a, 4Q214b, 4Q540, 4Q541
Bibliography: R. Eisenman, M. Wise, *DSSU*, 136-141; K. Beyer, *ATTME*, 71-78; Cf. 4Q213 and 4Q213b

Frag. 2 (= CTL Bodleian *col.* d; 4Q214b 2 - 6 1)   *1* [… to sprin]kle [the blood on the sides of the altar, and again wash] *2* [your hands and] your [fe]et fr[om the blood, and begin to offer] *3* [the sal]ted [portions. Offer] the head [first, and] *4* [cover it with] the [fat,] and not should be seen [on it blood of the slaughtered cow. And after it] *5* the [neck (?),] and after them, the forelegs, [and after them the breast with the ribs.] *6* [And afte]r them the thighs and the spine of [the loin. And after the thighs, the hind-legs] *7* [was]hed, with the entrails. And all of th[em salted with salt, in the way which is fitting] *8* [for the]m, according to their need. *Blank* And af[ter this, flour mixed with oil.] *9* [And] after everything, [pour] wine, [and burn incense over them] *10* [so that] your service may be in or[der and all your offerings …]

4Q214a (4QLevi^e ar) *4QAramaic Levi^e*

CTL, 1Q21, 4Q213, 4Q213a, 4Q213b, 4Q214, 4Q214b, 4Q540, 4Q541
Bibliography: R. Eisenman, M. Wise, *DSSU*, 136-141; K. Beyer, *ATTME*, 71-78; Cf. 4Q213

Frags. 2 - 3 *col.* I (= CTL Cambridge *col.* c)   *1* […] when *2* […] over him *3* [… In the fortieth year of my life she gave birth in the fou]rth [month,] *4* and once again I was with her, and she became pregnant and gave birth to a daughter for me.] And I called *5* [her Jochebed, I thought: «She has given birth to me the honour of Israel.] In the [sixty-fourth] year *6* [of my life she gave birth on the first day of the seven]th [month]

Frags. 2-3 ɪɪ   1 ומדיתא [ויבוזון כל מה די בהון אוצרי חכמתא לא
טביה ו]לא   3   [... ולא יעלון תרעיה ולא מטמוריה ישכחון] לא   2 יבוזון]
מ]וסר]   5   וכען בני ספר ו[...]פל מנה   4   [... ישכחון למכבש שוריה
[...]... חזית   6   [... חכמתא אלפו

4Q214b (4QLeviᶠ ar) *4QAramaic Leviᶠ*

M.E. Stone, J.C. Greenfield, *DJD XXII*, 61-72, pl. IV
PAM 43.260
ROC 370

Frags. 2-6 ɪ   1 [...] עעי]ן מצלחין   2 [ובקר אינון לקדמין מן תולעא
ובאדי]ן אסק] אנו]ן ארי [כדן חזית לאברה]ם]   3 [אבי מזדהר מן כל תרי
[די ריח תננ הון   4 ע]שר עעין א[מ]ר לי] די חזין ל[אסקה מנהון למדבחא
ואטו לא ושוחא]   5 בשים [סלק ואל]ן שמה]תהון ארזא ודפ]רנא וסיגדה
[רקתא [אל]ן אנון   6 ואורנא] ברותא ותככא] ועעא משחא ע]רא אדסה ועעי
[על מדבחא וכדי אסקת   7 די א]מר לי די חזין לאסקה מנהון [לתחות עלתא
[והא באדין תשרא   8 מן עעי]א אל ן למדבח]א ונורא ישרא לאדלקא בהון]
[ורגליך מן דמא ושרי   9 למזרק דמא [על כותלי מדבחא ותוב] רחע ידיך]
[... לאסקה א[ב]ריא] מ[ל]יחן רא[ש]א

4Q215 (4QTNaph) *4QTestament of Naphtali*

M.E. Stone, *DJD XXII*, 73-82, pl. V
PAM 43.237
ROC 368

Frags. 1-3   1 עם אחיות אבי בלהה א]מי ודוד]תה דבורה אשר הניקה
את רב]קה [...]   2 וילך בשבי וישלח לבן ויפרקהו ויתן לו את חנה אחת
מאמהותי]ו ותהר ותלד]   3 ראישונה את זלפה ויתן את שמה זלפה בשם

454

Frags. 2 - 3 *col.* ɪɪ (= CTL Cambridge *col.* f; cf. 4Q213 1 ɪɪ - 2)   *1* and of the province [and they steal everything there is in them, they cannot steal the treasure of wisdom,] *2* nor will they find [its secrets, nor enter its gates, nor …] *3* its goods, n[or will they be able to conquer its ramparts …] *4* from it … […] *5* And now, my son, reading and [the instruction of wisdom teach …] *6* I saw … […]

4Q214b (4QLevi^f ar) *4QAramaic Levi^f*

CTL, 1Q21, 4Q213, 4Q213a, 4Q213b, 4Q214, 4Q214a, 4Q540, 4Q541
Bibliography: Cf. 4Q213

Frags. 2 - 6 *col.* ɪ (= CTL Bodleian *cols.* c - d; 4Q214 2)   *1* [… the] split [woo]d; *2* [but scrutinise it first for all the worms, and the]n [offer] it. [For] thus I saw Abraha[m,] *3* [my father, looking out for any obstacle. Twe]lve (kinds of) wood did he s[ho]w me of those [which are fitting to be] offered upon the altar, *4* [whose aroma] rises, [pleasing.] And these are [their] name[s: cedar, juni]per, almond, *5* [tamarind, pine, ash,] cypress, fig, [olive, lau]rel, myrtle and *6* [balsam.] These are what he sh[owed me, from which one could make offerings] under the holocause *7* [upon the altar. When you offer any of] these [(kinds of) wood] upon [the] altar [and the fi]re st[arts to burn them] *8* [then you shall begin to sprinkle the blood] upon the sides of the altar. Again, [you shall wash your hands] *9* [and your feet from the blood and you shall begin to offer] the sal[t]ed [por]ti[ons, the] he[ad …]

4Q215 (4QTNaph) *4QTestament of Naphtali*

Bibliography: R. Eisenman, M. Wise, *DSSU*, 156-160; G. W. Nebe, 'Qumranica I: Zu unveröffentlichten Handschriften aus Höhle 4 von Qumran', *ZAW* 106 (1994) 315-322; *Wacholder-Abegg 3*, 6; M.E. Stone, 'The Hebrew Testament of Naphtali', *JJS* 47 (1996) 311-321

Frags. 1 - 3   *1* with Ahiyot, Bilhah's father, [my] mo[ther, and] her [aunt was] Deborah, who suckled Rebe[cca …] *2* And he went to captivity, but Laban went and freed him; and he gave Hana to him, one of [his] maidservants [and she conceived and gave birth] *3* first to Zilpah. He gave her the name of

העיר אשר נשבה אל[י]ה [...] 4 ותהר ותלד את בלהה אמי ותקרא חנה את

שמה בלהה כי כאשר נולדה[...] 5 מתבהלת לינוק ותואמר מה מתבהלת

היאה בתי ותקרא עוד בלההה[...] 6 *vacat* 7 וכאשר בא יעקוב אבי אל

לבן בורח מלפני עישיו אחיהו וכאשר [...] 8 אבי בלהה אמי וינהג לבן את

חנה אם אמי ואת שתי בנותיה] עמה ונתן אחת] 9 [ללאה]ואחת לרחל

וכאשר היתה רחל לוא ילדה בנים ...[...] 10 [... יעקו]ב אבי ונתון לו את

בלהה אמי ותלד את דן אח]י ... [...]...[...] 11

4Q215a (4QTime of Righteousness) *4QTime of Righteousness*

Wacholder-Abegg 3, 7-8
PAM 43.245
ROC 371

Frag. 1 II 1-2 [...]...[...]...[...] 3 וצרת מצוק ונסוי שחת ויצרופו

בם לבחירי צדק וימח [כו]ל פשע 4 בעבור חס[ד]יו כיא שלם קץ הרשע

וכול עולה ת[עבו]ר [כיא] 5 באה עת הצדק ומלאה הארץ דעה ותהלת אל

בימ[י ...] 6 בא קץ השלום וחוקי האמת ותעודת [ה]צדק להשכיל] כול]

7 בדרכי אל [ו]בגבורות מעשיו] ... ע]ד עולמי עד כול ל[שון] 8 תברכנו

וכול אנש ישתחוה לו[ן] והיה לב]בם אח[ד] כיא הואה [ידע] 9 פעולתם

בטרם הבראם ועבודת הצדק פלג גבולותם [*vacat?*] 10 בדורותם כיא בא

ממשל {הצדק} הטוב וירם כסא ה[...] 11 ומודה גבה השכל ערמה ותושיה

נבחנו במחש[בת] ק[ו]ל[ד]שו [... [...]...[...] 12

Frag. 2 1 קודשו יסדם ל[...]...[...] 2 בראם לחד[ש ... [...] 3 מימיו

וחושך[...] 4 למועדי ...[...] חושך[... 5 למועדים בטרם [...]

6 [...]...[...]

Frag. 3 1 [...]להחרים ארץ] ב]חרונו ולחדש [...] 2 [...]...[...]

מ]קור דעה כי [...] 3 [...]...[...]

Zilpah, the name of the city in which he had been prisoner. [...] *4* And she conceived and gave birth to Bilhah, my mother. Hana gave her the name of Bilhah, for when she was born [...] *5* hurried to suck. And she said: «How my daughter hurries!» And she called her Bilhah again [...] *6 Blank 7* When Jacob, my father, came to Laban fleeing away from his brother Esau, and when [...] *8* the father of Bilhah, my mother. And Laban led Hana, my mother's mother, and her two daughters, [with him; and he gave one] *9* [to Leah] and the other to Rachel. And as Rachel did not bear sons ... [...] *10* [... Jaco]b, my father. And he was given Bilhah, my mother, and she bore Dan, [my] brother [...] *11* [...] ... [...]

4Q215a (4QTime of Righteousness) *4QTime of Righteousness*

Bibliography: R. Eisenman, M. Wise, *DSSU*, 156-160; E.G. Chazon, M.E. Stone, '*4QTime of Righteousness* (4Q215ᵃ, Olim *4QTNaphtali*): A Preliminary Publication of Fragment 1 ii', in *Provo Conference*, 124-125

Frag. 1 *col.* II   *1-2* [...] ... [...] *3* and the dread of hardship, and the trial of the pit. And they will refine by them the chosen of justice and he will wipe out [al]l iniquity *4* on account of his pio[us] ones; for the age of wickedness is fulfilled and all injustice will [pass a]way. [For] *5* the time of justice has arrived, and the earth is filled with knowledge and the praise of God. In the da[ys of ...] *6* the age of peace has arrived, and the laws of truth, and the testimony of justice, to instruct [all] *7* in God's paths [and] in the mighty acts of his deeds [... f]or eternal centuries. Every t[ongue] *8* will bless him, and every man will bow down before him, [and they will be] of on[e mi]nd. For he [knows] *9* their actions before they were created, and (for) the service of justice he has divided their territories [*Blank?*] *10* in their generations. For the dominion {of justice} of goodness has arrived, and he will raise the throne of [...] *11* and very high. Intelligence, prudence and sound wisdom are tested by [his] h[o]ly desi[gn ...] *12* [...] ... [...]

Frag. 2   *1* (by) his holy (design) he established them for [...] ... [...] *2* he created them to ren[ew ...] *3* of his days. And darkness [...] *4* for their appointed times ... [...] darkness [...] *5* for the appointed times before [...] *6* [...] ... [...]

Frag. 3   *1* [...] to destroy the earth [with] his anger and to renew [...] *2* [... the w]ell of knowledge, because [...] *3* [...] ... [...]

4Q216 (4QJubᵃ) *4QJubilees^a*

J.C. VanderKam, J.T. Milik, *DJD XIII*, 1-22, pl. I-II

PAM 43.185, 43.186

ROC 384, 385

1Q17, 1Q18, 2Q19, 2Q20, 3Q5, 4Q176a,b, 4Q217, 4Q218, 4Q219, 4Q220,

Col. I   4 [...]אל ראש   [...יהוה] בדבר [...]3   [...ל]קחת [...]2-1

[ל]א יהוה דבר זה[...ישי] השל[ש בחוד]ח ...5   [...]י בנ[לצאת ...]ר[הה

[וה]יה כבוד]כ ... ותם]להור[...] 7 [ה]התור האבן[...]ה[ההר]...[6

אשר הדב]רים ... [12]ה[לתור העו]תים[חלקות]מ ...[11]...[10-8

כורת ונכי]א ...[עזבתים לא כי דורותם עו[ד]...[13]לך מגיד אנכי

[הם]משפטי ...[16 הדברים כל]ם ה[עלי]א בבו[...[15 היום וביניך ביני

האלה הדב]רים [ל]כ]ל[את ...[17   ]ו[ידע קללות]בכל ו]

Col. II   אתנה לזרע]כם לאמר 3   [ב]ויע]ק[...[ ]ר[בא 2   [...]1

... ים]אחר אלהים אחר 4   [ופנו]ו שב[ע]אכלו ו דב]ש חלב זבת ארץ

[אחר וכ]ויל וצו[א ... כ]י הזאת התעודה 5   [אל ה]תעודה]ונתנה ת]צוקו]מ

להם ויהיו ה[ם את אלהי ויעבודו חרפת]ם אחר ו]כ[מתם אחר ו]הג]וים 6

[כי אויב ביד[ונפלו ילכדו ם]רבי ואבדו מוקש]ל]ו[עני ול]ולצור 7

[ואת שבתותי ואת ברית]י מועד]י מצותי ואת[חקותי ואת]עזבו 8

אשר מקדש]י ואת משכני ואת וכם]בת לי הקדישו אשר 9   [קדשי

וישתחוו 11   [... עליו]ת שמי א]לשים הארץ 10   [בתוך] לי הקדשתי

4Q216

4Q216 (4QJub^a) *4QJubilees^a*

4Q221, 4Q222, 4Q223-4Q224, 4Q482?, 4Q483?, 11Q12
Bibliography: J.C. VanderKam, J.T. Milik, 'The First Jubilees Manuscript from Qumran Cave 4: A Preliminary Publication', *JBL* 110 (1991) 243-270

Col. I (= *Jub* 1:1-2.4-7)   *1-2* [...] *3* [Sinai, when he went up to] re[ceive the stone tablets, the Torah and the statute] by the word of YHWH [according to which he told him:] *4* [«Go up] to the top of the moun[tain». In the first year] of the son[s of Israel] leaving *5* [Egypt, in] the thir[d mon]th, [the sixteenth of] this [month] YHWH spoke t[o] *6* [Moses saying: «Come up to me] on the mountain [and I will give you the two tablets of] stone, the La[w] *7* [and the statute which I have written in order to te]ach [them». And Moses climbed the mountain of YHWH and the gl]ory of YH[WH settled] *8-10* [...] *11* [... And he showed him the di]visions [of the per]iods for the La[w] *12* [and for the testimony. And he said to him: «Pay attention to all the wo]rds which I tell you *13* [on this mountain and write them in a book so that] their generations [may kn]ow that I have not forsaken them *14* [for all the evil which they did by breaking the covenant which] I set up today between me and you *15* [for their generations on Mount Sinai. And when] all [these] things [happ]en to th[em] *16* [they will know that I have been just with them in all] their [judgments] and [in all] their curses and they will know *17* [that in truth I was with them. And you, write al]l these [wo]rds

Col. II (= *Jub* 1:7-15)   *1* [...] *2* in the l[a]nd [which I promised to their fathers, to Abraham and to Isaac and to Ja]c[ob,] *3* saying: «To [your] offspring [I will give a land which flows with milk and ho]ney». They will eat and ‹be replete›, [but they will turn] *4* after other gods [who did not save them from any tr]oubles. And the [testimony] will reply [to] *5* this testimony; bec[ause they will forget all my statutes, all that I] command you and they will g[o after] *6* [the nat]ions and [after their dis]gr[ace and after] their [shame. And they will serve [their] g[ods who to them will be a hindrance,] *7* trouble, [affliction] and [trap. Man]y [will be destroyed.] They will be captured and fall [into the hand of the enemy for] *8* [they have forsaken] my laws and [my statutes, the festival]s of my covenant [and my sabbaths and my holy things] *9* which they have dedicated to me in [their] mid[st and my tent and my] sanctuary [which I made holy for myself in the midst of] *10* the earth in order to place [my name] on it [and reside there. They made for themselves burial mounds, sacred woods and idols] *11* and bowed down in front of a[ll the wor]ks of [their]

459

13 ואת [... העיד]ל עדים ל[יהם] ואשלחה אל[יהם] 12 [... לכ]ל מע[שי תעות]ם

את אתם ונת[תי מהם פנ]י ואסתי[ר בעיני 14 [... ו]תורה ה[תורה ירדופ]ו מבקשי[ן

הגוי[ם] בכל ו]אפיצים ... [שמות]ולמ[15 לש[בי] הגוי[ם ביד

הגוי[ם ... אלי מתוך 17 [...]חו ושכ[תורותי ו]כל [... 16

[דה]ולתעו[ה ... לתור[4 [ם]ה[אחרני]ה...[3 [...] 1-2

מקדשי יבנה]ר[אש ... 7 [ה]פנים להכתיב ...[6 ם]ע[ושכנתי ... [5

[...] 17-11 [קדשה]ם[וירוש]ל ... [10 [ומלך]עקב[...]י 9]כל וידעו ... [8

[השביעי]ם[ו)בת בי(וישב...] 2 [שר]א[הבריה כ דב]רי ... [1

[...] [ק]העליונים ואת האר[ים]השמ[ם ... vacat 4 vacat]משו[...] 3

רוחות [ו]מל[א]כי ...[ם]הנושבי ... [ם]ומל[א]כי 6 [הקו]דש]הפנים ומל[א]כי

[...]ת[ו]ולמל[א]כי הרוח 8 [ת]ו]ורח ומל[א]כי הקו]לו[]פל ... ו]לער[7 [העננים

את [ובכל]ק[בא]ר ... [ת]ו]רוחות ברי 9 [ולכל]ולקי]ן[חום ולחרף]ול

[ברכהו]בד[עתו אז ראינו מעשיו ונ[...]אור[מאפלה ושחר ו 10 [מות]התהו

ביום]שה[מעשים גדולים ע]ולל לפניו כי שבעה]ל[עשיו]ונה[מ]על כל 11

עלו 13 [...]ם[בתו]ך ה[מי]עשה את הרקיע]ם[וביו השני 12 [הראשון

[...] 17-15 [...]]ק[האר 14 [... לה]למע

error. [And they will sacrifice their sons to the devils and to all the works of the error of their heart.] *12* I shall send to [them] witnesses to [testify against them, but they will not listen and will kill the witnesses.] *13* They will pursue those who study [the] Law [and they will alter everything and will start to do what is evil] *14* in my eyes. And I shall hid[e] my [face] from them and will gi[ve them into the hand of the people]s for cap[tivity,] *15* [for devas]tation [and so they can be consumed. I will remove them from the midst of the land and] scatter them among all the people[s.] *16* [They will forget all my laws and all my statutes] and all my teachings and they will for[get the month, the sabbath] *17* [the feast, the jubilee and the covenant. After this they will come back] to me from among the people[s …]

Col. IV (= *Jub* 1:26-28)   *1-2* […] *3* [… the first and the] last *4* [and what will come in all the divisions of the periods for the La]w and for the testimo[ny] *5* [and for the weeks and the jubilees for ever until I come down] and stay wi[th them] *6* [for all the centuries of centuries. And he told the angel of the] presence to dictate *7* [to Moses from the beginning of creation unti]l my sanctuary is built *8* [in their midst for all the centuries of the centuries. YHWH will reveal himself to the eyes of] everyone and they will [all] know *9* [that I am the God of Israel and the father of all the sons of Ja]cob and king *10* [on Mount Zion for all the centuries of centuries. And Zion and Jerusa]l[em will be holy] *11-17* […]

Col. V (= *Jub* 2:1-4)   *1* [And the angel of the presence told Moses at God's command: « Write all the wo]rds of the creation: h[ow] *2* [on the sixth day YHWH God finished all his works and all that he had created] and rested on the [seventh] day *3* [and made it holy for all the centuries and placed it as a sign for all] his works». *Blank 4* [*Blank* For on the first day he created the] upper [heaven]s, the ear[th,] *5* [the waters and all the spirits who serve before him: the angels of] the presence, the angels of ho[liness,] *6* the an[gels of the spirits of fire, the angels of the spirits of the current]s [and] the angels of the spirits of the [clouds], *7* of dark[ness, ice, frost, dew, snow, hail and hoar]frost; and the angels of thunder[s] *8* and the angels of the [storm-]winds [and the angels of the winds of cold and of] heat, of winter and of summer, [all] *9* the spirits of his creatures [which he made in the heavens and which he made in the ear]th and in everything, the aby[sses,] *10* darkness, dawn, [light, the dusk which he prepared with] his [know]ledge. Then we saw his deeds and [blessed him] *11* on account of all his [d]eeds and [we praised him in his presence because] he ma[de seven] great works [on the first day.] *12* And on the [second] da[y he made the vault in the midd]le of the [water]s, [and the waters were separated on that day. Half] *13* went up on to[p of the vault and half went down below the vault which was in its midst, on top of the face of all] *14* the earth […] *15-17* […]

Col. VI 1 [...] 2 [...]האג[מים ואת כל כל ט[ל ... 3 [... ה]יערים ואת

גן ע[ד]ן בעדן [...] 4 עשה <עשה> ביום השל[י]שי [...] 5 הש[מ]ש ואת

הירח ואת הכוכבים [ויתן] 6 [... ו]למשל ביום ובלילה ולהב[דיל בין]

7 [... גד]ול [על הארץ] לימ[ים] ול[ש]בתות ול[חדשים] 8 [... וליוב]לים

ולכל תק[ופת השנים] 9 [... ה]צמח וגדל בא[ר]ץ את 10 [...] *vacat*

11 [... הגדו]לים בתו[ך] תהומ[ו]ת המ[י]ם ... 12 [... ב]מים דגי[ם] ואת

[כל <ואת כ>ל< עוף] 13 [... ל]מרפה ועו]ל כל]אשר בא[רץ ...

14 [...] של[ו]שה המינ[י]ם הגד[ו]לים [... 15 [...] *vacat* 16-17 [*vacat*]

Col. VII 1 [ובי]ו[ם] הששי את כל חי[ת ...] 2 עשה את האדם זכר

ונק[בה ...] 3 ובחיה ובכל הרמש ה[רומש ...] 4 המנים האלה עשה ב[יום

...] 5 אשר בשמים ובארץ [...] 6 השבת אשר שבת ב[ו ...] 7 עשוים

ששת ימים[...] 8 ונשבותה ביום הש[ביעי ...] 9 המינים האלה אמ[ר ...]

10 עם בתוך עממי ו[שבתו ...] 11 ובחר בזרע יעקוב ב[כל ...]

12 לעולם ועד ואת היום ה[שביעי ...] 13 מכל הגוים ולהיות יחד[...]

Col. vi (= *Jub* 2:7-12) *1* […] *2* [… and the po]ols and all the d[ew of the earth] *3* [the seed for sowing with its seed, every shoot and tree that gives fruit, the] woods and the garden of E[de]n [in Eden] *4* [for pleasure and for eating. These four great kinds] he made <he made> on the thi[rd] day. *5* [*Blank* On the fourth day YHWH made the s]un, the moon and the stars. [He placed] *6* [them in the vault of the sky so that they could give light to the whole earth,] to regulate day and night and to separ[ate] *7* [light and darkness. And he placed the sun as a gre]at [sign above the earth] for the day[s], the [sa]bbaths, the [months], *8* [the feasts, the years, the weeks of years and the jubi]lees and for all the cyc[les of the years.] *9* [It separates light from darkness and is the vitality by which everything that] sprouts and grows in the ea[rth prospers.] *10* [These three great kinds he made on the fourth day.] *Blank* *11* [On the fifth day he created the gre]at [sea serpents] in the co[re of the abyss]es of the wa[ters, for these] *12* [were the first works of flesh by his hands; and everything that moves in the] waters, fish [and] all <and al[l> the birds] *13* [which fly and all their species. The sun shone over them for] vigour and ov[er everything] there was on the ea[rth, everything] *14* [that sprouted from the earth and every tree that yields fruit and all flesh. These] thr[ee] gre[at kinds] *15* [he made on the fifth day. *Blank*] *16-17* [*Blank*]

Col. vii (= *Jub* 2:13-24) *1* [On the] sixth [da]y [he made] all the anim[als of the earth and all the cattle and everything that creeps over the earth. After all these] *2* he made man, male and fem[ale he made them, and gave them control over everything there is on the earth and in the seas and over everything that flies] *3* over the animals and over all the creeping animals that [creep over the earth, and the cattle and over all the earth. Over all these he gave them con-trol.] *4* He made these [four] kinds on [the sixth day. And in all there were twenty-two kinds. And he finished all his works on the sixth day: everything] *5* there is in the heavens and on the earth [and in the waters and in the abysses, in the light and in the darkness and in everything. And he gave us a huge sign, the day of] *6* the sabbath on which he rested [from doing all the works which he had created over the six days …] *7* they were made in six days. […] *8* and we observe the sabbath on the sev[enth] day [(refraining) from all work. For we, all the angels of the presence and all the angels of holiness - these] *9* two kinds - he comman[ded us to observe the sabbath with him in the heavens and on the earth. And he said to us: «I am going to isolate for myself] *10* a nation among my nations. And [they will keep the sabbath and I will consecrate them as my people and I will bless them. They will be my people and I will be their God».] *11* And he chose the descendants of Jacob among [all those I saw. And I registered them for me as the first-born son and consecrated them to me] *12* for ever and ever. The [seventh] day [I will teach them so that they keep the sabbath on it above all. For I blessed them and consecrated them as an excep-

14 כל הימים [...] *vacat* [...] 15 מאדם עד אליו וש(נ)ים ועשרים מ]יני [...
16 וקדש וזה עם זה נעשו יחד לקדש] [... 17 וזאת התעודה והתורה
הראש]ונה [...

4Q217 (4QpapJub*b*?) *4QpapJubilees*b*?*

J.C. VanderKam, J.T. Milik, *DJD XIII*, 23-33, pl. III
PAM 43.261
ROC 586

Frag. 2   1 [...] [מחלקות העתים לתורה ול]תעודה...[2 [...]לכל ש]ני
[העולם מן הברי]אה [... 3 [...]ם וכל [הנ]ברא עד היום [...].
4 [...]...[...]...יר]ושלם ה]...[5 [...]ב את כל]...[6 [...]...[...]

4Q218 (4QJub*c*) *4QJubilees*c**

J.C. VanderKam, J.T. Milik, *DJD XIII*, 35-38, pl. IV
PAM 43.189
ROC 849
1Q17, 1Q18, 2Q19, 2Q20, 3Q5, 4Q176a,b, 4Q216, 4Q217, 4Q219, 4Q220,

Frag. 1   1 לקד]שו [... 2 קדוש הוא [מ]כל הימים כל [המחלל אתו
מות יומת] 3 [וכ]ל העשה בו מלאכה ונכרתה [לע]ו[ל]ם [ל]מ[ע]ן [ישמר]ו
4 [בני ישראל]את היום הז]ה לדורו]תם ולא יכרת]ו [מן הא]ר[ץ]

tional people] *13* among all the peoples so that together [with us] they keep [the sabbath. And he lifted up his statutes like a pleasant perfume which is acceptable in his presence] *14* every day. *Blank* [There are twenty-two patriarchs] *15* from Adam to him and twenty ‹two› ki[nds of works were done up to the seventh day. One is blessed and holy and the other is blessed] *16* and holy. One and the other were made together for holiness [and for blessing. To this one was granted to be blessed and holy forever.] *17* And this is the testimony and the fir[st] Law. [...]

4Q217 (4QpapJub^b?) *4QpapJubilees^b?*

1Q17, 1Q18, 2Q19, 2Q20, 3Q5, 4Q176a,b, 4Q216, 4Q218, 4Q219, 4Q220, 4Q221, 4Q222, 4Q223-4Q224, 4Q482?, 4Q483?, 11Q12

Frag. 2   *1* [...] the divisions of the times, for the law and for [the testimony ...] *2* [...] for all the y[ears of] eternity, from the crea[tion ...] *3* [...] and all [that is] created until the day [...] *4* [... Jer]usalem [...] *5* [...] all [...] *6* [...] ... [...]

4Q218 (4QJub^c) *4QJubilees^c*

4Q221, 4Q222, 4Q223-4Q224, 4Q482?, 4Q483?, 11Q12
Bibliography: J.C. VanderKam, J.T. Milik, '4QJub^c (4Q218) and 4QJub^e (4Q220): A Preliminary Edition', *Textus* 17 (1994) 43-56

Frag. 1   (= *Jub* 2:26-27)   *1* to sanc[tify it, not to do any work on it, and not to defile it, for] *2* it is holier [than] all the days. Anyone [who desecrates it, shall certainly die] *3* [and any]one who does work on it shall be cut off [for ev]er, in order [th]at *4* [the Israelites observe] thi[s] day, [throughout] their [generation]s and not be cut off from the ea[rth].

4Q219 (4QJub^d^) *4QJubilees^d^*

J.C. VanderKam, J.T. Milik, *DJD XIII*, 39-53, pl. IV
PAM 43.187
ROC 300
1Q17, 1Q18, 2Q19, 2Q20, 3Q5, 4Q176a,b, 4Q216, 4Q217, 4Q218, 4Q220,

Col. I   1-10 [...]   11 [...]   [... לי]ובל [השביעי   12 ויצווהו לאמור
אני זק[נתי ...]   13 ימי והנא אני בן שתים [...]   14 תמי[ד את א]לוהינו
ודרש[תי ...]   15-31 [...]   32 המזב[ח ...]   33 ה[מזבח ... תק]טיר
34 [... כו]ל ה[ח]לב   35 [... ו]כול החלב אשר עליהן ואת א[שר]   36 [...]
ה]כבד עם הכליות תסירנה וחקטרת[ה]   37 [... ה]אלוהי[ם עם מ[נח]תוה
ונסכוה לנ[יחוח] ל[הם]   38 [... ה]הואה וממוח]רת [...

Col. II   1-6 [...]   7-8 [...]...[...]   9-10 [...]   11 [... אל] השמים
vacat שמ[ור]   12 [... תי]שר בכול מעשיכה   13 [... ת]לך להקטיר
14-16 [...]   17 [...]   18 [... ה]ואה כי הדם הוא[ה ...]   [... אדם אשר ישפך ...]
19 [... וה]ארץ לו תוכל ל[הטהר ...]   20 [... ש]וחד *vacat* וכופר ב[דם ...]
21 [... יהו]ה אל עליון והייה משמרוה ע[ל ...]   22 [... ולהצ]ילך [מ]כול
רשף *vacat* [...]   23 [... מע]שי בני ה[אדם ...]   24 [... ונאצ]ה ותבל

466

4Q219 (4QJub^d) *4QJubilees^d*

4Q221, 4Q222, 4Q223-4Q224, 4Q482?, 4Q483?, 11Q12
Bibliography: J.C. VanderKam, J.T. Milik, 'A Preliminary Publication of a Jubi-lees Manuscript from Qumran Cave 4: 4QJub^d (4Q219)', *Biblica* 73 (1992) 62-83

Col. I (= *Jub* 21:1-2.7-10; 4Q220 1)   *1-10* […] *11* [And in the sixth year, in] the seventh [week] of [this jubilee, Abraham called Isaac, his son,] *12* and com-manded him saying: [I am] ol[d and I do not know the day of my death, for I have completed] *13* my days. Behold, I am [one hundred and seventy-]two [years, and throughout all the days of my life I have been remembering] *14* our [G]od always and [I] sought [him with all my heart …] *15-31* [… upon] *32* the alta[r with the finest flour of its offering mixed with oil and its libation. And you will burn everything upon] *33* the [altar, a fire-offering with a pleasant fragrance before God. And the fat of the thanksgiving sacrifice you will of]fer *34* [on the fire which is upon the altar, and the fat which is upon the belly, and al]l the [f]at *35* [which is upon the entrails and the kidneys and] all the fat which is upon them and that wh[ich] *36* [is on the loins and the appendix of the] liver with the kidneys you shall remove. You shall offer *37* [the whole for a pleasant fragrance before Go]d, with its of[fer]ing and its libation [for a pleasant (fragrance), the] br[ead] *38* [of the fire-offering to YHWH. You are to eat its flesh the] same [day] and the following mor[ning, and (the sun) will not set upon it.]

Col. II (= *Jub* 21:14-16.18 - 22:1; 4Q221 1)   *1-6* […] *7-8* […] … […] *9-10* […] *11* [… and the aroma of its fragrance goes up to] heaven. *Blank* Ke[ep] *12* [this commandment and carry it out, my son, so that you will be up]right in all your works. *13* [And at every time be pure in your flesh and wash yourself with water before] going to offer *14-16* […] *17* [You are not to eat blood any more] because the blood is [the life, and you are not to eat any blood. You are not to accept] *18* [a bribe for any blood of] men which is poured out [for no reason, without judgment, because the blood which is poured out] *19* [defiles the earth, and the] earth cannot be [purified from the human blood except with the blood] *20* [of the one who shed it. Do not take a br]ibe *Blank* or atonement for [human blood: blood for blood, and it will be acceptable] *21* [before YHW]H, God Most High. His guardianship will be ov[er the good, so that you will keep yourself from every] *22* [evil and He will pro]tect you [from] every pes-tilence. *Blank* […] *23* [My son: I see that all the] wor[ks of the sons of] man [are evil and sinful and all] *24* [their works are uncleanness, abominatio]n and filth,

ואין אמת אתם הש]מר *vacat* [... 25   ...] ות]צעד במסלותם ואשמתה

אשמת מות] [... 26   ...] ממכה ונתנכה בייד פשעיכה והכריתכ]ה [...

27 [ואת זרעכה מ]תחת השמים *vacat* ואבד שמכה וזכרכה מכו]ל הארץ]

28 [... מ]עשיהמה ומכול תועבותיהמה ו]שמ]ור משמ]רת אל] 29 [עליון

ועשה]רצונוה ותצלח בכול וברככה בכול מעשיכה ו]הקים] 30 [ממכה

מטעת ה]אמת בארץ לכול דורות הארץ ולו ישביתו שמי] 31 [ושמכה

מתח]ת השמים בכול היימים *vacat* הישר בני בשל]ום [... 32   ...] ע]ליון

אלוהי ואלו(ה)י)כה לעשות רצונוה ול]ברך את זרעכה] 33 ואת]שאר

זר]עכה לכול דורות עולמים בכול ברכו]ת האמת להיותכה] 34 לברכה]

בכול הא]רץ *vacat* ויצא מאתוה שמח *vacat* [...] 35 [...] *vacat* והיי]ה בשבוע

הרישון לשלושה וארבעים היובל בשנה] 36 [השנית בו היאה]השנה

אשר מת בה אברהם בא]ו [... 37   ...]...[...] 38 [...]

4Q220 (4QJub^e) *4QJubilees^e*

J.C. VanderKam, J.T. Milik, *DJD XIII*, 55-61, pl. V
PAM 43.189
ROC 849
1Q17, 1Q18, 2Q19, 2Q20, 3Q5, 4Q176a,b, 4Q216, 4Q217, 4Q218, 4Q219,

1 [חקותיו ו]מצות]יו ומשפטיו ואל תלך א]חר גלולים ואחר   *Frag. 1*

[פסילים ואחר] 2 [מסכות ו]אל ת]אכל כל ד]ם לחיה ולבהמה ולכל עוף

אשר] יעופף בשמים] 3 [ואם תז]בח עלה זב]ח] שלמים לרצון ת]ז]בחנו

ואת דמם תזרוק על המזבח] 4 [ואת כל]בשר העלה תקטי]י]ר על המז]בח

[עם סולת מנחתו בלולה ב]ש]מ]ן] 5 [עם נסכו ת]קטיר הכול על המזבח

אשה ריח ניחוח לפני האלהים [ואת חלב] 6 [זבח הש]ל]מ]ים תקטיר על

האש אשר על המזבח ואת החלב] אשר על] 7 [הקרב וא]ת ה]ח]לב אשר

על הקרבים ואת הכליות [ו]את ה]חלב אשר עליהן] 8 [ואת אשר על

הכסלים] ואת היותרת הכבד עם הכליות תסיר]נה והקטרת את] 9 [הכל

לריח ניחוח לפני הא]להי]ם] עם מנחתו ונסכו לריח נ(י)ח]וח לחם אשה]

and there is no truth with them. *Blank* Be[ware of walking] *25* [in their ways and] tread in their paths and get guilty of a deadly guilt [in front of God Most High] *26* [and He hide his face] from you, give you into the hands of your offences and cut you off [from the earth] *27* [and your progeny from] beneath the sky. *Blank* And your name and the memory of you will vanish from the who[le earth.] *28* [Refrain from all] their [w]orks and from all their abominations, and [ke]ep the obser[vance of God] *29* [Most High and do] His will, and you will be successful in everything. He will bless you in all your works, and [will raise] *30* [from you a plant of] truth in the earth for all the generations of the earth. And he will not bring to an end [my name] *31* [and your name from benea]th the sky for all the days. *Blank* Be upright, my son, in pea[ce. May he strengthen] *32* [you, the God Mo]st High, my God and your ‹God›, to perform his will and to [bless your offspring] *33* and the [remnant of] your [offsp]ring for all the eternal generations with all blessings [of truth so that you might become] *34* a blessing [in all the ea]rth. *Blank* And he went out from him rejoicing. *Blank* […] *35* [*Blank*] In the first week of the fo[rty-]third [jubilee, in its] *36* [second year, which is] the year in which Abraham died, [Isaac and Ishmael] came *37* […]…[…] *38* […]

4Q220 (4QJubᶜ) *4QJubilees*

4Q221, 4Q222, 4Q223-4Q224, 4Q482?, 4Q483?, 11Q12
Bibliography: J.C. VanderKam, J.T. Milik, '4QJubᶜ (4Q218) and 4QJubᵉ (4Q220): A Preliminary Edition', *Textus* 17 (1994) 43-56

Frag. 1 (= *Jub* 21:5-10; 4Q219 I)   *1* [his precepts, his] decrees [and his judgments; do not go af]ter idols or after [images or after] *2* [cast effigies. And] do not [eat any blo]od of an animal, cattle or any bird which [flies in the sky.] *3* [If you sacri]fice (as) a burnt-offering a peace-offe[ring], according to (his) will you shall [sac]rifice it and pour the blood over the alt[ar.] *4* [And all] the meat of the burnt-offering you shall offer upon the al[tar] with the finest flour of its offering mixed with [o]i[l], *5* [with its libation. You] shall offer everything upon the altar, a fire-offering with a pleasant fragrance before God. [The fat of] *6* [the pe]a[c]e-[offering] you shall offer on the fire which is upon the altar, and the fat [which is on] *7* [the intestines and] the [f]at which is on the entrails and the kidneys [and] the [fat which is upon them] *8* [and that which is on the loins] and the appendix of the liver with the kidneys you shall remove, [and you shall offer] *9* [it all as a pleasant fragrance before G]od with its offering and its libation for the ‹plea[sant› fragrance, bread of the fire-offering] *10* [for

10 [לאלהים ואת בשרו אכול ביום]ההוא ומחרת ול[א] תב[וא עליו
השמש [   ] 11 [...]ל[...]

4Q221 (4QJub^f^) *4QJubilees^f^*

J.C. VanderKam, J.T. Milik, *DJD XIII*, 63-85, pl. VI
PAM 43.188
ROC 361
1Q17, 1Q18, 2Q19, 2Q20, 3Q5, 4Q176a,b, 4Q216, 4Q217, 4Q218, 4Q219,

Frag. 1 1 [...]ותצעד מסלותי[הם ואשמתה] אשמת מות [... 2 [...
והסת[יר את [פ]נו ממכה וניתנכ]ה ביד פשעיכה] 3 [והכריתך מהארץ]
ואת זרעך [מתח]ת השמים [...] 4 [... ו]אבד שמך] ו]זכרך מכול הארץ]
[... 5 [מעשיהם ומכול תו]עבתם ושמור משמר]ת אל] עליון] ועשה]
6 [רצונו ותצלח בכול] {ומכול תועבתם וש]מור משמרת אל עליון]
7 [ועשה רצונו ות[צלח בכול} וברככ]ה] בכו]ל מעשיך והקים ממך]
8 [מטעת האמת באר]ץ לכול דור]ות האר]ץ ול]וא ישבית שמי ושמך]
9 [מתחת השמים בכו]ל הי]מים [...

Frag. 4 1 [...] שנית] ... [אביהו כי גל]ה] 2 כנף אביהו [... אמ]ן אמן
ואתה 3 צו את בני [... הז]ה כי משפט 4 מות הואה [ו]נאצ]ה ... לכ]פר
על 5 האיש אשר יעש]ה ... כי א]ם 6 להמיתו ולסקל]ו [... 7 [כי]א אין
לו לחיות {ים} [... 8 [אש]ר יעשנה בישראל [...] 9 [ואל י]אמרו
לרובן נעש]ו [... 10 [עם פילג]ש אביהו [...]

Frag. 5 1 [...] לאבי]הם] [... 2 בעת [א]שר ראה את בנו מחז]יקים

God. Eat its flesh the] same [day] and the following morning and not should s[et the sun on it]. *11* […] … […]

4Q221 (4QJub^f) *4QJubilees^f*

4Q220, 4Q222, 4Q223-4Q224, 4Q482?, 4Q483?, 11Q12
Bibliography: J.T. Milik, 'Fragment d'une source du Psautier (4QPs89) et fragments de Jubilés, du Document de Damas, d'un phylactère dans la grotte 4 de Qumrân', *RB* 73 (1966) 104, pl. II

Frag. 1 (= *Jub* 21:22-24; 4Q219 ii) *1* [in their ways and tread in] their [paths] and get guilty of [a deadly guilt in front of God Most High] *2* [and He hi]de his [fa]ce from you, give you [into the hands of your offences] *3* [and cut you off from the earth] and your progeny [from benea]th the sky. [*Blank* …] *4* [… And] your name [and] the memory of you will vanish from the whole earth. [Refrain from all] *5* [their works and from all their [abo]minations; keep the observance [of God] Most High, [and do] *6* [His will and you will be successful in everything.] {and from all their abominations; keep [the observance of God Most High,] *7* [and do his will and you will] be successful in everything.} He will bless you in all [your works, and will raise from you] *8* [a plant of truth in the ear]th for all the generation[s of the ear]th. And [he will] no[t bring and end to my name and your name] *9* [from beneath the sky for al]l the da[ys …]

Frag. 4 (= *Jub* 32:12-15) *1* [written] a second time: [«Cursed is he who sleeps with the wife of] his father, for he has uncover[ed] *2* the skirt of his father». [And all the holy ones of YHWH said: «Ame]n, amen!». And you, *3* command the children of [Israel to keep thi]s [word], for the penalty *4* is death [and] it is a disgrace, and there is no atonement to at]one for *5* the man who doe[s this evil for ever. Bu]t *6* one has to kill him and to sto[ne him and to kill him with stones and to cut him off from the midst of the nation,] *7* [fo]r not may live {…} [one day in the land, any man] *8* [wh]o does it in Israel, [for it is an abomination and a disgrace.] *9* [And they should not] say: «Reuben was granted [life and atonement after he slept] *10* [with the concu]bine of his father [Jacob» …]

Frag. 5 (= *Jub* 37:11-15) *1* [… and they said to] their [father: «Go out, lead them. Otherwise we will kill you». And he became filled with wrath and anger] *2* on the moment [th]at he saw that his sons for[ced him to go out first, to

471

[...] 3 את כול הרעות אשר הי[ו ...]   4 ולוא זכר את השבועה אשר[...]
5 ליעקוב ובכול זה לוא יד[ע ...]   6 היה מתאבל על אשתו עד [...]   7 גבור
למלחמה וישלחו א[ל ...]

4Q222 (4QJubᵍ) *4QJubileesᵍ*

J.C. VanderKam, J.T. Milik, *DJD XIII*, 87-94, pl. V
PAM 43.189
ROC 230
1Q17, 1Q18, 2Q19, 2Q20, 3Q5, 4Q176a,b, 4Q216, 4Q217, 4Q218, 4Q219,

1 [כול]ימי חי}א{ לא [...]   2 [עשה]אחי עשו אל תיראי אמי   *Frag.* 1
והחלמי[...]   3 [ול]א אשחית דרכי לעולם *vacat* אז נשא[ה ...]   4 י[]דיהא
ותפתח פיה ותברך את }ע{אל עליון [...]   5 [תו]דות ותהלה ות}ו{ᴬמר ברוך
יהוה אלוה[ים ...]   6 [עו]למים אשר נתן לי [א]ת יע[קוב ...]   7 [הוא]ה
ושלכ]ה [...]

4Q223-224 (4QpapJubʰ) *4QpapJubileesʰ*

J.C. VanderKam, J.T. Milik, *DJD XIII*, 95-140, pl. VII-IX
PAM 43.190-191
ROC 134, 135

...] 46   דאוה [...] 45   [...] 44-6 ...[...] 5-4 [...] 3-1   *Unit* 2 ı
אמ]י אם [... שנ]י לשני חי]י[ך]   47 [... מות]ᵀכי ותבו]א אל יצ[חק

lead them against his brother, and he remembered] *3* all the evil thoughts which we[re hidden in his heart against his brother Jacob,] *4* but not did he remember the oath which [he had sworn to his father and mother, that he would not seek, all his days, evil] *5* against Jacob. And while all this happened, [Jacob] did not kno[w that they were coming against him for battle, for he] *6* was mourning for his wife, until [they had drawn near to him, near the fortification, with four thousand] *7* heroes of war. And [the men of Hebron] sent [him] (the message): …]

4Q222 (4QJub^g) *4QJubilees^g*

4Q220, 4Q221, 4Q223-4Q224, 4Q482?, 4Q483?, 11Q12
Bibliography: J.C. VanderKam, J.T. Milik, '4QJubilees^g (4Q222)', *New Qumran Texts and Studies*, 105-114, pl. 7

Frag. 1 (= *Jub* 25:9-12)   *1* [all] the days of my life [I will] not [take for myself a wife from the daughters of Canaan, and I will not commit evil by doing like] *2* my brother Esau [did]. Do not fear, mother, and be reassured [for I will do your will, will walk in uprightness] *3* [and] will [no]t corrupt my ways ever. *Blank* Then [she] lifted [her face to heaven, stretched out the fingers of] *4* her [ha]nds, opened her mouth, blessed God Most High, [creator of heaven and earth, gave him] *5* [than]ks and praise, and said: «Blessed is YHWH, God, [and blessed is his name for everlasting] *6* [cen]turies, for he has given to me Ja[cob, a pure son and a holy offspring, for to you] *7* he [belongs,] and to you [will] belong [his offspring …]

4Q223-224 (4QpapJub^h) *4QpapJubilees^h*

1Q17, 1Q18, 2Q19, 2Q20, 3Q5, 4Q176a,b, 4Q216, 4Q217, 4Q218, 4Q219, 4Q220, 4Q221, 4Q222, 4Q482?, 4Q483?, 11Q12

Unit 2 col. 1 (= *Jub* 35:7-12; 1Q18)   *1-3* […] *4-5* […] … *6-44* […] *45* […] illness *46* [had not touched her all the days of her life. Then Jacob said to her: «I will be fortunate,] my [mother,] if my [years approach] the years of [your] life *47* [and my strength stays in me like your strength. You will not die, for you

473

48 [ותאמר אליו vacat אחת בקשה אבקש ממכה השבע את עי[שאו אשר
לו[א]ירע את יעקוב   49 [ולוא ירדפנו באיבה כי יודע אתה את יצר עישאו
אשר הואה ר[ע מן נעוריו וא[ין] עמו ישר כי   50 [... עש[ה] עמנו מיום
[ה]ליכת אחיהו   51 [... ועש[ה]ה עמנו רע את צואנכה נהג ואת כול 52 [...
עו[שה] עו[ד זמה כאיש   53 [... א[ין אתו רעה

Unit 2 II   [...] 2-1   [...] 3 vacat [...] גם אנוכי יוד[ע ...   4 הוא מכבדנו
ועושה רצוננו [...] עישאו הרבה [...]   5 ועתה אני אוהב את יעקוב
מ[עישאו כי הרב]ה הרע מעשיו ו[...]   6 [כו]ל דרכיו ח[מ]ס ורשע ואין ב[ו
אמת סביבותי[ו ועתה לב[י ...   7 [...]   8 ...[הנ]שים ואחר תעות הנ[ו]שים
[...]   9 ...[יע]ק[ב] אם ישמע לוא י[י]עמיד ולוא יע[שה]   10 [...] אחיהו
ביד vacat יעקוב ינתן   11 [...ואת]י אל תדאיגי [על יעקו]ב כי שומר
יע[קו]ב גדול וגבור   12 [... עיש[או כיא כאבק לפני רוח כ]ן כול שומרי
עישאו ל[פ]ני אלוהי   13 [... י]עקוב ב[ני התמים והי]קר אבל אנכי אה[ב
את העו]שה רצוננו   14 [...]אחותי בשלום ותשלח ר[בקה] ותקרא[...
22-15 [...]...[...] 47-23 [...] 53-48 ...[...]...[...]

Unit 2 III   2-1 [...]...[...] 8-3   [...]...[...]   9 ...[...]... ב]יניהמה ו[יצאו
מ[ן   10 א]צלו ... ביו[ם הזה שמח וישן ש]נת עולמים[11 וי]מות ...
[וש'מני]ם ... וע]שרים שבועי שנים [...] שנים   12 ויק[ברו ... ויל[ד] לוא
עישא[ו] לארק[ן הר]שעיר וישב   13 שמ[...] בארץ כנען באר[ץ א]ברהם
[...] 19-14 ...[...]... 54-20 [...]

474

speak without reason with me about] your death». But she fle[d to Isa]ac 48 [and said to him: *Blank* «One request I ask from you: Make E]sau [swear] that he will no[t] harm Jacob 49 [and will not persecute him with enmity - for you know Esau's inclination, which is ev]il from his youth, and uprightness is n[ot] with him, for 50 [he wants to kill him after your death. And you know all he di]d with us since the day of [the] departure of his brother 51 [Jacob to Haran, up to this very day, for with his whole heart he has forsaken us, and has act]ed wickedly with us. He has led away your flocks, and all 52 [your posses-sions he has stolen from you. And whenever we tried to question him about what belonged to us, he aga]in [act]ed mischievously, like someone 53 [who has compassion for us. And he has been bitter against you, because you blessed Jacob, your perfect and upright son, for there] is no evil with him

Unit 2 *col.* II (= *Jub* 35:13-18)   *1-2* […] *3* […] *Blank* «I, too, kno[w and see the behaviour of Jacob towards us, for with his whole heart] *4* he honours us and does our will. [At first I loved] Esau much [more than Jacob, after he was born,] *5* but now I love Jacob more [than Esau, for] he has acted [ver]y wick-edly, and [truth is not in him. For] *6* [al]l his ways are vi[ol]ence and wicked-ness, and there is no [truth] in [him, around] him. And now, [my] heart […] *7* […] *8* [… and he and his sons have gone after the impurity of the wo]men, and after the error of the wo[men. You said] *9* [to me that I should make him swear not to kill his brother Ja]c[ob]. If he swears, he will not maintain, and not d[o] *10* [good, but evil. And if he tries to kill Jacob] his brother, /he will be given/ into the hand of *Blank* Jacob. *11* [And he will not escape from his hand, but shall go down by his hand. But yo]u, do not worry [about Jaco]b, for the guardian of Ja[co]b is greater and mightier, *12* [more glorious and praised, than the guardian of Es]au, for like dust befor[e the wind, th]us are all the guardians of Esau before the God of *13* [Abraham, the God of Isaac, and the God of J]acob, [my perfect and pre]cious son. Truly, I lo[ve the one who do]es our will *14* […] my sister, in peace». And R[ebecca] sent and called […] *15-22* […] … […] *23-47* […] *48-53* … […] … […]

Unit 2 *col.* III (= *Jub* 36:17-20)   *1-2* […] *3-8* […] … […] *9* […] … [… be]tween them. And [they departed from] *10* [his] si[de. And they rested and slept that day. And Isaac slept on his bed] that [da]y, rejoicing, and he slept [the eternal] sl[eep] *10* and [died at the age of one hundred] and eighty [years, and he had completed tw]enty-[five] weeks of years [and five] years *11* and [his two sons, Esau and Jacob] bu[ried him. And] Esau [went] to the land of [the mountain of] Seir, and lived *12* there. [And Jacob lived in the mountainland of Hebron, in the fortress,] in the land of Canaan, in the lan[d of A]braham […] *14-19* … […] *20-54* […]

Unit 2 IV   1 [...] 2 [...] הטאת]ה בשבוע]ה[3 [...]אין לבני הא]דם[

4 [ולנ]חשים שבועה נא]מנה ... א[לה לאלה 5 [רע]ה היככה יהרוגו אי]ש

... [בני ע]ד[6 [עול]ם ואין לעשות עמכ]ה ... מ[דבר לך 7 [אם י]הפוך

החזיר את ע]ורו ... י]רך וי]עלו בראו]שו קר]נים כקרני א]יל[8 [וצאו]ן אז

אעשה עמכה] ... ל]וא היתה אח] לי ואם] יעשו 9]זאבי]ם שלם עם

הטלים ל]בלתי ...[יהיה}י{ לבם [...] 10 [עליה]ם אז יהיה בלבי]ן ... ל]שור

רע ומאמ]י]ן[[...] 11 [עמו ו]חרש עול אחד א]ז ... [העורבים כקא]ת אז[

דע כי 12 [...] ונכ]רתים בניכה ואי]ן לכ]ה שלום [...] 13 [...]להורג]ו[וב]א

ומדחק 14 [...]ממנו א]ז [אמר לבניו 15 [... יעק]וב אביהו 16 [...]

והשל]ך חצכה] ... האו]יב ויהי 17 [...]אחיכה הו]א ... הו]א וכמוכה הוא

18 [...] והשליך [...]עישאו 19 [... והשל]יך חץ שנ]י ... הא]רמי אל

20 [...]בני יעקו]ב ... נחל]קים לארבע 21 [...]ראשון ונפתלי וגד] ...

עמ]ם לדרום 22 [...]]ולוא נמלט מהם] ...]ודן ואשר 23 [... ע]מם

ויהרוגו את ג]בורי ...] ויצא ראובן 24 [... וחמ]שיהם עמם ויה]רוגו ...

פלשת 25 [...] ו]הרגו מאד]ום[26-33 [...]...[...] 34-54 [...]

Unit 2 col. IV (= *Jub* 37:17 - 38:8)   *1* [...] *2* [...] you [sinned] against the oath *3* [and at the time when you swore to your father you were judged. Then Esau answered and said to him:] «Neither the sons of m[an] *4* [nor sn]akes have a tru[stworthy] oath [which they swear for ever, but every day they seek, the o]nes against the others, *5* [evi]l, how [to kill one's enemy and oppressor. And you, you hate me and] my sons f[or] *6* [eve]r, and with you I can not behave [as a brother. Listen to these words of mine which I] speak to you: *7* [«If] the wild boar changes [its] sk[in, and makes its hair] soft [like wool], and [ho]rns rise up on [its] head, like the horns of a r[am] *8* [or shee]p, then I will behave with you [as a brother. The breasts have been separated from their mother, for no]t have you been a brother [to me. And if] *9* [/the/ wolve]s make peace with /the/ lambs, [not] to [eat and oppress them, and if] their heart is [intent to do good] *10* [towards th]em, then there will be in my heart [peace towards you. And if the lion becomes] a companion and confidant [of] the bull, [and is bound together] *11* [with him, and] plows (with) one yoke, th[en I will make peace with you. And if] the ravens [become white] like a pelican, [then] know that *12* [I love you, and will make peace with you. But you, be cut off, and] your sons are [cut] off, and yo[u will ha]ve no peace». *13* [And when Jacob saw that out of his heart and out of all his soul Esau was evil-minded towards him,] intent to kill him, and was coming and thrusting *14* [like a wild boar that comes to the spear which pierces and kills it, but not shrinks back] from it, th[en] he told his sons *15* [and his servants to attack him and all his companions. And after that Judah spoke to Jac]ob his father *16* [saying: «Draw, father, your bow, shoo]t your arrow, [fell the oppressor, kill the ene]my. May *17* [you have strength, for we will not kill your brother, because] he is your brother, and he [is similar to you], and like you he is *18* [honoured by us». Then Jacob draw his bow,] shot [the first arrow, hit] Esau *19* [his brother on the right breast, and killed him. And he sh]ot a second arrow, [hit Adurim, the Ara]mean *20* [on the left breast, threw him back and killed him. Then] the sons of Jaco[b went out, they and their servants, divi]ded to the four *21* [sides of the fortress. Judah went out] first, and [with him] Naphtali and Gad, [and their fifty with] them, to the south] *22* [of the fortress. And they killed all they found before them,] and no one, [not even one] could escape from them. [And Levi,] Dan and Asher *23* [went out to the east of the fortress and their fifty wi]th them, and they killed the he[roes of Moab and Ammon.] And Reuben went out, *24* [as well as Issachar and Zebulon to the north of the fortress, and] their [fi]fty with them and they ki[lled the heroes of] Philistia. *25* [And Simeon, Benjamin, and Enoch, the son of Reuben went out to the west of the fortress, and their fifty with them, and] killed of Ed[om] *26-33* [...] ... [...] *34-54* [...]

4Q225 (4QpsJub^a) *4QPseudo-Jubilees^a*

J.C. VanderKam, J.T. Milik, *DJD XIII*, 141-155, pl. X
PAM 43.251
ROC 311

Frag. 1　1 [...]ל מעוון הזנות [...]　2 [...].[...] הואה .[...]　3 [...]...
[...]. וימל אברהם עם נכרתה [אשר הברית ... 4　[...]ב אותם ויכא
מצרים ו^ימכור אותם אלוהים [...] 6 [...] *vacat* ואתה מושה בדברי 5 [...]ת
עמ[...]　7 [...]הבריאה עד יום הבריאה] החדשה [... 8 [...]ה עומד ויקם
...[...]　9 [...] וביום אשר [...]... 10 [...] ע[ל שפת ה[...].[...]
11-12 [...]...[...]

Frag. 2 ı　1 [...]ת תכרת הנ[פ]ש[ההיא 2 [מקרב ע]מיה] ... יש[ב
בחרן עשר[י]ם שנה 3 [ויאמר א]ברהם אל אלוהים אדני הנני בא ע[רירי
ואלי[עזר] 4 [בן ביתי] הואה וירשני *vacat* 5 [אמר אד]ני אל א[ב]רהם
שא צפא את הכוכבים וראה 6 [וספור את]ה{כ}^וול אשר על שפת הים
ואת עפר הארץ כי אם 7 [יהיו נמ]נים אלה וא[ף] אם לוא יהיה זרעכה
ויא[מין] 8 [אברהם] אלו[ה]י[ם ותחשב לו צדקה ויולד בן אח]רי [כן
9 [לאברה]ם ו[י]קרא את שמו יסחק ויבוא שר המ[ש]טמה 10 [אל
אל]והים וישטים את אברהם בישחק ויאמר א[לוהים 11 [אל אבר]הם קח
את בנכה את ישחק את יחיד[כה אשר] 12 [אותו אהב]תה והעלהו לי
לעולה על אחד ההרי[ם הגבוה]ים 13 [אשר אומר] לכה ויק[ום וי]ל[ך]מן
הבארות על .[...] 14 [...] [וישא אב]רהם את

Frag. 2 ıı　1 [...]...[...] 2 [ויאמר] ישחק אל אברהם [...]
3 ל[ע]ולה ויאמר אברהם אל[... 4 לו אמר ישחק אל אביו כ]...[
5 מלאכי ק[ו]דש עומדים בוכים על[... 6 את בניו מן הארץ ומלאכי
המ[שטמה ... 7 שמחים ואומרים עכשו יאבד ו[...] אם[8 ימצא כחש
ואם לא ימצא נאמן [...] 9 אברהם אברהם ויאמר הנני ויאמר ע[תה ידעתי

478

4Q225 (4QpsJub^a) *4QPseudo-Jubilees^a*

4Q226, 4Q227?
Bibliography: Wacholder-Abegg 2, 204-206

Frag. 1   *1* […] from the guilt of immorality … […] *2* […] he … […] *3* […] …
and he struck them with … […] *4* [… the covenant which] was made with
Abraham. And he circumcised […] *5* […] Egypt, /and/ God /sold/ them […]
6 […] *Blank* And you, Moses, when I speak with […] *7* […] the creation until
the [new] creation […] *8* […] standing, and he took vengeance (?) … […]
9 […] and on the day which … […] *10* [… o]n the shore of the […] … […]
11-12 […] … […]

Frag. 2 *col.* I   *1* […] that p[erson] shall be cut off *2* [from the midst of] his
[na]tion [… liv]ed in Haran twenty years. *3* [And A]braham [said] to God:
«My Lord, see that I am going ch[ildle]ss, and Eli[ezer] *4* is [the son of my
house], and he will inherit me». *Blank 5* [The Lo]rd [said] to A[b]raham: «Lift
up, observe the stars, and see *6* [and count] {it all} the sand on the shore of the
sea, and the dust of the earth, whether *7* these [can be coun]ted, or not. Thus
your offspring shall be». And [Abraham] tr[usted] *8* Go[d], and righteousness
was accounted to him. And af[ter] this a son was born *9* [to Abraha]m, And
[he] called him Isaac, and the Prince of A[ni]mosity came *10* [to G]od and
accused Abraham with regard to Isaac. And [G]od said *11* [to Abra]ham:
«Take your son, Isaac, [your] only one, [whom] *12* you [love], and offer him
to me as a burnt-offering on one of the [high] mountains *13* [which I will tell]
you». And he ar[ose, and we]n[t] from the wells up to […] *14* […] and
Ab[raham] lifted

Frag. 2 *col.* II (cf. 4Q266 7)   *1* […] … […] *2* [and] Isaac [said] to Abraham […]
3 for the [bur]nt-offering»? And Abraham said to […] *4* for himself». Isaac
said to his father: [«…» …] *5* the angels of holiness were standing weeping
above […] *6* his sons from the earth. And the angels of the An[imosity …]
7 were rejoicing and saying: «Now he will come to an end». And […
whether] *8* he would be found untruthful, and whether he would not be found
faithful […] *9* «Abraham, Abraham». And he said: «Here am I». And he said:

כי [...]   10 לא יהיה אהב ויברך אל יהוה את יש[חק כול ימי חיו ויולד את]

11 יעקוב ויעקוב הוליד את לוי ד[ור שלישי vacat ויהיו כול]   12 ימי

אברהם וישחק ויעקוב ולו[י ...]   13 ושר המשטמה vacat אסור [...].

14 שר המ[ש]טמה וישמע בליעל אל[...]

4Q226 (4QpsJub^b) *4QPseudo-Jubilees^b*

J.C. VanderKam, J.T. Milik, *DJD XIII*, 157-169, pl. XI
PAM 41.320, 43.234
ROC 811

מצוה ... [3   [...] מת[ו]ך[...]בלהבת אש[2   [...]...[...] 1   *Frag. 1*
[... ותשב] נ[תתי לך האותות] ...[...] 4   [...]עליך לרדת מצרים ולהוצי[א
[... הוא קדש כי הזה היובל]... 6   [...] י שנים עשית מן השבוע י[...] 5
[...]...[...] 8   [...]. עולמים ב[ע]ו[ו]לם קודש[מ[ל]אכי ...] 7

יהוה ויברך לרצון 2   [...]ה[א]ל[א]ל נאמן אברהם נמצא 1   *Frag. 7*
לוי 4   [את עקוב הוליד י]ויולד את vacat חיו 3   [ימי כל ישחק את]
[... ולוי אברהם וישחק ויע]קב 5   [ימי כל ויהיו vacat]ישי דור של[
[...שר] ...[...] 8   [...]צום שם[vacat? 7   [...]שר אל ...[...]ממלאכי הקדש 6

4Q227 (4QpsJub^c?) *4QPseudo-Jubilees^c?*

J.C. VanderKam, J.T. Milik, *DJD XIII*, 171-175, pl. XII
PAM 43.238
ROC 812

[...]. מושה לפני .[...] 2   [...] הצדיקים כול [...] 1   *Frag. 1*
[...שני]כו .[...] 5   [...] vacat [...] 4   [...] ימי כול את[...]א 3
[...]...[...] 6

«N[ow I know ...] *10* he will not be loving. And God YHWH blessed Isa[ac all the days of his live. And he begot] *11* Jacob, and Jacob begot Levi, a [third] ge[neration. *Blank* And all] *12* the days of Abraham, Isaac, Jacob and Lev[i were ...] *13* and the Prince of Animosity *Blank* Bind [...] *14* the Prince of An[im]osity, and Belial listened to [...]

4Q226 (4QpsJub^b) *4QPseudo-Jubilees^b*

4Q225, 4Q227?
Bibliography: Wacholder-Abegg 2, 207-210

Frag. 1   *1* [...] ... [...] *2* [...] in a flame of fire from the mi[dd]le of [...] *3* [... commanding] you to go down to Egypt, and to bring [out ...] *4* [...] ... the signs I [ga]ve to you, and you stayed [...] *5* [...] ... years you spent from the week [...] *6* [...] this jubilee, for it is holy [...] *7* [...] holy a[n]gels [in eter]nity of eternities [...] *8* [...] ... [...]

Frag. 7 (cf. 4Q225 2 II)   *1* Abraham was found faithful to [G]o[d ...] *2* acceptable. And YHWH blessed [Isaac all the days of] *3* his live. *Blank* And he begot J[acob, and Jacob begot] *4* Levi, a th[ird] generation. [*Blank* And all the days of] *5* Abraham, Isaac, Ja[cob and Levi were ...] *6* And the holy angels [...] *7* to the prince (?) *Blank?* Fast (?) there [...] *8* [...] ... [...]

4Q227 (4QpsJub^c?) *4QPseudo-Jubilees^c?*

4Q225?, 4Q226?
Bibliography: J.T. Milik, *The Books of Enoch*, 12, 14, 25, 60; *Wacholder-Abegg 2*, 211

Frag. 1   *1* [...] all the righteous [...] *2* [...] before Moses [...] *3* [...] all the days of [...] *4* [...] *Blank* [...] *5* [...] ... years [...] *6* [...] ... [...]

Frag. 2 1 [... ח]נוך אחר אשר למד־והו   2 [...]ששה יובלי שנים

3 [... א]רץ אל תוך בני האדם ויעד על כולם   4 [...] וגם על העירים

ויכתוב את כול 5 [...ש]מים ואת דרכי צבאם ואת] החוד]שים   6 [...

א]שר לוא ישגו הצ]דיקים [...

4Q228 *4QWork with citation of Jubilees*

J.C. VanderKam, J.T. Milik, *DJD XIII*, 178-185, pl. XII
PAM 43.232

Frag. 1 i 1 [...]   2 [... במחל]ק]ו]ת העתים   3 [...] כ]מה אשר תדעו

4 [...]ר לפנו מחלקת עתו וכל   5 [...מע]בה במשפט עתי עולה

6 [...]אש בוערת אוכלת בסוד רשעה   7 [...]ת במחלקת עתה ימצאנה

8 [...]מקשי שחת ומלאך שלומו   9 [...]י נצח כי כן כתוב במחלק]ת

10 העתים [...]למ ילכו [....]   [...] את כל   11 [...]יחזק אתכמה [....].

12-14 [...]...

Frag. 1 ii 1 [...]   [...]בשר ולוא   2 משפחת הגוי]ם [...   3 יעשו ואת

ישר מ.[.].   4 {.}עת עם טעיכם [...] 5-13 *vacat*

Frag. 2   *1* [… E]noch, after /we/ had taught him *2* […] six jubilees of years *3* [… of the ea]rth, among the sons of men and he gave witness against them all *4* […] and also against the Watchers and he wrote everything *5* [… of the he]avens and the paths of their armies and [the mont]hs *6* [… so t]hat the j[ust] would not stray […]

4Q228 *4QWork with citation of Jubilees*

ROC 309

Frag. 1 *col.* I   *1* […] *2* [… divisi]ons of the times *3* […] you(r), that you know *4* […] before him the division of his time, and all *5* […] … in the judgment of times of injustice *6* […] a blazing fire, consuming at the foundation of wicked-ness *7* […] in the division of its time he will find it *8* […] snares of destruction and the angel of his peace […] *9* […] everlasting. For thus is written in the division/s/ *10* [of the times …] … will walk […] all the *11* […] he will strengthen you […] … *12-14* […] …

Frag. 1 *col.* II   *1* … […] flesh and not *2* the race of the nation[s …] *3* […] they will do, and the upright of […] *4* time (?) with (?) your erring ones (?) *5-13 Blank*

4Q229 *4QPseudepigraphic work in Mishnaic Hebrew*

Details unknown

4Q230 *4QCatalogue of Spirits*[a]

Details unknown

4Q231 *4QCatalogue of Spirits*[b]

Details unknown

4Q232 (4QNJ?) *4QNew Jerusalem (?)*

4QJN[h] 1, 2 and 3 of the *Concordance* have been published as 4Q365a frags. 3, 2 and 4, but Milik seems to refer to yet another fragment.
Bibliography: Concordance, 5; J.T. Milik, *The Books of Enoch*, 59; S.A. Reed, *Catalogue*, xxxvii

4Q233 *4QFragments with place names*

Details unknown

4Q234 *4QGen 27:20-21 (Exercitium Calami)*

A. Yardeni, *DJD XXXVI* (forthcoming)
PAM 43.407
ROC 603

4Q235 *4QFragments of Book of Kings nabatean (?)*

A. Yardeni, *DJD XXVII*, 288, fig. 28, pl. LV (published not as 4Q235, but as *Unidentified Fragments* in an appendix to 4Q343)
PAM 41.687, 43.402
ROC 601

4Q236 (4QPs89) *4QPsalm 89* [now **4Q98g**]

J.T. Milik, 'Fragment d'une source du psautier (4Q Ps 89) et fragments de Jubilés, du Document de Damas, d'un Phylactère dans la grotte 4 de Qumrân', *RB* 73 (1966) 93-104, pl. 1
PAM 41.438. 43.399
ROC 304
Bibliography: U. Gleßmer, 'Das Textwachstum von Ps 89 und ein Qumran-fragment', *BN* 65 (1992) 55-73; P.W. Flint, *PTSDSSP 4A*, 40-45

4Q237

Cancelled (= 4Q97 Ps^q)

4Q238 (4QHab3) *4QHabakkuk 3 and songs*

Details unknown

4Q239 *4QPesher on the True Israel*

Details unknown

4Q240 *4QCommentary on Canticles* (?)

Details unknown

4Q241 *4QFragments citing Lamentations*

PAM 43.400

Frag. 1   1 [...][...]*vacat* [...] 2 [...]אנשי {איש}[...] 3 [...] גדול
כ]ים ... [4 ...] ו[לא גלות]ך ...[

Frag. 2   1 [...]לך מטעו[ן] ... [2 ... שכ]בו בת]לתי .[...]   3 [...
[תקרא ביו]ם ... [4 [...]...[...]

4Q242 (4QPrNab ar) *4QPrayer of Nabonidus ar*

J. Collins, *DJD XXII*, 83-93, pl. VI
PAM 42.265
ROC 248, 665
Bibliography: J.T. Milik, 'Prière de Nabonide et autres écrits d'un cycle de Dan-
iel', *RB* 63 (1965) 407-411, pl. I; R. Meyer, *Das Gebet des Nabonid. Eine in den
Qumran-Handschriften wiederentdeckte Weisheitserzählung* (Berlin: Akademie,
1962); A.S. van der Woude, 'Bemerkungen zum Gebet des Nabonid', in M.
Delcor (ed.), *Qumrân. Sa piété, sa théologie et son milieu* (BETL 46; Paris-
Gembloux: Duculot / Leuven: University Press, 1978) 120-129; P. Grelot, 'La

Frags. 1-3   1 מלי צ]ל[תא די צלי נבני מלך א]רעא די בב]ל' מלכא[
רבא כדי כתיש הוא[2 בשחנא באישא בפתגם א]להא עלי[א בתימן] אנה
נבני בשחנא באישא[3 כתיש הוית שנין שבע ומן] אנשיא[שוי א]נה
וצלית קדם אלהא עליא[4 וחטאי שבק לה גזר והוא] גבר]יהודי מ]ן בני
גלותא והוא אמר לי[5 החוי וכתב למעבד יקר ור]בו והד]ר לשם א]להא
עליא וכן כתבת כדי[6 כתיש הוית בשחנא ב]אישא ... [בתימן] בפתגם
אלהא עליא[7 שנין שבע מצלא הוי]ת קדם כל]אלהי כספא ודהבא [נחשא
פרזלא[8 אעא אבנא הספא מן די[ן] הוית סבי]ר די אלהין ה]מון ...[
[...]...[...] 9

486

4Q241 *4QFragments citing Lamentations*

ROC 303

Frag. 1   *1* [... *Lam 3:56?*] to my cry for help. *Blank* [...] *2* [...] men of {...} [...]
3 [...] *Lam 2:13-14?* wide as the [ocean ...] *4* [... and] not [your] exile [...]

Frag. 2   *1* [...] for you his plantation (?) [...] *2* [... *Lam 2:21-22*] my virgins [li]e
[...] *3* [...] you call on the da[y ...] *4* [...] ... [...]

4Q242 (4QPrNab ar) *4QPrayer of Nabonidus ar*

prière de Nabonide (4Q Or Nab). Nouvel essai de restauration', *RevQ* 9/36
(1978) 483-495; J.A. Fitzmyer, D. Harrington, *MPAT*, 2-5; F.M. Cross, 'Fragments of the Prayer of Nabonidus', *IEJ* 34 (1984) 260-264; F. García
Martínez, 'The Prayer of Nabonidus: A New Synthesis', in *Qumran and Apocalyptic. Studies on the Aramaic Texts from Qumran* (STDJ 9; Leiden: E.J. Brill,
1992) 116-136; É. Puech, 'La prière de Nabonide (4Q242)', in K.J. Cathcart,
M. Maher (eds.), *Targumic and Cognate Studies: Essays in Honour of Martin
McNamara* (Sheffield: Sheffield University Press, 1996)

Frags. 1 - 3   *1* Words of the pr[ay]er which Nabonidus, king of [the] la[nd of
Baby]lon, the [great] king, prayed [when he was afflicted] *2* by a malignant
inflammation, by decree of the G[od Most Hi]gh, in Teiman. [I, Nabonidus,]
was afflicted [by a malignant inflammation] *3* for seven years, and was banished far [from men, until I prayed to the God Most High] *4* and an exorcist
forgave my sin. He was a Je[w] fr[om the exiles, who said to me:] *5* «Make a
proclamation in writing, so that glory, exal[tation and hono]ur be given to the
name of [the] G[od Most High». And I wrote as follows: «When] *6* I was
afflicted by a ma[lignant] inflammation [...] in Teiman, [by decree of the God
Most High,] *7* [I] prayed for seven years [to all] the gods of silver and gold, [of
bronze and iron,] *8* of wood, of stone and of clay, because [I thoug]ht that
t[hey were] gods [...]

Frag. 4 1 [...] מ]לבר המון אחלמת 2 [...] מנה אח]ל]ף שלם של[...]
3 [...].[...].[...]נו רחמי לא יכלת] [... 4 [...] כמה דמא אנתה ל.[...]
5 [...]...[...]

4Q243 (4QpsDanᵃ ar) *4QPseudo-Danielᵃ ar*

J. Collins, P. Flint, *DJD XXII*, 97-121, pls. VII-VIII
PAM 43.247; 43.252
ROC 854, 855, 908
4Q244, 245
Bibliography: J.T. Milik, 'Prière de Nabonide et autres écrits d'un cycle de Daniel', *RB* 63 (1965) 411-415; J.A. Fitzmyer, D. Harrington, *MPAT*, 4-9;

Frag. 1 1 שאיל דניאל לממר בד[י]ל[...] 2 [...]ל[...]. ומנין ꝺ⅂ꝺᴸꟼ [...]ל[...]
3 יצלה ינ[...] 4 ע[...]

Frag. 6 1 [...].[...] 2 [...]ובה כתיב [...] 3 ... ד]ניאל די י[...]
4 ...] א]שתכח כתי]ב [...

Frag. 10 1 [...]...[...] 2 ... ע]ל מגדלא ושלח[...] 3 ... ל]בקרה
בבנין [...] 4 [...]...[...]

Frag. 12 1 ... שנין אר]בע מאה ומן 2 [...]סהון ויתון מן גוא 3 [...]
מעברהון ירדנא יובל]א [... 4 ...] ובניהון [...] 5 [...]...[...]

Frag. 13 1 ... ב]חרו בני ישראל אנפיה]ון מן אנפי אלוהין] 2 [והוו
דב]חין לבניהון לשידי [טעותא ורגז עליהון] 3 [אלוהין ואמר] למנתן אנון
ביד נב]כדנצר מלך בבל] 4 [ולאחרבא ארעה]ון מנה]ון מן די [ש]...[

Frag. 4   *1* [... a]part from (?) them. I was healed *2* [...] from it he caused to p[as]s. The peace of ... [...] *3* [...] ... my friends. I could not [...] *4* [...] how are you like [...] *5* [...] ... [...]

4Q243 (4QpsDanᵃ ar) *4QPseudo-Danielᵃ ar*

R. Eisenman, M. Wise, *DSSU*, 64-68; F. García Martínez, '4QPseudo Daniel Aramaic and the Pseudo Daniel Literature', in *Qumran and Apocalyptic. Studies on the Aramaic Texts from Qumran* (STDJ 9; Leiden: E.J. Brill, 1992) 137-161; K. Beyer, *ATTME*, 105-107; J.J. Collins, 'Pseudo-Daniel Revisited', *RevQ* 17/65-68 (1996) 111-136

Frag. 1   *1* He asked Daniel, saying: « [...] *2* your God, and a number [...] *3* he will pray ... [...] *4* ... [...]

Frag. 6   *1* [...] ... [...] *2* [...] and in it was written [...] *3* [... Da]niel who ... [...] *4* [... wa]s found writ[ten ...]

Frag. 10   *1* [...] ... [...] *2* [... o]n the tower and he sent [...] *3* [... to] examine a building [...] *4* [...] ... [...]

Frag. 12   *1* [... fo]ur hundred [years] and from [...] *2* [...] their [...] and they will depart from within *3* [...] he will cause them to cross the River Jordan [...] *4* [...] and their sons [...] *5* [...] ... [...]

Frag. 13 (= 4Q244 12)   *1* [...] the children of Israel [pre]ferred th[eir] presence above [God's presence,] *2* [and they sacrif]iced their sons to the devils of [delusion. God grew angry against them] *3* [and ordered] them to be given into the hand of Nebu[chadnezzar, king of Babylon,] *4* [and to make the]ir [land desolate] of th[em, because ...]

Frag. 16 1 [...] [ש]אין [...] בעין שנין [...] 2 [...] בי]דה רבתא ויושע
3 [...] חסנין ומלכות עממ]יא ... [...] 4 [...] היא מלכותא קד]ישתא
[...

Frag. 19 1 [...] ש]נין [...]. [...] 2 [...]רהוס בר[...] 3 [...]וס שנין ת[...]
4 [...]ימללון [...]

Frag. 21 1 [...]מלך שנין [...] 2 [...]... בלכרוס [...] 3 [...]...[...]

Frag. 24 1 [... רש]עא אטעו]ן [...] 2 [... בתר]דנה יתכנשון
3 [...]עממיא ולהוה מן יום [...] 4 [... קדי]שין ומלכי עממיא]
5 [... ע]בדין עד יומא] [...

4Q244 (4QpsDanᵇ ar) *4QPseudo-Danielᵇ ar*

J. Collins, P. Flint, *DJD XXII*, 123-131, pl. IX
PAM 43.249
ROC 853

Frag. 1 1 קודם רב בני מלכא ואשריא ל]...[

Frag. 8 2 [...]מן בתר מבולא [...] 3 [...]נוח מן לובר]טורא ...
4 [...]. קריה]...[

Frag. 12 1 [...] בחרו בני ישראל אנפיהון מן [אנפי אלוהין] 2 והוו]
דבחין לבניהון ל]שידי טעותא ורגז עליהון אלוהין וא]מר למנתן אנון]
3 [ביד נבכדנצר מלך ב]בל ולאחרבא ארע]הון מנהון מן די [...]
4 [...]...[...]...[...]. בני גלותא [...]

Frag. 16   *1* […] oppressed (for) [se]venty years […] *2* [… with] his great [ha]nd and he will rescue th[em …] *3* […] strong (ones) and the kingdom of [the] people[s …] *4* […] This is the fi[rst] kingdom […]

Frag. 19   *1* [… ye]ars […] *2* […]RHWS, son of […] *3* […]ws, years *4* […] they will speak […]

Frag. 21   *1* […] ruled […] years *2* […] BLKRWS […] *3* […] … […]

Frag. 24   *1* [… the children of si]n, have led […] astray […] *2* [… after] that (period) the called ones will be assembled […] *3* […] the peoples, and from the day of […] there will be […] *4* [… the hol]y ones and the kings of the peoples […] *5* [… sl]aves until the day […]

4Q244 (4QpsDan^b ar) *4QPseudo-Daniel^b ar*

4Q243, 4Q245
Bibliography: Cf. 4Q243

Frag. 1   *1* […] before the ministers of the King, and the Assyrians […]

Frag. 8   *1* […] … […] *2* […] after the flood *3* […] Noah from [Mount] Lubar […] *4* […] a city […]

Frag. 12 (= 4Q242 13)   *1* […] the children of Israel preferred their presence above [God's presence] *2* [and they sacrificed their sons to] the devils of delusion. God grew angry against them and or[dered them to be given] *3* [into the hand of Nebuchadnezzar, king of Ba]bylon, and to make their land desolate of them because […] *4* […] … […] the exiles […]

4Q245 (4QpsDanᶜ ar) *4QPseudo-Danielᶜ ar*

J. Collins, P. Flint, *DJD XXII*, 153-164, pl. X
PAM 43.259
ROC 247

Frag. 1 ו‏ 1 [...]אי‏ 2 [...]‏... ומה די‏ 3 [...] דניאל‏ 4 [...]כתב די
יהיב‏ 5 [...] קהת‏ 6 [...]בוקי עוז‏[י]‏ 7 ... צדו‏[ק א]בי‏[תר‏ 8 [...]
[ח]ל‏[ק]יה‏ 9 [...] וחוניה‏ 10 ... יונ[תן שמעון‏ 11 [...]דויד שלומוה
12 [...] א[חזי]ה‏ ... 13 [...].[...]

Frag. 2 1 [...]...[...]‏ 2 [...]למסף ר[ש]עא‏ 3 [...]אלן בעור וטעו
4 ... א]לן אדין יקומון‏ 5 ... ק]דיש[ת]א ויתובון‏ 6 [...] רשעא *vacat*

4Q246 *4QAramaic Apocalypse*

É. Puech, *DJD XXII*, 165-184, pl. XI
PAM 42.601, 43.236
ROC 209

Bibliography: J.T. Milik, *The Books of Enoch*, 60; D. Flusser, 'The Hubris of the Antichrist in a Fragment from Qumran', *Immanuel* 10 (1980) 31-37; É. Puech, 'Fragment d'une apocalypse en araméen (4Q246 = pseudo-Danᵈ) et le "royaume de Dieu"', *RB* 99 (1992) 98-131; J.A. Fitzmyer, 'The 'Son of God' Document from Qumran', *Biblica* 74 (1993) 153-174; F. García Martínez, 'The Eschatological Figure of 4Q246', in *Qumran and Apocalyptic. Studies on the*

Col. I 1 [...]ע[לוהי שרת נפל קדם כרסיא‏ 2 ... מ]לכא לעלמא אתה
3 [...].א חזוך וכלא אתה עד עלמא‏ 4 [... ר]ברבין עקה תתא
על ארעא‏ 5 [...] ונחשירון רב במדינתא‏ 6 [...] מלך אתור [ומ]צרין
7 [...] רב להוה על ארעא‏ 8 ... יע]בדון וכלא ישמשון‏ 9 ... ר]בא
יתקרא ובשמה יתכנה

4Q245 (4QpsDan^c ar) *4QPseudo-Daniel^c ar*

4Q243, 4Q244

Bibliography: Cf. 4Q243; P. Flint, '4Qpseudo-Daniel ar^c (4Q245) and the Restoration of the Priesthood', *RevQ* 17/65-68 (1996) 137-150

Frag. 1 *col.* I *1* […] … *2* […] … and what *3* […] Daniel *4* […] a book that was given *5* […] Qahat *6* […] Bukki, Uzz[iah] *7* [… Zado]k, A[bia]thar *8* […] Hi[l]kiah *9* […] and Onias *10* [… Jona]than, Simeon *11* […] David, Solomon *12* […] Ahazia[h …] *13* […] … […]

Frag. 2 *1* […] … […] *2* […] in order to eradicate wic[ked]ness *3* […] those in their blindness, and they have gone astray *4* [… th]ey then shall arise *5* […] the [h]oly, and they will return *6* […] wickedness. *Blank*

4Q246 *4QAramaic Apocalypse*

Aramaic Texts from Qumran (STDJ 9; Leiden: E.J. Brill, 1992) 162-179; É. Puech, 'Notes sur le fragment d'apocalypse 4Q246 — "le fils de dieu"', *RB* 101 (1994) 533-558; J.J. Collins, 'The Messiah as the Son of God', in *The Scepter and the Star* (New York: Doubleday, 1995) 154-172; F.M. Cross, 'Notes on the Doctrine of the Two Messiahs at Qumran and the Extracanonical Daniel Apocalypse (4Q246)', in D.W. Parry, S.D. Ricks (eds.), *Current Research and Technological Developments on the Dead Sea Scrolls* (STDJ 20; Leiden: E.J. Brill, 1996) 1-13

Col. I *1* […] settled [up]on him and he fell before the throne *2* [… k]ing for ever. You are angry, and have changed you *3* […] … your vision, and everything that shall come for ever. *4* [… mi]ghty ones, oppression will come upon the earth *5* […] and great slaughter in the provinces *6* […] king of Assyria [and E]gypt *7* […] and he will be great over the earth *8* […] they [will d]o, and all will serve *9* [… gr]eat will he be called and he will be designated by his name.

Col. II   1 ברה די אל יתאמר ובר עליון יקרונה כזיקיא   2 די חזיתא כן
מלכותהן תהוה שני[ן] ימלכון על   3 ארעא וכלא ידשון עם לעם ידוש
ומדינה למדני[נ]ה   4 *vacat*   עד יקום עם אל וכלא יניח מן חרב *vacat*
5 מלכותה מלכות עלם וכל ארחתה בקשוט ידי[ן]   6 ארעא בקשט וכלא
יעבד שלם חרב מן ארעא יסף   7 וכל מדינתה לה יסגדון אל רבא באילה
8 הוא יעבד לה קרב עממין ינתן בידה וכלהן   9 ירמה קדמוהי שלטנה
שלטן עלם וכל תהומי

4Q247 (4QApocWeeks?) *Apocalypse of Weeks* (?)

M. Broshi, *DJD XXXVI* (forthcoming)
PAM 43.248

Frag. 1   1 [...] קץ ח[ה]קוק [...]   2 ... ומאחריו יב[ו]א השבוע הח[מ]ישי
[...]   3 ... שנים שמונים ו[ארבע מאות שלו[מ]וה [... 4 ...] צד[ק]יה מלך
יהודה [...]   5 [...]לבני לוי ועם האר[ץ ... 6 [...] מל[ך] כתיים [...].
7 [...]ל[...] ...[...]א[...]

4Q248 *Acts of a Greek King*

E. Eshel, M. Broshi, *DJD XXXVI* (forthcoming)
PAM 43.248
ROC 815

1 [...]...[...]   2 [...]מצרים וביון ו[...]   3 [...]ם הגוי[ם]בכן יאכלו
[...]   4 [והיו ב]ניהם ובנותי[ה]ם במצור ב[...]   5 [וה]עביר **** רוח[ו
ב]חצרותיהם ו[...]   6 [ו]בא למצרים ומכר את עפרה ואת] ...   7 אל עיר
המקדש ותפשה עם כ[ל ...   8 והפך בארצות גוים ושב למצרי]ם ...
9 [ו]בבציר עם הק[...]   10 כל אלה ישובו בני[...]

494

Col. II *1* He will be called son of God, and they will call him son of the Most High. Like the sparks *2* that you saw, so will their kingdom be; they will rule several year[s] over *3* the earth and crush everything; a people will crush another people, and a province another provi[n]ce. *4 Blank* Until the people of God arises and makes everyone rest from the sword. *Blank 5* His kingdom will be an eternal kingdom, and all his paths in truth. He will jud[ge] *6* the earth in truth and all will make peace. The sword will cease from the earth, *7* and all the provinces will pay him homage. The great God is his strength, *8* he will wage war for him; he will place the peoples in his hand and *9* cast them all away before him. His rule will be an eternal rule, and all the abysses

---

4Q247 (4QApocWeeks?) *Apocalypse of Weeks* (?)

ROC 377
Bibliography: J.T. Milik, *The Books of Enoch*, 256; *Wacholder-Abegg 3*, 32

Frag. 1 *1* [… the de]termined [time …] *2* [… and after it shall co]me the fi[fth] week […] *3* […] four hundred [and eighty years] Solo[mon …] *4* [… Zede]kiah the king of Judah […] *5* […] for the Levites and the people of the la[nd …] *6* […] the kin[g] of the Kittim […] *7* […] … […] … […]

4Q248 *Acts of a Greek King*

Bibliography: Wacholder-Abegg 3, 33; M. Broshi, E. Eshel, 'The Greek King is Antiochus IV (4QHistorical Text = 4Q248)', *JJS* 48 (1997) 120-129

1 […] … […] *2* […] Egypt and in Greece and […] *3* […] the natio[ns]. Then they shall eat […] *4* [and] their [s]ons and [th]eir daughters [will be] besieged in […] *5* [and] **** will [cause his] spirit to pass through their settlements and […] *6* [and] he will come to Egypt and sell its soil and […] *7* to the city of the sanctuary and he will conquer it with a[ll …] *8* and he will turn back against the lands of the peoples and return to Egyp[t …] *9* [and] in the vintage time with … […] *10* these all shall return, the sons […]

495

4Q249 (4Qpap cryptA MSM) *4QCryptic A: Midrash Sefer Moshe*

S. Pfann, *DJD XXXV* (forthcoming)
PAM 40.637; 43.408-43.413
ROC 589, 590, 593, 596, 597
Bibliography: S.J. Pfann, '4Q249 Midrash Sefer Moshe', in M. Bernstein *et al.*

Frag. 1 *verso*   מדרש ספר מושה

Frag. 1 *recto*   1 [...]...[...]   2 [...]תחליף את [אבנים ...]   3 [...]בית
ונתצ[ו את הבית ...]   4 [... כ]ל אשר אין ב[ה נגע ...]   5 [... מש]פט אחד
vacat   6 [...]   7 [...]ר ואם בח[...].[...]ל תמות ובי.[...]   8-11 [...]...[...]
12 [...משפט]   13 [...]בבית[...]   14 [...]רמיה[...]

4Q249a-4Q249m (4Qpap crypt A texts) *4Qpap Cryptic A Texts*

S. Pfann, *DJD XXXV* (forthcoming)
PAM 43.408-43.412
ROC 590, 596, 598

4Q251 (4QHalakhah A) *4QHalakhah A*

E. Larson, M. Lehmann, *DJD XXXV* (forthcoming)
PAM 43.307, 43.308
ROC 702, 711

Frag. 1   1 [...]...[...]   2 [...ו]ת כול[...]   3 לש[...]בהמה ולמשוך
מים מבור   4 המשיכה ...[...] אל [יוצא איש ממקומו כל השבת   5 ומן
הבית אל הח[ו]ץ[...]לו לדרוש ולקרא בספר ב[שב]ת   6 [...ל]החיל א[ת
... הט[מ]יא נדה בש[ר]ו ביום [ה]שבת   7 [...בי[ו]ם חששי בשר ער[וה]

4Q249 (4Qpap cryptA MSM) *4QCryptic A: Midrash Sefer Moshe*

(eds.), *Legal Texts and Legal Issues. Proceedings of the Second Meeting of the International Organization for Qumran Studies Cambridge 1995. Published in Honour of Joseph M. Baumgarten* (STDJ 23; Leiden: Brill, 1997) 11-18, pl. 4

Frag. 1 *verso*   Interpretation of the Book of Moses

Frag. 1 *recto*   *1* […] … […] *2* […] you shall pull out [the stones …] *3* […] house, and [t]he[y] shall tear down [the house …] *4* [… al]l in [which] there is no [blemish …] *5* […] one [ordi]nance *Blank* […] *6* […] you shall kill and … […] *7* […] and if … […] *8-11* […] … […] *12* […] ordinance […] *13* […] in the house […] *14* […] deceit […]

4Q250, 4Q250a-b (4Qpap cryptA texts) *4Qpap Cryptic A Texts*

S. Pfann, *DJD XXXV* (forthcoming)
PAM 40.636, 43.313, 43.414
ROC 593

4Q251 (4QHalakhah A) *4QHalakhah A*

Bibliography: J.T. Milk, *DJD* III, 300; J.M. Baumgarten, '4QHalakah[a], the Law of Hadash, and the Pentecontad Calendar', *JJS* 27 (1976) 36-46; *Wacholder-Abegg 3*, 34-40

Frag. 1   *1* […] … […] *2* […] … all […] *3* to […] cattle, and to draw water from a well. *4* The drawing [… No] one should go out from his place the entire Sabbath, *5* neither from his house to out[si]de […] … to study or to read in the Book on [the Sabba]th *6* [… to] profane [… to de]file the impurity of his fle[sh] on the Sabbath day *7* […] on the sixth d[a]y. Nak[ed] flesh

Frag. 4   1 [...] עין[ ] בעין [...]   2 [...]. ונתן שב[תו ורפו]א ירפא
3 [... כי יגח שור איש או א]שה והומת השור יסקלהו   4 [... ואם שור נ]גח
הוא מאתמול   5 [שלשום ... והמית אי]ש או אשה   6 [...]...[...]

Frag. 5   1 [אל יאכל איש דגן ותיר]וש ויצהר כי אם [הניף הכוהן]
2 ראשיתם הבכורים והמלאה אל יאחר איש כי [...]   3 היאה ראשית
המלאה [ו]דגן הואה הדמע [...]. ולחם   4 בכורים הוא חלות החמץ אשר
יביאו [בי]ום ה[בכורים]   5 בכורים הם אל יאכל א[י]ש חטים חדשים[...]
6 עד יום בא לחם חבכורים אל [...].

Frag. 6   1 [...]..[...]   2 [... מ]עוט אל ימעי[ט ...]   3 [...]ת העשרון
ל[...]   4 [... בכור הא[דם והבהמה הטמא]ה [...]   5 [...] בכור האדם
והבהמה הטמאה   6 [... ה]שו[ר ו]הצאן והמקדש מן   7 [... הו]א כבכור
ותבואת עץ   8 [... והר]מון והזית בשנה הרביעית   9 [...]תרומה כל חרם
לכוהן

Frag. 7   1 [...] שור [ו]כבש ועז אשר לא שלמו [...]   2 [...]אש[ר
במעי]ן אמו ואל יאכל בשרו כי [...].   3 [... ה]יא אל יאכל איש בשר בהמה
4 vacat [... נב]לות וטרפה אשר לא חיה כי [...]   5 [...]... לנכרי וחלבה
לעש[ות ...]   6 [...] ול[ז]בחה ממנו הכ[...]   7 [...]...[...]

Frag. 9   1 [... ו]אם[ ]כל [הבהמה הטמאה אשר] [...]   2 [... לא י]גאלו
ושדה החרם תהיה אחזת [...]   3 [...]ת נפשו לשמ[ל]
[...]

Frag. 10   1 [... קודש קוד]שים הוא והי[ה ...]   2 [... וה]חרימו לכוהן
לעוברו[ן ...]   3 [...]לו לכוהן והאיש אש[ר ...]   4 [... לא] יאכל איש[...]

Frag. 11   1 [...]. את לחם אישה   2 [...] יאכלו בלחמו רק זונה

Frag. 4 (cf. *Exod* 21 : 19, 28 - 29)   *1* [… an eye] for an eye […] *2* […] he will compensate for [his enforced unem]ployment and defray the cost of the treatment. *3* [… If a bull gores a man or a wo]man and (s)he dies, they shall stone the bull *4* [and its meat is not to be eaten; but the owner will be acquitted. But if the bull had been gor]ing in the past *5* [and, the owner having been warned, had not restrained it and it should kill a ma]n or a woman *6* […] … […]

Frag. 5   *1* [No-one is to consume grain, wi]ne or oil until [the priest has waved] *2* their first fruits. And no-one is to separate the must, for [… wine] *3* is the first of the must, [and] the grain is the best part of [… And the bread of] *4* the first fruits are the leavened cakes which they have to bring [on the d]ay of the [first fruits.] *5* These are the first fruits. No-o[n]e is to eat the new wheat […] *6* until the day of the bread from the first fruits arrives. Not […]

Frag. 6   *1* […] … […] *2* […] not shall he pay le[ss …] *3* […] the *issaron* […] *4* [… the first-born of m]an and of an unclean animal […] *5* […] the first-born of man and of an unclean animal, *6* [… the bu]ll [and] ram, and what has been consecrated of *7* [… i]s like the first-born. And the produce of a tree *8* [… and the pome]granate and the olive in the fourth year *9* […] offering, all is banned for the priest.

Frag. 7   *1* […] a bull [or] ewe or she-goat which are not perfect […] *2* [… whi]ch is in the belly [of] its mother. And you shall not eat its flesh, for […] *3* [… i]t. No-one is to eat the meat of an animal *Blank* *4* [… and de]ad [animal]s or a torn animal which is not alive, for […] *5* […] … to the foreigner, and its fat, to ma[ke …] *6* […] and to [sa]crifice from it … […] *7* […] … […]

Frag. 9   *1* [… And] if (the vow concerns) [any] unclean animal which […] *2* [… not shall] they redeem, and the devoted field shall be the property of […] *3* […] his life for … […]

Frag. 10   *1* […] it is [most ho]ly; and wh[en …] *2* [… and] he shall [d]evote it to the priest to pass it on […] *3* […] … for the priest, and the man wh[o …] *4* [… not] shall a man eat […]

Frag. 11   *1* […] the bread of her husband *2* […] shall eat from his bread, only a

בעל[...] 5 [לאכול כי תועבה...] איש[4 כל המעל אשר ימעל .[...] 3
אשר אין לו גואל

Frag. 12 1 על העריות[...] 2 אל יקח איש את .[...] 3 את בת אחיו
ואת בת א[...] 4 איש את ערות אחות א[מו ...] 5 אביה ולאחי אמה[...]
6 אל יגל איש ערות [...] 7 אל יקח איש בתו נ[...]

Frag. 13 1 [...] אי[ש ברעהו [...] 2 [...] תחת]האילן לטמאה [...].
3 [... כיא ימצא] חלל אשר יפול ב[...] 4 [... וערפו שם את עגל]ה ב[נח]ל
חלף הנפש את [...] 5 [...].ה חליפה היא כל אשר הכרת ע[...] 6 [...]כול
אשר לא נפש עליו מות בק[בר...] 7 [...]...[...]

4Q252 (4QcommGen A) *4QCommentary on Genesis A*

G. Brooke, *DJD XXII*, 185-207, pls. XII-XIII
PAM 43.253, 43.381
ROC 668, 670
4Q253, 4Q254, 4Q254a
Bibliography: J.M. Allegro, 'Further Messianic References in Qumran Litera-
ture', *JBL* 75 (1956) 174-176, pl. 1; H. Stegemann, 'Weitere Stücke von 4Q
Psalm 37, von 4Q Patriarchal Blessings und Hinweis auf eine unedierte
Handschrift aus Höhle 4Q mit Exzerpten aus dem Deuteronomium', *RevQ*

Col. I 1 [ב]שנת ארבע מאות ושמונים לחיי נוח בא קצם לנוח
ואלוהים 2 אמר לא ידור רוחי באדם לעולם ויחתכו ימיהם מאה ועשרים
3 שנה עד קץ מי מבול ומי מבול היו על הארץ *vacat* בשנת שש מאות שנה
4 לחיי נוח בחודש השני באחד בשבת בשבעה עשר בו ביום ההוא
5 נבקעו כול מעינות תהום רבה וארבות השמים נפתחו ויהי הגשם על
6 הארץ ארבעים יום וארבעים לילה עד יום עשרים וששה בחודש
7 השלישי יום חמשה בשבת ויגברו המים על הארץ חמשים מאות יום
8 עד יום ארבעה עשר בחודש השביעי בשלושה בשבת ובסוף חמשים
9 ומאת יום חסרו המים שני ימים יום הרביעי ויום החמישי ויום 10 השישי

prostitute *3* […] All the unfaithfulness with which [one] is unfaithful *4* […] to eat, for it is an abomination. *5* […] an owner (and) has no-one to ransom him

Frag. 12　*1* Concerning prohibited marriages: […] *2* A man is not to take […] *3* his brother's daughter or the daughter of […] *4* a man the nakedness of [his] mo[ther's] sister […] *5* her father and to her mother's brother […] *6* A man is not to expose the nakedness of […] *7* A man is not take his daughter […]

Frag. 13　*1* [… on]e another […] *2* [… under] the tree, to the unclean […] *3* [… when one finds] a wounded man who has fallen in […] *4* [… and they shall break there the heif]er's [neck] in [the ravi]ne in return for (his) life … […] *5* […] it is a substitution; everyone who has been brought to death […] *6* […] everyone who has no life inside is dead, in a gr[ave …] *7* […] … […]

4Q252 (4QcommGen A) *4QCommentary on Genesis A*

6/22 (1967) 211-217; J.T. Milik, 'Milkî-ṣedeq et Milkî-resaᶜ', 138; T. H. Lim, 'The Chronology of the Flood Story in a Qumran Text (4Q252)', *JJS* 43 (1992) 288-298; *Wacholder-Abegg* 2, 212-215; U. Gleßmer, 'Antike und moderne Auslegungen des Sintflutberichtes Gen 6-8 und der Qumran-Pesher 4Q252', *Forschungsstelle Judentum Mitteilungen und Beiträge* 6 (1993) 3-79; G.J. Brooke, 'The Thematic Content of 4Q252', *JQR* 85 (1994) 33-59; .- '4Q252 as Early Jewish Commentary', *RevQ* 17/65-68 (1996) 385-401

Col. I　*1* [*Gen 7:10 - 8:13* In] the year four hundred and eighty of Noah's life, Noah reached the end of them. And God *2* said: «My spirit will not reside in man for ever. Their days shall be fixed at one hundred and twenty *3* years until the end of the waters of the flood». And the waters of the flood burst over the earth. *Blank* In the year six hundred *4* of Noah's life, in the second month, on the first (day) of the week, on its seventeenth (day), on that day *5* all the springs of the great abyss were split and the sluices of the sky opened and rain fell upon *6* the earth forty days and forty nights, until the twenty-sixth day of the third *7* month, the fifth day of the week. One hundred and fifty days did the wate[rs] hold sway over the [ea]rth, *8* until the fourteenth day in the seventh month, the third (day) of the week. At the end of *9* one hundred and fifty days, the waters came down (during) two days, the fourth day and the fifth day, and the *10* sixth

נחה התבה על הרי הוררט ה[וא יו]ם שבעה עשר בחודש השביעי

11 והמים הי[ו] הלוך וחסור עד החודש[הע]שירי באחד בו יום רביעי

12 לשבת נראו ראשי ההרים ויהי מקץ ארבעים יום להראות ראשי

13 ההר[ים ויפ]תח נוח את חלון התבה יום אחד בשבת יום עשרה

14 בעש[תי עשר] החודש וישלח את היונה לראות הקלו המים ולוא

15 מצאה מנוח ותבוא אליו [אל] התבה ויחל עוד שבעת ימים א[חרים]

16 ויוסף לשלחה ותבוא אליו ועלי זית טרף בפיה [הוא יום עשרים]

17 וארבעה לעשתי עשר החודש באחד בשב[ת ויד]ע נוח כי קלו המים

18 מעל הארץ vacat ומקץ שבעת ימים אחר[ים שלח א]ת ה[יונה ולוא]

19 יספה לשוב עוד הוא יום א[חד לשנים עשר] החודש[באחד]   20 בשבת

ומקץ שלושי[ם יום לשלח את היונ]ה אשר לוא יספ[ה]   21 שוב עוד חרבו

המ[ים מעל הארץ ו]יסר נוח מכסה התבה   22 וירא והנה [חרבו יום רביעי

לשבת] באחד בחודש הריאשון

1 באחת ושש מאות שנה לחיי נוח ובשבעה עשר יום לחודש   *Col.* II

השני 2 יבשה הארץ באחד בשבת ביום ההוא יצא נוח מן התבה לקץ שנה

3 תמימה לימים שלוש מאות ששים וארבעה באחד בשבת בשבעה 4 *vacat*

אחת ושש *vacat* נוח מן התבת למועד שנה   5 תמימה *vacat* ויקץ נוח מיינו

וידע את אשר עשה   6 לו בנו הקטן ויומר ארור כנען עבד עבדים יהייה

לאחיו ולוא   7 קלל את חם כי אם בנו כי ברך אל את בני נוח ובאהלי שם

ישכון   8 ארץ נתן לאברהם אהבו *vacat* בן מאה ואר[ב]עים שנה תרח

בצאתו   9 מאור כשדיים ויבוא חרן ואב[רם בן ש]בעים שנה וחמש שנים

ישב 10 אברם בחרן ואחר יצא [אברם אל]ארץ כנען ששי[ם וחמש שנה]

11 העגלה והאיל והע[ז ...] אברם לא[...]   12 האש בעברו[...]צה לקח

לו[...]   13 לצאת אב[רם אל ארץ] כנען ל[...]   14 *vacat*   [...]

1 כאשר כתוב [...]שנים   2 עשר אנשי[ם ... עמו]רה וגם   *Col.* III

3 העיר הזואת[...] צדיקים   4 אנוכ[י] לא[ ]אשחית ...[.]ים לבדם יחרמו

5 ואם לוא ימצא שם[... וכל] הנמצא בה ושלל'ה   6 וטפ'ה ושאר [.]

[עולם וישלח   7 אבר'ם את ידו] ... הש[מ]ים   8 ויומר אליו עת]ה [...

502

day, the ark rested in the mountains of Hurarat, i[t was] the seventeenth [da]y of the seventh month. *11* And the waters continu[ed] diminishing until the [te]nth month, on its first (day), the fourth day *12* of the week, the peaks of the mountains began to be visible. And at the end of forty days, when the peaks of the mountain[s] had become visible, *13* Noah [op]ened the window of the ark the first day of the week, which is the tenth day *14* of the el[eventh] month. And he sent out the dove to see whether the waters had diminished, but it did not *15* find a place of rest and returned to him, [to] the ark. And he waited yet a[nother] seven days *16* and again sent it out, and it returned to him, and in its beak there was a newly plucked olive leaf. [It was day twenty-] *17* four of the eleventh month, the first (day) of the wee[k. And Noah knew that the waters had diminished] *18* from upon the earth. *Blank* And at the end of another seven days, [he sent] the [dove out, but it did not] *19* come back again. It was the fi[rst] day [of the twelfth] month, [the first day] *20* of the week. And at the end of the thir[ty days after having sent out the dov]e which did not come back *21* again, the wat[ers] dried up [from upon the earth and] Noah removed the cover of the ark *22* and looked, and behold [they had dried up on the fourth day of the week,] on the first (day) of the first month

Col. ii (cf. 4Q254 1)   *1* in the year six-hundred and one of Noah's life. On the seventeenth day of the second month *3* the land dried up, on the first (day) of the week. On that day, Noah went out of the ark, at the end of a complete *3* year of three-hundred and sixty-four days, on the first (day) of the week. On the seventh *4* *Blank* one and six *Blank* Noah from the ark, at the appointed time of a complete *5* year. *Blank Gen 9:24-27* And Noah awoke from his wine and knew what *6* his youngest son had done. And he said: «Cursed be Canaan; he will be, for his brothers, a slave of slaves!» But he did not *7* curse Ham, but only his son, for God had blessed the sons of Noah. And in the tents of Shem he may dwell. *8* He gave the land to Abraham, his beloved. *Blank* Terah was one hundred and fo[r]ty years old when he left *9* Ur of the Chaldees and came to Haran, and Ab[ram was se]venty years old. Abram lived five years *10* in Haran, and afterwards [Abram] went [to] the land of Canaan. Six[ty five years (?).] *11* The heifer, the ram and the he-g[oat …] Abram … […] *12* the fire when it passed […] … he took for him […] *13* for Ab[ram] to go [to the land of] Canaan […] *14* *Blank* […]

Col. iii   *1* As it is written: […] twe- *2* lve me[n … Gomor]rah and also *3* this city. […] just ones *4* I [will] not [destroy …] only … they will exterminate. *5* If there are not found there [… and all] that is found in it and its booty *6* and its children. And the remnant […] forever. *Gen 22:10-12* And Abra/ha/m *7* stretched out his hand [… the hea]ven *8* And he told him: «No[w …] *9* your beloved

9 יחידכה מ]מני [... 10-11 [...]. 12 אל שדי יב]רך [... 13 [א]ת ברכת
אביכה] אברהם [... 14 [...]לם תהי]ה [...

Col. IV 1 תמנע היתה פילגש לאליפז בן עשיו ותלד לו את עמלק הוא
אשר הכ]הו[ן 2 *vacat* כאשר דבר למושה באחרית ה]מים תמחה את
זכר עמלק 3 מתחת השמים *vacat* ברכות יעקוב ראובן בכורי אתה
4 ורישית אוני יתר שאת ויתר עוז פחזתה כמים אל תותר עליתה 5 משכבי
אביכה אז חללתה יצועיו עלה *vacat* פשרו אשר הוכיחו אשר 6 שכב עם
בלהה פילגשו ו]א[מר בכו]רי [א]תה [... ראובן הוא 7 ראשית [...]...

Col. v 1 [... לו]א יסור שליט משבט יהודה בהיות לישראל ממשל
2 [לוא י]כרת יושב כסא לדויד כי המחקק היא ברית המלכות 3 [ואל]פי
ישראל המה הדגלים *vacat* עד בוא משיח הצדק צמח 4 דויד כי לו ולזרעו
נתנה ברית מלכות עמו עד דורות עולם אשר 5 שמר י]... [התורה עם
אנשי היחד כי 6 [...]. היא כנסת אנשי 7 [...] נתן

Col. vi 1 יתן מעדני [...]. 2 שפר ע].[...] 3 את ה]... 4 [...]...

4Q253 (4QcommGen B) *4QCommentary on Genesis B*

G. Brooke, *DJD XXII*, 209-212, pl. XIV
PAM 42.360, 43.258
ROC 819

Frag. 1 1 [...]...[...] 2 [... י]שראל ו.[...] 3 [...] מן התבה[...]
4 [...]וק להודיע לנו]ח [...

Frag. 2 1 ה.[...] 2 טהורים מן הבריאה] [... 3 עולתו לרצון כאשר
נקח]...[...] 4 לו שערי המרום כאש]ר [...

f[rom me …] *10-11* […] *12* El-Shaddai will bl[ess …] *13* the blessing of your father [Abraham …] *14* […] … you wi[ll …]

Col. IV *1* Timnah was the concubine of Eliphaz, Esau's son, and she bore him Amaleq. It was he who[m] Saul sl[ew], *2 Blank* as he said to Moses: «In the last days *Deut 25:19* you will erase the memory of Amaleq *3* from under the heavens». *Blank* Blessings of Jacob: *Gen 49:3-4* «Reuben, you are my first-born *4* and the first-fruits of my manhood, pre-eminent in stature and pre-eminent in strength; you seethe like water; you shall not enjoy supremacy. You mounted *5* your father's bed; then you defiled it, he had lain in it». *Blank* Its interpretation: That he reproved him, because *6* he lay with Bilhah, his concubine. And he [s]aid: «Y[ou are my] first[-born» …] Reuben was *7* the first-fruits of … […]

Col. V *1* […] *Gen 49:10* The sceptre shall [no]t depart from the tribe of Judah. While Israel has the dominion, *2* there [will not] be cut off someone who sits on the throne of David. For «the staff» is the covenant of royalty, *3* [and the thou]sands of Israel are «the standards». *Blank* Until the messiah of righteousness comes, the branch *4* of David. For to him and to his descendants has been given the covenant of the kingship of his people for everlasting generations, which *5* he observed […] the Law with the men of the Community, for *6* […] it is the assembly of the men of […] *7* […] He gives

Col. VI *1 Gen 49:20* He will give the pleasures of […] *2* beauty. … […] *3* the […] *4* … […]

4Q253 (4QcommGen B) *4QCommentary on Genesis B*

4Q252, 4Q254, 4Q254a
Bibliography: Wacholder-Abegg 2, 216-217; G.J. Brooke, '4Q253: A Preliminary Edition', *JSS* 40 (1995) 227-232

Frag. 1 *1* […] … […] *2* [… I]srael and […] *3* […] from the ark […] *4* […] … to make known to No[ah …]

Frag. 2 *1* …[…] *2* pure (animals) from the creation […] *3* his holocaust for acceptance, as we shall take […] *4* for him the highest gates, a[s …]

Frag. 3 1 [...][הים] [...] 2 [...]. בליעל וכא[שר ...] 3 [...]יעזוב
[...]את

4Q253a (4QcommMal) *4QCommentary on Malachi*

G. Brooke, *DJD XXII*, 213-215, pl. XIV
PAM 43.258
ROC 819

Frag. 1 i 1 [... אז נדברו יראי יהוה איש אל רעה]ו ויקשב 2 יהו[ה
וישמע ויכתב ספר זכרון לפניו ליראי יהוה ולחשבי שמו] והיו לי 3 [אמר
יהוה צבאות ליום אשר אני עושה סגלה וחמלתי ע]ליהם כאשר 4 [יחמול
איש אל בנו העובד אותו ושבתם וראיתם]בין צדיק לרשע 5 [בין עובד
אלוהים לאשר לוא עבדו פשרו על ...]הצדק ועל ...

Frag. 1 ii 1 וא'ש{ר} מישראל אשר יא[...] 2 יגיש את דמו אל [...]
3 ההוא[...] 4 ...[...]

4Q254 (4QcommGen C) *4QCommentary on Genesis C*

G. Brooke, *DJD XXII*, 217-232, pl. XV
PAM 43.233
ROC 113
4Q252, 4Q253, 4Q254a
Bibliography: G.J. Brooke, '4Q254 Fragments 1 and 4, and 4Q254a: Some Pre

Frag. 1 1 אשר אמר[...] 2 על הפתחים והח[... ויקץ נוח מיינו]
3 וידע את אש[ר עשה לו בנו הקטן ויאמר ארור כנען] 4 עבד עבדים [יהיה
לאחיו ...] 5 [...]...[...]

4Q253, 4Q253a, 4Q254

Frag. 3   *1* […] … […] *2* […] Belial, and a[s …] *3* […] he will abandon […]

4Q253a (4QcommMal) *4QCommentary on Malachi*

Bibliography: Wacholder-Abegg 2, 217; G.J. Brooke, '4Q253: A Preliminary Edition', *JSS* 40 (1995) 233-239

Frag. 1 *col.* I   *1* [… *Mal 3:16-18* «Then those who feared YHWH spoke with one anoth]er, and [YHWH] paid attention *2* [and listened, and a book of remembrance was written before him of those who feared YHWH and kept his name in mind.] And they shall be mine, *3* [says YHWH of Hosts, a possession on the day that I prepare. I will have pity o]n them, as *4* [a man has pity on the son who serves him. You shall again differentiate] between the just and the wicked, *5* [between who serves God and who does not serve him». Its interpretation concerns the … of] righteousness and …

Frag. 1 *col.* II   *1* and {he who} /a man/ of Israel who … […] *2* (he) brings its blood to […] *3* that […] *4* … […]

4Q254 (4QcommGen C) *4QCommentary on Genesis C*

liminary Comments', in *Proceedings of the Eleventh World Congress of Jewish Studies. Jerusalem, June 22-29, 1993. Division A: The Bible and its World* (Jerusalem: World Union of Jewish Studies, 1994) 185-188; *Wacholder-Abegg 2*, 218-222; C.A. Evans, '"The Two Sons of Oil": Early Evidence of Messianic Interpretation of Zechariah 4:14 in 4Q252 4 2', in *Provo Conference*, 566-575

Frag. 1 (cf. 4Q252 II)   *1* what he said: […] *2* concerning the doors and the … [… And Noah awoke from his wine] *3* and knew wha[t his youngest son had done. And he said: «Cursed be Canaan;] *4* a slave of slaves [he will be for his brothers!» …] *5* […] … […]

507

Frag. 4   1 [...]להם ...עם [...].   2 [...] שני בני היצהר אשר] ...[

3 [...]שומרי מצות אל[...]   4 [...]. כיא אנשי הי]וח[ד ...]...[

Frags. 5-6   1 ויט] שכמו לסבול ויהי למס]עובד[*vacat* [...]   2 אשר

[...]ן הגדולים] ...[3 עובד]... דן ידין ע]מו כאח[ד שבטי ישראל[4 ויהי

דן נח]ש עלי דרך שפי]פון עלי או]רח הנושך[5 עקב]י[סוס [...]

6 ישר]אל ...[

Frag. 7   1 [...].[...]   2 ... ותש]ב באיתן קשת]ו ...[3 ... רוע]ה

אבן ישראל] ...[4 ... ברכות שמים] ממ]ע[ל]...[5]...[ל].[...]

Frag. 8   1-2 ...[...]   3 וללחמו ול]...[4 פניכה לא]...[5 *vacat*

[...] 6 אשר לקח]...[7]ו[הבדיל בי]ן ...[8]...[...]...[

4Q254a (4QcommGen D) *4QCommentary on Genesis D*

G. Brooke, *DJD XXII*, 233-236, pl. XVI
PAM 43.239
ROC 820

Frags. 1-2   1 [...]היונה [...].   2 וזה חשבון מעשה ה]תבה שלוש

מאות אמה אור]ך התבה וחמ]שים אמה[3 רוחבה ושלשים] אמה קומתה

...[מה וש]...[4 ומדת התבה ...]...[5-6]...[...].[...]

Frag. 3   1 [...] ב]שבעה *vacat* עשר *vacat* לחודש   2]השני ...[... נוח

יצא מן התבה למועד ימים ימימה   3 [...] *vacat*   4 ... וישלח את העו]רב

ויצא יצוא וישוב להודיע לדורות הא]חרונים[5]...[... לפניו כי העו]רב

]יצוא יצא ויש]וב ...[

Frag. 4   *1* [...] to them, ... [...] *2* [...] the two sons of the oil who [...] *3* [...] those who observe God's precepts [...] *5* [...] because the men of the com[mun]ity ... [...]

Frags. 5 - 6   *1* *Gen 49:15* And he bent [his shoulder to the burden and] submitted [to forced labour]. *Blank* [...] *2* which [...] the great [...] *3* servant ... [... *Gen 49:17* Dan will judge] his [peo]ple like on[e of the tribes of Israel.] *4* And Dan will be a ser[pent on the path, an as]p on the w[ay which bites] *5* the horse's heel[s ...] *6* Isra[el ...]

Frag. 7   *1* [...] *2* [... *Gen 49:24-25* And his] bow [remain]ed steady [...] *3* [... the Shepher]d, the Stone of Israel. [...] *4* [... blessings of the heaven] from ab[ov]e, [...] *5* [...] ... [...]

Frag. 8   *1-2* ... [...] *3* and for his bread and for [...] *4* your countenance does not [...] *5* *Blank* [...] *6* what he took [...] *7* [and] he distinguished betwe[en ...] *8* [...] ... [...]

4Q254a (4QcommGen D) *4QCommentary on Genesis D*

4Q252, 4Q253, 4Q254
Bibliography: G.J. Brooke, '4Q254 Fragments 1 and 4, and 4Q254a', 188-192; *Wacholder-Abegg 2*, 222

Frags. 1 - 2   *1* [...] the dove [...] *2* And this is the plan of the construction of the [ark: three hundred cubits the leng]th of the ark, and fi[fty cubits] *3* its width, and thirty [cubits its height ...] ... and [...] *4* And the measurement of the ark ... [...] *5-6* [...] ... [...]

Frag. 3   *1* [... on the] seven *Blank* teenth *Blank* of the [second] month *2* [...] ... Noah went out of the ark at the appointed time year by year *3* [...] *Blank* *4* [... And he sent out the ra]ven and it went out, and returned, to show to the la[st] generations *5* [...] ... before him, for the ra[ven] had gone out, and ret[urned ...]

4Q255 (4QpapSᵃ) *4QRule of the Communityᵃ*

P. Alexander, G. Vermes, *DJD XXVI*, 27-38, pl. I
PAM 43.254
ROC 177
1QS, 4Q256, 4Q257, 4Q258, 4Q259, 4Q260, 4Q261, 4Q262, 4Q263, 4Q264,
5Q11, 11Q29?

Frag. 1   1 [...]מ[...]ם ל[ח]יו ספר סרך היחד   2 [לדרוש אל בכול לב
ובכ]ול נפש לעשות   3 [הטוב והישר לפניו כאשר] צוה ביד מושה   4 [וביד
כול עבדיו הנביאים ולא]הוב כו[ל]ל [אשר בחר]   5 [ולשנוא את כול אשר
מא]ס לר[חוק מכול רע]   6 [ולדבוק בכול מעשי טוב] ולעשו[ות אמת]

Frag. 2   1 וברוח קודשו ליחד באמת[ו] יטה[ר מכול]   2 עונתו וברוח
ישר וענו[ה תכופ[ר חט[אתו ובענות]   3 נפשו לכול חוקי אל יטהר בש[ורו
להזות עליו]   4 מי נדה ולהתקדש במי דוכי ופ[עמיו יהכין]   5 להלך תמים
בכול דרכ[י]ו אל כאש[ר צוה]   6 למועדי תעדתו ו[לא לסור] ימין
7 וש[מאו]ל ואין לצעו[ד] על אחד [מכול דבריו]   8 אז ירצה ב[כפו]רי
ניח[וח והיתה לו לברית]   9 [יחד [עולמים] [vacat]

Frag. A   1 [...].[...].[...]   2 [...]דרכי איש   3 [...]רת.להשכיל
4 [...].ל רוחות בני איש   5 [...]אור וי...[...]. חושך

4Q256 (4QSᵇ) *4QRule of the Communityᵇ*

P. Alexander, G. Vermes, *DJD XXVI*, 39-64, pls. II-V
PAM 43.240, 43.250
ROC 905, 907
1QS, 4Q255, 4Q257, 4Q258, 4Q259, 4Q260, 4Q261, 4Q262, 4Q263, 4Q264,
5Q11, 11Q29?

4Q255 (4QpapSᵃ) *4QRule of the Community*ᵃ

Bibliography: J.T. Milik, review of P. Wernberg-Møller, *The Manual of Discipline*, *RB* 67 (1960) 412-416; *Wacholder-Abegg 3*, 41-42; E. Qimron, J.H. Charlesworth, *PTSDSSP I*, 58-59; C. Martone, *"Regola"*, 162, 176-177; S. Metso, *Textual Development*, 18-21

Frag. 1 (= 1QS I *1-5*)   *1* […] for his [li]fe. Book of the Rule of the Community. *2* [In order to seek God with all (one's) heart and with a]ll (one's) soul; in order to do *3* [what is good and just in his presence, as] he commanded through the hand of Moses *4* [and through the hand of all his servants the Prophets; in order to lo]ve eve[ry]thing [which he selects] *5* [and to hate everything that he reje]cts; in order to keep oneself at a dis[tance from all evil,] *6* [and to become attached to all good works;] in order to d[o truth]

Frag. 2 (= 1QS III *7-12*)   *1* And it is by his holy spirit of the community, in [its] truth, that he is clea[nsed of all] *2* his iniquities. And by the spirit of uprightness and of humility his s[in is atoned. And by the compliance of] *3* his soul with all the laws of God [his] fle[sh] is cleansed [by there being sprinkled upon it] *4* cleansing waters and being made holy with the waters of repentance, and [may he steady his] s[teps] *5* in order to walk with perfection on all the path[s of] God, a[s he has decreed] *6* concerning the appointed times of his assemblies. [He should not turn aside,] (either) right *7* or l[ef]t, nor infri[nge] even one [of all his words.] *8* In this way he will be admitted by means of plea[sing atone]ment [and for him it will be the covenant of] *9* [an] everlasting [Community. *Blank*]

Frag. A   *1* […] … […] … *2* […] the paths of man *3* […] … to instruct *4* […] … the spirits of /the sons of/ man *5* […] light and /…/[…] darkness

4Q256 (4QSᵇ) *4QRule of the Community*ᵇ

Bibliography: J.T. Milik, 'Numérotation des feuilles des rouleaux dans le scriptorium de Qumrân', *Semitica* 27 (1977) 75-81, pl. X; *Wacholder-Abegg 3*, 43-47; E. Qimron, J.H. Charlesworth, *PTSDSSP 1*, 60-67; C. Martone, *"Regola"*, 162-164, 177-80; S. Metso, *Textual Development*, 22-31

Col. II   [...] וכול הבאים [בסרך היחד יעבורו] בבר[ית]   2 [לפני
אל לעשות ככול אשר צוה ולוא לשוב מאחרו [מכול פ[חד וא]ימה ומצרף
3 [נסוים בממשלת בליעל ובעוברם בברית יהיו הכוהני]ם והל[וים מברכים
את אל]   4 [...]   5 [... את צדקות אל במעשי]ו גבורת[ו ומשמיעים כול
חסדי]   6 [רחמים על ישראל והלוים מספרים את ע]וונות בני [ישראל ...]
7-11 [...]   12 [...]והלוים [מקללים את כול אנשי גורל]   13 [בליעל וענו
ואמרו ארור אתה בכול מעשי רש]ע[אשמתכה ...]

Col. III   1 [...] ויפקיד אחריכה כל[ה ביד כול] משלמי גמולים אר[ור
אתה לאין רחמים כחושך   2 [מעשיכה וזעום אתה באפלת אש]עולמים
לוא] יחונכה אל בקור[אכה ולוא יסלח לכפר עוונכה   3 [ישא פני אפו
לנקמתכה ולוא יהיה לכה שלום בפי כול אוחזי אבות] וכול העוברים בברית
4 [אומרים אחר המברכים והמקללים אמן אמן vacat והוסיפו הכוהנים
והלוים ואמרו [ארור

Col. IX   1 מדרש למשכיל על] אנשי התורה המתנדבים להשיב מכול
רע ולהחזיק בכול]   2 אשר צוה ולהבד[ל] מעדת א[נשי העול ולהיות יחד
בתורה ובהון ומשובים]   3 על פי הרבים לכול דבר לתורה] ולהון ולעשות
ענוה וצדקה ומשפט ואהבת]   4 חסד והצנע לכת בכול דרכיהמה אשר] לוא
ילך איש בשרירות לבו לתעות]   5 כי אם ליסד מסד אמת לישראל ליחד
לכול] המתנדב לקודש באהרון ובית]   6 אמת לישראל והנלוים עליהם
ליחד וכול הבא [לעצת היחד יקים על נפשו]   7 באסר לשוב אל תורת משה
בכול לב ו[בכול נפש כול הנגלה מן התורה על פי]   8 עצת אנשי היחד
ולהבדל מ[כו]ל[] אנ[שי העול [ואשר לוא יגעו לטהרת אנשי]   9 הקודש ואל
יוכל אתו [בי]חד ואשר ל[וא ישוב איש מאנשי היחד על פיהם]   10 לכול
תורה ומשפט ואשר לוא יבו ... [...] בהון ובעבודה ואל יואכל]   11 [איש

Col. ɪɪ (frags. 2a-c; = 1QS ɪ *16-19; 21-23;* ɪɪ *4-5;* 4Q257 ɪɪ; 5Q11 1 ɪ)   *1* [… And all those who enter] in the Rule of the Community shall establish /…/ a coven[ant] *2* [before God in order to carry out all that he commanded and in order not to stray from following him] out of any fe[ar, dr]ead or testing *3* [(that might occur) during the dominion of Belial. When they enter the covenant, the priest]s and the le[vites shall bless the God of] *4* […] *5* [… the just deeds of God in his] mighty [works, and they shall proclaim all his merciful favours] *6* [towards Israel. And the levites shall recite the ini]quities of the children of [Israel …] *7-11* […] *12* […] And the levites [shall curse all the men of the lot of] *13* [Belial. They shall begin to speak and shall say: «Accursed are you for all] your [wick]ed, blameworthy [deeds …]

Col. ɪɪɪ (*frag.* 3a-b; = 1QS ɪɪ *6-11;* 4Q257 ɪɪ; 5Q11 1 ɪ)   *1* [… May he bring upon you destruc]tion by the hand of all [those who accomplish retributions. Acc]ursed are you, without mercy, according to the darkness *2* [of your deeds, and sentenced to the gloom of] everlasting [fire. May God] not [be merciful when] you [entre]at him. May he not forgive by purifying your iniquities. *3* [May he lift the countenance of his anger to avenge himself on you, and may there be no peace for you in the mouth of those who intercede».] And all those who enter the covenant *4* [shall say, after those who pronounce blessings and those who pronounce curses: «Amen, Amen». *Blank* And the priests and the levites shall continue, saying:] «Accursed

Col. ɪx (*frag.* 4; = 4Q258 ɪ; cf. 1QS v *1-20*)   *1* Midrash for the Instructor concerning [the men of the law who freely volunteer to revert from all evil and to keep themselves steadfast in all] *2* he commanded. They should keep apa[rt from the congregation of the m[en of injustice in order to constitute a Community in law and possessions, and acquiesce] *3* to the authority of the Many in every affair involving the law [and possessions. They must exercise humility, justice and right,] *4* compassionate [love] and seemly behaviour in all their paths. [No-one should walk in the stubbornness of his heart in order to go astray] *5* but one should establish a foundation of truth for Israel, for the Community for all [who freely volunteer for holiness in Aaron and for the house of] *6* truth in Israel and for those who join them for the Community. And whoever enters [the council of the Community shall make a binding promise] *7* to revert to the Law of Moses, with whole heart and [whole soul, all that has been revealed from the Law, in accordance with] *8* the council of the men of the Community; and to be segregated from [al]l [the me]n of injustice; [and they are not to approach the pure food of the] *9* holy [men], and he shall not eat it [in the Com]munity. And n[ot one of the men of the Community is to be subject to their authority] *10* in any law or precept. And no one is to enter … [… with possessions or with work, and not shall eat] *11* [any of the] holy [m]en *Blank*

מא[נשי הקודש vacat ...] ולוא ישענו על כול[12 [מעשי ההבל כי הבל

כול] אשר לוא י[דעו את בריתו וכול מנאצי דברו להשמיד] 13 [מתבל

ומעשיהם לנ[ג]דה לפ[ני]ו [...]

Col. xi 5 [...אל]ידבר[...] 6 [...]הרבים אל יד[בר איש ...] 7 [...

וכול] איש אשר יש [אתו דבר ...] 8 [...]ידבר וכול המת[נדב מישראל ...]

9-10 [...] 11 [...] הכול] על דבריו [... 12 ...] לוא יגע ב[טהרת הרבים

עד מ[לאות לו...] 13 [...]ובמלאות [ל]ו [ ]שנה תמימה ישא[לו הרבים ...]

Col. xviii 1 [...] איש כרוחו וכת[כון העת להנחותם בדעה וכן

לה]שכילם[2 [ברזי פלא ואמת בתוך אנשי היח]ד להלך תמים איש את

רעהו [בכול] 3 [הנגלה להם היאה עת פנות הדרך למד]בר להשכילם בכול

הנמצא לעשות 4 [בעת הזואת והבדל מכול איש ולוא הסיר דר]כו מכול

עול [וא[ל]ה vacat 5 [תכוני הדרך למשכיל בעתים האלה לאהבתו עם

שנ[אתו שנאת [עולם עם 6 [אנ]שי השחת ברוח הסתר ולעזוב למו הון

ובצע כעבד למ[ושל בו] וענוה לפני[7 הר[ודה בו ...]

Col. xix 1 מאורות מזבול קודשו עם האספם למעון כבוד במבוא

מועדים לימ' חדש יחד 2 תקופותיהמה עם מסרו[ת[ם] זה לזה בהתחדשם

יום גדול לקודש קודשים ואות 3 למפתח חס[דיו עו]ל[ם לר]אשי מועדים

בכול קץ נהיה בר"שית ירחים למועדיהם 4 וימי] קודש בתכונם לז[כרון

במועדיהם תרומת שפתים אברכנו כח[ו]ק [חרות לעד 5 [בראשי שנים

ובתקופו[ת מועדים בהשלם חוק תכונם יום מ[שפטו זה לזה] 6 [מועד קציר

לקיץ ומועד זרע [מ[וע]ד דשא מועדי ש[נים ... 7 [...]...[...]...[...]

[*Blank* And they are not to support on any] *12* [deed of futility, for all those] who do not k[now his covenant are futility. And all those who scorn his word, shall be obliterated] *13* [from the earth, and all their works are uncle]anness be[fore] him […]

Col. xi (*frags.* 5a-b; cf. 1QS vi *10-13; 16-18*; 4Q258 iii)   *5* [… not] should speak […] *6* […] of the Many, no[-one] should spe[ak …] *7* [… and any]one who has [something to say …] *8* […] he should speak. And anyone [from Israel] who freely volun[teers …] *9-10* […] *11* […] all (of them) [concerning his affairs …] *12* [… he must not touch the] pure food of the Many until [he has] com[pleted …] *13* [… When] he [has completed] a full year [the Many] will be quest[ioned …]

Col. xviii (*frags.* 6a i, 6b; = 1QS ix *18-23*; 4Q258 viii; 4Q259 iii-iv)   *1* [… each one according to his spirit, and according to the regula]tion of the time. He should lead them with knowledge and in this way te[ach them] *2* [the mysteries of wonder and of truth in the midst of the men of the Commun]ity, so that they walk perfectly, one with another, [in all] *3* [that has been revealed to them. This is the time for making ready the path to the de]sert and he will teach them about all that has been discovered so that they can carry it out *4* [in this moment and so they will be detached from anyone who has not withdrawn] his [pa]th from all injustice. [*Blank* And th]es[e are] *5* [the regulations of behaviour for the Inspector in these times, concerning his love and] his [hat]red. [Everlasting] hatred [for *6* the m[en of the pit in clandestine spirit. To them he should leave goods and profit like a servant to] his [mas]ter and like one oppressed before] *7* someone do[mineering him …]

Col. xix (*frag.* 6a ii; = 1QS x *3-7*; 4Q258 ix; 4Q260 ii)   *1* the lights from his holy vault, when they retire to the abode of glory. At the entry of the seasons /in the days/ of the new moon together *2* with their rotations during their stations renewing each other. It is a great day for the holy of holies, and a sign of *3* the opening [of his everlasting] mer[cies for the be]ginnings of the seasons in every future age. At the commencement of the months in their seasons, *4* and of the [holy] days [in their sequence, as a re]minder in their seasons. With the offering of lips I shall bless him, in accordance with the dec[ree] recorded for ever. *5* [At the commencement of the years and in the turnin]g of the seasons, when the decree of their disposition is carried out, on [its] pre[scribed] day, [one after another;] *6* [the season of the harvest up to summer, the season of seed-time up to] the se[as]on of the grass, the season of the ye[ars …] *7* […] … […]

Col. xx   1 [...] ברישי]ת משלח ידי ורגלי]   2 [אברך שמו ברישית
צאת ובוא לשבת וקום ועם משכב יצועי] ארננה לו וא[ברכנו]   3 [תרומת
מוצא שפתי במערכת אנשים ובטרם ארים ידי] להדשן בעדני תנובת
4 [תבל ברישית פחד ואימה ובמכון צרה עם בוקה אברכ]נו בהפלא מודה
ובגבורתו   5 [אשוחח ועל חסדיו אשען כול היום וא[דעה כ]י בי]דו משפט
כול חי ו[א]מת   6 [כול מעשיו ובהפתח צרה אהללנו ובישוע[תו [ארננ]ה]
יחד לוא אשיב לאיש]   7 [גמול רע וטוב ארדף גבר כיא את אל]משפט כול
חי והואה] ישלם לאיש]

4Q257 (4QpapS^c) *4QRule of the Community*

P. Alexander, G. Vermes, *DJD XXVI*, 65-82, pls. VI-IX
PAM 43.256 (recto); 43.262
ROC 858, 859
1QS, 4Q255, 4Q256, 4Q258, 4Q259, 4Q260, 4Q261, 4Q262, 4Q263, 4Q264,

Col. II   1 והלויים מקללים את כול אנשי גורל [בלי]על וענו ואמרו
ארור   2 [א]תה [בכול מעשי רשע [אשממתכה יתנכה אל [ז]עות ביד כול
נוקמ]י]   3 [נקם ויפקיד אחריכה כלה ביד כול משלמי גמו]ל[ים א]רור אתה
4 [לאין רחמים כ]חושך[מעשיכה ... וזעום אתה]באפלת   5 [אש עולמים
[לוא י]חונכה אל בקוראכה ולוא יסלח לכפר עו]ונכה   6 [ישא פני אפו
לנקמתכה ולוא יהיה לכה [שלום [בפי כול אוחזי אבות]   7 [וכול העוברים
בברית אומרים אח]ר המברכים] והמקללים אמן אמן]   8 [...].[...]

Col. III   1 לוא י]עבור ביח[ד אמ]תו] כ[י]א ג[ע]לה נפשו] ביסורי
דעת]   2 משפט]י צדק לוא [חזק] ל[משוב חיו ועם י]שרים לוא] יתח[שב]
3 ודעתו וכוח]ו והונו]ל[וא]יבואו [בעצת יחד כי]א ב]סאון רש[ע]

Col. xx (*frags.* 7a-c; = 1QS x *13-18*; 4Q258 x; 4Q260 IV)   *1* [... When I] sta[rt to stretch out my hands and my feet] *2* [I shall bless his name.] When (I) sta[rt to go out and to come in, to sit and to stand up, and lying down in my bed] I shall extol him; I shall [bless him] *3* [with the offering that issues from my lips in the row of men. And before stretching out my hand] to get fat on the tasty fruit of *4* [the earth, at the onset of fright and dismay and in the place of distress and grief, I shall bless] him for (his) great marvels, on his power *5* [I shall meditate and shall rely on his compassion the whole day. I] realize th[at in] his [ha]nd lies the judgment of every living thing, and [tr]uth *6* [are all his deeds. When distress is unleashed I shall praise him, just as I shall sing to him for] his [deliverance. I] shall [not repay anyone] *7* [with an evil reward; with goodness I shall pursue man. For to God (belongs)] the judgment of every living being, and it is he [who pays man]

4Q257 (4QpapS^c) *4QRule of the Community^f*

5Q11, 11Q29?

Bibliography: Wacholder-Abegg 3, 48-50; E. Qimron, J.H. Charlesworth, *PTSDSSP 1*, 68-71; C. Martone, *"Regola"*, 165-166, 180-181; S. Metso, *Textual Development*, 31-36

Col. II (*frags.* 1a II, 1b-c; = 1QS II *4-10*; 4Q256 II-III; 5Q11 1 I)   *1* And the levites shall curse all the men of the lot of [Beli]al. They shall begin to speak and shall say: «Accursed are *2* [y]ou [for all] your [wicked,] blameworthy [deeds.] May God hand you over to [te]rror into the hands of those carrying out acts of *3* [vengeance. May he bring upon you destruction by the hand of all those who accomplish retributions. Ac]cursed are you, *4* [without mercy, for the] darkne[ss of your deeds, ... and sentenced] to the gloom *5* [of everlasting fire.] May [God] not [be merciful when you entreat him. May he not forgive by purifying] your [in]iquity. *6* [May he lift the countenance of his anger to avenge himself on you, and may there be no] peace [for you by the mouth of all those who intercede».] *7* [And all those who enter the covenant shall say aft]er those who pronounce blessings [and those who pronounce curses: «Amen, Amen».] *8* [...] ... [...]

Col. III (*frags.* 1a III, 2a-g; = 1QS II *26* - III *4 (10)*; 4Q262 1)   *1* shall not [enter the Commun]ity of [his] tru[th,] since his soul lo[ath]es [the disciplines of the knowledge of] *2* [just] judgment[s. He has not] the strength [to] convert his life and shall [not] be co[unted] with the up[right.] *3* His knowledge, [his] energy [and his wealth shall] n[ot] enter the council of the Community

4 מחרשו וגא[ו]לי[ם בש[ו]בתו ו[ו]לוא יצדק במתו[ר [שרירות 5 לבו
וחושך י[ביט לדרכי] אור בעין תמימים לוא יתח[שב] 6 לוא יזכה
בכפו[רים ולו]א יטהר במי נדה ולוא יתקד[ש] 7-14 [...]...[...]

Col. v 1 [...] ומחשבת ק[ו]דש 2 [ביצר סמוך ורוב חסדים על כול
בני אמת וטהר]ת כבוד מתעבת כול גלולי 3 [נדה והצנע לכת בערמת כול
וחבא לאמת רזי] דעת אלה סודי רוח 4 [לבני אמת תבל ופקודת כול הולכי
בה למרפא ורו]ב שלום באו[רך ימים]ופ[ר]ות זרע 5 [עם כול ברכות עד
ושמחת עולמים בחיי]נצח[ו]כליל כבוד ע[ם מדת הדר] 6 [באור עולמים
7a [*vacat?*] *vacat* [*vacat*]ולרוח עולה רחוב נפש ושפול ידים בעבודת
[צדק [*vacat?*] *vacat?* 7 רשע ושקר גוה ורום לב]ב כחש ורמיה
אכז[רי ורוב חנף] 8 [קצור אפים ורוב אולת וקנאת זד]ון מעשי תו[עבת
[... 9-11 [...] 12 [... וכול קציהם לדורותם ב]אבל יגון 13 [ורעת
מרורים בהווה חושך עד כלותם לאין שרית ופליט[ה למו 14 [...]ל[...]

4Q258 (4QS^d) *4QRule of the Community^d*

P. Alexander, G. Vermes, *DJD XXVI*, 83-128, pls. X-XIII
PAM 43.244, 43.246
ROC 140, 141
1QS, 4Q255, 4Q256, 4Q257, 4Q259, 4Q260, 4Q261, 4Q262, 4Q263, 4Q264,
5Q11, 11Q29?
Bibliography: J.T. Milik, review of P. Wernberg-Møller, *The Manual of Discipline*, *RB* 67 (1960) 412-416; G. Vermes, 'Preliminary Remarks on Unpub-

Col. I 1 מדרש למשכיל על אנשי התורה המתנד(ב)ים להשיב מכל רע
ולהחזיק בכל אשר צוה 2 ולבדל מעדת אנשי העול ולהיות י[ח]ד בתור[ה]
ובהון ומשובים על פי הרבים לכל דבר 3 לתורה ולהון ולעשות ענוה

be[cause] he ploughs [in] the mud of wicked[ness] *4* and there are sta[in]s on his con[ver]sion. He shall not be justified while he mainta[ins] the stubborn ness of *5* his heart, since he [regards] darkness [as paths of] light. In the source of the perfect he shall not be cou[nted.] *6* He will not become clean by the acts of aton[ement, no]r shall he be purified by the cleansing waters, nor shall he be made ho[ly] *7-14* […] *(a few letters per line corresponding to 1QS* III *5-10)* […]

Col. v *(frags.* 3a I, 3b; = 1QS IV *4-10; 13-14)* *1* […] and ho[l]y plans *2* [with firm purpose, of generous compassion with all the sons of truth, of] magnificent [puri]ty which detests all [unclean] idols, *3* [of careful behaviour in wisdom concerning everything, of concealment concerning the truth of the mysteries of] knowledge. These are the foundations of the spirit *4* [of the sons of truth (in) the world. And the reward of all those who walk in it will be healing, plenti]ful peace in a lo[ng life,] fr[ui]tful offspring *5* [with all everlasting blessings, eternal enjoyment with] endless [life, and] a crown of glory wi[th majestic raiment] *6* [in eternal light. *Blank*] *Blank* [*Blank?*] *7a* [However, to the spirit of deceit belong greed, sluggishness in the service of] justice, *Blank?* [*Blank?*] *7* [*Blank?* wickedness, falsehood, pride, haughtiness of hea]rt, dishonesty, trickery, crue[lty, much insincerity,] *8* [impatience, much foolishness, impu]dent [enthusiasm] for app[alling] acts […] *9-11* […] *12* [… And all the ages of their generations (they shall spend) in] bitter weeping *13* [and harsh evils in the abysses of darkness until their destruction, without there being a remnant or a survivo]r for them. *14* […] … […]

4Q258 (4QS^d) *4QRule of the Community^d*

lished Fragments of the Community Rule from Qumran Cave 4', *JJS* 42 (1991) 250-255; E. Qimron, 'Manuscript D of the Community Rule from Qumran Cave 4: Preliminary Publication of Columns 7-8', *Tarbiz* 60 (1991) 334-343 (Hebrew); *Wacholder-Abegg 3*, 51-57; E. Qimron, J.H. Charlesworth, *PTSDSSP 1*, 72-83; C. Martone, *"Regola"*, 166-169, 181-185; S. Metso, *Textual Development*, 36-47

Col. I *(frags.* 1a I, 1b; = 4Q256 IX; cf. 1QS V *1-20)* *1* Midrash for the Instructor concerning the men of the law who ‹freely volunteer› to revert from all evil and to keep themselves steadfast in all he commanded. *2* They should keep apart from the congregation of the men of injustice in order to constitute a Com[mun]ity in law and possessions and acquiesce to the authority of the Many in every affair *3* involving the law and possessions. They must exercise

וצדקה ומשפט ואהבת] חסד וה[צנע לכת בכל דרכיהם 4 [אשר [לא ילך
איש בשרירות לבו לתעות כי אם ליסד] מוסד [אמת לישראל ליחד לכל
5 המתנדב לקדש באהרן ובית אמת לישראל והנלוי[ם] על[י]ה]ם ליחד vacat
וכל הבא לעצת 6 [ה]י[ח]ד יק[י]ם על נפשו באסר ל[שוב א]ל [ת]ורת
מש[ה] בכל לב ובכל נפש כל הנגלה מן 7 התו[רה ע]ל[פי] עצת אנש[י
[היחד] ולהבדל מכל אנשי] העול [ו]אשר לא יגעו לטהרת אנשי 8 [הקד]ש
ואל יוכל אתו ב[יחד ואשר לא ישוב א[יש מאנשי היחד על פיהם לכל
9 [תורה] ומשפט ואש[ר לא ... בע[בודה ואל יואכל איש מאנשי הקדש
10 [...][ל]ל[...] ולא ישענו על כ[ל מע]ש[י ההבל כי הבל כל אשר [לא ידעו
את] 11 [בריתו וכל מנאצ]י דברו להשמיד מתבל ומעשיהם לנד[ה] ל[פניו
וטמא בכ]ל [הונם] 12 [...]ם גוים ושבעות וחרמים ונדרים בפיהם [...
13 [...]...[...]...[...]

Col. ii 1 ואת מעשיהם בתורה על פי בני אהרון המתנדבים להקים את
בריתו ולפקוד את כל חקיו אשר צוה 2 לעשות על פי רוב ישראל
המתנדבים לשוב ביחד ולהכתב איש לפני רעה בסרך איש לפי שכלו
3 ומעשיו בתורה להשמע הכול איש לרעה הקטן לגדול ולהיות פוקדים את
רוחם ומעשיהם 4 בתורה שנה בשנה ל^לעלות איש כפי ש[כלו] ולאחרו
כנעותיו להוכיח איש את רעהו ואהבת חסד 5 ואל ידבר איש אל רעהו
באף או בתלונה או בקנאת רשע וגם אל יבא איש על רעהו דבר לרבים
6 אשר לא בהוכח לפני ע[דים] ובאלה יתהלכו בכול מגוריהם כל הנמצא
את רעהו וי[שמעו הקטן 7 [ל]גדול למלאכה ולה]ון ויחד יוא[כלו י[ח]ד
יברכו ויחד יועצ[ו ו]ב[כ]ל[מקום אשר יהיה שם עשרה] 8 אנשים מ[עצת
היחד אל ימש מ[אתם כו]הן וא[י]ש כתכונו יש[בו לפניו וכן ישאלו לעצתם
לכל דבר] 9 והיה כי[ן יערוכו השולחן לאכול או הת[י]רוש] לשתות ה]כוהן
יש[לח ידו לרשונה להברך בראשית הלחם] 10 והתירוש] [...]...[...]

humility, justice and right, [compassionate] love [and se]emly behaviour in all their paths. *4* [N]o-one should walk in the stubbornness of his heart in order to go astray, but one should establish [a foundation of] truth for Israel, for the Community for all *5* who freely volunteer for holiness in Aaron and for the house of truth in Israel and for those who join them for the Community. *Blank* And whoever enters the council of *6* [the] Com[mun]ity shall make a binding promise to [revert t]o the [L]aw of Mos[es] with whole heart and whole soul, all that has been revealed from *7* the L[aw in accordance] with [the opinion of the council of the men [of] the Community [and to be segregated from all the men of] injustice, [and] they are not to approach the pure food of [the hol]y *8* men. And he shall not eat it in [the Community. And] not one of the men of the Community [is to be subject] to their authority in any *9* [law] or precept, and [… in wo]rk, and no-one of the holy men is to eat *10* […] And they are not to support on a[ny de]ed of futility, for futility are all those who [do not know] *11* [his covenant. And all those who scorn] his word, shall be obliterated from the earth; their works are unclean[ness] be[fore him, there is uncleanness in al]l [their possessions.] *12* […] the peoples. Oathes, adjurations and vows in their mouths […] *13* […] … […]

Col. II (*frag.* 1a II; = 1QS V *21* - VI *6*; 4Q261 1; 4Q263)   *1* and his deeds in law, under the authority of the sons of Aaron, those who freely volunteer in the Community to set up his covenant and to follow all his decrees which he commanded *2* to fulfil, and under the authority of the majority of Israel, those who freely volunteer to be converted within the Community. And they shall be recorded in order, one before the other, according to one's insight *3* and one's deeds in the law, in such a way that each one obeys another, the junior the senior. And their spirit and their deeds in the law must be tested, *4* year after year, in order to upgrade each one to the extent of [his] in[sight,] or to demote him according to his failings. One should reproach one another (in …) and compassionate love. *5* And no-one should speak to his fellow in anger or muttering, or with spiteful intent. And in addition, no-one should raise a matter against his fellow in front of the Many *6* unless it is with reproof in the presence of wit[nesses.] In this way shall they behave in all their places of residence. Whenever one fellow meets another, [the junior shall obey] *7* the senior in work and in mo[ney. They shall] ea[t together,] to[ge]ther they shall bless and together they shall take counsel. In [eve]ry [place where there are ten] *8* men of the [Community council, there should not be missing] a prie[st amongst] them. [And eve]ry one shall si[t] according to his rank, [before him, and in this way they shall be asked for their counsel in every matter.] *9* And when [they prepare the table to dine or the] new wine [for drinking, the] priest shall stre[tch out his hand as the first to bless the first fruits of the bread] *10* and the new wine […] … […]

Col. III   1 איש את מד[עו לעצת היחד אל ידבר איש בתוך דברי רעהו
טרם יכלה אחיהו לדבר ... ובמושב]   2 הרבים אל ידב[ר איש כל דבר אשר
לא להפץ הרבים וכי האיש המבקר על הרבים וכל איש יש אתו דבר
לדבר]   3 לרבים אשר [...]   4 .[.]...[...]

Col. VI   1 [... ול]השיב לרשעים 2 [גמולם היא חומת הבחן פנת יקר
בל יזדעזעו יסודותיהו ובל יחישו ממ[קומם מעון קודש קודשים
3 [לאהרון בדעת עולם לברית משפט ולקריב ריח ניחוח ובית תמים ואמת
בישרא]ל להקים ברית לחקות עולם   4 [והיו לרצון לכפר בעד הארץ
ולחרוץ משפט רשעה ואין עולה בהכון אלה בי]סוד היחד שנתים ימים
5 [בתמים דרך יבדלו קודש בתוך עצת אנש]י היחד[וכל דבר ה]נ[סתר
מי]שראל ונמצא   6 לאיש] הדורש אל יסתרהו מאלה מיראת רוח נסוגה]
vacat   ובהיות אלה] בישראל [יבדלו מ]תוך מושב]   7 אנשי[ן העול ללכת
למדבר לפנות שם את דרכו היא מדרש התור]ה אשר צוה בי[ד משה
לע]שות כל[הנגלה]   8 ע]ת בעת וכאשר גלו הנביאים ברוח קדשו וכל
אי]ש מאנשי ברית ה[י]חד [... 9-10 [...] 11-12 [...]...[...]

Col. VII   1 והבדילהו מן הטהרה ומן העצה ומן המשפט שנת]ים ימי[ם
ושב במדרש ובעצה אם לא הלך עוד   2 בשגגה עד מלאות לו שנתים כי על
שגגה אחת יענש שנתים וליד הרמה לא ישוב עוד אך   3 שנתים [י]מים
יבחן לתמים דרכו ולעצתו על פי הרבים ונכתב בתכונו ליחד קודש vacat
4 [בהיו]ת אלה בישראל ליחד כתכונים האלה ל[י]סד רוח קודש לאמת
עולם לכפר על אשמת פשע vacat [5 [ומעל הטא]ת ולרצון לאר[ץ מבשר]
עלות וחלבי זבחים ותרומות ונדבת שפתים ל[משפ]ט כניחוח   6 [צדק

Col. III (*frag.* 1a III (= 1QS VI *9-12*; cf. 4Q256 IX) *1* each can impart [his] know[ledge to the council of the Community. No-one should talk during the speech of his fellow before his brother has finished speaking … And in the session of] *2* the Many no-one should ut[ter anything without the consent of the Many, save the Inspector of the Many. And anyone who has something to say] *3* to the Many but […] *4* […] … […]

Col. VI (*frags.* 3a-d; = 1QS VIII *6-17 (19-21)*; 4Q259 II-III) *1* [… and to] render the wicked *2* [their retribution. This is the tested rampart, the precious cornerstone whose foundations do not shake or tremble from] their [p]lace. (It will be) the most holy dwelling *3* [for Aaron with eternal knowledge of the covenant of justice and in order to offer a pleasant aroma; and (it will be) a house of per-fection and truth for Israe]l; in order to establish a covenant in compliance with the everlasting decrees. *4* [And these, will be accepted, to atone for the earth and to decide the judgment of the wickedness and there will be no iniq-uity. When these have been established in the fou]ndation of the Community for two full years *5* [in perfect behaviour they will be segregated (like) holy ones in the midst of the council of the me]n of the Community. [And every matter hidden from I]srael, but which has been found out *6* by the Inter[preter, he should not keep hidden from them for fear of a spirit of desertion.] *Blank* And when these exist [in Israel] they are to be segregated from [within the dwelling] *7* of the men of [sin to walk to the desert in order to open there His path. This is the study of the la]w which he commanded through the ha[nd of Moses, in order to d]o all [that has been revealed] *8* from a[ge to age, and according to what the prophets have revealed through his holy spirit. And anyone] of the men of the covenant of the [community …] *9-10* […] *11-12* […] (*a few letters corresponding to 1QS* VIII *19 and 21*) […]

Col. VII (*frag.* 4a I; = 1QS VIII *24* - IX *10*) *1* he should be excluded from pure food and from the council and the judgment for two [ful]l years. And he may return to the interpretation and to the council if he does not go *2* sinning through oversight until two years have passed. Because for one sin of oversight he will be punished two years; but for impertinence he shall not go back again. Only *3* two [f]ull years shall he be tested in respect of the perfection of his behav-iour and in respect of his counsel according to the authority of the Many and then he will be enrolled according to his rank in the Community of holiness. *Blank 4* [When] these have become a community in Israel in compliance with these arrangements in order to establish the spirit of holiness in truth eternal, in order to atone for the guilt of iniquity *5* [and for the unfaithfulness of si]n and for approval for the ear[th without the flesh] of burnt offerings and with-out the fats of sacrifice — the offerings and the free-will offering of the lips in compliance with the decree will be like the pleasant aroma *6* [of justice and

ותמים] דרך כנדב]ת מנחת ר]צון vacat בעת ההיא יבדלו בית אהרן לקודש

לכל .[...].ל   7 [יחד ליש]ראל ההלכים בת^מי]ם רק בני אה]רן[ימש]ל]ו

ב]משפט ובהון vacat והון] אנשי הקודש] 8 [ההלכ]ים בתמים אל יתע]רב

הונם עם] הון [אנשי הרמיה]אשר לא הזכ]ו דרכם [... 9 [...]ת[...]

להתהלך ב]...] ונשפטו במ]שפטים ...]

1 ולפי שכלו להגישו וכן אהבתו עם שנאתו ואשר לא יוכיח   Col. VIII

איש ולא יתרובב עם אנשי ה^ש]דע}חת   2 ולסתר עצתו בתוך אנשי העול

ולהוכיח דעת אמת ומשפט צדק לבחירי דרך איש כרוחו וכתכון

3 העת ל]הנחות]ם בדעה וכן להשכילם ברזי פלא ואמת בתוך אנשי היחד

להלך תמים איש את   4 [רעהו בכל ה]נגלה להם היא עת פנות הדרך

ל]מדבר [ו]להשכילם בכל הנמצא לעשות vacat בעת   5 [הזאת והבדל]

מכל איש אשר לא הסיר דרכיו מכול עול vacat ואלה תכוני הדרך למשכיל

בעת]ים]   6 [האלה לאהבתו עם] שנאתו שנאת עולם עם אנשי השחת ברוח

הסתר לעזוב למו הון ובצע   7 [ועמל כפים כעבד למוש]ל בו וענוה לפני

הרודה בו ולהיות איש מקנא לחוק ועתו ליום [נקם ל]עשות]   8 [רצון בכל

משלח כפים וב]כל ממשלו כאש]ר צוה וכ]ל הנעשה בו ירצה בנדבה וזולת

רצון [^לᴦ]   9 [לא יחפץ ובכל אמרי פיהו ירצה ולא יתאוה בכל אשר ל]א

צוה למשפ]ט^לᴦ יצפה ת]מ]יד]   10 [... ותרומת שפתים י]ברכנו עם [קצים]

11 [אשר חקק^לᴦ בראשית ממשלת אור עם תקופתו ובה]אספו על מעון

חק]ו [בראשית] אשמורי]   12 [חושך כי יפתח אוצרו וישיתהו עלת

ובתקופתו עם האספו מ]פני אור בהופע] מאורות מזבול]   13 [קודש עם

האספם למעון כבוד במבוא מועדים לימי חודש יחד תקופתם עם מסרותם

זה לזה]

524

the perfection of] behaviour will be accept[able] like a freewill offering. *Blank* At this time they shall set the house of Aaron apart for holiness, for all […] *7* [Community for Is]rael, those who walk in perfect[ion. Only the sons of Aa]ron [will have authority in] the matter of judgment and of goods. *Blank* And the goo[ds of the holy men] *8* [who wa]lk in perfection. [Their goods] must not be con[fused with the] goods [of the men of deceit] who have not puri[fied their path …] *9* […] to walk in […] shall be governed by the dir[ectives …]

Col. VIII (*frags.* 4a II, 4e; = 1QS IX *15* - X *3*; 4Q256 XVIII; 4Q259 III-IV; 4Q260 I, II) *1* and according to his intellect promote him. And thus shall be his love and thus shall be his hatred. He should not reproach anyone or argue with the men of {knowledge} /the pit/ *2* but instead hide his counsel in the midst of the men of injustice. He should reproach (with) truthful knowledge and (with) just judgment those who choose the path, each one according to his spirit, and according to the regulation *3* of the time. He should [lead] them with knowledge and in this way teach them the mysteries of wonder and of truth in the midst of the men of the Community, so they walk perfectly, one *4* [with another, in all that has been revealed to] them. This is the time for making ready the path in the desert to teach them about all that has been discovered so that they can carry it out. *Blank* In this time *5* [they will be detached] from anyone who has not withdrawn his path from all injustice. And these are the regulations of behaviour for the Instructor in [these] time[s,] *6* [concerning his love and] his hatred. Everlasting hatred for the men of the pit in clandestine spirit. To them he should leave goods and profit *7* [and hand-made items like a servant to] his [mast]er and like one oppressed before someone domineering him. He should be a man enthusiastic for the decree and for his time, for the day of [revenge.] He should [perform] *8* [(God's) will in all that his hand should tackle and in] all that he controls, as [he commanded. And a]ll that happens to him he should welcome freely and [be gratified by nothing] except [God's] will. *9* [He should relish all the words of his mouth, wish for nothing that he has not commanded and be ever alert to the precep]t of God. […] *10* [… and with the offering of his lips he] shall bless him during [the periods] *11* [which God decreed: at the commencement of the dominion of light, during its rotation and at] its [re]tirement to [its] appointed abode. At the commencement of [the vigils of] *12* [darkness when he opens his store and stretches them upwards and during its rotation, when they retire] before the light. When [the lights] shine out [of the holy vault], *13* [when they retire to the abode of glory. At the entry of the seasons in the days of the new moon together with its rotations during its stations,]

Col. ix 1 בהתחדשם יום גדול לקודש קודשים ואות למפתח חסדי

עולם 2 לראשי מועדים בכל קץ נהיה בראשית ירחים למועדיהם וימי

3 קודש בתכונם לזכרון במועדי[הם תרומת [שפת]ים] אברכנו כחק

4 [ח]רות לעד בראשי שנים ובתקו[פת מועדיהם בהש]לם חוק 5 תכונם

יום משפטו זה לזה מוע[ד] קציר לקיץ ומועד ז[רע למועד 6 דשא מועדי

ש[ני]ם לשביעיה[ם ובראש ש[ב]עיהם למועדי דרור 7 ובכל היותי חוק

[ח]רות ב[ל]שוני לפרי [תהלה ומ]נת] שפתי אזמרה 8 בדעת וכל נגינתי

לכבוד ᴸF אכה נבל[י]י לתכון [קדשו וחליל] 9 [שפתי א]שא בקו מ[שפטו

[עם מבוא] יום] ו[ל]י]ל]ה] אבואה בברית ᴸF] 10 ועם מוצא ערב ובוקר

אמר חוקיו]ובהיותם אשיב 11 [גבולי לבלתי שוב ומשפטו אוכיח כנעוותי

ופ]שעי לנגד עיני 12 [כחוק חרות ולᴸF אומר צדקי ולעליון]מכון טובי

מק[ור] 13 [דעת ומעון קודש רום כבוד וגבורת כל לתפארת עולם

אבחרה]

Col. x 1 באשר יור]ני וארצה כאשר ישופטני בראשית משלח ידי]

2 ורגלי אברך] שמו ואברכנו בתרם אריס ידי להדשן] 3 בעדני תנ]ובת

תבל בראשית פחד ואימה ובמכון צרה] 4 ע[ם בוקה אברכנו בהפלא מודה

ובגבורתו אשוחח ועל חסדיו] 5 אשע]ן כל היום ואדעה כי בידו משפט כל

חי ואמת כל מעשיו] 6 ובה]פתח צרה אהללנו ובישועתו ארננה יחד לא

אשיב לאיש] 7 גמול] רע וטוב ארדף גבר כי את ᴸF משפט כל חי והוא]

8 ישלם [לאיש גמולו ...]

Col. IX (*frag.* 5 I; = 1QS X *4-12*; 4Q256 XIX; 4Q260 II-III)   *1* renewing each other. It is a great day for the holy of holies, and a sign of the opening of everlasting mercies, *2* for the beginnings of the seasons in every future age. At the commencement of the months in their seasons, and of the holy *3* days in their sequence, as a reminder in [their] seasons. [With the offering of] lip[s] I shall bless him, in accordance with the decree *4* [re]corded for ever. At the commencement of the years and in the tu[rning of their seasons, when] the decree *5* of their disposition [is carr]ied out, on its prescribed day, one after another; the sea[son of the harvest up to summer, the season of seed-]time up to the season of *6* the grass, the season of y[ear]s up to their seven-year periods. [At the commencement of the se]ven-year periods, up to the moments decided for deliverance. *7* And in all my existence the precept will be [en]graved on [my tongue to be a fruit of] eulogy and a por[tion] (of offering) of my lips. I will sing *8* with knowledge and for the glory of God shall all my music be, the playing of my harp to [his holy] order, [and the whistle] *9* [of my lips I shall] tune to its [co]rrect mea[sure. At the onset of] day [and ni]ght I shall enter the covenant *10* [of God, and when evening and morning depart I shall repeat his precepts;] and while they last I shall turn back *11* [my limit without turning away. I acknowledge his judgment to be right according to my pervertedness;] my [s]ins are before my eyes, *12* [like an engraved decree. To God I shall say: «My justice», and to the Most High:] «Establisher of my well-being», «sou[rce of] *13* [knowing», «place of holiness», «peak of glory», «all-powerful one of eternal majesty». I shall choose]

Col. X (*frag.* 5 II; = 1QS X *12-18*; 4Q256 XX; 4Q260 IV)   *1* what he teaches [me, I shall be pleased in how he might judge me. When I start to stretch out my hands] *2* and my feet I shall [bless his name, I shall bless him before stretching out my hand to get fat] *3* on the tasty fr[uit of the earth. At the onset of fright and dismay, in the place of distress] *4* an[d grief, I shall bless him for (his) great marvels and shall meditate on his power, on his compassion] *5* I shall rel[y the whole day. I realize that in his hand lies the judgment of every living thing, and all his deeds are truth.] *6* When [distress is unleashed I shall praise him, just as I shall sing to him for his deliverance. I shall not repay anyone with an evil] *7* reward; [with goodness I shall pursue man. For to God (belongs) the judgment of every living being, and it is he who] *8* pays [man his wages ...]

4Q259 (4QSᵉ) *4QRule of the Community*ᵉ
+ 4Q319 (4QOtot) *4QOtot*

4Q259:

P. Alexander, G. Vermes, *DJD XXVI*, 129-152, pls. XIV-XVI
PAM 43.263, 43.264
ROC 810, 818
1QS, 4Q255, 4Q256, 4Q257, 4Q258, 4Q260, 4Q261, 4Q262, 4Q263, 4Q264, 5Q11, 11Q29?

4Q319:

Wacholder-Abegg 1, 96-101
PAM 43.283-43.286
ROC 683, 695, 696, 708
Bibliography: J.T. Milik, *The Books of Enoch*, 61-64; M. Albani, 'Die lunaren Zyklen im 364-Tage-Festkalender von 4QMischmarot/4QSᵉ', *Forschungsstelle Judentum Mitteilungen und Beiträge* 4 (1992) 3-47; R. Eisenman, M. Wise, *DSSU*, 128-133; U. Gleßmer, 'Investigation of the Otot-Texts (4Q319) and Questions about Methodology', in M. Wise *et al.* (eds.), *Methods of Investigation of the Dead Sea Scrolls and the Khirbet Qumran Site* (New York: Academy of Sciences, 1994) 429-440; C. Martone, 'Un calendario proveniente da Qumran

Col. ɪ   4 [ששה חוד]שים] וכן לנוקם לנפשו כול דבר ואשר ידבר
בפיהו] 5 [דבר נבל שלושה חודשים ולמדבר בתוך דברי רעהו עשרת]
6 [ימים] ואשר ישכב [וישן במושב הרבים שלושים ימים וכן לאיש]
7 הנפטר ממוש(ב) הרבים אש]ר לוא בעצה והנם עד שלוש פעמים] 8 על
מושב אחד ונענש עש]רת ימים ואם יזקפו ונפטר] 9 ונענש שלושים יום
ואשר יה]לך לפני רעהו ערום ולוא] 10 היה אנוס] ונע]נש [ש]שה
חו]דשים ואיש אשר ירוק אל תוך מושב] 11 הרבים ו]נענש שלוש]ים
יום] *vacat?* ואשר יוציא] 12 את [ידו מתחת] בגד[ו] והוא]ה פוח ונראתה
ערותו] 13 ונענש ששים יום ואשר ישח]ק בסכלות להשמיע] 14 ק]לו
ונענש שלשים [יום והמוציא את יד שמאולו] 15 לשוח בה] [...]

Col. ɪɪ   3 [... יש]ב ובמלאות] לו] 4 [שנתים ימים ישאלו הרבים על
דבריו ואם יקרבהו ונכתב בתכ]ונ'{.} ואחר ישאל 5 [אל המשפט *vacat?*

528

4Q259 (4QS^e) *4QRule of the Community^e*
+ **4Q319** (4QOtot) *4QOtot*

4Q259:

Bibliography: J.T. Milik, 'Le travail d'édition des manuscrits du désert de Juda' *Volume du Congrès de Strasbourg* (SVT 4; Leiden: E.J. Brill, 1957) 25; C. Martone, *"Regola"*, 169-171, 185-187; S. Metso, *Textual Development*, 48-54; E. Qimron, J.H. Charlesworth, *PTSDSSP 1*, 84-89; É. Puech, 'L'alphabet cryptique A en *4QS^e (4Q259)*', *RevQ* 18/71 (1998) 429-435

4Q319:

recentemente pubblicato', *Henoch* 16 (1994) 49-75; .- *"Regola"*, 171-173, 187-190; U. Gleßmer, *Die ideale Kultordnung: 24 Priesterordnungen in den Chronikbüchern, den kalendarischen Qumrantexten und in synagogalen Inschriften* (Habitilationsschrift Hamburg, 1995); .- 'The Otot-Texts (4Q319) and the Problem of Intercalations in the Context of the 364-Day Calendar', in H.-J. Fabry *et al.* (eds.), *Qumranstudien: Vorträge und Beiträge der Teilnehmer des Qumranseminars auf dem internationalen Treffen der Society of Biblical Literature, Münster, 25.-26. Juli 1993* (Schriften des Institutum Judaicum Delitzschianum 4; Göttingen: Vandenhoeck & Ruprecht, 1996) 125-164; F. García Martínez, 'Calendarios en Qumrán (I)', *Est Bib* 54 (1996) 327-348

Col. I (= 1QS VII *8-15*; 4Q261 5) *4* [six mon]ths. [And likewise for anyone retaliating for any reason. Whoever utters with his mouth] *5* [futile words, three months; and for talking in the middle of the words of his fellow, ten] *6* [days] And whoever lies down [and goes to sleep in the session of the Many, thirty days. And the same applies to whoever] *7* [leaves] the ‹session› of the Many with[out permission, or falls asleep up to three times] *8* during a session, he shall be punished for te[n days; however, if they raise up (?) and he withdraws,] *9* he shall be punished for thirty days. And whoever wa[lks about naked in front of his fellow, without] *10* needing to, [shall be puni]shed for [s]ix mon[ths. And the person who spits in the course of a meeting of] *11* the Many shall [be punished thir]ty days. [*Blank?* And whoever takes] *12* out ["his hand" from under his] clothes, or if these are [rags which allow his nakedness to be seen,] *13* he will be punished sixty days. And whoever gigg[les inanely causing] *14* his voice [to be heard] shall be sentenced to thirty [days. And whoever takes out his left hand] *15* to gesticulate with it [...]

Col. II (= 1QS VII *20* - VIII *10*; 4Q258 VI) *3* [... he shall si]t. And when [the days of two years] are complete *4* [the Many shall be questioned concerning his affairs; if they admit him, he shall be enrolled in] his [ra]nk; and later he will be questioned *5* [in connection with judgment. *Blank?* However, anyone who

וכול איש אשר יהיה בעצ]ת היחד עד מלאות לו 6]עשר שנים ושבה רוחו
לבגוד ביחד ויצא מלפני] הרבים ללכת   7]בשרירות לבו לוא ישוב אל
עצת היחד עוד ואיש מ]אנשי היחד אשר   8]יתערב עמו בטהרתו או בהונו
אשר ... הרבים] והיה משפטו   9]כמוהו לשלח ... בעצת היחד שנים עשר
]אנשים]ו]כוהנים שלושה   10]תמימים בכול הנגלה מכול התורה לעשות
]אמת צדקה ומשפט   11]ואהבת חסד והצנע לכת איש עם רעהו לשמור
א]מונה בארץ ביצר סמוך ובענוה   12]ורוח נ]שברה ולרצות ע]וון בעושי
משפט וצרת] מצרף ו](ל)התהלך עם כול   13]במדת] האמת ובתכון] העת
בהיות אלה ב]ישרא]ל] נכונה עצת היחד   14]באמת למ]שפט עול]ם בית
קודש לישראל וסוד] קדש קדשים לאה{}ת{}ר{}ו   15 עדי אמת למשפט ובחירי
רצ]ון לכפר בעד] הארץ] ו]ל]השי]ב לרשעים 16 גמולם היאה חומת הבחן
פ]נת יקר ב]ל] יזדעזעו וב]ל יחושו ממקומם   17 מעוז קודש קו]ד]שים
לאהר]ון בדעת עולם]לברי]ת משפט ולקריב]^לם   ניחוח ובית
18 תמים ואמת ב]ישראל להקים ברית לחוקות עו]לם בהכון אלה
vacat [vacat] vacat 19

Col. III   1]ביסוד היחד שנתים ימים בתמים דרך יבדלו]לקדש בתוך
עצת אנ]שי]   2]היחד וכול דבר הנסתר מישראל ונמצ]א לאיש הדורש אל
י]ס]תרה]ו]   3]מאלה מיראת ר]וח נסו]גה ובהיות] אלה {ביחד} בישרא^ל
יבדלו ממ]ו]שב   4 אנ^שי העו]ל] ללכת המדבר]לפנות שמ]ה את דרך האמת
כאש]ר]   5 כתוב] במד]בר פ]נו דרך יהוה יש]רו בערבה מסלה לאלוהינו
6 הואה]מדרש התורה אשר]צוה ביד משה אלה הח]וקים]
7 למ]שכיל להתהלך בהם] עם כול חי לתכון עת]ועת]   8 ולמש]קל איש
ואיש לע]שות רצון אל ככול הנגלה]לעת בעת]   9]ולמוד את כול השכל]
הנמצא לפי העתים ואת]חוק]   10 העת] להבדיל ול]שקול בני הצדק לפי
ר]ו]חמה   11 ו]בבחירי העת להחזיק] על פי רצונו כאשר צוה ואיש

has been in the] Community [counc]il until completion of *6* [ten years and whose spirit reverts to betray the Community and go away from the presence of] the Many in order to walk *7* [in the stubbornness of his heart, will never return to the Community council. And the person from among] the men of the Community who *8* [fraternizes with him with regard to his purity or his goods, who … the Many,] and his sentence will be *9* [like his, he shall be expelled … In the Community council (there shall be) twelve] men [and] three priests, *10* [perfect in everything that has been revealed from all the law to implement] just truth, judgment, *11* [compassionate love and unassuming behaviour of one to another to preserve fa]ithfulness in the land with firm purpose and with simplicity *12* [and re]pentant [spirit,] in order to atone for s[in by doing justice and] undergoing [trials,] and ‹to› walk with everyone *13* [in the measure of] the truth and the regulation [of the time. When these things exist in] Israe[l,] the Community council shall be founded *14* [on truth for an] everlast[ing jud]gment, [a holy house for Israel and the foundation of the] holy of holies for Aaron, *15* true witnesses for the judgment and chosen by the wi[ll (of God) to atone for] the land [and] to [rend]er the wicked *16* their retribution. This is the tested rampart, [the precious] cor[nerstone, who do not shake or] tremble from their place. *17* It will be the most holy stronghold for Aar[on with eternal knowledge] of the coven[ant of justice and in order to offer] /for them/ a pleasant (aroma); and it will be a house *18* of perfection and truth in [Israel; in order to establish a covenant in compliance with the] everlasting [decrees.] When these have been established *19* Blank [Blank] Blank

Col. III (= 1QS VIII *11-15* + IX, *12-20*; 4Q258 2 VI, VIII; 4Q256 XVIII) *1* [in the foundation of the Community for two full years in perfect behaviour they will be segregated] for holiness in the midst of the council of the me[n of] *2* [the] Community. And every matter hidden from Israel but which has been foun]d out by the Interpreter, he should not [keep] hidden *3* [from them for fear of a spi]rit of deser[tion. And when] these [are] {in the Community} in Israel *(written in Cryptic A letters)* they are to be segregated from the dwe[ll]ing of *4* the men of si[n] *(written in Cryptic A letters)* to walk to the desert [in order to prepare] the path of truth. As *5* it is written: [*Isa 40:3* «In the des]ert, [prepare the way of YHWH, straigh]ten in the steppe a roadway for our God». *6* This is [the study of the law which] he commanded through the hand of Moses. These are the regu[lations] *7* for the Ins[tructor, by which he shall walk] with every living being in compliance with the regulation of [every] period *8* and in compliance with the wor[th of each man: he should ful]fill the will of God in compliance with all revelation [for every period;] *9* [he should acquire all the wisdom] that has been gained according to the periods and [the decree of] *10* the period; [he should separate and] weigh the sons of justice according to their spirits; *11* [he should keep hold of the chosen ones of the period] according to his will, as he

12 [כרוחו כן לעשות משפטו]ואיש כבור כפיו לקרבו ל[פי]   13 [שכלו

להגישו וכן אה]בתו עם שנאתו ואשר לוא [להוכיח]   14 ול[וא להתרובב

עם א]נשי השחת ולסתיר את ע[צת]   15 התורה] בתוך אנשי העול

ו]להוכיח דעת אמת ומשפט   16 צדק לבח]ירי דרך איש [כרוחו וכתכוני

העת להנחותם   17 בדעה] וכן להשכילם ב]רזי פלא ואם תיתם דרך סוד

18 [ה]יחד לה]לך תמים איש [את רעיו בכל הנגלה להם   19 היאה]עת

פנות הדרך]למדבר ולהמשילם בכול

1   *Col.* IV   [הנמצא לעשות] בעת ה[זואת ו]ה[ב]דל מכול איש אשר לוא

הסיר]   2 [דרכו מכול עול] ואלה תכוני [הדר]ך למשכיל [בעתים האלה

לאהבתו]   3 עם שנא]תו שנאת עו[ל]ם ע[ם] [אנשי שחת ברוח]הסתר

לעזו]ובו   4 למו הון] ועמל כפים כעבד למושל בו וענוה]לפני הרודה בו

ו[להיות]   5 איש [מקנא לחוק ועתו ליום נקם לעשות רצון בכ]ול משל[ח

כפים   6 ובו]כו[ל] [...] 9-7 [...] 10 [...]אורה בארבעה בשב[וע ...]

11 [... ה]בריאה בארבעה בג]מול אות שכניה ברביעית אות גמול בשמטה

או]ת   12 [שכניה בשלי]שית אות [ג]מול בששית אות [שכניה בשנית אות

ג]מול   13 [בחמישית או]ת שכניה אחר השממטה אות גמו]ל ברביעית אות

שכ]נ]י]ה   14 [בשממטה או]ת גמול בשלישית את שכנית [בששית אות

גמ]ול   15 [בשנית או]ת ש]כניה] בחמישית אות גמו]ל אחר השמט]ה אות

16 [שכניה בר]ביעית אות גמול בשממטה אות ס]וף היובל אתות הי]ובל

17 [השני] אתות 17 מזה בשממטה אתות[... 3 ...]. הבריאה   18 [... או]ת

שכ]נ]י]ה בשנה השלישית אות גמו]ל בששית א]ות שכניה   19 [בשנית אות

ג]מול בחמישית אות שכניה אחר הש]מטה אות ג]מול

1   *Col.* v   [ברביעית אות שכניה בשמטה אות גמול בשלישית אות

שכניה]   2 [בששית אות גמול ב]שנ]י]ת א]ות שכניה בחמישית אות גמול]

has commanded; of each man *12* [in accordance with his spirit he should carry out the judgment;] he should include each one according to the purity of his hands; according [to] *13* [his intellect he should promote him. And thus shall be] his [lo]ve and thus shall be his hatred. He should not [reproach] *14* no[r argue with the m]en of the pit but instead hide the cou[nsel] *15* of the law [in the midst of the men of injustice.] He should reproach (with) truthful knowledge and (with) just *16* judgment those who cho[ose the path, each one] according to his spirit and according to the regulation of the time. He should lead them *17* with knowledge [and in this way teach them the] mysteries of wonder and of truth and give them the secret pa[th of the men of] *18* the Community, so that they wa[lk perfectly, one] with another, in all that has been revealed to them. *19* This is [the time for making ready the path] to the desert and he will teach them about all

Col. IV (= 1QS IX *20-24*; 4Q256 VIII; 4Q258 VIII; 4Q260 I)   *1* [that has been discovered so that they can carry it out] in th[is] moment [and so they will be] deta[ched from anyone who has not withdrawn] *2* [his path from all injustice.] And these are the regulations of [behavio]ur for the Inspector [in these times, concerning his love] *3* and [his] hatr[ed. Everlasting hatred for the men of the pit in] clandestine [spirit.] To them he should le[ave] *4* goods [and hand-made items like a servant to his master and like one oppressed] before someone domineering him. [He should be] *5* a man [enthusiastic for the decree and for its time, for the day of revenge. He should perform (God's) will in a]ll that [his hand] should tack[le] *6* and in [al]l […] *7-9* […] *10* […] its light on the fourth (day) of the we[ek …] *11* [… the] creation. In the fourth (day) Ga[mul; the sign of Shecaniah in the fourth (year); the sign of Gamul in (the year of) the Release; the sig]n of *12* [Shecaniah in the thi]rd; the sign of [Ga]mul in the sixth; the sign of [Shecaniah in the second; the sign of Ga]mul *13* [in the fifth; the sig]n of Shecaniah (in the year) after the Release; the sign of Ga[mul in the fourth; the sign of Shecan]iah *14* [in (the year of) the Release; the sig]n of Gamul in the third; the sign of Shecaniah [in the sixth; the sign of Gam]ul *15* [in the second; the si]gn of She[caniah] in the fifth; the sign of Ga[mul (in the year) after the Relea]se; the sign of *16* [Shecaniah in the fo]urth; the sign of Gamul in (the year of) the Release, the sign of the e[nd of the jubilee. The signs of the second j]ubilee *17* are seventeen signs. Of these are [three] in (the years of) the Release […] the creation *18* [… the sig]n of Shecaniah in the third year; the sign of Gamu[l in the sixth; the si]gn of Shecaniah *19* [in the second; the sign of Ga]mul in the fifth; the sign of Shecaniah (in the year) after the Re[mission; the sign of Ga]mul

Col. V   *1* [in the fourth; the sign of Shecaniah in (the year of) the Release; the sign of Gamul in the third; the sign of Shecaniah] *2* [in the sixth; the sign of Gamul in the se]cond; the sig[n of Shecaniah in the fifth; the sign of Gamul]

3 [אחר השמט]ה אות שכניה בר[ביעית אות גמול בשמטה אות] 4 [שכניה
בשלי]שית אות גמול בש[שית אות] שכני]ה בשנית אות סוף] 5 היובל
השיל]י]שי אתות היובל [השלישי אתות 6]1 מזה בשמטה 6 אתות 2 שכניה
[בשנה השנית או]ת [גמו]ל בחמישית אות שכניה 7 אחר השמטה או]ת
גמול ברביעית או]ת שכניה בשמטה אות 8 גמול בשלישית אות [שכניה
בששית אות ג]מול בשנית אות 9 שכניה בחמישית אות [גמול אחר]
השמטה אות שכניה 10 ברביעית אות גמול] בשמטה אות] שכניה
בשלישית אות גמול 11 בששית אות שכ]נית בשנית אות] גמול בחמישית
אות שכניה 12 אחר השמטה א]ות סוף היובל אתו]ת היובל אתות 17
13 מ[ז]ה בשמטה אותות 2 [*vacat?*] גמול] בשנה הרביעית אות שכניה
14 [בש]מטה אות גמול ב]שלישית אות שכניה בששית אות גמול]
15 בשנ[י]ת אות שכניה בחמ]ישת אות גמול אחר השמטה אות שכניה]
16 ברביעית אות [ג]מול ב]שמטה אות שכניה בשלישית אות גמול]
17 בשש[י]ת א]ות ש]כניה בשנית אות גמול בחמישית אות שכניה]
18 [אחר ה]שמטה אות ג]מול ברביעית שכניה בשמטה אות סוף]
19 [היובל החמיש]י בישיב אב [אתות היובל החמשי 17 מזה בשמטה]

1   *Col.* vi   [אתות 3 גמול בשנה השלילית אות שכניה בששית אות]
2 [גמול ב]שנית אות שכניה ב]חמישית אות גמול אחר השמ]טה 3 [או]ת
שכניה ברביעית אות גמ]ול בשמטה אות שכניה] בשלישית 4 אות גמול
בששית אות שכניה [בשנית אות] גמול 5 בח]מי]שית אות שכניה אחר
[השמטה] אות 6 גמול ב[ר]ביעית אות שכניה בשמ]טה אות גמול
ב]שלישית 7 אות [שכניה בש]שית אות סוף [ה]יו]בל [ה]ששי אתות]
8 יובל [הששי אתות 6]1 מזה ב]שמטה [אתות 2 ...] 9 הח]מישי
[ביובל ...] 10 וליובל]ל גמול בשנה השנית אות שכניה בחמישית אות
גמול אחר] 11 השמט]ה אות שכניה ברביעי]ת אות גמו]ל ב]שמטה]
12 [אות שכניה בשלישית אות] גמול בששית או]ת שכניה] 13 [ב]שנית
או]ת גמול] בחמישית אות שכניה [אחר] 14 השמט]ה אות ג]מול ברביעית

534

3 [(in the year) after the Relea]se; the sign of Shecaniah in the fou[rth; the sign of Gamul in (the year of) the Release; the sign of] *4* [Shecaniah in thc thi]rd; the sign of Gamul in the s[ixth; the sign of] Shecani[ah in the second, the sign of the end of the] *5* th[ird] jubilee. The signs of the [third] jubilee are [six]teen. Of these are in (the years of) the Release *6* two signs. (The sign of) Shecaniah [in the second year; the sign of Gamu]l in the fifth; the sign of Shecaniah *7* (in the year) after the Release; the si[gn of Gamul in the fourth; the si]gn of Shecaniah in (the year of) the Release; the sign of *8* Gamul in the third; the sign of [Shecaniah in the sixth; the sign of Ga]mul in the second; the sign of *9* Shecaniah in the fifth; the sign of [Gamul (in the year) after] the Release; the sign of Shecaniah *10* in the fourth; the sign of Gamul [in (the year of) the Release; the sign of] Shecaniah in the third; the sign of Gamul *11* in the sixth; the sign of Shec[aniah in the second; the sign of] Gamul in the fifth; the sign of Shecaniah *12* (in the year) after the Release, the s[ign of the end of the jubilee.] The /jubilee/ has seventeen signs. *13* Of these are in (the years of) the Release two /signs/. [*Blank?* Gamul] in the fourth year; the sign of Shecaniah *14* [in (the year of) the Re]lease; the sign of Gamul in [the third; the sign of Shecaniah in the sixth; the sign of Gamul] *15* in the second; the sign of Shecaniah in the fif[th; the sign of Gamul (in the year) after the Release, the sign of Shecaniah] *16* in the fourth; the sign of [Ga]mul in [(the year of) the Release; the sign of Shecaniah in the third; the sign of Gamul] *17* in the six[th, the sig]n of Sh[ecaniah] *18* [(in the year) after the] Release; the sign of Ga[mul in the fourth; the sign of Shecaniah in (the year of) the Release; the sign of the end of] *19* [the fif]th [jubilee] is in Jeshebeab. [The signs of the fifth jubilee are seventeen. Of these are in (the years of) the Release]

Col. VI *1* [three signs. Gamul in the third year; the sign of Shecaniah in the sixth; the sign of] *2* [Gamul in the] second, the sign of Shecaniah in [the fifth; the sign of Gamul (in the year) after the Rel]ease; *3* [the sig]n of Shecaniah in the fourth; the sign of Gam[ul in (the year of) the Release; the sign of Shecaniah] in the third; *4* the sign of Gamul in the sixth; the sign of Shecaniah [in the second; the sign of] Gamul *5* in the fifth; the sign of Shecaniah (in the year) after [the Release;] the sign of *6* Gamul in the [f]ourth; the sign of Shecaniah in (the year of) the Rele[ase; the sign of Gamul in the] third; *7* the sign of [Shecaniah in the six]th; the /sign/ of the end of the [sixth] jubilee. [The signs of] *8* the [sixth] jubilee [are six]teen. Of these are in [(the year of) the Release] two signs […] *9* the f[ifth (?) …] in the jubi[lee …] *10* and to the jub[ilee. Gamul, in the second year; the sign of Shecaniah in the fifth; the sign of Gamul (in the year) after] *11* the Relea[se; the sign of Shecaniah in the four]th; the sign of Gamu[l in] (the year of) the Relea[se;] *12* [the sign of Shecaniah in the third; the sign of] Gamul in the sixth; the si[gn of Shecaniah] *13* [in] the second; the sig[n of Gamul] in the fifth; the sign of Shecaniah [(in the year) after] *14* the Release; [the sign of Ga]mul in the fourth; the sign of

אות שכניה בש[מטה אות]   15 גמול [בשלי]שית אות שכניה בששית אות]

גמול]   16 בש[נית אות שכניה] בחמישית אות סוף היוב[ל ה]שביעי

17 [אתות היובל ה]שביעי אתות 16 מזה בש[מ]טה   18 [אתות 2 [אות

הי[ו]בלים [ש]נת יובלים לימ]י...[19]...[במימן השלישי י]דעיה]

1 גמול] אלישיב מעוזיה חופה בריאשונה]   2 ידעיה [בלגה   *Col.* VII

שעורים חזיר בשנית]   3 מימין [פתחיה אביה יכין בשלישית]   4 שכניה

[דליה יקים יויריב ברביעית]   5 ישבאב [חרים אמר מלכיה בחמישית]

6 הפצץ [הקוץ יחזקאל ישוע בששית]   7 גמול]...[

1]... [הפסח [השני ב.]...[2]...[. בחזי]ר ... [3]...[...   *Col.* VIII

בחזיר] ... [4]... ב[מעוזיה הפסח] ... [5]... [יום הזכר]ון [...

1]... [גמ]ול מימן   2]... יד]עיה שכניה   3]...[שכניה   *Col.* IX

4]...[ל שכניה   5]...[...

4]...[. [ם [ול]שבתות   5]ימיה[ם]... [ול]חג]י[6]ימי]הם   *Col.* X

[ול]ח[ו]דש]י שניהם ו[לאותות   7 [ש]מט]יה[ם וליובליהם בשבת   8 [בנ]י

גמו]ל בי[ו]ם הרבי[עי]

4Q260 (4QS^f) *4QRule of the Community^f*

P. Alexander, G. Vermes, *DJD XXVI*, 153-167, pl. XVII
PAM 43.265
ROC 366
1QS, 4Q255, 4Q256, 4Q257, 4Q258, 4Q259, 4Q261, 4Q262, 4Q263, 4Q264, 5Q11, 11Q29?

1]... [לעשות רצון בכו]ל משלוח   2 [כפים ובכול ממשלו   *Col.* I

כאשר צוה]וכול הנעשה

Shecaniah in (the year of) the Re[lease; the sign of] *15* Gamul [in the th]ird;
the sign of Shecaniah in the sixth; the sign of [Gamul] *16* in the se[cond; the
sign of Shecaniah] in the fifth; the sign of the end of the [se]venth jubilee.
17 [The signs of the] seventh [jubilee] are sixteen. Of these are in (the years
of) the Release *18* [two signs.] The sign of the jubilees, the [y]ear of the jubilees, according to the days [of ...] *19* [...] in Mijamin, the third Ye[daiah ...]

Col. VII   (cf. 4Q328 1; 4Q329 1 - 2)   *1* Gamul, [Eliashib, Maaziah, Huppah in
the first (year);] *2* Yedaiah, [Bilgah, Seorim, Hezir in the second (year);]
3 Mijamin, [Pethahiah, Abiah, Jachin in the third (year);] *4* Shecaniah,
[Delaiah, Jakim, Jehoiarib in the fourth (year);] *5* Jeshebeab, [Harim, Immer,
Malkiah in the fifth (year);] *6* Aphses, [Hakkoz, Jehezekel, Jeshua in the sixth
(year).] *7* Gamul [...]

Col. VIII   *1* [... on the ... of ...] the second [Passover]; on the [... of ...] *2* [... on
the ...] of Hezir [...] *3* [... on the ...] of Hezi[r ...] *4* [... on the ... of] Maaziah
the Passover; [...] *4* [... on the ... of ...] the day of remembr[ance ...]

Col. IX   *1* [... Gam]ul, Mijamin *2* [... Yeda]iah, Shecaniah *3* [...] Shecaniah
4 [...] Shecaniah *5* [...] ...

Col. X   *4* [... and about] the sabbaths *5* [and the]ir [days ... and about] the feast[s
of] *6* their [days, and about the] month[s of their years and] about the signs of
7 [the]ir [Re]lease[s] and about their jubilees. On the sabbath of *8* [the son]s of
[Gamu]l, on the fou[rth] d[a]y

4Q260 (4QS^f) *4QRule of the Community^f*

Bibliography: J.T. Milik, review of P. Wernberg-Møller, *The Manual of Disci-
pline*, RB 67 (1960) 412-416; *Wacholder-Abegg 3*, 62-64; E. Qimron, J.H.
Charlesworth, *PTSDSSP 1*, 90-93; C. Martone, *"Regola"*, 173-174, 190-191;
S. Metso, *Textual Development*, 55-58

Col. I (= 1QS IX *23-24*; 4Q258 VIII; 4Q259 IV)   *1* [... He should perform (God's)
will in al]l that [his hand] should tackle *2* [and in all that he controls, as he
commanded.] And all that happens

Col. II   1 בראשית א[ש]מורות [חושך כי יפתח אוצרו וישיתהו עלת]
תקופתו   2 עם האספו מ[פני אור בהופיע מאורות מזבול קודש עם האס]פם
למעון   3 כבוד ובבוא[מועדים לימי חודש יחד תקופתם עם מסרותם ז]ה
לזה   4 בהתחד[שם יום גדול לקודש קודשים ואות למפתח חסדי ע]ולם
5 ...[...].

Col. III   1 אכה נבל[ו]י] ל[תכון קודשו וחליל שפתי א[שא בקו משפטו
2 ע[ם מבוא יום ולילה אבואה בברית אל ועם] מוצא   ערב
3 ובוקר א[ומר חוקיו ובהיותם אשים גבולי ל[בלתי שוב

Col. IV   1 [בר]אשית פחד ואימה [ובמכון] צרה עם בוקא [אברכנו]
2 בהפלא מאדה ובגבורו[תיו א[שוחח ועל חסד]יו אשען]   3 כול היום
משפט כול חי[בידו ואמת מ[עש]יו [ובה]פתח]   4 צרה אהללנו ובישועת[ו
ארננה י]חד לוא אש[יב]   5 לאיש גמול רע לטוב [ארדוף [גבר כ]י] את אל]
משפט   6 כול חי הוא ישלם לא[יש גמו]לו לוא אק[נא ברוח]   7 רשעה
ולהון חמ]ס לוא תאוה [נפשי ור]יב אנש]   8 שחת ל[ו]א אתפוש ע[ד יום
נקם ו]אפי לו]א אשיב]   9 מאנשי עולה ול[ו]א] ארצה עד הכי]ן משפט
[לוא]   10 אטור לש[ב]י פשע [...][אנשי ...] ולוא]

Col. V   1 [אר]חם על כול סוררי דרך לוא אנחם בנכוחים עד תום
2 ד[רכ]ם ובליעל לוא אשמור בלבבי ולוא ישמע בפי   3 נבלות וכחש עוון
[ומ]רמות וכזבין לוא ימצאו בשפתי *vacat*   4 ופרי קודש בלשוני ושקוצים
לוא ימצא   5 בה בהוד[ות אפתח] *vacat* פי[ו]צדקות אל תס[פר]   6 לשוני
תמ]יד ומעל [אנשים [עד ת]ום פשעם   6 [...].[...]

4Q260

Col. II (= 1QS x *1-4*; 4Q258 VIII-IX; 4Q256 XIX)   *1* At the commencement of the vigils of [darkness when he opens his store and stretches them upwards and during] its rotation, *2* when it retires be[fore the light. When the lights shine out of the holy vault, when] they [reti]re to the abode *3* of glory. At the entry of [the seasons in the days of the new moon together with their rotations during their stations] renewing *4* [ea]ch other. [It is a great day for the holy of holies, and a sign of the opening of the ever]lasting [mercies.] *5* … […] …

Col. III (= 1QS x *9-11*; 4Q258 IX)   *19* the playing of [my] harp according to [his holy order, and the whistle of my lips I shall t]une to its correct measure. *2* At the [onset of day and night I shall enter the covenant of God, at the] onset of evening *3* and morning I [shall repeat his precepts; and while they last I shall set them as my limit,] with no backtracking.

Col. IV (= 1QS x *15-20*; 4Q256 XX; 4Q258 X)   *1* [At the on]set of fright and dismay, [in the place] of distress and grief, [I shall bless him] *2* for (his) great marvels and shall meditate on [his] mighty deed[s] and [shall rely] on [his] compassion *3* the whole day. The judgment of every living thing [is in his hand and his d]eed[s are truth.] When *4* distress is [unleashed] I shall praise him, [j]ust as [I shall sing to him] for [his] deliverance. I shall not rep[ay] *5* anyone with an evil reward; with goodness [I shall pursue] man. For to God (belongs) [the judgment] *6* of every living being, and it is he who pays m[an] his [wage]s. I shall not be je[alous with] a wicked *7* [spirit], and my soul [shall not crave] wealth by violence. [In the dispute with the men] *8* of the pit I shall not be involved un[til the day of vengeance. However, I shall] no[t remove] my anger *9* from unjust men, nor [shall I be appeased, until he has carried out] the judgment. [I shall not] *10* sustain angry resentment for those who convert from iniquity; […] of men. [… and not]

Col. V (= 1QS x *20-24*)   *1* [shall I have mer]cy for all those who turn aside from the path. I shall not comfort the oppressed until their p[ath] is *2* perfect. I shall not retain Belial within my heart. From my mouth no *3* vulgarity shall be heard or wicked deceptions; sophistries or lies shall not be found on my lips. *4* The fruit of holiness will be on my tongue, *Blank* profanity shall not be found *5* on it. With hymn[s shall I open] *Blank* my mouth, [and] the just acts of God *6* my tongue will ev[er reco[unt] and the unfaithfulness] of men [until] their iniquity [is com]plete. *6* […] … […]

539

4Q261 (4QSᵍ) *4QRule of the Community*ᵍ

P. Alexander, G. Vermes, *DJD XXVI*, 169-187, pls. XVIII-XIX
PAM 43.266
ROC 705
1QS, 4Q255, 4Q256, 4Q257, 4Q258, 4Q259, 4Q260, 4Q262, 4Q263, 4Q264,
5Q11, 11Q29?

Frag. 1   1   [את ברי]תו ול[פקוד את כול חו]קו אשר צוה לע[שות]
2 [ועל פי רו]ב יש[ראל המתנדבים]לשבת יחד ולכת[ב]   3   [איש לפנ]י
רע]הו בסרך לפי]שכלו ומעשו בתור[ה]   4   [להשמע] הקטן] לגדול ולהיות
פוקדי]ם א[ת רוחם]   5   [ומעשי]הם ב[תורה שנה בשנה להעלות איש לפי
שכלו]   6   [ולאחרו כ]נעוות]ו ...[

Frag. 3   1   [...   ע]צתו ליח]ד ומשפטו [*vacat*]   2   [ואלה המשפטים
א]שר ישפטו על פי] הדברים אם ימצא בם]   3   [איש אשר ישקר במ]מון
והוא יודע וה]בדילוהו מתוך טהרת]   4   [רבים שנה אחת ונענש את רבי]עית
לח]מו ...[

Frag. 5   1   [...].[...]   2   [... ואשר ישכב ו]ישן במ[וש]ב   3   [הרבים
שלושים ימים כן לאיש הנפטר במושב הר]בי[ם]אשר לא ב״צה   4   [וחנם
עד שלוש פעמים על מושב אחד ונענ]ש] עש[ר]ת [ימים   5   [ואם יזקפו
vacat? ונפטר ונענש ש[לושי]ם י]ום ואשר   6   [יהלך לפני רעהו ערום ...
ול]א היה אנוש   7   [ונענש ששה הודשים ואיש אשר ירוק אל תוך מו]שב
הרבים   8   [ונענש שלושים יום ואשר יוציא את ידו מת]חת בגדו
9 [...]...[...]

Frag. 6   1-2 [...].[...]   3 [... י]שלחוהו מא[ת]ם ול[א ...]   4 [...
יסו]ד היחד לשלח ול[א ...   5 [...]...[...]

4Q261 (4QS^g) *4QRule of the Community^g*

Bibliography: J.T. Milik, review of P. Wernberg-Møller, *The Manual of Discipline*, *RB* 67 (1960) 412-416; *Wacholder-Abegg* 3, 65-67; E. Qimron, J.H. Charlesworth, *PTSDSSP 1*, 94-97; C. Martone, *"Regola"*, 174-175, 191-192; S. Metso, *Textual Development*, 59-61

Frag. 1 (= 1QS v 22-24; 4Q258 II)   *1* his [cove]nant and to [follow all] his [decr]ees which he commanded to fu[lfil,] *2* [and under the authority of the major]ity of Is[rael, those who freely volunteer] to dwell together. And they shall be reco[rded] *3* [one be]fore the oth[er, in order, according to one's insight and one's deeds in the law.] *4* The junior [shall obey the senior. And their spirit must be tested,] *5* [and] their [deeds] in [the law, year after year, in order to upgrade each one to the extent of his insight,] *6* [or to demote him according to his] failings […]

Frag. 3 (= 1QS vi 22-25)   *1* […] his [ad]vice will be for the Commu[nity as will his judgment. *Blank*] *2* [And these are the regulations] by which they shall judge him depending on [the case. If one is found among them] *3* [who has lied] knowingly [concerning mo]ney, he shall be [excluded from the pure food] *4* [of the Many for one year and shall be sentenced to a quar]ter of [his] bre[ad. …]

Frag. 5 (= 1QS vii 10-13; 4Q259 I)   *1* […] … […] *2* [… And whoever lies down and] goes to sleep in the se[ssi]on *3* [of the Many, thirty days. The same applies to whoever leaves the session of the Ma]ny without cause, *4* [or falls to sleep up to three times during a session, shall be punis]hed [ten] days; *5* [however, if they raise up (?) *Blank?* and he withdraws, he shall be punished for th]ir[ty d]ays. And whoever *6* [walks about naked in front of his fellow …] without needing to, *7* [shall be punished for six months. And the person who spits in the course of a ses]sion of the Many *8* [shall be punished thirty days. And whoever takes out his 'hand' from und]er his clothes, *9* […] … […]

Frag. 6 (cf. 1QS vii 16-17)   *1-2* […] … […] *3* […] they shall expel him from their midst and no[t …] *4* [… foundat]ion of the Community shall be expelled and n[ot …] *5* […] … […]

4Q262 (4QSʰ) *4QRule of the Communityʰ*

P. Alexander, G. Vermes, *DJD XXVI*, 189-195, pl. XX
PAM 43.267
ROC 105
1QS, 4Q255, 4Q256, 4Q257, 4Q258, 4Q259, 4Q260, 4Q261, 4Q263, 4Q264,
5Q11, 11Q29?

Frag. 1   2 [יתקד]ש בימים   1 [בכפורי]ם ולא יטהר ב[מי נדה ולא]

4 [ימי   3 [בכל מי]רחיצה טמ[א טמא יהיה כל]   ונהרות] ולא יטהר]
מוא]סי ב[משפטי אל ...]

Frag. A   1 נכ{.}סו לכול ק.[...]   2 רום נושים]...]   3 במפץ אבן[...]

4Q262 frag. B

P. Alexander, G. Vermes, *DJD XXVI*, 193-195, pl. XX
PAM 41.280, 43.267

Frag. 1   1 [...] תחת דליתו ישתו עד] [...]   2 [... עד]שחקים ודליותו
עד] [...   3 [... מו]רי מרום ינובב פרי[ו ...]   4 [...]ם שבעה בזוהרו[...]
5 [...]שמי טוהר .[...]   6 [...]מלקוש]...]

4Q263 (4QSⁱ) *4QRule of the Communityⁱ*

P. Alexander, G. Vermes, *DJD XXVI*, 197-200, pl. XXI
PAM 43.267
ROC 251
1QS, 4Q255, 4Q256, 4Q257, 4Q258, 4Q259, 4Q260, 4Q261, 4Q262, 4Q264,
5Q11, 11Q29?

1 [...]. [וגם]אל יבא[איש על רעהו דבר לפני הרבים]
2 [אשר לוא בהו]כח לפני עדים ובאלה יתהל]כו בכול מגוריהם כול הנמצא

542

4Q262 (4QS^h) *4QRule of the Community^h*

Bibliography: J.T. Milik, review of P. Wernberg-Møller, *The Manual of Discipline*, *RB* 67 (1960) 412-416; *Wacholder-Abegg 3*, 68; E. Qimron, J.H. Charlesworth, *PTSDSSP 1*, 98-99; C. Martone, *"Regola"*, 175, 192; S. Metso, *Textual Development*, 61-62

Frag. 1 (cf. 1QS III *4-6*; 4Q257 III; 5Q13 4)   *1* [by the acts of aton]ement, nor shall he be purified by [the cleansing waters, nor] *2* [shall he be made hol]y by the seas or rivers, [nor shall he be purified] *3* [by all the water of] the ablutions. Defil[ed, defiled shall he be,] *4* [all the days he spur]ns the [decrees of God,...]

Frag. A   *1* his wealth for all ... [...] *2* the haughtiness of creditors [...] *3* by the shattering blow of a sto[ne ...]

4Q262 frag. B

ROC 105
Bibliography: Wacholder-Abegg 3, 69S. Metso, *Textual Development*, 62

Frag. 1   *1* [...] beneath its branches they drink up to [...] *2* [... up to] the clouds, and its branches up to [...] *3* [... the early r]ain (?) of the height makes [its] fruits flourish [...] *4* [...] seven, in its splendour [...] *5* [...] clear heavens (?) [...] *6* [...] late rain [...]

4Q263 (4QS^i) *4QRule of the Community^i*

Bibliography: J.T. Milik, review of P. Wernberg-Møller, *The Manual of Discipline*, *RB* 67 (1960) 412-416; *Wacholder-Abegg 3*, 70; E. Qimron, J.H. Charlesworth, *PTSDSSP 1*, 100-101; C. Martone, *"Regola"*, 175, 192-193; S. Metso, *Textual Development*, 63

(= 1QS VI *1-4*; 4Q258 II)   *1* [... And in addition,] no-one should raise [a matter against his fellow in front of the Many] *2* [unless it is with repro]of in the

איש 3 [את רעהו וישמ]ע הקטן לגדול למלכאה (למלאכה) ולה[ון ויחד
יואכלו ויחד יברכו] 4 [ויחד יועצו ובכול [מ]ק[ו]ם אשר יהיה שם [עשרה
אנשים מעצת היחד אל ימש] 5 [מאתם איש כוהן ואי]ש כת[כונו ישבו
לפניו ...]

4Q264 (4QS^j) *4QRule of the Community*

P. Alexander, G. Vermes, *DJD XXVI*, 201-206, pl. XXI
PAM 43.267
ROC 297
1QS, 4Q255, 4Q256, 4Q257, 4Q258, 4Q259, 4Q260, 4Q261, 4Q262, 4Q263,
5Q11, 11Q29?

1 [ברחמיו הגישני ובחסדיו יביא משפטי בצדקת [אמתו שפטני
וברוב טו[בו] 2 [יכפר בעד כל עונותי ובצדקתו יטהרני מנדת אנ] וש
וחטאת בני אדם להודות 3 [לאל צדקו ולעליון תפארתו ברוך אתה אלי
הפותח לדעה]לב עבדך הכן ב[צד]ק כל מעש[יו] 4 [והקם לבן אמתך
כאשר רצית לבחירי אדם להתי]צב לפניך לעד כי מבלעדיך 5 [לא תתם
דרך ובלא רצונך לא יעשה כל אתה ה]ורית כל דעה וכל הנהיה 6 [ברצונך
היה ואין אחר זולתך להשיב על עצ]תך ולהשכיל בכל מחשבת 7 [קדשך
ולהביט בעומק רזיך ולהתבונן ב]כל נפלאותיך עם כוח [ג]בורתך 8 [ומי
יכול להכיל את כבודך ומה אף הוא בן ה]אדם במעשי פלאך וילוד אשה
9 [מה יחשב לפניך והוא מעפר מגבלו ולחם רמ]ה מדורו והוא מצירוק חמר
10 [קרץ ולעפר תשוקתו מה ישיב חמר ויוצר יד]ולעצת מה יבין *vacat*

presence of witnesses. And in this way shall they beha[ve in all their places of residence, whenever one fellow meets] *3* [another,] the junior [shall obc]y the senior in <work> and in wea[lth. They shall eat together, together they shall bless] *4* [and together they shall take counsel. In every] p[la]ce where there are [ten men of the Community council, there should not be missing] *5* [amongst them a priest. And every]one [shall sit before him] according to [his] r[ank ...]

4Q264 (4QSⁱ) *4QRule of the Community*ʲ

Bibliography: J.T. Milik, review of P. Wernberg-Møller, *The Manual of Discipline*, *RB* 67 (1960) 412-416; *Wacholder-Abegg 3*, 71; E. Qimron, J.H. Charlesworth, *PTSDSSP 1*, 102-103; C. Martone, *"Regola"*, 175-176, 193; S. Metso, *Textual Development*, 63-64

(= 1QS XI *14-22*)   *1* [he will draw me near in his mercies, and by kindnesses set in motion my judgment;] he will judge me [in the justice] of his truth, and in [his] plentiful good[ness] *2* [always atone for all my iniquities; in his justice he will cleanse me from the uncleanness of the hu]man being, and from the sin of the sons of man, so that I can give *3* [God thanks for his justice and The Highest for his majesty. Blessed be you, my God, who opens] the heart of your servant [to knowledge!] Establish all his deeds in [just]ice, *4* [and raise up the son of your handmaid to st]and everlastingly in your presence, [as you have cared for the selected ones of humankind.] For without you *5* [no behaviour is perfect, and without your will, nothing comes to be.] You have taught all knowledge, and all that exists *6* [is so by your will. Beyond you there is no-one to oppose your counsel,] to understand any of [your holy] thoughts, *7* [to gaze into the abyss of your mysteries, to fathom] all your marvels or the strength of your [m]ight. *8* [Who can endure your glory? What, indeed, is ma]n, among all your marvellous deeds? [As what shall] one born of woman *9* [be considered in your presence? Shaped from dust has he been, maggots' food] shall be his dwelling; he is spat saliva, [moulded] clay, *10* [and for dust is his longing. What will the clay reply and the one shaped by hand?] And what advice will he be able to understand? *Blank*

4Q264a (4QHalakhah B) *4QHalakhah B*

J.M. Baumgarten, *DJD XXXV* (forthcoming)
PAM 42.412, 43.310
ROC 110

Frag. 1   1 [... כי אם אל]ף באמה אל יקח איש   2 [...] גם הכוהנים
בני 3 [אהרון ... כול] העולות והזבחים אשר   4 [... מגל]ת ספר ל[קרו]א
בכתבו ביום [השבת ...]   5 [... יקרא]ו וילמדו בם אל יחשב איש] בפיהו]
6 [...]בכול דברי עבודה או בהון או [בבצע ...]   7 [...]ביום הש]ב]ת ואל
יד]בר ד]בר כי אם ל]דבר דברי]   8 [קודש כחוק יד]בר לברך אל אך ידבר
[דבר]לאכול ולש]תות ...]

Frag. 3   1 [...]...[2 אחריהם ל.[...]   3 ועץ וכול איש] ...   4 בבית
א]ו] בעיר] ... [5 להלחם עמו .[...]

4Q265 *4QMiscellaneous Rules*

J.M. Baumgarten, *DJD XXXV* (forthcoming)
PAM 43.304-43.306
ROC 306, 307, 308
Bibliography: Wacholder-Abegg 3, 72-78; J.M. Baumgarten, 'Purification after Childbirth and the Sacred Garden in 4Q265 and Jubilees', in G.J. Brooke, F.

Frag. 1 i   1 [...]...[...]   2-1 [...]...[...]   3 ...]ע]שרת י]מ]ים   4 [...] *vacat*   [...]
[שלושים יום ...] ונענש [בם   5 את מחצית לחמו חמשה ע]שר יום ...]
6 ונענש שלושה הודשים א]ת מחצית לחמו ואיש אשר ידבר לפני] 7 רעהו
הכתוב לפניו והבדיל]הו ... ונענש] *vacat* 8 בם את מחצית לחמו ואיש
אשר יצ]חה ...] *vacat* 9 שלושים יום ואיש אשר יכחש במ]דעו ...]
10 חודשים ונענש במה את מחצית לחמו]*vacat* [...] 11 בדעתו בכול דבר
ונענש שלושים יום]*vacat* [...] 12 בדע]תו ו]הבדילהו ששה הודשים *vacat*
[...]

546

4Q264a (4QHalakhah B) *4QHalakhah B*

Bibliography: Wacholder-Abegg 3, 375-376; E.J.C. Tigchelaar, 'Sabbath Halakha and Worship in 4QWays of Righteousness: 4Q421 11 and 13+2+8 par 4Q264a 1-2', *RevQ* 18/71 (1998) 359-372

Frag. 1 (= 4Q421 13+2+8) *1* [… except for one thousa]nd cubits. A man should not take *2* […] Also the priests, the sons of *3* [Aaron … all] the burnt-offerings and the sacrifices which *4* […a scroll] of a book to [rea]d its writing on the day [of sabbath …] *5* […they shall rea]d and they shall teach them. Let no-one plan [aloud] *6* […] about all matters of work or about wealth or [about gain …] *7* […] on the day of sa[bba]th. And one shoud not sp[eak a wor]d except to [speak] *8* [holy words. According to the precept one shall spe]ak to praise God. Indeed one may speak [a word] regarding eating or dr[inking …]

Frag. 3 *1* … […] *2* after them to […] *3* and wood. And everyone […] *4* at home [or] in the city […] *5* to fight with him […]

4Q265 *4QMiscellaneous Rules*

García Martínez (eds.), *New Qumran Texts and Studies*, 3-10, pl. 1; .- 'Scripture and Law in 4Q265', in M.E. Stone, E.G. Chazon (eds.), *Biblical Perspectives: Early Use and Interpretation of the Bible in Light of the Dead Sea Scrolls* (STDJ 28; Leiden: Brill, 1998) 25-33

Frag. 1 *col.* I *1-2* […] … […] *3* [… t]en days. *Blank* […] *4* […] thirty days [… and shall be punished] because of them *5* to half his bread, for fifte[en days …] *6* he shall be punished for three months [to half his bread. And anyone who speaks before] *7* his fellow who is listed before him, shall be excluded [… and he shall be punished] *8* because of them to half his bread. *Blank* And whoever in[sults …] *9* thirty days. *Blank* And whoever cheats k[nowingly …] *10* months and shall be punished because of them to half his bread *Blank* […] *11* knowingly in any matter, shall be punished for thirty days. *Blank* […] *12* know[ingly,] shall be excluded for six months. *Blank* […]

יום] 2 [וישׁ]ן במושב הרב[ים] וׁנׁעׁנשׁ שׁלושׁ[ים] 1 [... *Frag. 1* ɪɪ

[...].להׁ[יבוא אשׁר ואׁי]ש ... [3 ואם פׁעמים עד [שׁ]לושׁ [יׁ]נׁוׁם הׁספר...[

...] 5 שׁנה ידׁרׁשׁו [שׁ]כׁלׁו לו נׁפל אם הרבים [... 4 ד]הׁיׁחׁ עׁצת אל

[נאמן ... 6 המבקר על היחד ימצא לא ואם [עלׁי]וׁ וׁנׁשׁאׁלׁו הרבים [פׁ]נׁי [ל

[...] שׁנׁת לו [ובׁמׁלׁאׁוׁ]ת תמׁימה שׁנה [עׁוׁד] 7 [...] יׁ ולא התורה ב[פׁרוׁש]

[...].הוא יבׁוׁא [כׁ]אׁשׁ[ר]... 9 [...]רׁבׁים הׁ על הׁמׁבׁקׁר שׁ[... 8

כתוב [כׁאשׁר ... 3 [...] כׁ]אׁשׁר כׁתׁובׁ[2 [...] מׁ.[...] 1 *Frag. 2*

כׁי חׁלׁה לא וׁ[צׁהׁלׁי רׁנׁה פׁצׁחׁי ילׁדה לא עׁקׁרׁה רׁנׁי] 4 הׁנׁבׁיׁא ישׁעׁיׁה בׁס[פׁר

[לׁדׁ]ךׁ אׁוׁה[בׁי מׁ]קׁום הׁרׁחׁי[בׁי והׁוׁה אׁמׁר בׁעׁולׁה מׁבׁנׁי שׁוׁמׁמׁה] 5 בׁנׁי רׁבׁים

[...]...[...] 6

בׁרׁאׁנׁו 2 אׁחׁד אׁל הׁלׁוׁא לׁכׁלׁנׁו אׁחׁד אׁב הׁלׁוׁא [...].[...] 1 *Frag. 4*

זׁעׁטׁוׁט נׁעׁר יׁוׁאׁכׁל 3 [אׁל אׁבׁוׁתׁיׁנׁו בׁרׁיׁת לׁחׁלׁל [אׁחׁיׁהׁו בׁ]אׁ[יׁ]שׁ נׁבׁגׁוׁד מׁדׁוׁעׁ

[... הׁפׁסׁחׁ]גׁ[בׁחׁ] וׁאׁשׁה

בׁגׁדׁי]ם עׁלׁיׁו יׁקׁח [אׁל הׁשׁבׁת בׁיׁום 3 [...] הׁשׁ]בׁת 2 [...] 1 *Frag. 7* ɪ

בׁיׁום 5 [...] אׁוׁ [בׁהׁם עׁפׁר אׁ]שׁר בׁבׁגׁדׁים אׁישׁ [...].[...] אׁל 4 [...] צׁואׁים

בׁיׁום 6 [לׁ]וׁמׁאׁכׁל כׁלׁי מׁאׁהׁלׁו אׁיׁ[שׁ יׁוׁ]צׁיׁא אׁל *vacat* הׁשׁבׁת *vacat*

וׁאׁם הׁשׁבׁת בׁיׁום הׁמׁים]אׁל 7 תׁפׁול אׁשׁר בׁחׁמׁה אׁישׁ יׁעׁל אׁל הׁשׁבׁת *vacat*

בׁגׁדׁו אׁת לׁו יׁשׁלׁחׁ הׁשׁבׁת [בׁיׁום] 8 הׁמׁים אׁל תׁפׁול אׁשׁר הׁיׁא אׁדׁם נׁפׁשׁ

[...]צׁבׁא[וׁאׁם הׁשׁבׁת] בׁיׁום ... 9 ישׁא לׁא וׁכׁלׁי בׁו לׁהׁעׁלׁוׁתׁו

[... וׁלׁא הׁ]שׁבׁת בׁיׁום ... 2 [...] הׁ]שׁבׁת בׁיׁום אׁ[...] 1 *Frag. 7* ɪɪ

[יׁכׁב]סׁו 4 [אׁל וׁגׁם אׁל יׁרׁחׁצׁו וׁגׁם הׁשׁבׁת בׁ]יׁום אׁהׁרׁון מׁזׁרׁע אׁישׁ זׁ[יׁ אׁ]לׁ 3

[...הׁ]מׁאׁ אׁלׁפׁים יׁלׁך בׁהׁמׁה אׁ[תׁ] 5 [...] הׁכׁפׁורׁים בׁיׁום] וׁצׁום גׁדׁול [בׁיׁ]וׁם

חׁמׁשׁה הׁיׁחׁד בׁעׁצׁת [בׁ]הׁיׁוׁת 7 [...] יׁמׁ[וׁשׁ אׁל רׁסׁ שׁלׁושׁים קׁדׁשׁ]הׁמׁ 6

רׁצׁון 9 [בׁחׁיׁרׁיׁ ... בׁאׁמׁת הׁיׁחׁ]ד עׁצׁת נׁכׁונׁה בׁיׁ]אׁים הׁנׁ[8 [... אׁישׁ עׁ]שׁר

עׁולׁה קׁצׁי בׁמׁשׁפׁט וׁסׁפׁה 10 [... שׁמׁטׁה מׁאׁ]רׁץ הׁ[אׁ]על לׁכׁפׁר נׁיׁחׁוׁח וׁרׁיׁח

הׁובׁא לׁא אׁשׁר 12 [עׁד ... אׁדׁם נׁבׁרׁא וׁן]הׁראׁישׁ בׁשׁבׁוע *vacat* 11 [...]הׁמׁ]וׁ

Frag. 1 *col.* II *1* [… and goes to sle]ep in the session of the Many, shall be punished for thir[ty] *2* [days …] of the book sleeps up to three times; and if *3* [… And] whoever enters to […] the council of the [communi]ty *4* […] the Many, if his [ins]ight (?) is allotted to him, they shall investigate for a year […] *5* […] be[fo]re the Many, and they shall be questioned [with regard to hi]m. And if he is not found *6* [trustworthy …] the Inspector of the community with regard to [the interpretation of] the law and not shall he […] *7* […] yet another full year. [And when] the year of [… is comp]lete […] *8* […] the Inspector of the Many […] *9* [… w]hen he enters […]

Frag. 2 *1* […] … […] *2* [… a]s is written […] *3* [… as] is written in the b[ook] of the prophet Isaiah: *4* [*Isa 54:1-2* «Sing, o barren woman, who never bore a child, burst into song and] shout, who have never been in labour. For more numerous will be the children of *5* [the deserted one, than the children of the wedded one, says YHWH.] Enlar[ge the s]ite of [your] ten[t,] *6* […] … […]

Frag. 4 *1* […] … [… *Mal 2:10* «Do we not all have the same father? Has not one God] *2* created us? Then why would we act faithless on[e to] another [by profaning the covenant of our fathers?» Not should] *3* an under-age boy or a woman eat the Passover [fea]st […]

Frag. 7 *col.* I *1* […] *2* the sa[bbath …] *3* on the sabbath day. No-one should [wear] dirty [clothe]s […] *4* […] No-one […] with clothes wh[ich] have dust on them or […] *5* on the sabbath *Blank* day. *Blank* No-[on]e should [take out] of his tent a vessel or foo[d] *6* on the sabbath *Blank* day. *Blank* No-one should take out an animal which has fallen *7* in[to] water on the sabbath day. But if it is a man who has fallen into water *8* [on] the sabbath [day,] he may throw his garment to him to lift him out with it. No-one should carry a vessel *9* [… on] the sabbath [day]. And if an army […] …

Frag. 7 *col.* II *1* […] on the [sabbath] day […] *2* [… on the] sabbath [day]. And not […] *3* [N]o-one from the seed of Aaron may sprinkle on [the sabbath day, and also they should not wash nor] *4* [bat]he [on] the great fasting [d]ay, on the day [of Atonement …] *5* [wi]th animals shall walk two thousand cubi[ts …] *6* [the te]mple, thirty stadia. Do not rem[ove …] *7* [When] there are in the community council fifte[en men …] *8* [the pr]ophets, the commun[ity] council will be [firmly] established [… those chosen of] *9* (his) will, and it shall be an aroma of a pleasant fragrance to atone for the land (cleansing it) from [its] g[uilt …] *10* shall end in the judgment of the times of injustice and […] *11* *Blank* In the fir[st] week [Adam was created … be-] *12* fore he was brought

אל גן עדן *vacat* ועצם [מעצמיו ...] 13 [ה]יה לה עד אשר לא הובאה
אצלו[ן] בשבוע השני [...] 14 [כי]קדוש גן עדן וכול האב אשר בתוכו קודש
על כ[ן] אשה כי תזריע וילדה זכר] 15 וטמאה שבעת ימים כימי נדת דותה
תטמא ושל[ושים יום ושלושת ימים תשב על דם] 16 ט[ו]הרה *vacat* ואם
נקבה תלד וטמאה[ן] שבועים כנדתה וששים יום וששת ימים] 17 [תש]ב
בדם טוהרה בכול קודש [לא תגע ...]

CD-A *Damascus Document*[a]

E. Qimron in M. Broshi (ed.), *The Damascus Document Reconsidered* (Jerusalem, 1992)
Cambridge University Library
CD-B, 4Q266, 4Q267, 4Q268, 4Q269, 4Q270, 4Q271, 4Q272, 4Q273, 5Q12, 6Q15
Bibliography: S. Schechter, *Documents of Jewish Sectaries. Vol. 1: Fragments of a Zadokite Work* (Cambridge, 1910; New York, 1970); L. Ginzberg, *Eine unbekannte jüdische Sekte* (New York, 1922); .- *An Unknown Jewish Sect* (New York, 1967); S. Zeitlin, *The Zadokite Fragments. Facsimile of the Manuscripts in the Cairo Genizah Collection in the Possession of the University Library, Cambridge,*

Col. I 1 *vacat* ועתה שמעו כל יודעי צדק ובינו במעשי 2 אל כי ריב
לו עם כל בשר ומשפט יעשה בכל מנאציו 3 כי במועלם אשר עזבוהו
הסתיר פניו מישראל וממקדשו 4 ויתנם לחרב ובזכרו ברית ראשנים
השאיר שארית 5 לישראל ולא נתנם לכלה ובקץ חרון שנים שלוש מאות
6 ותשעים לתיתו אותם ביד נבוכדנאצר מלך בבל 7 פקדם ויצמח מישראל
ומאהרן שורש מטעת לירוש 8 את ארצו ולדשן בטוב אדמתו ויבינו בעונם
וידעו כי 9 {אנשים} אשימים הם ויהיו כעורים וכימגששים דרך 10 שנים
עשרים ויבן אל אל מעשיהם כי בלב שלם דרשוהו 11 ויקם להם מורה
צדק להדריכם בדרך לבו *vacat* ויודע 12 לדורות אחרונים את אשר עשה
בדור אחרון בעדת בוגדים 13 הם סרי דרך היא העת אשר היה כתוב עליה

into the garden of Eden. *Blank* And bone [from his bones ...] *13* [w]as for her before she was brought to his side [in the second week ...] *14* [for] holy is the garden of Eden. And every shoot which is in its middle, is holy. Therefo[re *Lev 12:2-5* a woman who conceives and bears a male child] *15* shall be impure for seven days; as in the days of her menstrual impurity, she shall be impure. And th[irty-three days she shall remain in the blood of] *16* her purification. *Blank* But if she gives birth to a baby girl, she shall be impure [for two weeks, as in her menstruation, and sixty-six days] *17* [she shall rem]ain in the blood of her purification. [No] holy thing [shall she touch ...]

CD-A *Damascus Document*[a]

England (Philadelphia, 1952); C. Rabin, *The Zadokite Documents* (Oxford, 1954); O.J.R. Schwarz, *Der erste Teil der Damaskusschrift und das Alte Testament* (Diest: Lichtland, 1965); P.R. Davies, *The Damascus Covenant. An Interpretation of the "Damascus Document"* (Sheffield, 1983); J.M. Baumgarten in *PTSDSSP 2*, 17-29, 39-57; H. Stegemann, 'Das Gesetzeskorpus der 'Damaskusschrift' (CD IX-XVI)', *RevQ* 14/55 (1990) 409-434; Ch. Hempel, *The Laws of the Damascus Document. Sources, Traditions, and Redaction* (Leiden: Brill, 1998); *bibliographical data in* J.A. Fitzmyer, 'Prolegomenon', in S. Schechter, *Fragments of a Zadokite Work* (New York, 1970) 25-34; *and* F. García Martínez, 'Bibliography', in M. Broshi (ed.), *The Damascus Document Reconsidered*

Col. I (= 4Q266 2 I-II; 4Q268 1) *1 Blank* And now, listen, all those who know justice, and understand the actions of *2* God; for he has a dispute with all flesh and will carry out judgment on all those who spurn him. *3* For when they were unfaithful in forsaking him, he hid his face from Israel and from his sanctuary *4* and delivered them up to the sword. But when he remembered the covenant with the forefathers, he saved a remnant *5* for Israel and did not deliver them up to destruction. And at the period of wrath, three hundred and *6* ninety years after having delivered them up into the hand of Nebuchadnezzar, king of Babylon, *7* he visited them and caused to sprout from Israel and from Aaron a shoot of the planting, in order to possess *8* his land and to become fat with the good things of his soil. And they realised their iniquity and knew that *9* they were guilty {men}; but they were like blind persons and like those who grope for a path *10* over twenty years. And God appraised their deeds, because they sought him with an undivided heart, *11* and raised up for them a Teacher of Righteousness, in order to direct them in the path of his heart. *Blank* And he made known *12* to the last generations what he had done for the last generation, the congregation of traitors. *13* These are the ones who stray from the

כפרה סוררה   14 כן סרר ישראל בעמוד איש הלצון אשר הטיף לישראל
15 מימי כזב ויתעם בתוהו לא דרך להשח גבהות עולם ולסור   16 מנתיבות
צדק ולסיע גבול אשר גבלו ראשנים בנחלתם למען   17 הדבק בהם את
אלות בריתו להסגירם לחרב נקמת נקם   18 ברית בעבור אשר דרשו
בחלקות ויבחרו במהתלות ויצפו   19 לפרצות ויבחרו בטוב הצואר ויצדיקו
רשע וירשיעו צדיק   20 ויעבירו ברית ויפירו חוק ויגודו על נפש צדיק
ובכל הולכי   21 תמים תעבה נפשם וירדפום לחרב ויסיסו לריב עם ויחר
אף

1   אל בעדתם להשם את כל המונם ומעשיהם לנדה לפניו   Col. II
2 vacat ועתה שמעו אלי כל באי ברית ואגלה אזנכם בדרכי   3 רשעים
vacat אל אהב דעת חכמה ותושייה הציב לפניו   4 ערמה ודעת הם ישרתוהו
ארך אפים עמו ורוב סליחות   5 לכפר בעד שבי פשע וכוח וגבורה וחמה
גדולה בלהבי אש   6 בי(ד) כל מלאכי חבל על סררי דרך ומתעבי חק לאין
שאירית   7 ופליטה למו כי לא בחר אל בהם מקדם עולם ובטרם נוסדו ידע
8 את מעשיהם ויתעב את דורות מדם ויסתר את פניו מן הארץ
9 מי(שראל) עד תומם וידע את שני מעמד ומספר ופרוש קציהם לכל
10 הוי עולמים ונהיית (ונהיות) עד מה יבוא בקציהם לכל שני עולם
11 ובכולם הקים לו קריאי שם למען התיר פליטה לארץ ולמלא   12 פני
תבל מזרעם vacat ויודיעם ביד משיחו (משיחי) רוח קדשו וחוזי   13 אמת
ובפרוש שמו שמותיהם ואת אשר שנא התעה vacat   14 vacat ועתה בנים
שמעו לי ואגלה עיניכם לראות ולהבין במעשי   15 אל ולבחור את אשר
רצה ולמאוס כאשר (באשר) שנא להתהלך תמים   16 בכל דרכיו ולא לתור
במחשבות יצר אשמה וע(י)ני זנות כי רבים   17 תעו בם וגבורי חיל נכשלו
בם מלפנים ועד הנה בלכתם בשרירות   18 לבם נפלו עירי השמים בה
נאחזו אשר לא שמרו מצות אל   19 ובניהם אשר כרום ארזים גבהם

path. This is the time about which it has been written: *Hos 4:16* «Like a stray heifer *14* so has Israel strayed», when «the scoffer» arose, who poured out over Israel *15* waters of lies and made them stray into a wilderness without path, causing the everlasting heights to sink down, diverging *16* from tracks of justice and removing the boundary with which the forefathers had marked their inheritance, so that *17* the curses of his covenant would adhere to them, to deliver them up to the sword carrying out the vengeance *18* of the covenant. For they sought easy interpretations, chose illusions, scrutinised *19* loopholes, chose the handsome neck, acquitted the guilty and sentenced the just, *20* violated the covenant, broke the precept, banded together against the life of the just man, their soul abominated all those who walk *21* in perfection, they hunted them down with the sword and provoked the dispute of the people. And kindled was the wrath of

Col. II (= 4Q266 2 II) *1* God against their congregation, laying waste all its great number, for their deeds were unclean in front of him. *2 Blank* And now, listen to me, all who enter the covenant, and I will open your ears to the paths of *3* the wicked. *Blank* God loves knowledge; he has established wisdom and counsel before him; *4* prudence and knowledge are at his service; patience is his and abundance of pardon, *5* to atone for those who repent from sin; however, strength and power and a great anger with flames of fire *6* by the ‹hand› of all the angels of destruction against those turning aside from the path and abominating the precept, without there being for them either a remnant *7* or survivor. For God did not choose them at the beginning of the world, and before they were established he knew *8* their deeds, and abominated the generations on account of blood and hid his face from the land, *9* from ‹Israel›, until their extinction. And he knew the years of existence, and the number and detail of their ages, of all *10* those who exist over the centuries, ‹and of those who will exist›, until it occurs in their ages throughout all the everlasting years. *11* And in all of them he raised up men of renown for himself, to leave a remnant for the land and in order to fill *12* the face of the world with their offspring. *Blank* And he taught them by the hand of ‹the anointed ones› with his holy spirit and through seers of the *13* truth, and their names were established with precision. But those he hates, he causes to stray. *Blank 14 Blank* And now, sons, listen to me and I shall open your eyes so that you can see and understand the deeds of *15* God, so that you can choose what he is pleased with and repudiate what he hates, so that you can walk perfectly *16* on all his paths and not allow yourselves to be attracted by the thoughts of a guilty inclination and lascivious eyes. For many *17* have gone astray due to these; brave heroes stumbled on account of them, from ancient times until now. For having walked in the stubbornness *18* of their hearts the Watchers of the heavens fell; on account of it they were caught, for they did not heed the precepts of God. *19* And their sons, whose height was like that of cedars and whose bodies were like mountains,

וכהרים גויותיהם כי נפלו   20 כל בשר היה אשר היה בחרבה כי גוע ויהיו כלא
היו בעשותם את   21 רצונם ולא שמרו את מצות עשיהם עד אשר חרה אפו
בם

Col. III   1 *vacat* בה תעי (תעו) בני נח ומשפחותיהם בה הם נכרתים
2 אברהם לא הלך בה ויעל אוהב בשמרו מצות אל ולא בחר   3 ברצון רוחו
וימסור ליצחק וליעקב וישמרו ויכתבו אוהבים   4 לאל ובעלי ברית לעולם
vacat בני יעקב תעו בם ויענשו לפני   5 משגותם ובניהם במצרים הלכו
בשרירות לבם להיעץ (להועץ) על   6 מצות אל ולעשות איש הישר בעיניו
ויאכלו את הדם ויכרת   7 זכורם במדבר (וידבר) להם בקדש עלו ורשו את
(הארץ ויבחרו את רצון) רוחם ולא שמעו   8 לקול עשיהם מצות יוריהם
וירגנו באהליהם ויחר אף אל   9 בעדתם ובניהם בו אבדו ומלכיהם בו
נכרתו וגיבוריהם בו   10 אבדו וארצם בו שממה בו הבו (חבו) באי הברית
הראשנים ויסגרו   11 לחרב בעזבם את ברית אל ויבחרו ברצונם ויתורו
אחרי שרירות   12 לבם לעשות איש את רצונו *vacat* ובמחזיקים במצות אל
13 אשר נותרו מהם הקים אל את בריתו לישראל עד עולם לגלות   14 להם
נסתרות אשר תעו בם כל ישראל *vacat* שבתות קדשו ומועדי   15 כבודו
עידות צדקו ודרכי אמתו וחפצי רצונו אשר יעשה   16 האדם וחיה בהם
vacat פתח לפניהם ויחפרו באר למים רבים   17 ומואסיהם לא יחיה והם
התגוללו בפשע אנוש ובדרכי נדה   18 ויאמרו כי לנו היא ואל ברזי פלאו
כפר בעד עונם וישא לפשעם   19 ויבן להם בית נאמן בישראל אשר לא
עמד כמהו למלפנים ועד   20 הנה המחזיקים בו לחיי נצח וכל כבוד אדם
להם הוא כאשר   21 הקים אל להם ביד יחזקאל הנביא לאמר הכהנים
והלוים ובני

Col. IV   1 צדוק אשר שמרו את משמרת מקדשי בתעות בני ישראל
2 מעליהם (מעלי הם) יגישו לי חלב ודם *vacat* הכהנים הם שבי ישראל

554

fell. *20* All flesh which there was on the dry earth expired and they became as if they had never been, because they had realized *21* their desires and had failed to keep their creator's precepts, until his wrath flared up against them.

Col. III (= 4Q269 2)   *1 Blank* Through it, the sons of Noah and their families strayed, through it, they were cut off. *2* Abraham did not walk in it, and was counted as a friend for keeping God's precepts and not following *3* the desire of his spirit. And he passed (them) on to Isaac and to Jacob, and they kept (them) and were written up as friends *4* of God and as members of the covenant for ever. *Blank* Jacob's sons strayed because of them and were punished in accordance with *5* their mistakes. And in Egypt their sons walked in the stubbornness of their hearts, plotting against *6* God's precepts and each one doing what was right in his own eyes; and they ate blood, *7* and their males were cut off in the wilderness. ‹And He spoke› to them in Qadesh: *Deut 9:23* «Go and possess ‹the land›. But they preferred the desire› of their spirit, and did not listen to *8* the voice of their creator, the precepts he had taught them, and murmured in their tents. And the wrath of God flared up *9* against their congregation. And their sons died through it, and through it their kings were cut off, and through it their warriors *10* perished, and through it their land was laid waste. Through it, the very first to enter the covenant made themselves guilty and were delivered up *11* to the sword, for having deserted God's covenant and having chosen their whims, and having followed the stubbornness *12* of their heart, each one doing (what was) his desire. *Blank* But with those who remained steadfast in God's precepts, *13* with those who were left from among them, God established his covenant with Israel for ever, revealing to them *14* hidden matters in which all Israel had gone astray: *Blank* his holy sabbaths and his *15* glorious feasts, his just stipulations and his truthful paths, and the wishes of his will which *16* man must do in order to live by them. *Blank* He disclosed (these matters) to them and they dug a well of plentiful water; *17* and whoever spurns them shall not live. But they had defiled themselves with human sin and unclean paths, *18* and they had said: «For this is ours». But God, in his wonderful mysteries, atoned for their iniquity and pardoned their sin. *19* And he built for them a safe home in Israel, such as there has not been since ancient times, not even till *20* now. Those who remained steadfast in it will acquire eternal life, and all the glory of Adam is for them. As *21* God swore to them by means of Ezekiel the prophet, saying: *Ez 44:15* «The priests and the levites and the sons of

Col. IV (= 6Q15 1)   *1* Zadok who maintained the service of my temple when the children of Israel strayed *2* far away from me; they shall offer me the fat and the blood». *Blank* The priests are the converts of Israel *3* who left the land of

3 היוצאים מארץ יהודה והנלוים (והלוים הם הנלוים) עמהם vacat ובני
צדוק הם בחירי 4 ישראל קריאי השם העמדים באחרית הימים הנה פרוש
5 שמותיהם לתולדותם וקץ מעמדם ומספר צרותיהם ושני 6 התגוררם
ופירוש מעשיהם vacat הקודש (הם הרא)שונים אשר כפר 7 אל בעדם
ויצדיקו צדיק וירשיעו רשע וכל הבאים אחריהם 8 לעשות כפרוש התורה
אשר התוסרו בו הראשנים עד שלים 9 הקץ השנים האלה כברית אשר
הקים אל לראשנים לכפר 10 על עונותיהם כן יכפר אל בעדם ובשלום
הקץ למספר השנים 11 האלה אין עוד להשתפח לבית יהודה כי אם לעמוד
איש על 12 מצודו נבנתה הגדר רחק החיק (החוק) ובכל השנים האלה
יהיה 13 בליעל משולח בישראל כאשר דבר אל ביד ישעיה הנביא בן
14 אמוץ לאמר פחד ופחת ופח עליך יושב הארץ vacat פשרו 15 שלושת
מצודות בליעל אשר אמר עליהם לוי בן יעקב 16 אשר הוא תפש בהם
בישראל ויתנם פניהם לשלושת מיני 17 הצדק הראשונה היא הזנות
השנית ההין (ההון) השלישית 18 טמא המקדש העולה מזה יתפש בזה
והניצל מזה יתפש 19 בזה vacat בוני החיץ אשר הלכו אחרי צו הצו הוא
מטיף 20 אשר אמר הטף יטיפון הם ניתפשים בשתים בזנות לקחת
21 שתי נשים בחייהם ויסוד הבריאה זכר ונקבה ברא אותם

Col. v 1 ובאי התבה שנים שנים באו אל התבה vacat ועל הנשיא
כתוב 2 לא ירבה לו נשים ודויד לא קרא בספר התורה החתום אשר
3 היה בארון כי לא {נפ.} נפתח בישראל מיום מות אלעזר 4 ויהושע
ויושׁ'ע והזקנים אשר עבדו את העשתרת ויטמון 5 נגלה עד עמוד צדוק
ויעלו מעשי דויד מלבד דם אוריה 6 ויעזבם לו אל וגם מטמאים הם את
המקדש אשר אין הם 7 מבדיל כתורה ושוכבים עם הרואה את דם זובה
ולוקחים 8 איש את בת אחיה{ם}'י ואת בת אחותו vacat ומשה אמר אל
9 אחות אמך לא תקרב שאר אמך היא ומשפט העריות לזכרים 10 הוא
כתוב וכהם כהנשים ואם תגלה בת האח את ערות אחי 11 אביה והיא שאר
vacat וגם את רוח קדשיהם טמאו ובלשון 12 גדופים פתחו פה על חוקי

Judah; and ‹the levites are› those who joined them; *Blank* and the sons of Zadok are the chosen of *4* Israel, the men of renown, who stand (to serve) at the end of days. Here is the detailed list *5* of their names, according to their genealogies and the age of their standing and the number of their miseries and the years of *6* their residence, and the detailed list of their deeds. *Blank* of holiness ‹are the forefathers›, for whom *7* God atoned, and who declared the just man as just, and declared the wicked as wicked, and all those who entered after them *8* in order to act according to the exact interpretation of the law in which the forefathers were instructed until *9* the period of these years is complete. According to the covenant which God established with the forefathers, in order to atone *10* for their iniquities, so will God atone for them. But when the period corresponding to the number of these years is complete, *11* there will no longer be any joining with the house of Judah but rather each one standing up on *12* his watchtower. The wall is built, the boundary far away. And during all these years *13* Belial will be set loose against Israel, as God has said by means of the prophet Isaiah, son of *14* Amoz, saying: *Isa 24:17* «Panic, pit and net against you, earth-dweller». *Blank* Its explanation: *15* They are Belial's three nets about which Levi, son of Jacob spoke, *16* by which he catches Israel and makes them appear before them like three types of *17* justice. The first is fornication; the second, wealth; the third, *18* defilement of the temple. He who eludes one is caught in another and he who is freed from that, is caught *19* in another. *Blank* The builders of the wall who go after Zaw - Zaw is the preacher *20* of whom he said: *Mic 2:6* «Assuredly they will preach» - are caught twice in fornication: by taking *21* two wives in their lives, even though the principle of creation is *Gen 1:27* «male and female he created them»,

Col. v (= 4Q266 3 ɪɪ; 4Q267 2; 6Q15 2, 3)   *1* and the ones who went into the ark *Gen 7:9* «went in two by two into the ark». *Blank* And about the prince it is written: *2 Deut 17:17* «He should not multiply wives to himself». However, David had not read the sealed book of the law which *3* was in the ark, for it had not been opened in Israel since the day of the death of Eleazar *4* and of Jehoshua, and Joshua and the elders who worshipped Ashtaroth. One had hidden *5* the public (copy) until Zadok's entry into office. And David's deeds were praised, except for Uriah's blood, *6* and God forgave him those. And they also defiled the temple, for they did not *7* keep apart in accordance with the law, but instead lay with her who sees the blood of her menstrual flow. And each man takes as a wife *8* the daughter of his brother and the daughter of his sister. *Blank* But Moses said: *Lev 18:13* «Do *9* not approach your mother's sister, she is a blood relation of your mother». The law of prohibited marriages, *10* written for males, applies equally to females, and therefore to the daughter of a brother who uncovers the nakedness of the brother of *11* her father, for he is a blood relation. *Blank* And also they defile their holy spirit, for with *12* blasphemous tongue they have opened their mouth against the statutes

ברית אל לאמר לא נכונו ותועבה   13   הם מדברים בם כלם קדחי אש
ומבערי זיקות קורי   14   עכביש קוריהם וביצי צפעונים ביציהם הקרוב
אליהם   15   לא ינקה כהר ביתו (כהרבותו) יאשם כי אם נלחץ כי אם
למילפנים פקד   16   אל את מעשיהם ויחר אפו בעלילותיהם כי לא עם בינות
הוא   17   הם גוי אבד עצות מאשר אין בהם בינה כי מלפנים עמד   18   משה
ואהרן ביד שר האורים ויקם בליעל את יחנה ואת   19   אחיהו במזמתו
בהושע ישראל את הראשונה   vacat   20   vacat   ובקץ חרבן הארץ עמדו
מסיגי הגבול ויתעו את ישראל   21   ותישם הארץ כי דברו סרה על מצות
אל ביד משה וגם

Col. VI   1   במשיחו (במשיחי) הקודש וינבאו שקר להשיב את ישראל
מאחר   2   אל ויזכר אל ברית ראשנים *vacat* ויקם מאהרן נבונים ומישראל
3   חכמים וישמיעם ויחפורו את הבאר באר חפרוה שרים כרוה   4   נדיבי
העם במחוקק הבאר היא התורה וחופריה *vacat* הם   5   שבי ישראל
היוצאים מארץ יהודה ויגורו בארץ דמשק   6   אשר קרא אל את כולם שרים
כי דרשוהו ולא הושבה *vacat*   7   פארתם בפי אחד והמחוקק הוא דורש
התורה אשר   8   אמר ישעיה מוציא כלי למעשיהו *vacat* ונדיבי העם הם
9   הבאים לכרות את הבאר במחוקקות אשר חקק המחוקק   10   להתהלך
במה בכל קץ הרשיע וזולתם לא ישיגו עד עמד   11   יורה הצדק באחרית
הימים *vacat* וכל אשר הובאו בברית   12   לבלתי בוא אל המקדש להאיר
מזבחו חנם ויהיו מסגירי   13   הדלת אשר אמר אל מי בכם יסגור דלתי
vacat ולא תאירו מזבחי   14   חנם אם לא ישמרו לעשות כפרוש התורה לקץ
הרשע ולהבדל   15   מבני השחת ולהנזר מהון הרשעה הטמא בנדר ובחרם
16   ובהון המקדש ולגזול את עניי עמו להיות אלמנ[ו]ת שללם   17   ואת
יתומים ירצחו ולהבדיל בין הטמא לטהור ולהודיע בין   18   הקודש לחול
ולשמור את יום השבת כפרושה ואת המועדות   19   ואת יום התענית
כמצאת באי הברית החדשה בארץ דמשק   20   להרים את הקדשים
כפירושיהם לאהוב איש את אחיהו   21   כמהו ולהחזיק ביד עני ואביון וגר
vacat ולדרוש איש את שלום

of God's covenant, saying: «they are unfounded». They speak abomination *13* against them. They are all igniters of fire, kindlers of blazes; webs *14* of a spider are their webs, and their eggs are vipers' eggs. Whoever comes close to them *15* will not be unpunished; ‹the more he does it›, the guiltier he shall be, unless he has been compelled. For already in ancient times *16* God visited their deeds, and his wrath flared up against their actions, for it is not an intelligent people; *17* they are folk bereft of advice, in that there is no intelligence in them. For in ancient times there arose *18* Moses and Aaron, by the hand of the prince of lights and Belial, with his cunning, raised up Jannes and *19* his brother during the first deliverance of Israel. *Blank 20 Blank* And in the age of devastation of the land there arose those who shifted the boundary and made Israel stray. *21* And the land became desolate, for they spoke of rebellion against God's precepts (given) through the hand of Moses and also

Col. vi (= 4Q266 3 ii; 4Q267 2; 4Q269 4 ii; 6Q15 3, 4)   *1* of the holy anointed ones. They prophesied deceit in order to divert Israel from following *2* God. But God remembered the covenant of the forefathers. *Blank* And he raised from Aaron men of knowledge and from Israel *3* wise men, and made them listen. And they dug the well: *Num 21:18* «A well which the princes dug, which *4* the nobles of the people delved with the staff». The well is the law. And those who dug it *Blank* are *5* the converts of Israel, who left the land of Judah and lived in the land of Damascus, *6* all of whom God called princes, for they sought him, and their renown has not been repudiated *7* in anyone's mouth. *Blank* And the staff is the interpreter of the law, of whom *8* Isaiah said: *Isa 54:16* «He produces a tool for his labour». *Blank* And the nobles of the people are *9* those who came to dig the well with the staves that the sceptre decreed, *10* to walk in them throughout the whole age of wickedness, and without which they will not obtain it, until there arises *11* he who teaches justice at the end of days. *Blank* But all those who have been brought into the covenant *12* shall not enter the temple to kindle his altar in vain. They will be the ones who close *13* the door, as God said: *Mal 1:10* «Whoever amongst you will close my door *Blank* so that you do not kindle my altar *14* in vain!». They should take care to act in accordance with the exact interpretation of the law for the age of wickedness: to keep apart *15* from the sons of the pit; to abstain from wicked wealth which defiles, either by promise or by vow, *16* and from the wealth of the temple and from stealing from the poor of his people, making widows their spoils *17* and murdering orphans; to separate unclean from clean and differentiate between *18* the holy and the common; to keep the sabbath day according to its exact interpretation, and the festivals *19* and the day of fasting, according to what was discovered by those who entered the new covenant in the land of Damascus; *20* to set apart holy portions according to their exact interpretation; for each to love his brother *21* like himself; to strengthen the hand of the poor, the needy and the foreigner; *Blank* for each to seek the peace

Col. VII 1 אחיהו ולא ימעל איש בשארו להזיר מן הזונות
2 כמשפט להוכיח איש את אחיהו כמצוה ולא לנטור 3 מיום ליום ולהבדל
מכל הטמאות כמשפטם ולא ישקץ 4 איש את רוח קדשיו כאשר הבדיל אל
להם כל המתהלכים 5 באלה בתמים קדש על פי כל יסורו ברית אל
נאמנות להם 6 לחיותם אלף דור vacat ואם מחנות ישבו כסדך (כסרך)
הארץ ולקחו 7 נשים והולידו בנים והתהלכו על פי התורה vacat וכמשפט
8 היסורים כסרך התורה כאשר אמר בין איש לאשתו ובין אב 9 לבנו וכל
המואסים בפקד אל את הארץ להשיב גמול רשעים 10 עליהם בבוא הדבר
אשר כתוב בדברי ישעיה בן אמוץ הנביא 11 אשר אמר יבוא עליך ועל
עמך ועל בית אביך ימים אשר 12 (לא) באו מיום סור אפרים מעל יהודה
בהפרד שני בתי ישראל 13 שר אפרים מעל יהודה וכל הנסוגים הᵒסגרו
לחרב והמחזיקים 14 נמלטו לארץ צפון vacat כאשר אמר והגליתי את
סכות מלככם 15 ואת כיון צלמיכם מאהלי דמשק vacat ספרי התורה הם
סוכת 16 המלך כאשר אמר והקימותי את סוכת דוד הנפלת vacat המלך
17 הוא הקהל וכיניי הצלמים וכיון הצלמים הם ספרי הנביאים 18 אשר
בזה ישראל את דבריהם vacat והכוכב הוא דורש התורה 19 הבא דמשק
כאשר כתוב דרך כוכב מיעקב וקם שבט 20 מישראל השבט הוא נשיא כל
העדה ובעמדו וקרקר 21 את כל בני שת vacat אלה מלטו בקק הפקודה
הראשון

Col. VIII 1 והנסוגים הסגירו לחרב וכן משפט כל באי בריתו אשר
2 לא יחזיקו באלה לפוקדם לכלה ביד בליעל הוא היום 3 אשר יפקד אל
היו שרי יהודה אשר תשפוך עליהם העברה 4 כי יחלו למרפא וידקמום
(וידבק מום) כל מורדים מאשר לא סרו מדרך 5 בוגדים ויתגוללו בדרכי
זונות ובהון רשעה ונקום וניטור 6 איש לאחיו ושנוא איש את רעהו
ויתעלמו איש בשאר בשרו 7 ויגשו לזמה ויתגברו להון ולבצע ויעשו איש
הישר בעיניו 8 ויבחרו איש בשרירות לבו ולא נזרו מעם ויפרעו ביד רמה

560

Col. VII (cf. CD-B XIX; = 4Q266 3 III)   *1* of his brother and not to be unfaithful against his blood relation; to refrain from fornication *2* in accordance with the regulation; for each to reprove his brother in accordance with the precept, and not to bear resentment *3* from one day to the next; to keep apart from every uncleanness according to their regulations, without anyone defiling *4* his holy spirit, according to what God kept apart for them. For all those who walk *5* according to these matters in holy perfectness, in accordance with all his teachings, God's covenant is a guarantee for them *6* that they shall live a thousand generations. *Blank* And if they reside in camps in accordance with the rule of the land, and take *7* women and beget children, they shall walk in accordance with the law *Blank* and according to the regulation *8* of the teachings, according to the rule of the law, as he said: *Num 30:17* « Between a man and his wife, and between a father *9* and his son ». But (for) all those who despise: when God visits the earth in order to empty over them the punishment of the wicked, *10* when there comes the word which is written in the words of Isaiah, son of Amoz, the prophet, *11* who said: *Isa 7:17* « There shall come upon you, upon your people and upon your father's house, days such as *12* have ‹not› come since the day Ephraim departed from Judah ». When the two houses of Israel separated, *13* Ephraim detached itself from Judah, and all the renegades were delivered up to the sword; but those who remained steadfast *14* escaped to the land of the north. *Blank* As he said: *Am 5:26-27* « I will deport the Sikkut of your King *15* and the Kiyyun of your images away from my tent to Damascus ». *Blank* The books of the law are the Sukkat *16* of the King, as he said *Am 9:11* « I will lift up the fallen Sukkat of David ». *Blank* The King *17* is the assembly; and the Kiyyune of the images ‹and the Kiyyun of the images› are the books of the prophets, *18* whose words Israel despised. *Blank* And the star is the Interpreter of the law, *19* who will come to Damascus, as is written: *Num 24:13* « A star moves out of Jacob, and a sceptre arises *20* out of Israel ». The sceptre is the prince of the whole congregation and when he rises he will destroy *21* all the sons of Seth. *Blank* These escaped at the time of the first visitation

Col. VIII (cf. CD-B XIX; = 4Q266 3 III)   *1* while the renegades were delivered up to the sword. Thus will be the judgment of all those entering his covenant but who *2* do not remain steadfast in them; they shall be visited for destruction at the hand of Belial. This is the day *3* when God will make a visitation. The princes of Judah are those upon whom the rage will be vented, *4* for they hope to be healed but ‹the defect sticks (to them)›; all are rebels because they have not left the path of *5* traitors and have defiled themselves in paths of licentiousness, and with wicked wealth, avenging themselves, and each one bearing resentment *6* against his brother, and each one hating his fellow. Each one became obscured by blood relatives, *7* and approached for debauchery and bragged about wealth and gain. Each one did what was right in his eyes *8* and each one has chosen the stubbornness of his heart. They did not keep apart

9 ללכת בדרך רשעים אשר אמר אל עליהם חמת תנינים יינם   10 וראש
פתנים אכזר vacat התנינים הם מלכי העמים vacat ויינם הוא   11 דרכיהם
וראש הפתנים הוא ראש מלכי יון הבא לעשות   12 בהם נקמה ובכל אלה
לא הבינו בוני החוץ (החיץ) וטחי התפל כי   13 שוקל רוח ומטיף כזב הטיף
להם אשר חרה אף אל בכל עדתו   14 ואשר אמר משה לא בצדקתך ובישר
לבבך אתה בא לרשת   15 את הגוים האלה כי מאהבתו את אבותך ומשמרו
את השבועה   vacat 16 וכן המשפט לשבי ישראל סרו מדרך העם באהבת
אל את   17 הראשנים אשר היעירו (היעידו) אחריו אהב את הבאים
אחריהם כי להם vacat 18 ברית האבות ובשונאי (ובשונאו) את בוני החוץ
(החיץ) חרה אפו vacat וכמשפט 19 הזה לכל המואס במצות אל ויעזבם
ויפנו בשרירות לבם vacat 20 הוא הדבר אשר אמר ירמיהו לברון בן
נרייה vacat ואלישע 21 לגחזי נערו vacat כל האנשים אשר באו בברית
החדשה בארץ דמשק

Col. xv   1 [יש]בע וגם באלף ולמד וגם באלף ודלת כי אם שבועת
הבנים   2 באלות הברית vacat ואת תורה משה אל יזכור כי בה כל פרוש
השם   vacat 3 ואם ישבע ועבר וחלל את השם vacat ואם באלות הברית
ישב[יעו]   4 השפטים vacat אם עבר אשם הוא והתודה והשיב ולא ישא
חטאה   5 [וי]מות vacat והבא בברית לכל ישראל לחוק עולם את בניהם
אשר יגיעו   6 לעבור על הפקודים בשבועת הברית יקימו עליהם vacat וכן
7 המשפט בכל קץ הרשע לכל השב מדרכו הנשחתה ביום דברו   8 עם
המבקר אשר לרבים יפקדוהו בשבועת הברית אשר כרת   9 משה עם
ישראל את הברית לש[וב] אל תורת משה בכל לב ו[ב]כ[ל]   10 נפש אל
הנמצא לעשות בכ[ל]קץ ק[ר]בו ואל יודיעהו איש את   11 המשפטים עד
עמדו לפני המבקר עומד יתפתה בו בדרשו אתו   12 וכאשר יקים אותו עליו
לשוב אל תורת משה בכל לב ובכל נפש   13 [נק]יאים הם ממנו אם ימעל
vacat וכל אשר נגלה מן התורה לרוב   14 המחנה והוא שגה בו יוד[יעה]ו
המבקר אותו וצוה עליו ויל[מד]   15 עד שנה תמימה ולפי דעתו (יקרב וכל)

562

from the people and have rebelled with insolence, *9* walking on the path of the wicked ones, about whom God says: *Deut 32:33* «Their wine is serpents' venom *10* and cruel poison of asps». *Blank* The serpents are the kings of the peoples *Blank* and their wine is *11* their paths, and the asps' poison is the head of the kings of Greece, who comes to carry out *12* vengeance against them. But the builders of the wall, have not understood all these things, nor those who daub with whitewash, for *13* one who weighs wind and preaches lies, has preached to them, so that God's wrath has been kindled against his entire congregation. *14* And what Moses said: *Deut 9:5* «Not because of your justice, or for the uprightness of your heart are you going to possess *15* these nations, but because he loved your fathers and keeps the oath». *16 Blank* And thus is the judgment of the converts of Israel, who turned aside from the path of the people: on account of God's love for *17* the forefathers who ‹testified› following him, he loves those who come after them, because to them belongs *18* the fathers' covenant. *Blank* And because of ‹his› hatred for the builders of the wall his anger is kindled. *Blank* And like this judgment *19* will be that of all who reject God's precepts and forsake them and move aside in the stubbornness of their heart. *20 Blank* This is the word which Jeremiah spoke to Baruch, son of Neriah, *Blank* and Elishah *21* to Gehazi his servant. *Blank* All the men who entered the new covenant in the land of Damascus

Col. xv (= 4Q266 8 i)   *1* [He will not sw]ear by Aleph and Lamed ('el = God) nor by Aleph and Daleth ('adonai = The Lord), but by the oath of the youths, *2* by the curses of the covenant. *Blank* Neither should one mention the law of Moses, for in it is the full enunciation of the name. *3 Blank* And if he swears and transgresses, he profanes the name. *Blank* If the judges adju[re] (someone) by the curses of the covenant. *4 Blank* If he transgresses, he will be guilty and will have to confess and make amends, and (then) he shall not be liable for sin *5* [and] die. *Blank* Those who enter the covenant, for all Israel for an eternal law, must impose upon their sons who have reached (the age) *6* to go over to the enrolled, the oath of the covenant. *Blank* And such is *7* the regulation, throughout all the age of wickedness, for whoever reverts from his path of corruption. On the day when he talks *8* to the Inspector of the Many, they shall enrol him with the oath of the covenant which Moses established *9* with Israel, the covenant to rev[ert to] the law of Moses with the whole heart and [with] the who[le] *10* soul, to what is found (therein) to do during the com[plete] period of his app[roach]. But no-one should make him know *11* the precepts before he stands in front of the Inspector: when he stands he should be persuaded by him when he tests him. *12* But when he has imposed upon himself to return to the law of Moses with all his heart and all his soul *13* they will [exact re]venge from him if he should become unfaithful. *Blank* All that has been revealed of the law for the multitude *14* of the camp — if he inadvertently fails, the Inspector should tea[ch h]im and give orders concerning him,

היותו אויל ומשוגע (אל יבא) וכל פת]י[ש]ו[גה   16   וכהה עינים לבל]תי
ראות]וחגר[או]פסח א]ו חרש[ונער ז]עטו[ט אל   17   יביא אי]ש מאלה אל
תוך העדה כי מלאכי הקודש]... ...[... 18-20 ...]...[

Col. XVI   1   עמכם ברית ועם כל ישראל על כן יקום (יקים) האיש על
נפשך (נפשו) לשוב אל   2   תורת משה כי בה הכל מדוקדק vacat ופרוש
קציהם לעורון   3   ישראל מכל אלה הנה הוא מדוקדק על ספר מחלקות
העתים   4   ליובליהם ובשבועותיהם וביום אשר יקום (יקים) האיש על
נפשו לשוב   5   אל תורת משה יסור מלאך המשטמה מאחריו אם יקים את
דבריו   6   על כן נימול]ב{ אברהם ביום דעתו vacat ואשר אמר מוצא
שפתיך   7   תשמור להקים vacat כל שבועת אסר אשר יקום (יקים) איש על
נפשו   8   לעשות דבר מן התורה עד מחיר מות אל יפדהו vacat כל אשר
9   ]יק[ים איש על נפשו לסור א]ת התו[רה עד מחיר מות אל יקימהו
10   ]ע[ל שבועת האשה אשר אמ]ר [לא]י[שה להניא את שבועתה אל
11   יניא איש שבועה אשר לא]י[דענה הם להקים היא vacat ואם להניא
12   אם לעבור ברית היא יניאה ואל יקימנה vacat וכן המשפט לאביה
13   על משפט הנדבות אל ידור איש למזבח מאום אנוס וגם   14   ה]כ[הנים
אל יקחו מאת ישראל vacat]אל[יקדש איש את מאכל   15   פיהו]לא[]ל[כי
הוא אשר אמר איש את רעיהו יצדו חרם vacat ואל   16   יקד]ש[איש מכל
א]...[...[... ...[ואם מ]שדה אחזתו   17   ]י[קדש ל]א[ל ג]ם ה[משפט הזה]...
נענש   18   הנודר[את ... ששית כסף ערכו ...[19   לשופט]ים לשפט צדק
... אחר המודר]...   20   אם[אנוס הוא ... ושלם האונס אם לא דבר אמת
עם רעהו]...

Col. IX   1   כל אדם אשר יחרים אדם מאדם בחוקי הגוים להמית הוא
2   ואשר אמר לא תקום ולא תטור את בני עמך וכל איש מביאי   3   הברית
אשר יביא על רעהו דבר אשר לא בהוכח לפני עדים   4   והביאו בחרון אפו
או ספר לזקניו להבזותו נוקם הוא ונוטר vacat   5   ואין כתוב כי אם נוקם

and he should le[arn] *15* for a full year. And in accordance with (his) knowledge ‹he will approach. And no-one› who is stupid or deranged ‹should enter›; and anyone feeble[-minded and insane,] *16* those with eyes too weak t[o see,] the lame [or] one who stumbles, o[r a deaf person,] or an un[der-a]ge boy, none *17* of these should one allow to enter [the congregation, since the holy angels …] … *18-20* […] …

Col. xvi (= 4Q266 8 ii; 4Q270 6 iii; 4Q271 4 ii)   *1* with you a covenant and with all Israel. Therefore, one will impose upon ‹him›self to return to *2* the law of Moses, for in it all is defined. *Blank* And the exact interpretation of their ages about the blindness *3* of Israel in all these matters, behold, it is defined in «The book of the divisions of the periods *4* according to their jubilees and their weeks». And on the day on which one has imposed upon himself to return *5* to the law of Moses, the angel Mastema will turn aside from following him, should he keep his words. *6* This is why Abraham circumcised himself on the day of his knowledge. *Blank* And as for what he said: *Deut 23:24* «What issues from your mouth, *7* keep it to carry it out». *Blank* Every binding oath by which anyone imposes upon himself *8* to fulfil a letter of the law, he should not annul, even at the price of death. *Blank* Anything by which *9* he might impose upon himself to turn away fr[om the la]w, he should not fulfil, not even when the price is death. *10* [Concern]ing the oath of a woman. What he sai[d:] *Num 30:7-9* «Her hus[ba]nd may annul her oath», *11* no-one should annul an oath if he does not know whether it should be carried out *Blank* or annulled. *12* If it would violate the covenant, he should annul it and should not carry it out. *Blank* And the regulation applies also to her father. *13* Concerning the regulation for freewill-offerings. No-one should dedicate anything, obtained by unjust means, to the altar. Neither *14* should the [pr]iests take from Israel (anything obtained by unjust means). *Blank* [No-]one should consecrate the food *15* of his mouth [for G]od, for this is what he said: *Mic 7:2* «Each one traps his fellow with anathema». *Blank* And no-[on]e should *16* consecr[ate] anything of […] and if] *17* [he] consecrates a field of his possession to [God, then al]so th[is regulation applies …] will be punished *18* he who dedicates [… the sixth part of the money which corresponds …] *19* for the judge[s in order to judge with justice … And then the dedicated thing …] *20* If [it is appropriated by violence,… the violator shall pay; if he has not spoken the truth to his fellow …]

Col. ix (= 4Q266 8 ii; 4Q267 9 i; 4Q270 6 iii-iv; 5Q12)   *1 Blank Lev 27:29* «Every man who vows anyone else to destruction» shall be executed according to the laws of the gentiles. *2* And what he said: *Lev 19:18* «Do not avenge yourself or bear resentment against the sons of your people»: everyone of those brought to *3* the covenant who brings an accusation against his fellow, unless it is with reproach before witnesses, *4* or brings it when he is angry, or tells it to his elders so that they might despise him, he is «the one who avenges himself and

הוא לצריו ונוטר הוא לאויביו 6 אם החריש לו מיום ליום ובחרון אפו בו
דבר בו בדבר מות 7 ענה בו יען אשר לא הקים את מצות אל אשר אמר לו
הוכח 8 תוכיח את רעיך ולא תשא עליו חטא vacat על השבועה אשר
9 אמר לא תושיעך ידך לך איש אשר ישביע על פני השדה 10 אשר לא
לפנים השפטים או מאמרם הושיע ידו לו וכל האובד 11 ולא נודע מי גנבו
ממאד המחנה אשר גנב בו ישביע בעליו 12 בשבועת האלה והשומע אם
יודע הוא ולא יגיד ואשם vacat 13 כל אשם מושב אשר אין בעלים
והתורה (והתודה) המישב (המשיב) לכהן 14 והיה לו לבד מאיל האשם
vacat {וכל} וכן כל אבדה נמצאת ואין 15 לה בעלים והיתה לכהנים כי לא
ידע מוצאיה את משפטה 16 אם לא נמצא לה בעלים הם ישמרו vacat כל
דבר אשר ימעל 17 איש בתורה וראה רעיהו והוא אחד אם דבר מות הוא
וידיעהו 18 לעיניו vacat בהוכיח למבקר והמבקר יכתבהו בידו עד עשותו
19 עוד לפני אחד ושב והודיע למבקר אם ישוב וניתפש לפני 20 אחד שלם
משפטו vacat ואם שנים הם והם מעידים על 21 דבר אחר והובדל האיש
מן הטהרה לבד vacat אם נאמנים 22 הם וביום ראות האיש יודיעה למבקר
ועל ההון יקבלו שני 23 עידים נאמנים vacat ועל אחד להבדיל הטהרה ואל
יקובל

1 עוד (עיד) לשופטים להמית על פיהו אשר לא מלאו ימיו   Col. x
לעבור 2 על הפקודים ירא את אל vacat אל יאמן איש על רעהו 3 לעד
עובר דבר מן המצוה ביד רמה עד זכו לשוב vacat 4 וזה סרך לשפטי העדה
עד עשרה אנשים ברורים 5 מן העדה לפי העת ארבעה למטה לוי ואהרן
ומישראל 6 ששה מבוננים בספר ההגי וביסודי הברית מבני חמשה
7 ועשרים שנה עד בני ששים שנה ואל יתיצב עוד מבן 8 ששים שנה
ומעלה לשפוט את העדה כי במעל האדם 9 מעטו ימו ובחרון אף אל
ביושבי הארץ אמר לסור (לסיר) את 10 דעתם עד לא ישלימו את ימיהם
על הטהר במים אל 11 ירחץ איש במים צואים ומעוטים מדי מרעיל איש

bears resentment». *5 Blank* Is it not perhaps written that only *Nah 1:2* «he (God) avenges himself on his foes and bears resentment against his enemies»? *6* If he kept silent about him from one day to the other, and then, when he was angry, accused him of a capital offence, *7* he has testified against himself, for he did not fulfil the commandment of God who said to him: *Lev 19:17* «You shall *8* reproach your fellow so as not to incur sin because of him». *Blank* Concerning the oath. What *9* he said: *1 Sam 25:26* «You shall not do justice with your (own) hand»: whoever forces the making of an oath in the open field, *10* not in the presence of judges or at their command, has done justice for himself with his hand. Every lost object *11* about which it is not known who stole it from the property of the camp in which it was stolen - its owner should make a maledictory *12* oath; whoever hears it, if he knows and does not say it, is guilty. *13 Blank* (If there is) any debt due to be given back, but there are no creditors, then the debtor should confess to the priest *14* and it will be for himself, apart from the ram of the sin-offering. *Blank* And in the same way, every lost object which has been found and has *15* no owners, will be for the priests, for he who found it does not know the regulation in its regard; *16* if its owners are not found, they shall keep it. *Blank* Any matter in which a man sins *17* against the law, and his fellow sees him and he is alone: if it is a capital matter, he shall report it *18* in his presence, *Blank* with reproach, to the Inspector; and the Inspector shall personally record it, until he does it *19* again in the presence of someone, and he too reports it to the Inspector; and if he is caught again in the presence of *20* someone, his judgment is complete. *Blank* But if there are two, and they testify about *21* a different matter, the man is only to be excluded from the pure food *Blank* on condition that *22* they are trustworthy, and that on the same day on which he saw him, he reported him to the Inspector. And concerning riches, they shall accept two *23* trustworthy witnesses. *Blank* And on the (basis of) one, to exclude from the pure food. A witness is not to be accepted

Col. x (= 4Q266 8 III; 4Q270 6 IV - v) *1* by the judges to condemn to death on his word, if he has not completed his days to pass *2* among those who are enrolled, fearful of God. *Blank* Not is to be believed as a witness against his fellow, *3* someone who has deliberately transgressed any precept until he has been purified to return. *4 Blank* And this is the rule of the judges of the congregation. Ten men in number, chosen *5* from among the congregation, for a period: four from the tribe of Levi and of Aaron and six from Israel, *6* learned in the book of HAGY and in the principles of the covenant, between *7* twenty-five and sixty years. And no-one over *8* sixty years should hold the office of judging the congregation, for on account of man's unfaithfulness *9* his days were shortened, and because of God's wrath against the inhabitants of the earth, he ordered ‹to remove› *10* their knowledge before they completed their days. Concerning purification with water. No- *11* one should bathe in water which is

12 *vacat* אל יטהר במה כלי וכל גבא בסלע אשר אין בו די 13 מרעיל אשר
נגע בו הטמא וטמא מימיו במימי (כמימי) הכלי 14 על הש[ב]ת לשמרה
כמשפטה *vacat* אל יעש איש ביום 15 {מל} השישי מלאכה מן העת אשר
יהיה גלגל השמש 16 רחוק מן השער מלואו כי הוא אשר אמר שמור את
17 יום השבת לקדשו וביום השבת אל ידבר איש דבר 18 נבל ורק אל
ישה ברעהו כל אל ישפוט על הון ובצע 19 אל ידבר בדברי המלאכה
והעבודה לעשות למשכים *vacat* 20 אל יתהלך איש בשדה לעשות את
עבודת חפצו (ביום) 21 השבת אל יתהלך חוץ לעירו {א} על אלף באמה
vacat 22 אל יאכל איש ביום השבת כי אם המוכן ומן האובד 23
בשדה ואל יאכל ואל ישתה כי אם היה במחנה

Col. xi 1 בדרך וירד לרחוץ ישתה על עומדו *vacat* ואל ישאב אל
2 כל כל(י) אל ישלח את בן הנכר לעשות את חפצו ביום השבת 3 *vacat*
אל יקח איש עליו בגדים צואים או מובאים בגז כי אם 4 כיבסו במים או
שופים בלבונה *vacat* אל יתערב איש מרצונו 5 בשבת *vacat* אל ילך איש
אחר הבהמה לרעותה חוץ מעירו כי 6 אם אלפים באמה *vacat* אל ירם את
ידו להכותה באגרוף *vacat* אם 7 סוררת היא אל יוציאה מביתו *vacat* אל
יוציא איש מן הבית 8 לחוץ ומן החוץ אל בית ואם בסוכה יהיה אל יוצא
ממנה 9 ואל יבא אליה אל פתח כלי טוח בשבת *vacat* אל ישא איש 10
עליו סמנים לצאת ולביא (ולבוא) בשבת *vacat* אל יטול בבית מושבת 11
סלע ועפר *vacat* אל ישא האומן את היונק לצאת ולבוא בשבת 12 *vacat*
אל ימרא איש את עבדו ואת אמתו ואת שוכרו בשבת 13 *vacat* {אל} אל
יילד איש בהמה ביום השבת *vacat* ואם תפיל (תפול) אל בור 14 ואל פחת
אל יקימה בשבת *vacat* אל ישבית (ישבות) איש במקום קרוב 15 לגוים
בשבת *vacat* 16 אל יחל איש את השבת על הון ובצע בשבת *vacat* וכל
נפש אדם אשר תפול אל {מים} מקום מים ואל מקום (מקוה) 17 אל יעלה
איש בסולם וחבל וכלי *vacat* אל יעל איש למזבח בשבת 18 כי אם עולת
השבת כי כן כתוב מלבד שבתותיכם *vacat* 19 אל ישלח איש למזבח עולה
ומנחה ולבונה ועץ ביד איש טמא באחת 20 מן הטמאות להרשותו לטמא

dirty or which is less than the amount which covers a man. *12 Blank* No-one should purify a vessel in it. And every cavity in the rock in which there is not the amount *13* which covers, if an impure person has touched it, he has defiled its water ‹like› the water of a vessel. *14* Concerning the sa[bba]th, to observe it in accordance with its regulation. *Blank* No-one should do *15* work on the sixth day, from the moment when the sun's disc is *16* at a distance of its diameter from the gate, for this is what he said: *Deut 5:12* «Observe the *17* sabbath day to keep it holy». And on the day of the sabbath, no-one should say a *18* useless or stupid word. He is not to lend anything to his fellow. He is not to take decisions with regard to riches or gain. *19* He is not to speak about matters of work or of the task to be carried out on the following day. *20 Blank* No-one is to walk in the field to do the work which he wishes ‹on› *21* the sabbath ‹day›. He is not to walk more than one thousand cubits outside his city. *22 Blank* No-one is to eat on the sabbath day except what has been prepared; and from what is lost *23* in the field *Blank* he should not eat, nor should he drink except of what there is in the camp.

Col. XI (= 4Q270 6 v; 4Q271 5 I) *1* On the road, if he goes down to bathe, he should drink where he stands. *Blank* But he is not to draw (water) with *2* any vessel. He is not to send a foreigner to do what he wishes on the sabbath day. *3 Blank* No-one is to wear dirty clothes or (clothes) which are in a chest, unless *4* they have been washed with water or rubbed with incense. *Blank* No-one should intermingle voluntarily *5* on the sabbath. *Blank* No-one should go after an animal to pasture it outside his city, except for *6* two thousand cubits. *Blank* He is not to raise his hand to strike it with the fist. *Blank* If *7* it is stubborn, he should not bring it out of his house. *Blank* No-one should remove anything from the house *8* to outside, or from outside to the house. Even if he is in a hut, he should remove nothing from it *9* nor bring anything into it. He is not to open a sealed vessel on the sabbath. *Blank* No-one should wear *10* perfumes, to go out ‹or come in› on the sabbath. *Blank* In his dwelling no-one should lift *11* a stone or dust. *Blank* The wet-nurse should not lift the baby to go out or come in on the sabbath. *12 Blank* No-one should press his servant or his maidservant or his employee on the sabbath. *Blank* {Not} No-one should help an animal give birth on the sabbath day. *Blank* And if ‹it falls› into a well *14* or a pit, he should not take it out on the sabbath. *Blank* No-one ‹should stay› in a place close *15* to gentiles on the sabbath. *Blank* No-one should profane the sabbath for riches or gain on the sabbath. *16 Blank* And any living man who falls into a place of water or into a ‹reservoir›, *17* no-one should take him out with a ladder or a rope or a utensil. *Blank* No-one should offer anything upon the altar on the sabbath, *18* except the sacrifice of the sabbath, for thus is it written: *Lev 23:38* «except your offerings of the sabbath». *Blank* No-one should send *19* to the altar a sacrifice, or an offering, or incense, or wood, by the hand of a man impure from any *20* of the impurities, so allowing him to defile the altar, for it

את המזבח כי כתוב זבח   21 רשעים תועבה ותפלת צדקם כמנחת רצון

וכל הבא אל   22 בית השתחות אל יבא טמא כבוס ובהרע חצוצרות *vacat*

הקהל   23 יתקדם או יתאחר ולא ישביתו את העבודה כולה [כ]י בית

Col. XII   1 קודש הוא *vacat* אל ישכב איש עם אשה בעיר המקדש

לטמא   2 את עיר המקדש בנדתם *vacat* כל א^{יש} אשר ימשלו בו רוחות

בליעל   3 ודבר סרה כמשפט האוב והידעוני ישפט וכל אשר יתעה

4 לחלל את השבת ואת המועדות לא יומת כי על בני האדם   5 משמרו ואם

ירפא ממנה ושמרוהו עד שבע שנים ואחר   6 יבוא אל הקהל *vacat* אל

ישלח את ידו לשפוך דם לאיש מן הגוים   7 בעבור הון ובצע *vacat* וגם אל

ישא מהונם כל בעבור אשר לא   8 יגדפו כי אם בעצת חבור ישראל *vacat*

אל ימכר איש בהמה   9 ועוף טהורים לגוים בעבור אשר לא יזבחום *vacat*

ומגורנו   10 ומגתו אל ימכר להם בכל מאדו ואת עבדו ואת אמתו אל ימכור

11 להם אשר באו עמו בברית אברהם *vacat* אל ישקץ איש את נפשו

12 בכל החיה והרמש לאכל מהם מעגלי הדבורים עד כל נפש   13 החיה

אשר תרמוש במים והדגים אל יאכלו כי אם נקרעו   14 חיים ונשפך דמם

וכל החגבים במיניהם יבאו באש או במים   15 עד הם חיים כי הוא משפט

בריאתם *vacat* וכל העצים והאבנים   16 והעפר אשר יגואלו בטמאת האדם

לגאולי שמן בהם כפי   17 טמאתם יטמא הנ[ו]גע בם *vacat* וכל כלי {מסמר}

מסמר או יתד בכותל   18 אשר יהיו עם המת בבית וטמאו בטמאת אחד כלי

מעשה   19 *vacat* סרך מושב ערי ישראל על המשפטים האלה להבדיל בין

20 הטמא לטהור ולהודיע בין הקודש לחול *vacat* ואלה החקים

21 למשכיל להתהלך בם עם כל חי למשפט עת ועת וכמשפט   22 הזה

יתהלכו זרע ישראל ולא יוארו *vacat* וזה סרך מושב   23 המח[נ]ו]ת

המתהלכים באלה בקץ הרשעה עד עמוד משוח (משיח) אהרן

Col. XIII   1 וישראל עד עשרה אנשים למועט לאלפים ומיאיות

וחמשים   2 ועשרות ובמקום עשרה אל ימש איש כהן מבונן בספר ההגי על

3 פיהו ישקו כולם *vacat* ואם אין הוא בחון בכל אלה ואיש מהלוים בחון

is written: *Prov 15:8* «the sacrifice *21* of the wicked ones is an abomination, but the prayer of the just ones is like an agreeable offering». *Blank* And everyone who enters *22* a house of prostration should not enter with impurity requiring washing; and when the trumpets of the assembly sound, *23* he may advance or retreat, but they should not stop the whole service, [f]or

Col. XII (= 4Q266 9 II; 4Q271 5 I)   *1* it is a holy house. *Blank* No-one should sleep with a woman in the city of the temple, defiling *2* the city of the temple with their impurity. *Blank* Every /man/ over whom the spirits of Belial dominate, *3* and who preaches apostasy, will be judged according to the regulation of the necromancer or the diviner. But every one who goes astray, *4* defiling the sabbath and the festivals, shall not be executed, for it is the task of men *5* to guard him; and if he is cured of it, they shall guard him for seven years and afterwards *6* he may enter the assembly. *Blank* He is not to stretch out his hand to shed the blood of one of the gentiles *7* for the sake of riches and gain. *Blank* Neither should he take any of their riches, lest they *8* blaspheme, except on the advice of the company of Israel. *Blank* No-one should sell clean animals *9* or birds, to the gentiles lest they sacrifice them. *Blank* *10* And he should not sell them anything from his granary or his press, at any price. Neither should he sell his servant and his maidservant *11* to them, for they entered the covenant of Abraham with him. *Blank* No-one should defile his soul *12* with any living or creeping animal, by eating them, from the larvae of bees to every living *13* being which creeps in water. And fish they should not eat unless they have been opened up *14* alive, and their blood poured away. And all the locusts, according to their kind, shall be put into fire or into water *15* while they are still alive, as this is the regulation for their species. *Blank* And all the wood and the stones *16* and the dust which are defiled by man's impurity, while with stains of oil in them, in accordance with *17* their uncleanness will make whoever touches them impure. *Blank* And every utensil, {nail} nail or peg in the wall *18* which is with a dead person in the house will be unclean with the same uncleanness as tools for work. *19* *Blank* Rule for the assembly of the cities of Israel. In accordance with these regulations, to keep *20* the unclean apart from the clean, and distinguish between holy and profane. *Blank* And these are the ordinances *21* for the Instructor, so that he walks in them with every living thing, according to the regulation for every time. And in accordance with this regulation *22* shall the seed of Israel walk and it will not be cursed. *Blank* And this is the rule of the assembly *23* of the cam[ps]. Those who walk in them, in the time of wickedness until there arises the ‹messiah› of Aaron

Col. XIII (= 4Q266 9 III; 4Q267 9 IV, V)   *1* and Israel, shall be ten in number as a minimum to (form) thousands, hundreds, fifties *2* and tens. And in a place of ten, a priest learned in the book of HAGY should not be lacking; by *3* his authority all shall be governed. *Blank* And if there should not be an expert in

4 באלה ויצא הגורל לצאת ולבוא על פיהו כל באי המחנה vacat ואם

5 משפט לתורת נגע יהיה באיש ובא הכהן ועמד במחנה והבינו 6 המבקר

בפרוש התורה vacat ואם פתי הוא הוא יסגירנו כי להם 7 המשפט vacat

וזה סרך המבקר למחנה ישכיל את הרבים במעשי 8 אל ויבינם בגבורות

פלאו ויספר לפניהם נהיות עולם בפרתיה (בפתריהם) 9 וירחם עליהם

כאב לבניו וישקה לכל מדהובם (מרהוב בם) כרועה עדרו 10 יתר כל

חרצובות קשריהם לבלתי היות עשוק ורצוץ בעדתו vacat 11 וכל הנוסף

לעדתו יפקדהו למעשיו ושוכלו וכוחו וגבורתו והונו 12 וכתבוהו במקומו

כפי נחלתו בגורל האור vacat אל ימשול איש 13 מבני המחנה להביא איש

אל העדה זולת פי המבקר אשר למחנה vacat 14 ואיש מכל באי ברית אל

אל ישא ואל יתן לבני השחר כי 15 אם כף לכף vacat ואל יעש איש דבר

למקח ולממכר כי אם הודיע 16 למבקר אשר במחנה ועשה בעצה ולא

יש[וגו וכן] ל[כ]ל ל[ו]ק[ח אש]ה] 17 וה]...[...].ב]עצה וכן למגרש והוא

ייס[ר את בניהם ... [...] 18 [וטפם ברוח]ענוה ובאהבת חסד אל יטור להם]

באף] 19 [ועברה על פ]שעיהם ואת אשר איננו נקשר ב.[...].[...] 20 [...]

vacat וזה מושב המחנות לכל ז[רע ישראל] 21 [ואשר לא מחזיקים בא]לה

לא יצליחו לשבת בארץ ב[...] 22 [...]ו]אלה המ[שפט]ים למשכיל

[להתהלך בם] 23 [במועד פקוד אל את הארץ בבוא הדבר אשר יבואו

על עמך ימים]

1 אשר לא באו מיום סור אפרים מעל יהודה וכל המתהלכים

באלה 2 ברית אל נאמנות להם להנצילם מכל מוקשי שחת כי פתאום

(פתאים עברו) ונענש[ו] 3 vacat וסרך מושב כל המחנות יפקדו כלם

בשמותיהם הכהנים לראשונה 4 והלוים שנים ובני ישראל שלשתם והגר

רביע ויכתבו בשמותיהם 5 איש אחר אחיהו הכהנים לראשונה והלוים

שנים ובני ישראל 6 שלושתם והגר רביע וכן ישבו וכן ישאלו לכל והכהן

אשר יפקד 7 א(י)ש (בראש) הרבים מבן שלושים שנה ועד בן ששים

them all, and one of the levites is an expert *4* in them, the decision about the going out and coming in is his authority (with regard to) all the members of the camp. *Blank* But if *5* there is a judgment against anyone about the law of leprosy, the priest shall take his place in the camp *6* and the Inspector shall instruct him in the exact interpretation of the law. *Blank* Even if he is a simpleton, he is the one who shall intern him, for theirs is *7* the judgment. *Blank* And this is the rule of the Inspector of the camp. He shall instruct the Many in the deeds of *8* God, and shall teach them his mighty marvels, and recount to them the eternal events with ‹their explanations›. *9* He shall have pity on them like a father on his sons, and will heal all the ‹afflicted among them› like a shepherd his flock. *10* He will undo all the chains which bind them, so that there will be neither harassed nor oppressed in his congregation. *11 Blank* And everyone who joins his congregation, he should examine, concerning his actions, his intelligence, his strength, his courage and his wealth; *12* and they shall inscribe him in his place according to his inheritance in the lot of light. *Blank* No-one *13* of the members of the camp should have authority to introduce anyone into the congregation without the permission of the Inspector of the camp. *14 Blank* And none of those who have entered the covenant of God should buy or sell to the Sons of Dawn, *15* except hand to hand. *Blank* And no-one should make a deed of purchase or of sale without informing *16* the Inspector of the camp; he shall proceed in consultation lest they e[rr. And likewise] with regard to [any]one who ma[rr]ies a wom[an] *17* and [… in] consultation. And likewise, with regard to anyone who divorces; he shall ins[truct their children …] *18* [and their small children with a spirit of] modesty and with compassionate love. He should not bear resentment against them [in anger] *19* [and rage because of] their [s]ins. And that which is not determined by […] *20* […] *Blank* And this is the assembly of the camps for all the s[eed of Israel.] *21* [And those who do not remain steadfast in th]ese (things) shall not succeed in dwelling in the land […] *22* […] These are the re[gulation]s for the Instructor, [to walk in them] *23* [in the appointed time when God visits the earth, when the word will be fulfilled which said: *Isa 7:17* «There shall come upon your people days]

Col. xiv (= 4Q266 10 i; 4Q267 9 v) *1* such as have not come since the day on which Ephraim became separated from Judah»; and (to) all those who walk in them, *2* the covenant of God is faithful to save them from all the nets of the pit, but *Prov 27:12* «‹the ignorant walk on› and are punished». *3 Blank* Rule of the assembly of all the camps. All of them shall be enlisted by their names: the priests first, *4* the levites second, the children of Israel third, and the proselyte fourth; and they shall be inscribed by their [na]mes, *5* each one after his brother; the priests first, the levites second, the children of Israel *6* third and the proselyte fourth. And thus shall they sit and thus shall they be questioned about everything. And the priest who is named *7* ‹at the head› of the Many will

מבונן בספר 8 ה]ה[גי ובכל משפטי התורה לדברם כמשפטם vacat
והמבקר אשר 9 לכל המחנות מבן שלשים שנה ועד בן חמשים שנה בעול
בכל 10 סוד אנשים ולכל לשון רמ].פריה על פיהו יבאו באי העדה
11 איש בתרו ולכל דבר אשר יהיה לכל האדם לדבר למבקר ידבר 12 לכל
ריב ומשפט vacat וזה סרך הרבים להכין כל חפציהם שכר 13 שני ימים
לכל חדש לממעיט ונתנו על יד המבקר והשופטים 14 ממנו יתנו בעד
פ]צ(ו)ע(י)ם וממנו יחזיקו ביד עני ואביון ולזקן אשר 15 יכר]ע ולאיש
אשר ינו]ג[ע ולאשר ישבה לגוי נכר ולבתולה אשר 16 אי]ן לה ג]וא[ל]
ו]ל(נ)ער] א[שר אין לו דורש כל עבודת החבר ולא 17 יכרת בית החבר
מיד]ם vacat וזה פרוש מושב המ]חנות (ואלה)י]סו[ד]ו[ת] 18 או]שי
הק]הל vacat וזה פרוש המשפטים אשר]ישפטו בהם] 19 עד מעמוד
משי]ח אהרן וישראל ויכפר עונם [ממנחה וחטאת] 20 vacat] והאי]ש
א]ש[ר (יש)קר בממון והוא יודע וה]בדילוהו מן הטהרה] 21 [... ונ]ענש
ימים ששה ואשר ידב]ר [... 22]ואשר יטור לרעהו אשר] לא במשפט
ונענ]ש חו]דשים [...] 23 [...]...[...]

CD-B *Damascus Document[b]*

E. Qimron in M. Broshi (ed.), *The Damascus Document Reconsidered*
Cambridge University Library
CD-A, 4Q266, 4Q267, 4Q268, 4Q269, 4Q270, 4Q271, 4Q272, 4Q273,

נאמנות להם לחיותם לאלפי דורות: כך שומר הברית 1 Col. xix
והחסד 2 לאהב(יו) ולשמרי מצותי (מצותו) לאלף דור: vacat ואם מחנות
ישבו כסרך 3 הארץ אשר היה מקדם ולקחו נשים כמנהג התורה וה]ו[לידו
בנים 4 ויתהלכו על פי התורה: vacat וכמשפט היסודים (היסורים) כסרך
התורה 5 כאשר אמר בֿי[ז] איש לאשתו ובין אב לבנו וכל המאסים במצות

be between thirty and sixty years old, learned in the book of *8* H[A]GY and in all the regulations of the law, to formulate them in accordance with their regulations. *Blank* And the Inspector who is *9* over all the camps will be between thirty years and fifty years of age, mastering every *10* secret of men and every language ... On his authority, the members of the assembly shall enter, *11* each one in his turn; and any matter which any man needs to discuss, should be told to the Inspector, *12* in connection with any dispute or judgment. *Blank* And this is the rule of the Many, to provide for all their needs: the salary *13* of two days each month at least. They shall place it in the hand of the Inspector and of the judges. *14* From it they shall give to the ‹[in]jured› and with it they shall support the needy and poor, and to the elder who *15* [is ben]t, and to the af[flic]ted, and to the prisoner of a foreign people, and to the girl who *16* has [n]o re[dee]mer, [and] to the ‹youth› [w]ho has no-one looking after him; everything is the task of the association, and *17* [the house of the association shall] not [be deprived of] its [means]. *Blank* And this is the exact interpretation for those who live in the c[amps, and ‹these› are the fou]nda[tion] *18* [walls of the as]sembly. *Blank* And this is the exact interpretation of the regulations by which [they shall be ruled] *19* [until there arises the messia]h of Aaron and Israel. And their iniquity will be atoned [through meal and sin-offerings] *20* [*Blank* And the ma]n who ‹lies› knowingly with regard to riches, they shall ex[clude from the pure food] *21* [... and he shall be] punished for six days. And he who spe[aks ...] *22* [and he who bears resentment against his fellow] without justification, [shall be puni]shed for [...] mo[nths ...]

CD-B *Damascus Document^b*

5Q12, 6Q15
Bibliography: J.M. Baumgarten in *PTSDSSP 2*, 30-39; cf. CD-A

Col. XIX (cf. CD-A VII - VIII)   *1* guarantees for them that they shall live for thousands of generations. *Blank* As it is written: *Deut 7:9* «He keeps the covenant and favour *2* for ‹those› who love ‹him› and keep ‹his› precepts for a thousand generations». *Blank* And if they reside in camps in accordance with the rule of *3* the land, as it was since ancient times, and take women in accordance with the custom of the law, and beget children, *4* they shall walk in accordance with the law. *Blank* And according to the regulation of the ‹teachings›, according to the rule of the law *5* as he said: *Num 30:17* «/Between/ a man and his wife, and between a father and his son». But (over) all those who despise the precepts

6 ובחקים להשיב גמול רשעים עליהם בפקד אל את הארץ   7 בבוא הדבר
אשר כתוב ביד זכריה הנביא חרב עורי על   8 רועי ועל גבר עמיתי נאם אל
הך את הרעה ותפוצינה הצאן   9 והשיבותי ידי על הצוערים: והשומרים
אותו הם עניי הצאן   10 אלה ימלטו בקץ הפקדה והנשארים ימסרו לחרב
בבוא משיח   11 אהרן וישראל: כאשר היה בקץ פקדת הראשון אשר אמר
{יחזקאל}   12 ביד יחזקאל *vacat* {והתוי} להתות התיו על מצחות נאנחים
ונאנקים   13 והנשארים הסגרו לחרב נוקמת נקם ברית: וכן משפט לכל
באי   14 בריתו אשר לא יחזיקו באלה החקים לפקדה לכלה ביד בליעל
15 הוא היום אשר יפקד אל כאשר דבר היו שרי יהודה כמשיגי   16 גבול
עליהם אשפך כמים עברה: כי באו {באו} בברית תשובה   17 ולא סרו
מדרך בוגדים ויתגללו בדרכי זנות ובהון הרשעה   18 ונקום ונטור איש
לאחיהו ושנא איש את רעהו ויתעלמו איש   19 בשאר בשרו ויגשו לזמה
ויתגברו להון ולבצע ויעשו {א...}   20 איש הישר בעיניו ויבחרו איש
בשרירות לבו ולא נזרו מעם   21 ומחטאתם: ויפרעו ביד רמה ללכת בדרכי
רשעים: אשר   22 אמר אל עליהם חמת תנינים יינם וראש פתנים אכזר:
התנינים   23 מלכי העמים ויינם הוא דרכיהם וראש פתנים הוא ראש
24 מלכי יון הבא עליהם לנקם נקמה ובכל אלה לא הבינו בוני   25 החיץ
וטחי תפל כי הולך רוח ושקל {ספת} סופות ומטיף אדם   26 לכזב אשר
חרה אף אל בכל עדתו: *vacat* ואשר אמר משה   27 לישראל לא בצדקתך
וביושר לבבך אתה בא לרשת את הגוים   28 האלה כי מאהבתו את אבותיך
ומשמרו את השבועה: כן   29 משפט לשבי ישראל סרו מדרך העם באהבת
אל{:} את הראשנים   30 אשר העידו על העם אחרי אל ואהב את הבאים
אחריהם כי להם   31 ברית אבות *vacat* ושונא ומתעב אל את בוני החיץ
וחרה {אב} אפו בם ובכל   32 ההלכים אחריהם וכמשפט הזה לכל המאס
במצות אל ...וע   33 ויעזבם ויפנו בשרירות לבם *vacat* כן כל האנשים

6 and the ordinances, may be emptied over them the punishment of the wicked, when God visits the earth, *7* when there comes the word which is written by the hand of the prophet Zechariah: *Zech 13:7* «Wake up, sword, against *8* my shepherd, and against the male who is my companion - oracle of God - strike the shepherd, and the flock may scatter, *9* and I shall turn my hand against the little ones». Those who revere him are *Zech 11:11* «the poor ones of the flock». *10* These shall escape in the age of the visitation; but those that remain shall be delivered up to the sword when there comes the messiah *11* of Aaron and Israel. As happened in the age of the first visitation, as {Ezekiel} he said *12* by the hand of Ezekiel: *Blank Ez 9:4* « {...} To mark with a tau the foreheads of those who sigh and groan». *13* But those who remained were delivered up to the sword, which carries out the vengeance of the covenant. Thus will be the judgment of all those entering *14* his covenant, who do not remain steadfast in these precepts; they shall be visited for destruction at the hand of Belial. *15* This is the day when God will make a visitation, as he said: *Hos 5:10* «The princes of Judah will be like those who move *16* the boundary, upon them he will pour out his fury like water». For they entered the covenant of conversion, *17* but have not left the path of traitors and have defiled themselves by paths of licentiousness and with wicked wealth, *18* avenging themselves, and each one bearing resentment against his brother, and each one hating his fellow. Each one became obscured *19* by blood relatives, approached for debauchery and bragged about wealth and gain {...} *20* Each one did what was right in his eyes and each one has chosen the stubbornness of his heart. They did not keep apart from the people *21* and from their sins. And they have rebelled with insolence, walking on the path of the wicked ones, *22* about whom God said: *Deut 32:33* «Their wine is serpents' venom and cruel poison of asps». The serpents *23* are the kings of the peoples and their wine is their paths, and the asps' poison is the head *24* of the kings of Greece, who comes upon them to execute vengeance. But the builders of *25* the wall have not understood all of these things, nor those who daub with whitewash, because of one who follows the wind, weighs storms, and preaches *26* lies to mankind, the one against whose congregation God's wrath has been kindled. *Blank* And what Moses said *27* to Israel: *Deut 9:5 and 7:8* «Not because of your justice, or for the uprightness of your heart are you going to possess these nations, *28* but because he loved your fathers and keeps the oath». So is *29* the judgment of the converts of Israel, who turned away from the path of the people: on account of God's love for the forefathers *30* who testified against the people, following God, he loves those who come after them, because to them belongs *31* the fathers' covenant. *Blank* And God hates and detests the builders of the wall and his anger is kindled against them and against all *32* those who follow them. And like this judgment will be that of all who reject God's precepts ... *33* and forsake them and move aside in the stubbornness of their heart. *Blank*

אשר באו בברית 34 החדשה בארץ דמשק ושבו ויבגדו ויסורו מבאר מים

החיים: 35 לא יחשבו בסוד עם בכתבם לא יכתבו מיום האסף {יור מורה}

Col. xx {...} 1 מורה היחיד עד עמוד משיח מאהרן ומישראל *vacat*

וכן המשפט 2 לכל באי עדת אנשי תמים הקדש ויקוץ מעשות פקודי

ישרים 3 הוא האיש הנתך בתוך כור: *vacat* {ה} בהופע מעשיו ישלח מעדה

4 כמו שלא נפל גורלו בתוך למודי אל כפי מעלו {יח} יוכיחוהו אנשי

5 דעות עד יום ישוב לעמד במעמד אנשי תמים קדש {אשר אין} 6 {גורלו

בתוך א} ובהופע מעשיו כפי מדרש התורה אשר יתהלכו 7 בו אנשי תמים

הקדש אל {ית} יאות איש עמו בהון ובעבודה 8 כי אררוהו כל קדושי עליון

וכמשפט הזה לכל המאס בראשונים 9 ובאחרונים אשר שמו גלולים על

לבם {וישימ}וילכו בשרירות 10 לבם אין להם חלק בבית התורה: *vacat*

כמשפט רעיהם אשר שבו 11 עם אנשי הלצון ישפטו כי דברו תועה על

חקי הצדק ומאסו {.} 12 בברית {.} ואמנה אשר קימו בארץ דמשק והוא ברית

החדשה: 13 ולא יהיה להם {ו} ולמשפחותיהם חלק בבית התורה *vacat*

ומיום 14 האסף יורה היחיד עד תם כל אנשי המלחמה אשר שבו 15 עם

איש הכזב כשנים ארבעים: *vacat* ובקץ ההוא יחרה 16 אף אל בישראל

כאשר אמר אין מלך ואין שר ואין שופט ו[אין] 17 מוכיח בצדק {.} ושבי

פשע יעקב שמרו ברית אל אז נדברו איש 18 אל רעהו להצדיק איש את

אחיו לתמך צעדם בדרך אל ויקשב 19 אל אל דבריהם וישמע ויכתב ספר

זכרון [לפני]ו ליראי אל ולחושבי 20 שמו עד יגלה {.} ישע וצדקה ליראי

אל ושבתם וראיתם בין צדיק 21 ורשע בין עבד אל לאשר לא עבדו: ועשה

חסד [לאלפים] לאהביו 22 ולשמריו לאלף דור: [...] מבית פלג אשר יצאו

מעיר הקדש: 23 וישענו על אל בקץ מעל ישראל ויטמאו את המקדש ושבו

עוד 24 אל דרך העם בדברים מעטי[ם כו]לם אי"ש לפי רוחו ישפטו בעצת

Thus, all the men who entered the new *34* covenant in the land of Damascus and turned and betrayed and departed from the well of living waters, *35* shall not be counted in the assembly of the people, they shall not be inscribed in their lists, from the day of the gathering in {of the teacher}

Col. xx   *1* {…} of the unique teacher until there arises the messiah out of Aaron and Israel. *Blank* And thus is the judgment *2* of everyone who enters the congregation of the men of perfect holiness and is slack in the fulfilment of the instructions of the upright. *3* This is the man who is melted in the crucible. *Blank* When his deeds are evident, he shall be expelled from the congregation, *4* like one whose lot did not fall among the disciples of God. In accordance with his unfaithfulness, all the men *5* of knowledge shall reproach him, until the day when he returns to take his place in the session of the men of perfect holiness {for} *6* {his lot is not in the midst of m}. But when his deeds are evident, according to the explanation of the law in which *7* the men of perfect holiness walked, no-one should associate with him in wealth or work, *8* for all the holy ones of the Most High have cursed him. And (proceed) according to this judgment, with all those who despise, among the first *9* as among the last, for they have placed idols in their heart {and have placed} and have walked in the stubbornness of *10* their heart. For them there shall be no part in the house of the law. *Blank* They shall be judged according to the judgment of their companions, who turned round *11* with insolent men, for they spoke falsehood about the just regulations and despised *12* the covenant {…} and the pact which they established in the land of Damascus, which is the new covenant. *13* And neither for them nor their families shall there shall be a part in the house of the law. *Blank* And from the day *14* of the gathering in of the unique teacher, until the end of all the men of war who turned back *15* with the man of lies, there shall be about forty years. *Blank* And in this age the wrath *16* of God will be kindled against Israel, as he said: *Hos 3:4* «There shall be no king, no prince, no judge, no-one who *17* reproaches in justice». But those who revert from the sin of Jacob, have kept the covenant of God. *Mal 3:16* «They shall then speak», each *18* to his fellow, acting just with one's brother, so that their steps become steady in the path of God, and God «will pay attention» to *19* their words. «And he will listen; and it will be written in a book of remembrance [before hi]m for those who fear God and think on *20* his name», until salvation and justice are revealed to those who fear God. *Mal 3:18* «And they shall distinguish again between the just *21* and the wicked, between whoever serves God and whoever does not serve him». *Exod 20:6b & Deut 7:9* «He shows mercy to [thousands,] to whoever loves him *22* and whoever is faithful to him, for a thousand generations». […] from the house of Peleg, who left the holy city *23* and leaned on God in the age of Israel's unfaithfulness; but defiled the temple and turned back *24* to the path of the people in some things. [All] of them, /each one/ according to his spirit, shall be judged in the holy *25* council.

579

25 הקדש vacat: וכל אשר פרצו את גבול התורה מבאי הברית בהופע
26 כבוד אל לישראל יכרתו מקרב המחנה ועמהם כל מרשיעי 27 יהודה
בימי מצרפותיו vacat וכל המחזיקים במשפטים האלה ל[צ]את 28 ולבוא
על פי התורה וישמעו לקול מורה ויתודו לפני אל חטאנו 29 רשענו גם
אנחנו גם אבותינו בלכתנו קרי בחקי הברית צד]ק[30 ואמת משפטיך בנו:
ולא ירימו יד על חקי קדשו ומשפט]י[31 צדקו ועדוות אמתו: והתיסרו
במשפטים הראשונים אשר 32 נשפטו בם אנשי היחיד והאזינו לקול מורה
צדק: ולא יעזבו 33 את חקי הצדק בשמעם אתם ישישו וישמחו ויעז לבם
ויתגברו 34 על כל בני תבל וכפר אל בעדם וראו בישועתו כי חסו בשם
קדשו

4Q266 (4QD^a) *4QDamascus Document^a*

J.M. Baumgarten, *DJD XVIII*, 23-93, pls. I-XVII
PAM 43.269-43.278, 43.281
ROC 680, 686, 687
CD-A, CD-B, 4Q267, 4Q268, 4Q269, 4Q270, 4Q271, 4Q272, 4Q273

Frag. 1 a-b 1 [... ב]ני אור להנזר מדר]כי ...[2 [...עד תום ה מועד
פקודה ב]...[3 [...ד אל את כול מעשיה להבי כל]ה[4 בת]...[למסיגי
גבול וכלה יעשה [לפועלי] 5 רשעה [... ועתה שמע]ו לי ואודיעה לכם
מח]...[6 הנורא]...[פלאו {.} א ספר]ר}ה לכ]ם ...[7 מאנוש [...]מים
אשר חי ... [...] 8 בעמקת [...]... [...] 9 חתם [...]... [...] 13-10 [...]
14 במצו]ת ...[15 בתרומ]ת ... שמעו] 16 לקול מושה [...]
17 רכיל בחוקי] ומצות אל[...] 18 קטנה וגדולה ל.[...] 19 הודיענו נא
[...] 20 שיחתך אם [...] 21 עמדתה ותתבונן [...] 22 {אפר} ישיבו את
[...]... עפר] 23 ואפר ומי]...[ק ...[...]... לא [א]...[24 התבונ]נתה
[...]... 25 [...].

Frag. 2 i 1 [...]עד[אשר 2 [יבוא בם ... [כי אין [להת]ק]ד[ם
ולהתאחר ממועדיהם 3 [...]א... חקוק קץ חרון לעם לא ידעהו 4 [והוא

Blank And all, among those who entered the covenant, transgressing the limits of the law, when *26* the glory of God is manifested to Israel, shall be cut off from amongst the camp, and with them all who acted wickedly against *27* Judah in the days of its chastenings. *Blank* But all those who remain steadfast in these regulations, [co]ming *28* and going in accordance with the law, and listen to the Teacher's voice, and confess before God: «Assuredly *29* have we sinned, both we and our fathers, walking contrary to the ordinances of the covenant; just[ice] *30* and truth are your judgments against us»; and they do not raise their hand against his holy regulations and his just *31* judgment[s] and his truthful stipulations; and they are instructed in the first ordinances, *32* in conformity with which the men of the Unique One were judged; and they lend their ears to the voice of the Teacher of Righteousness; and do not reject *33* the just regulations when they hear them; these shall exult and rejoice and their heart will be strong, and they shall prevail *34* over all the sons of the world. And God will atone for them, and they shall see his salvation, for they have taken refuge in his holy name.

4Q266 (4QD^a) *4QDamascus Document^a*

5Q12, 6Q15
Bibliography: J.T. Milik, 'Fragment d'une source du Psautier', 103, 105, pl. III; J.T. Milik, 'Numérotation', 78-79, pl. XI; J.M. Baumgarten, 'The 4Q Zadokite Fragments on Skin Disease', *JJS* 41 (1990) 153-154; *Wacholder-Abegg 1*, 3-22

Frag. 1 a - b (= 4Q267 1)   *1* [… the so]ns of light to keep apart from the pa[ths of …] *2* […] until the completion of the appointed time of visitation … […] *3* […] God […] all its deeds, bringing destruc[tion] *4* upon … […] to those who move the boundary, and he shall wreak destruction [upon those who act] *5* wickedly [… And now, lis]ten to me and I will inform you of … […] *6* the terrible […] his marvel (?), I will tell you […] *7* from man […] … who lives … […] *8* in the depth of […] *9* seal […] *10-13* […] *14* by the precept[s …] *15* by the offering [… they did not listen] *16* to the voice of Moses […] *17* slander /against the law[s]/ and precepts of God […] *18* small and great … […] *19* Inform us, then, […] *20* your concern, if […] *21* you stood and considered […] *22* {ashes} they shall bring back the [… dust] *23* and ashes, and whoever [… not] *24* understand […] *25* … […]

Frag. 2 *col.* I (= CD-A I *1-21*; 4Q268 1)   *1* […] until *2* [there comes upon them …] for there is no [adva]n[ci]ng or delaying their festivals. *3* […] … There is

הכין מועדי רצון לדור]שי מצוותו ולה[ל]כים בתמים דרך   5 [ויגל עיניהם
בנסתרות וא[וזנם פתחו וישמעו עמוקות ויבינו 6 [בכול נהיות עד מה יבוא
בם [vacat vacat

ועתה שמעו כול יודעי   7 [צ]דק ו[בינו במעשי אל כי ריב לו עם [כל
בשר ומשפט יעשה   8 בכול מנא[צו כי במעלם אשר עזבוהו]הסתיר פ]נו
מי]שראל וממקדשו 9 ויתנם [לחרב ובזכרו ברית רישונים השאיר שארית
[לישראל ולא   10 נתנם ל[כלה ובקץ חרו]ן שנים שלו[ש מאות ותשעים]
לתתו אותם ביד   11 נב[וכדנא[צר מל[ך]בבל פקדם] ויצמח מישראל[
ומאהר[ו]ן שו[ר]ש   12 [מט]עת לירוש א[ת א]ר[צו ולדשן בטוב אדמתו
ויבינו [ב[ע]ונם וידעו   13 כי אשימים המה [ויהיו כעוורים וכמגששים
דרך] שנ[י]ם עשר[ים]   14 ויבן אל אל מעש[י]הם כי בלב שלם דרשוהו
ויקם להם מורה צדק]   15 להדריכם ב[ד]ורך לב[ן]vacat ויודע לדורות
אחרונים את אשר[16 עשה בד[ור א]חרון [בעדת בוגדים המה סוררי דרך
והיאה העת]   17 אשר היה [כתו]ב עליה[ן vacat ?] כפרה סוררה כן סרר
ישראל[18 בעמוד איש הל[צו]ן אשר הטיף לישראל מימי כזב [ויתעם
בתהו   19 ול[ו]א דרך להשח גבהו[ת עולם ולסור מנתיבות צדק ו]לסיע גבול
20 אשר גבלו רישו[נים בנחלתם למען הדבק בהם את א]לות בריתו
21 להסגירם לחר[ב נוקמת נקם ברית בעבור אשר דרשו]בחלקות
22 [וי]בחרו [ב]מה[תלות ויצפו לפרצות ויבחרו בטוב ה]צור ויצדיקו
23 [רשע וירשיעו צדיק ויעבירו ברית ויפרו חוק ו]יגו[ד]ו על   24 [נפש
צדיק vacat ? ובכול הולכי תמים תעבה] נפשמה   25 [וירדפום בחרב ויסיסו
לריב עם [vacat ?

1   ויחר אף אל ב[ע]דתם [להשם את כול המונם ומעשיהם   Frag. 2 II
לנדה]   2 לפנו vacat
ועתה שמ[עו אלי כול באי ברית ואגלה אזנכם בדרכי רשעים] 3 ומכול
שבילי חט[א]ים אזיר אתכם אל אהב דעת חוכמה ותושייה[]   4 הציב לפנו
וערמ]ה ודעת הם ישרתוהו ורוב סליחות עמו לכפר[5 בעד כל שבי פ]שע

582

determined a moment of wrath for a nation that does not know him, *4* [and he has established times of favour for those who exa]mine his precepts and walk on the perfect path. *5* [He uncovered their eyes for hidden things and] they opened their [e]ars and heard profound things and understood *6* [everything that happens before it comes upon them. *Blank*] *Blank* And now, listen, all those of you who know *7* [ju]stice, and [understand the actions of God; for he has a dispute with] all flesh and will carry out judgment *8* on all those who spu[rn him. For when they were unfaithful in forsaking him,] he hid his fa[ce from I]srael and from his sanctuary *9* and deliv[ered them up to the sword. But when he remembered the covenant with the forefathers, he saved a remnant] for Israel and did not *10* deliver them up to [destruction. And at the period of wrath,] thr[ee hundred and ninety] years after having delivered them up into the hand *11* of Neb[uchadne]zzar, kin[g] of Babylon, he visited them [and caused to sprout from Israel] and from Aa[ro]n a shoot *12* [of the plan]ting, in order to possess [his land and to become fat with the good things of his soil. And they realised] their [iniqu]ity and knew *13* that they were guilty; [but they were like blind persons and like those who grope] for a path over twen[ty] years. *14* And God appraised [their] deed[s, because they sought him with a undivided heart and raised up for them a Teacher of Righteousness,] *15* in order to direct them /in the [p]ath of [his] heart/. [*Blank* And he made known to the last generations what] *16* he had done to the [l]ast gener[ation], [the congregation of traitors. These are the ones who stray from the path. This is the time] *17* about which it has been [writ]ten: [*Blank? Hos 4:16* «Like a stray heifer so has Israel strayed», *18* when «the scof[fer» arose, who poured out over Israel waters of lies] and made them stray into a wilderness *19* without path, causing the everlasting [heights] to sink down, [diverging from tracks of justice and] removing the boundary *20* with which the forefa[thers] had marked [their inheritance, so that the cur]ses of his covenant [would adhere to them,] *21* to deliver them up to the swo[rd carrying out the vengeance of the covenant. For they sought] easy interpretations, *22* chose illu[sions, scrutinised loopholes, chose the handsome] neck, acquitted *23* [the guilty and sentenced the just, violated the covenant broke the precept,] ban[d]ed together against *24* [the life of the just man, *Blank*?] their soul [abominated all those who walk in perfection,] *25* [they hunted them down with the sword and provoked the dispute of the people. *Blank?*]

Frag. 2 col II (= CD-A I *21*- II *21*)   *1* And kindled was the wrath of God against their [con]gregation, [laying waste all its great number, for their deeds were unclean] *2* before him. *Blank* Now, then, lis[ten to me, all who enter the covenant, and I will open your ears to the paths of the wicked] *3* and from all the tracks of the s[inners I shall divert you. God loves knowledge; wisdom and counsel] *4* has he established before him; pruden[ce and knowledge are at his service; patience is his and abundance of pardon to atone] *5* for those who

[...] 6 לאין שרת [ופליטה ... כי לא בחר אל בהם] 7 מקדם עולם [ובטרם

נוסדו ידע את מעשיהם ויתעב את דורות מדם] 8 ויסתר את [פנו מן הארץ

עד תומם וידע את שני מעמד] 9 ומספר {...} [ופרוש קציהם לכול הווי

עולמים ונהיות] 10 עד מה [יבוא בקציהם לכול שני עולם ובכולם הקים

לו] 11 קריאים [למען הותיר פליטה לארץ ולמלא פני תבל] 12 מזר[עם

vacat [ויודעם ביד משיחי רוח קודשו וחוזי אמת] 13 בפרוש שמותי[הם

ואת אשר שנא התעה vacat ועתה בנים שמעו] 14 [א]ל[י ואג]ל[ה עיניכם

לראות ולהבין במעשי אל ולבחור את] 15 [אשר] רצה ולמאוס באשר

שנא vacat? להתהלך] 16 [ת]מים [ב]כול [דרכו ולא לתור במחשבות יצר

אשמה ועיני זנות כי] 17 גבורי חיל נכש[לו בם מלפנים ועד הנה בלכתם

בשרירות לבם נפלו] 18 עירי ה[שמים בה נאחזו אשר לא שמרו מצות אל

ובניהם אשר כארזים גבהם] 19 [וכ]הרים [גויותיהם כי נפלו כול בשר

אשר היה בחרבה כי גוע ויהיו] 20 כלו ה[יו בעשותם את רצונם ולא שמרו

את מצות עשיהם עד אשר חרה] 21 אפה [בם בה ...]

Frag. 3 II 1 [מדברים ב]ם כו]לם קודחי אש ומבערי זיקות קורי

עכביש קוריהם] 2 [וביצי צפע]ונים ב[י]ציה]ם הקרוב אליהם לא ינקה

כהרבותו יאשם] 3 [כי אם נל]חץ כי למ[ל]פנ]ים פקד אל] את מעשי]הם

ויחר אפו בעלילותיהם] 4 [כי עם [בלא בינות הוא] גוי אוב]ד עצות [המה

מאשר אין בהם] 5 [בינה כי מלפ]נים עמ]ד מושה ואה]רון ביד ש]ר

ה]אור]ים ויקם 6 [בליעל את י]חנה ו]את אחיהו במזמ]תו {ב]רשעה}

בהר[שע ישראל] 7 [את הרישו]נה [ובקץ חרבן הארץ ע]מדו מסגי גבול

[ויתעו את] 8 [ישראל ותשם הארץ כי דברו עצה סרה על] מצוות אל ביד

[מושה וגם] 9 [במשיחי הקודש וינבאו שקר להשיב] את ישראל [מ]אחרי

[אל ויזכר] 10 [אל ברית רישונים ויקם מאהרון נ]בונים ומישראל [ח]כמים

ויש]מיעם ויחפורו את הבאר] אשר אמר מוש]ה באר] 11 [חפרוה שרים כרוה

repent from s[in …] *6* without there being a remnant [or survivor … For God did not choose them] *7* at the beginning of the world, [and before they were established he knew their deeds, and abominated the generations on account of blood,] *8* and hid his [face from the land until their extinction. And he knew the years of their existence,] *9* and the number {…} [and detail of their ages, of all those who exist over the centuries, and of those who will exist,] *10* until it [occurs in their ages throughout all the everlasting years. And in all of them he raised up for himself,] *11* men of renown, [to leave a remnant for the land and in order to fill the face of the world] *12* with [their] offsp[ring.] *Blank* [And he taught them by the hand of the anointed ones with his holy spirit and through seers of the truth.] *13* With precision [their] names [were established. But those he hates, he causes to stray. *Blank* And now, sons, listen] *14* to [me and I shall o]p[en your eyes so that you can see and understand the deeds of God, so that you can choose] *15* [w]hat [he is pleased with and repudiate what he hates *Blank?* so that you can walk] *16* [per]fectly [on] all [his paths and not allow yourselves to be attracted by the thoughts of a guilty inclination and lascivious eyes. For] *17* brave heroes stum[bled on account of them, from ancient times until now. For having walked in the stubbornness of their hearts] *18* the Watchers of the [heavens fell; on account of it they were caught, for they did not follow the precepts of God; in the same way their sons fell, whose height was like that of cedars] *19* [and whose bodies were like] mountains. [All flesh which there was in the dry earth expired and became] *20* as if they had never [been, for having realized their desires and failing to keep their creator's precepts, until] *21* his wrath [flared up against them …]

Frag. 3 col. II (= CD-A V *13*-VI *18*; 4Q267 2)   *1* [They speak (abomination) against] them. [They are] al[l igniters of fire, kindlers of blazes; webs of a spider are their webs,] *2* [and the]ir eggs are [vi]pers' [eggs. Whoever comes close to them will not be unpunished; even more so, if the fault is greater,] *3* unless he has been comp]elled. For since ancient [times God visited their] deeds, [and his wrath flared up against their actions, *4* [for it] is not an intelligent [people, they are a nation be]reft of counsels [in that there is no] *5* [intelligence in them. For in ancient] times there aro[se Moses and Aa]ron, by the hand of the pri[nce of li]ght[s, and] *6* [Belial, raised up Jan]nes and [his brother with] his [cunning] {during the wickedness} when he acted [wickedly against Israel] *7* [the fir]st (time). [And in the age of devastation of the land there a]rose those who shifted the boundary [and made] *8* [Israel stray. And they razed the countryside, for they spoke of rebellion against] God's precepts through the hand of [Moses and also] *9* [of the holy anointed ones. They prophesied deceit in order to divert] Israel [from] following [God. But God] *10* [remembered the covenant of the forefathers. And he raised from Aaron] men of knowledge /and from Israel [wi]se men, and made them lis[ten. And they dug the well] /as Moses said: [*Num 21:18* «A well] *11* [which the princes

נדיבי העם במחו[קק הבאר היא הת]ורה וחופריה]   12 [המה שבי ישראל
היוצאים מ]ארץ יהודה ויגורו[בארץ דמשק]   13 [אשר קרא אל את כולם
שרים כי כ]ול[ם דרשוהו] ול[א הושבה פארתם]   16-14 [...] 17 [...] ו]כול
אשר הובא   18 [בברי]ת לבל[תי בוא אל המקדש להאיר מזבחו הו]א
מס׳גר}ת הדלת   19 [א]שר אמר] אל מי בכם יסגור דלתי ולא תאי]רו
מזבחי חנם   20 [אם]לא יש]מרו לעשות כפרוש התורה לקץ הר]שע
ל[הבדל] מבני   21 [הועו]ל ו[להנזר מהון הרשעה הטמא ב]נדר וב]חרם
ובהון[22 [המקד]ש ול[גזול את עניי עמו להיות אלמנ]ות שללם ואת
יתומים[23 [ירצחו] להבד]יל בין הטמא לטהור ולהודיע בין הקודש לחול]
24 [ולשמור]את]יום השבת [...

18 [...] המלך הוא הק[הל] וכיניי הצלמי]ם המה ספר]י   *Frag. 3* III
[הנבא]ים   19 [אשר בזה ישראל א[ת ד[בריהם והכוכב] הוא דור]ש
ה[תורה   20 [הבא אל] דמשק {כאשר} [כאש]ר כתוב דרך[כוכב מיעקוב]
21 [וקם שב]ט מישראל השבט ה[וא נ]שי [כו]ל [העדה ובעומדו]
22 [וקרקר א]ת כול בני שית אל]ה מ]ל]טו בקץ] *vacat*   23 [הפקודה]
הריש]ון *vacat* והנסוגים ה]סגיר]ו לחרב [וכן מ]שפט   24 כול באים
בברי]תו אשר לו יחזיקו [באלה]ל[פ]קדים [לכלה ב]יד   25 [ב]ליעל [הוא
הי]ום אשר יפקדו [אל] כאשר] דבר [היו]שרי]

18 [...] המחזי[קים בשם קוד]שו ה]ם   10 [...].ה כי ביהודה נמ]צא קש]ר
Frag. 5 I b   9 [...] ...[...] 8 [...] ואמיצי כוח בנגל]ה [...] 7
11 [לשוב ...]לישראל בעומד [...].   12 [...]שלו]ם *vacat* וכול הנשא]רים
[...]   13 [...].[... איש]ל} לפי רוח]ו יקר]בו   14 [...]וח יר חק}ו לפי
המבקר וכו]לל   15 [... יתהל]כו בם *vacat* כול שבי ישראל].[...]   16 [...]
ב]ני צדוק הכהנים הנה המ]ה[17 [...] מדרש ה]תורה האחרון *vacat* ואלה
החוו]ק]ים למש]כיל[18 [...]בם לכול ישראל כ׳ לו יוש]יע אל [...]...[...]א[
19 [...] ... להתהלך [...]...

1 [...]...[...]ם[2 [...]כי לכול ישרי לבב בי[ש]ראל   *Frag. 5* I c-d
3 [...]את חוקו הצדיקו ב[...]   4 [...].יעו ל[...]

dug, which the nobles of the people delved with the sta]ff». The well is the l[aw. And those who dug it] *12* [are the converts of Israel, who left the] land of Judah and lived [in the land of Damascus,] *13* [all of whom God called princes, for they a]ll [sought him, and their renown] has no[t been repudiated] *14-16* [...] *17* [... But] all those who have been brought *18* [into the covena]nt shall not [enter the temple to kindle his altar.] He will be the one who closes the door, *19* as [God] said: [*Mal 1:10* «Whoever amongst you will close its door so that you do not kind]le my altar in vain!». *20* [They] should [take] care [to act in accordance with the exact interpretation of the law for the a]ge of wicke[dness: to be keep] apart from the sons of *21* [injust]ice; [to abstain from wicked wealth which defiles, either by] promise or by [vow, and from the wealth of the] *22* [temp]le and from [stealing from the poor of his people, from making their widow]s [their] spoils,] *23* [and murdering orphans;] to separ[ate unclean from clean and differentiate between the holy and the common;] *24* [to keep] the [sabbath day ...]

Frag. 3 col. III (= CD-A VII *16*-VIII *3*) *18* [The King is the as]sembly; [and the Kiyyune of the imag]es are the book[s of] the prophet[s,] *19* [whose] wo[rds Israel despised. And the star] is the Interp[reter of the] law, *20* [who will come to] Damascus, {as is written} [as is writ]ten: *Num 24:13* «[A star] moves out [of Jacob] *21* [and a scep]tre [arises] out of Israel». The sceptre is the [pr]ince [of the wh]ole [congregation and when he rises] *22* [he will destroy] all the sons of Seth. *Blank* The[se will escape in the age of] *23* the first [visitation.] *Blank* And the renegades will [be delivered up] to the sword. [Thus will be the ju]dgment of *24* all those entering his covenant but do not remain steadfast [in these;] they shall be [vis]ited [unto destruction at] the hand of *25* [Be]lial. [This is the d]ay which [God] will appoint, as [he says:] «[The princes (of Judah)] were

Frag. 5 col. I b (= 4Q267 5 II) *7* [...] ... [...] *8* [...] and those of firm power in what has been reveal[ed ...] *9* [... those who hold] fast to [his] ho[ly] name [... a]re *10* [...] ... for in Judah there is fo[und a conspir]acy *11* [to return ...] to Israel when arises [...] *12* [... peac]e. *Blank* And all those who are le[ft ...] *13* [...] each one according to [his] spirit they [shall let appr]oach *14* [...] ... they shall be removed by order of the Inspector, and a[l]l [...] *15* [... shall wal]k in them. *Blank* All the converts of Israel [...] *16* [... the s]ons of Zadok, the priests. Behold, they [are ...] *17* [...] the last [interpretation] of the law. *Blank* And these are the ordina[nce]s for the Ins[tructor ...] *18* [...] in them for all Israel, for [God] shall not sa[ve ...] ... *19* [...] ... to walk ... [...]

Frag. 5 col. I c - d *1* [...] ... [...] ... *2* [...] ... for all the upright of heart in I[s]rael *3* [...] they declared his regulations to be just with [...] *4* [...] ... [...]

Frag. 5 II   1 [וכול אשר אינו ממהר להב]ין וכול א[שר נקל בלשונו או
בקול טרוד]   2 [דבר לו ו]לא פצל דברו להשמיע [קולו איש מאלה לא
יקרא בספר]   3 [התורה]למה ישוג בדבר מות [...]   4 [...]. אחו הכהנים
בעבודה [ואל]...[איש]   5 מבני אהרון אשר ישבה לגואים [...] 6 לחללה
בטמאתם אל יגש לעבודת [...]   7 מבית לפרוכת vacat ואל יי'כל את קודש
ה]קודשים [...   8 איש מבני אהרון אשר ינדד לעב]וד [... 9 להורות עמו
בישוד עם וגם לבגו(ד)]...[איש מבני]   10 אהרון אשר ה'פיל שמו מן
האמ˂י˃ת ו]...[להתהלך]   11 בשרירות לבו לאכול מן הקודש] ...
12 מישראל את עצת בני אהרון המ.[...]   13 את האוכל {וחבו} vacat וחב
בדם [...]   14 ביחש{י}ם [...] vacat וזה סרך מושב [...]   15 הקוד]ש במחני]הם
ו]עריהם בכ]ול [...   16 [...]. מו]שב א[...]

Frag. 6 I   1 [...]...[...]   ו]א[ם] [שפל ה]שת [א]ו השפח]ת [2 [מן העור ...
הכ]הן וראה הכהן אותו כמראי הבשר החי וכ[...]   3 [... צרעת] היאה
האוחז]ת}ה בעור החי וכמשפט הזה [...]   4 [...] וראה הכוהן ביום השביעי והנא
נוסף מן החי   5 [אל המת ... צ]רעת ממארת היא ומשפט נתק הרוש והזקן]
6 [... ו]ראה הכוהן וה]נא באה הרוח ברוש ו{י}אⁱ בזקן באוחז]ת]ה   7 בגיד
ופר]ח הנגע מתחת הש]ער והפך מרא{ת}ה לדק צוהב כי כעשב   8 הוא
אשר [י]ש הרחש תחתו vacat ויקיץ שורשו ויבש פרחו ואשר   9 אמר וצ'ה
הכוהן וגלחו את ה{ב}ר'ש}ר} ואת הנתק לא יגלחו למען אשר
10 י{ש}ספור הכוהן את השערות המיתות והחיות וראה אם יו}סף מן
11 {כ} החי אל המת בשבעת הימים טמא הואה ואם לו ליוסף מן הח]יות]
12 על המיתות והגיד נמלא [ד]ם ור]ו]ח החיים עולה וי'רדת בון נרפא]
13 הנגע זה משפט [תור]ת הצרעת לבני אהרון להבדיל ל[...]   14 vacat]
מ]שפט הזב את זובו כול איש א]שר זו]ב יז]וב] 15-16 [...]...[...]

Frag. 6 II   1 [...]...[...]... ו]א[יש [א]שר י]קרב   2 [אליה ע]ו]ן נדה עלו
ואם ראתה] עו]ד והיאה לו] בעת]   3 [נדתה]שבעת ימים והיאה אל תוכל
קודש ואל ת]בו]   4 אל המקדש עד בו השמש ביום השמיני vacat   5 ואשה

Frag. 5 col. II (= 4Q267 5 III)   *1* [And anyone who is not quick to under]stand, and anyone w[ho speaks weakly or staccato], *2* [with]out separating his words to make [his voice] heard, [such men should not read in the book of] *3* [the Torah], so that he will not lead to error in a capital matter [...] *4* [...] his brothers, the priests, in service. [And no]t [... Anyone] *5* of the sons of Aaron who has been a captive among the gentiles [...] *6* to defile it with their impurity. He should not approach the service of [...] *7* from the house of the veil. *Blank* And he should not eat of the [most] holy things [...] *8* Whoever of the sons of Aaron emigrates to se[rve ...] *9* /to teach/ his people in the council of the people, and also to ‹betray› ... [... And whoever of the sons of] *10* Aaron has allowed his name to fall from the ‹truth› [... walking] *11* in the stubbornness of his heart to eat of the holy [...] *12* of Israel the council of the sons of Aaron ... [...] *13* he who eats *Blank* shall incur the fault of the blood [...] *14* in their genealogy (?). *Blank* And this is the rule of the session of [...] *15* of holine[ss in] their [camps and] their cities in a[ll ...] *16* [... the ses]sion of [...]

Frag. 6 col. I (= 4Q269 7; 4Q272 1 I - II; 4Q273 4 II)   *1* [... But i]f [the] tumour or the ras[h is deeper] *2* [than the skin ... the prie]st, and the priest sees in it something like living flesh, or like [...] *3* [...] it is [leprosy] which has taken hold of the living skin. And in accordance with this regulation, *4* [...] The priest shall examine it on the seventh day; if something live has been added *5* [to the dead, ...] it is malignant [le]prosy. And the regulation for ringworm of the head or of the bear[d:] *6* [... the priest shall examine whe]ther the spirit has come into the head {and} /or/ the beard, taking hold of *7* the artery, and [the disease has] spro[uted from underneath the ha]ir, changing its appearance to yellowish - for it is like a plant *8* under which there [is] a worm, *Blank* which cuts its root so that its fruit turns pale. And what he *9* said: *Lev 13:33* «The priest shall order them to shave their {flesh} head, but not to shave their ringworm», it is so that *10* the priest can count the dead and living hairs, and see whether *11* living (hairs) have been added to the dead ones during the seven days, (then) he is impure; but if liv[ing] (hairs) have not been added *12* to the dead ones and the artery is full of [blo]od, and the sp[ir]it of life goes up and down through it, *13* that disease [is healed]. This is the regulation of the law of leprosy for the sons of Aaron, so that they can differentiate [...] *14* *Blank* [Re]gulation concerning the man with a discharge. Every man w[ith a di]sch[arge] *15-16* [...] ... [...]

Frag. 6 col. II   *1* [...] ... [and a] m[an] w[ho] approaches *2* her, the ini]quity of impurity is upon him; and if she sees (it) [aga]in, whilst she is not [in the period] *3* [of her impurity of] seven days, she shall not eat anything holy or [enter] *4* the temple until sunset on the eighth day. *Blank* *5* And the woman who

אשר] תזרי[ע וילדה זכר [וטמאה א[ת שבעת [הימים   6   [כ]י[מי] נדת[
...[...   7   [...] 8   [...]אותה ו[...   9   [...]לא תוכל[...   10   ...]מ[שפט
מות הו[אה ...   11   [הי]לד למנקת בטוה[רה ...   12   [ו]אם לוא ה^שיגה
יד]ה   [...   13   [ו]המירה [א]ת ה[שה ...

Frag. 6 iii   1   [...]...[...]   2   [...] את מי הנדה [...]   3   אל [...] *vacat* ...]
[על}   4   [...]ועללות הכ]רם עד עשרה גרגרי[ם [העל]לת   5   [...]וכול
הלקט] עד סאה לבית ה[סא]ה]   6   [והיא] אשר זרעה אין בה] תרומה ו[פרט
[...]   7   [...]ובעוללתו עד עשרה ג[רגרים] ובנק[וף]   8   [הזית ופר]י
תבואותו אם [...]   9   ...[...]...[...]

Frag. 6 iv   1   [...].[...]   2   נטעי הכר[ם ו]כול {עצי הפרי} וכל עצי ה...
[...]   3   כמשפטם [באדמ]ת הקודש ובארץ מגורים ואחר ימכו[רו]   4   ומהם
לקנ[ה...[... ...]   ואם י[טע איש בשנה הרב'עית ל[ו יוכ]ל   5   [כי]קדשו בש[נה
הזאות   [...].[...   6   [...]...   7   [...]...[...]   8   [להו]סיף לו .[... ...]
9   [...]...[...]

Frag. 7 i   1   [...]...[...]   2   [...]...[...] אבד אליה[ם .[...   3   [ו]מעלו
אל יטור איש אל[... בנ[י עמו כי א[ם]   4   בהוכח ענות צדק אליה[ם ...
[ונושה עוו[ן]   5   [...] ול[ו] אבה [...]...[...]

Frag. 7 ii   6   [...] כול המחנה]   7   [...] רובעו *vacat* [...]
8   [...]...[...]   9   [...] א[שר לו במש[פט ...   10   ...]ו[האיש אשר] ...[

Frag. 7 iii   1   בוא.[...]   2   לפני ה[מבק[ר ה]...]   3   למבק[ר א]שר על
המחנה [...] *vacat* [...]...   4   [...]... [י]דרוש מידו[... ...]   5   [...] את המוא[ס בת[ורה]
[...   6   [...]...[...]... מ[עשים] ...[...]   7   [...] [הוא]ה
[...]...[...]

Frag. 8 i   1   [...]...[...]   2   עמדו לפני המבקר למה [יתפ]תה בה
בדרשה אותו וכא[שר]   3   יקים עלו לשוב אל תורת מוש[ה]בכול לב ובכול

is [pregna]nt and gives birth to a male [she shall be impure] during seven [days,] *6* [as in] the d[ays of] impurity [...] ... *7* [...] *8* [...] her and [...] *9* [...] she shall not eat [...] *10* [... it] is a [ca]pital offense [...] *11* [the ch]ild to a wet-nurse in puri[ty ...] *12* [And] if [her] means do not stretch [...] *13* [and] she may substitute the [lamb ...]

Frag. 6 col. III (= 4Q267 6; 4Q270 3 II)   *1* [...] ... [...] *2* [...] the lustral water [...] *3* [...] God (?) *Blank* [...] {concerning} *4* [...] and the grapes of the vine[yard: up to ten berrie]s [the gra]pe. *5* [...] and all the gleanings [up to one seah per bu]sh[el.] *6* [And that] in which (is only) its seed, in it there is not [sacred offering nor] fallen grapes [...] *7* [...] and in its grapes are up to ten b[erries,] and at the bea[ting] *8* [of the olive and frui]t of its produce, if [...] ... *9* [...] ... [...]

Frag. 6 col. IV   *1* [...] ... [...] *2* plants of the vine[yard, and eve]ry {fruit tree} and all trees ... [...] *3* in accordance with their regulation [on] the holy [soil] and in the land of residence, and afterwards they shall se[ll] *4* from them to b[uy ...] And if a man plants, in the fourth year [he may] n[ot ea]t (of it) *5* [but] he shall consecrate it in [that] y[ear ...] *6* ... [...] *7* [...] ... [...] *8* [to a]dd for him [...] *9* [...] ... [...]

Frag. 7 col. I   *1* [...] ... [...] *2* [...] destroys th[em ...] *3* [and] his unfaithfulness. No-one should bear resentment towards [... the childr]en of his nation, exc[ept] *4* with reproof of just humility of th[em ...] and bearing iniqui[ty] *5* [...] and n[ot] did he desire ... [...]

Frag. 7 col. II   *6* [...] the whole camp [...] *7* [...] its quarter. *Blank* [...] *8* [...] ... [...] *9* [...] which is not according to the regu[lation ...] *10* [... and] he who [...]

Frag. 7 col. III   *1* enter [...] *2* in front of the [Inspec]tor [...] *3* to the Inspect[tor w]ho is over the camp. *Blank* [...] *4* [...] he shall ask from him [...] *5* [...] who spu[rns the l]aw [...] *6* [...] ... [... d]eeds [...] *7* [...] /he/ ... [...]

Frag. 8 col. I (= CD-A xv *11-17*)   *1* [...] ... [...] *2* he stands in front of the Inspector, lest he [appears si]mple when he examines him. But wh[en] *3* he has imposed upon himself to return to the law of Mos[es] with all his heart and all his

נפש נקיאים   4 הם] ממנו [אם ימעל וכול אש]ר [נגלה מן התורה לרוב
המחנה   5 והו[א שג]ה בה יודיעהו המבקר אותו ויצוהו עלו וילמד   6 עד
שנה תמימה ולפי דעתה יקרב וכול היותו אויל   7 [ומ]שוגע אל יבו וכול
פתי ושוגה וכה עינים לבלתי ראות   8 [ו]חגר או פסח או חרש או נער
זעטוט א[ל יבו [איש   9 [מ]אלה אל תוך העדה כי מלאכ[י] הקוד[ש ...]...
10 [...]...[...]

Frag. 8 II   1 [...]   2 גם   המשפט ה[זה ... ונענש הנודר ...]ששית
3 כסף ערכו [...]   [להמשפט] [לשופטים} vacat   4 לשפוט צד[ק ...]ד אחר
המ[ודר ... א[ם אנוס   5 הוא [ע]ד אשר ... ושלם ה[אונס אם לו]דבר
6 אמת עם רעה vacat ועד [...]...[...]   7 [...]... כמוה כי לו ה]קים את
דברו [...] vacat   8 ואשר אמר vacat [כול אדם אשר יחרים א[דם   9 מאדם
בחוקי [הגואים להמית הואה ...   10 ואש]ר אמר [...

Frag. 8 III   1-2 [...]   3 [דבר מן המצוה בי]ד ר]מה עד זכו ל[שוב
vacat [vacat]   4 ו]זה סרך לשופטי[העדה [עד עשרה אנ]שים ברורים מן
העד[ה] לפי העת   5 ארב[עה למטה לוי ו]אהרון ומ[ישרא]ל[ל ששה
מבו]ננים vacat בספר ההגי   6 ובישו]די הברית מב[ני חמש [ו]עשרים]
שנה ועד] בן ששים שנה ואל ית[יצ]ב]   7 עוד [מבן ששים שנה ומע]לה
לשפוט את] העדה כ]י במעל האדם מעט[ו ימו]   8 [ובחרון אף אל ביושבי
הארץ אמר] לה]סיר את דעתם עד לו ישלימו את]   9 [ימיהם vacat על
הטהר במים אל ירחץ איש במים צואים ומו]עטים   10 [מדי מרעיל איש
אל יטהר במה כלי וכול גבא בסלע [אשר אין בו vacat

Frag. 9 II   1 [... או במי]ם עד הם ח[יים]   2 [כי הוא משפט בריאתם
וכול העצים והאבני[ם והעפר א[שר]   3 [יגואלו בטמאת האדם לגאולי שמן
בהם כפי ט[מאתם יט[מא]   4 [הנוגע בם וכול כלי מסמר או יתד בכותל
אשר יהי]ו עם   5 [המת בבית וטמאו בטמאת אחד כלי מעשה סרך מוש[ב
ערי ישראל   6 [על המשפטים האלה להבדיל בין הטמא לטהור ול[ה]ודיע

4Q266

soul they will exact revenge *4* [from him] if he should become unfaithful. All that has been revealed of the law for the multitude of the camp *5* — if h[e inadvertently fa]ils, the Inspector should teach him and give orders concerning him and he should learn *6* for a full year. And in accordance with (his) knowledge he will approach. And no-one stupid *7* [or de]ranged should enter; and anyone feeble-minded and insane, those with eyes to weak to see, *8* [and] the lame or one who stumbles, or a deaf person, or an under-age boy, none *9* [of] these [shall enter] the congregation, for the ho[ly] angels [...] ... *10* [...] ... [...]

Frag. 8 col. II (= CD-A XVI *17*- IX *2*)   *1* [...] also *2* th[is] rule (applies) [... will be punished he who dedicates ...] the sixth part of *3* the money which corresponds [...] {by the regulation} [... For the judges,] *Blank 4* in order to judge with jus[tice ...] then the dedi[cated thing ... I]f it is appropriated by violence *5* [un]til ... and the [violator] shall pay; [if he has not] spoken *6* the truth to his fellow, *Blank* and until [...] *7* ... [...] like it, because he has not k[ept his word ...] *8 Blank* And as for what he said: *Blank* [*Lev 27:29* «Every man who vows to destruction any]one *9* else», [shall be executed] according to the laws of [the gentiles. ...] *10* And wha[t he said: ...]

Frag. 8 col. III (= CD-A X *3-12*)   *1-2* [...] *3* [any precept, deli]bera[tely, until he has been purified to] return. *Blank* [*Blank*] *4* And [this is the rule of the judges of] the congregation. [Ten me]n [in number,] chosen from among the congregation, for a period: *5* fo[ur from the tribe of Levi and of] Aaron and [six] from [Israe]l, [lea]rned *Blank* in the book of HAGY *6* and in the princi[ples of the covenant; between] twenty-five and sixty years. And no-one *7* over [sixty years should h]old the office of judging [the congregation, f]or on account of man's unfaithfulness [his days] were shortened, *8* [and because of God's wrath against the inhabitants of the earth, he ordered] to re[move knowledge from them before they completed] *9* [their days. *Blank* Concerning purification with water. No-one should bathe in water which is dirty or which is l]ess *10* [than the amount which covers a man. *Blank* No-one should purify a vessel in it. And every cavity in the rock] in which there is no

Frag. 9 col. II (= CD-A XII *14-22*)   *1* [... or into w]ater while they are still al[ive,] *2* [as this is the regulation for their species. And all the wood and the stone]s and the dust w[hich *3* are defiled by man's impurity, while with stains of oil in them, in accordance with] their [unc]leanness will make *4* [whoever touches them] im[pure. And every utensil, nail or peg in the wall which i]s with *5* [a dead person in the house will be unclean with the same uncleanness as tools for work. Rule for the asse]mbly of the cities of Israel. *6* [In accordance with these regulations, to keep the unclean apart from the clean, and]

7 [בין הקודש לחול *vacat* ואלה החקים למשכיל לה[ת]ה[ה]לך 8 [בם עם
כול חי למשפט עת ועת וכמשפט הזה יתהלכו זרע יש[ראל

1 [ואל י]עש[ה] איש למקח ולממכר] 2 [ד]בר כי אם] הודיע *Frag. 9* III
למבקר] 3 [א]שר במחנ]ה ועשה בעצה] 4 ולו ישוגו וכן לכול לוק[ח
אשה] 5 והואה בעצה וכן יבן ל[מגרש] 6 וה[ואה י]יסר את בניהם] [...]
7 וטפם] ברו[ח ע[נ]וה ובא[הבת חסד] 8 אל יטור לה[ם] באף וע[ברה]
9 [ע]ל פשעיהם] וא[ת אשר איננו 10 [נק]ש[ר ... מ]שפטיהם 11 [וזה
מושב המחנות לכו]ל זרע

1 [ובכול משפט]י ה[תורה לדבר]ם כמשפ[טם *vacat* *Frag. 10* I
וה]מבקר שלכול 2 [המחנות מבן] שלשים] שנה עד ב[ן חמשים [שנה
בעול ב[כול ס[ו]ד 3 [אנשים ו]לכול לשו[ן ... על פי]הו יבאו [באי
[הע[ד]ה 4 [איש בתרו]וכול הד[בר אשר י]היה לכול [האד]ם לדבר לעדה
5 [למבקר ידבר]לכול ר]יב ומשפט ו]זה סרך הרבי]ם [להכין כול
6 [חפציהם שכר] שני [ימים לממעי]ט וינתן [על יד] המבקר והשופטים
7 [ממנו ית]נו בעד פצ]ועים וממנו י]חזקו בעד] הע]ני והאביון 8 [ולזקן
א]שר יכרע ו]ל[איש אשר ינוגע ולאשר ישבה לגי נכר 9 [ולבתולה אש]ר
אין ל]ה [גואל ולנער אשר אין ול (לו) דורש ולכול 10 [עבודת החבר ו]לו
יכרת בית החבר מידם זה פרוש 11 [מושב המחנות וא]לה יסדות אוש[י]
הקהל וזה פרוש 12 [המשפטים אשר יש]פטו בם עד ממוד (מעמוד) משיח
אהרון וישראל 13 [ויכפר עוונם ממנ]חה וחטת [...] *vacat* 14 [והאיש
אשר ישקר בממון והוא יודע והבדילו]הו מן הט[הרה]

1 [מאת]ים ימים ונענש מאה יום ואם בדבר מות ינטור *Frag. 10* II
ולו] י]שוב 2 [עוד ואש]ר [יצ]חה את רעהו שלו בעצה [והו]בדל שנה אחת
ונע[נ]ש 3 ש]שה חודשים] ואשר ידבר בפיה]ו [דבר נבל ונענש ע]שר]ים
4 [יום והובדל]שלושה חודשי]ם ואשר י]דבר בתוך דב]רי רעהו ו]פרע

594

distinguish *7* [between holy and profane. *Blank* And these are the ordinances for the Instructor, so that he w]alks *8* [in them with every living thing, according to the regulation for every time. And in accordance with this regulation shall the seed of Is]rael [walk.]

Frag. 9 *col.* III (= CD-A XIII *15-20*)   *1* [And no-one should] make [a purchase or sell] *2* [any]thing, without [informing the Inspector] *3* [o]f the cam[p; he shall proceed in consultation] *4* lest they err. And likewise with regard to anyone who mar[ries a woman:] *5* it should be with consultation. And likewise he shall pay attention to [anyone who divorces;] *6* he shall instruct their children [...] *7* and their small children [with a spir]it of mo[de]sty and with [compassionate] l[ove]. *8* He should not bear resentment against them in anger and ra[ge] *9* because of their sins. And that which is not *10* [deter]mi[ned ...] their [ju]dgments [...] *11* [And this is the assembly of the camps for al]l the seed of

Frag. 10 *col.* I (= CD-A XIV *8-20*; 4Q267 9 v)   *1* [and in all the regulation]s of the [law, to formulate] them in accordance with [their] regu[lations. *Blank* And the] Inspector who is over all *2* [the camps will be between] thirty [years] and fifty [years of age, mastering] every secret *3* [of men and] every langua[ge ... On] his [authority, the members of] the ass[em]bly shall enter, *4* [each one in his turn;] and any ma[tter which] any [ma]n needs to say to the assembly, *5* [should be told to the Inspector,] in connection with any disp[ute or judgment.] This is the rule of the Many, to provide for all *6* [their needs: the salary] of two [days at leas]t. It shall be placed [in the hand] of the Inspector and of the judges. *7* [From it they shall g]ive to the inju[red, and with it they shall] support [the ne]edy and the poor, *8* [and to the elder] who is bent, and [to] the afflicted, and to the prisoner of a foreign people, *9* [and to the girl who] has no redeemer, and to the youth who has no-one looking after him, and for all *10* [the task of the association; and] the house of the association shall not be deprived of its means. This is the exact interpretation *11* [of those who live in the camps, and the]se are the foundation walls of the assembly. And this is the exact interpretation *12* [of the regulations by which they shall be r]uled until the rise of the messiah of Aaron and Israel. *13* [And their iniquity will be atoned through meal] and sin-offerings [...] *Blank* *14* [And the man who lies knowingly with regard to riches they shall exclude] from the pu[re food]

Frag. 10 *col.* II (cf. 1QS VII)   *1* two [hundred] days, and he shall be punished for one hundred days. And if he bears resentment in a capital matter, he may not return *2* [anymore. And whoever in]sults someone else inadvertently, [shall be] excluded for one year, and he shall be pun[is]hed *3* for si[x months.] And whoever utters a senseless word with his mouth, shall be punished for t[we]nty *4* [days, and he shall be excluded] for three months. [And whoever] speaks in the middle of [a fellow's] wor[ds, and] is deranged, *5* [shall be pun-

5 [ונענש עשרת]ימים [ואשר ישכ]ב [ו]ישן ב[מו]ש[ב הרבים ...]ה

6 [והובדל]שלושים יום [ו]נענש עשרת ימים[וכן לאיש הנפ]טר   7 [אשר

[לו בעצת הר[ב]י]ם ו[ה]נ[מ] ^{עד} שלוש פע]מים על מושב[אחד   8 ו[נענש

[עשרה ימים ^יאם] יזקפו [ונפטר] במושב ונענש שלושים[9 יו[ם] ואשר

יהלך לפני רע]הו ערום בבית או בשדה הלך ערום לפני[10 ה[ב]ריאות

והובדל ששה] חדשים ונענש שלושים יום ואשר[11 [יו]צא {את} ידו

מתחת בגד]ו [...] ...[...]   12 [יו]ם ונענש עשרה

וה{ש}[ס]ו[ח]ק בסכלו]ת להשמיע קולו ו[הובדל]   13 [ש]לושים ונענש

חמש[ת] עשר] ימים [והמוציא את י]דו השמ[א]לית]   14 [לש]ח בה ונענש]

עשרה ימים והאיש א[שר ילך] רכיל]   15 [בר]ע[ה]ו [...]

1 על הרבים וקבל את משפטו מרצונו כאשר אמר ביד   *Frag. 11*

2 מושה על הנפש אשר תחטא בשגגה אשר יביאו את   3 חטתו[ו]את

אשמו ועל ישראל כתוב אלכה לי   4 אל קצי[ן ה]שמים ולו אריח בריח

ניחוחכם ובמקום אחר   5 כתוב לשוב אל אל בבכי ובצום ובמקו[ם אח]ר כתוב

קרעו לבבכם ואל בגדיכם וכול המואס במשפטים   6 האלה על פי כול החוקים

הנמצאים בתורת מושה לו יחשב   7 בכול בני אמתו כי געלה נפשו ביסורי

הצדק במרד מלפני   8 הרבים ישתלח וידבר בו הכוהן המופקד] ע[ל הרבים

וענה   9 [וא]מר ^{את} ברוך אונו הו הכול ובידיך הכול ועושה הכול אשר

יסדתה   10 [ע]מים למשפחותיהם ולשונות לאומותם ותתעם בתהו ולו

11 <ולו> דרך ובאבותינו בחרתה לזרעם נתתה חוקי אמתכה   12 ומשפטי

קודשכה אשר יעשה האדם וחיה וגבולות הגבלתה   13 לנו אשר את

עובריהם ארותה ואנו עם פדותכה וצון מרעיתך^ה   14 אתה ארותה את

עובריהם ואנו הקימונו ויצא המשתלח והאיש   15 אשר יוכל מהונם ואשר

ידרוש שלומו {והמשתלח} ואשר יאות עמו   16 ונכתב דברו על יד המבקר

כחרת ושלים משפטו וכול {יו}   17 [יושבי]המחנות יקהלו בחודש השלישי

ואררו את הנוטה ימין   18 [ושמאול מן ה]תורה והזה פרוש המשפטים אשר

ished for ten] days. And whoever lies do[wn and] goes to sleep during the [meet]in[g of the Many …] 6 [shall be excluded] for thirty days [and] shall be punished for ten days. [And thus with whoever goes] away, 7 [with]out the permission of the Man[y, and that] /up to/ three ti[mes in] one [session,] 8 [he shall be punished] for ten days; and if [they raise up (?)] and he withdraws [from the session he shall be punished for thirty] 9 da[ys.] And whoever walks [naked] in front of [his] fel[low in a house, or walks naked in the field in front of] 10 the [cr]eatures, shall be excluded for six [months and shall be punished thirty days. And whoever] 11 [ta]kes out {the} "his hand" from under [his] clothes, […] … [… he shall be excluded thi]rty 12 days, and shall be punished for ten; and whoever giggles inanely, [causing his voice to be heard, shall be excluded] 13 for [th]irty and shall be punished for fif[teen] days. [And he who takes out] his le[ft hand] 14 [to gestic]ulate with it, shall be punished [for ten days. And whoev]er goes around [defaming] 15 his [fe]llow […]

Frag. 11 (= 4Q270 7 i - ii)   1 over the Many and he will readily receive his judgment, as he said through the hand of 2 Moses about the person who sins through oversight: *Lev 4:27* «they should present 3 his sin-offering [or] their guilt-offering»; and about Israel it is written: *Lev 26:31* «I shall go 4 to the edges of the heavens, and I shall not smell the aroma of your pleasant fra-grances». And in another place 5 it is written: *Joel 2:12* (?) «to return to God in tears and in fasting». /And in [anoth]er pla[ce] it is written : *Joel 2:13* «Tear your heart and not your clothes»/. And anyone who despises these regulations 6 according to all the precepts which are found in the law of Moses, shall not be considered 7 among all the sons of his truth, for his soul has loathed the disciplines of justice. In rebellion, he will be expelled from the presence of 8 the Many. And the priest who governs [ov]er the Many will speak to him; he will begin to speak, 9 [sa]ying: /«Blessed are you,/ who art everything, in your hands is everything, you do everything, you have founded 10 the [na]tions according to their families, and according to their languages, and according to their tribes, and you have led them astray in a trackless 11 wilder-ness. You chose our fathers and gave their descendants your truthful regula-tions 12 and your holy precepts, so that man could carry them out and live. And you established frontiers 13 for us, and you curse those who cross them. And we are the people of your ransom and the flock of your pasture. 14 You curse those who cross them but us you have raised up». And the one who has been expelled will leave, and the man 15 who eats from his riches, and the one who seeks his peace, {the one who has been expelled} and the one who is agreement with him. 16 And his sentence will be written down by the Inspec-tor's hand, as an engraving, and his judgment will be complete. And all 17 [those who dwell in] the camps will assemble in the third month and will curse whoever tends to the right 18 [or to the left of the] law. This is the exact

יעשו בכול קץ   19 [הפקודה את אשר יפק]ידו [בכו]ל קצי החרון ומסעיהם
לכול   20 [...]...[...]

Frag. 13   1 [...]. הקודש [...]   2 [...] כמדת [...].   3 ... [...]ה[גואים
עובד א[ת ... אשר   4 ל[ו יעיד את רעה]ו [...   5 הדם vacat ה.[...]
6 אשר לא י.[...]...[...]   7 [...]

4Q267 (4QDᵇ) *4QDamascus Documentᵇ*

J.M. Baumgarten, *DJD XVIII*, 95-113, pls. XVIII-XXI
PAM 43.293, 43.294
ROC 106, 107
CD-A, CD-B, 4Q266, 4Q268, 4Q269, 4Q270, 4Q271, 4Q272, 4Q273, 5Q12,

Frag. 1   1 [...].   2 [...] שיחתכה [אם ...   3 [...]עמ[דתה   4 [ותתבונן
...[...]   5 [ישיבו את ...]ה עפר ואפר   6 [...]ה לוא הבינותה
7 [...]...יתכה   8 [...]ד כול בשר ובר[יאה]

Frag. 2   1 [מלפני]ם [עמד מושה ואהרון ביד [שר האו]רים ויקם]
2 [בליעל [את יחנה וא[ת אחי]הו במזמ]תו [בהושע י]שראל את]
3 [הריאש]ונה vacat   4 [ובקץ חורבן [הא]רץ עמדו] מסיגי [ג]בול ויתעו
את יש[ראל]   5 [ותשם ה]א[ר]ץ כי דברו עצה סרה על מצוות אל ב[י]ד
6 [מוש]ה vacat וגם במשיחי הקודש וינבאו שקר לה[ש]יב את   7 [ישר]אל
מאחרי אל ויזכור אל ברית רי[אשו]נים ויקם   8 [מאה]רון נבונים ומישראל
חכמים ו[ישמ]יעם ויחפ[ו]ר[ו]   9 [א]ת הבאר באר אשר אמר מושה באר
חפ[ר]וה שרים כרוה   10 נדיב[י] העם [במחוקק vacat   11 הבאר] הי[א]ה
התור]ה וחופריה [המה שבי י]שרא[ל   12 היוצ[א]י[ם מארץ י]הוד]ה
וי[גורו במגו]ר' [דמשק אשר קרא]   13 אל א[ת כ]ולם שרי[ם]כי כול[ם
דרשוהו ולוא הושבה פארתם]   14 בפי אחד vacat   15 [והמחוקק הואה
דור]ש התו]רה [...

598

interpretation of the regulations which they are to observe in the whole age of
19 [visitation, with which they will be visi]ted (?) [in al]l the ages of wrath and
their routes, to all *20* [...] ... [...]

Frag. 13   *1* [...] of holiness [...] *2* [...] according to the measure of [...] *3* [...
the] nations, doing [... who] *4* does [no]t warn his fellow [...] *5* the blood *Blank*
[...] *6* who does not [...] *7* [...] ... [...]

4Q267 (4QDᵇ) *4QDamascus Documentᵇ*

6Q15

Bibliography: J.M. Baumgarten, 'The 4Q Zadokite Fragments on Skin Disease',
JJS 41 (1990) 157-158; *Wacholder-Abegg 1,* 28-35

Frag. 1 (= 4Q266 1 a - b)   *1* [...] *2* [... your concern] if *3* [...] you stood *4* [and
considered ...] ... *5* [they shall answer bring back the ...] dust and ashes *6* [...]
you did not understand *7* [...] your ... *8* [...] all flesh and cre[ature]

Frag. 2 (= CD-A v *17*- vi *7*; 4Q266 3 ii; 6Q15 3)   *1* [in ancient time]s [there arose
Moses and Aaron, by the hand of the] prince of lig[hts,] *2* [and Belial,] with
[his] cunning, [raised up] Jannes and his [brother] during the fi[rst] deliverance of *3* [Israel]. *Blank* *4* [And in the age of devastation of] the la[nd there
arose] those who shifted the [bo]undary and made Is[rael] stray. *5* [And the]
l[a]nd [became desolate], for they counselled a rebellion against God's precepts (given) through the hand of *6* [Mose]s *Blank* and also of the holy
anointed ones. They prophesied deceit in order to di[ve]rt *7* [Isra]el from following God. But God remembered the covenant with the fore[fath]ers, and
raised *8* [from Aa]ron men of knowledge and from Israel wise men, and made
them [li]sten. And they dug *9* the well, a well about which Moses said: *Num
21:18* «A well which the princes d[u]g, which *10* the nobles [of the people]
delved with the staff». *Blank* *11* The well is the law. [And those who dug it] are
the converts of I[srae]l, *12* who lef[t] the land of J[uda]h and [lived in the
dwell]ing/s/ of [Damascus, al]l of whom *13* God [called] princes, for [they] all
[sought him, and their renown has not been repudiated *14* in anyone's mouth.
Blank *15* [And the spade is the interpreter] of the la[w, ...]

Frag. 5 II   1 [ואמ]יצי כו[ח בנגלה ... המחזיקים בשם]   2 [קוד]שו
המה א[נשי ... כי ביהודה]   3 [נמצא] קשר לשוב[...]   4 [ליש]ראל
בעומד[...]   5 [...] vacat שלום [...]   6 וכ[ו]ל[ל] הנ[שארים [...]   7 [איש לפ]י
רוחו[יקרבו ...]

Frag. 5 III   1 [... וכ]ול א[שר ...]   2 [...] וכול כהה [עיני]ם או ...]
וכול אשר אינו[3 ממהר לה[ב]ין]וכול אשר נקל בל[שונו או בקול]
4 טרוד דבר לו לוא פצל[דב]ריו ל[השמיע קולו איש מאלה]   5 לוא יקרא
בס[פר התורה ... 6-9 [...]...[...]

Frag. 6   1 [...]...[...]   2 [...ואם [...] ועללות הכרם] עד עשרה גרגרים
העוללת   3 [... א]שר זרעה אין בה תרומה   4 [...] vacat   5 [... נק]פו אחד
משלושים vacat וכול   6 [... ואם רפוס הש[ד]ה או קדה בשרף ונפרס
7 [מסאה לבית סאה מעשרה בה ו]אם תלקוט נפש אחת

Frag. 9 I   1 [...]   2 [מחודש לחודש [ובחרון אפו בו דבר בו בדבר מות
ענה בו יען אשר לוא]הקים את מצות   3 [אשר אמר לו הוכח תוכיח את
רעכה ולוא תשא עליו]חטא vacat   4 [על השבועה אשר אמר לוא
תושיעכה ידכה לכה אי[ש אשר]יש[ב]יע [ע]ל   5 [פני השדה אשר לוא לפני
השופטים או מאמרם הושיעה י]דו לו [וכו]ל   6 [האובד ולוא נודע מי גנבו
ממאוד המחנה אשר גנב בו יש[ב]יע ב[על]יו   7 [בשבועת האלה והשומע
אם יודע הוא ולוא יגיד ואשם כו]ל[אשם   8 [מושב אשר אין בעלים והתודה
המשיב לכוהן והיה לו] לב[ד מא[י]ל

Frag. 9 IV   1 [...] ואם משפט לתורת נ[גע יהיה] באיש ובא הכהן
ועמד[2 [במחנה והבינו המבקר]בפרוש התו[רה ואם פתי הוא]   3 [הוא
יסגירנו כי להם ה]משפט vacat [וזה סרך המבקר]   4 [למחנה ישכיל את
הרבים במ[עשי] ויבינם בגבורות]   5 [פלאו ויספר לפניהם נהיות

Frag. 5 *col.* II (= 4Q266 5 I b)   *1* [and those of fi]rm pow[er in what has been revealed ... those who hold fast to] *2* his [hol]y [name] are the m[en of ... for in Judah] *3* [there is found] a conspiracy to return [...] *4* [to Is]rael when arises [...] *5* peace. *Blank* [...] *6* And all [those who r]emain [...] *7* [each one accor]ding to his spirit [they shall let approach ...]

Frag. 5 *col.* III (= 4Q266 5 II)   *1* [... and any]one w[ho ...] *2* [...] and anyone with week [eye]s or [... And anyone who is not] *3* quick to under[stand,] and anyone who spe[aks] weakly [or] *4* staccato, without separating his [wor]ds to [make his voice heard, such men] *5* should not read in the bo[ok of the Torah ...] *6-9* [...] ... [...]

Frag. 6 (= 4Q266 6 III; 4Q270 3 II)   *1* [...] and if *2* [... and the grapes of the vineyard:] up to ten berries the grape *3* [...] in which (is only) its seed, in it there is not sacred offering *4* [...] *Blank* *5* [...] its [beat]ing is one from every thirty. *Blank* And all *6* [... And if the fi]eld [was trampled] or scorched by fire, but there remains *7* [up to a seah per bushel, there is tithe in it. And] if a person gleans

Frag. 9 *col.* I (= CD-A IX *6-14*; 5Q12 1)   *1* [...] from one month to the other, *2* [and then, when he was angry, accused him of a capital offence, he has testified against himself, for he did not] fulfil the commandment of God *3* [who said to him: *Lev 19:17* «You shall reproach your fellow so as not to incur] sin [because of him».] *Blank 4* [Concerning the oath. What he said: *1 Sam 25:26* «You shall not do justice with your (own) hand»: wh]oever forces the making of an oath in *5* [the open field, not in the presence of judges or at their command, has done justice] for himself with his hand. [Eve]ry *6* [lost object about which it is not known who stole it from the property of the camp in which it was stolen -] its ow[ner should] make a maledictory *7* [oath; whoever hears it, if he knows and does not say it, is guilty. If there is any] debt *8* [due to be given back, but there are no creditors, then the debtor should confess to the priest and it will be for himself,] apa[rt from the r]am

Frag. 9 *col.* IV (= CD-A XIII *4-14*)   *1* [... But if there] is [a judgment against anyone about the law of] leprosy, [the priest shall take his place] *2* [in the camp, and the Inspector shall instruct him] in the exact interpretation of the la[w. Even if he is a simpleton,] *3* [he is the one who shall intern him, for theirs is the] judgment. *Blank* [And this is the rule of the Inspector] *4* [of the camp. He shall instruct the Many in the de]eds of God, [and shall teach them his mighty marvels,] *5* [and recount to them] the eternal [eve]nts [with] their

[עולם] בפ[תריהם וע]לי[הם   6 [ירחם כאב לבניו וישקה לכל מרהוב [בם

כרעה עדרו יתר   7 [כול חרצובות קשריהם לבלתי ה]יות עשוק ורצוץ

[בעדתו] 8 [וכול הנוסף לעדתו יפקדהו [למעשיו ושכלו ו[כוחו] 9 [והונו

וכתבוהו במקומו כפי נח]לתו בגורל האו[ר] vacat   אל   10 [ימשול איש

מכול בני המחנה ל]הביא איש אל [הע]דה   11 [זולת פי המבקר אשר

למחנה ואיש מכל באי ברית [אל אל

Frag. 9 v   1 [...] ואלה המשפטים למשכיל להת]הלך בם   2 [במועד

פקוד אל את ה]ארץ בבו[א ה]דבר אשר דבר יבואו   3 [על עמכה ימים

אש]ר לוא באו [מ]יום סור א[פ]רים מעל   4 [יהודה וכול המתה]ל[כי]ם

באל]ה] ברית $^{\angle F}$ נאמנת   5 [להם להנצילם מכול מו[קשי [הש]חת כי^{א}

פ[ת]אי[ם] עבר[ו]   vacat ויענשו   6 [וסרך מושב כ]ול המ[ח]נות יפקדו

[כו]ל[ם] בשמ[ות]יהם   7 הכוהנים [לרא]יש[ו]נה והלויים] שניים ובני

ישראל   8 [ש]לשיים ויכתבו [בשמותיהם אי]ש אחר אחיהו הכוהנים

9 ל]ראישונה] והלויים שניים ובני] ישראל של'שיים   10 [ו]הגר רביעי

ו]כן י]שבון וכן ישאלו] לכול vacat והכוהן אשר   11 [יפ]קד ברואש

ה]רב]ים מבן שלושים שנה ועד בן ששים   12 [שנ]ה מבונן [בספר] הה'גי

ובכול משפטי התורה לדבר'ם   13 [כ]משפטם וה[מבקר אשר] ל[כו]ל

מחנות מבן [ש]לושים [ש]נה   14 [וע]ד בן חמש[י]ם שנה בעול בכול סו]ד

אנשי]ם ולכול לשו]ן[

Frag. 9 vi   1 [...] ו]האיש אש]ר ימאס [2 [את משפט הרבים ויצא

ולוא ישו]ב עוד vacat   3 [ואשר לקח אוכלו חוצה מן המשפ]ט והשיבו

לאיש   4 [אשר לקחו ממנו ... ו]אשר יקרב לזנות   5 [לאשתו אשר לוא

כמשפט ויצא ו]ל]וא ישו]ב עוד

602

[explan]ations. He shall have pity *6* [on them like a father on his sons, and shall heal all the afflicted] among them like a shepherd his flock. He will undo *7* [all the chains which bind them, so that there] will be [neither] harassed nor oppressed in his congregation. *8* [And everyone who joins his congregation, he should examine] concerning his actions, his intelligence, [his strength,] *9* [and his wealth; and they shall inscribe him in his place according to] his [inher]itance in the lot of lig[ht]. *Blank* No *10* [one of all the members of the camp should have authority to] introduce anyone into [the con]gregation *11* [without the permission of the Inspector of the camp. And] no[ne of those who have entered the covenant] of God

Frag. 9 col. V (= CD-A XIII 22-XIV 9)   *1* [... These are the regulations for the Instructor, to wal]k in them *2* [in the appointed time when God visits the] earth, when [the] word will be fulfil[led] which said: *Isa 7:17* «There shall come *3* [upon your people days such a]s have not come [since] the day on which Ephraim became separated from *4* [Judah»; and (to) all those who wal]k in them, the covenant of God is faithful *5* [to save them from all the ne]ts of [the p]it, but *Prov 27:12* «the ig[no]rant walk on *6* and are punished». *Blank* [Rule of the assembly of a]ll the c[a]mps. [Al]l [of them] shall be enlisted by their names: *7* the priests [first, the levites] second, the children of Israel *8* third; and they shall be inscribed [by their names, each o]ne after his brother: the priests *9* [fi]rst, [the levites second, the children of] Israel third *10* [and the pro]selyte fourth. And [thus shall they] sit [and thus shall they be questioned] about everything. *Blank* And the priest who *11* [is na]med at the head of the M[an]y will be between thirty and sixty *12* [years old,] learned [in the book of] H/W/GY, and in all the regulations of the law, to formulate them *13* [in accordance with] their regulations. And the [Inspector who] is over [al]l the camps will be between [th]irty [y]ears *14* and fif[ty years of age, mastering every secr]et of me[n and every language]

Frag. 9 col. VI (= 4Q270 7 I)   *1* [... And] whoever [despises] *2* [the judgment of the Many, shall leave and n]ever [retu]rn. *Blank 3* [And whoever takes his food contrary to the regulat]ion, is to give it back to the one *4* [from whom he took it ... And] whoever approaches to have illegal sex *5* [with his wife, not in accordance with the regulation, shall leave and] never [retu]rn. *Blank*

4Q268 (4QD^c) *4QDamascus Document^c*

J.M. Baumgarten, *DJD XVIII*, 115-121, pl. XXII
PAM 43.268
ROC 373
CD-A, CD-B, 4Q266, 4Q267, 4Q269, 4Q270, 4Q271, 4Q272, 4Q273, 5Q12,

Frag. 1 1 [...] [אחרונות הלוא כן תבואינה] [...] 2 [...]ה איזה תחלתו
ואיזה סופו וא[יזה ... 3 [... עד] אשר יבוא במה כי .[...] 4 [... כי אי]ן
לקדם [ו]ל[א]חר ממועדיה]מה [... 5 [.] ...*vacat* ... חקק קצי ח[רון לעם
לוא ידעהו] 6 והוא הכין [מועדי] [רצון לדורשי מצוותיו ול]הולכים
בתמים] 7 דרך ויגל ע]יני]מה בנסתרות ואוזנמה פתח ו[ישמעו עמוקות]
8 ויבינו בכול נהיות עד מה יבוא במה *vacat* [*vacat*] 9 [ו]עתה שמעו לי
כול יודעי צדק ובינו במעש]י [כי ריב] 10 [לו עם כול בשר ו]משפט
יעשה בכול מנאציו כי ב[מע]לם [אשר] 11 [עזבוהו] הסת]יר פניו
מ]ישראל [ו]ממקדשו ויתנם] לחרב ובזכרו] 12 [ברית]ראישונים ה]שאיר
ש]ארית לישראל ולוא] נתנם לכלה ובקץ] 13 [חרון ש]נים שלוש מאות
ותשע[ים לתתו]א[ותמה ביד נבוכדנאצר] 14 [מלך בבל]פקדם וי[צמח
מישרא]ל ומא[הרו]ן שור[ש מטעת לירוש] 15 [את ארצו ולדשן בט]וב
אדמתו [ויב]ינו בעוו[נמה וידעו כי] 16 [אשמים המה ויהיו כעוורים
וכמגש]שים ד]רך שנים עשרים] 17 [ויבן אל מעשיהמה כי בלב שלם
דרשו]הו [...]

4Q269 (4QD^d) *4QDamascus Document^d*

J.M. Baumgarten, *DJD XVIII*, 123-136, pls. XXIII-XXV
PAM 43.300, 43.301
ROC 220, 221

Frag. 2 1 [... עלו ור]שו את] הארץ] 2 [... ולוא שמעו לקול עשיהם
ולוא האזינו]למצוות] 3 [יוריהם וירגנו באוהליהם ויחר אף]אל בעדתם

4Q268 (4QD^c) *4QDamascus Document^c*

6Q15

Bibliography: Wacholder-Abegg 1, 1-2; J.M. Baumgarten, 'A "Scriptural" Citation in 4Q Fragments of the Damascus Document', *JJS* 43 (1992) 95-98; R. Eisenman, M. Wise, *DSSU*, 212-219

Frag. 1 (= CD-A I *1-10*; 4Q266 2 I)   *1* […] the final things, should they not surely come? […] *2* […] which is its beginning and which its end and w[hich …] *3* [… until] there comes upon them, for … […] *4* [… for there is n]o before [or] after in th[eir] festivals […] *5 Blank* … He determined the moments of wr[ath for a nation that does not know him,] *6* and he has established [times of] favour for those who examine his precepts and [walk on the perfect] *7* path. He uncovered their e[yes] for hidden things and opened their ears and [they heard profound things] *8* and understood everything that happens before it comes upon them. *Blank* [*Blank*] *9* Now, then, listen to me, all you who know justice, and understand the action[s of] God; [for he has a dispute] *10* [with all flesh, and] will carry out judgment on all those who spurn him. For when they were [unfaith]ful [in] *11* [forsaking him, he hi[d his face from] Israel [and] from his sanctuary, and delivered them [up to the sword. But when he remembered] *12* [the covenant] with the forefathers, he s[aved a re]mnant for Israel and did not [deliver them up to destruction. And at the moment of] *13* [wrath,] three hundred and nin[ety ye]ars [after having delivered them up into the hand of Nebuchadnezzar,] *14* [king of Babylon,] he visited them and cau[sed to sprout from Israe]l and from A[aro]n a sho[ot of the planting, in order to possess] *15* [his land and to become fat with the goo]d things of his soil. [And they rea]lised their s[in and knew that] *16* [they were guilty; but they were like blind persons and like those who gro]pe for the pa[th over twenty years.] *17* [And God appraised their deeds, because they sought] him […]

4Q269 (4QD^d) *4QDamascus Document^d*

CD-A, CD-B, 4Q266, 4Q267, 4Q268, 4Q270, 4Q271, 4Q272, 4Q273, 5Q12, 6Q15

Bibliography: Wacholder-Abegg 1, 48-53; H. Stegemann, 'More Identified Fragments of 4QD^d (4Q269)', *RevQ* 18/72 (1998) 497-509, pl. I

Frag. 2 (= CD-A III *7-11*)   *1* [… *Deut 9:23* «Go and pos]sess [the land»….] *2* [… and they did not listen to the voice of their creator] and did not pay attention [to the precepts] *3* [he had taught them and murmured in their tents. And the

ובנ[יה]ם ב[ו] 4 [אבדו ומלכיהם בו נכרתו וגבוריה]ם בו אבדו וארצם בו
שממה 5 [... בו חבו] באי הברית הראישונים 6 [ויסגרו לחרב בעוזבם
את ברית אל ויבחרו] ברצונם ויתורו אחר[י]

Frag. 4 II 1 [...]...[...] 2 כפרושיהם לאה[ו]ב איש את אחיהו כמוהו]
3 [ו]ל[החז]יק בע[ד עני ואביון וגר ולדרוש] 4 א[י]ש בש[לום אחיהו ולוא
ימעל איש בשאר] 5 בשר[ו] להזיר מן הזונות כמשפט להוכיח] 6 איש
את] אחיהו כמצוה ולוא לנטור מיום ליום] 7 [ו]ל[.].הב]דל [...

Frag. 7 1 [...]מה היא והספחת מכת עץ] 2 [ואבן וכול מכה בבוא
הרוח וא[חזה בגיד ו[ש]ב הדם 3 [למעלה ולמטה והגיד ...[. אחר הדם
4 [... וראה הכוהן את עור החי [ואת ה]מת [... *vacat* 5 [... ב]שבעת]
הימי[ם [... 6 [... ואחר י]שוה [ב[ו] כאשר [אמר והס]גירו הכוהן]
7 [שבעת ימים עד אשר יצ]מח הבשר וראה הכוהן [ביום ה]שביעי] והנה]
8 [רוח החיים עולה ו]יורדת והבשר] צמח נרפא הנגע [... 9 [הספחת לוא
יראנה הכוהן] לעור הב[שר ... 10 [... ואם שפ]ל השת או [הספחת מן
העור [... 11 [... וראה הכוהן א[ו]תו כמ[ראי] הבש[ר החי ... 12 [צרעת
היא אוחזה] בעור הח[י וכמשפט הזה [... 13 [... וראה [הכוהן ב]יום
השביעי [...

Frag. 8 II 1 [... אל יביא [איש את ...[...] ... בדם זבחם [...]
2 [בטהרתו ומכול הזהב ו]הכסף והנחושת] והבדיל והעופרת א[שר עשו
הגואים פ]סל] 3 [אל יביאהו כיא אם] מן החדש] הבא מן הכור] אל יבא
איש כול ע[ור ובגד] 4 [ומן כול הכלי אשר יעשה מ]לאכה ב]הם אשר
יטמאו ל]נפש אדם כיא אם הוזו כמ]שפט] 5 [הטהרה במי הנדה ב]קץ
הרש[ע איש טהור מ]כול טמא]ה] אשר יעריב א[ת] 6 [השמש ...[.].[...]

Frag. 9 1 [כול מומיה יספר לו למה יביא עליו את משפט האר]רה

wrath] of God [flared up] against their congregation. And their son[s] *4* [died] through [it,] and through it their kings were cut off, and their warriors perished] through it, and through it their land was laid waste. *5* [... Through it] the very first to enter the covenant [made themselves guilty] *6* [and were delivered up to the sword, for having deserted God's covenant and having chosen] their whims and having followed

Frag. 4 col. II (= CD-A VI *20*-VII *3*) *1* [...] ... [...] *2* according to their exact interpretation; to lo[ve, each one, his brother like himself;] *3* to [streng]then [the poor, the needy and the foreigner; to seek,] *4* ea[ch] one, the pe[ace of his brother and not to be unfaithful against] *5* [his] blood [relation; to refrain from fornication in accordance with the regulation; to reprove] *6* each one, [his brother in accordance with the precept, and not to bear resentment from one day to the next;] *7* to keep ap[art ...]

Frag. 7 (= 4Q266 6 I; 4Q272 1 I; 4Q273 4 II) *1* [...] ... and the rash is (from) a blow by wood *2* [or stone, or any wound. When the spirit comes and takes h]old of the artery and the blood re[tu]rns *3* [upwards or downwards, and the artery ...] after the blood *Blank 4* [The priest shall examine the live skin and] the d[ead ...] *5* [... during] the seven [days ...] *6* [... and then he] shall compare it, [as] he said, and [the priest] shall quaran[tine him] *7* [seven days, until] the flesh [gr]ows. /The priest/ shall examine him [on the] seventh [day; if] *8* [the spirit of life goes up and] goes down and the flesh [has grown the disease is healed ...] *9* [the rash. The pries]t [shall not examine] the skin of the fl[esh ...] *10* [... But if] the tumour or [the rash is dee]per [than the skin ...] *11* [... and the priest sees in] it something li[ke living] fle[sh ...] *12* [it is leprosy which has taken hold] of the living skin. [And in accordance with this regulation] *13* [...] The priest [shall examine it] on [the seventh day ...]

Frag. 8 col. II (= 4Q270 3 III; 4Q271 2) *1* [... No]-one [should bring in ...] with the blood of their sacrifice [...] *2* [in its purity; and of any gold and] silver and copper [and tin and lead] with which the gentiles made im[ages,] *3* [one should not bring it except] from the new [that has come from the furnace.] No-one should bring in any s[kin, or clothing *4* [or any utensil] with [which w]ork [has been done which defiles the] soul of man, unless they were sprinkled according to the re[gulation] *5* [of purification with lustral water during] the age of wicked[ness by man purified from] all impurity who should wait for *6* [sundown ...] ... [...]

Frag. 9 (= 4Q270 5; 4Q271 3) *1* [all her blemishes he should recount to him, lest he bring upon himself the judgment of the cur]se which he said *2* [(regarding)

אשר אמר 2 [משגה עור בדרך וגם אל יתנהה לאשר לוא הוכן לה] כיא

הוא כלאים 3 [... שור וחמור ולבוש צמר ופשתים יחדיו] 4 vacat vacat

אל יבא איש אשה ...[.[.[...]קוד]ש [אשר]ידעה] 5 [לעשות מעשה בדבר

ואשר ידעה מעשה בבית אב]יה או אלמנה אשר 6 [נשכבה מאשר

התארמלה וכול אשה אשר עליה ש]ם רע בבתולי]ה 7 [בבית אביה vacat

אל יקחה איש כיא אם בראו]ת נשים נאמנ]ות[8 [...]...[...]

4Q270 (4QD^e) *4QDamascus Document^e*

J.M. Baumgarten, *DJD XVIII*, 137-168, pls. XXVI-XXXVI
PAM 43.295-43.299
ROC 685, 690, 697, 698, 703
CD-A, CD-B, 4Q266, 4Q267, 4Q268, 4Q269, 4Q271, 4Q272, 4Q273, 5Q12,

משׁ[...].ישל או יעבוד [אשר ...] 9 [...] 8-4 [...] 3-1 *Frag. 2* i

10 [... שע]ירים או ידרוש באוב ובידעונים 11 [...].[...]. או אשר יחלל

את השם 15-12 [...] 16 [... או אשר עליה שם רע ב]בתוליה בבית

17 [אביה ... או אלמנה אשר]ישכב אחר עמה 18 [... או יק]רב אל אשתו

ביום 19 [...]ה או אשר י]...[20 [...] 21 [...]כל

---

1 על ק]...[2 .את הק].[...].[...].[... *Frag. 2* ii 3 אל מקום]

...[...].[...] 4 [ו]אל[ו...] 5 [...].[...].[... 6 [...מחא להרים [...] 7 [...לבני

אהרון המטעת[...] 7 [...]ת כל אשר להם ומעשר בה]מתם מן הבקר]

8 והצון ופדו]י בכור הבה]מה הטמאה ופדוי בכ]ור ... [9 הצון וכסף

הערכים לפדוי נפשם vacat [...] 10 אין להשיבה וחומשה עליה או י]...[

11 בשמותם לטמא את רוח קודשו .[...] 12 או ינוגע בנגע צרעת או זוב

טמא]ה ... וכל] 13 אשר יגלה את רז עמו לגואים או יקלל א]ת עמו או

ידבר] 14 סרה על משיחי רוח הקדש ותועה ב]...[15 את פי אל או ישחט

בהמה וחיה עבר]ה או אשר ישכב עם] 16 אשה הרה מקיץ דמ]ו או יקרב

א]ל בת] אחיו או ישכב עם זכר] 17 משכבי אשה vacat עוברי

Deut 27:18 «whoever leads a blind man astray from the path». And also he should not give her to anyone who is not fit for her,] because that is «two kinds». *3* [... an ox and an ass, and woollen and linen clothing together.] *Blank* *4* [*Blank* No-one should bring a woman ...] hol[y] who [has experience] *5* [in doing the act, who either has done the act in the house of] her [fath]er, or as a widow who *6* [slept (with someone) after she was widowed. And every woman who] has had a bad [repu]tation during [her] maidenhood *7* [in her father's house, *Blank* no-one should take her, unless on inspecti]on by trust-worthy women *8* [...] ... [...]

4Q270 (4QDᶜ) *4QDamascus Documentᵉ*

6Q15

Bibliography: Wacholder-Abegg 1, 36-47; J.M. Baumgarten, 'A Fragment on Fetal Life and Pregnancy in 4Q270', in D. Wright *et al.* (eds.), *Pomegranates*, 445-448

Frag. 2 col. ɪ *1-3* [...] ... *4-8* [...] *9* [... who] worships or ... [...] ... *10* [... goat-de]mons, or consults a necromancer or diviners *11* [...] ... [...] or who curses the name *12-15* [...] ... *16* [... or who had a bad reputation during] her maiden-hood in the house of *17* [... or a widow] with whom some-one else sleeps *18* [... or who app]roaches his wife on the day of *19* [...] or who [...] *20* [...] *21* [...] all (?)

Frag. 2 col. ɪɪ (= 6Q15 5) *1* concerning [...] *2* ... [...] *3* to the place of [...] *4* [and] to [...] *5* [...] ... to raise (?) [...] *6* [...] to the sons of Aaron the planta-tion [...] *7* [...] all that they have, and a tenth part of [their] ani[mals, of the cattle] *8* and of the flocks, and the ransom for [the firstborn of the] unclean [anim]al and the ransom for the first[born ...] *9* the flocks, and the money of the assessments for the ransom of their souls. *Blank* [...] *10* without returning it, and on top of that a fifth part or [...] *11* by their names, defiling his holy spirit [...] *12* or infected by the disease of leprosy or one with an impu[re] discharge. [... And whoever] *13* divulges the secret of his people to the pa-gans, or curses [his people or preaches] *14* rebellion against those anointed with the spirit of holiness and error [...] *15* God's word, or slaughters an ani-mal carrying a live foetus, [or who sleeps with] *16* a pregnant woman because of the heat (?) of [his] blood [or approaches] the daughter [of his brother, or sleeps with a male] *17* the way one sleeps with a woman. *Blank* The trangres-

[...]...[...]א 18 [...] בם חקק אל להעביר ...[...].[...] 19 ועתה שמעו לי כל
יודעי צדק ו[שימו תור]ת אל [... 20 לכם דרכי חיים ונתיבות שחת
אפתחה ל[...] 21 אל תתפשו ובהבינכם במעשי דור ודור[...]

Frag. 3 II 1-11 [...] 12 ... ועול[לות הכרם [ע]ד עש[רה גרגרים[
13 [הע]וללת [וכל הלקט] עד סאה לבית הסאה והיא אשר ז[רעה] 14 אין
בה תרו[מה ופרט מן הכרם] ובעוללה עד עשרה ג[רגרים] 15 [וב]נקוף
הזית [ופרי תבואתו אם] שלמה היא נקפה[אחד] 16 [משלו]שים ...[נו
ואם רפוס השדה או[יקדה] 17 [בשרפה ונפרס] מסאה לבית סאה מעשדה
(מעשרה) בה ואם תלקוט 18 [נפש אחת סאה] אחת ממנו ביום אחד
תרומה בה עשרון 19 [אחד ... על שתי] חלות התרומה לכל בתי ישראל
אוכלי לחם 20 [הארץ ... ל]הרים אחת בשנה עשרון אחד תהיה האחת
[...] 21 השלמו לישראל אל [י]רם איש

Frag. 3 III 16-13 [...]...[...] 17 [...] 18-19 ... (?) [...]
20 [...]...[בטה]רתו ומכל הזהב ו[הכסף והנחשת והבדיל והעפרת אשר
עשו] 21 [ה]גואים פסל אל יבא איש אל טהרת[ו ...]

Frag. 4 1 [...]יבא איש אשה להאלותה 2 [...]הרואה אם יראה אשת
3 [רעהו ... אם] אמרה אנוסה היתי 4 [... לא יב]יאה כי אם דמה יצוא
5 [לא יצא ... יביאה לפני אי]ש [מן] הכהנים ופרע 6 [הכהן את ראשה
והשביע את [האשה והשקה את 7 [האשה את מי המרים המאררים [לא
תקח מיד]ו כ[ל ...] 8 [... המים [הקדושים 9 [... א]ל יתן איש א[ת]
10 [...].[...] 11 [...]...[...]12 [...]המלכים 13 [... א]ל ישכב איש] עם
אשה 14 [...] ה[שופחה ה**חרופה** ... 15 [... שבע שנים כאשר] אמר לא
ת[...] 16 [... י]קחנה או לב[נו] 17 [...]ה את אשר ל[...] 18 [...]...
19 [...מן הקד]ש[לחמו 20 [...]ישכב עם

Frag. 5 14 [ואם את בתו ית]ן איש לאיש] את כל מומיה יספר לו למה
יביא[15 [עלו א]ת משפט הארו אשר אמר משגה עור בדרך וגם אל

sors of […] … […] *18* against them God has determined to let pass […] *19* And now, listen to me all you who know justice and [fulfil the] law [of God …] *20* to you paths of life, but the ways to the pit I shall open for […] *21* you shall not be caught and in your understanding of the deeds of each generation […]

Frag. 3 *col.* II (= 4Q266 6 III; 4Q267 6)   *1-11* […] *12* [… And the gra]pes of the vineyard: up to te[n berries] *13* [the gr]ape. [And all the gleanings] up to one seah per bushel. And that in which (is only) [its] s[eed], *14* in it there is not sacred off[ering] nor fallen grapes from the vine …] and in its grapes are up to ten b[erries.] *15* [And at] the beating of the olive [and fruit of its produce, if] the gathering is complete. The beating [is one] *16* [from every th]irty […] And if you the field [was trampled or scorched] *17* [by fire, but there remains] up to one seah per bushel, there is tithe in it. And if *18* [a person gleans] one [seah] from it on one day, the sacred offering shall be [one] tenth. *19* [… Concerning the two] loaves of the sacred offering, it is for all the houses of Israel which eat the bread *20* [of the land … to] raise once a year. One tenth shall be each one […] *21* […] its completion for Israel. No-one should raise

Frag. 3 *col.* III (= 4Q269 8 II; 4Q271 2)   *13-16* […] … […] *17* […] *18-19* … (?) […] *20* […] … [in] its [pu]rity, and of any gold and [silver] *21* [and copper and tin and lead with which the] gentiles made images, no-one should bring into [its] purity […]

Frag. 4   *1* […] a man brings a woman to curse her *2* […] he who sees, if he sees the wife of *3* [his fellow … if] she said: «I have been raped», *4* [… he shall not br]ing her unless her blood absolutely *5* [does not come forth … he shall bring her before on]e [of] the priests, and [the priest] shall untie *6* [her hair, put] the woman [on oath] and make [the woman] drink *7* [the bitter water of the curse.] She shall not take from [his] hand [a]ny *8* […] the holy [water] *9* [… No]t should anyone give *10-11* […] *12* […] the kings *13* [… not should anyone sleep] with a woman *14* […] the slave girl /who has been assigned/ … *15* [… seven years as he] said: «You shall not […] *16* […] he shall take her, or for [his] s[on] *17* […] which […] *18* […] … *19* […] from the hol[y] his bread […] *20* […] sleep with

Frag. 5 (= 4Q269 9; 4Q271 3)   *14* [and if] a man [giv]es [his daughter] to some-one else [he should recount all her blemishes to him, lest he bring] *15* [upon himself] the judgment of the curse [which he said: (regarding) *Deut* 27:18

יתננה]   16   [לאשר לא הו]כן לה כי ה[ו]א כלאים ... שור וחמור ולבוש

צמר]   17   [ופשתים יחד]ו vacat אל יבא איש] אשה ...[ת הקוד[ש]

18   [אשר י]דעה לעשות מעשה בד[בר ואשר ידע]ה מעשה [בבית]

19   [אבי]ה vacat או אלמנה אשר נשכב]ה מאשר התארמ]ל[ה   20   [וכל

אשר] עליה שם רע [בבתוליה בבית אביה אל יקחה]   21   [איש כי א[ם

בראות נש[י]ם [נאמנות ...]

13   [...] לשופ[טים לשפוט [צד]ק [...]...[...]   14   [...] ו[שלם   Frag. 6 III

האונס אם לא דבר א[מת ע[ם רעהו עד אש[ר ...]   15   [...]כי לו הקים את]

דברו לדבר א[מת vacat וא[שר אמר]   16   [כל אדם אשר יחרים אד[ם

מאדם [בח]וקי הגואים להמית הוא vacat וא[שר אמר]   17   [לא תקום ולא]

תטור את בני עמך כל [א]יש מבאי הב[רית אשר י]ביא על רעהו [דבר אש[ר

18   [לא בהוכח ע]ל פי עדים והביאו בח[רון] אפו או ספר [לזקנו להב]זתו

נוקם הוא [ונו]טר   19   [ואין כתוב כי א]ם נוקם הוא ל[צרו ו]נוטר ^{הוא}

לאויבו אם החריש לו מיום ליום ובחר[ו]ת אפו   20   [...] דבר כן ...[...]

והיו [...]   21   [...]...[...]...[...ע]נה [...]

11   [...] והובדל [האי]ש מן הטהרה לבד]   12   [א[ם]   Frag. 6 IV

נאמני[ם] הם וביום ראות האיש יודיעהו למבקר ועל ההו[ן] יקבלו ש[ני

עדים נאמנ]ים]   13   ועל פי עד אחד לה[בדיל מן הטהרה ואל יקובל ע[ד

לשופט[ים ל]המית על פיהו על א[שר]   14   לא מלאו ימו לעבור] על הפקודים

ירא א[ת אל vacat אל יאמן איש על רעה[ו לעד]   15   [עו]בר דבר מן

המצו[ה ביד רמה עד זכו לשוב] vacat וזה סרך לשופטי העדה [עד]

16   עשרה אנשים ברורי[ם מן הע]דה לפי העת א[רבע]ה למטה לוי ואהרון

ומישר[א]ל [ששה]   17   מבוננים בספר ההג[י וביסו]רי הברית [מבן ח]מש

ועשרים שנה וע[ד בן ששים] שנה   18   ולא יתיצב עוד מבן ששים שנה

[ומעלה לשפו]ט את העדה כי במועל [ה]אדם] מע]טו   19   ימו ובחרון אף

«whoever leads a blind man astray from the path». And also he should not give her] *16* [to anyone who is not f]it for her, because th[at is «two kinds». ... an ox and an ass, and woollen and linen clothing] *17* [togeth]er. *Blank* No-one should bring [a woman ...] the hol[y ...] *18* [who has] experience in doing the act, [who either has don]e the act [in the house] *19* [of her father *Blank* or as a widow who slept (with someone) after she was widowed.] *20* [And every woman who] has had a bad reputation [during her maidenhood in her father's house, no] *21* [one should take her, unle]ss on inspection by [trustworthy] women [...]

Frag. 6 *col.* III (CD-A XVI *19-* IX *7*; 4Q266 8 II; 4Q267 9 I; 5Q12 1) *13* [... for the jud]ges in order judge [with justice ...] *14* [... and] the violator shall pay; if he has not spoken the tr[uth to] his fellow, until [...] *15* [...] for he has not kept [his word to speak the tr]uth *Blank* And wh[at he said] *16* [*Lev 27:29* «Every man who vowes any]one else to destruction» shall be executed [according to the la]ws of the gentiles. *Blank* And [what he said:] *17* [*Lev 19:18* «Do not avenge yourself or] bear resentment against the sons of your people» - everyone of those brought to the cove[nant, who] brings [an accusation] against his fellow, *18* [not on the tes]timony of witnesses, or brings it when he is an[gry,] or tells it [to his elders] so that they might des]pise him, he is «the one who avenges himself [and bears rese]ntment». *19* [Is it not perhaps written that on]ly *Nah 1:2* «he (God) avenges himself on [his foes and] bears resentment against his enemies»? If he kept silent about him from one day to the other, and then, when he was angry *20* [...] the matter. Thus [...] and they were [...] *21* [...] ... [...] he has testified (?) [...]

Frag. 6 *col.* IV (= CD-A IX *21-* X *12*; 4Q266 8 III) *11* [...] the ma[n is only to be excluded from the pure food,] *12* [on condition that they are trustworthy, and that on the same day on which he saw him, he reported him to the Inspector. And concerning riche]s, [they shall accept t]wo trustworthy witnesses. *13* [And] on the testimony of one, to ex[clude from the pure food. A wit]ness [is not to be accepted] by the judge[s to] condemn to death on his word, [if he has] *14* not completed his days to pass [among those who are enrolled, fearful of] God. Not is to be believed [as a witness] against his fellow, anyone *15* [who has deliberately trans]gressed any precept, [until he has been purified to return.] *Blank* And this is the rule of the judges of the congregation. *16* Ten men in number, chosen [from among the con]gregation, for a period: f[our] from the tribe of Levi and of Aaron and [six] from Israel; *17* learned in the book of HAG[Y and in the princi]ples of the covenant; [between] twenty-five and [sixty] years. *18* And no-one [over] sixty years should hold the office [of judg]ing the congregation, for on account of man's unfaithfulness *19* his days [were shor]tened, and because of God's wrath against the inhabitants of the

אל ביושבי הארץ [אמר להסיר א]ת דעתם עד אשר לא [ישלי]מו א[ת
ימ]יהם 20 vacat על הטהר במים אל [ירחץ איש במים צואים ומעוטים
מ]די [מרעיל איש] 21 אל יטהר בם כל כלי וכל גבא [...]

Frag. 6 v 1 [...]מ[לאכה] 2 [מן העת אשר יהיה גלגל השמש רחוק
מן השער מלואו כי הו]א אשר א[מר] 3 שמור את יום השבת לקדשו וביום
השבת אל ידבר איש[ ]דבר נבל ורק [אל] 4 [ישה ברעהו כל אל ישפוט על
הון ובצע אל ידבר בדברי המ]לאכה וה[עבודה] 5-11 [...] 12 בא[מה
vacat אל ירם את ידו להכותה באגרוף אם סוררת היא[ ] 13 אל [יוצי]א[ה
מביתו אל יוציא] איש[ ]מן הבית לחוץ ומן החוץ לבית ואם בסוכה]
14 יהיה אל [י]וצא ממנה ואל יבא [אליה אל יפתח כלי טוח בשבת אל ישא
15 א[י]ש עלו סמנים לצת ולבוא בש[בת אל יטול בבית מושבת סלע ועפר]
16 [א]ל ישא האומן את היונ[ק לצת ולבוא בשבת vacat אל ימר איש
17 את עבדו ואת אמ[ת]ו ביום השבת[אל יילד איש בהמה ביום השבת]
18 ואם יפול אל בור ואל פחת אל [יקימה בשבת אל יחל את השבת על]
19 הון ובצע בשבת וכל נפש אד[ם אשר תפול אל מקום מים ואל מקוה אל]
20 יעלה אי^ש בסולם וחבל וכלי אל[ ]יעל איש למזבח בשבת כי אם עולת
השבת כי כן[ ]21 כתוב מלבד שבתותיכם vacat [...]

Frag. 7 i 1 [...]... ונ[...] [ואשר יהלך] 2 [לפני רעהו ערו]ם בבית או
בשדה ה[לך] ע[רום לפני הבריאות] [והובדל ששה חודשים ונענש שלושים יום
3 [ואשר יוצא את] ידו מתחת בגדו והו[א פוח ונראתה ערותו והובדל
שלושים יום] 4 [ונענש עשרה והסוח]ק בסכלות לה[ש}רים{שמיע [קולו
והובדל שלושים יום ונענש חמשה עשר] 5 [והמוציא את ידו הש]מאלית
לשח בה ונע[נש עשרת ימים והאיש אשר ילך רכיל] 6 [ברעהו והבדילה]ו
מן הטהרה שנ[ה]ה אחת ... ואיש ברבים ילך] 7 [רכיל לשלח הוא ולא] ישוב
ע[וד ואם על רעהו ילון אשר לא במשפט ונענש ששה] 8 [חודשים והאי]ש
אשר תזוע [רוחו לבגוד באמת וללכת בשרירות לבו אם ישוב]

614

earth, [he ordered to remove] their knowledge before [they comple]ted their [day]s. *20 Blank* Concerning purification with water. No-[one should bathe in water which is dirty or which is less than] the amount [which covers a man] *21* No-one should purify a vessel in it. And every cavity [...]

Frag. 6 *col.* v (= CD-A x *15-19*; xi *6-18*; 4Q271 5 1)   *1* [...] w[ork] *2* [from the moment when the sun's disc is at a distance of its diameter from the gate, for th]is is what he sa[id: *3 Deut 5:12* «Observe the sabbath day to keep it holy». And on the day of the sabbath, no-one should say] a useless or stupid word. [He is not] *4* [to lend anything to his fellow. He is not to take decisions with regard to riches or gain. He is not to speak about matters of wo]rk or of the [task] *5-11* [...] *12* cub[its. *Blank* He is not to raise his hand to strike it with the fist. If it is stubborn *13* [he should] not bring it out of his house. No-]one [should remove anything from the house to outside, or from outside to the house. Even if] *14* he is [in a hut,] he should remove nothing from it or bring [anything into it. He is not to open a sealed vessel on the sabbath. No-one should wear] *15* perfumes on the sa[bbath,] to go out or come in. [No-one should lift, in his dwelling, a stone or dust.] *16* The wet-nurse should [no]t lift the baby [to go out or come in on the sabbath. *Blank* No-one should press] *17* his servant or his maidservant on the sabba[th. No-one should help an ani-mal give birth on the sabbath day.] *18* And if it falls into a well or a pit, he should not [take it out on the sabbath. No-one should profane the sabbath for] *19* riches or gain on the sabbath. And any living ma[n who falls into a place of water or into a reservoir, no-] *20* /one/ should take him out with a ladder or a rope or a utensil. No-[one should offer anything upon the altar on the sabbath, except the sacrifice of the sabbath, for thus] *21* is it written: *Lev 23:38* «except your offerings of the sabbath». *Blank* [...]

Frag. 7 *col.* I (= 4Q266 10 II - 11; 4Q267 9 VI; cf. 1QS VII)   1 [...] ... [... and whoever walks] *2* [nake]d [in front of his fellow] in the house or /w[alks] n[aked in front of the creatures]/ in the field, [shall be excluded for six months, and shall be punished for thirty days.] *3* [And whoever takes out] "his hand" from under his clothes or th[ese are rags which allow his nakedness to be seen, shall be excluded for thirty days,] *4* [and shall be punished for ten; and whoever giggles inane]ly, {raising} /making/ [his voice] /heard/, [shall be excluded for thirty days and shall be punished for fifteen.] *5* [And he who takes out his le]ft [hand] to gesticulate with it, shall be pun[ished for ten days. And whoever goes around defaming] *6* [his fellow they shall exclude] from the pure food for [one] year [... however, whoever goes round defaming the Many] *7* [shall be expelled and] shall [not] come back ever a[gain; if he com-plains against his fellow *20* without cause he will be punished six] *8* [months. The pers]on [whose spirit] turns aside [to betray the truth and walk in the

9 [ו]הו[ן]בדל שתי שנים מן קו[דש [ונ]ענש ששים [יום ובמלואת לו שנתים
ימים ישאלו הרבים] 10 על דב[רו ואם יקרב] ויכתו[בוהו בתכונו ואחר
ישאל אל המשפט [vacat 11 [vacat [והאיש] אשר ימאס [א]ת משפט
הרבים ויצא ו[לא ישוב עוד ואשר יקח] 12 אוכלו חוצה מן המשפט
והשיבו לאיש אשר לקחו מ[מנו [vacat ואשר יקר[ב] 13 לזנות לאשתו
אשר לא כמשפט ויצא ולא ישוב עוד [vacat ואשר ילו]ן על האבות
14 [ישלח] מן העדה ולא ישוב [ואם] על האמות ונענש עשר[ת] ימים כי אין
לאמ[ו]ת רוקמה בתוך [העדה] vacat 15 [ואלה המ]שפטים א[שר ישפטו
[בם כל המתיסרים כל אי[ש] אשר 16 [...]ר יבוא וידיעהו לכוהן
[המ]ופקד ע[ל הרבים וקב]ל את משפטו מר[צונ]ו כ[א]שר 17 א[מ]ר ביד
משה על הנפש אשר תח[טא בשגגה אשר יביאו] את חטאתו ו[את אשמו
וע[ל 18 ישראל כתוב אלכה לי אל קצה הש[מים ולא אריח בריח
ני[חוח]ם ובמ[קום אחר כתוב] 19 קרעו לבבכם ואל בגדיכם וכ[תוב לשוב
אל אל בבכי ובצום] וכל המו[אס במשפטי]ם 20 האלה על פי כל החוקים
ה[ל]מצ[ו]{א}[י]ם בתורת משה לא יחשב בכל ב[ני אמת]ו כי געלה נפשו]
21 ביסורי הצדק vacat וב[מרד [...

11 [...] 10 *Frag.* 7 II [וכל יושבי המחנות יקהלו ב[חדש
השלישי ואר[רו את] 12 [הנוטה ימין ושמאול מן התורה] vacat זה פרוש
המשפטים אש[ר] 13 [יעשו כל] קץ [הפקודה א]ת אשר [יפ]קידו בכל קצי
החרון 14 ומס[עיהם] לכל ישב [מ]חניהם וכל י[שב ערי]הם הנה הכול
כ[תוב] 15 על מדרש [ה]תורה האחרון vacat 16-21 vacat

4Q271 (4QDᶠ) *4QDamascus Documentᶠ*

J.M. Baumgarten, *DJD XVIII*, 169-183, pls. XXXVII-XXXIX
PAM 43.279, 43.280
ROC 357, 362

stubbornness of his heart, if he comes back] *9* [he shall] be [excluded for two years /from anything h]oly/ [and shall be pu]nished for sixty [days. When the days of the two years are complete the Many shall be questioned] *10* concerning [his] affa[ir, and if he may approach] they will enro[ll him in his rank, and later he will be questioned in connection with judgment. *Blank*] *11 Blank* [And whoever] despises the judgment of the Many shall leave and [never return. And whoever takes] *12* his food contrary to the regulation, is to give it back to the one fr[om whom] he took it. *Blank* And whoever approac[hes] *13* to have illegal sex with his wife, not in accordance with the regulation, shall leave and never return. [*Blank* And whoever complai]ns against the fathers, *14* [shall be expelled] from the congregation and not come back again. [But if] against the mothers, he shall be punished for ten days because for mothers there is no mingling (?) in the midst of *15* [the congregation.] *Blank* [And these are the reg]ulations by which [shall be ruled] all those disciplined and everyone who *16* […] shall enter and inform the priest [who is appo]inted ov[er the Many and he will] rea[di]lly [recei]ve his judgment, as he] *17* s[a]id through the hand of Moses about the person who si[ns through oversight: *Lev 4:27* «they should present] his sin-offering and [his guilt-offering»; and ab]out *18* Israel it is written: *Lev 26:31* «I shall go to the edges of the hea[vens, and I shall not smell the aroma of] your [ple]asant fragrances»; and in ano[ther place it is written:] *19 Joel 2:13* «Tear your heart and not your clothes» and it is writt[en: *Joel 2:12* (?) «to return to God in tears and in fasting».] And anyone who des[pises these regulations] *20* according to all the precepts which are found [in the law of Moses, shall not be considered among all the so]ns of [his] truth, [for his soul has loathed] *21* those disciplined by justice. *Blank* And in re[bellion …]

Frag. 7 col. II (= 4Q266 11)   *11* [And all those who dwell in the camps will assemble in] the third month and will cu[rse] *12* [whoever tends to the right or to the left of the law.] *Blank* This is the precise interpretation of the regulations which *13* [they are to observe in the whole] age [of visitation] with which they [will be vi]sited (?) in all the ages of anger *14* and their routes, to all those who dwell in their [c]amps and all [who dwell] in their [cities.] And so, then, all this is w[ritten] *15* with regard to the last interpretation of [the] law. *Blank* *16-21 Blank*

4Q271 (4QD^f) *4QDamascus Document^f*

CD-A, CD-B, 4Q266, 4Q267, 4Q268, 4Q269, 4Q270, 4Q272, 4Q273, 5Q12, 6Q15
Bibliography: Wacholder-Abegg 1, 23-27

Frag. 2   1   [...] מגורן יורד את העשרון מן הח[ומר היא הא]יפה

2   [...] [האיפה והבת{ב} תכון אחד שניהן ומן] החטים ש[שית   3   [האיפה

לחמר ... ה[ע]ץ אל יבדל איש להרים לשה[ד מן המאה   4   ואל י]אכל

איש [... ומן הגנה טרם ישלחו [הכוה]נים את ידם   5   [לבר]ך לריאשונה]

[... בית לאיש ימכור ובחס.[...]ח ואז ינקה   6   [...].[...]...[...] ואת ה.[...]שדה

המעורב   7   [...].[...]חד שלוש פעמים   8   אל יבא] איש את ... בדם זבחם ...

[תו בטהרתו ומכו]ל[9   הזהב והכסף [והנחושת וה]בדיל והעו]פרת אשר

עשו הגוים פ[סל אל יביאהו   10   איש אל טהר]תו כי אם מן החד]ש הבא מן

הכב[ש]ן ... אל יב]א איש [כול עור ובגד ומן   11   כול הכל]י אשר יעשה

מ]לאכה בהם אשר יטמאו לנפש] אדם כי [אם הוזו כמשפט   12   [הטהרה ...

במי]הנדה בקץ הרשע איש טו]הר מכול טמא]תו אשר   13   י]עריב את

השמש וכול נער אשר לו]א מלאו ימיו לעבור על הפ]קודים [...

[...]...[...]   14

Frag. 3   1   [...] בכסף [...]...[...]   2   [... וידו לוא ה]שיגה דיו לה[שיב

לו] והגיש]ה [שנת ה]יובל [...   3   [...].[. ואל יעזוב ל]ו כול] עוונותיו *vacat*

אל [...]...[4   [...] כאחת כי תועבה היא *vacat* ואשר אמר כי] תמכור

ממכר]   5   [לעמיתך או קנה מיד [עמיתך לוא תונו איש את עמיתו וזה *vacat*

פרו]ש [... .[...]...ת.[...]   6   [...] בכול אשר הוא יודע אשר ימצא   7   [...] .תן

והוא יודע אשר הוא מועל בו ובאדם ובהמה ואם   8   [את בתו יתן איש

לאי]ש את כול מומיה יספר לו למה יביא עליו את משפט   9   [הארור אשר

אמ]ר משגה עור בדרך וגם אל יתנהה לאשר לוא הוכן לה כי   10   [הוא

כלאים ... ש]ור וחמור ולבוש צמר {.}ופשתים יחדיו *vacat* אל יבא איש

11   [אשה ... הקו]דש אשר ידעה לעשות מעשה {מ}²דבר ואשר ידעה

12   [מעשה בבית] אביה או אלמנה אשר נשכבה מאשר התארמלה וכול

13   [אשר עליה ש]ם רע בבתוליה בבית אביה אל יקחה איש כי אם

14   [בראות נשים] נאמנות וידעות ברורות ממאמר המבקר אשר על

15   [הרבים ואח]ר יקחנה ובלוקחו אותה יעשה כמשפ]ט ולוא] יגיד עלי]ה

[...]...[...]   16

Frag. 2 (= 4Q269 8 II; 4Q270 3 III)   *1* [...] from the threshing floor he shall deduct the tenth of the ho[mer, which is an e]phah *2* [...] the ephah and the bath are both the same measure, and from [the wheat a si]xth *3* [of an ephah per homer ...] tree. Not should separate himself to offer of the lambs, [on]e from every hundred. *4* [No-]one should eat [...] and from the garden before [the pri]ests have stretched out their hands *5* [to ble]ss (it) first [...] a house to someone sells and with ... [...] and then he is innocent *6* [...] ... [...] and the [...] the mortgaged field *7* [...] ... three times. *8* No-one should bring in [... with the blood of their sacrifice ...] ... in its purity, and of an[y] *9* gold and silver [and copper and] tin and le[ad with which the gentiles make im]ages, one should only bring *10* to [its] purit[y from the ne]w that has come from the furnace ... No-[one] should bring in any skin, or clothing or *11* any utensil with which [w]ork [has been done] which defiles the soul of [man, un]less they were sprinkled according to the regulation *12* [of purification ...] with lustral [water] during the age of wickedness by man puri[fied from all] his [impur]ity *13* [who has waited for sundown. And any young man] who has not yet reached the age to pass to those en[rolled ...] *14* [...] ... [...]

Frag. 3 (= 4Q269 9; 4Q270 5)   *1* [...] with money [...] ... [...] *2* [... he did not ha]ve enough to re[pay him] and the [Jubilee] year approaches [...] *3* [...] and God will forgive [him all] his sins. *Blank* Not ... [...] *4* [...] as one, for it is an abomination. *Blank* And what he said: *Lev 25:14* «Whether [you make a sale] *5* [to your fellow, or purchase from the hand of] your fellow, none of you is to harm his fellow». *Blank* And this is the exact interpre[tation ...] *6* [...] in everything that he knows that has been found ... [...] ... *7* [...] and he knows that he is committing fraud towards him, whether concerning man or animals. And if *8* [a man gives his daughter to some-one] else, he should recount all her blemishes to him, lest he bring upon himself the judgment *9* [of the curse which he sai]d: (regarding) *Deut 27:18* «whoever leads a blind man astray from the path». And also he should not give her to anyone who is not fit for her, because *10* [that is «two kinds». ... an o]x and an ass, and woollen and linen clothing together. *Blank* No-one should bring *11* [a woman ... the ho]ly [...], who has experience in doing the act, who has either done *12* [the act in] her father's [house,] or as a widow who slept (with someone) after she was widowed. And every *13* [woman who has had] a bad [reput]ation during her maidenhood in her father's house, no-one should take her, unless *14* [on inspection by] trustworthy and knowledgeable [women], selected by the command of the Inspector who is over *15* [the Many; then] he may take her and if he takes her, he should proceed in accordance with the regulati[on. And he should not] announce about [her] *16* [...] ... [...]

Frag. 4 II   1 [...][...]...[...][ויא]מר [...]   2 יכרות [את בית ישראל ואת

בית יהודה] ברית ועל הבר[י]ת ה[זות דבר ביד מושה]   3 לאמור] על [פי

הד[ברי]ם האלה כרתי עמכם ברית ועם] כול ישראל על כן יקים האיש]

4 על נפשו לשוב א[ל [תורת מושה {כי} כי בה הכול מד]וקדק ופרוש קציהם

לעורון]   5 ישראל מכול אלה הנה הוא] מדו[קדק על ספר] מח]ל[קות

העתים ליובליהם ובשבועותיהם]   vacat 6 וביום אשר יקים] האיש ע[ל

נפשו לש[וב אל תורת] מושה] יסור מלא[ך ה[מ]שטמה] 7 מאחריו אם יקים

את [דבריו על [כן נמול] אברהם בי[ום דע[תו ואש]ר אמר מוצא 8 שפתיך

תשמור להקים כול שב[ועת אסר אשר יקי]ם א[יש ע]ל נפשו לעשות

9 דבר מן התורה עד מחיר מות אל] יפדהו כול אשר יקים אי]ש על נפשו

לסור   10 את התורה עד מחיר מות אל יקי]מהו על שבועת האשה [א]שר]

אמר לאישה   11 להניא את שבועתה אל ינא איש ש[בועה אשר לוא ידענה

א]ם להקים היא ואם   12 להניא אם לעבור ברית היא יניא]ה ואל יקימנה

וכן המשפט] לאביה vacat על   vacat 13 משפט הנדבות אל ידור איש

למ[זבח מאום אנוס וגם] הכוהנים אל יקחו מיד vacat 14 ישראל אל יקדש

איש את מא[כל פיהו לאל כי הוא] אשר אמר איש א[ת [רעהו   15 יצ]ודו]

חרם vacat אל יקדש איש] מכול [...] vacat. ואם מש[דה]   16 [אחזתו יקדש

לאל [גם המשפט[...] הנודר א[ת]

Frag. 5 I   1 [בגז כי אם כב]סו במים או שופים בלבונה אל יתערב]

איש מר[נצונו   2 [בשבת אל ילך א]יש אחר בהמה לרעותה חוץ מעירו כי]

אם אלפים] באמה   3 [אל ירם איש את] ידו להכותה באגרוף אם סוררת

הי]א אל יוצי[אה   4 [מביתו אל יוצא [איש מן הבית לחוץ ומן החוץ לבית

וא[ם בסו]כה יהיה   5 [אל יוצא ממנה וא]ל יב[י]א אל[יה] אל יפתח כלי

טוח בשבת] אל [ישא איש   6 [עליו סמנים לצא]ת ולבוא [ב]שבת אל יטול

בבית מושבת סלע ועפר אל   7 [ישא האומן את]היונק לצאת ולבוא בשבת

אל ימר את עבדו ואת   8 [אמתו ואת שוכרו ב[ש]בת א]ל ייל[ד איש בהמה

בשבת ואם תפול אל בור   9 [ואל פחת אל יקימה בש]בת אל ישבות איש

Frag. 4 *col.* II (= CD-A XVI *1-18*)   *1* […] … […] and he s[aid …] *2* and he will conclude a the covenant [with the house of Israel and the house of Judah]; and about th[is] cov[e]nant [he spoke through Moses] *3* saying: [*Exod 34:27* «In accor]dance with these w[ord]s I established with you a covenant and with [all Israel». Therefore one will impose upon himself] *4* to return t[o] the law of Moses, {for} for in it all is def[ined. And the exact interpretation of their ages about the blindness of] *5* Israel in all these matters, behold, [it is defi]ned in «The book [of the divisions of the periods according to their jubilees and their weeks».] *6* *Blank* And on the day on which [one] has imposed upon himself to re[turn to the law of] Moses, [the ang]el [Ma]stema will turn aside *7* from following him, should he keep [his words. This is w]hy [Abraham] circumcised himself [on the d]ay of [his] know[ledge. And as for wha]t he said: *Deut 23:24* «What issues *8* from your mouth, keep it and carry it out». Every [binding] oa[th by which] any[one impos]es [up]on himself to fulfil *9* a letter of the law, he should not [annul], even at the price of death. [Anything by which he might impose] upon himself to turn away *10* from the law, he should not ful[fil,] not even when the price is death. [Concerning the oath of a woman. What] he said: *Num 30:7-9* «Her husband *11* may annul her oath», no-one should annul an o[ath if he does not know whet]her it should be carried out or *12* annulled. If it would violate the covenant, he should annul [it and should not carry it out. And the regulation applies also] to her father. *Blank* Concerning *13* the regulation for freewill-offerings. *Blank* No-one should dedicate [anything, obtained by unjust means,] to the al[tar. Neit]her should the priests take from *14* Israel (anything obtained by unjust means). *Blank* No-one should consecrate the fo[od of his mouth for God, for this is] what he said: *Mic 7:2* «Each one *15* tr[aps] his fellow with anathema». *Blank* And no-one should consecrate [anything of …] and if he *16* [consecrates] a fi[eld of his possession to God] then also this regulation applies […] he who dedicates th[e]

Frag. 5 *col.* I (= CD-A XI *3*-XII *7*)   *1* [in a chest, unless they have been wa]shed with water or rubbed with incense. No-[one] should intermingle[vol]untarily *2* [on the sabbath. No]-one should go after an animal to pasture it outside his city, exce[pt for two thousand] cubits. *3* [He is not to raise] his hand to strike with the fist. If it is stubborn, [he should not bring] it out *4* [of his house. No-]one [should remove] anything from the house to outside, or from outside to the house. Eve[n if] he is [in a h]ut, *5* [he should remove nothing from it nor] bring anything into [it.] He is not to open a sealed vessel on the sabbath. [No-]one should wear *6* [perfumes, to go] out or come in on the sabbath. In his dwelling no-one should lift a stone or dust. *7* [The wet-nurse should] not [lift] the baby to go out or come in on the sabbath. Do not press one's servant *8* [or one's maidservant or one's employee on the sabbath. No]-one should help an animal give birth on the sabbath day. And if it has fallen into a well *9* [or a pit, he should not take it out on the sa]bbath. No-one should stay in a place close

במקום קרוב לגוים בשבת   10   [אל יחל איש את השב]ת על הון ובצע

בשבת וכול נפש אדם אשר תפול   11   [אל מקום מים ואל בו]ר אל יעלה

[אי]ש בסולם וחבל וכלי אל יעל איש   12   [למזבח בשבת כי אם עו]ל[ת

השבת כי כן כתוב מלבד שבתותיכם אל [יש]ל[ח   13   [איש למזבח עולה

ומנחה ולבונה] ועץ בי[ד   [איש [טמא באח]ת מן הטמאות לה[רשותו

14   [לטמא את המזבח כי   [כתוב זבח רשעים תעובה] ותפלת [צדיקים

כמנחת   15   [רצון *vacat* וכול הבא   [אל בית ההשתחוות אל יבוא טמא כבוס

וב[הרע]   16   [חצוצרות הקהל י]תקדם או יתאחר ולוא ישביתו את

העבודה] כולה]   17   [כי בית קודש הוא אל [ישכב איש עם אשה בעיר

המקדש לטמא את] עיר]   18   [המקדש בנדתם כו]ל [איש אשר ימשולו בו

רוחות בליעל ודבר סרה כ[משפט]   19   [האוב והידעוני י]שפט וכול אשר

יתעה לחלל את השבת ואת המו[עדות]   20   [לוא יומת כי על בני] האדם

משמרו ואם ירפא ממנה ושמרוהו עד] שבע]   21   [שנים ואחר יב]וא לקהל

אל ישלח איש את ידו לשפוך [דם לאיש מן]

4Q272 (4QD*g*) *4QDamascus Document*

J.M. Baumgarten, *DJD XVIII*, 186-191, pl. XL

PAM 43.302

ROC 219

CD-A, CD-B, 4Q266, 4Q267, 4Q268, 4Q269, 4Q270, 4Q271, 4Q273, 5Q12,

[...] 1   *Frag.* 1 i   שאת א[ו ספחת או ב]הרת [...   2   [והספחת מכת עץ

ו]אבן וכול מכה מכה בבוא הרו[ח ואחזה]   3   [בגיד ושב הדם למ]עלה ולמטה

והגיד [...]...[...   4   [... אחר הדם ...[...]...[...   5   [וראה הכוהן את עור]החי

ואת המת] ואם שפל [המת מן   6   [החי והסגירו עד] אשר יצמח [הבשר]עד

אשר י]שוב הדם לגיד [ואח]ר ישוה [בו וראה]הכוהן ב[יום   7   [השביעי והנה

רו]ח החיים עולה ויירדת   8   [הבשר צמח ו]נרפא הנגע ... ה]ספחת לוא

יראנה הכוהן לעור הבש[ר]   9   [...] ואם] שפ]ל השאת או הס[פחת מן]

10   [העור ... וראה הכוהן]אותו כמראי הבשר החי ו[...]   11   [צרעת היא

to gentiles on the sabbath. *10* [No-one should profane the sabba]th for riches or gain on the sabbath. And any living man who falls *11* [into a place of water or a we]ll, no-[on]e should take him out with a ladder or a rope or a utensil. No-one should offer anything *12* [upon the altar on the sabbath, except the sacrifice of the sabbath, for th]us is it written: *Lev 23:38* «except your offerings of the sabbath». No-[one] should [se]nd *13* [to the altar a sacrifice, or an offering, or incense,] or wood, by the ha[nd of] a man [impure from a]ny of the impurities, so al[lowing him] *14* [to defile the altar, for] it is written: *Prov 15:8* «the sacrifice of the wicked ones is an abomination, [but the prayer] of the just ones is like an agreeable *15* [offering». *Blank* And everyone who enters] the house of prostration should not enter with impurity requiring washing; and when *16* [the trumpets of the assembly sound,] he may advance or retreat, but they should not stop the [whole] service, *17* [for it is a holy house. No]-one should sleep with a woman in the city of the temple, defiling [the city of the] *18* [temple with their impurity. Ev]ery man over whom the spirits of Belial dominate, and who preaches apostasy, will be judged according to [the regulation] *19* [of the necromancer or the diviner.] But every one who goes astray, defiling the sabbath and the fes[tivals,] *20* [shall not be executed, for it is the task of] men him to guard him; and if he is cured of it, they shall guard him for [seven] *21* [years and afterwards he may en]ter the assembly. No-one is to stretch out his hand to shed [the blood of]

4Q272 (4QDᵍ) *4QDamascus Documentᵍ*

6Q15

Bibliography: J.M. Baumgarten, 'The 4Q Zadokite Fragments on Skin Disease', *JJS* 41 (1990) 157-158; *Wacholder-Abegg 1*, 54-56

Frag. 1 *col.* I (= 4Q266 6 I; 4Q269 7; 4Q273 4 II) *1* [... a tumour, o]r a rash, or a wh[ite spot ...] *2* [and the rash is (from) a blow by wood or] stone, or any wound. When the spir[it] comes [which takes hold] *3* [of the artery and the blood returns] upwards or downwards, and the artery ... [...] *4* [... after the blood ...] ... [...] *5* [The priest shall examine] the live [skin,] and the dead. [And if] the dead (skin) [is deeper] than *6* [the living (skin) he shall confine him until] the flesh grows, /[until] the blood returns to the artery, [and th]en he shall compare [it]./ The priest shall [examine him] on *7* [the seventh day: if the spir]it of life goes up and down [and] the flesh has grown *8* [the disease is healed ... the] rash. The priest shall not examine the skin of the fle[sh] *9* [...] But if the tumour or the rash is [dee]per [than] *10* [the skin ... and the priest

האוחזה] בעור החי וכמשפט[הזה כאשר א]מר והסגיר[ו הכוהן שבעת ימים]

12 [... וראה הכוהן ביום השב]יעי [ו]הנה נוסף מ[ן החי]   13   [אל המת ...

צרעת מ]מארת היא   *vacat*   14   [ומשפט נתק הראש והזקן ... ור]אה הכוהן

וה]נה]   15   [באה הרוח בראש או בזקן באוחזה בגיד ופרח הנג]ע מתחת

השער]ר[16   [והפך מראה לדק צוהב כי כעשב] הוא אשר] י]ש הרחש

17   [תחתו ויקיץ שורשו ויבש פרחו] *vacat* ואשר א]מר וצוה הכוהן]

18 [וגלחו את הראש ואת] הנתק לוא יגלחו [למען יספ]ור [הכוהן]   19   [את

השערות המתות והחיות וראה אם יוסף] מן החי אל המ[ת]   20   [בשבעת

הימים טמא הוא ואם לוא ליוסף מן]החיות אל [המתות]

1   [ו]הגיד נמלא דם ורוח החיים עולה וי[ורדת בו נרפא]   *Frag.* 1 ⅱ

2 [הנ]גע זה] משפט הצרעת לב[ני אהרון [להבדיל ל...]   3 *vacat* [vacat]

ומש]פט הזב את זו]בו כ]ול איש]   4   [אשר י]זו]ב מבשרו או אשר יעלה

עליו מ]חשבת זמה או אשר   5   [...] מגעו כמגע ה...   6   וכבס בג[ד]יו [...]

7 בו הנוגע בו ו.[... ו]משפט [הזבה כול אשה]   8   הזבה דם שב[עת ימים

תהיה בנד]תה ב[...]   9   [ו]שבעת הימים[...]   10   [הנו]גע בה[...]

11 ובע..[...]   12 תקוץ [...]   13 המים [...]   14 [...]   15 ובמי הנדה[...

המים[16   החיי]ם[17 ידה[...]   18   [...]

4Q273 (4QpapD^h) *4QpapDamascus Document^h*

J.M. Baumgarten, *DJD XVIII*, 193-198, pls. XLI-XLII
PAM 43.303
ROC 108

1   [...] .[...]   2 אמר ... [... עד אשר יצמח הבשר וראה]   *Frag.* 4 ⅱ

3 הכה[ן בי]ום השביע]י והנה רוח החיים עולה וירדת]   4   [ו]הבשר צמח

נרפא מן [הנגע ... ה]ספחת [לא יראנה הכהן]   5 לעור ה[ב]שר ...[... וא]ם

ישפל [השאת]   6   או הספחת בשפה ...[... ורא]ה הכהן אותו כמראי]

sees in] something like living flesh and [...] *11* [it is leprosy which has taken hold] of the living skin. And in accordance with [this] regulation /[as he sa]id: [the priest] shall confine [him seven days]/ *12* [... The priest shall examine him] on the [sev]enth [day;] if something [live] has been added *13* [to the dead ... it is mal]ignant [leprosy.] *Blank 14* [And the regulation for ringworm of the head or of the beard: ...] the priest shall examine it, and if *15* [the spirit enters the head or the beard taking hold of the artery and the dise]ase [has sprouted] from underneath the hai[r] *16* [changing its appearance to yellowish — for] it is [like a plant under] which there is a worm: *17* [which cuts its root so that its fruit turns pale.] *Blank* And what he sa[id: *Lev 13:33* «The priest shall order] *18* [them to shave their head, but] not to shave their ringworm», [it is so that the priest can co]unt *19* [the dead and living hairs, and see whether] living (hairs) [have been added] to the dead ones *20* [during the seven days, (then) he is impure; but if] living (hairs) [have not been added] to [the dead ones]

Frag. 1 *col.* II (= 4Q266 6 1) *1* and the artery is full of blood and the spirit of life goes up and d[own through it,] *2* [the dis]ease [is healed.] This is [the regulation of leprosy for the so]ns of Aaron, [so that they can differentiate ...] *3 Blank* [*Blank*] Regula[tion concerning the man with a disch]arge. Eve[ry man] *4* [with a di]scha[rge from his flesh, or who brings upon himself a] lustful thought or who *5* [...] his contact is like the contact of the ... *6* and he shall wash his clothes [...] *7* him (?). He who touches him, and [...] Regulation [concerning the woman who has a discharge. Any woman] *8* who has a discharge of blood. Se[ven days she shall be in] her [impuri]ty [...] *9* [and] seven days [...] *10* [he who to]uches her [...] *11* and in ... [...] *12* stir up [...] *13* the water [...] *14* ... [...] *15* and with the lustral water [...] *16* living [waters] ... [...] *17* her hand [...] *18* ... [...]

4Q273 (4QpapD^h) *4QpapDamascus Document^h*

CD-A, CD-B, 4Q266, 4Q267, 4Q268, 4Q269, 4Q270, 4Q271, 4Q272, 5Q12, 6Q15
Bibliography: Wacholder-Abegg 1, 57-59

Frag. 4 *col.* II (= 4Q266 6 1; 4Q269 7; 4Q272 1 1) *1* ... [...] *2* said ... [... until the flesh grows. And] *3* the priest [shall examine him on the] seventh [d]ay: if the spirit of life goes up and down] *4* [and] the flesh has grown, he is cured of [the disease ... the] rash. [The priest shall not examine] *5* the skin of the [fl]esh [... and i]f [the discolouration] *6* or the rash are deep in the surroundings ... [...

7 הבשר [החי ...   8 [...]   9 [ו]הנה [נוסף מן ה]חי אל [המת ... צרעת
ממארת] 10 היא ומשפט נתק הר[וש והזקן ... וראה] 11 הכהן והנה באה
הרו[ח ...]

Frag. 5 1 [...]...[...]   2 [...] ...אחרונה [...] כי שבה וכסתה [...]
3 [...]...נה היא אשר הוא י[...]   4 [...]ות עולם המה אל יקח איש את
האש]ה [...   5 [...]מימי ספרה את דם ... עד אשר י[...]

Frag. 6 1 [...]לא בעצת התורה ה[...]   2 [...]א הואה אשם והכה
[...]

and the priest sees in it something like] *7* [living] flesh […] *8* […] *9* if some-thing live [has been added] to the [dead …] it is [malignant leprosy] *10* And the regulation for ringworm of the he[ad or of the beard …] *11* the priest [shall examine it,] and if the spi[rit] enters […]

Frag. 5   *1* […] … […] *2* […] … last […] for she covered again […] *3* […] … it is what he […] *4* […] are […] eternal. No-one should take the wom[an …] *5* […] from the days she counted the blood of … until […]

Frag. 6   *1* […] not by the counsel of the law […] *2* […] he is guilty and strikes […]

Made in the USA
Las Vegas, NV
23 February 2022